AN INTRODUCTION TO CRIMINAL LAW

AN INTRODUCTION TO CRIMINAL LAW

SECOND EDITION

Graham Parker
Osgoode Hall Law School
York University

METHUEN

Toronto New York London
Sydney Auckland

Canadian Cataloguing in Publication Data

Parker, Graham, 1933-
An introduction to criminal law
Bibliography: p.
Includes indexes.
ISBN 0-458-95340-7

1. Criminal law—Canada. 2. Criminal procedure—Canada.
I. Title.

KE 8809.P37 1983 345.71 C83-094152-5

Printed and bound in Canada
1 2 3 4 5 83 88 87 86 85 84

CONTENTS

PREFACE
to the Second Edition

The scope of this book has been considerably broadened. In the first edition, it covered fewer offences. The Illustration chapter now includes more cases on property and sexual offences.

The book is still aimed at high school and undergraduate university students who are taking courses in law. In the first edition, I suggested that first-year law students might find the book a useful introduction and this expanded version should prove more valuable, but I would repeat the advice to law students that an introductory text is no substitute for reading the cases.

The literature on the Canadian criminal law has been enriched in the past five years. A text for lawyers has been published and a scholarly treatise is forthcoming. In addition, I recommend the excellent reports of the Law Reform Commission of Canada; everyone can profit from reading *Our Criminal Law*, and there are more specialized reports on specific offences and procedure matters.

This book does not aim to be a technical, nuts-and-bolts, black-letter treatment of the subject. No statement will be found at the end of this introduction that the "law is stated as of June 30, 1982." While I admire the certitude and confidence of such authors, I have only emulated them to the extent of giving basic definitional information. Instead, the criminal law is examined in a broader social, historical and cultural context. If this book were meant to be useful to the practitioner in the magistrates' or provincial courts, it would concentrate on radar traps, drunk driving, shoplifting and common assault. Similarly, on the procedure side, I have not overburdened the text with very technical matters which are best left to the attention of specialist volumes. In place of such complicated lawyers' law, I have tried to describe the trial process in the social context of Canada and the United States. This seems appropriate and necessary if only because Canadians have such misconceptions about the rights of the accused and the power of the State which they pick up by watching the wrong television programs. The potential of the Charter of Rights is taken into account in the Evidence and Procedure part of this book, but at this stage, the remarks are closer to prophecy than reporting.

I am most grateful to the teachers and reviewers who have given me useful suggestions. I have added to the illustrations, and the text provides a few more tentative answers to them. I have resisted the suggestion that the illustrations should be interspersed throughout the book. I view the illustrations as a casebook of facts for discussion in class, and I do not believe an instant answer is conducive to learning. In addition, it may give the false impression that the law is more certain than it is.

Others have wanted more sociological theories about crime, but I have not expanded that part of the book because this is a book about law, not a book about crime.

Complaints were also made about the use of technical language. I hope neither edition is overburdened with legalese of the "whereas" and "theretofore" variety, but I did not feel I could avoid legal terms if I were talking about the law. A short glossary is now included.

I have prepared a teaching guide that can be made available to those who adopt this book.

Finally, a stylistic note. Rather than resort to the cumbrous device of his/her or he-or-she, I seek refuge in section 26(6) of the Canadian Interpretation Act which states "words importing male persons include female persons" and *vice versa,* of course.

Graham Parker
Toronto 1982

1/INTRODUCTION

Looking at Crime in Its Legal Context

A crime can be defined as any form of human activity that the law defines as a crime. That statement seems circular and not very informative, but it is difficult to think of a better one. It would be so simple if we could say that only human activity that we instinctively consider to be "wrong" should be a crime. Our immediate thought might be that murder, rape, arson, theft and fraud would be common ground between us in defining at least some of the "worst" crimes. Yet, if we tried to be a little more specific and attempted a definition of murder, we might think that "the killing of any human being" is both wrong and a crime, but we would very soon have to start making exceptions so that the definition would now read "murder = the killing of any human being so long as the killer was not a soldier, hangman, prison guard, police officer or doctor engaged in their lawful duties or a householder defending his home or his body against deadly force." The definition is still not complete because we would have to make a distinction between killings that were intentional (or reckless) and those that were done only negligently or accidentally. And even if the killing appeared to have been done intentionally, the killer may have a defence—insanity, duress, self-defence, etc. How do we arrive at these definitions? By making laws, and therefore, we are back where we started. We could go through the same process with all those other crimes or wrong acts about which we felt so certain.

At one level, the law is engaged with making definitions and trying to draw distinctions between activities that should be controlled by criminal law and punishment and those that are "innocent" but nevertheless might result in a civil action or some other form of control. On a broader perspective, the law is a self-contained system of social control. No one suggests it is the only or the best system; it reflects the values of the dominant political power groups in society, at least to the extent that those values can be translated into legal terms and are capable of enforcement.

Law school might aptly be described as a secular seminary. Inside the four walls of the law seminary, students are taught a legal dogma that has its own terminology and liturgy. If students wish to become high priests of the law, they must be prepared to recognize the limits (and limitations) of the system and accept the fact that they must operate within that context to achieve certain purposes.

For instance, legal evidence does not present the "real" facts of an event but only an expression of legal truth that is admissible in a court deciding the guilt or innocence of an accused. The procedure of the court does not cater for an exhaustive examination of the facts but only relevant and admissible data that will be recognized in the stylized and symbolic trial. In a complex, heterogeneous and anonymous society, this seems to be the best effort we can make in fact-finding and truth-telling.

The law has been variously described as an art and a science. The lawyers of the eighteenth and nineteenth centuries believed (rather than discovered) that law was a science and that eternal principles governing society did exist. At the same time these lawyers, and notably Blackstone, believed that there was a mystical quality to the law which had its origins in the traditions of the profession, the folklore of the people and the abilities of English judges to discover these immutable, if evasive, truths in the science of reconciling cases and precedents of the common law; that is, the accumulation of experience found in law reports, digests of past cases and the wisdom of ancient commentators. Today we are a little more cynical and realize that we no longer live in a static society, but in a very complicated one, and the content of the law is influenced by many social, economic and political factors.

The law has its own peculiar logic. Because it is a folk art (or folk science) that must deal expeditiously with everyday problems involving real people, it cannot be an intellectually or conceptually perfect system of science or philosophy. Lawyers must solve problems, make urgent practical decisions and predict. These tasks have required them to be generalists and pragmatists and to be subject to a logic of their own.

Our Criminal Law: Proposals for Reform

In 1977, the Law Reform Commission of Canada published a remarkable document, *Our Criminal Law,* which was at once lucidly and simply stated and, at the same time, an important statement of principle. The recommendations were not revolutionary; they were affirmations of fundamentals. The following is a summary of the Commission's views:

> Man is a social being who has to live in a society. Society means cooperation, a common life, a sharing of fundamental values. To hold a value sincerely, a person must react when it is violated. To share a fundamental value genuinely, society too must react publicly when it is violated, condemn the violation and take steps to reaffirm the value. One way of doing this is by the criminal law.
>
> Criminal law operates at three different stages. At the law-making stage it denounces and prohibits certain actions. At the trial stage it condemns in solemn ritual those who commit them. And at the punishment stage it penalizes the offenders. This, not mere deterrence and rehabilitation, is what we get from criminal law—an indirect protection through bolstering our basic values.
>
> But criminal law is not the only means of bolstering values. Nor is it necessarily always the best means. The fact is, criminal law is a blunt and costly instrument—blunt because it cannot have the human sensitivity of institutions like the family, the school, the church or the community, and costly since it imposes suffering, loss of liberty and great expense.
>
> So criminal law must be an instrument of last resort.

The Commission was not drafting a document that would result in instant reform of the criminal law; instead, it was trying to create a climate of reform in a very balanced consideration of the problem. This is well expressed when they say that in a just society not coping with crime is unjust to the victim but wrongly coping with the criminal is equally unjust because the criminal law is "always on the cutting edge of the abuse of power." In creating a better criminal law, the Commission accentuates three factors. First, the criminal law must be humane so that punishment is not cruel, and the offender must be treated as a human being "not a robot to be reprogrammed." Secondly, there is an ingredient of freedom—presumption of innocence and the burden of proof on the Crown to prove the criminal act. Finally, justice demands that guilt only be determined by proper evidence, punishment should be appropriate to the offence and the offender and "like cases should be treated alike and different cases differently." These were the ideals, but of course, the Commission found the reality somewhat different. It saw the criminal justice system as resembling "a vast machine sucking people in one end, spewing them out the other and then sucking them back in again—a self-generating mechanism, certainly not a human process." Freedom was also infringed because so many crimes or quasi-crimes could result in conviction without proof of fault. The presumption of innocence was often illusory because of the appearance, clothing, speech or lack of education of the accused. Justice also seemed to be badly served because the prison population contained "a quite unrepresentative proportion of poor, of disadvantaged and of native offenders." In summary of these statements of concern, the Commission stated:

> Theoretically, we demonstrate our public disapproval of certain types of conduct; in practice all we do is process an interminable series of recurring cases along the dreary assembly line of dime-store justice. Judges, Crown attorneys, defence lawyers, police and all concerned in the operation of the system grow daily more disillusioned and discouraged. Small wonder many think our criminal law a hollow mockery.

The Commission wanted a minimal criminal law. The law's business was not the enforcement of morals ("making sin reap its own reward is not a fit enterprise for mere mortal men and women"). The law cannot make people moral. Instead, the Commission wanted a society where "people think they *ought* not to be criminals." The criminal law was a system of applied morality but only those values should be enforced that are fundamental and essential, such as the sanctity of life. The law must limit itself to "real" crime, and the prime duty for teaching values must be put back where it belonged—with the family, school, churches, and other socializing agencies.

What did the Commission mean by "real" crime? First, such crimes would include protection of such values as "the sanctity of life, the inviolability of the person, the virtue of truth and the necessity of order." These would include violent crimes, fraud and offences against peace, order and good government. Secondly, a "real" crime would protect freedom, justice, tolerance, human dignity and equality. These would include false imprisonment, interfering with justice and false arrest.

The Commission resisted suggestions that the legal notion of guilt should be abandoned in favour of a concept of dangerousness. It wanted to maintain the test of personal fault or "moral notion of guilt" which differentiated between "intentional and unintentional, deliberate and accidental, careful and careless." In other words, the problem of crime, at least real crime, should be subject to legal tests.

Non-Legal Approaches to Crime

Before we embark on an examination of the criminal law and its treatment of the social phenomenon known as crime, we should consider the alternative methods of looking at and dealing with crime, deviance, wrongdoing, evil, immorality or whatever we choose to call it. There are many other disciplines that have studied crime, and their contributions cannot be ignored. At the same time, students of the law must be made fully aware of the limited legal use of these extra-legal concepts and should recognize the occasions on which disciplines such as philosophy, psychology and sociology have a contribution to make. It must be remembered that these extra-legal disciplinary contributions are considered legally valid only after they have been converted into concepts that the law recognizes (and puts to its own use).

The Relationship between Law and Religion: Law and Morals

There are strong historical connections between law and religion, particularly organized religion. We like to think that in most of the newer democracies there is a clear separation of Church and State. In England, the Anglican church is still established and bishops sit in the House of Lords, but their real power is limited to the control of the church and its clergy. This was not always the case. For instance, up to the fifteenth century, the most powerful legal administrator, the Lord Chancellor, was the chief official of the law and also an important clergyman. Literacy was almost a monopoly of those in Holy Orders, and it was inevitable that the administration of the law should be the responsibility of the clerics (or clerks). At this time the canon law and the secular law were frequently intermingled. The Inquisition (and, in England, the Court of Star Chamber) fulfilled the double role of protecting the citizens from religious unorthodoxy by punishing heresy, blasphemy, witchcraft and immorality and, in doing so, ensuring the internal security of the State.

In recent decades there has been much debate about the relationship between law and morals. Particular attention has been given to homosexual behaviour (notably of the private, consensual variety), pornography, prostitution and abortion. The legal idea of crime and the theological concept of sin are not coincident and are becoming less so. Few people would want to live in a theocracy where all sins were crimes; perhaps Calvin's Geneva, the New England of the Puritans, and the ayatollahs' Iran came closest to being societies of this kind. Yet we could say that law in general and crime in particular have always been a reflection of the mores of the community. This is not restricted to sexual mores, and the administrators of the legal system (which would include legislators, judges, prosecutors and police officers) are intent on perpetuating the values of the dominant forces in society.

Heresy and witchcraft are no longer punished by temporal authority. The legal treatment of immorality is subject to the shifting tides of public opinion. Blasphemy has not totally disappeared. In his *Digest of the Criminal Law of Canada,* Burbidge described the criminal law in 1889. Under the heading of offences against religion, he listed blasphemy, which included any publication relating to God, the Bible, etc. "... intended to wound the feelings of mankind ..." or "to promote immorality." The article makes it an offence to deny the existence of God, to "deprave" the Lord's Supper or the *Book of Common Prayer.* Today we protect religious freedom by means of human rights legislation.

When the Canadian Parliament enacted the 1892 Code, blasphemous libel continued as an offence under Canadian law. Although prosecutions have been rare, this offence is still found in the Code (s. 260). The offence is not defined except in a negative way by saying that a person shall not be convicted "for expressing in good faith and in decent language ... an opinion upon a religious subject." The crime seemed a dead letter in Canada and in England, but in the last decade an Englishman was successfully prosecuted and jailed for suggesting in a poem that Jesus may have had homosexual tendencies. Adultery was a crime in the United States until recent years, and was also an offence in the Maritimes before Confederation. For instance, in New Brunswick, adultery could be punishable by a fine of $400 or two years in prison. The drafters of the Canadian Criminal Code were encouraged in 1892 to punish such behaviour as a crime, but they withstood the temptation. Although it is still a matrimonial "offence" in the divorce courts, it has lost much of its stigma.

The Court of Star Chamber was abolished in 1641, but it permanently enlarged the criminal law by creating the offences of perjury, forgery, riot, maintenance, libel and conspiracy. The inquisitorial procedure of this prerogative court also made important changes in the mode of trial and the methods of compelling the attendance of witnesses and their examination. The wide definition given to the crime of conspiracy in the controversial case of *Shaw* v. *D.P.P.* has its roots in the jurisdiction of the Star Chamber. (This case, which is a very important landmark in the law-and-morals debate, will be discussed later.)

While the direct intervention of the Church has ceased, the moral beliefs of the more influential denominations continue to have a strong influence on the legislators and the courts. In recent years, there have been attempts, meeting with some success, to inject morality into public affairs. In the last two decades there have been lengthy debates on the dichotomy of law and morals. The crucial question: what are the appropriate areas for criminal law intervention to control (or at least punish) behaviour which a significant section of the population looks upon as a matter of private morality? We shall see, in a later chapter, that this was sparked by the Wolfenden Report which examined the feasibility and advisability of making criminal, and punishing, public prostitution and private adult consensual homosexuality. This debate has included other "morals" offences—attempted suicide, obscenity, drug addiction (including the use of alcohol), gambling and abortion.

The dichotomy of law and morals will require more elaborate debate, but at this stage, students of the law should realize that the standards of behaviour that are expected from a practising religionist or from a dutiful son or daughter have very limited application in the criminal law. We will soon discover that the Seven Deadly Sins and the Ten Commandments are poorly represented in the definition of crime. At least we can say that infractions of holy laws are enforced rather selectively in the statute books and law courts. Despite the decision in *Shaw* v. *D.P.P.* the current view is that the State should keep out of the bedrooms of the nation and the courts should not see themselves as the custodians of public morals.

The Wolfenden Report was the work of an official government committee; it recommended that it was not the "function of the law to intervene in the private lives of citizens or to seek to enforce any particular pattern of behaviour." John Robinson has been a bishop in the Anglican church and the liberal theologian who wrote *Honest to God*. On behalf of the Sexual Law Reform Society, he has said that the law's function was "not to prohibit but to protect, not to enforce morals but to safeguard persons, their privacies and freedoms." The Sexual Law Reform Society issued a report in 1974; it was not an official document, but its findings are worth examining because they reflect the avant-garde view. The Working Party rejected the idea that "the law has a duty, for the sake of society at large, to prevent behaviour—however morally dubious—which is freely chosen and indulged in private by some citizens."

The group's overall recommendation was that the criminal law should be entitled to restrict or punish sexual activity only when (1) there is no true consent, (2) where there is not full responsibility on the part of one or more of those engaging in it or (3) where offence is caused to identifiable members of the public who give evidence that they have witnessed or been involved in such activity against their will.

The most important recommendation concerns the age of consent for sexual activity. The group considered the choice of a legal age arbitrary, nonsensical and a fiction. They would have preferred to protect young persons who are irresponsible or "in moral danger" by intervening in their lives as children and young persons in need of "care and control" under welfare legislation. The reasons put forward were:

1. The present age of sixteen has no biological justification; it does not take into account the attitudes or actual behaviour of young people.
2. It is not a function of the law to make people compulsorily chaste, even though their behaviour might be immoral.
3. The criteria of "harm" should be judged by commonsense standards.

The group recommended that incest should no longer be an offence. Incest has only been an offence in the criminal statutes of England since 1908; before that time it was solely an ecclesiastical offence. Someone suggested that it makes as much sense to charge a person with incest as to charge him with living in inadequate housing or being a partner in an unhappy marriage. The Working Party suggested that incest committed by two persons under fourteen years should be ignored by the law but anyone under eighteen years could, in appropriate circumstances, be treated as in the need of "care and control."

The English reformers also wished to abolish most of the crimes associated with prostitution. The State should not try to regulate prostitution in any way except to punish assaults, protect the immature and prevent public annoyance. This means that pimping or keeping a common bawdy house would no longer be offences, but procuring any person under eighteen years for the purposes of prostitution would be an offence. Any kind of street activity, by either sex, that was "overtly indecent or annoying" would also be an offence so long as those who have been annoyed are identified.

The Working Party also made recommendations about the crime of rape which will be examined later. Most sexual offences were once the preserve of the Church which was responsible for the moral welfare of the people, but with the secularization of society, the State has taken over the responsibility for policing lust.

Criminal Law and the Judeo-Christian Ethic

The criminal law is based on a concept of blameworthiness which has its foundation in the Judeo-Christian ethic and the notion of free will, that normal adult humans can make a choice between good and evil. If they choose to do wrong, then they deserve to be punished. The law seldom listens to arguments that a defendant's actions were determined by some social or psychological forces. In *Powell* v. *Texas,* the United States Supreme Court refused to act on the suggestion that the appellant, who was charged with public drunkenness, was criminally irresponsible and incapable of controlling his behaviour because he was an alcoholic. The majority took the narrow view that he had the conscious will to take the first drink each day, although he may have thereafter been subject to an uncontrollable urge to drink. Similarly, an accused would not be excused from liability because he claimed that his social or criminal irresponsibility was a product of a deprived childhood or because he was a member of an oppressed minority.

The criminal law is based on a free will concept of responsibility and will punish intentional and reckless behaviour that shows conscious wrong-doing, or at least a conscious disregard of consequences that would be foreseen by the notional "reasonable man." As we shall see presently, *mens rea,* or the mental element in the criminal law, only applies to the minority of the work of the courts. Most charges concern acts that are decided on strict or absolute liability; that is, the intention or blameworthiness of the actor is considered irrelevant. The most common of these offences involve the use of automobiles on public highways. Most of the offences described in the Criminal Code, however, require proof by the prosecution of *mens rea.*

If we examine the law laid down in Exodus, we find that society has always recognized gradations of guilt and has recognized mitigation for behaviour that was not blameworthy or was less blameworthy.

The criminal law is still based on a system that requires blameworthiness before the determination of guilt and the application of punishment. The law of murder refers to the mental element (or *mens rea*) of that crime as "malice aforethought" and has gradations of crime such as the "planned and deliberate" nature of murder in the first degree. (This type of murder also includes killings, not necessarily planned and deliberate, where the victim is a police officer, prison guard or other official employee in the administration of justice.) Other forms of blameworthy homicide are either murder in the second degree or manslaughter; in theory, at least, the degree of homicide will depend on the blameworthiness of the accused and the presence or absence of any mitigations or excuses.

These gradations are found in all offences and have always existed. They exist in our everyday transactions with our friends, fellow workers or on the sports field; as Justice Holmes said, even a dog knows the difference between being kicked and accidentally tripped over.

Theoreticians of the law argue that ordinary negligence should not be sufficient *mens rea* for a crime, because a negligent person cannot foresee (or advert to) a merely negligent act; punishment, therefore, makes no sense. Opponents of this view suggest that the negligent person should be punished because this will make him more careful in the future. Therefore, in utilitarian terms, they argue that punishment will deter negligent behaviour.

There are relatively clear distinctions between religious concepts of responsibility, blame or accountability and the meaning of similar terms in the secular criminal law. For instance, the law does not punish persons for merely having evil thoughts. In most cases the law requires an act (*actus reus*) that is coincident with the evil intent (*mens rea*). The law says it is usually not concerned with motive as part of the definition of crime, although it may be part of the admissible evidence; for example, the fact that Jean Valjean, in Hugo's *Les Miserables,* stole a loaf of bread to feed his starving child did not excuse him from criminal liability. The law does not make moral judgements about the accused's past wickedness, bad character, or previous convictions in assessing guilt (although they may be taken into account in sentencing).

Murder is a peculiar crime because society views it with special solemnity because of the sanctity of human life. No matter how much the drafters try to make clear definitions, the old notion of "malice" tends to retain some of its old meaning. J.F. Stephen was one of the most important commentators on the criminal law in the nineteenth century. He drafted the laws that eventually became our Criminal Code. He tried to bring reason to the law and was influenced by Bentham, the father of codification. He was, however, also a moralist who strongly believed in the desert theory of punishment. The State had a duty to punish those who transgressed the laws. He said that words such as "malice" carry a moral connotation and may therefore produce confusion and uncertainty; the administration of justice, however, is "based on morality" and "its general correspondence with the moral sentiments of the nation." He continued:

> It is therefore absolutely necessary that legal definitions of crimes should be based upon moral distinctions, whatever may be the difficulty of ascertaining with precision what those distinctions are; and it will be found in practice impossible to attach to the words "malice" and "malicious" any other meaning than . . . wickedness and wicked.

Religion also has relevance to the way in which the facts of a crime are proved in court. With a few exceptions, a court will not accept evidence that is not on oath because it is assumed that a person who is not sworn "to tell the truth, the whole truth, etc." will be less likely to be a trustworthy witness. This may seem illogical to some but in earlier times when people were more afraid of eternal damnation in a life hereafter, or were more superstitious, the oath had more force. We have all heard fictional lawyers say to witnesses, "Now remember, you are still under oath"; this implies that people are less likely to tell lies when under oath and, therefore, subject to being charged with the crime of perjury. The criminal trial, particularly when there is a jury, has many of the attributes of a morality play. In other words, there is an uneasy truce between law and religion. Religion does not have a direct influence on the law but the religious content of the law is implied and pervasive.

Law and Philosophy

The law, a peculiar amalgam of art and science, does not proceed by syllogistic reasoning. Words are used very loosely as the quotation from Stephen shows. Lawyers seem to take pride in describing their *modus operandi* as "pragmatic." Law students are often shocked when it is suggested that judges arrive at their decision intuitively and then proceed to find a rationalization to explain that decision in legal terms. This does not mean that judges are particularly cynical. They are not dealing with abstract questions about which they can cogitate for years. They must reach decisions affecting people's rights. They have a gut-feeling about justice and decide accordingly.

Persons trained in philosophy are somewhat frustrated by the law's imprecise use of language. They will sometimes find that lawyers examine the concepts of criminal law in a very mechanical or idiosyncratic manner. For instance, the legal definitions of "act," "will," "intention," "motive," "cause" and "ought" will not satisfy the philosopher because they appear superficial and seem to be based on expediency.

The lawyer must use words with as much precision as he can muster, but those words must be applied in the public arena to an urgent practical problem that involves the actions, thoughts, motives and emotions of a human being. Debates about the nice or logical use of words are often forgotten in the pragmatism and expediency of legal practice and the social demands for an immediate solution to a real-life problem. Furthermore, the criminal law approach to the problems of human behaviour inherent in words such as "intend" or "ought" incorporates a moral ingredient inherent in the free will concept of the Judeo-Christian ethic.

Philosophy has not made a significant contribution to the technical definition of crime, partly because lawyers and courts treat that part of the law as their peculiar expertise.

The greatest contribution has been made by the philosopher H.L.A. Hart who was a professor of jurisprudence. The basic question Hart confronts is "a scepticism about the whole idea that the courts can usefully enquire into whether or not a person could have done what he did not do, and to them the enlightened policy seems to be the one in which we by-pass this question: we should neither assert nor deny that the accused could have done otherwise than he did. Instead we should look upon his act merely as a symptom of the need for either punishment or treatment." Hart is preparing to answer the argument of Barbara Wootton, a social scientist, that the lawyers' verbal games about *mens rea* and blameworthiness were senseless and the crucial issue was what should be done with the offender after the lawyers had decided that the accused had factually committed the act. Wootton argued that the real question of responsibility was limited to the issue of disposition of the person who had shown himself in need of social adjustment. Hart makes some persuasive counter-arguments. He said: ". . . a primary vindication of the principle of responsibility could rest on the simple idea that unless a man has the capacity and a fair opportunity or chance to adjust his behaviour to the law, its penalties ought not to be applied to him." Hart also argued in favour of the legal view of crime because it gave citizens the opportunity "to predict and plan the future course of our lives within the coercive framework of the law." In addition, the law that makes liability to punishment depend on a voluntary act calls for the exercise of powers of self-control. Finally, he makes this most persuasive argument:

> Human society is a society of persons; and persons do not view themselves or each other merely as so many bodies moving in ways which are sometimes harmful and have to be prevented or altered. Instead persons interpret each

> other's movements as manifestations of intention and choices, and these subjective factors are often more important to their social relations than the movements by which they are manifested or their effects.

Philosophy has played an important part in persuading lawyers and legislators to re-examine the relationship between law and morals. The Wolfenden Report in England and the LeDain Commission in Canada created heated debates between the adherents of J.S. Mill and those who believed that the law should enforce morality.

Punishment has received most attention from philosophers. Beccaria, writing in the eighteenth century, was responsible for a new attitude toward punishment. He believed that certainty of punishment was more important than very harsh penalties. He wanted punishment to be proportioned to the seriousness of the offence. His work influenced John Howard, William Eden, Samuel Romilly and Jeremy Bentham who improved prison conditions, helped reduce the number of crimes that could be punished by hanging and tried to make the laws not only more humane but also more rational.

Many of the ideas of the philosophers have not been incorporated in the Criminal Code because of political expediency, the innate conservatism of the legal profession and the courts or hostile and irrational public opinion. Before we condemn the law for its self-satisfied and narrow attitude toward social problems, perhaps we should take note of the comments of historian Hugh Stretton:

> ... other social scientists ... dismiss law as if it were a primitive "natural history" of ungeneralized detail, or as if prescription were unrelated to description, understanding and prediction. In fact, prescription is thickly textured with prediction. In common prudence, the level of generalization of such a skilled profession should attract respectful attention, and some inquiry into its reasons.

The Relevance of Psychology and Psychiatry

Psychiatrists and psychologists are interested in problems of human behaviour and many of them seriously question the basis of the criminal law liability being free will rather than determinism. The law's attitude toward intention, necessity, coercion or responsibility generally is very artificial and, in the eyes of many psychologists, is just plain wrong. The law has most difficulty with the behavioural scientists when the defence of the accused is that he lacks criminal responsibility because he is mentally abnormal. Psychologists and psychiatrists argue that the law has an obsolete test of "insanity" that does not take account of modern knowledge and thus precludes the application of psychiatric expertise to the accused's problem. The law's answer is that the question of criminal responsibility is to be examined in a court of law with strict rules of relevance; the trial is not a clinical conference. The law is saying, in effect, that the behavioural scientist is only a guest in the legal preserve. The law will make the rules and decide how much behavioural science will be injected into the system of criminal justice. Some accused persons who are mentally incompetent are not even tried because they are "unfit to plead" in that they are incapable of properly instructing counsel or would not understand the import of a criminal trial. Others who are legally insane can be found not guilty by a jury because of their inability to understand their acts or to control the actions that led to the charge against them.

On the other hand, irresponsibility due to intoxication provides only a partial defence, reducing murder to manslaughter. Acts that are committed while under the influence of drugs other than alcohol are not always excused or mitigated. Some accused who were on an LSD trip or heavily dosed with amphetamines have been given a partial defence; others have been convicted of the full offence, admonished by judges for befouling their brains and punished for this behaviour.

We still seem to be a long way from the law's acceptance of a more "scientific" approach to abnormal behaviour.

The Sociological View of Crime

Of all the non-legal disciplines, sociology has the greatest current interest in crime. The most durable interest has been in criminology which is concerned with the description and explanation of criminal behaviour. In the nineteenth and the early part of the twentieth century special attention was paid to biological and psychological explanations for criminal behaviour. Lombroso and Healy are two of the best-known practitioners and theorists. Lombroso's attempts to identify a criminal type by biological means have fallen into disrepute. Psychological explanations for criminal behaviour have not been treated as unkindly, but recently sociologists have dominated the field of criminology. In particular, theories "explaining" juvenile delinquency have proliferated; the work of Sutherland, Glueck, Merton, Cohen, Cloward and Ohlin and Matza are the best known in a very long list. These theories, which have not shown great practical value, are neither formulated nor discussed much at the moment.

In the past decade or so, there has been a revived interest in the sociology of law which has led to a closer sociological examination of the criminal justice system. Skolnick was a pioneer with his *Justice Without Trial,* a study of the actual operations of a city police department and an examination of the "low-visibility" decisions of officials in the lower echelons of the criminal justice system. This "critical criminology" concerns itself with crime as a "function of who is doing the defining, how people who are able to make definitions stick on a legislative level and are able to carry out these definitions on an administrative level." Consequently, we also have studies on the legal profession, the jury, plea bargaining, the office of the prosecutor, bail and the function of the judiciary.

Critical criminology has also relied on labelling theory, and Becker is one of the best known of the labelling theorists. He certainly did not limit application of this theory to criminals but included all forms of deviance. In Becker's words:

> Social groups create deviance by making rules whose infractions constitute deviance, and by applying those rules to particular people and labelling them as outsiders . . . deviance is not a quality of the act the person commits, but rather a consequence of the application by others of rules and sanctions to an "offender." The deviant is one to whom the label has been successfully applied; deviant behaviour is behaviour that people so label.

Of course, this approach is very different from the seemingly tautological legal definition of crime, that is, crime is any behaviour so described by law. Or is it?

Critical criminology is not only concerned with narrow studies of how a particular bail system works *in fact* in a particular jurisdiction; it is also concerned with an examination of the very nature of the criminal law. Something like cyclic history is at work here. The Classical School of criminology, founded by Bentham and Beccaria, was attempting to reform the legal system and to minimize the discretionary nature of the definition of crime and the amount of punishment being imposed by repressive regimes. The Positive School of Lombroso and Ferri did not concern itself with the definition of the crime, but with the scientific study of the criminal. Now we are back to the study of crime.

The present sociological interest in crime as a social phenomenon has its roots in the work of Durkheim, who believed that crime was inevitable and indeed necessary. According to Durkheim, crime would only disappear when the "collective sentiments" in a community reached such an intensity that all persons concurred in the same common values; this, however, was probably neither desirable nor possible. Durkheim saw crime as providing a means of self-expression, although of a low order. Laws to control crime are an expression of the societal disapproval of such deviant behaviour.

Marx had a different theory about crime and saw law as an institution created by the ruling elite to further its own interests. Critical criminologists are indebted to Marxist theory when they attribute criminal laws to the interaction of competing interest groups in the political process, but these interest groups necessarily exclude "that group whose behaviour the law is intended to control." The powerless and the poor, the argument goes, are victimized by the criminal justice system. The history of the law, particularly in the past three hundred years, suggests some support for this view. Authority has invariably constructed laws and institutions to control the "deviant"—the poor, the orphan, labourers trying to organize themselves, the delinquent, the heretic, the nonconformist, the epileptic, the mentally disturbed and the criminal.

Yet, before we completely accept the views of the new criminology, we should consider further the history of the last one hundred and fifty years. At the beginning of the nineteenth century, more than two hundred offences attracted the death penalty. By mid-century, this number had been very drastically reduced. Prison conditions improved, and probation, parole and juvenile courts had been established by the end of century.

With the passage of the Reform Acts of 1832 and 1867, the vote had been extended to a much wider segment of society so that the interests of the average citizen should have been better protected. It would appear that the average citizen turned out to be equally intolerant of the deviant. Paraphrasing some illustrious thinkers, the new criminologists could be answered by saying that the deviant is always with us, or if the deviant did not exist, it would be necessary to invent him. And in one sense, the law, reflecting society, invented deviance, or more particularly, crime.

On the other hand, even if democratic ideals had been triumphant and the citizen, through his representative, had been willing and able to protect the poor, the powerless and the deviant, the administration of criminal justice was not conducted by elected officials. The police, the prosecutor and the judge are appointed functionaries of the law and in deciding to arrest, to lay a particular charge and to reach a verdict of guilty, the officials use their discretion. These officials are instruments of the power structure of society. No one is suggesting that they are corrupt or consciously biassed, but they have no more love of the deviant than has the average citizen. Max Weber put this in a different fashion but with the same message. He pointed out that the poor want law to serve the social purpose of equalization of economic and social opportunities, but they inevitably come "into conflict with the formalism and the rule-bound, detached objectivity of bureaucratic administration." Richard Quinney, an industrious Marxist criminologist, suggests the alternative of "popular justice," so that people could ignore the legal institutions of the capitalist state and would attempt "to resolve conflicts between themselves in their own communities and work places."

The Law Reform Commission of Canada could hardly be viewed as a Marxist front, but in *Our Criminal Law,* the Commissioners argue that not all crime is caused by a "wrongful preference of self-interest." Much crime results from boredom, frustration, a need for identity and social injustice. Many property offences are "the product of the unjust distribution of property in our society." Yet theft is given great importance in the criminal law, and the Commission questions this:

> Sometimes ... paradigms need changing. Pollution, depletion of resources, poverty, unemployment, inflation, race conflicts, terrorism, alienation—all these throw doubts on the adequacy of our older criminal law paradigm.
>
> We must chart the proper place of property offences in our law. What is the interest to be protected—ownership, possession or personal space? What relevance has it to peace, order and good government? How should we weigh ownership as against human dignity? How should we rate property as compared with persons?

Roscoe Pound was a lawyer and the most prominent proponent of sociological jurisprudence in the 1930s. He viewed law as a neutral system that fulfilled societal aims. His ideas took a middle ground that was more legal than sociological. Law, he said, attempted "to satisfy, to reconcile, to harmonize, to adjust those overlapping and often conflicting claims and demands, either through securing them directly and immediately or through securing certain individual interests or through delimitations or compromises of individual interests, so as to give effect to the greatest total of interests that weigh most in our civilization with the least sacrifice of the scheme of interests as a whole."

No doubt, the classic crimes of murder, rape, arson and robbery reflect the consensus of society that its members wish to be protected from such depredations. Criminal legislation, however, is full of offences and punishments that reflect special interests, for example, public drunkenness, vagrancy, prostitution, the gaming laws in England a century or so ago, the conspiracy laws which penalized workers for trying to form unions or organize strikes and, in Canada, the offence in the 1927 (and earlier) Code which could impose life imprisonment for interfering with railroad equipment "to endanger the safety" of passengers. In contrast to the nineteenth-century offence of conspiracy aimed at trade unionists is s. 367 of the 1954 Code which now makes it an offence for an employer to refuse to hire a trade unionist. In all these cases, an interest group has placed its own particular brand on the definition of crime. The classic crimes reflect the functional or consensus theory, that crime offends against "strong collective sentiments" and the criminal law is the "embodiment of moral consensus in society." The other crimes described illustrate the conflict theory, that crime offends and threatens powerful groups in society and the criminal law is an expression of the "interest of elites and criminal behaviour is a manifestation of non-elite interests."

Andrew Hopkins, a perceptive commentator, has properly pointed out that sociologists interested in the criminal law might be employed profitably in trying to reconcile the conflict and consensus theories of the law rather than constructing competing models. The first step would be "to make a distinction between theories about the creation of criminal law and descriptions of it once it is in operation." Hopkins continues, "Once we have made the distinction between the genesis and nature of criminal law, it is immediately apparent that interest group theorists are concerned primarily with the processes by which criminal law comes into existence and evolves, while consensus theorists are more interested with the analysis of existing law."

Sociologists have also examined judicial decision-making and have decided that the judge's opinion is not formulated on a basis of reason and logic alone. In addition, the personality, sociological background and political allegiances of the jurists have all played their parts in the decision reached. These sociological insights have undoubted merit. They are important if we are trying to understand the criminal justice system. However, the contributions of the sociologists must play a subsidiary role while we study the closed system of criminal law theory. In the long run, of course, we hope the sociologists will aid in the reform of the criminal law so that injustices can be minimized.

Leroy Powell: Legal versus Social Policy

The case of *Powell* v. *Texas* provides an apt illustration of the contrast between the notion of responsibility viewed by the law and how it is interpreted by the social or behavioural scientist.

Powell was found on a public street and "smelled strongly of alcoholic beverages, staggered when walking, speech incoherent." He was charged under a Texas law which provided that, "Whoever shall get drunk or be found in a state of intoxication in any public place or at any private house except his own, shall be fined not exceeding one hundred dollars."

Powell's lawyers argued that the following were the proper findings in the case:

1. Chronic alcoholism is a disease that destroys the afflicted person's will to resist the constant, excessive consumption of alcohol.
2. A chronic alcoholic does not appear in public by his own volition, but under a compulsion symptomatic of the disease of chronic alcoholism.
3. Leroy Powell is a chronic alcoholic who is afflicted with the disease of chronic alcoholism.

Justice Marshall wrote the majority judgement. He characterized the first premise as covering a multitude of sins and thought that the proposed findings "utterly" failed to make a crucial distinction originally made by Dr. Jellinek, the most reputable authority on problems of alcoholism. Jellinek had said that "conceptual clarity [relating to the problems of alcoholism] can only be achieved by distinguishing carefully between 'loss of control' once an individual has commenced to drink and 'inability to abstain' from drinking in the first place."

The defence based its case on the expert evidence of a psychiatrist, Dr. Wade, who had a special interest in alcoholism. Dr. Wade acknowledged that there is no generally accepted definition of alcoholism. He referred to the debate in the medical profession over whether alcohol is actually physically "addicting," or merely psychologically "habituating," and gave the opinion that under either interpretation the chronic alcoholic is an "involuntary drinker" who is "powerless not to drink" and who loses self-control over his drinking. After examining Powell he had reached the conclusion that the appellant was a chronic alcoholic who "by the time he had reached [the state of intoxication] . . . is not able to control his behaviour and . . . has reached this point because he has an uncontrollable compulsion to drink." He also added that the appellant lacked "the will power to resist the constant excessive consumption of alcohol." Finally, in his expert opinion, jailing people like Powell would neither rehabilitate them nor lessen their desire for alcohol. The psychiatrist's evidence was therefore not unequivocal, and this was the weakness in the appellant's case; it is not difficult to imagine the responses that the doctor was forced to make on cross-examination. Dr. Wade admitted that, when sober, Powell knew the difference between right and wrong and also conceded that when the appellant took the first drink on the day on which he was eventually arrested for public drunkenness, Powell had exercised "voluntary exercise of his will." In further explanation of this answer, the expert stated, "These individuals have a compulsion [which] . . . while not completely overpowering, is a very strong influence, and this compulsion, coupled with the firm belief in their mind that they are going to be able to handle it from now on, causes their judgement to be somewhat clouded." The damage caused by this cross-examination was compounded by the cross-examination of the accused himself. He was asked:

Q: You knew you had to be here this afternoon, but this morning you took one drink and then you knew that you couldn't afford to drink any more and come to court; is that right?
A: Yes, sir, that's right.
Q: So you exercised your will power and kept from drinking anything except that one drink?
A: Yes, sir.

This was further explained on re-examination:

Q: Leroy, isn't the real reason why you just had one drink today because you just had enough money to buy one drink?
A: Well, that was just give to me.
Q: In other words, you didn't have any money with which you could buy any drinks yourself?
A: No sir, that was give to me.
Q: And that's really what was controlling the amount you drank this morning, isn't it?
A: Yes, sir.
Q: Leroy, when you start drinking, do you have any control over how many drinks you can take?
A: No, sir.

The decision of the court, and in particular the judgement of Marshall J., provides a microcosm of the criminal law. He decided the following points, either explicitly or implicitly: first, that public drunkenness was not a status offence. Second, that

> . . . facilities for the attempted treatment of indigent alcoholics are woefully lacking throughout the country. It would be tragic to return large numbers of helpless, sometimes dangerous and frequently unsanitary inebriates to the streets of our cities without even the opportunity to sober up adequately which a brief gaol term provides. . . . Yet the medical profession cannot, and does not,

> tell us with any assurance that, even if the buildings, equipment and trained personnel were made available, it could provide anything more than slightly higher-class gaols for our indigent habitual inebriates. Thus we run the grave risk that nothing will be accomplished beyond hanging of a new sign—reading "hospital"—over the wing of the gaol house.

The defence claimed that Powell lacked capacity to commit the offences of public drunkenness because he was unable to control his actions when he ventured on to a public street in an inebriated state. The majority disagreed with this submission. The dissenting opinion, delivered by Fortas J. (and concurred in by Justices Douglas, Stewart and Brennan), first argued that the offence of public drunkenness did not involve the question of whether an alcoholic is responsible for criminal acts. The dissent addressed itself to the question of "the 'condition' of being intoxicated in public." Fortas J. took the view that the "appellant's being intoxicated in public was part of the pattern of his disease and due to a compulsion symptomatic of that disease." The dissent promptly added that this defence or excuse would not apply to "offences such as driving a car while intoxicated, assault, theft or robbery." With rather shaky logic, Fortas J. said these can be differentiated because "such offences require independent acts or conduct and do not typically flow from and are not part of the syndrome of the disease of chronic alcoholism." Finally, Fortas J. said:

> If an alcoholic should be convicted for criminal conduct which is not a characteristic and involuntary part of the pattern of the disease as it afflicts him, nothing herein would prevent his punishment.

The minority was much more certain than most experts are about the identification of the "quality" of alcoholism. They were sure, it seems, that the scientists know a good deal about the problem, that they are capable of curing or containing it, that it is a disease and clearly identified. Even if, for the moment, we accept the above quotations from Fortas J., one wonders how carefully the judge chose his offences. One would imagine, for instance, that if a man became inebriated and staggered to his car and drove away he would be performing these acts with as much volition as he had in buying the fourth, fifth, sixth (or first?) drink. To decide to leave the tavern or to venture out "in public" (in the terms of the impugned legislation) is not of a different quality from the decision to venture out and step on the accelerator of an automobile. Similarly, the volition required to commit an assault applies just as strongly to a man who has the "condition" of being a chronic will-less alcoholic.

The last sentences anticipate the judgement of Marshall J. on this question. He and his concurring colleagues took the view that the evidence of Dr. Wade and the appellant (particularly under cross-examination) showed that the appellant was not totally lacking in volition. Marshall J. was of the opinion that if Powell could not be convicted of public intoxication, it was difficult to see how an accused could be convicted of murder if the actor, "while exhibiting normal behaviour in all other respects, suffers from 'a compulsion' to kill, which is an exceedingly strong influence, but 'not completely overpowering.'" Therefore the plea of Powell was refused because Marshall J. could not see how the theory propounded by the dissent could be limited in any way. The core of the judgement is found in the following statement:

> We are unable to conclude, on the state of this record on the current state of medical knowledge, that chronic alcoholics in general, and Leroy Powell in particular, suffer from such an irresistible compulsion to drink and to get drunk in public that they are utterly unable to control their performance of either or both of these acts and thus cannot be deterred at all from public intoxication.

Finally, Marshall J. said in a most important statement that preserved the integrity of the criminal law as a closed system:

> We cannot cast aside the centuries-long evolution of the collection of interlocking and overlapping concepts which the common law has utilized to assess the moral accountability of an individual for his antisocial deeds. The doctrines of *actus reus, mens rea,* insanity, mistake, justification and duress have historically provided the tools for a constantly shifting adjustment of the tension between the evolving aims of the criminal law and changing religious, moral, philosophical and medical views of the nature of man.

Marshall J. expressed the fear that the extension mooted by the dissent would have to include the defence of insanity, and he used this as a further example of the stultifying effect that a constitutional principle relating to criminal liability would have on the law. He believed that this would stop experimentation and would hinder attempts to inject into the criminal law principles that could evolve from new discoveries in the field of criminology and, more particularly, the behavioural sciences.

The dissent decided that chronic drunkenness, which has its source in a life-time drinking problem, is a special case that can be taken out of the criminal law, despite the logistical problem of curing the presently incurable alcoholic and despite the lack of facilities even if a cure were in sight. They also decided that this inroad on the Judeo-Christian ethic was a proper one, although free will (or lack of it) in Leroy Powell was not much clearer than in the case of a young man who could say that inadequate parental discipline had resulted in his becoming a bank robber. (Or that life in a Harlem slum with improper food, inadequate housing and the bad influence of evil companions were the factors that led to the offence with which he was charged.) The next logical step would be for the dissent to attack the convictions of those criminals commonly known as psychopaths, or shoplifters who are suffering from personality disorders, or persons who kill their children during post-partum depression or child batterers who injure their children because they are inevitable victims of an iniquitous welfare system.

The final step, perhaps a little Utopian, will be for the court to declare that all the criminal law is aberrational, that it merely attaches stigma to persons who are caught and that the status of "criminal" must be abolished by constitutional fiat.

Punishment and Penology

Sociologists also have a deep interest in prisons and other "total institutions." They have shown that certain underprivileged groups, such as Canadian Indians, are grossly overrepresented in the nation's prisons, that the sentencing practices of our judges exhibit little consistency or rationality, that terms of imprisonment do not deter criminality, that prisons are repressive institutions that breed further crime rather than rehabilitate criminals and teach them law-abiding, industrious and frugal habits.

While lawyers, as humanitarians, may have a serious concern for penal reform, the inadequacies of prison or systems of punishment have no relevance to the definition of a crime or to an assessment of the guilt or innocence of the accused. This state of affairs may seem incredible, but the strict view of the criminal law treats these factors as only relevant at the post-guilt determination state. In *Powell* v. *Texas* Marshall J. used the lack of treatment facilities as an additional reason for denying relief to Powell; the justices of the majority viewpoint, however, would certainly insist that the *ratio decidendi* of the case (that is, the rule for which the decision is authority) concerns the criminal law theory of *mens rea* and not the broader questions of penal policy. And before we condemn the majority decision, let us also remember that Marshall J. expressed his serious misgivings about finding Powell not guilty because of his alcoholism and then compulsorily treating him in an institution that might seem much like a prison to Powell despite the sign *Hospital* or *Treatment Centre* over its portals.

Law students should be familiar with penal theory and the various rationales of punishment. They should know that Beccaria was the founder of the Classical School of criminology on which much of our criminal law is based—that there should be a maximum of certainty in the criminal law and a minimum of judicial discretion, that punishment should be fair and certain. They should also know the work of the positivists (such as Garafolo and Ferri), who were determinists and who believed that social dangerousness and rehabilitation were important criteria.

Similarly, students of the criminal law should not be ignorant of the history of penal methods. They should know that, until one hundred and fifty years ago, hundreds of offences could be punished by ghastly forms of capital punishment (including hanging, drawing and quartering), that branding and other forms of mutilation used to be common and that corporal punishment was abolished in Canada only in the last decade or so. They should read of the pioneering work of John Howard, Elizabeth Fry, Alexander Maconochie, Walter Crofton, Eden and Romilly who tried to alleviate the miserable prison conditions, to reform Draconian criminal laws and to introduce some humanitarian principles into the retributive criminal justice system. Remission of jail sentences for good behaviour, parole, probation, work release, gradual release, weekend jail and psychiatric treatment are some of the ameliorative and rehabilitative methods that have been introduced in the last century and are a legacy of these reformers.

Three theories of punishment are usually mentioned—retribution, deterrence and rehabilitation. Retribution can loosely be described as revenge or the *lex talionis* or Mosaic law—an eye for an eye. Stephen said that criminal law and punishment have the same relationship as sexual appetite has to marriage. He meant that punishment is perfectly legitimate but only permissible when sanctioned by law. Little is heard about retribution nowadays except from those who want to bring back the gallows or the lash. A chaplain to the Metropolitan Toronto Police once argued that murderers of police officers deserve to die, and we should hang them "zestfully." Deterrence is either special or general—that punishment can stop a particular criminal or the world at large from committing further crime. At times of social panic, it is usual to hear that there is too much of crime X, and we should crack down hard, and this will deter others. Unfortunately, studies on deterrence do not prove this argument. The theory of rehabilitation is that we can reform criminals by enlightened penal methods. Once again, the evidence is rather pessimistic of success. Instead we imprison many criminals for long periods on the false promise that we will make them good or train them for the work place. Denunciation is a phrase that is heard frequently now—that the imposition of punishment is an expression of societal disapproval.

Unfortunately, these punishment theories are too frequently stated as if they were mutually exclusive explanations of criminal law and penal policies. Retributivists have argued that man has free will and, therefore, moral responsibility and that society should show its condemnation and take its revenge. Adherents of the deterrent school, steeped in Benthamite utilitarianism, see man as a free agent who chooses between good and evil and who must be taught, by means of punishment, to choose the former. The rehabilitationists, influenced by positive criminology, deny free will and argue that the criminal has no moral responsibility (and therefore *mens rea* is irrelevant) and that society should treat rather than punish the criminal. In recent years, commentators such as Ross of Denmark and Packer of the United States have argued for an integrative philosophy that denies the watertight quality of the categories mentioned above.

Packer sums up his integrated theory of punishment in these words:

1. It is a necessary but not a sufficient condition for punishment that it is designed to prevent the commission of offences.
2. It is a necessary but not a sufficient condition of punishment that the person on whom it is imposed is found to have committed an offence

> under circumstances that permit his conduct to be characterized as blameworthy.

Ross argues that disapproval (or social condemnation) is one, but not the only, legitimate function of punishment; to say this does not necessarily mean that the criminal justice system is being retributive. Disapproval can also fulfil a preventive role because it "is in itself a form of behavioural reaction with a conduct-influencing (preventive) function." Criminal legislation and the moral stigma of punishment can influence societal attitudes. So far, we can see that the old isolated notions of retribution and deterrence are interdependent.

Ross goes on to offer a convincing criticism of the rehabilitative school that denies the validity of condemnation and of general prevention (as well as negating the use of *mens rea* as explained below). Ross says that the anti-punishment school is wrong because of the false assumptions:

> 1. ... that moral disapproval, and punishment as an expression of it, are incompatible with scientific thinking on a deterministic basis.
> 2. ... that moral disapproval, and punishment as an expression of it, are irrelevant once it is assumed that the aim of the penal system is prevention ... arising from the ... confused view that 'prevention' and 'retribution' express alternative aims of punishment.
> 3. ... that it is impossible to formulate and apply a criterion of mental responsibility, an error stemming from exaggerated demands on the knowledge needed to make moral and legal judgements.

As Packer and Ross both point out, a scientific criminological approach to crime and criminals may be valid but the logical basis (as shown above) is not proved, and the state of the science of human behaviour is still far from exact. In such circumstances, the substitution of therapy and indefinite terms of treatment are untrustworthy and dangerous to human liberty.

Packer, Hart and Ross argue in favour of *mens rea* or moral and mental responsibility because they see it as an expression of the principle of legality (or rule of law) and as a human rights guarantee against the State's unlimited right to impose punishment. Later discussion will examine this legal concept of *mens rea* and the forms of human behaviour that the criminal law recognizes as defences to the Crown allegation that the accused is criminally responsible for his act.

The Law Reform Commission of Canada has suggested a much more widespread use of diversion. Of course, in the past, police officers and prosecutors have often exercised their discretion and have not arrested, charged or proceeded to trial where they have decided that a warning is sufficient, that the young suspects will be dealt with by their families or peer groups or that the incident is too trivial or has been satisfactorily adjusted in some informal manner. The new view of diversion encourages the use of non-penal, informal adjustment of antisocial behaviour. The wider use of diversion would, of necessity, institutionalize the process to some extent but this would be avoided as much as possible. Offender and victim would try to reconcile their differences, and restitution of property and reparation of damages would be ordered where appropriate. The offender would avoid the trauma of arrest, time spent in jail awaiting trial and the trial itself. The stigma of a criminal record (which creates disabilities for travel, bonding or employment) would also not occur.

Diversion in the above sense is an extra-legal process and does not involve consideration of the niceties of criminal law theory. Instead, it obviates the problems of the law student who would otherwise have to wrestle with the technicalities of *mens rea* and theories of punishment.

The Relevance of Evidence

Someone may have witnessed a crime or been involved, in some peripheral way, in the perpetration or detection of a crime. That person may be very surprised to attend the trial or to read an account of the case in a law report, because his idea of the "real" facts may differ substantially from the evidence admitted at the trial. The most obvious reason for this factual discrepancy is that the trial judge will not allow criminal responsibility to be proved by facts that are based on hearsay, rumour, hunch or innuendo.

The law of evidence provides the rules for the conduct of trials in our justice system. The trial is conducted in an adversarial manner (compared with the European inquisitorial method) and is sometimes colloquially described as a system of "fair play." This has several facets: (1) the prosecution has the burden of proving, beyond a reasonable doubt, the guilt of the accused; (2) the accused may remain silent and is under no obligation to incriminate himself; (3) it is better that nine guilty men go free than that one innocent man be convicted.

The Canadian Bill of Rights states the concept of fair play and the rules of evidence and procedure more explicitly. An accused's fundamental rights are guaranteed—right to counsel, to confront one's accuser, to apply for bail, to be secure from illegal arrests and searches and to be entitled to a speedy trial. These rights are characterized under the general concept "due process," which also ensures that a suspect cannot be subjected to police interrogations that are overbearing or unfair. Due process ensures that police behaviour adheres to acceptable standards. The law of evidence has strict rules about admissibility. Often facts may seem relevant to the issue that the prosecution wishes to prove, but the judge rules them inadmissible because they would be unfair to the accused or their relevance is out of proportion to their prejudicial qualities (such as the bad character of the accused). Furthermore, the rules of evidence are designed to test the trustworthiness of the data that the prosecution (or the defence) wishes to present to the court (such as hearsay evidence which is second- or third-hand evidence that cannot be tested on cross-examination because the person who originally perceived the data is not present in court).

The criminal law trial is therefore not after the "truth" or "real" facts at any price. The law is interested in ascertaining the truth within narrow guidelines of fact-finding. While some guilty men may go free because they have clever lawyers who create doubts in the mind of the fact-finder, this is a more satisfactory situation than a system where the accused is presumed guilty until he proves the contrary or is convicted because the judge is biassed against him on some irrational, legally irrelevant basis.

In other words, the criminal trial is more interested in proof than truth, although everyone would hope that they could coincide. Therefore, the age-old question asked of lawyers, "How can you defend a person you *know* is guilty?" is quite properly answered by "I don't know he is guilty until he is *proved* to be guilty according to law."

2/An INTRODUCTION to the HISTORY of the CRIMINAL LAW

The Relativity of Crime

We are all so accustomed to the idea of crime that it is difficult to imagine a time when there was no crime. This is not an allusion to a perfect state of man found in some Garden of Eden. Man has always sinned, committed wicked acts or been antisocial—at least as long as there has been a family, tribe, community or society living together to judge his actions. As long as there have been governors and governed, those with power, security and property and those who would deprive them of these privileges, there have been demands for control and coercion to preserve the status quo, and to create rules of definition, enforcement and punishment. There was a time, however, when deviant acts were not described by labels such as murder, arson, rape or theft. The antisocial acts that were considered most serious were not killings or rapes. The community may have become much more upset about the breach of some custom or taboo thought fundamental to its well being. We must also imagine a time when there were no policemen, no prisons and no criminal trials as we know them, when a killing or a rape was dealt with by the law as a strange hybrid of what we call criminal law and tort law. (The latter provides compensation or damages for wrongs performed negligently or carelessly against persons or property to whom we owe some duty of care. The most common example is a civil action between two car-drivers where the plaintiff is claiming damages for the death of a relative, or for injury to the plaintiff or his passengers or for property damage or loss of earnings.)

Although it may have appeared to us to be a typically evasive lawyer's answer, we have already discovered that the only tenable definition of crime is any act that the law so defines as a crime. A little reflection will show that no other definition is possible because the ruler—whether a despot, an elite governing body, a democratic majority, elected representative or a judge—decides what acts will be considered by law to be criminal. We have already seen the relativity of crime in the way in which sins and immoral acts have alternated, being crimes and merely private acts that may not have been approved but were not subject to penalty at the hands of the State.

A look at the Canadian criminal law of 1890 will give us some insight into the values considered by society to be in need of the penal protection of the criminal law. Of course, some of the crimes were peculiarly Canadian because they circumscribed some unlawful behaviour in the forestry and fishing industries and prohibited certain acts that would interfere with the running of the railroad. This is to be expected because a society decides to protect the interests that are considered to be most important. Those interests change as the structure of society changes. For instance, "unlawful drilling" concerned military parades, not oil wells. In 1892, the memory of the 1837 rebellions were still sufficiently vivid that the government did not want dissidents creating private armies. This may seem far-fetched in 1982, and it is impossible to justify the offence's continued existence in the current Code. Similarly, the 1892 Code made it an offence to challenge someone to a duel. Although there had been duels in Canadian colonies until the mid-nineteenth century, the fact that it is still on the statute book of today must be due to government inefficiency or oversight.

Other offences have not changed their definitions in the past eighty years, although their usefulness has lessened. If they once filled a social need, this is no longer the case because prosecutions are rare. The offences of "common nuisance" and "spreading false news" provided a useful method of control over minor troublemakers at a time when society was cohesive and homogeneous but that is no longer true. Common nuisance was and is (in s. 176) defined as the doing of an unlawful act or failure to discharge a legal duty that thereby "endangers the lives, safety, health, property or comfort of the public" or "obstructs the public in the exercise or enjoyment of any right that is common to all subjects." This is only a minor indictable offence, attracting a maximum penalty of two years. It is also a vague offence, and vagueness should always trouble us when found in criminal law.

Burbidge's Digest also cites specific instances of nuisance—by offensive trades, to highways, to bridges, to navigable rivers—but now we have only common nuisance. The specific nuisances are akin to public torts, and they have not disappeared. They are now found in all those regulatory or public welfare offences that control so much of our life. They regulate such everyday concerns as automobiles, health, pollution, education, pure foods and garbage collection.

The Canadian criminal law of 1890 also sought to protect society and perpetuate social values by elaborate provisions to control "loose, idle or disorderly persons" otherwise known as vagrants. The work ethic is well expressed in the definitions of vagrants as being those who:

(a) not having visible means of maintaining themselves, live without employment,
(b) being able to work and thereby or by other means to maintain themselves and families, wilfully refuse or neglect to do so. . . .
(c) without a certificate signed, within six months, by a . . . clergyman . . . or two JPs., residing in the municipality where the alms are being asked, that he or she is a deserving object of charity, wander about and beg, or go about from door to door, or place themselves in any . . . public place to beg or receive alms.

The 1890 laws describe other types of behaviour that come within the definition of "loose, idle or disorderly"—loitering, causing a disturbance, making noise, being drunk or otherwise "impeding or incommoding peaceable passengers," discharging firearms, riotous conduct on the street, "wantonly or maliciously disturb the peace and quiet," breaking windows, defacing signs, being a common prostitute, keeping or being found in a bawdy house and, finally, "having no peaceable profession or calling to maintain themselves by, for the most part support themselves by gaming or crime, or by the avails of prostitution." Most of these provisions were continued in the 1892 Code. They reflect a preoccupation with public order. Indeed, the history of criminal law is very largely a series of reactions to actual or perceived breaches of public order and panic responses to emergencies that threatened private property and social stability. With two exceptions, the behaviour described no longer constitutes vagrancy. Of course, some of those acts are minor offences now found elsewhere in the Code or in municipal by-laws and provincial legislation. The economic form of vagrancy—unemployed, refusing to work, begging or drunkenness—has been removed from the Criminal Code. We may be less entranced with the work ethic, and in addition, we may have decided that there are more appropriate, efficient and non-punitive methods of dealing with drop-outs from the economic system.

The Code today has only two definitions for vagrancy—the person who supports himself by gaming or crime, and a new provision that makes it an offence to be a convicted sex offender found loitering in a school yard or playground. Protection of society is still the rationale, but the theme is crime control rather than the explicit control of the economically underprivileged.

Prostitution has not been entirely removed from the control of the criminal law. There are provisions about bawdy houses. The new s. 195.1 concerns itself with the prostitute soliciting in public. Public attitudes toward prostitution have changed; the law is no longer interested in the act of prostitution (unless it is performed in a common bawdy house). Instead, the concentration is on the exploitation of prostitutes by pimps and others who perpetuate the system. Of course, the criminal justice system may still be misguided in thinking that some indirect control over community mores is better than none.

In a later chapter, we shall see how the criminal law tries to control homosexual and heterosexual behaviour. At this point, the relativity of crime can be exemplified by one section that has remained unchanged for ninety years. Seduction of an unmarried female under twenty-one years of age by a male over that age is an offence if the female is of previously chaste character and the seduction was accompanied by a promise to marry. There has been no prosecution for more than forty years. In many places in Canada, a prosecution would be laughed out of court.

The law's treatment of trade unions is the final article of comparison in this brief survey of the state of the criminal law in the nineteenth and twentieth centuries. A conspiracy in restraint of trade is an agreement between two or more persons to do any unlawful act in restraint of trade. It is an offence that could be committed by a group of merchants who combined to force out a competitor. In the past any combined action by workers to strike or seek better conditions by "going slow" was an offence. This situation had changed, in part, by the time of Burbidge's Digest, which exempted trade unions, in part, from the offence of conspiracy in restraint of trade. The union, however, could be convicted if the members conspired to limit unduly the facilities for transporting, producing or dealing in any article of trade or commerce or to limit unduly or lessen the manufacture or production of any such article or commodity. Guilt could result in a fine of up to $4,000 or two years in prison.

Another provision from the nineteenth century, criminal breach of contract, could be and was used against trade unions who sought to press their claims for better wages and working conditions.

This situation is changed in the present Code. Section 425 provides that no person can be convicted of the offence of conspiracy by reason only that he (a) refuses to work with a workman or for an employer or (b) does any act or causes any act to be done for the purpose of a trade combination.

Similarly, under s. 380 of the Code, which describes criminal breach of contract, a person does not wilfully break a contract merely because he stops work owing to a failure in negotiations on working conditions so long as the laws relating to industrial relations are honoured.

While the criminal law has given more recognition to the rights of the trade unions, the State has been imposing some controls on the entrepreneurs. Anti-combines legislation has tried to control monopolistic and oligopolistic practices. Freedom of contract should be available to all sectors of the economy—within reason.

Consumerism has also sought to control business practices. These measures did not begin with Ralph Nader; Magna Carta in 1215 demanded of the king honest weights and measures. In more recent times, there has been legislation prohibiting or controlling deceptive advertising and unfair lending practices and regulating the quality of foodstuffs.

Sometimes we find that a multinational corporation will be fined a few hundred dollars for some act of corporate fraud, while some unfortunate anonymous citizen will be sent to jail for some small theft from a supermarket.

In the nineteenth century, slavery and the exploitation of child factory workers were not condemned by the law, civil or criminal. At the same time, however, the larceny of an article worth a few shillings was a capital offence, and wealthy men could procure young girls of thirteen from their parents for a small payment. Perhaps these illustrations give some inkling of the relativity of crime and show that its definition depends on political, social and economic mores.

Law and Custom in Primitive Societies

In primitive societies existing at the present time, we find in some instances that the most serious offence in the eyes of the group or the offender's peers is a violation of some taboo. This may be based on sexual, religious or property customs. A man may live in a society where extramarital sexual intercourse is common, or even encouraged, but it may be an outrageous infraction of the society's mores for him to have sexual relations with his wife while she is pregnant or menstruating or for him ever to have such relations with his wife's sister or his niece.

In these sparse introductory remarks, we cannot make a study of legal anthropology, but the comment of Paul Radin, a practitioner in the field, should be noticed:

> ... customs are an integral part of the life of primitive peoples. There is no compulsive submission to them. They are not followed because the weight of tradition overwhelms a man ... a custom is obeyed because it is intimately intertwined with a vast living network of interrelations, arranged in a meticulous and ordered manner.

Problems arise when these customs come into conflict with European values. In Canadian society this is well illustrated by the potlatch of West Coast native peoples that was subjected to disapproval and abolition by government administrators. The seemingly wasteful largesse was viewed by Indian agents as a socially disruptive influence, although it seems remarkably similar to the conspicuous consumption that Veblen noticed in North American society.

In many social groups invasions of property rights often attracted more condemnation than physical injury or death. Even today, in some primitive societies which need to be self-sufficient for food and shelter, the destruction of a hunting weapon or of a digging stick may offer the most serious threat to the members of the group. The flavour of this property taboo is seen in the decision of an enlightened Canadian judge, who has heard cases involving indigenous people such as the Innuit. In a case decided by Judge Sissons in the Northwest Territories, the two accused Innuit had felt compelled to kill an insane woman who was destroying hunting equipment, thus threatening the security of the group. Although they were not acquitted, Judge Sissons, in assessing their criminal responsibility, took into account the customs of the group and imposed a relatively light sentence.

The Influence of Religion

In these so-called primitive societies, religious taboos play what seems to us a disproportionately important role in the life of the community. An unauthorized member of the tribe who invades a holy place or touches a holy object may be more severely ostracized by the community than a man who kills another. Sometimes the revenge or retribution does not come from the tribe but will emanate from supernatural forces. Readers familiar with the Old Testament will remember the story of the man who disobeyed orders and touched the Ark of the Covenant. He was struck down, although he did the forbidden act from the best of motives.

In Anglo-Saxon times, when society was often in a state of anarchy, the Church played an important stabilizing role and indeed was an equal partner in dealing with what we call crime. For instance, the religious system of doing penance for sins applied to many acts that, at various times, have been treated as crimes—homicide, rape, usury, fornication, adultery, perjury, arson, robbery, soothsaying, magic and incest. The more serious the sin, the more likely that the Church would demand public penance with weeping, wailing and the donning of sackcloth and ashes. The sinner was ex-communicated, and this was a close analogue to the idea of outlawry which was the secular method of treating the worst wrongdoers. The ex-communicant was ostracized and deprived of the offices of the Church. The outlaw was cast out of the community and could be killed on sight. Sometimes penance consisted of money payments, similar to the idea of compensation or wergild. Sometimes the penitent who, for instance, had wounded another had to work for the victim until the wounds had healed. The penance was frequently graded according to the seriousness of the offence; premeditated murder could require seven to fifteen years of "severe penance." It is little wonder therefore that the confession became an important ingredient of later medieval trials.

Today's laws relating to the sanctity of marriage, legitimacy, suicide and Sunday trading are illustrations of religious taboos that still have a tenuous hold on the group consciousness. Until the Reformation, and to a lesser extent even as late as the English revolution of the seventeenth century, the Church, as an established organ of society, maintained strong control and even legal jurisdiction over citizens. Of course, the most obvious control was over religious non-conformists who committed acts of blasphemy or heresy. These offences included: (1) statements against God, denying his being or providence, (2) all profane scoffing at the Holy Scripture, (3) terrifying or abusing the People with Impostures in Religion, (4) all open lewdness, (5) seditious words in derogation of the established religion. As late as the eighteenth century, the courts were saying "an offence against religion is an offence against the common law" and "To say that an attempt to subvert the established Religion is not punishable by those Laws upon which it is established, is an Absurdity." These laws and cases are the basis for the secular law that controls pornography and obscenity.

The ecclesiastical courts had jurisdiction over adultery, fornication and other forms of "incontinence" as well as perjury, defamation, drunkenness, disorderly conduct and all human behaviour that intruded on the Church—unseemly behaviour in church, for example. These courts also had total jurisdiction over priests and others in Holy Orders who committed any kind of offence, sacred or secular.

In John Gregory Dunne's *True Confessions,* two brothers, one a priest and the other a detective, made the comment that they were both in the "confessions business." The Church has always used the very effective psychological device of the confession. The medieval Church took an active part in the criminal process by superintending the ascertainment of guilt—*by peine forte et dure,* trial by ordeal and trial by battle (which will be more fully examined).

The Emerging Concept of Crime

A separate law of crime did not actually emerge until after the Norman Conquest. Before the eleventh century there were various acts that were looked upon with disfavour by the community, the tribe or some other social unit, but there was little concept of criminal responsibility as distinct from community responsibility, or civil responsibility leading to a demand for compensation. This does not mean that a miraculous transformation occurred immediately after 1066, although William the Conqueror was an exceptionally competent administrator. The Anglo-Saxon kings ruled parts of the country only and did not achieve central authority. They did, however, formulate crude codes of law that attempted to regulate relationships between subjects and the subject's dealings with the king and his advisors.

Before this stage of sophistication was reached, there were tribes and chieftains with a tenuous control over the members of the community. Redress was often the crudest form of revenge, meted out peremptorily without trial or proof. In the era of the blood feud, the party injured or the kin of the party killed would seek revenge by further killing, by maiming or by seizing goods. The feud was not only limited to a life for a life but was also applied to sexual assaults upon kinswomen, to attacks upon property and to insults to family members.

Feud and Peace

Gradually tribes came to realize that if they wanted to be prepared for attacks by external enemies or if they wanted to create a stable society, feuds were disruptive and wasteful of manpower and resources. The feud was gradually but spasmodically replaced by "composition." By this procedure, the aggrieved parties accepted a fixed tariff of compensation for the loss or damage suffered. The compensation process became a relatively peaceful substitute for the bloody feud. (The modern trial, using the adversary system, could also be seen as a stylized battle.)

At first, the tariff for a wrong, particularly a killing, was no doubt a crude measure. If the tariff, or wergild, were not paid, the kin of the slain person resorted to the self-help of the feud. Further refinements occurred. The slayer was given twelve months to pay the wergild, and his kin were not considered implicated or "responsible" unless they harboured him, thereby acknowledging his misdeed. Compensation varied depending on the rank and power of the injured or deprived party. At this stage of legal development there was no differentiation between what we know as crime or criminal law and tort or civil liability for damage inflicted. All injuries to persons or property were considered as "wrongs." The seriousness of the wrong depended upon the disruption caused to the community or the actual or perceived affront to the injured parties.

Slowly, a distinction emerged between wrongs that were private disputes and required payment to the injured party or his kin and wrongs that had a public quality and required compensation to the whole group. We also find distinctions being drawn between behaviour that could be paid for and behaviour that was so heinous (and therefore unemendable, i.e., could not be compensated with money) that the wrongdoer was no longer considered fit to be a member of the group and was outlawed. No doubt, the first wrong that became unemendable was treason which is the most serious crime in any society. This is not surprising because the crime consists of the overthrow of the constituted authority and in its original form would have been the literal murder of authority, the chief of the tribe.

The Anglo-Saxon community had a concept of "peace" or societal order. The group became concerned only when the peace between the parties was not settled reasonably or in a reasonable time. The group was trying to prevent an unresolved personal quarrel from disturbing the peace of everyone. A wrong became a community concern much more quickly if it had a direct effect on the community at large.

The early English kings started to enforce the "peace" on behalf of the tribes. The gradation of offences according to rank (and, to some extent, according to social harm) is seen in the following:

> The property of God and the Church is to be paid for with a twelvefold compensation: a bishop's property with an elevenfold compensation . . . a deacon's property with a sixfold compensation . . . the peace of the Church with a twofold compensation. . . .
>
> If the King calls his people to him, and anyone does them injury there, he is to pay a twofold compensation and fifty shillings to the King. . . .
>
> The breach of the King's protection, fifty shillings.
>
> The breach of a ceorl's protection, six shillings.
>
> If anyone kills a man, he is to pay as ordinary wergild one hundred shillings. . . .
>
> If hair pulling occur . . . fifty sceattas [equal to two and a half shillings] are to be paid as compensation.

William the Conqueror imposed his will on the whole country and created a central authority. He exploited the notion of the king's "peace"—a term we still use today in "justice of the peace" and "breach of the peace." The king's peace, like so many effective and useful legal concepts, was essentially a fiction and initially a semantic device. The king alleged (or perhaps pretended) that the disturbances caused by the "wrong," and its repercussions, were an affront to the peace of the king and therefore disruptive of communal harmony. As the ruler, he had a right (or perhaps a duty) to minimize friction among his subjects and to maximize the peaceful conduct of the affairs of the kingdom.

The sovereign realized that royal interference in the composition process and in supervising the resolution of disputes over wrongs had three salutary effects. First, it accelerated the process of centralizing power, an essential aim of a ruler who wished to impose his will on the recalcitrant tribes of England and to keep control over the powerful, ambitious and potentially rebellious Norman nobles who had been granted large fiefs by their king.

Second, royal justice not only contributed to stability but also could be used to fill the royal coffers. The populace was encouraged to apply to the Royal Court for justice because the king dispensed a fairer form of justice than did the local nobles. The king provided this service by means of itinerant judges as well as the court at Westminster and in return extracted fees and compensations for the harm done to society or supposedly done in disturbing the king's peace. In due course, the forfeiture of property by those who had committed serious wrongs became another form of revenue and control.

Starting with the Norman kings of England, the community was required to "combined themselves in associations of ten" so that they could be held fiscally responsible for the "good behaviour of the rest." Eventually this frankpledge system (which was a combination of modern concepts of bail, probation and insurance) became too unwieldy. When the king seized the lands and goods of felons, that made sense under a feudal system where the king had granted tenure in land in the first place. These two systems of raising revenue and maintaining order could be called fines and forfeitures.

The third effect, though slower to evolve, proved most important in the long run: the king's central authority would receive its greatest impetus if royal justice replaced tribal justice, communal justice or justice in manorial courts. To obtain a monopoly over the administration of justice, the king had to ensure that he could offer faster, more certain and fairer justice than his competitors. In this he was successful and the stability of British society is evidence of his success. The king had to tread a fine line between ensuring royal supremacy and curtailing his natural ambition to be too autocratic. The problems encountered by King John in 1215, and his reluctant signing of Magna Carta, show that the nobles were not prepared to forfeit all their powers and privileges to the king's court.

Legal history cannot provide us with a precise date at which crime and tort became separate legal concepts. For a time, composition and feud co-existed in varying degrees. Royal justice and private justice overlapped; royal retribution and private feud lived side by side. Eventually two jurisdictions developed, one for wrongs that were deemed "public" (or crimes) and one for wrongs that were deemed "private" (or torts). Even today there is some overlap between criminal and civil justice; assault, trespass and libel are both crimes and torts.

When wrongs between private citizens became subject to litigation in constituted courts, the remedies sought were usually pecuniary damages payable to the successful aggrieved party. In contrast to these private actions were actions of a more public nature requiring intervention by the king or the State as a form of collective condemnation of the wrong allegedly done. The separation between crime and tort is always somewhat arbitrary and is subject to public opinion, current mores, the character and disposition of the victim, the nature of the trial process and the penalties that could be imposed.

Slowly, crime and tort developed differing forms and standards of behaviour that would attract liability. The criminal law concept of responsibility (incorporating *mens rea,* the guilt mind, intention, recklessness or advertence) became distinct from the standard of tortious liability (which eventually was based on negligence and inadvertence).

All criminal acts can lead to the victim suing the offender in tort for damages for any behaviour that led to harm to property or person. In many modern states victims of crime can obtain some compensation for injuries caused by criminals. The victims are paid from government funds. In addition, a sentencing judge has always had the power to order an offender to make some restitution to the victim.

The Evolution of Criminal Responsibility

Human beings have always differentiated acts that are intentional from those that are accidental. Gradations of responsibility are obvious in the Mosaic law:

> Whoever strikes another man and kills him shall be put to death.
>
> But if he did not act with intent, but they met by act of God, the slayer may flee to a place which I shall appoint for you. But if a man has the presumption to kill another by treachery, you shall take him even from my altar to be put to death. . . .
>
> When men quarrel and one hits another with a stone or with a spade, and the man is not killed but takes to his bed; if he recovers so as to walk outside with a stick, then the one who struck him has no liability, except that he shall pay for loss of time and shall see that he is cured. . . .
>
> When an ox gores a man or a woman to death, the ox shall be stoned, and its flesh may not be eaten; the owner of the ox shall be free from liability. If, however, the ox has for some time past been a vicious animal, and the owner has been duly warned but has not kept it under control, and the ox kills a man or a

> woman, then the ox shall be stoned, and the owner shall be put to death as well. . . .
>
> If a burglar is caught in the act and is fatally injured, it is not murder; but if he breaks in after sunrise and is fatally injured, then it is murder. . . .
>
> You shall not deprive the poor man of justice in his suit. Avoid all lies, and do not cause the death of the innocent and the guiltless; for I the Lord will never acquit the guilty.

The second paragraph quoted above introduces the concept of "treachery" which became an important element in grading wrongs in early English law. Wrongs, particularly killing and theft, that were done by stealth, by lying in wait or by means of a preconceived plan have always been dealt with in a more severe fashion. In a small self-contained society where everyone knew everybody else's business, and social stability depended on nipping in the bud any wrongdoing, then secret wrongdoing had a very unstabilizing effect. A wrong done openly was more forgiveable or more easily dealt with than having a mysterious and anonymous wrongdoer in the group.

The concept of the "peace" also contributed to the gradation of wrongs, although in this instance royal discretion was the deciding factor. For example, should anyone fight or draw weapons in the king's hall it was for the king to decide whether he should be put to death or permitted to live. We have already seen that the tenth century graded wrongdoing according to the status of the victim. A lord was worth more (in wergild) than a peasant. Abducting a female was probably only a wrong if she was an heiress.

In literally laying down the law, the king (or his councillors) were recognizing some crude conception of moral blameworthiness. Laws of the same period include the following provision:

> Let the man who slayeth another wilfully perish by death. Let him who slayeth another of necessity or unwillingly or unartfully . . . and for whom he has not lain in wait, be worthy of his life, and of lawful *bot*, if he seek an asylum. If, however, anyone presumptuously and wilfully slay his neighbour through guile, pluck thou him from my altar, to the end that he may perish by death.

This passage shows a clear distinction between intentional and other forms of killing. It allowed a defence of self-defence or accident but only when the slayer had protected himself by seeking asylum in a sanctuary. In due course, the person who killed by accident or in self-defence would not be found liable but must seek the king's pardon. Even today these categories are found in the law of homicide where some killings are justifiable and others excusable. The former were automatically lacking in responsibility (e.g., killing a thief found stealing by night) while the latter required a royal intervention to satisfy the king that the case was one of legitimate self-defence or killing merely in the heat of the moment. In this way, the royal court maintained control over law and order.

If the criminal law originated from the blood-feud-vengeance relationship and the subsequent royal preoccupation with "peace" and authority, it is natural that the criminal law concerned itself with those wrongs that were highly provocative and disruptive. The most provocative injuries were usually those that were intentional. In addition, human vengeance tends to seek a perpetrator who has exhibited evil design or fault rather than one who is innocent or merely foolish. The influence of the Church and its preoccupation with sin also accentuated the blameworthiness factor in wrongdoing.

Today, students of the criminal law devote much of their time to an analysis of *mens rea* and *actus reus* and of judicial interpretations of these elements of the criminal law in relation to the alleged behaviour of the accused. In examining the history of the criminal law, it is too easy to believe that the criminal trial of the fifteenth or sixteenth century was preoccupied with long discussions of *mens rea* and learned analyses of criminal law. Nothing could be farther from the truth. Trials were summary affairs and proof of guilt was not determined by a full airing of the facts. The presumption of innocence by the prisoner was unknown. Instead, the burden of proof seemed to have been on the prisoner rather than on the prosecution. The community had a hunch who did the crime and the "trial" consisted mostly of making the prisoner confess by the process of *peine forte et dure*. He had no lawyer and could not furnish his own witnesses. The gradations of guilt or responsibility seem to have been decided at what would be called, in civil suits, the pleadings stage. Furthermore the literature of the law was extremely sparse. There were a few commentaries on the law but these were usually little more than digests of cases. (In the case of the great commentator Coke, we do not so much have a digest of cases but Coke's views on what law should be.) The reports of cases contained recitals of facts and more or less accurate regurgitations of the trial judge's charge to the jury. Review of cases by appeal tribunals was almost unknown and therefore very little jurisprudence of the criminal law was developed. The authoritative books from the sixteenth to the eighteenth centuries consisted of terse statements of principles culled from the reports of trials that contained a few facts and even less law.

Clemency in a Rigid System

The law was a formal and rigid system. Clemency was injected into the process by procedural devices. Royal pardons provided the first precedents (using that term loosely) for excusing an accused from criminal responsibility or punishment, but this was an extra-judicial remedy.

Throughout the history of the criminal law, there has always been a tendency for the law to advertise more than it delivered. The law was very harsh on paper but was never as Draconian in practice. The law threatened, but often applied clemency; this started with the royal prerogative of mercy, and now we have parole.

Originally the benefit of clergy was used as a means of preserving the jurisdiction of the Church over priests who committed crimes. The privilege was extended to members of the laity who were first offenders. The clergy were still subject to the jurisdiction of the ecclesiastical courts, but lay persons who pleaded their "clergy" escaped punishment. If a person charged with a crime was not in Holy Orders but would recite the "neck verse" ("Miserere mei, Deus"), then he was freed after being branded on the thumb, so he could only claim this benefit once. The benefit of clergy existed as a form of clemency until 1827. Some serious offences were not clergyable; the list of such offences varied over the centuries, reflecting society's desire to protect itself from this evil or that.

When guilt was tried by such religiously based methods as trial by ordeal, the law could affect the likelihood of the prisoner being convicted by varying the stringency of the ordeal and thus injecting some clemency into the system. When ordeal was replaced by trial by jury, the legal system was still rigid and harsh, but clemency was achieved by legal fictions that allowed the letter of the law to remain intact, although its spirit was modified. For instance, at a time when legal formalism was crucially important, the accused who had aroused some sympathy might be acquitted because there was a flaw in the indictment. For instance, a jury was instructed to acquit when the charge alleged that the accused had hit the victim with an axe, cutting open the head, but the indictment did not state that the victim died. Sometimes juries were encouraged to make improbable findings of fact. A common example was the drastic deflation of the value of goods stolen in order to reduce a larceny from a capital offence to a misdemeanour.

Although juries were not independent and impartial until the eighteenth century (as a result of the landmark decision in *Bushell*), recent research shows that the good sense and compassion of the jury sometimes provided a system of "criminal equity." If the jury were sympathetic, excuses were provided for the accused, although these decisions did not readily become part of the jurisprudence of criminal law. The formalism of the criminal trial continued to be dominant, and of course, isolated jury verdicts were hardly precedents for future cases.

The intellectual apparatus of the criminal law remained essentially unchanged until the methods of proof were changed. The jury became a truly impartial fact-finding body when the accused was allowed to testify on his own behalf and to have counsel to conduct his own defence. Some of these reforms did not emerge until the end of the nineteenth century.

Some History of Criminal Responsibility

When feud and composition were discussed in the early history of crime and tort, we noticed that from the earliest times, human beings asked to judge the behaviour of their neighbours have always differentiated between acts that were intentional or accidental and have created degrees of heinousness. The influence of the Judeo-Christian ethic of free will was also noted. Now the history of liability will be further traced through the crime of murder (and other forms of unlawful homicide). The mental element of every crime is different and what can be said about the *mens rea* of murder is not necessarily true of the *mentes reae* of rape, theft or arson. Murder is chosen because it has had most attention from the courts and the law-writers.

Until the nineteenth century, the law of murder was very simple. Murder was defined as a killing of another human being done with malice aforethought. All other killings were manslaughter or not criminal at all. That was almost the sum of the knowledge on the law of the mental element of murder. The law seemed to be saying "We all know murder when we see it. Sometimes we might be dissuaded from that view, but we shall have to be persuaded." Murder comes from *murdrum* which meant the money "fine" imposed on a community for a non-accidental death in its environs. Later it meant the worst form of unlawful death—a secret, uncompensatable killing. From the time of Bracton, in the thirteenth century, to the end of the nineteenth, the law of homicide did not develop clearly enunciated principles. Bracton, one of the first important commentators on the law, divided killings into (1) homicide *ex justitia,* for example, the lawful sentence of the court or the killing of an outlaw; (2) homicide *ex necessitate* or *se defendendo,* for example, a justifiable killing, either inevitable out of necessity or in defence of one's house from a housebreaker or trespasser; and (3) homicide *per infortunium,* an excusable killing occurring through misadventure. Bracton offered no definition of murder, only of exceptions to the law of murder. This implies that all other wrongful killings were murder, and the second and third categories were notionally treated as murder punishable by death, until the king's pardon was obtained. In this way, royal authority hoped to maintain close control over violence in the realm. This system proved too cumbersome and the Statute of Gloucester (1278) laid down that no writ (to initiate the "criminal" action against the accused) should issue from that writ-factory, the Chancery, if a person killed by misadventure or in self-defence. If such a person had been arrested and was in jail, the king would pardon him after the grand jury found that the death occurred through accident or in self-defence. The jury was obliged to find that the prisoner had acted in self-defence and not "of malice aforethought." In the time of Henry VIII, killings done with malice aforethought were not only unpardonable but also could not be subject to benefit of clergy.

That phrase "malice aforethought" (or sometimes rendered in Law French as *malice prepense*) has proved a mischievous one. Lawyers have always treated it as a shorthand, but its inherent vagueness has allowed it to be very flexible so that in times of social panics, the crime of murder has been expanded without giving much thought to the fact that malice aforethought meant premeditation or a killing done by lying-in-wait (or ambush). For instance, in 1604, the Statute of Stabbing was enacted because there was too much killing by "inhuman and wicked persons in the time of their rage, drunkenness, hidden displeasure, or other passion of mind." This law-and-order statute decreed that if two persons fight and one dies, it would be treated as if done with malice aforethought. The courts soon discovered that the law was too wide and ignored it by announcing that it really made no change in the common law, which of course was a bare-faced lie, but done to prevent injustice. At other times, the courts wanted to extend the law of murder, and they achieved this by a legal fiction—implied or constructive malice. The great English jurist Coke created categories of murder that have haunted us for more than three hundred years. In Coke's time, the law of homicide was:

1. Petit treason—killing of husband by wife, master by servant and bishop by priest. This was really only murder despite its name but the penalties were sometimes more stringent.
2. Felonious Homicide—which should be further subdivided into (a) with malice aforethought, express or implied, i.e., not clergyable and was murder—also included was suicide, although the only punishment that could be imposed was refusal to bury the criminal in hallowed ground; and (b) without malice aforethought i.e., manslaughter which was clergyable.
3. Non-felonious Homicide—in self-defence in a quarrel or by accident while doing an unlawful act. The actor had to seek a pardon that was usually forthcoming, but his goods were forfeited to the king.
4. Justifiable Homicide—in advancement of justice or self-defence against a robber or burglar. These were completely lacking in any kind of liability.

The gradations of liability were clearly seen, with two exceptions—the meaning of "implied malice" and the significance of "unlawful act." Coke gave some illustrations. If a man were hunting on his own property and shot at a deer and hit and killed a person hidden in a bush, this was a mere accident. If a man were out hunting and shot at a wild pheasant and missed and killed someone hidden in the bushes, this would also be an accident because it was not unlawful to shoot at a wild pheasant. But if he had shot at a domestic fowl, intending to kill it and instead killed a person similarly hidden, that would be murder because the original act was unlawful and the law implied malice. This was a very far-ranging extension of murder and much broader than implied malice or intent arising from the status of the victim (e.g., the death of a constable in the course of duty) or from the situation of the person killing. ("If A assaults B to rob him, and in resisting, A killeth B, this is murder by malice implied.")

A later commentator, Hawkins, described malice as a "formed design of doing mischief" which showed the heart to be "pervertly wicked." Murder could also be committed indirectly by implied malice where the accused was "wilfully and deliberately doing a thing which apparently endangers another's life." The "thing" was sometimes not "apparently" dangerous but merely a felony that, in the eighteenth and nineteenth centuries, could be almost any serious crime and by no means limited to an inherently violent act. Hawkins was therefore putting forward the felony-murder rule under the head of implied malice, and as we shall see later, this remains a matter of controversy.

The essence of constructive crime is that the law is more interested in the consequences of the accused's acts rather than in his actual intentions. If a death has occurred and the accused was doing something wrong, although it was only remotely connected with the death, then the law would still call it murder (or culpable homicide). The law was presuming *mens rea* in an attempt to place stringent controls on wrongdoing. This seems to make nonsense of the idea of free will or consciously chosen wrongdoing which the law preferred to take as its ethical basis. The law of murder was a crude and ineffectual attempt to impose law and order.

For a century after Hawkins wrote his treatise, other authorities on the criminal law described the law of murder in very similar terms. There was no great learning in the criminal law, and lawyers and judges did not give careful thought to formulating general principles. The treatises were usually only digests of the trials that were reported very cryptically. The law of crime was not seriously discussed, and there were hardly any appeals in criminal cases that would build up a jurisprudence on the law of homicide.

The reformers of the nineteenth century wanted to clear away this legal bric-a-brac and make sense and order out of the legal accretions of seven hundred years. They wanted to have a criminal law that proportioned the punishment to the seriousness of the harm done to society by the crime and wanted to define crime so that the *actual* intention of the accused was taken into account. The first half of the nineteenth century was preoccupied with reducing the number of capital offences. Bentham inspired the codification of the law in the second half. Edward Livingston, in the United States, was the first codifier. He was very critical of the common law and the scores of criminal statutes that prescribed the death penalty for small larcenies and many other offences that contained very little or no threat to life. He considered that "the English nation have submitted to the legislation of its courts, and seen their fellow subjects hanged for constructive felonies . . . with a patience that would be astonishing, even if their written laws had sanctioned the butchery." His definitions of homicide tried to limit criminal liability to behaviour that the accused intended. Has Livingston solved the problem and excluded Coke's oppressively broad test of liability when his code stated "If the act which caused the death had no connexion with the injury intended to be offered or committed, it does not come within the definition"? "Connexion" is a rather vague term and the Crown could easily argue that the killing of the victim was connected with the attempt to shoot and steal the fowl.

The most imaginative code was drafted by T.B. Macaulay, who is best remembered today as an historian. His code for India defined murder as including acts done with intent to cause death, to cause "such bodily injury as the offender knows to be likely to cause death," or if the person "knows that it is so imminently dangerous that it must in all probability cause death." All of these definitions looked to the intention of the accused and tried to minimize the constructive approach to homicide. Macaulay said in explanation of his code: ". . . to punish a man whose negligence has produced some evil which he never contemplated as if he had produced the same evil knowingly and with deliberate malice, is a course which . . . no jurist has ever recommended in theory, and which we are confident that no society would tolerate in practice." The commissions of enquiry that examined the law of England agreed, but their recommendations were not heeded. Instead, the task of preparing laws fell to J.F. Stephen who drafted a liberal homicide bill in 1872, but it was ignored. He then drafted the Draft Code of 1879 which became the basis for the Canadian Criminal Code. Stephen wanted accuracy in language and wanted the elements of every crime to be "so worded as to denote by the mere literal sense of the words every action intended to be punished, and no other." Unfortunately Stephen also believed that morality was an indispensable ingredient of the criminal law which should be in "general correspondence with the moral sentiments of the nation." As a result we have such provisions in the Canadian Criminal Code as s. 212(c) which makes it murder "where a person for an unlawful object does anything that he . . . *ought to know* is likely to cause death . . . *notwithstanding that he desires* to effect his object without causing death or bodily harm to any human being." The italicized words are morality-laden and give the courts the opportunity to convict a person when he never intended to kill or never foresaw the likelihood of death or harm. This section is still law, although it was passed at a time when the accused was not able to give sworn evidence on his own behalf. Therefore, it made less sense to have a test of criminal liability that was based on the accused's intention or foresight. Furthermore, the nineteenth century was a time when there was much less attention paid to the presumption of innocence and the burden of proof being on the prosecution. At that time, the definition of murder seemed to presume that every killing was murder until the accused showed that it was done in self-defence, under provocation or by accident. There was in fact a presumption of guilt, and this would have been aggravated at a time when the accused could not give sworn evidence, was often not represented by counsel and the juries were relatively uneducated (at least on today's standards). Trials were not the exhaustive affairs that we know today when the adversary system is truly tested.

The crime of murder is a peculiar one. Human life is sacred and therefore the unnatural and involuntary ending of a life tends to attract emotional rather than rational responses from the public and the law. This is particularly so when the death penalty applies to murder; capital punishment can lead to blind retribution and the distortion of the legal rules to obtain convictions. The use of a legal fiction, constructive crime, has been the device to effect this policy. We have already seen that the trend in general criminal law policy has been to de-emphasize the moral ingredient of the criminal law. This at least is true in the delineation of the substance of criminal offences so that merely "immoral" behaviour should not necessarily be crimes. When we are speaking of making moral decisions about whether the accused's behaviour should attract criminal liability for murder, the moral ingredient is a different matter. If a death occurs in circumstances that are peripherally criminal, then it is often easy for human beings to make value judgements and say the accused "ought to" have known that his behaviour could result in the actual fatal consequences.

Some Further History of the Criminal Law

The English legal historian Milsom has written an excellent general history of the law and yet only devotes one short chapter to the history of the criminal law. He describes the history of the subject as "miserable," and unfortunately, this seems a just description. Criminal laws and statutes did not attract the attention of the best legal minds (either as legislative drafters or as counsel). Panic was often the major ingredient in formulating new laws that were hurriedly passed to prevent (or try to prevent) some currently urgent social problem. Similarly, the rise of mercantilism resulted in the creation of many new property offences. The conceptual straitjacket of the old offences of larceny and burglary proved incapable of protecting merchants against dishonest servants and carriers. The use of commercial documents to facilitate commercial transactions also allowed or invited fraud which did not come within traditional definitions. The history of the criminal law up to 1820 was the history of a search for order and stability and, quite frequently, repression that resulted in patchwork legislation and increasingly severe penalties. This is well expressed by Douglas Hay in *Albion's Fatal Tree*:

> . . . the law did not enforce uniform obedience, did not seek total control; indeed it sacrificed punishment when necessary to preserve the belief in justice. The courts dealt in terror, pain and death, but also in moral ideals, control of arbitrary power, mercy for the weak. . . . the gentleman accepting an apology from the man in his power, the thief or the rioter, would have been gratified to know that the contrition was absolute, from the soul. But provided that the act of contrition was public and convincing, that it served to sustain general belief in the justice of the social order, it sufficed.

Most of the work of the criminal courts was handled by amateur justices. The books from which they learned their law were mere catalogues of offences and punishments. Little thought was given to the intellectual content of the criminal law or of the underlying social philosophy that should have guided our legislators and judges.

Most histories of the criminal law also tend to be catalogues of offences that devote most of their pages to a dismal history of the punishments that were imposed. Descriptions of crimes other than murder show, in the early stages, a preoccupation with severe punishments for crimes against property committed by stealth or by invasion of that sanctum sanctorum, the English home; that is, larceny and burglary. In later stages, the criminal law was extended to protect the dominant sectors of society. For instance, in addition to the proliferation of "religious" offences, the seventeenth century also saw a great expansion of treason and similar offences against the established public order.

In the early nineteenth century, the influence of Bentham and philosophical radicalism initiated an era of remarkable reform. At the political level, of course, the passage of the 1832 Reform Act enfranchised many more English males (with a much increased suffrage in 1867, but the females had to wait until the twentieth century). Influential men such as Brougham and Romilly started on wholesale law reform. The latter was partly responsible for reducing the numbers of offences that could be punished by death, which numbered more than one hundred. The reform of punishment, inspired by Beccaria, had to take precedence over the reform of procedure and the definitional parts of the criminal law. Bentham was also responsible for advocating the reform of the law. He detested the common law with all its uncertainties and wanted it replaced by codification where the law was certain. He viewed the common law as a "fathomless and boundless chaos made up of fictions, tautology and inconsistency." He believed that the law should be rational and intelligible to the general populace. He was not successful in his own attempts to draft whole codes of law for the United States or Russia, but his disciples were luckier. Livingston drafted a code for Louisiana, and his efforts had great influence in the United States. Thomas Babington Macaulay drafted a code for India and simplified the law. Canada was an heir to this crusade for codification because its Code of 1892 was adapted from the English Draft Code which had been drafted by James Fitzjames Stephen, whom we have previously mentioned. Unfortunately, it was an incomplete code because it did not pay sufficient attention to general principles (some of which are found in Part I, s. 3-45) of the law. In addition, the Canadian judges have not devoted their energies to interpreting the Canadian Criminal Code as a cohesive body of law. Instead, they have usually resorted to common law principles to apply to Canadian criminal law. Perhaps practitioners and judges brought up in the common law tradition are incapable, by training and instinct, of construing a code of law. Instead, the judges, even those of the Supreme Court of Canada, have had a cultural cringe resulting in the citation and use of English case precedents to the neglect of Canadian cases and authorities. A good argument could be made for abolishing the use of precedents in all criminal cases because the words of the Code should be interpreted with the predicament of *this* accused only in mind. The case law system of *stare decisis* (or precedent) is too embedded for that to happen; instead, the particular circumstances of the accused's case are often only taken into account at the sentencing stage. The Canadian Criminal Code is only a partial code; all offences (descriptions of criminal behaviour) are included in the Code, but s. 7(3) provides that the common law may be resorted to for any defence. Until this is remedied, the courts will continue to seek instruction in the sources of the common law.

Punishment

The above description of homicide shows that for many centuries a killing was either murder, and automatically punishable by death, or was excusable or justifiable and was pardoned. We have also seen that the automatic punishment of death for murder tended to distort the interpretation of the law.

Punishment for arson, robbery, burglary or larceny (if of a sufficient amount) was also nominally death. Punishment for lesser offences was not usually imprisonment. It could range from banishment through corporal punishments such as whipping, mutilation, the pillory and the stocks, to the imposition of large and small fines.

In medieval society, an enemy of the State was more likely to be exiled permanently than executed. Imprisonment was usually only used as a means of temporary disposal of the king's enemies, or as a place of safekeeping for those few who could not be trusted to remain in the community while they were awaiting trial.

The use of banishment or the stocks shows the real nature of punishment in the medieval period. These penal measures reflected communal disapproval of the offender who had transgressed the social mores to such an extent that collective social condemnation was necessary. Private tort action would have been ineffective or would have led to greater disruptions. Mutilation, branding and the stocks were also useful ways of identifying offenders and recidivists. These punishments gave notice to the community at large of the wrongdoing of the accused who could easily be identified in the days before criminal records were kept.

In the transition from the medieval world to the more complicated world of Tudor times, the State became unable to handle social unrest with communal punishments. Capital offences started to proliferate and accelerated in the eighteenth century. The courts, juries and the executive found it difficult to apply the letter of these laws. Many of those sentenced to death had their sentences remitted and were transported to the American, African or Australian colonies. Ironically, the use of the prison only became the common form of punishment because the reformers succeeded in curtailing the number of capital offences and because the colonies refused to accept any more transported convicts. The irony is that the prison was meant to be more humane than the earlier forms of punishment. Prisons really started in Pennsylvania because the Quakers saw it as a vast improvement on capital punishment. Prisoners would become penitent and would be redeemed from their wrongful ways. The prison would eliminate crime because the criminal would be reformed and rehabilitated. The reformers of the nineteenth century spent far too much time squabbling among themselves as to whether the criminal was more likely to be reformed by the Separate Pennsylvania System or the Silent Auburn System. The reformers had no doubt as to their ultimate success—whether they believed the prisoner would be rehabilitated by contemplating his sins in the solitude of his own cell or by congregating with fellow prisoners but forbidden to communicate with them. The prison system has been a failure. We are now convinced that most prisoners are not reformed by incarceration. We also know that there is a small percentage of prisoners who are dangerous and should be kept out of public circulation for the safety of society. Unfortunately, we have some difficulty in identifying that small percentage of intractable criminals.

Prison reformers had been inspired by the *philosophes* of the Enlightenment. In particular, Beccaria's treatise on crimes and punishments had argued for certain rather than merely harsh penalties and had also criticized the wide discretion that resided in the judiciary and the administrators of the criminal justice system. His work also contained the seeds of what we now call the principle of legality or the rudiments of due process—no retroactive crimes; fixed penalties for offences that are clearly defined; the right to a speedy and fair trial, which would be the right to confront one's accuser, to prepare a defence, to be represented by counsel and to be presumed innocent until found otherwise. The law-and-order lobby is still critical of the legacy of Beccaria. The criminal is acquitted because of the procedural niceties. They want to restore police and judicial discretion. They want to restore the death penalty. They want prison to be a place of great hardship.

The Continuing Relationship of Tort and Crime

By the sixteenth century, the categories of crime had become established in a mould that still exists today—at least in relation to serious crime. If we read the statutes and commentaries of that period, we find that treason, murder, rape, arson, robbery and theft were the most stringently condemned acts. They were condemned because they threatened the internal security of the group; treason and murder most obviously of all.

This group solidarity was not developed overnight. In any emerging society, there is a period when the struggle for power is constantly at odds with the average citizen's thirst for peace and security. A successful "traitor," of course, becomes the new leader. The man who murders a person in power similarly takes over the authority and the property of the victim and, if the victim is sufficiently powerful or wealthy, the murderer may also become the dominant member of the group. The other serious crimes listed above may not have had such a decisive effect on the community. They gained prominence, however, because they also threatened various forms of property rights that had become increasingly important as a result of the rise of a bourgeoisie in industrial and mercantile society. In the simpler agricultural communities, the peasants in a feudal or post-feudal society were not particularly concerned with property because they had nothing but the most rudimentary belongings. The earlier agricultural community was more concerned with the maintenance of order.

The historical sketch given above shows how private vengeance in the form of blood feuds between aggrieved parties (or their survivors) slowly evolved into the concepts of crime and tort. Today we know that there are clear categories of law and obvious remedies when those laws are breached. If a citizen drives his automobile in a negligent fashion and causes damage to another automobile or to its occupants, those suffering damage to property or person sue in civil court and, if successful, recover a sum of money as damages. This is an attempt by the law to compensate the injured party. Some damages, such as automobile repair, medical expenses or loss of wages, can be computed. Obviously, money is not a true recompense for a broken or severed limb, for "pain and suffering," impaired health, shortened life expectancy or loss of prospective income, but it is a symbolic accommodation for the real loss. Other forms of damage, such as nervous shock or the loss of the services and affection of a wife or mother, cannot be measured with any accuracy. Some successful tort actions do not result in money damages. A court may issue an injunction against a defendant to desist from injurious or annoying acts. For instance, a factory may be required to stop its chimney polluting the air. A court might forbid a slaughterhouse to be built in a residential area or may stop a rock band from practising at three in the morning.

The traditional criminal action is an attempt to stop an offender from continuing acts that are contrary to the criminal law. In most instances, however, this is only a secondary aim. The first task of the criminal law is to punish the offender for an act he has already committed. The idea of compensation is only ancillary. The purposes of punishment are retribution (as an embodiment of societal condemnation or revenge), deterrence (either of a general variety that will stop others from following the offender's example or special deterrence that should ensure that the offender does not repeat his offence) and rehabilitation (in the hope that treatment will reform the criminal).

In recent years, there has been something of a renewal of the ancient interrelationship between tort and crime. For instance, some governments have established compensation boards that provide government funds to pay the expenses of victims of crime, particularly where the injury has been physical and medical expenses and loss of employment have resulted. In other instances, society has discovered that some acts, previously treated as torts, have such serious consequences that they cannot be adequately dealt with as private law suits. The barrier between the public and private sectors has become blurred. Furthermore, government has played an increasing role in controlling society. In some instances society has become so complicated that a *laissez-faire* policy by the law no longer can be tolerated. The most obvious example is air and water pollution. Fishermen, whose livelihood is threatened by a pulp mill that allows effluent to pollute a lake or river, can sue in tort for loss of income. Acid rain is causing similar problems. The elected representatives of the State, representing present and future generations, have decided, however, that private initiative is sometimes not enough. The fishermen may not pursue a tort claim because of inertia or lack of funds, and the State wants to deter pollution in any event. Therefore, a prosecution is brought against the polluter. The penalty is not corporal or capital punishment but a substantial fine that may be imposed for every infraction, or an injunction to prevent future operation of the mill until the pollution is stopped. Such an action is sometimes called quasi-criminal law—the act of air pollution does not fall within the categories of classical crimes (such as murder or theft) and is more in the nature of a public tort. The fine is some compensation to the State for the expense it will incur in remedying the damage done by water pollution. One is reminded of the earlier time when the king started interfering in the composition process and demanded that the wrongdoer not only pay compensation to the victim or his kin but also suffer a royal pecuniary penalty for the disturbance of the king's peace.

Sometimes the damage done by a corporation or individual cannot be measured in dollars and cents. Indeed the very existence of any "damage" may depend upon a particular political philosophy as to the ideal nature of a society. These attempts to penalize offenders against the norms of society provide some of the most interesting problems in quasi-criminal law or public torts. In the United States there have been many administrative offences of this kind since the New Deal. There are armies of civil servants in numerous administrative agencies in Washington laying down policy, investigating complaints and prosecuting alleged offenders. Many of these administrative offences are based on an application of economic philosophy that is meant to be a compromise somewhere between a *laissez-faire* viewpoint and a totally planned economy. For instance, the anti-trust, price-fixing or unfair competition laws attempt to regulate the economy, to stimulate competition in a free enterprise system or to impose a socialistic dictatorship on honest businessmen, depending on one's point of view. In a famous case in the United States, the Department of Justice was able to prove that some of the largest electrical corporations in the United States had conspired (or agreed) to take the competition out of bidding on defence contracts by taking turns, in effect, at submitting the lowest bid. The government had been cheated out of millions of dollars because of these unfair tendering practices. The corporations were forced to pay monetary penalties for their dishonesty. They were also forced to pay treble damages to the innocent corporations that had submitted honest, and unsuccessful, bids on contracts. The most striking outcome of the "G.E. conspiracy cases" was the prosecution and jailing of some senior executives of the offending corporations. These men, pillars of their communities, were hardly stereotype criminals. They were, nevertheless, fined thousands of dollars and jailed for periods of up to three months. Society was showing its disapproval of unethical business practices, and the G.E. case was a notorious instance of corporate dishonesty. Three months' imprisonment is a remarkably mild indication of communal disapproval when compared with the much longer sentences imposed for minor thefts and assaults committed by persons who do not happen to be business executives. (Canada has had a similar experience with the Hamilton dredging trials.)

Many cases are not so obvious and reflect a more hairsplitting construction of economic philosophy. When has a corporation employed tactics that have unfairly lessened competition? When does a corporation have a dangerously large (or monopolistic or oligopolistic) share of the market? Is the newspaper industry different from, and more in need of, legal controls than, say, the manufacturer of shoes? When is a share prospectus misleading to an illegal degree? Is connivance or mere neglect evidence of a conspiracy to fix prices or drive out competition in an unfair manner? When is advertising so misleading as to be actionable under quasi-criminal law? When should gullible consumers be protected from their own stupidity and when should the doctrine of *caveat emptor* apply? What are the lawful and bearable limits of lobbying and influence peddling? What duties have directors to their stockholders and to the economy as a whole? All of these questions are considered by administrative agencies in the United States, and many of the problems are now being considered by Canadian governments at the federal and provincial levels. Some have caused much discussion in recent years. What policy should the federal government pursue about capital gains? Is a radio or television station injecting too much advertising in its programs? What is a proper definition of "Canadian content" in radio or television programming? What is taxable income? Does it include living and entertainment expenses? What is the dividing line between tax evasion and tax avoidance? When (and how) should a trade union be penalized for an unlawful strike or for secondary picketing? What controls should the government have over foreign investment in Canada? Should the Canadian governments prohibit or control the sale of natural resources to foreign countries?

All of these questions must be decided by law makers. If legislation is passed to control the above situations, a quasi-criminal law will develop to penalize those corporations or individuals who commit infractions of the rules laid down. The offenders will hardly be typical criminals. No one is plunging a knife into the heart of a hated enemy. There is no rape or armed robbery—except in a symbolic sense. Yet, the harm caused by pollution of the atmosphere, by the foolhardy dissipation of Canadian assets or resources, or the erosion of Canadian culture may cause more harm than the classic crimes.

One day the citizens of Canada and their elected representatives may be persuaded of these dangers and old taboos may be replaced by new ones. Furthermore, the old concept of breach of the peace may be reflected, not in the aberrational behaviour of murderers or rapists whose acts affect a few victims, but in the actions of those who deplete a whole country's resources or threaten the stability of a nation. Once again the borderline between tort and crime would be blurred, although the original rationale of crime, namely, the safeguard of a nation's security, would remain unchanged.

The Expansion of Crime

The use of penal laws to circumscribe the impugned acts mentioned above has expanded the scope of the criminal law. The criminal law has drastically increased its coverage in the last few decades. Some of the expansion is a result of the desire by authority to have control over human behaviour it considers to be deviant. This may appear to be an unlikely statement in our so-called permissive society, but this is the major reason why the criminal law has attempted to impose further controls. As citizens have sought further freedom in their personal and professional lives in modern democracies, governments have reacted by imposing more definitions of crime and tougher penalties for offenders. This has continued despite abject failure to maintain the desired control. The most infamous example is the attempt to prohibit the sale and consumption of alcohol in the 1920s. There is a second, and related, reason for the expansion of the scope of the criminal law. While no one but a confirmed anarchist could say that we live in a police state, there seems to be an increasing tendency to regulate any and all human activity. While the sexual emancipationists seem to be gaining some ground in their fight against repressive Mrs. Grundyism and outdated taboos, the social regulators seem to be making net gains in controlling our lives. This tendency is rationalized on the basis of the complicated nature of modern technological society, the growth of cities and conurbations and, paradoxically, the increased freedom enjoyed (and demanded) by a growing proportion of an educated and affluent population.

The complexity of society is certainly the most valid of these explanations. For each new invention in modern industrial society, there is an endless stream of legislation, regulations and by-laws to control its use. The use of the automobile and the invention of the credit card, to take two random examples, have expanded the criminal law and have swelled the ranks of those charged with offences and occupying prison cells. There is another body of quasi-criminal law that has added alarmingly to the criminal statistics in the last fifty years. These regulations and laws affect such matters as foods and drugs, weights and measures, and the keeping of pets. They do not often result in jail sentences or disabling criminal records, but they tend to affect the ordinarily law-abiding citizen in a way in which the crimes of arson or larceny, for instance, are not likely to be of concern to him. The penalty is usually a monetary fine and conviction is recorded against him even when his mind was not blameworthy.

The most obvious expansion of the criminal and regulatory quasi-criminal law has arisen from the use of the automobile on the highway. A Canadian committee reported that in 1901 there were 42,148 convictions for all offences, while the 1965 figure was 4,066,957. Before the law-and-order advocates start using this increase as a sure sign that modern society is disintegrating as a result of disrespect for law enforcement, it might be well to point out that ninety-eight per cent of the increase was in summary (or less serious) offences that attract a maximum sentence of six months and/or a five hundred dollar fine. Of these summary offences, ninety per cent were for breaches of the traffic laws.

In addition, there are other regulatory offences in relation to firearms, hunting, fishing and boating which have swelled the total. In 1928 Hewart, later a Chief Justice of England, wrote a book protesting the increase in social welfare or regulatory offences. We called his book *The New Despotism.* If he were alive today, he would be hard put to find a suitable title to express the indignation he would undoubtedly feel at the plight of the harassed citizen who is regulated (as well as cared for) by the State from the cradle to the grave.

Yet the plight of the offender convicted of a "classic" crime has not changed very much. There may be more humane prisons than existed in Canada in 1901, but the stigma attached to a conviction for an offence under the Criminal Code remains equally strong. Those of us who are convicted of speeding on the highway, evading tax, selling unsanitary meat or kilogram bags of sugar that contain only seven hundred and fifty grams, dodging customs duties, failing to obtain a permit to drive a taxi or failing to install a proper drainage system at the cottage do not see ourselves as criminals. We think that we are very different from the miscreants who steal a packet of cigarettes from the corner store or who have a brawl with their drinking companions. These "hardened" criminals are the ones who are ostracized and the ones who suffer serious disabilities as citizens—they cannot obtain passports, pursue certain professions or be bonded. Yet perhaps this is not so unreasonable; we have decided that there is little or no shame in being caught cheating on our income tax returns or in being convicted of careless driving. On the other hand, the tax delinquent would be horrified if a colleague suggested that he should steal money from his employer. Society has decided on its values. The protection of private property is considered sacrosanct, and its invasion seems more of a threat than dishonesty in dealings with the government or driving in a manner that endangers the lives or safety of other highway users. So long as society is satisfied with this arrangement of its affairs, the classic criminal law will remain in its present state.

3/LAW and MORALS

The criminal law became a distinct legal entity—with its own special rules and procedures—when society wanted protection from antisocial acts that threatened internal security but could not be resolved by money payments or the chaotic private "justice" of the feud. A central authority (usually the king) assumed the role of protector of the people and guardian of the *status quo*. The criminal law was an expression of the State's disapproval of acts that were contrary to current values. When the Church played a more central role in government, crime included blasphemy, heresy and adultery as well as murder, treason and theft.

A Marxist penal philosopher would claim that a capitalist system used the criminal law to keep the worker in his place. Experiments in applying Marxist philosophy (or bowderlized versions of it) show that the criminal law did not wither away. Treason, ranging from attempted assassination to revisionism, continued to be the most serious crime because it was a direct threat to the regime. The Soviet codes also circumscribed hooliganism in many ways in an effort to control even minor attempts to undermine the system. The next most serious offences were acts of private gain, for example, practising capitalism or corrupting public officials.

Therefore, the Church in medieval England, the industrial-capitalist interests in the West of the nineteenth and twentieth centuries and the State in modern Russia or China wanted to impose their values on the society that they dominated. The Church has lost its predominance, and now some of its values are not so readily accepted as properly injected into the political secular State. In the West the debate on law and morals primarily has concerned sexual mores. While we could attribute the interest in such reform to a backlash against the hypocrisy and repression of the Victorian era, the emancipation of women, the convulsive effects of two world wars or the youth revolution, the most identifiable cause is the report of the Wolfenden Committee in 1957. This committee examined the law relating to two "crimes without victims"—adult homosexuality and public prostitution. It recommended that adult, private, consensual homosexuality should no longer be subject to criminal prosecution; in the words of the Report, some private human acts are simply not the law's business. Prime Minister Trudeau, when minister of justice, introduced a bill proposing similar amendments to the Canadian Criminal Code and commented that the government had no business in the bedrooms of the nation.

The act of prostitution, in itself, was never a crime. There were peripheral offences such as keeping a common bawdy house or living off the earnings of prostitution. The English Vagrancy Act of 1824 made it an offence punishable with one month's hard labour if a "common prostitute was wandering in the public streets or public highways, or in any place of public resort, and behaving in a riotous or indecent manner." This was replaced, after the Wolfenden Report, by the Street Offences Act of 1959 which made it an offence (punishable by fine) for "a common prostitute to loiter or solicit in a street or public place for the purpose of prostitution."

The Canadian Criminal Code had also sought to control prostitution by the vagrancy laws. A "common prostitute" found in a public place and unable to give a good account of herself was guilty of a form of vagrancy. This was repealed and replaced by s. 195.1 of the Code which now makes it a minor offence for "every person who solicits any person in a public place for the purpose of prostitution."

The Hart-Devlin Debate

The views on homosexuality expressed in the Report caused a lively debate. Lord Devlin, an English judge (and a prominent Catholic layman), published "The Enforcement of Morals," in which he criticized the recommendation of the Wolfenden Committee and urged that society protect itself against moral breakdown and cultural suicide. He argued that morals and religion were "inextricably joined" and that any Christian country should enforce its morals legally. Not all immoral activities should be enforced through the criminal law, but "the smooth functioning of society and the preservation of order require a number of activities should be regulated." He believed that the suppression of vice was as much "the law's business as the suppression of subversive activities." He also said:

> You may argue that if a man's sins affect only himself it cannot be the concern of society. If he chooses to get drunk every night in the privacy of his own home, is any one except himself the worse for it? But suppose a quarter or a half of the population got drunk every night. What sort of society would it be? You cannot set a theoretical limit to the number of people who can get drunk before society is entitled to legislate against drunkenness. The same may be said of gambling. . . .

Devlin had many critics but his chief protagonist was Professor H.L.A. Hart who did not see morals as being as homogeneous as Devlin had suggested. Of course, some moral values—such as individual freedom, safety of life and protection from deliberately inflicted harm—were universal and had to be legally protected or enforced. Hart did not agree, however, that societies collapsed because the legal regulation of their morals was relaxed. He said:

> The use of legal punishment to freeze into immobility the morality dominant at a particular time in a society's existence may possibly succeed, but even where it does, it contributes nothing to the survival of the animating spirit and formal values of social morality and may do much to harm them.

A philosopher, Richard Wollheim, agreed with Hart:

> It is, for instance, arguable that a morality, if enforced, ceases to be respected, and once it loses respect its existence is in danger. And, again, it can be argued that for a code of morals to preserve respect, it must sometimes be broken, and if it is rigorously enforced it runs the risk of never being broken. Historical examples confirm this abstract reasoning. Sumptuary laws may provide a reasonable system of taxation, but they have done little to inculcate a moral aversion to waste and extravagance; and the relation between Prohibition and Temperance has been the inverse of that desired by reformers.

Hart argued for a moral pluralism and believed that Devlin took too little account of "argument, advice and exhortation" as alternative methods of enforcing morality. He agreed with J.S. Mill who had said:

> It would be a great misunderstanding . . . to suppose . . . that human beings have no business with each other's conduct in life, and that they should not concern themselves about the well doing or well being of another unless their own interest is involved. . . . Human beings owe to each other help to distinguish the better from the worse and encouragement to choose the former and avoid the latter.

Most of the "moral" offences discussed in the Hart-Devlin debate have been removed from the criminal law. Homosexual acts between consenting adults in private is no longer a crime in Britain, Canada and in some parts of the United States. Abortion laws have been liberalized in many of the same jurisdictions. Attempted suicide laws have been amended. The censorship of "obscene" books and films has been successfully challenged on many occasions.

Shaw v. *Director of Public Prosecutions* and Prostitution

In *Shaw* v. *D.P.P.*, the House of Lords examined the law resulting from the recommendations of the Wolfenden Report on prostitution. The decision has been almost universally condemned, and yet the principle laid down is so broad and nebulous that it could be applied at any time in many different circumstances. The case raised two important issues. First, should a nation's highest court base a conviction on an obscure and tenuous precedent? (Justice Holmes had said that if the sole argument in favour of a rule was that it was the law in 1383, it was insufficient reason for upholding that law.) Secondly, should Shaw's activities be circumscribed by law? The House of Lords saw its role as custodian of public morals. If the court, as a final arbiter, failed to enforce morality then Lord Devlin's worst fears might be realized.

Clearly, Shaw was trying to subvert the Street Offences Act that made it illegal for prostitutes to solicit in a public place. They were therefore forced to advertise—either by off-the-street personal displays or, more frequently, by posting small advertisements on public noticeboards. Shaw decided that these activities could be better organized. He published *The Ladies' Directory*, listing the names of prostitutes who paid a fee for inclusion in this advertising brochure. His directory also gave the prostitutes' addresses, telephone numbers, photographs and any "specialties" that they might perform.

Shaw was charged with obscenity, living off the earnings of prostitution and conspiracy to corrupt public morals. He was convicted on the second and third charges, but we are mostly concerned with the conspiracy charge. Conspiracy is a very vague crime and "conspiracy to corrupt morals" is the most vague of this genus.

The scandalized Law Lords obviously wanted to punish Shaw and were not satisfied with the conviction for living off the earnings of prostitutes. The House of Lords had two problems: the crime of conspiracy and the concept of public indecency are very vague, and there were very few precedents. The House of Lords relied upon one precedent from this century (which concerned a conspiracy to make illegal sales of pottery) and four others from the eighteenth and nineteenth centuries in which the accused were charged with conspiring to seduce a girl under twenty-one years of age or induce her to become a prostitute. In addition, there was the ancient precedent of the *Sedley* case in which the defendant had "shewed his naked body in a balcony in Covent Garden to a great multitude of people and there did such things, and spoke such words ... throwing down bottles (pissed in) *vi et armis* among the people." On convicting Sir Charles Sedley of public indecency, the court noted that the defendant "was a gentleman of a very ancient family," fined him two thousand marks (roughly thirteen hundred English pounds), declared that he was to be imprisoned a week without bail and to be of good behaviour for three years. Shaw was more severely punished and was imprisoned for one year.

There was virulent criticism of the Shaw decision, based on the tenuous precedent used to convict the defendant and the dubious use of the crime of conspiracy to control sexual mores. The determination of the House of Lords to act as guardians of the morality of the nation was also viewed as a little reactionary at a time when sexual standards were being relaxed.

Their Lordships would have been better advised to state honestly that the policy of the statute was to drive prostitution off the streets and that Shaw was openly flouting that law. The obvious answer to such an argument would be that if Shaw had found a loophole in the Street Offences Act, then it was the responsibility of the legislature to plug the gap. English judges frequently protest that they are powerless to reform the law because that is the role of the legislature. The House of Lords decided on the more devious route of resurrecting an obsolete common law offence of dubious ancestry to convict someone when it was impossible to do so directly under a statute passed in the last half of the twentieth century.

The offence of conspiracy to corrupt public morals was discussed again in *Regina* v. *Knuller (Publishing) Ltd.* where the accused published a magazine that contained advertisements by homosexuals seeking sexual partners. This case arose after the enactment of the reforms suggested by the Wolfenden Report.

The accused's conviction was upheld by the House of Lords but some of the judges in *Knuller* appear to have retreated a little from the position in *Shaw* v. *D.P.P.* One judge said that policy decisions are best left to Parliament rather than being subjected to judicial legislation and he did not believe the courts had a residual power to create new offences. The courts did not have a "general superintendence of morals," but he did not think that "conspiracy to corrupt public morals invites a general tangling with codes of morality."

Another judge tried to answer criticism of the *Shaw* decision:

> ... it has been suggested that there is an element of uncertainty which attaches to the offence of conspiracy to corrupt public morals. It is said that the rules of law ought to be precise so that a person will know the exact consequences of all his actions and so that he can regulate his conduct with complete assurance. This, however, is not possible under any system of law.... Those who skate on thin ice can hardly expect to find a sign which will denote the precise spot where they may fall in.

These two statements are hardly compatible nor do they answer the contention of critics of *Shaw* and *Knuller* that the crime of conspiracy to corrupt public morals breaches the principle *nullum crimen sine lege* (i.e., a citizen is entitled to expect the law to be defined with some precision and to have prior notice of its existence so that he can regulate his behaviour accordingly). The decisions of the House of Lords fail to satisfy this fundamental test.

The Limits of the Law

Precedent was used more prudently by Piper J. of the Supreme Court of South Australia in *Todd.*

Todd was married and the father of two children; his wife was expecting a third. He was unhappy in his marriage and decided that he would run away from his responsibilities. He faked a suicide by running his car off a road, through a fence and into a river. He walked away from the scene and travelled to another state. The police spent many hours investigating the "accident" and dragging the river for a body. In due course he was found and returned to his home city where he was charged with the crime of "effecting a public mischief." This crime has had a few modern applications and is almost as nebulous as conspiracy to corrupt public morals.

The prosecution had based its case on two recent English cases. One of these was *R.* v. *Manley* where the court had resurrected the ancient common law offence of "effecting a public mischief" (which, incidentally, is made statutory under s. 128 of the Canadian Code). The accused had made false complaints to the police that a crime had been committed against her. The police force wasted time and resources seeking the fictitious criminal. Mrs. Manley was convicted.

Todd's lawyer argued that effecting a public mischief was not a crime under the common law of South Australia because it was not part of the law introduced into the state when it was set up as a British colony more than one hundred years before. The presiding judge agreed with the defence counsel's contentions and wrote a carefully researched and reasoned judgement that held that it would have been improper for a judge to attempt to legislate new offences.

The "sin" of Todd was more private than that of Shaw because it was limited to the suffering caused to his immediate family (if we ignore public expense and inconvenience for police engaged in a fruitless search). Shaw was trying to circumvent national policy on a moral issue. From a moral viewpoint, however, a judge might be forgiven for feeling that Todd's behaviour was more in need of immediate social retaliation than Shaw's whose conviction held only a tenuous hope for beneficial effects on traffic in prostitution.

In any case, the policy behind the prostitution legislation is extremely hypocritical. The law is saying, "We know that prostitution exists, we might even be convinced that it is inevitable, but we will drive it off the streets and that will at least appear to be a solution to a social problem." In fairness, the legislation had some social hygienic value by stopping prostitutes actively soliciting on the streets, annoying law-abiding citizens who did not wish to do business with them. A vice squad rationalizes its crusade against prostitution as a fight against venereal disease, although there is little evidence that prostitutes are the major carriers of the disease, that they receive treatment or that venereal disease is decreasing. (Note that s. 253 of the Code makes it an offence to knowingly transmit V.D.) The policy of sentencing prostitutes often seems pointless; the women are fined and given time to pay. It does not take much imagination to guess how they raise the money.

The dilemmas raised by *Shaw* and *Todd* must be resolved by Parliament. Do we want more (or any) legal controls over prostitution and its subsidiary industries? Should the criminal law be so defined as to include behaviour similar to Todd's? Piper J.'s decision was correct because he refused to legislate to deprive a defendant of his freedom when there was no pre-existing law forbidding Todd's act. The judge's position was peculiarly difficult because another man, Copley, was sitting in jail awaiting the outcome of the *Todd* case. No one can say that Copley was inspired by Todd's acts. Fake suicides by misunderstood, distraught or disenchanted husbands are not uncommon. Copley's shoes were found on a rock ledge frequented by fishermen. The man's family and the police presumed that he had been swept from the ledge by high seas. A widespread search ensued. Two of the volunteer searchers were brothers who were prosperous farmers in the area.

They each had four children. While searching in their own small plane, they flew into a hillside and were killed. Copley later surrendered to the police. Copley's case caused great public outcry for vengeance but as soon as Todd was acquitted, there was no charge to lay against Copley. Todd's acquittal says much for Piper J.'s judicial discretion and restraint in such circumstances. He had to make a difficult moral decision and showed a preference for the rule of law over the public pressure for vengeance.

Abortion

The abortion debate is not over but important reforms have been achieved. There has been violent opposition from some religious (and other) groups who, although a minority, want to impose their moral beliefs on the rest of society. The history of the laws relating to abortion and the arguments for and against reform tell us much about the legal process, the interrelationship of law and morals, the influence of pressure groups and current social values.

Most of the reform of the law was in the 1960s. Before that time liberal abortion laws existed only in some Iron Curtain countries, Japan and Scandinavia. Since 1968, many jurisdictions in the United States and the Commonwealth (including Canada) have made quite broad changes. The statistics on abortion are widely speculative. Four recurring facts emerge from even conservative studies: more married than single women have their pregnancies terminated; there are many more illegal abortions than legal ones; there are probably more abortions than natural births; and amateur abortionists kill many of their clients every year.

Women obtain illegal abortions in one of two ways: by going to a modern, sterile—but underground—abortion "mill" run by skilled professionals or by risking their lives with a backyard abortionist who helps "girls in trouble." Abortion law reformers claim that there is another method that is on the borderline between legitimate medical practice and crime—a woman has an abortion disguised as a gynecological operation or exploratory examination. Doctors usually deny the frequent use of this method because of the restraints imposed by hospital procedures—obligatory tissue samples and surgeons' reports and the danger of losing hospital privileges.

Until the recent reforms there was only one legal method in the Anglo-American medico-legal world. The Canadian law was typical. There is little case law on it. While many amateurs have been convicted and punished, no reported case of a doctor challenging the legality or morality of the Code section or sections can be found. One obvious exception is the case of Dr. Henry Morgentaler (but this case comes under the revised Code provision).

The 1954 Canadian Criminal Code provided by s. 237(1) that:

> Everyone who, with intent to procure the miscarriage of a female person, whether or not she is pregnant, uses any means for the purpose of carrying out

his intention is guilty of an indictable offence and is liable to imprisonment for life.

Any layman reading this section might think that there was no legal way to procure a miscarriage, although he may have heard lawyers and doctors talking about therapeutic abortions as falling outside the criminal law. Section 237(1) is identical to s. 303 of the 1927 version of the Code except that in the earlier Code, the word "unlawfully" implied that there were *lawful* ways of procuring a miscarriage, and therefore, its omission meant that there could be no legal abortions. (If "unlawfully" had been included in s. 237, it would have qualified the word "uses.") Legislative draftsmen have always used adverbs to describe, qualify or modify the active verbs used in penal statutes. For instance, "maliciously," "knowingly," "wilfully," "recklessly," "inadvertently" are some of the more common ones that not only imply that the act could be done non-maliciously, unknowingly, unwillingly, et cetera but also suggest that one of the basic ingredients of crime—a guilty mind or *mens rea*—had to be present. Some lawyers—those who do not believe that statutes are written by infallible draftsmen or who have a limited regard for the immutability of the wording of statutes as Holy Writ—think this pedantic attitude toward statutory language a trifle ridiculous. A criminal provision of any importance must always carry the criterion of *mens rea* unless the exclusion of a guilty mind is made quite clear.

This would seem a commonsense attitude if it had not been for the legal *legerdemain* of Mr. Justice Macnaughten in the case of a gynecologist, Mr. Bourne. While the law construed in *R.* v. *Bourne* (and s. 237(1)) is no longer in force, the legal problems raised are still pertinent for two reasons: because they explain the legal process in action and because the amended abortion laws will no doubt require judicial interpretation.

Bourne was charged under the English Offences Against the Person Act, 1861 with "unlawfully procuring the abortion of a female. . . ." The maximum penalty under that statute (and in the 1954 Canadian Code) was life imprisonment. Bourne was one of England's most respected gynecologists. A girl of fourteen had been violently raped by some soldiers, and the doctor decided that it would do the girl irreparable harm to carry the foetus full term. He informed the prosecuting authorities that he intended to terminate the pregnancy, thus challenging the abortion laws. The Crown accepted the challenge and, after the operation had been performed, charged Bourne with unlawful abortion.

Bourne was supported by his colleagues, some of whom appeared as witnesses and testified as to the dangers to the life and health of a fourteen-year-old girl if she were forced to bear a child in such circumstances. The trial judge, Macnaughten J., who addressed the jury in terms sympathetic to Bourne, pointed out the inevitable uncertainty of medical diagnoses and that the distinction between danger to life and danger to health was not absolute but only relative. The expert witnesses did not suggest that the girl would face instant death at confinement but pointed out she could easily suffer psychic or physical harm.

These medical indications did not seem to offer Bourne a defence under the 1861 Act but the judge—at the invitation of defence counsel—resorted to a legal subterfuge that eventually led to an acquittal. Sometimes it is necessary to crush the skull of a child being born to protect the life of the mother. No one, legal or medical, suggests that this comes within the category of miscarriage. This is covered in Canada by s. 209 "killing an unborn child" and in Bourne's case by the Infant Life (Preservation) Act, 1929. This Act provided that child destruction was not unlawful unless "the act which caused the death of the child was not done in good faith for the purpose only of preserving the life of the mother." Although this had nothing to do with aborting a foetus several weeks old, Macnaughten J. used it as analogous to the 1861 Act (under which Bourne was charged) and explained to the jury that the words in the Infant Life (Preservation) Act had "always been the law with regard to the procuring of an abortion, and although not expressed in . . . the Act of 1861, they are implied by the word 'unlawful' in that section. No person ought to be convicted under . . . the Act of 1861 unless the jury are satisfied the act was not done in good faith for the purpose only of preserving the life of the mother." As stated earlier, the trial judge instructed the jury that the fine line between preservation of life and protection of health was a delicate medical judgement that was not susceptible to precise legal definition. The analogy that the judge drew between the two statutes based on the use of the word "unlawful" explains the concern over the omission of the word "unlawfully" in the 1954 revision of the Canadian Criminal Code.

Bourne won a victory for the medical profession and for women who had good reason for not wanting to be pregnant. The decision, however, may well have caused a postponement of almost three decades in the general reform of the abortion laws. In those intervening years a truce seemed to develop between the medical profession and the police; if the doctors kept within reasonable limits, the law would not interfere—providing there were only a moderate number of discreetly performed "therapeutic" abortions. The doctors kept their own house in order by creating informal abortion committees that ruled on the therapeutic quality of the abortion within the terms of the "preservation of life/preservation of health" test (using many of the criteria found in Illustration 49). Although the trial judge in *Bourne* tried to give the impression that "preservation of life" was the criterion, no one was fooled by that limitation. If questioned informally, doctors would admit the need for some legal controls, would have serious reservations about abortion on request and yet were often content with the state of the abortion market. The word "market" is used advisedly because the availability of an abortion was governed by economic factors; there were (and are) great inequities for poor women who wished to terminate their pregnancies. The police did not worry respectable, reputable doctors; the governing body of the medical profession was perfectly aware of abortionists among its members but had no intention of de-registering them unless they were very indiscreet.

This cosy situation could not continue when women started campaigning for "rights over their own bodies." Some doctors, male and female, became crusaders for reform, and of course, the debate over the separation of law and morals had its effect. Anyone with lots of money could get an abortion; the indications for "preservation of life and health" became thin and, in some instances, spurious. Many of the physical indications were no longer dangerous to life or health because of advances in medical science. The most foolproof method was to obtain a certificate from a psychiatrist declaring that the patient would likely kill herself if the pregnancy continued. The women's rights movement also claimed that there was discrimination on the basis of ability to pay and that the expensive hospital abortion was the privilege of the rich while the poor took real physical risks by using the services of the careless, unskilled, unhygienic amateur.

Despite great opposition from the Catholic church and other right-to-life adherents, the laws were eventually changed. The successful reformers claimed that if anyone had moral scruples about abortion, the question was one of private morals and should not interfere with the legal reform desired by the majority.

The new s. 251 provides that abortion is still an offence punishable by life imprisonment unless a doctor procures a miscarriage in "good faith" after the therapeutic abortion committee of a hospital has reviewed the case. A majority of the members of the committee must decide whether the "continuation of the pregnancy . . . would or would not be likely to endanger . . . life or health." The therapeutic abortion committee must be comprised of no less than three members of the medical profession. The medical indications as to danger to life or health are left to the professional discretion of the abortion committee.

Similar changes have occurred in Britain and some parts of the United States. Most of the new laws require official abortion committees in the hospitals that can now, quite legitimately, permit abortions to preserve the health as well as to save the life of the mother. These laws have not worked particularly well in California because there are indications that some committees have been dominated by conservative doctors. Law and morals clash again. What criteria should an abortion committee apply? If the medical or psychiatric indications are weak, should the fact that the applicant is a single woman or a young married woman with ample means to support a child be decisive in denying the abortion application? In California, where medical care is more free enterprise than it is in Canada, demand has caused a great increase in the price of abortion. Often hospitals have had too few beds to handle the demand. Once again, welfare patients and other women of limited means have not been able to obtain professional abortions.

Scandinavia, Japan and several Iron Curtain countries have had "liberal" abortion laws for a generation or more. In all but one of these countries—Norway—the liberalization of the abortion laws has not effectively eliminated illegal abortions. If liberalized abortion laws placed any limitations on the grounds or indications for granting a therapeutic abortion, there were many women who were disappointed and consequently sought out an illegal or unofficial abortionist. In all countries but Norway the number of illegal abortions either remained stable or increased. Norway's illegal abortion rate appears to have declined, probably as a result of the broad "social" indication included in their law. The only law that clearly would cover Illustration 49(u) is the Norwegian one.

Is there any alternative to granting abortion on request? If abortion were granted on request, would it mean that Lord Devlin's worst fears for the downfall of Western society would be realized? Abortion, like prostitution, is a service demanded by citizens. The reasons for seeking an abortion (or a prostitute) are frequently less than "moral," but there appears to be no way to stem public demand. A professional abortion "mill" would be preferable to the dangerous methods of self-help. (Similarly, state supervised hygienic brothels would be preferable to pretending that prostitution does not exist.)

Attempts to legislate morality will not work and perhaps we must rely on "exhortation," as H.L.A. Hart calls it, or education in the broadest sense. For instance, abortion might be less of a problem if birth control methods were more accessible or if the stigma of illegitimacy were alleviated. Once again, the aura of sexual mores seems to have disproportionate importance. Abortion, moreover, has only an indirect relationship with sexual mores; perhaps the moralists want to punish pregnant women because they were *caught* in "wrongdoing."

Regina v. *Morgentaler*: A Story About a Miscarriage

The Supreme Court of Canada, in a 6-3 decision, dismissed Dr. Morgentaler's appeal and made legal history. The case provides an important discussion of the law relating to abortion; it also illustrates the unusual legal situation, which exists in Canada, allowing the prosecution to appeal from an acquittal. Dr. Morgentaler had been acquitted by a Montreal judge and jury, but the Quebec Court of Appeal substituted a conviction and jail term under s. 251 of the Code. A majority of the Supreme Court of Canada decided not to disturb this appellate decision.

Morgentaler was a qualified doctor who specialized in abortions. He pioneered the use of the vacuum aspiration method in Canada. He was paid fees for his services. He was charged with performing an abortion on P., who was a student from Sierra Leone. She had no family in Canada. Her general practitioner and gynecologist confirmed that she was pregnant but refused to help her procure a miscarriage. P. called five Montreal hospitals but she decided she could not afford the high cost of the abortion. One hospital offered to set up an appointment for her case to be referred to the therapeutic abortion committee, but by then she would have been at least eight to ten weeks pregnant. One of the hospitals suggested that P. call Morgentaler. He interviewed P. and obtained her medical history. He decided that an abortion was "reasonable, necessary and ... indispensable," because (quoting his evidence at the trial):

> ... she was single, ... studying, ... a stranger here, her boyfriend was a student, and they were not ready to get married and take on the responsibilities of a child. So she was in a state of psychological distress; ... she was not sleeping, she was not eating, she was very upset and losing sleep; and, in psychosomatic terms, I am well aware that a state of psychism like that can cause very serious physical disorders, and, if I had not done it, there was always the danger that she would give up hope and go to a quack, that she would perform the abortion herself, that it was absolutely necessary, in order to protect her life and her health, for me to perform this abortion.

Morgentaler argued that he was protected from criminal responsibility under s. 45 of the Code as he had performed a surgical operation under "reasonable" circumstances "having regard to the state of health" of the patient.

In addition, he claimed the defence of necessity which was the basis of the decision in *Bourne.* There was a related argument that Morgentaler could act under the defence of necessity because s. 251 of the Code contained no exceptional provision similar to s. 1(4) of the English Abortion Act. Section 1(4) allowed the decision of a single practitioner (instead of the more usual opinion of two doctors) to perform an abortion in "a case where he is of the opinion, formed in good faith that the termination is immediately necessary to save the life or to prevent grave permanent injury to the physical or mental health of the pregnant woman."

The majority decided that s. 45 of the Code was no longer relevant (as a similar statutory provision had been in *Bourne*) because, in the words of Dickson J., "Section 251 contains a comprehensive code on the subject of abortions." That judge also decided that if the defence of necessity does exist, "it can go no further than to justify non-compliance with the law which is demonstrably impossible. No system of positive law can recognize any principle that would entitle a person to violate the law because on his view the law conflicted with some higher social value."

In his dissent, Laskin C.J. did not suggest that the court should approve abortion on demand. He did hold, however, that s. 45 could still apply to an abortion situation, partly because the additional ground in s. 1(4) of the English Abortion Act was not found in the Canadian Criminal Code and partly because of the particular merits of the case. In an alien city a friendless young woman from another country, "frightened by her pregnancy and without the means or access to means to be able to invoke the elaborate procedures of s. 251(4) and who in desperation seeks the assistance of a qualified surgeon who in his honest judgement feels that immediate abortional surgery should be performed, and carried it out to preserve the young woman's mental health, if not also her physical health."

While Laskin C.J. denied the arguments on the Bill of Rights, the question of "access" was raised by the advocates of a Bill of Rights approach. They pointed out that the trial judge had taken notice of the following facts:

(a) There are no approved hospitals in the province of Quebec.
(b) Of the two hundred and ten accredited hospitals in the province of Quebec, only twenty-three have established therapeutic abortion committees. Twelve of these are French language hospitals and eleven are English language hospitals.
(c) Almost all the accredited hospitals that have therapeutic abortion committees are located in the Montreal metropolitan area. There are, in consequence, vast geographical areas of the province in which therapeutic abortion is not available.
(d) Among those hospitals that have established therapeutic abortion committees, there is wide variance in practice and in the application of the very general criteria laid down by the law.
(e) Many, if not most, of the hospitals having therapeutic abortion committees require that the applicant for a therapeutic abortion be a resident of the area served by the hospital.
(f) A wealthy person who is using the services of a physician in private practice is more likely to obtain approval of a requested therapeutic abortion in useful time than is a poor person applying to a hospital clinic. In the latter case, the delay between application and approval may be as long as eight weeks, thereby rendering the abortion procedure itself, when performed, more difficult and dangerous.
(g) Among the various provinces, there is a wide variation in the number of abortions practised. In 1971, the rate of abortions in Ontario was some forty times higher than in Newfoundland.

Therefore, it was argued that not all women in Montreal, or in Canada for that matter, had equal access to abortion under Canadian law.

Homosexuality

Homosexuality upsets just as many, if not more, "moral" citizens than does abortion but the reform of the law was more quickly achieved. The abortion problem was more complicated because some of the opponents of reform conscientiously believed that abortion was legalized murder (albeit giving too little thought to the women who died at the hands of illegal abortionists). Proponents of homosexual law reform showed that police often resorted to entrapment and *agents provocateurs.* Members of the vice squad were often placed in the ridiculous situation of hiding in broom closets in public toilets in order to catch homosexuals. Attractive young police officers propositioned homosexuals to obtain incriminating evidence. Enterprising young men

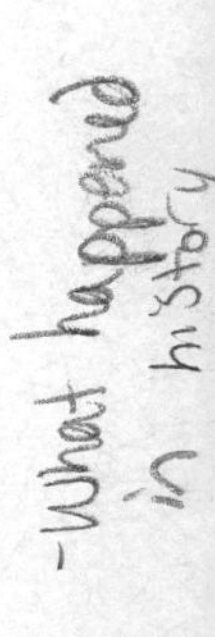

exploited aging homosexuals, accepting money and hospitality and then informing on them. Many homosexuals who were prominent citizens complained of blackmail. Some psychiatrists argued that homosexuals needed treatment not punishment. Penologists said that sending a homosexual to prison made as much sense as sentencing a drunkard to a brewery. Some of these arguments seem a little old-fashioned in these days of Gay Liberation.

One of the few problems remaining in the present criminal law on homosexuality is the definition of a "consenting adult in private." Few in favour of reform were prepared to legalize homosexual behaviour where "youths" were concerned. Should "youth" end at fourteen years, as the token age of puberty, sixteen (or eighteen) years, as the age of adult criminal responsibility, or twenty-one years, as the customary start of adulthood (and the age of marriage without parental approval)? The Canadian law decided on the last criterion and by s. 158(1) both participants in the "indecent act" had to be over twenty-one years of age. This of course was a very arbitrary figure and has no relationship to biological or social realities. (See Illustration 46(b)) The Law Reform Commission of Canada produced a report on sexual offences and had some difficulty in arriving at a sensible age of consent. They chose fourteen years for both genders for all sexual behaviour, but this is not yet law. English studies made similar recommendations with an equal lack of legislative success. Society is not prepared to approve of changes in sexual mores even if they know that they are inevitable and reasonable. Society just *feels* that homosexuality is wrong. A more thoughtful approach is found in *I Know What I am* prepared by an English group concerned about teenage homosexuals. This report was a response to a government document that had recommended an age of consent for male homosexuals at eighteen and females at sixteen. The gay teenagers argued:

> The strong disapproval of homosexual relations ... spills over into acts of physical violence against gay people.... It is under these sorts of pressures that young gay people have to grow up. More often than not they feel themselves unable to talk to anyone at all about their emotions and needs, and live lives of almost total repression and isolation. Many have adopted, at least partially, society's negative valuation of their sexuality. Their sexual relationships and general contact with other gay people, in these circumstances, are necessarily restricted to ones that are furtive and unsatisfactory to themselves.

The group suggested that young gay people needed advice not laws. They added: "It would be wholly unsatisfactory if the law, even with a minimum age of sixteen, still made it risky for support and counselling services, gay and non-gay, to offer help and advice to self-defined gay people younger than sixteen. The only humane and logical step would be to abolish the concept of a minimum age altogether for homosexuals of both sexes and to rely instead on the laws dealing with common assault where there is evidence that a sexual act was not consensual."

The "private" quality of the new law has not yet been defined by the courts, but presumably it would not be considered "private" if two men were found committing homosexual acts in the locked cubicle of a public toilet—even if the only reason for their discovery was the inquisitive policeman in the next cubicle. A rented cubicle in a bath house also seems to be public. "Private" does not include a couple performing acts in a car or in a public park at night. In strict terms, such acts performed by heterosexuals could be legally indecent but prosecutions are very rare in such circumstances. The gay community does not enjoy such *de facto* immunity and has some justification for feelings of discrimination (see Illustration 46(c)).

When considering homosexuality one should not ignore lesbianism. The criminal law of the Victorian era did not circumscribe sexual behaviour between two females. The 1954 revision of the Canadian Criminal Code de-gendered the offence of gross indecency. Section 157 which had read (in the old s. 206) "any male person" who commits acts of gross indecency now reads "every one who commits an act of gross indecency with another person."

Heterosexual Crime

In other chapters we shall see the attitude of the criminal law toward heterosexual behaviour, particularly when it involves women under certain specified ages. The law aims to protect the innocence of the young, both male and female. In the case of girls and young women, however, there is the added factor that men have looked upon females as chattels, and the virgin, in particular, had a special value as a sexual object and item in the marriage market.

As a general rule no man can lawfully have sexual intercourse with a female under sixteen years of age unless the female is his lawful wife. The punishment—which used to include whipping—increases as the age of the girl decreases. If the female is under fourteen years, the maximum punishment is life imprisonment. If she is between fourteen and sixteen years, the convicted male may be sentenced to up to five years in prison. The male cannot claim reasonable grounds for believing the girl was over fourteen or sixteen as a defence. Dale in Illustration 21(a), therefore, would have no defence based on his belief as to Viva's age or based on her consent. The law has decided that protection of females is more important than allowing an accused a full defence based on lack of *mens rea.* He cannot say that he thought she was over fourteen or sixteen or whatever is the age of consent, and of course, it is quite irrelevant for him to say that the female was a willing party. His only chance of acquittal is found in s. 146(3) that allows the court to find Dale not guilty if it is "of opinion that the evidence does not show that, as between the accused and the female person, the accused is wholly or chiefly to blame." The law is making a moral statement—we are prepared to protect innocent girls but if she were the temptress, she is a "bad," not a "good," girl. The same values can be seen expressed in s. 151 (seduction of female between sixteen and eighteen) and s. 152 (seduction under promise of marriage where male is over twenty-one and female under twenty-one) because there would be no conviction unless the female was of "previously chaste character." There have been very few prosecutions under these sections since the 1920s, but before then, the courts had some difficulty in defining "previously chaste character" which was meant to separate the "good" from the "bad." In one case, a young couple had "kept company" for eighteen months, and "illicit connection" under promise of marriage took place weekly until the female was pregnant. The court had some difficulty believing that the female was still being "seduced" after eighteen months. They defined previously chaste character as indicating "those acts and that disposition of mind which constitutes an unmarried woman's virtue or morals." The court was not prepared to define the phrase as *virgo intacta* and suggested that a female could be seduced more than once as long as, in the meantime, she had exhibited "such conduct and behaviour as to imply reform and self-rehabilitation in chastity." The following passage from a Canadian judgement is not typical but it does reflect an attitude toward sexual morals that some readers might have some difficulty believing in the 1980s:

> Chastity is a virtue which makes one abstain from the prohibited carnal pleasures and repel even the thought of it.
>
> Purity is the most perfect chastity. As far as the words honour, wisdom, virtue are applicable to a woman, it supposes the determination to remain estimable to the eyes of the world; wisdom brings the idea of prudence with which a woman must avoid the dangerous occasions; virtue suggests the courage with which a woman shall resist the seducer's attacks.

The rule (in s. 146) refusing a defence of honest belief that the girl is older than fourteen or sixteen derives generally from the rule that young girls are to be protected and specifically from the 1875 case of *Prince*.

Prince was convicted of taking a girl under sixteen years out of the care and control of her father. He claimed in his defence that he thought that the girl was over that age. The court, composed of many judges, refused to grant him a defence (that is, a negation of *mens rea*). Some judges said that if he had been under the misconception that the girl's father had consented to the girl's going away with Prince, they would have allowed him a defence based on lack of *mens rea* because of mistake; however, his actual behaviour did not show such misconception and the judges agreed he should be convicted because his acts were inherently wrong or immoral. The judges' decision is difficult to follow in moral terms. It suggests that the real immorality was not so much abducting (and presumably seducing) the female as taking the "property" of the father. No court would possibly take that view today. On the other hand, Dale in Illustration 21(a)(*b*) would not have a defence today because the father consented to the sexual behaviour practised by the young couple.

The *Prince* case must be related to the legislation under which he was charged and, more particularly, to the mores and social climate of the time. In the Canadian case of *Rees,* decided some eighty years later, the Supreme Court of Canada determined that the accused, who had been charged with contributing to the delinquency of a minor by having sexual intercourse with her, should be acquitted when he convinced the court that he was of the honest belief that the girl was above the age of consent. *Rees* was fortunate that the prosecution decided to charge him with contributing because the offence under s. 146 is an offence of absolute liability on the issue of age of the female.

On the other hand, Illustration 43(b) shows a court assuming paternalistic control over corruptible youth, even where the corruption was more notional than real. Drago was convicted not for sleeping with the girl but for sleeping with the girl's mother. The court convicted Drago of contributing to the delinquency of a minor because of potential harm. Why? Because he made the mother an immoral woman? Because the child *may* have witnessed the act of sexual intercourse and *may* have become a delinquent? Or because it was plainly wrong?

In a few isolated jurisdictions adultery is still a crime. Until recently interracial fornication and marriage had been proscribed by some southern states in the United States, but that country's Supreme Court has now declared such laws unconstitutional. Of course the criminal law is not the only method for attempted control of human behaviour, sexual or otherwise. A few years ago, an employee of the federal government was fired because he had become engaged to an Innuit woman and that was contrary to government employment practices.

What is Abnormal Sexual Behaviour?

In Illustration 47 we see one of the three recent cases in which "abnormal" sexual behaviour was subjected to criminal prosecution. Here the court decided that there are some forms of human behaviour that are outside the law's concern. Dickson J.A. said in *R.* v. *P.*:

> ... it would require words much plainer than appear in s. 149 to persuade me that Parliament suddenly decided to enter the portals of the home to require courts to sit in judgement upon what passes in private between consenting adult spouses or persons living together, whether married or not, or, for that matter upon any heterosexual act ... done in private between consenting adults.

Yet in the case of *Le François,* decided three years earlier, the Chief Justice of Manitoba determined that similar acts performed in an automobile by a couple on a casual date made the *male* guilty of a crime. There was some question of force being used but it seems to have been irrelevant to the decision by Miller C.J.M. who found the accused guilty of gross indecency and regretted that he could not increase the penalty. The conduct was judged "so repugnant to ordinary standards of morality and decency that it cannot be called other than grossly indecent." Defence counsel argued that fellatio was an ordinary mode of love making. This was denied by Miller C.J.M., but perhaps the lawyer made a bad tactical error in using the analogy of animal behaviour. There was no reference in the judgement to the Kinsey Report, and perhaps Le François would have had a slightly better chance of acquittal if it had been shown that such abnormal behaviour was practised by many members of the human population.

In another prairie case, decided in 1957, a couple had been discovered performing acts similar to those in *R.* v. *P.* and *R.* v. *Le François.* In *R.* v. *J.* they were acquitted, presumably because they were engaged and "very much in love." The latter decision would agree with that of Meredith J.A. in *Menary:*

> Zeal against immorality is natural and commendable, but it is quite misplaced in any effort to bring an act quite without the criminal law within its penalties.

The charges in these cases of "abnormal" sexual behaviour show the regrettable influence of a Mrs. Grundy mentality. Those who argue that these acts should not come within the criminal law assume that the police have more important work than acting as official Peeping Toms.

Obscenity, Pornography, Smut and Filth

Voyeuristic Grundyism is most persistent in the law's attempt to control obscene materials—pornography, smut, dirty books, sexy postcards or whatever might be deemed to come within the censor's jurisdiction.

The 1960s saw a great assault on censorship and the statutes that tried to define obscenity. The legislators have made numerous attempts to define the concept, but they have been remarkably ineffectual. Perhaps it would be better to emulate former U.S. Supreme Court Justice Clark who said he could not define obscenity but he knew it when he saw it. Or we might use Kurt Vonnegut's definition of obscenity in *God Bless You, Mr. Rosewater* as being "any picture or phonograph record or any written matter calling attention to reproductive organs, bodily discharge, or bodily hair. ... The difference between pornography and art is bodily hair."

The classical legal test of obscenity lasted for almost one hundred years. In *Hicklin,* that test was "whether the tendency of the matter ... is to deprave and corrupt those whose minds are open to such immoral influence, and into whose hands a publication of this sort may fall." The book involved contained a scandalous attack on the Catholic church, supposedly describing the behaviour of members of Holy Orders. In recent years the censors have been more interested in what the critics might call "quality literature" or "serious art." Celebrated trials have concerned Joyce's *Ulysses,* Miller's *Tropic of Cancer,* Kauffman's *The Philanderer,* Lawrence's *Lady Chatterley's Lover,* Hall's *Well of Loneliness,* Cleland's *Fanny Hill* and Selby's *Last Exit to Brooklyn.* While some of these works can hardly be considered enduring classics, all received serious critical attention. In recent years, concerned parents have tried to persuade school boards that it would be injurious for senior high school students to read Salinger's *Catcher in the Rye* or Margaret Laurence's *The Diviners*.

The *Hicklin* rule was paternalistic and characteristically Victorian. The essence of the rule—depravity and corruption—is so nebulous that proof of such "tendency" is difficult or impossible. With the exception of Sir Basil Blackwell in the *Last Exit to Brooklyn* trial, no prosecution witness has ever admitted that a particular book tended to deprave and corrupt him. Furthermore, these two qualities, in addition to being tautological, are self-fulfilling because a person who lays the charge is the only one in a position to say what he means by depravity and corruption. The test is completely subjective. If the offended person is narrow-minded or paternalistic, he will find parts of all books dangerous and believe they should be banned. Presumably, the person nearest to depravity and corruption in the first place would be the first to be affected by the book. Or was the test meant to be applied to the person who is youngest, most innocent or most pure? This point is answered, in part, by the last portion of the rule that declares that the book will be banned only if the potentially depravable or corruptible person is the person into "whose hands a publication of this sort may fall." Obviously, a medical textbook will not be sold in drugstores or found in cheap paperback format. Similarly, some of the encyclopedias on sex practices and customs can escape censorship because they are too expensive for the average book buyer or are sold discreetly.

Prosecutions under the *Hicklin* rule were often initiated by police officers and tried by old patrician judges or magistrates, neither of whom could be described as discriminating literary critics or average members of society. A happy exception was Mr. Justice Stable who presided over *R.* v. *Martin Secker and Warburg* when Kauffman's *The Philanderer* was on trial. (Of course, we must remember that this book was extremely mild compared to such recent books as Philip Roth's *Portnoy's Complaint* or Gore Vidal's *Myra Breckinridge* or *The Story of O* by Pauline Réage. Obviously the question of obscenity is relative as well as subjective.)

In contrast to many supporters of Comstockery, Stable J. was not prepared to "take our literary standards as being the level of something that is suitable for the decently brought-up young female age fourteen." He admitted that there were many books unsuitable for adolescents. After explaining that the book, which dealt with human passion and sexual intercourse, had been called "sheer filth" by the prosecution, he added, "Is the act of sexual passion sheer filth? It may be an error of taste to write about it. It may be a matter in which, perhaps, old-fashioned people would mourn the reticence that was observed in these matters yesterday, but is it sheer filth?" The book was acquitted by a liberal, enlightened judge. Unfortunately one atypical decision did not make a new rule of obscenity.

The revisers of the Canadian Criminal Code may have had *R.* v. *Martin*

Secker and Warburg in mind when they changed the law in 1959. Until that time there had been no definition of obscenity in the Canadian Criminal Code, and the courts had applied the *Hicklin* rule. In 1959, subsection (8) of s. 150 was added:

> For the purposes of this Act, any publication, a dominant characteristic of which is the undue exploitation of sex, or of sex and any one or more of the following subjects, namely, crime, horror, cruelty and violence, shall be deemed to be obscene.
>
> (Note: This is now s. 159.)

The "dominant characteristic of which is the undue exploitation of the sex" was some improvement and did not suggest that the consumer must be affected in some particular way. It also referred to the pornography of violence, which was the current liberal taboo. (The amendments of 1959 also included special provisions regarding "crime comics" that no doubt were inspired, in part, by Dr. Frederic Wertham's *Seduction of the Innocents,* a book that attacked the insidious influence of such publications on the minds of children.) The test, however, was still close to *Hicklin* because it was totally subjective and the trier of fact had to decide on the meaning of "undue" and "exploitation." Some people may believe that any advertising that uses sexual symbols to sell products is "undue exploitation." Similarly, Mrs. Grundy may decide that *any* mention or description of the "private parts" of the human body is obscene. In other words, we are faced with the old problem of demarcation between law and morals. The definitions we have examined thus far are probably useless because any rule is going to amount to nothing more than the gut reaction of the trier of fact, who is a product of his environment and upbringing and may be a poor judge of current mores. The cultural lag between a writer's expression of "outrageous" ideas and the popularization of those ideas was once decades (witness the slow official acceptance of *Lady Chatterley's Lover* and *Ulysses*); today the cultural lag is much shorter. Public mores can change in a matter of months.

Canadian courts have made no pioneer decisions on obscenity. No important decision occurred between the *National News* case of 1953 and the trial of *Lady Chatterley's Lover* in 1962, by which time Lawrence's book had been defended successfully in England. The trial judge in that case advised the jury that even if they had decided that the book was, on face value, obscene, there was an additional question they must decide:

> . . . have the defendants established the probability that the merits of the book as a novel are so high that they outbalance the obscenity, so that its publication is for the public good? In other words, in my view, it was not the intention of Parliament by that section to say, "Well, if somebody who is a skilful author is prepared to write filth, and write it very well, he will escape conviction." What has to be established, . . . is that the merits of the book are so high they outbalance the obscenity so that its publication is for the public good.

Byrne J. also referred to the relevance of the forum (and the format) of the book. The book was not going to be subjected to the rarified atmosphere of academe where professors would study its true inner meaning. This book, published by Penguin Books in paperback, would be available for the price of a packet of cigarettes at bookstalls and would be read at public libraries. (In the first year after *Lady Chatterley's Lover* was acquitted, Penguin sold two million copies of the book.)

In a 5-4 decision the Supreme Court of Canada upheld the acquittal in a judgement that was based largely on the English experience. Speaking for the majority, Judson J. thought the 1959 amendment provided a more objective test that did not "so much depend ... upon the idiosyncracies and sensitivities of the tribunal of fact." The book was not to be judged on isolated words or passages but examined as a whole. The writer's intention, which had been considered irrelevant under the *Hicklin* rule, could also be examined. (In the English trial many famous literary figures gave evidence for the book and gave their interpretation of the author's artistic aims.) Judson J. said:

> What was he trying to do, actually doing, and intending to do? Had he a serious literary purpose or was his purpose one of basic exploitation? . . . One cannot ascertain a dominant characteristic of a book without an examination of its literary or artistic merit. . . .

Judson J. decided that Lawrence was not trying to exploit sex for mere titillation and commented that the book:

> . . . has none of the characteristics that are often described in judgements dealing with obscenity—dirt for dirt's sake, the leer of the sensualist, depravity in the mind of an author with an obsession for dirt, pornography, an appeal to a prurient interest, etc.

Fauteux J., in dissent, did not agree and commented: "Whatever the outstanding position held by Lawrence as a writer, this book offers no evidence that an expert in literature necessarily qualifies, for that reason, as a *custos mores*." Taschereau J. also dissented and agreed that:

> In order to improve the social conditions in England, if they have to be improved, I have more faith and hope in sound legislation enacted by Parliament, than in the adulterous scenes described by Lawrence in his book.

He also added a statement that was later echoed in the controversial *Ginzburg* decision of the U.S. Supreme Court:

> The diffusion of these patriotic ideas, cherished by Lawrence, are surely not forbidden by law. What in my view is objectionable is not the aim pursued by the author, although I find it an illusory promise of future happiness, but the means employed for the demonstration of this thesis.

In the next few years, there were numerous prosecutions and most of them failed. *Fanny Hill, Tropic of Cancer* and *The Story of O* were all cleared. The Canadian courts went along in most instances. One of the few exceptions was *Cameron* which did not prosecute a book but a series of drawings by the Canadian artist Robert Markle. Cameron was unlucky. (Illustration 25(c)) Three years later, the erotic drawings of Picasso and John Lennon were shown in Toronto without legal challenge; perhaps this was because the drawings were by better-known artists. To some extent there is some snobbery and cowardice among censors. If a painting is a superb piece of craftsmanship—and done by someone less famous than Picasso—there is every chance of its being banned because a policeman from the vice squad does not appreciate the depiction of bodily hair in the "wrong" places. (Hugh Hefner used to air brush the *Playboy* centrefolds, thus making them more presentable, more hygienic and less lifelike.)

Perhaps we should accept the average member of the vice squad, with his high school education, as a proper representative of the general populace. His interpretation of what is obscene may be more representative—of the Burnaby truck driver, the Lethbridge housewife, the Brandon miner, the Toronto subway driver, the Montreal butcher or the Halifax fisherman—than the so-called intelligensia and art critics. (Vice squad members can make mistakes, but one doubts whether they would seize two titles that caught the eye of Australian morality protectors, Koestler's *Act of Creation* and A.A. Milne's *Winnie the Pooh*.)

There is a peculiar situation in Canada as a result of federal-provincial allocation of powers. Federal customs officials can grant entry to a book that is then banned by a provincial attorney general prosecuting under a federal statute, s. 159 of the Canadian Criminal Code.

The Nova Scotia Appellate Court has recently decided in *McNeil* v. *Attorney General of Nova Scotia* that the province's Amusements Regulation Board does not have the power to prohibit or censor films. The court decided that the board was concerned with public morality, an aspect of criminal law which is an exclusive power of the federal government. A citizen had challenged the power of the board to refuse showing the film *Last Tango in Paris*. The Supreme Court of Canada upheld the view of the Nova Scotia court, although the court dealt more with constitutional than moral issues. The Manitoba Court of Appeal in *R.* v. *Odeon Morton Theatres* found the film was not obscene.

The case of *McAuslane* (Illustration 25(a)) shows that the position of the bookseller can be precarious. The defendant was charged under s. 150(1) with having in his possession for the purposes of circulation or sale certain "obscene written matter." He claimed that he should be acquitted because he had not read the books and, therefore, had no way of knowing that their contents were obscene. His case was not helped by s. 150(b) stating that:

> . . . the fact that the accused was ignorant of the nature or presence of the matter . . . is not a defence to the charge.

This would seem to put an end to any argument for acquittal, and yet the criminal law has always operated on the principle that no man can be convicted of a criminal offence unless he had *mens rea* or a guilty mind. We shall see that in the case in Illustration 7, *Beaver,* the accused, was acquitted because he had a *bona fide* belief that the substance in his possession was not heroin. Given the social dangers of heroin addiction, one would think that a more stringent rule should apply to possession of a narcotic than to selling an allegedly obscene book. The Ontario Court of Appeal in *McAuslane* was stringent because the criminal law is usually reluctant to impose a punishment depriving an accused of his liberty for a strict or absolute liability offence. (McAuslane was given a six months' sentence.)

The rule in *Beaver* was somewhat inaccurately stated in *McAuslane* as:

> A *bona fide* honest and reasonable belief based on reasonable grounds of the existence of circumstances which, if true, would make the act for which the prisoner is indicted an innocent act is a good defence.

The court distinguished *Beaver* and decided that McAuslane had no defence based on negation of *mens rea.* Presuming for a moment that we want to punish citizens under obscenity laws, we could still have a rule that differentiated innocent purpose from guilty knowledge. If the Crown had been able to prove that McAuslane had a reputation for peddling pornography or that the books in question had been previously declared obscene and banned, then a conviction would have been more reasonable. If the prosecution had been able to prove that McAuslane would sell anything that the wholesaler sent him without reading any of his titles, then he might be considered reckless and a conviction would have been more reasonable.

In the more recent case of *Lee,* similar facts arose but on this occasion the bookseller could not read English, and he was given a defence of mistake of fact. No amount of foresight, care or caution on Lee's part could have saved him from possession of the obscene material unless he had hired an interpreter (and literary critic) to read the books before they were displayed. (Illustration 25(b))

We should be very careful about allowing laws that convict without *mens rea,* particularly where the alleged offence concerns one of the basic freedoms—the freedom to read or the freedom of the press. This constitutional freedom was the basis of the defence contentions before the U.S. Supreme Court in *Ginsberg* v. *State of New York.* The question of *mens rea* was not fully discussed. The accused ran a variety store that sold paperbacks and magazines. He was charged with selling a "girlie" magazine to a boy under seventeen years of age. (There was some evidence that a group of "decency" advocates had instructed the boy to buy the magazine.) Girlie magazines already had been ruled not obscene for adults, but they could not be sold to minors under seventeen. The Court upheld the conviction, primarily on the ground that adults have a right to supervise youthful activities such as marriage, voting and reading matter. The Court denied his plea that he lacked *mens rea.* The statute was not so narrowly drawn as the Canadian legislation; it provided:

> Section 484, section 1
> (g) "knowingly" means having general knowledge of, or reason to know, or a belief or ground for belief which warrants further inspection or inquiry of both;
> (1) the character and content of any material described herein which is reasonably susceptible of examination by the defendant.

Justice Brennan commented that:

> . . . only those who are in some manner aware of the character of the materials they attempt to distribute should be punished.

The U.S. Supreme Court has nevertheless decided against most obscenity laws in recent years. The legislators have had great difficulty in drafting laws that the highest court of the United States has not found legally vague or an encroachment on the First Amendment, freedom of speech. The court brought these pro-defendant cases to a temporary halt in *Ginzburg* v. *U.S.* Whatever one may think of the behaviour of Ginzburg or the materials he circulated, there is no doubt that a jail term of five years was totally unreasonable (or, as Charles Rembar described it, "grotesque").

Ginzburg had been the publisher of *Eros, Liaison,* a biweekly newsletter, and *The Housewife's Handbook on Selective Promiscuity.* The contents of these publications are not important to the decision. Their avowed intent was to "keep sex as an art and to prevent it from becoming a science." *Eros* had some artistic and literary pretensions and the *Handbook* was, in effect, a sex manual. (Copies of *Eros* are now collectors' items, and today, a moderate advocate of censorship would have difficulty understanding the fuss caused by this publication.)

The court decided that Ginzburg was in the "sorbid business" of pandering, "the business of purveying textual or graphic matter openly advertised to appeal to the erotic interest of their customers." Ginzburg sought to circulate *Eros* from post offices in Intercourse and Blue Ball, Pennsylvania, but they were too small to handle the anticipated volume of mail so he had to settle for mailing privileges from Middlesex, New Jersey. The court gave a further description of what it saw as pandering:

> The "leer of the sensualist" also permeates the advertising for the three publications. The circulars sent for *Eros* and *Liaison* stressed the sexual candor of the receptive publications and openly boasted that the publishers would take full advantage of what they regarded as unrestricted licence allowed by law in the expression of sex and sexual matters. The advertising for the *Handbook,* apparently mailed from New York, consisted almost entirely of a reproduction of the introduction of the book written by one Dr. Albert Ellis. Although he alludes to the book's informational value and its putative therapeutic useful-

ness, his remarks are preoccupied with the book's sexual imagery. The solicitation was indiscriminate, not limited to those, such as physicians or psychiatrists, who might independently discern the book's therapeutic worth.

The court held that this evidence was relevant and helped prove that the publications were appealing to prurient interest and that the transactions were "sales of illicit merchandise, not sales of constitutionally protected matter." The court also said:

The deliberate representation of petitioners' publications as erotically arousing, for example, stimulates the reader to accept them as prurient; he looks for titillation, not for saving intellectual content. Similarly, such representation would tend to force public confrontation with the potentially offensive aspects of the work; the brazenness of such an appeal heightens the offensiveness of the publications to those who are offended by such material. And the circumstances of presentation and dissemination of materials are equally relevant to determining whether social importance claimed for material in the courtroom was, in the circumstances, pretence or reality—whether it was the basis upon which it was traded in the market place or a spurious claim for litigation purposes. Where the purveyor's sole emphasis is on the sexually provocative aspects of his publications, that fact may be decisive in the determination of obscenity.

In other words, Ginzburg's publications may not have been considered obscene in another context but they were obscene under the circumstances. Although this case has been criticized severely—and although the punishment remains abhorrent—the decision does not seem unreasonable *if* we want to maintain any controls over obscenity, which is doubtful. In fact, the pandering idea is the only possible limitation that should be imposed, unless we except sales to children. If we do not want undue exploitation of sex, pandering is the only illustration that fits the definition of obscenity. This assumes that control over undue exploitation of sex (or some similar definition of obscenity) is viable. If we are to be ruled by Platonic guardians, perhaps this assumption might be true, but we are driven back to the definition of Rembar that "pornography is in the groin of the beholder." No definition will work unless we can be assured that the arbiters of obscenity—whether they be police, customs officials or members of the judiciary—are as impartial as a set of scales, as wise as Solomon and as efficient as a computer. We cannot have this assurance. Police may not reflect "good," or *avant-garde,* taste: judges may be old and reactionary; and customs officials may be too cautious.

It all comes back to the questions of taste and control. The forbidden fruit syndrome means that we cannot keep the public from wanting these saucy, sexy, titillating, sordid pieces of trash. We cannot deter the booksellers from making profits in proportion to the risks they take. We cannot prevent citizens—whether masturbating fourteen-year-old boys, middle-aged "dirty old men" or potential sexual perverts—from reading materials that may provide an erotic outlet. Furthermore, the free publication of anything and everything may well lead to a satiety in the market. There are indications that this is happening in Denmark and that the Danes are no longer particularly interested in pornography—except for the revenue it earns from sales to foreigners. Once again, we are back to H.L.A. Hart's argument in favour of exhortation rather than legal repression.

The only answer lies in education and self-censoring. The question of taste must guide the future market. If the trash (and let us not quibble, there *is* trash) is freely and cheaply available, perhaps both curious readers and connoisseurs of pornography may become a little more discriminating.

One reservation in advocating total freedom from control of obscenity is the question raised by the *Ginzburg* decision. Does the average citizen have any right to privacy that is subverted by the panderers? Is there any way of controlling the packaging of obscenity? Probably not, unless a self-censoring public penalizes the panderers by its failure to buy. The advertiser or panderer will then be forced to be more subtle—or perhaps risk further governmental penalties for misleading advertising.

The answer usually given by the hard-sell panderer is that the consumer is not obliged to read the advertising copy and can react by refusing to buy the product. Yet there is also soft-core pornography that is not exactly subliminal advertising but very close to it—the advertising campaign that suggests (but *only* suggests) that you cannot really be a success in bed if you do not drink this brand of whiskey, smoke that brand of cigarette, or wear the right clothes or cosmetics. Many of these ads are titillating and are promoting values that are thought by some to be just as deleterious in their influence as dirty books. Once again it is a question of waste. We have no right to stop this form of advertising but hope that the public may deter the pandering advertiser by refusing to buy his merchandise. The advertiser, of course, will never suffer this because he will ensure that his message is subtle and does not offend the literal-minded. The advertiser is hardly likely to say "Want to get laid? Then wear XQY jeans!" If he becomes crass or is in advance of current tolerance, the public will react and the advertiser will go broke or, more likely, change his advertising campaign.

The Continuing Search for a Definition

The search for a definition goes on but to no avail. We are unlikely to reach a stage where a majority of the population wants complete freedom from censorship. Both the pro- and anti-censorship supporters argue their positions with passion. The intellectuals, "longhairs" and artistic types have contempt for those less "liberated." Staunch religionists, who may be Catholics or fundamentalists, find that the banning of dirty books is one cause on which they can agree. The pro-censorship forces have many weapons in their arsenal; they can apply economic pressure by asking members of their group to boycott a particular magazine, bookstore or theatre. The authorities can gag an author, film director, producer or exhibitor by threatening to withhold a permit or by cancelling licences. The censor is often the sponsor of the mediocre and mundane and, in effect, helps define the avant-garde. Until recently the censors have had the peculiar habit of penalizing quality works, while the hastily prepared pulp magazine or book which may be more explicit, and is certainly less subtle, is left unmolested by the morality squad. Perhaps the authorities and those who draft and enforce our censorship laws take the attitude that vices should be taxed and that a bestseller (such as *Portnoy's Complaint,* with sales in the millions) does not deserve such rewards. Yet there is a curious relationship here: in a hard-core pornography store books with titles such as *I Was a Sex Kitten in a Ski Lodge* or *Dolls Love Leather* or *Nympho Nights* are often three or four times the price of a volume by Apuleius, Updike, Roth, Rabelais, Miller, Zola, or an English translation of the *Kama Sutra.* Perhaps the morality squad is satisfied if the price is high enough to deter youths and delighted if the volume is encased in plastic.

The forces of Comstockery seemed to be losing ground in many parts of Canada. There are still those complaints from the prairies when a play on the CBC uses some phrase stronger than "pshaw," but there was little censorship of books or films in the sixties and seventies, but the book-burners and film censors seem to be re-emerging in the eighties. They will censor a film such as *The Tin Drum* which has an important message or restrict admission for an excellent film such as *The Devil's Playground.* The latter contains some scenes of full frontal nudity and is a sensitive portrayal of the sexual explorations of pubescent boys, but they are the very ones who are not allowed to see it. A documentary such as *Not a Love Story* cannot be shown commercially but many of the pornographic films that it condemns can be shown or bought for home consumption. The censors seem to be giving up on the so-called good books. The occasional raid on a hard core bookstore is often in token response to the protests of the Aunt Ednas who demand that "something be done on behalf of God-fearing taxpayers."

The differential application of the obscenity laws to the various media is difficult to understand. The censors presumably apply some aesthetic judgement so that the millions who watch television will be protected from everything but the most harmless pap. Perhaps this is partly because of the influence it *may* have on children. The hundreds of thousands who visit cinemas must be protected from some of the explicit scenes that can be described in words but cannot be depicted on film. Only tens of thousands read books readily available in variety stores, drug stores or bookshops, and more freedom will usually apply here as long as the expression is in words rather than pictures. Finally, only a few hundred read technical journals such as medical magazines and sexology periodicals where there may be clinical detail. Therefore, the basis seems to be accessibility, size of audience and type of media.

There are scenes described in words in *Portnoy's Complaint,* for instance, that may never be portrayed explicitly in the commercial cinema. Some of these topics might be filmed for instructional purposes in schools of psychiatry or institutes of criminology or for the underground or stag film market. Why should either be banned? There may be a self-censoring process here. The average movie goer will not tolerate these scenes at his local Bijou, and he is not likely to be interested in buying a stag movie version of them on the underground market. Instead of banning them, we could impose a tax on stag movies and devote the proceeds to behavioural research on the psychic effects of explicitly sexual or violent scenes on various segments of society.

The mode of presentation can also provide a means of controlling allegedly obscene material. Films can be graded according to age or other criteria. Children can be kept out of films that are rated unsuitable for them. In the future, we should appoint film censors on the basis of their knowledge and relative sophistication; the present incumbents seem to have a narrow view of the community's standards and tastes. The rating system is such that there are few films children under fourteen years of age can see without being accompanied by an adult.

Television is easily controlled but at the present time it is more subject to stupid controls than any other media. Once again, the censor seems to be more interested in mediocrity than quality. The networks are prepared to allow *double entrendres* in the vaudeville tradition but are reluctant to allow serious discussion of controversial or explicit topics.

There is little hope of controlling literature except, perhaps, by limiting the age at which children can buy specific titles. Perhaps there should be a labelling process whereby a reader can tell by a code what category a magazine or book belongs to and make his own decision to purchase or read. The last argument in favour of censorship is that obscene materials are an affront to personal privacy. If, however, a brochure advertising Scandinavian pornography, a "skin" magazine or a scatalogical book had marked on its cover, "Anyone likely to be offended by sexually explicit materials is advised not to read the contents," then there should be no problem.

The U.S. Supreme Court has retreated somewhat from its role as protector of the First Amendment, freedom to read. The Court has not produced any new definitions but it has suggested that "the community standards" should be just that—the local community has the right to apply the test to local conditions, rather than being forced to adhere to some broad national test of obscenity.

There seem to be few taboos remaining. Certainly the conventional ones, relating to religion and sex, are now considerably eroded. Perhaps we shall invent new ones. There are indications that materials that make deleterious statements about race or that glorify violence are the new pornography. Canada has passed a statute making race hatred propaganda an offence. Yet laws against hatred or violence do not make any more sense than strictures on the undue exploitation of sex in movies or books.

The search for definition goes on in vain. One of the more thoughtful efforts at drafting a new definition is the Model Penal Code. The definition provides:

> Material is obscene if, considered as a whole, its predominant appeal is to prurient interest, that is a shameful or morbid interest in nudity, sex or excretion and if in addition it goes substantially beyond customary limits of candor in describing or representing such matters. Predominant appeal shall be judged with reference to ordinary adults unless it appears from the character of the material or the circumstances of its dissemination to be designed for children or other specifically susceptible audience. Undeveloped photographs, molds, printing plates and the like shall be deemed obscene notwithstanding that processing or other acts may be required to make the obscenity patent or to disseminate it.

We have to go on living with the censors, and they make it very difficult because they keep changing the ground rules. One of the cardinal principles of law, and particularly the criminal law, is that the citizen can rely on the rule of law. He has a right to a government of laws, not a government of men. He must have prior notice of laws. He must have certainty in his laws, and the laws must not be retroactive. The laws must not be ambiguous or vague so that it is possible for him to know whether his behaviour falls within the limits of the law. As was shown in *McAuslane,* it is contrary to the rule of law to convict a man (and imprison him for six months) when it is impossible for him to know beforehand which books in his stock would be considered obscene by the morality squad.

This situation continues today. No definition of obscenity, even if updated every year to match social mores, can answer the problem. Every book, picture or film seized becomes a potential case to be taken to the Supreme Court of Canada. The most sensible, and provocative, antidote to this perpetual process of attack and counter-attack has been proposed by the Australian critic Donald Horne who would challenge the authorities to state what *they* mean by the term "deprave and corrupt":

> Thus, if the State wishes to ban the description or portrayal of some or all sexual acts it should say so. If the State decides that certain parts of the human body are obscene it should name them. If it doesn't want people to use certain words it should write them down. . . . It would be fascinating to find out what words, what sexual acts and what parts of the body the State found obscene.

The nearest answer to Horne's demand is in the New York Penal Law (s. 484-h) which was used in the *Ginsberg* (girlie magazine sale to a minor) case. In part, the legislation stated:

> (b) "Nudity" means the showing of the human male and female genitals, pubic area or buttocks with less than a full opaque covering, or the showing of the female breast with less than a fully opaque covering of any portion thereof below the top of the nipple, or the depiction of covered male genitals in a discernibly turgid state.

(f) "Harmful to minors" means that the quality of any description or representation, in whatever form, of nudity, sexual conduct, sexual excitement, or sadomasochistic abuse, when it:
  (1) predominately appeals to the prurient, shameful or morbid interest of minors,
  (2) is patently offensive to prevailing standards in the adult community as a whole with respect to what is suitable material for minors,
  (3) is utterly without redeeming social importance for minors.

Is this any more satisfactory? Is it too vague? Finally, is it necessary?

In 1970, the Report of the Commission on Obscenity and Pornography was issued by the United States Congress. The Report was a liberal document but far from unanimous. The dissenters, the moral minority, offered the following definitions:

> A thing is "obscene" if, by contemporary community standards, and considered as a whole, its predominant appeal is to the prurient interest. As a matter of public policy, anything which is obscene by this definition shall be conclusively deemed to be utterly without redeeming social importance. Any slight social value in such obscenity shall be deemed outweighed by the social interest in order and morality.
>
> "Prurient interest" is defined as a shameful or morbid interest in nudity, sex or excretion which goes substantially beyond customary limits of candor in description or representation of such matters. If it appears from the character of the material or the circumstances of its dissemination that the subject matter is designed for, or directed to a specially susceptible audience, the subject matter shall be judged with reference to such audience. When the subject matter is distributed or exhibited to minors who have not attained their eighteenth birthday, the subject matter shall be judged with reference to an average person in the community of the actual age of the minor to whom such material is distributed or exhibited. In all other cases, the subject matter shall be judged with reference to the average person in the community.

The majority believed that "much of the 'problem' regarding materials which depict explicit sexual activity stems from the inability or reluctance of people in our society to be open and direct in dealing with sexual matters." Therefore the Commission called for a "massive" program of sex education for adults and children and a full and open discussion of obscenity and pornography. A majority of twelve out of seventeen recommended that all legislation prohibiting the sale and distribution of sexual materials to consenting adults be repealed. This was based on the following grounds:

1. Extensive empirical investigation, both by the Commission and by others, provides no evidence that exposure to or use of explicit sexual materials play a significant role in the causation of social or individual harms such as crime, delinquency, sexual or nonsexual deviancy or severe emotion disturbances.
2. On the positive side, explicit sexual materials are sought as a source of entertainment and information by substantial numbers of American adults. At times these materials also appear to serve to increase and facilitate

constructive communication about sexual matters within marriage. The most frequent purchaser of explicit sexual materials is a college educated married male, in his thirties or forties, who is of above average socio-economic status. Even where materials are legally available to them, young adults and older adolescents do not constitute an important portion of the purchasers of such materials.

3. Society's attempts to legislate for adults in the area of obscenity have not been successful. Present laws prohibiting the consensual sale or distribution of explicit sexual materials to adults are extremely unsatisfactory in their practical application.
4. Public opinion in America does not support the imposition of legal prohibitions upon the right of adults to read or see explicit sexual materials.
5. The lack of consensus among Americans concerning whether explicit sexual materials should be available to adults in our society, and the significant number of adults who wish to have access to such materials, pose serious problems regarding the enforcement of legal prohibitions upon adults, even aside from the vagueness and subjectivity of present law.

The majority were not prepared to repeal all laws affecting children and pornography. While there is little empirical data showing any harmful effects from sexual materials, the Commission bowed to the commonly held belief that children should not be so exposed and preferred to leave the availability of pornography for children to the discretion of their parents. The age limit was left for the decision of the state jurisdictions. The draft legislation provide

(b) Offences Defined. A person is guilty of a misdemeanor if he
  (i) knowingly disseminates explicit sexual material, as hereinafter defined, to young persons or
  (ii) if he knowingly displays explicit sexual material for sale in an area to which young persons have access, unless such material has artistic, literary, historical, scientific, medical, educational or other similar social values for adults.

  "Explicit sexual material" means any pictorial or three-dimensional material including, but not limited to, books, magazines, films, photographs and statuary, which is made up in whole or in dominant part of depictions of human sexual intercourse, masturbation, sodomy (i.e., bestiality or oral or anal intercourse), direct physical stimulation of unclothed genitals, or flagellation or torture in the context of a sexual relationship, or which emphasizes the depiction of uncovered adult human genitals; provided however, that works of art or of anthropological significance shall not be deemed to be within the foregoing definition.

The Law Reform Commission of Canada studied the problem of obscenity and took the following criteria as the starting point:

1. no act should be criminally prescribed unless its incidence, actual or potential is substantially damaging to society

2. no act should be criminally prohibited when it can be adequately controlled by other social forces, such as public opinion, and
3. no law should give rise to social or personal damage greater than that it was designed to prevent.

The Canadian Commission recognized that there was a "hard core minority" who would still favour censorship even if obscene materials did *not* cause any social harm, and the Commission admitted that it was very difficult to "prove a negative." Finally, it commented:

> It may well be that recommendations for liberalization of the law can rest simply on a policy decision to withdraw the criminal law from all areas of conduct except those that threaten substantial harm. In the field of private morals this would allow minorities the freedom to remain pluralistic instead of coercing them to conformity.
>
> If, on the other hand, extended anti-obscenity legislation and a vigorous campaign of law enforcement is to be recommended, attention should at least be given to whether the community is willing to pay the costs in manpower, money and invasions of privacy. The question of monetary costs and manpower might be easily tested by recommending that each new offence created should be accompanied by an allocation of funds for its enforcement.
>
> Ultimately the problem to be resolved is whether, in Canada in the 1970s, the state through the vehicle of the criminal law must maintain its role as *custos morum* over consenting adults. Are there to be any circumstances in which one willing adult will legally be permitted to purchase, from another, access to any sexual material he or she desires?

Since that Report, the debate has been complicated by the persuasive writings of many feminists. The first pertinent comment comes from D.H. Lawrence who is not usually viewed by feminists as one of their heroes. He did not want any "good" literature censored, but he felt differently about pornography which he viewed as an "attempt to insult sex, to do dirt on it." He thought it was an "insult to the human body, . . . to a vital human relationship." Its purveyors made nudity and the sexual act "ugly, cheap, degraded, trivial and nasty." Gloria Steinem would obviously agree with this assessment of pornography. She has said:

> Consider also our spirits that break a little each time we see ourselves in chains or full labial display for the conquering male viewer, bruised or on our knees, screaming a real or pretended pain to delight the sadist, pretending to enjoy what we don't en oy, to be blind to the images of our sisters that really haunt us—humiliated oiten enough ourselves by the truly obscene idea that sex and the domination oi women must be combined.

Most feminists are not in favour of censorship partly because they are making political rather than legal statements. This is very well put by Andrew Dworkin in *Pornography: Men Possessing Women:*

> This is not a book about the First Amendment. By definition the First

> Amendment protects only those who can exercise the rights it protects. Pornography by definition—"the graphic description of whores"—is trade in a class of persons who have been systematically denied the rights protected by the First Amendment and the rest of the Bill of Rights. The question this book raises is not whether the First Amendment protects pornography or should, but whether pornography keeps women from exercising the rights protected by the First Amendment.

Dworkin's powerful book and the Canadian film *Not a Love Story* contain important messages. Women must wield political power to end that debasement and general powerlessness that is merely exemplified, crudely but so dramatically, in pornography. Men must be made to recognize the loss to *all* humans if they objectify and brutalize women as mere sex symbols. H.L.A. Hart's methods of education and exhortation seem more appropriate than attempting to use the criminal law to control pornography and disputes between the sexes. A dialogue seems a better idea than the legal harangues of the adversary system. If a problem of sexual harassment can be solved peaceably in the work place by mediation, it is better than assault charges in the courts. If a human rights commission can arbitrate and make findings of sex discrimination, this is a victory for all women and that is not as true if one woman sues one man and gets a damage award or lays an information in criminal court against one individual. Of course, the criminal laws of rape or indecent assault must still exist but they should be used as last resorts. In the best of all worlds, pornography would, as a consequence, disappear.

Law and Economic Morals

When Lord Devlin fulminated against the inevitable evils of the Wolfenden Report, he gave little thought to nonsexual morals. He did not suggest, for instance, that the Deadly Sins were clearly present in a world where millions in Asia and Africa were starving while farmers in the United States were paid not to grow wheat. Devlin did not comment on the fact that a shoplifter may spend months' in jail for stealing a few cents' worth of merchandise while a swindler who made millions of dollars was not deprived of that money and spent less than three months in prison. A mentally ill arsonist was originally given twenty-four years in the penitentiary because he destroyed other people's property, while the crooked businessmen who only cheated on government contracts received three months' imprisonment from the trial judge.

Jail terms are probably no more effective in deterring cheats on Bay Street than in stopping neurotic shoplifters or psychotic arsonists. Longer terms of imprisonment are not the answer. These illustrations of economic crime were simply raised to show that we live under an economic system where the entrepreneur is more important than the individual. Lord Devlin's attitude is not atypical. Whenever the courts discuss "morals," they are usually talking about sex. There are a few exceptions which show the clash of the law with religious or political morals. The defendants in Illustrations 14 and 43(a) are likely to be penalized because the law of the majority does not agree with the views of religious or ideological minorities. Moreover, the strictures against Communists in the 1950s show that the law can be used to enforce conformity to a political morality. Although it was not a criminal case, George Martin suffered the very severe penalty of not being able to follow his chosen profession of law because the Law Society and Court of Appeal of British Columbia decided that a Communist could not be admitted. The judgement was written in the 1950s at the time of the McCarthy witch-hunts.

Yet it would be a distortion to suggest that the economic mores of the law are still strictly *laissez-faire*. While the underprivileged continue to be overrepresented in the criminal courts and prisons—indeed, in the very contents of the Criminal Code—the business community has not been left unscathed. Anti-monopoly and anti-price-fixing laws try to prohibit one corporation from obtaining a predominant share of the market, but what exactly is a "monopolistic tendency," how big is "too big," when does Mega Corporation have so much of the market that the economic system is being undermined? Similar problems exist when we try to define price fixing and tax evasion (which is not to be confused with tax avoidance). Part of the problem is that we find it so difficult to define economic immorality, but a more serious allegation is that the enforcers of those laws are rather half-hearted in their enforcement efforts against powerful big business who can afford high priced lawyers to obstruct and obfuscate.

Vagrancy and Economic Morals

Most of the provisions about the crime of vagrancy were repealed in 1972, but it is still worth considering as an illustration of the law's attempt to control and penalize those persons who fell below society's accepted standards of economic morality. A vagrant was defined (in the old s. 164(1)) as anyone who (a) "not having any apparent means of support is found wandering abroad or trespassing and does not, when required, justify his presence in the place where he is found" *or* (b) begs from door to door or in a public place *or* (c) "being a common prostitute or night walker is found in a public place does not, when required, give a good account of herself." Illustrations 48(a) and 48(c) show the distinction between the "common prostitute" and the call-girl. The former is a criminal while the latter seldom comes within the law. The ingredients of the crime of the old "Vag (c)" were its public quality ("found in a public place") and the fact that the street walker is a nuisance ("does not, when required, give a good account of herself"). Both the prostitute and the call-girl fulfil an economic and social function, but the call-girl does it without upsetting our sense of propriety and decorum.

Similarly there is no essential difference between the alcoholic playboy and the drunken bum. With the possible exception of his inherited investments, the playboy makes no more contribution to society than the bum, but he leads a quiet, discreet life of debauchery while the other man advertises his plight on Skid Row—a public place where he is seen panhandling by the patrolling policeman.

There are only two forms of vagrancy left in the Code: a person who supports himself, in whole or in part, by gaming or crime and "has no lawful profession or calling by which to maintain himself"—164(1)(d)—and a previously convicted sex offender found "loitering or wandering in or near" a school yard, playground, public park or bathing area. The most common offence of vagrancy was s. 164(1)(a). This type of crime was criticized and eventually repealed because it penalized a citizen on the basis of a status. Opponents of such offences argued that the status offence was unjust because it made a man a criminal when he was powerless to change his condition. The United States Supreme Court struck down a California law that made it an offence to be addicted to a narcotic and another that required previously convicted persons to register when taking up residence. In *Powell* v. *Texas* a conviction for public drunkenness registered against a chronic alcoholic was unsuccessfully attacked on the same basis. The *Drybones* decision of the Supreme Court of Canada decided that the Canadian Bill of Rights protected the Canadian Indian from inferior status under our liquor laws.

The crime of vagrancy under s. 164(1)(a) served many purposes. Sometimes it was used as a means of stopping a full crime from being committed. If two men were found in a blind alley behind a warehouse at two o'clock in the morning and gave questioning police officers the unlikely explanation that they were having a discussion about baseball, the police sometimes charged them with vagrancy if there was insufficient evidence for a charge of attempted crime. This gave the police a chance to fingerprint and photograph them (although strictly illegal in many instances) and to find out if there were any outstanding charges against them. Their arrest may also have averted a breaking and entering. This is similar to the familiar "holding" or "material witness" arrests used in the United States.

Subsection (b), concerning begging, was commonly used aginst hippies, panhandlers and drunks who needed the price of another drink. The rationale of the offence was very similar to that for prostitution—social hygiene. Clean-living, law-abiding citizens, it was said, have a right to walk on public thoroughfares without being waylaid by dishevelled citizens who are importuning or otherwise making a nuisance of themselves. There is no need in our economy for anyone to beg because we have established charities, transient hostels, welfare payments and unemployment insurance. In other words, these beggars were breaching current economic morals. They were deviants who refused to believe in the Canadian dream.

Section 164(1)(a) was also used against hippies and other "undesirables" even when they did not fulfil all the criteria. For instance, a longhaired youth may have had money in his pocket and a permanent address, but if the police believed they should clear the streets of unsightly hippies or bums, they booked him for vagrancy. In some country towns the local police used the vagrancy charge in an illegal way, not intending to lay a charge. They would arrest the vagrant, keep him in jail overnight and tell him that no charge would be laid if he was out of town within the hour.

Both types of vagrancy—the "no apparent means of support" and begging "from door to door or in a public place"—have interesting historical backgrounds. These offences have been in existence for more than a thousand years. When communities were smaller and financed on a local level, any non-productive person was a drain on the taxpayer or ratepayer. If a stranger to the township or parish were found using local charitable resources (usually the church or workhouse), he was sent away or returned to his own neighbourhood where his own people were responsible for his support. There was another reason for penalizing beggars and vagrants: a wandering band of desperate, penniless, hungry or idle men was a threat to communal peace, and in times of acute unemployment, disease or famine, these men were feared because of the crimes they might commit. Hard-working, law-abiding citizens took the view that hippies and bums added nothing to the gross national product. If they would not work, they should not be supported. If they persisted in their behaviour, they should be punished so that they would be deterred in the future—even if they were unable to work or find work. (Section 164(3) exempted the aged or infirm from the provisions of the "apparent means of support" provision.)

In the seventeenth and eighteenth centuries vagrants were treated stringently. They were incarcerated for indefinite periods in workhouses where they did busywork. In the nineteenth century it was decided that workhouses were not solving the problem and were breeding criminals (particularly when children were kept there). When the social reformers addressed themselves to the problem, there were great debates on the relative merits of indoor relief (in workhouses), outdoor relief (through handouts from charitable agencies) and no relief at all (encouraging work and self-help). We still have drop-outs but have decided to abandon vagrancy as a crime. Jails did not turn vagrants into "productive" citizens. These institutions did not reduce unemployment. They have not converted disillusioned men into adherents to the Protestant work ethic.

Vagrancy, however, was not an altogether iniquitous law. Drunks and bums who slept in doorways were rounded up so that they could be "dried out," given medical attention, a meal and some clothing. In jail they would not freeze to death, would not suffer from malnutrition and would be safe from muggings by juvenile delinquents or other vagrants. If vagrancy laws were used against able-bodied men and women who resolutely refused to work and who had shown that no amount of coercion (short of a penal sanction) would move them from that resolve, then the use of the criminal law might make sense. Unfortunately, many vagrants are physically unfit and cannot work. Furthermore, many of them are ineligible for unemployment assistance or welfare payments.

If it is proper for us to apply criminal sanctions to those members of society who fall below the norm of prosperity or ability and, therefore, are unable to take care of themselves, should we also take a similar penal attitude toward citizens who are, in effect, too successful and have more than their share? One hundred years ago the idea would have been considered preposterous. English courts in the nineteenth century believed in total freedom of contract not only between business entrepreneurs of equal power but also between an employer and an employee so that the latter could claim no compensation if injured on the job. (The fathers of the Russian Revolution would be shocked to find that, instead of the law "withering away," the Soviet Criminal Codes now have many offences for the punishment of profiteering and other capitalistic aberrations.)

The economy is being regulated with increasing assiduity. These controls include regulation of weights and measures, the purity of food and drugs, safety standards in factories, pollution, child labour and minimum wages. These measures protect the health and welfare of the public, and few would quarrel with the need for them, although many of the laws were achieved only after long struggles.

At the end of the nineteenth century, during the era of the robber barons, governments in North America, though previously dedicated to *laissez-faire*, introduced legal limitations on business enterprises. Today entire government departments devote their energies to the protection of consumers, the regulation of competition, the prosecution of breaches of the anti-trust laws, the supervision of trading in stocks and securities and the control of foreign investment.

We have already discussed the G.E. price-fixing conspiracy. The convicted corporation executives had two answers to the charges: they argued that they were simply following the natural entrepreneurial dictate of maximizing profits for the stockholders and, furthermore, that in so doing they were obeying the explicit or implicit orders of their superiors. (Compare Illustration 36.) In other words, this was an attempt by the law to interfere in the economic life of the United States.

Perhaps the case is not quite analogous to vagrancy. Surely, though, the vagrant should argue (with Anatole France) that the rich, like the poor, have a perfect right to sleep under the bridges of Paris and that society has no right to stop them. The executives might well argue that the government is being too paternalistic and that if a mining stock promoter hoodwinks the public into buying worthless stock in a mining venture, then *caveat emptor* applies, and the government has no business interfering. They argue that economic morals are no more the concern of the government than are sexual morals; that economically "immoral" acts are no different from sharp or dishonest practices of private citizens that nonetheless fall short of larceny or criminal fraud, as defined in the criminal law.

This is hardly the forum for an analysis of economic theory, but at least it can be said that the activities of a giant conglomerate produce greater effects on the community than the acts of one thousand crooked travelling salesmen, confidence tricksters and other swindlers. For instance, the collapse of the Atlantic Acceptance financial empire had a direct effect on the level of foreign investment, mortgage rates and the lives of thousands of modest investors on fixed incomes. Obviously, not all "immoral" economic acts are as blatantly criminal as the activities of some executives of Atlantic Acceptance. It is equally clear that pure monopoly is undesirable for everyone but the monopolists. The most difficult decision is to draw the line between free enterprise applying the ethics of the market place and the government trying to create a totally planned economy.

Conclusion

We have covered most of the obvious questions about the relationship of law and morals. We have looked at morals in a slightly broader context than that of homosexuality and prostitution. There are no easy answers. Students of the criminal law spend much of their time deciding where to draw the line between law and morals, between effective social control and unvarnished retribution, between defining blameworthiness and subscribing to the behavioural view. Criminal law must regulate the human acts we consider harmful to the type of society in which we want to live. Of course, we must decide what we mean by social harm. The control of antisocial acts must be effective; if ineffective, it will not deter the harmful acts. The attempt to prohibit the sale and manufacture of alcoholic beverages is a good example of legal farce. In the debate on law and morals we must be sure—even before talking of deterrence—that members of society consider the behaviour antisocial or that they want the power of the criminal law focussed on such behaviour. In the end the dilemma is a political one, because the final profile of the criminal law will be based on the type of the society for which the law is drafted.

In the following chapter, we will discover that morality plays a part in the determination of guilt. In this context morality in the law does not concern itself with strictures on particular forms of human vice and corruption. Instead, morality is injected into the decisions of judges who must decide whether the accused exhibited *mens rea,* criminal intention, recklessness, malice aforethought, evil intent or whatever label we might apply to it. The criminal law certainly does not restrict its definition of criminal responsibility to those acts of the accused that he says he intended to do. Frequently, the law looks objectively at allegedly criminal behaviour and, in effect, says to the accused, "You ought to have known that your initial acts could have led to that disastrous, dangerous or harmful consequence. Any reasonable man would have foreseen that consequence, and therefore, we will impose an external standard of responsibility on your behaviour." In this sense morality has an extremely important role to play in the criminal law. Yet all this is to say no more than that the criminal process is not a valueless system and deals with human beings, not laboratory specimens.

4/Illustrations

The following pages provide narratives of criminal acts. There is no immediate attempt to solve the legal or social problems presented. Some solutions are suggested in the following chapters.

Some questions have been appended that point to what are thought to be the most obvious problems raised. The reader will note that these illustrative cases contain many instances of the classic crimes such as larceny, rape and murder. A visit to the magistrates' courts in any city would show that the offences and surrounding circumstances described in the ensuing pages present a distorted picture of a typical court calendar. Some of the simpler highway traffic offences are grossly underrepresented as are the thousands of simple property offences where the accused has been caught red-handed with the goods and has confessed to the investigating or arresting police officer.

While some solutions will be suggested in the chapters of this book, the reader should be warned that there are not necessarily clear-cut answers to all of the questions presented. Persons who are not legally trained seem to suffer from the misconception that the law is carved on tablets of stone and is certain, immutable and unchanging. No doubt this confusion has been caused in part by the unfortunate tendency of lawyers to give the impression that they are omniscient and utterly confident of their opinions. These less than lovable qualities are symptoms of the disease of being a lawyer, and the intelligent layman, particularly one who is paying a fee, must not be fooled by these posturings.

Even where the stated problems do not reflect a grey, uncertain area of the law, the answer may not be a satisfactory one and may again offer corroboration to the suspicion that:

the law is "a ass" (as Dickens suggested); or

the law has lost touch with social reality; or

the law is in drastic need of revision but the lawyers in court and Parliament are so conservative, reactionary or obtuse that reform will not be achieved for two more generations.

On occasion, the plots may seem a little skimpy and the language may sound very close to the notes found in a policeman's notebook. The plots could have been filled out a little; this would have added elegance but no more relevance. The fact-situations are seldom ridiculous and in most instances are based on actual cases. A safe guess would be that the most unlikely plot lines are the authentic ones. To repeat: there are no correct answers unless the reader is so rule-oriented that he believes the pronouncement of one judge on one case is the embodiment of what the criminal law is and should be.

Non-lawyers should also be warned that the legal answers may not make much sense to those trained in sociology, psychology, psychiatry, social work, political science, philosophy or English literature. The law is a closed system with its own peculiar logic, rationalizations and dogmas. You will remember that the suggested definition of a crime is "an act so defined by law." The law makes the rules and binds members of society to those rules. The law strives to be certain, and rationality or logic to many lawyers is reflected in rules that aim at certainty. Finally, we must remember that the law is an exercise in power—to define crime and punishment, to convict or acquit the criminal, to apply punishment to that convicted criminal. These functions are to be achieved through fixed procedures which, we hope, will be fair—that is, in accordance with due process. In short, the law of criminal procedure is interested in proof rather than truth (although we hope they will coincide as often as possible).

The Elements of the Offence

Coincidence of Actus Reus and Mens Rea

Note: D (or a name starting with D) will usually signify the defendant and V will usually signify the victim.

1. Donald and Victor have always been sworn enemies. On more than one occasion Donald has said he would like to see Victor dead. One night Donald's car collides with a taxi in which Victor is an occupant. Independent witnesses are able to show that the collision was purely accidental.

   (a) Is D criminally responsible for V's death?
   (b) What if D had left a party half an hour before the collision, vowing to kill V that very night?
   (c) Would it make a difference if D were very drunk when he was driving his car?

2. David and Vince hate each other and each has made death threats against the other. One night D's mother, who is very nervous about many recent burglaries in the neighbourhood, tells him there is a prowler downstairs. D takes his shotgun and creeps down the staircase. He sees a movement behind a curtain and hears the click of a firearm being cocked. D fires both barrels at the curtain. To his astonishment, D sees V's dead body drop from behind the curtain.

   Is D guilty of any criminal offence in relation to V's death?

3. Drew has been involved in a brawl outside a tavern. He picked up a rock intending to hit one of his adversaries. The rock misses its human target

but breaks a window in the tavern. Should Drew be charged and convicted for

(a) damaging the window; or
(b) some other offence; or
(c) acquitted entirely?

4. Dick is arguing with Vikki. He takes off his belt intending to hit Vikki. He misses but the belt buckle hits and wounds Vanda who is a stranger.
   What offence, if any, has D committed?

5. Dan is parking his car on a city street. Constable Vickers is guiding him into the space. One of the rear wheels of D's car comes to rest on the constable's foot. At that moment, the car's engine stops but the evidence does not make it clear whether this was because the engine stalled or because D switched off the ignition. V pointed out to D that the wheel was on his foot. D made an offensive remark and told the constable he could wait. V made further requests and finally D moved the car. D was charged with assaulting a police officer in the execution of his duty.
   Can you imagine why there was any question of D being found guilty? Would the problem be different if D were charged with obstruction of Constable Vickers in the execution of his duty?

6. Delius visited Veronica's apartment where he found her on the couch in a state that D took to be sleep. He had sexual relations with V who, at the time, was in fact dead. D was charged under s. 178 of the Code, with offering an indignity to a human corpse. His defence was that he did not know V was dead. In his own defence, he tried to explain his behaviour by saying that the dead woman was a drug addict and was often found in a comatose state.
   Should he be convicted?

What is Mens Rea?

7. A man was charged with possession of a narcotic drug. He claimed that he thought the substance in his possession was harmless and not a narcotic. He claimed that he had a quantity of sugar of milk (which had the same physical appearance as heroin) that he intended to pass off as heroin because he wanted to hoodwink his intended victim. He said he was very surprised when the analysis showed that the substance was in fact heroin. The prosecution argued that the trade in heroin was so dangerous to society that liability for possession should be absolute.
   Should he be acquitted?

8. (a) Doreen arrived at Vancouver airport from Asia and was clearing her baggage through customs. The RCMP became suspicious of a scuba tank that seemed abnormally heavy. When D was approached by a man

she took to be a customs official, she said, "Oh, oh, looks as if I am in for it now." The man was from the RCMP, and he discovered that the tank contained a large amount of hashish. On being questioned by police officers, D replied that she did not know the scuba tank contained hashish, she did not know that it contained a drug, she suspected that the tank contained something illegal, and she refused to divulge the address to which she was supposed to deliver the tank. She was charged with importation of a narcotic contrary to the Narcotic Control Act.

(a) Would you convict her on the evidence given?
(b) Would your answer be different if the trial judge had allowed the prosecution to admit evidence that the hashish had a street value of many thousands of dollars?
(c) What if she thought the scuba tank contained:
  (i) pornography;
  (ii) counterfeit money;
  (iii) jewellery;
  (iv) heroin; or
  (v) amphetamines?

(b) Dingle is sitting in a tavern shouting his wares, "Speed, acid, MDA or hash." M, a police officer working undercover, approached D and asked for hash or acid. D said he was sold out of those drugs but offered mescaline. M offered to buy mescaline; a deal was struck and drugs and money changed hands. Analysis showed that the drug was LSD not mescaline. D was charged with trafficking in a restricted drug, namely, LSD.

(c) Dorothy owns a house in the country. She rented it to a group of young people who might be described with the rather loose label of hippies. She retained the right to use a bedroom and the kitchen in the house when she came for the occasional weekend. Otherwise she had no control over the premises except the landlady's usual right under a lease to inspect the premises with reasonable notice and at reasonable times. The police raided the premises and found various drugs. D was charged with possession of those drugs.

Note: Also see Illustration 31(e) for other drug cases.

Some Homicide Cases

9. *Malice Aforethought*

Darcy and Duggan decide to hold up a gas station. They agree to take along a gun but no bullets. They hope that the sight of the gun, presumably loaded, will scare their victim into handing over the cash. They pull into the gas station and Darcy points the gun at the attendant Van and demands money. While Duggan empties the cash register,

Darcy keeps Van covered. Unknown to the robbers, Ted, the owner of the gas station, has been working on his books in a back room. He grabs a loaded revolver from his desk drawer and takes a shot at Darcy but misses, killing instead his employee Van.

(a) Should Darcy and Duggan be convicted of murder under s. 213 of the Criminal Code?
(b) What difference would it make if D's gun had actually been loaded?
(c) Should Darcy be charged with murder if Ted shot and killed Duggan instead of Van?
(d) If the police had been called and a police officer had exchanged shots with the two robbers and one shot from a police revolver had killed Duggan, should Darcy be convicted of murder?
(e) If a third man waited outside in the getaway car, should he also be charged with murder in any, or all, of these circumstances?

10. *The Intent To Kill—Express or Implied*
Dillon was driving an automobile on a busy street. In the back seat he had a quantity of stolen goods. He reached an intersection where Constable Vail was on point duty. The policeman was an acquaintance of D. V had a conversation with D, saw the goods in the back of the car and asked D to pull over to the side of the road. The constable followed the car to a convenient place but, as V started to question D, D panicked and started to accelerate. V found a handhold on the side of the car and, draped over the car, held on while D speeded up. Witnesses said that the car was swerving from side to side. The prosecution claimed that D was trying to dislodge V, but the accused claimed that V's presence on the car made it unstable. Some distance down the road when D had reached thirty miles per hour, V fell off and under the wheels of a passing car. The constable was killed. D drove around the block, dumped the stolen goods, and came back to the place where V lay dead, claiming that he had no intention of hurting V. D was charged with murder.

Look at ss. 212 and 213 of the Criminal Code. Would he be convicted under any of these provisions?

11. (a) Dinah was jealous because her boyfriend had deserted her in favour of Verna. D thought that she would win back her lover if she could intimidate V. D went to V's house and thrust paper through the mail slot, splashed gasoline over the door step and started a fire. D claimed she only wanted to scare V, but unfortunately V's house was burned and two of V's children (aged seventeen and eleven) died of asphyxiation in the blaze.

Is D guilty of murder under ss. 212 or 213?

(b) Dante and Bert agreed to organize an "accidental" fire in a supermarket so that its owners can collect the insurance money. D and B carry out some field research and satisfy themselves that if a fire is started on a Saturday night, there will be no one on adjacent premises for at least four doors on either side of the supermarket. The arsonists are not as expert as they might be. They poured gasoline on the floor of the store, but they used too much and left it there so long before ignition that an explosion occurred as well as a fire. B was killed and D barely escaped. On the night of the explosion the next-door offices were not vacant; Vulcan, the cleaner, was performing his duties there. V was killed by the explosion.

Should D be convicted of murder under ss. 212 (c) or 213 of the Code?

12. Virgil was a very large, strong man. He went to a party and became very obnoxious. He accused Irwin, a small, shy man, of making passes at V's wife, and threw him down the stairs. The host Wade remonstrated with him for his bad behaviour; V threw him down the stairs. Then he picked up Wanda, the hostess, and held her over the balcony, threatening to drop her. Someone threatened to call the police and V went home. Irwin went over to the house of Dominic and told him and Dwight about Virgil's behaviour. Dominic and Dwight decided to go to V's place and have a chat with him. They were confronted at V's door by V armed with a crutch and a knife. He was very menacing and they left. Dominic ran home and came back armed with a loaded revolver. He could not at first find Dwight and thought he may have been attacked by V. They again went to V's door and started remonstrating with V who lunged at them with the crutch. D and D said that the crutch hit the revolver in Dominic's hand, making it discharge. The bullet entered V's armpit and then his heart and killed him. D and D panicked and were picked up in their car some hundreds of miles from home. A young boy had a different version of the second visit at V's door. He said D and D kicked open V's door and challenged him and fired the gun.

    Consider the liability of D and D, particularly under s. 212(c) of the Code.

More Homicide Cases

In the next two illustrations there is no question of the intention of the accused, but was it criminal intention?

13. *Euthanasia and the Law*

    Derek's mother was sixty-six years old. She had incurable cancer of a kind that caused a very painful, lingering death. He did not want to place her in a hospital and she was cared for by D and his wife in their own home. D was a loving and dutiful son, and he and his wife gave the dying woman the most solicitous care. After three months of suffering, D could no longer stand the agony that his mother was obviously experiencing. D dosed his mother's coffee with a lethal quantity of sleeping pills and she died.

    (a) Should D be convicted of murder?

(b) What if D simply made it possible for his mother to take the pills herself?

14. *Killing for Conscience*
Dennis is a member of a religious sect that believes that human life depends on God's will and therefore it is contrary to scriptural teaching to take curative drugs or seek medical advice and assistance. D's baby is born with a congenital heart defect. He is advised that the child will die within three months if an operation is not performed. The baby died without having the operation.

Consult ss. 205, 212 and 213 of the Code to decide D's criminal liability, if any.

Would it make any difference if expert medical evidence at the trial gave the opinion that an operation would not necessarily have been successful?

Homicides Falling Short of Murder—When is a Tort More Than a Tort?

15. *Professional Standard of Care*
The accused doctor was a public health medical officer. He was on a routine visit to a school where he meant to innoculate eighty first-grade children against whooping cough. He chose the wrong ampoules of serum, and five children died from the effects.

(a) Should this be a matter for the criminal law?
(b) If he is charged with a criminal offence, should the law demand a higher standard of behaviour from a medical practitioner than from a nurse, a medical orderly or the storeman in charge of medical supplies?

16. *The Demon Alcohol*
A bootlegger, with a large and dedicated clientele, usually produced good liquor. On one occasion his method of production was inferior, and his moonshine liquor was extremely dangerous because it contained wood alcohol. Two of his more thirsty clients died of the effects of drinking the tainted liquor. He was charged with manslaughter.

(a) Should he be criminally responsible?
(b) Would it make any difference if the accused were a lawful manufacturer of orange pop and, on one occasion, his product was lethal because his bottling equipment had become contaminated and two little girls died of drinking the orange drink?

17. *Death and Inattention*
Davinia, who was an unemployed spinster, lived with her elderly aunt, Violet. She paid no board but, in return for free food and board, she acted as companion to her aunt. Her aunt became ill and was so weak that she

could not prepare food for herself or give herself her medicines. D simply ignored her. After a week or so her aunt died from a combination of the original illness, malnutrition and lack of attention. D was charged with manslaughter. Would it make a difference if

(a) D were not related to V;
(b) D were paid by V to be a companion;
(c) D would benefit under V's will?

18. *The Dividing Line Between Stupidity and Wickedness*
Dyson was standing on a pier. He noticed a large wooden packing case near him. The crate belonged to a refreshment kiosk nearby. For no apparent reason, D picked up the heavy crate and threw it into the water. Unknown to D, Veronica was swimming in the water below. The crate hit V and she drowned. D was charged with manslaughter under s. 205 of the Code.
Would you convict?

19. *The Hunter and the Hunted*
Dudley and Verity went deer-hunting together. They separated during their search for venison. Toward dusk, when they had both been unsuccessful, D heard a rustle in a clump of bush and in his excitement fired into the bush killing V instead of some antlered beast. D is charged with manslaughter. How would any of the following factors change your decision:

(a) It was D's first experience in deer-hunting;
(b) It was V's first experience in deer-hunting;
(c) D, V (or both) failed to wear distinctive clothing recommended by most competent authorities;
(d) They were hunting out of season;
(e) They had failed to obtain a hunting licence;
(f) They were hunting in season and they had the necessary licences but were in a national park where hunting is always prohibited;
(g) D was using soft-nosed bullets that were prohibited by law?

20. *Law and Order on the Highway*
Devlin had an automobile accident at an intersection. A child was killed. It is possible that the death was a pure accident or a piece of very bad luck. More frequently, a charge would be laid because there was some attributable blame. The offence could range from a speeding offence, following too close, failing to keep a proper look-out, careless driving, dangerous driving, impaired driving or criminal negligence. The last offence can carry a maximum penalty of five years' imprisonment. Most of the others would result in a moderate fine. Some may result in cancellation of driving privileges for a specific or indefinite period. (No doubt a civil suit would be brought by the child's parents. D would have

to pay part of the cost of repairing the damages to his automobile, and his insurance rates would probably rise.) How would the following facts affect the criminal liability that D should incur:

(a) D was travelling five, ten, fifteen, thirty or fifty miles over the speed limit;
(b) He had had one, two, five or ten whiskies *or* two, four, ten or twenty beers, within six hours of the accident;
(c) He had failed to have his car tested when requested to do so by the Department of Motor Vehicles. His untested car was
  (i) in perfect condition; or
  (ii) needed attention to steering, brakes and headlights;
(d) He had no driver's licence;
(e) He was driving an automobile while his licence was suspended;
(f) He had failed to slow down at
  (i) an unmarked intersection;
  (ii) a pedestrian crosswalk;
(g) He had failed to observe a "slow" sign, a "stop" sign, a flashing amber light, a stop light or a policeman on point duty;
(h) He had failed to yield right of way;
(i) Investigation shows that he was only partly to blame. Arithmetic seems inappropriate to such a human event but a coroner's jury decided that D was only sixty per cent to blame, because another driver had failed to signal a left turn and obscured D's vision for a short time;
(j) He had recently been convicted of two speeding offences;
(k) He has defective eyesight and
  (i) he does not wear spectacles; or
  (ii) his licence is properly endorsed for use of an automobile with prescribed spectacles.

Note: The facts above can be treated as alternatives or various combinations that might exist.

Further Problems of Mens Rea
(With Particular Emphasis on Mistake)

Mistake could be treated as a defence (or a rule subordinate to the general principles of the criminal law) but it is placed here because mistake is not a true defence but a negation of *mens rea*. In the usual case where a defence is raised, the accused is saying "*Yes,* I did the act *but* I have an explanation." With mistake of fact, he says "No, I did not do the act as charged *because*. . . ."

21. Mistake (a) Sex in the Permissive Society

Dale is a young man of about twenty-three years and he is friendly with Viva. They have been going out for about six months. D and V want to get married but must wait until D has graduated. In the meantime, they start having sexual relations. V told D that she was seventeen and from her physical appearance D had no reason to doubt her. V's mother discovers that her daughter is having sexual relations with D and is so outraged that she reports the matter to the police. V is in fact only fifteen years and ten months. D is charged with an offence under s.146(2) of the Criminal Code, for having sexual intercourse with a female under sixteen years of age. His defence was that he did not know that she was that young and believed she was of the age of consent.

(a) Is D guilty?
(b) Would you change your decision if V were living with her father and he gave D every indication that he did not mind the young people having sexual relations?

Note: There are other cases on sex offences later in the illustrations.

(b) How Innocent a Mistake?
Drake was a spectator at a street fight. An off-duty policeman, Vidal, saw the event and decided to intervene. V claims that he identified himself, but the court tended to believe D's story that V stayed incognito until after the event. When it appeared that V was about to enter the fray, D restrained him. D claimed that he simply pushed V, although the plainclothes policeman said that D had used more violence than that. D's defence to the charge (of assaulting a police office in the execution of his duty) was that he did not know V was a police officer.

Should he be acquitted on that charge? Should he be convicted of the lesser offence of common assault?

22. *Theft in the Acquisitive Society*
Note: More illustrations of property offences at Illustration 50.

(a) Dogwood was a lumber beachcomber. With the use of a motor boat he searched out and retrieved logs, which he salvaged. He received a reward from the lumber company whose mark was on the log. One day he noticed a log that, he claimed, was floating free outside a log boom. There was no legislation on this point, but the convention of the lumber industry was that any logs outside a boom could be salvaged by a beachcomber. There was a brochure, published by the British Columbia Department of Forestry, that advised beachcombers that they must not steal logs but it made no specific mention of log booms. The lumber company claimed the language of the brochure was too broad but even if it were accurate, witnesses had seen D go inside the boom to retrieve the log. D claimed that the log had been floating free, and a wave had driven it inside the log boom by the time he reached it. The company therefore demanded the return of their log. D promised to do so when he was paid the customary reward. The company caused D to be charged with larceny. Should Dogwood have a defence based on

(a) a mere convention of the industry;
(b) his perception of the location of the log; or
(c) the witnesses' perception of the location of the log?

Also consider the following cases that contain similar problems:

(b) One day, a scrap-metal dealer went to an army firing range situated on some wilderness land near the town where he lived. He found there a large number of metal bomb casings. He loaded them on his truck and sold them. He was charged with larceny. He claimed that "everyone" went onto the bombing range, although it was government property. He said he took the casings because he thought they had been abandoned and were of no use to anyone else.

(c) A civilian cook on an armed services base baked some cakes for the evening meal in the mess. A large slab of cake was left after the personnel had dined. He knew that the cake would only be thrown into the garbage so he took it home for his wife and children. The army sold the garbage from the kitchen to a pig farmer. He was charged with larceny.

23. *Mistake of Law*

(a) Dobson had lost his driver's licence on being convicted of driving an automobile while impaired. He had a job driving vehicles on federal property—the Halifax International Airport. His employer advised him that they would prefer him not to drive at the airport until his status was clarified. D called the Registrar of Motor Vehicles and was told by a senior official there that he could drive at the airport without a current licence so long as his employer approved. D drove at the airport and was involved in a collision. At that stage, D was charged with driving a vehicle while unlicensed. The charge was based on an obscure regulation that provided that a valid licence was needed to drive on federal property.
Should D be acquitted?

(b) Daisy rented an apartment in an old house, and she was delighted to discover that it had a fireplace. She thought she would brighten up the place a little and she bought from an antique store some beautiful old tiles that she used to decorate the surrounds of the fireplace. She attached the tiles with an adhesive. When her lease expired, D decided to take the tiles with her. Her landlord had her charged with larceny because he said that all "fixtures" belong to the landlord. (In strict law, the landlord may well have been correct in treating the tiles as fixtures.) D insisted that she should be acquitted because she did not know they were "fixtures." Do you agree?

(c) Derby came to Canada as an immigrant from a country that was not Anglo-Saxon in origin. He is questioned by the police for alleged criminal behaviour, but his defence was that in his country of birth his acts were not criminal or unlawful. Indeed what he did was standard behaviour among the people of his village. Imagine that D had committed one of the following:

(a) He regularly beats his wife because, he says, she is lazy, disobedient and sometimes talks with strange men in the supermarket.
(b) He quite seriously wounded a twenty-three-year-old man when he discovered that the man had been having sexual intercourse with D's twenty-one-year-old unmarried daughter.
(c) He wanted to add an extension to his house and offered bribe money to a building inspector from city hall.
(d) He played cards for money in a cafe near his home.
(e) He has a still in his basement where he makes liquor.

Or let us suppose that D is not from another country but is a Canadian, an Innuit or a Canadian Indian from a remote reserve in northern Saskatchewan. Would that affect your verdict?

(d) Dalton is an impecunious university student who works part-time as a waiter. His boss is not a very principled person; he owed D money for a night when the student-waiter worked over-time. D has asked the restaurant owner at least once weekly for the last ten weeks but he has received no money. D finally lost patience and simply took the money from the cash register and left a note explaining his action. D was charged with larceny.

24. *Marriage as a Crime: Was it Mistake of Fact or Mistake of Law? What's the Difference?*

(a) Dwight had been married to Agnes in 1966. She left him in 1970, and he had not seen her since. He met Florence in 1974 and now wants to marry her. He decided to save money by filing his own divorce papers. He obtained a decree *nisi* on the basis of Agnes's desertion. He thought that this meant he was free to remarry. As a precaution, he asked a young law student whom he knew if a decree *nisi* meant he was able to remarry. Unfortunately, the law student had failed his course in Family Law I and gave D incorrect advice. D went through a form of marriage with Florence without waiting for a decree absolute and was subsequently charged with bigamy.

(b) Darius was married to Ethel. After a time, she got sick of him and left but told him that although they went through a wedding ceremony, they were never actually married because she had been previously married to Charles and had never obtained a divorce. On the strength of this story, and making no further investigation, D went through a form of marriage. Later, D discovered that E's story was false and she was divorced when she married D. Can D be convicted of bigamy?

(c) Deeble, a near illiterate, consults a lawyer about a divorce and the lawyer starts proceedings. There is little doubt that D will be granted his divorce as he has adequate grounds. After a few weeks, D receives a letter that is simply a notice of the date of the hearing of this petition. D misunderstands the import of the letter and is jubilant because he thinks he is a free man. He rushes over to Gloria's place. Gloria is a wealthy widow. She accepts his proposal and D goes through a form of marriage with Gloria. Soon after, he is charged with bigamy.

(d) Debbie was married to a sailor named Toby. She hears in 1961 that his ship has foundered in a tropical storm off Sumatra and all hands are presumed dead. In 1966 she married again. Two months later Toby arrived home with stirring tales of shipwrecks and coral islands. D is charged with bigamy. The prosecution claimed that D was only entitled to marry after Toby had been continuously absent for seven years when the law would presume that he was dead (see s. 254(2) of the Code).

25. *Dirty Books and Clean Literature*

(a) A bookseller in Toronto was raided by the vice squad which made a quick perusal of the shelves and storeroom and seized fourteen titles. They informed him that he would be charged with possessing, and offering for sale, obscene books. At his trial his defence lawyer argued that the bookseller stocked 3,500 different titles and he had no way of knowing which books were likely to be declared obscene and which were acceptable because he found it impossible to read all of them. (He also argued that, in any case, he could not make a prejudgement about the legal definition of obscenity.)

(b) This is a similar case to (a) except that the accused D owned a neighbourhood variety store. His small collection of paperbacks was stocked and serviced by a publisher's representative and D had no say in the choice of titles. Furthermore D argued that he could not be convicted of obscenity because he could neither read nor write English, the language in which the books were written.

(c) Dolores owned an art gallery. One day the vice squad raided her premises and confiscated six paintings and she was charged with obscenity. At her trial, she said that she knew nothing about art but knew what her customers liked.

The Relationship between Intent and Motive

26. *From the Best Motives*

Dupuis, who was partly a public-spirited citizen, partly a busybody, was convinced that the mayor of his town was a corrupt man. He wanted to test his hypothesis and persuaded his friend Albert, a road-building contractor, to try to bribe the mayor in exchange for a lucrative contract.

The mayor may have been dishonest but he was not stupid. He smelled a rat and reported Albert's attempted bribe to the police. Albert told the police the whole story and D was charged with attempting to bribe a public official. In his defence, D argued that he was a public-spirited citizen who wanted to keep city hall honest. What would the verdict be if

(a) subsequent events showed that D's suspicions were well founded; or
(b) D were head of the fraud squad of the city police?

The Borderland of Mens Rea

27. *Strict and Absolute Liability—and Due Diligence*

Sometimes the law decides that some forms of social behaviour are so trivial (or so socially significant) that *mens rea* and procedural safeguards are not appropriate. The law does not require any proof (or perhaps not full proof by the Crown beyond a reasonable doubt) that the accused intended to do the act. The trivial cases may concern regulation of everyday problems such as traffic, liquor, pure foods, pollution, health or safety. These are public torts and not really criminal. The penalties will usually be fines or short terms of imprisonment. The idea of creating these quasi-criminal offences is based on expediency and deterrence.

There are a few serious offences that attract liability without full proof of intent; these include some narcotics offences and possession of many items that are potentially dangerous or very difficult for the prosecution to prove under ordinary evidential rules. These offences include possession of recently stolen goods, burglars' tools, counterfeiting equipment, or explosives. Should the following cases come within the definition of absolute liability offences?

(a) Drug control legislation provides that everyone who traffics in a narcotic drug or what is held out to be a narcotic drug shall be guilty of an offence and subject to severe punishment. D claims that he had been persuaded, against his better judgement, to sell heroin to a seventeen-year-old girl who wanted to find out what it was like. To protect her from becoming hooked, he substituted a mixture of milk powder and aspirin for the heroin which was originally in the capsule.

(b) Dobie and Dorion were driving on a city street at 2:20 a.m. when they were stopped by a police cruiser. A search by the police produced a crowbar, four screw-drivers, three credit cards, two flashlights, three pairs of gloves and two pairs of nylon stockings. They were charged under s. 309(1) of the Code which makes it an offence for anyone who "without lawful excuse, the proof of which lies upon him, has in his possession any instrument suitable for house-breaking . . . under circumstances that give rise to a reasonable inference that the instrument has been used or is or was intended to be used for house-breaking. . . ."

(c) Dane's hobby was tinkering about with cars. He particularly liked restoring English sportscars. He obtained from a wrecker a 1968 Aston Martin but unfortunately the engine was beyond repair. He was having a beer in a pub one night and a man whom he had not previously met and whom he only knew as "Mike" offered him an engine from a 1979 Aston Martin. This engine could be adapted for use in his 1968 Aston Martin chassis. M wanted only $150 for the engine which D thought was a very low price but he could not resist the bargain. Of course the engine had been stolen, but D, in his enthusiasm, had not given any thought to such a possibility. D picked up the engine and noticed that the identification number on the engine block had been partly obliterated with acid or some other corrosive substance. D did not give it another thought until he was charged with possession of property obtained by crime under s. 312 of the Code. Subsection (2) of that provision states "evidence that a person has in his possession ... part of a motor vehicle identification number of which has been wholly or partly ... obliterated ... is, in the absence of any evidence to the contrary, proof that the motor vehicle or part" was obtained by crime.

The following are examples of the "public torts" or quasi-criminal and social welfare offences. In most instances, the accused is facing a fine. Sometimes on a second or subsequent conviction, the accused may face a jail term or the loss of a licence, both of which would affect his livelihood. The question in each case will be, Should the accused be convicted when there is some (or a clear) indication that he did intend to do the act or lacked knowledge that would have enabled him to avoid committing the act? In many instances, the prosecution will argue that it would be impossible to make the law effective if lack of *mens rea* (or knowledge or intent) were a defence.

(d) Dorey owned a tavern. There was a local law that no on-duty policeman could be served with liquor in a public bar. Policemen wore a checkered band on their left sleeves when they were on duty. Constable Abbott was on the beat on a very hot day. He felt very thirsty. He removed his on-duty band and entered D's bar where he bought a drink. One of A's superiors noticed him in the bar and D was charged with an offence under the local law. D claims that he thought it was lawful to serve A as he had no band on his sleeve.

(e) On another occasion Dorey was charged with serving liquor to a man who was drunk. D claimed that he did not know the man was drunk—he seemed to be speaking clearly and was able to sit on his stool.

(f) Dixie lived in a town where the killing of domestic pigeons was an offence. D saw two plump pigeons in a field and killed them. When the police officer arrived with a summons at D's house, she discovered that the pigeons were prized homing pigeons being trained for the Annual Trans-Canada Pigeon Race. D claimed that she did not know the difference between a wild pigeon and a domestic one.

(g) Dominic ran a corner grocery. He sold bags of sugar that were marked "Net Weight: Five Kilograms." One of his customers bought such a bag and discovered, on weighing it on her kitchen scales, that it contained only four kilograms. D was charged under the Weights and Measures Regulation Act. He claimed that it was simply an honest mistake.

(h) Dent was driving a truck along a highway when he was stopped by a policeman for speeding. D explained that he did not realize he was exceeding the speed limit because he suspected his speedometer was not working properly. The police officer tested his speedometer and discovered that it was indeed faulty. He nevertheless charged D with speeding. (In that jurisdiction it was not required by law to have a speedometer on a motor vehicle.)

(i) Dulcie went duck-hunting. The Wildlife Protection Act made it an offence to shoot ducks within fifty yards of a feeding station (where food was left for migratory ducks). D shot a duck in circumstances that would come within that prohibition. She said she did not know where the feeding stations were located.

28. *Vicarious Liability*

Is the situation any different in these strict and absolute liability offences if the accused did not actually do the act himself but it was done by a relative, an employee, an independent contractor or some other person (including the legal "person" of a corporation) with whom the accused has some legal relationship?

(a) Dickens ran a tavern. He went on vacation and left Otto, his head barman, as manager. Before leaving, he reminded Otto that the city police vice squad had warned the tavern owner that prostitutes must not gather in the saloon bar. After D had been on holidays for only five days, the vice squad visited D's bar and discovered seven prostitutes in the bar. D was charged with the relevant offence. In his defence, he argued that he had no knowledge of the presence of the prostitutes and had warned his manager against this very eventuality.

(b) The City of Delray made a contract with the Acme Trash Company to dispose of the city's garbage. The company leased a site and dumped the garbage there but effluent from that site found its way into the Delray River causing serious pollution to the city's water supply. The city was charged under the provincial pollution control legislation. The penalties were $1000 per day for every day on which the pollution continued.

(c) ABC Limited, a corporation, was the incorporated business of Mr. A.B. Cox. He had been advised by his lawyer that he could minimize his tax burden by this legal subterfuge. He was the sole director and the sole shareholder (except for the one share he had given his wife). ABC Limited was charged with an offence under the Sales Tax Act with falsifying its sales tax returns.

Should Cox also be charged with an offence under the Act?

Other General Principles

The common law of crime developed from case precedents. Until this century, those precedents consisted of reports of trials and the reports were very short, quite often inaccurate and contained little discussion of the underlying intellectual content of the law. Making law by collecting past court decisions is not a very satisfactory method of creating a system of legal thought. A code of criminal law should change all that but the Criminal Code does not have a comprehensive General Part that would set out the principles of the law. Those general principles would provide a firm foundation upon which subordinate rules could be built. Principles would include fundamentals such as guaranteeing a presumption of innocence, prohibition of retroactive laws and, of course, a description of *actus reus* and *mens rea,* the physical and mental elements of a crime. We have already had many illustrations about *mens rea* (including some offences where it is not included, at least not to a full extent). Some of the illustrations have hinted at problems of *actus reus,* and it is often impossible to separate *actus reus* and *mens rea* despite the best efforts of some theorists. After we have looked at some cases of *actus reus,* we shall look at some cases illustrating other principles such as causation and accountability of persons who were secondary participants in crime.

29. When is an Act a Willed Act?

(a) Docherty had been a sleepwalker all his life. This night, he had gone to bed worrying about the fact that his mother had withdrawn from the bank a large sum in cash to use as a deposit on a house the following day. While in a somnambulistic state, he had gone to his mother's handbag and taken the roll of money and returned to his bed and hid the money under the pillow.

(b) Dallas was charged with criminal negligence because his car had crossed the centre line and crashed into an oncoming car, killing two people. He had not been drinking but he claimed that he could not recollect any of his journey which had been for five miles and had involved some difficult manoeuvres, such as steering his vehicle around traffic islands, etc.

(c) Danby went to an oral surgeon for the removal of two teeth. Sodium pentothal was administered to him. Two days before the extractions D had signed the consent form which the surgeon required of all his patients. The form contained the following warning: "Patients are cautioned not to drive after anaesthetic until head clears." When D had apparently regained consciousness, he paid the bill and was dismissed by the nurse who testified that he appeared quite normal. She reminded him not to drive a car until his head was clear. He said he felt fine but intended to walk anyway. At his trial, D could not recollect any of this conversation. When he left the office, D immediately walked to his car and drove away. One block from the office he allegedly suffered a "blackout" and crashed into a parked car. When arrested he showed signs of lack of coordination. D had had no alcohol and it was conceded that his condition was solely due to the drug. He was charged with driving a motor vehicle while his ability to drive was impaired by a drug.

Should D be held criminally responsible?

(d) Dunlop was the mother of a child of seven years. One day, D called her daughter, Vera, to the window of their second-floor apartment to see a parade passing by. V was found on the pavement outside the apartment with a fractured skull. D was later stopped by the police as she drove through the city streets. She could not remember doing anything to her child, although she did express a vague concern about V's welfare, as if she were trying to recall something. Clinical examination proved that D was suffering from a brain tumour that was no doubt the cause of her attack on V whom D had pushed out of the window.

Is there any criminal responsibility here?

30. Who or What Killed the Victim—A Problem of Legal Causation

(a) Devine and Voss were drinking together in a tavern. After a couple of beers, they started quarrelling about a girl. They started wrestling and finally D drew a knife and V sustained a wound on the arm which required stitches but was far from a fatal injury. He was taken to hospital where he was kept overnight for observation. During the night a young intern ordered penicillin injections for V. The patient showed a very strong reaction to penicillin, and the duty nurse marked his chart with a warning that the patient was not to be given any further injections of the drug. Unfortunately a change of staff occurred and the new nurse and doctor did not notice the warning on the chart. V was given further large doses of penicillin and he died.

Should D be convicted of the murder of V? If not, under what changed circumstances would a conviction be warranted?

(*a*) If D had stabbed V as mentioned in (a) and V proved to be a haemophiliac and bled to death, should D be convicted of murder?

(*b*) Devine and Voss had a fist fight and D knocked V unconscious. If D then left V lying in the street and V had died of exposure and loss of blood, would that be murder if the death had occurred in July (or January) in Whitehorse?

(b) There had been a violent drunken brawl on an army base. Vogel was injured. His drunken friends carried him to the medical station, dropping him several times on the way. The medical staff was overburdened with the victims of the brawl. Consequently, they decided to practice a form of triage. V was placed in the group whose injuries were thought the least serious. Eventually V was given artificial respiration and a saline drip. In fact, V was seriously injured, having sustained a bayonet wound to the lung. Expert evidence showed that the medical treatment was completely inappropriate in the circumstances. Duncan, who had wielded the bayonet that injured V, was charged with murder.

Had D legally caused V's death?

(c) Dyer and Diaz were sitting in a tavern and they noticed Vallance who seemed to be very drunk. They decided that when V left the tavern, they would follow V and "roll" him. They undertook their plan and relieved V of his wallet, and they threw him over a wall into an open storm drain that contained about eight inches of water. Because of both his extreme state of drunkenness and the very steep sides of the storm drain, V died there from drowning. He tried to get out but he kept falling back and finally fell face down into the water.

(d) Dube and her three companions beat up Verrill. V was quite badly hurt and had lost consciousness. D thought that they had killed V and decided they had to dispose of the body. They threw V's weighted body into a lake. An autopsy on the body showed that V had died of drowning rather than the wounds inflicted by D and her friends.

(e) Dolly was the wife of Steve, a well-known gangster. She came home very late one night. She had been out on the town with her lover. She was very afraid of Steve and when his questions became a little too insistent, she told him that Steve's friend Vinton had taken her up to his apartment and would not let her go and had made a pass at her. Of course all this was untrue but Steve rushed from the house and killed Vinton. Did D legally cause V's death?

31. The Parties to an Offence

(a) Day tried to persuade Pan to kidnap his enemy Vanek. P pretended to go along with the plan but reported the incident to the police.

Should D be convicted of some criminal offence?

(b) Pater is an elder statesman of crime. He provided a car for his protégé, Dome, so that D could hold up a bank. What would be P's criminal liability if either of the following events happened:

(a) D used the car to commit rape; or
(b) D held up the bank and killed a bank guard in the process?

(c) Adam, Badger and Cade decided that they would rob Vita, who ran a store. They agreed that they would not carry a gun and would only use as much force as was necessary. They did not expect much resistance as V was a frail, old man. C drove the car and waited outside V's store. A and B entered the store and demanded money. V proved to be much more intractable than expected. He would not hand over his money and refused to tell them where he had hidden it. A hit V on the head with a can of pet food. V did not fall down or become unconscious. Then A looked for the money while B held V. The old storekeeper kept yelling. A became scared of the noise V was making and asked B to "shut him up." B hit V with his fist and the old man fell to the ground. B placed his knee on V's throat. V died of asphyxiation. All three men were charged with murder. A's lawyer argued that his client was not guilty because B had used more force than was necessary and more than was agreed upon. C also argued that he was not liable because he did not know what was happening in the store and only agreed to drive the car.

If Dud had loaned the other three his car (and knew of their plans), would he be guilty of murder?

(d) Dover met Prince in a hamburger joint. They were both drifters and decided to drift together. That day P bought a large and dangerous-looking knife. Toward dusk, D and P had stopped at a gas station and struck up a conversation with Vezina. They noticed that she had a fair amount of cash with her. They asked her for a lift. When they had driven a short way, P drew his knife and told V to turn on to a quiet side-road. P and V got out of the car and went into the bush. P told D to turn the car around and wait. Later P came back and D helped P move V's badly wounded body further into the trees where she died. Was D a party to the murder of V?

(e) Is Dulcinea a party to the offence of possession of a drug under the Narcotic Control Act in any of the following situations:

(a) D lives with Perry who is a heroin addict. She is not an addict but she loves P and wants to go on living with him. One day the police raid their apartment and find P with some heroin that he was just about to inject into himself.

(b) D is hitchhiking through the Rockies and is picked up by three people who have been smoking dope. The ashtray of the car is full of roaches—the butts of marijuana cigarettes. A policeman stops them and charges all four with possession of cannabis on the basis of the butts in the ashtray.

(f) Pratt and Potter were members of a motorcycle gang. The gang had taken Vonnie, a sixteen-year-old girl, to an isolated site. They ripped off her clothes and eighteen men had sexual intercourse with her without her consent. Pratt did not have sexual intercourse with V; he merely watched as others did so. There was evidence that Potter was seen with his pants down waiting for his turn but there was no evidence that he had had sexual intercourse with V. Could either or both be convicted of being parties to the offence of rape?

(g) Davis was charged with setting fire to a school along with Pedder. The two had been together from late afternoon until they had been apprehended. During that time both took a ride in D's car out to the area in which the school was situated. On the way D stopped and purchased a can of gasoline at a filling station and placed it in the car behind the seat in which P was sitting. Eventually the car was parked across from the school, the can taken from the car and the fire set. Assuming P remained at all times in the car, does non-accidental presence at the commission of a crime, as in these circumstances, justify a jury making an inference of abetting?

(h) Dulles and Palmer were travelling together in a car. Dulles was driving negligently or recklessly and had an accident causing property damage and injury to other people. Is P a party to an offence in relation to the accident? How would the following facts affect your answer:

(a) P knew D was an habitually careless driver;
(b) D was intoxicated;
(c) D was intoxicated and had become so while P was drinking with him;
(d) D and P had jointly borrowed the car without permission?

(i) When D entered his hotel room he found three provincial police officers questioning several of his guests in regard to an alleged liquor offence. D, on learning this, did no other act than shouting out to his friends not to give the officers their proper identity. All of D's friends on being questioned followed D's advice and thus hampered the officer's investigation. Was D a party to his companions' alleged offence?

(j) D, D1 and D2 joined together in a common purpose to rob V. During the attempted robbery D struck down and killed V with an iron bar. D1 and D2, who, up to this time, had performed the tasks assigned to them, on seeing the iron bar raised, decided they wanted no further part in the crime and fled the scene. Are D1 and D2 parties to the killing of V along with D?

(k) Polly's husband, Dwayne, had stolen money in a bank holdup. He hid in the attic of their house. P misled the police by telling them she had not seen her husband. D's best friend, Upton, lent D a driving licence and a car so that he could escape. P and U were charged with being accessories after the fact to bank robbery.

Would it make any difference if P and D were not married but simply:

(i) engaged; or

(ii) living "common law"?

Similarly, would it make any difference if U were D's brother or father?

32. *The Anachronism of the Inchoate Crime of Attempt*

Note: It may seem a little strange to have two offences under General Principles but these inchoate crimes have qualities that seriously affect the principles of the criminal law and the elements of *mens rea* and *actus reus* in particular.

The crime of attempt, like conspiracy, is an inchoate crime. More than enough ink has been wasted in concocting theories to rationalize the law of attempt or to destroy someone else's theory. No catalogue of crimes and legal conundrums would be complete without the old chestnuts greatly loved by law professors and defence lawyers desperate for an argument. Perhaps it would only be fair to add at this point that there is supposed to be a distinction between attempts that are factually impossible and those that are legally impossible. Is it a crime:

(a) to attempt to steal from an empty pocket?

(b) to attempt to kill your enemy by shooting into his bed when he is

(i) not home yet;

(ii) in the bathroom ten feet away;

(iii) next door;

(iv) in another city; or

(v) already dead?

(c) to attempt to abort a woman who, in fact, is not pregnant?

(d) to attempt to steal an article that, unknown to you, is really yours?

(e) Finally, there is the famous case of Lady Eldon who had been on a trip to Paris. She returned to England with six pairs of gloves. She thought they were made from a rare and very expensive Brussels lace which would make them dutiable. She tried to smuggle them through customs. What if:

(i) the gloves were cheap imitations and not subject to customs duty; or

(ii) the gloves were authentic, but the day before (and unknown to Lady Eldon) the duty on lace gloves had been lifted?

(f) Is it attempt if:

(i) A, B and C want to rob a bank messenger. They drive around the streets looking for him, drive past the bank several times; they are armed and want the money but they never find the messenger.

(ii) Two men, wearing balaclavas pulled down over their heads, knocked on the door of a fast-food outlet. The manager told them it was closed. The manager noticed that one of the men had a gun in his hand. The two men walked away. The manager phoned the police. The police found the men, and before they were apprehended, one of the men threw into a snowbank an article that turned out to be a balaclava. The police also discovered that both men were armed. They were charged with attempted robbery.

(g) A person is found with a box of matches and a can of petrol alongside the haystack of a farmer. Is that attempted arson?

What if the person was known to have a strong hatred of the farmer?

Can you imagine any circumstances under which his behaviour would be considered quite innocent?

(h) A jeweller's business has been going badly. He decided to fake a robbery hoping to claim the insurance. He hides his valuable jewels and watches, and he ties himself in a chair. The police discover his ruse.

Can he be convicted of attempted crime and, if so, what crime?

(i) A man asks a little boy to carry his bags and promises him some candy and "some fun" if he will accompany the man to a park. After a short conversation the boy runs home to his parents. The prosecution is able to have admitted in evidence that the man has previous convictions for pedophilia.

Can he be convicted of attempted indecent assault?

(j) There has been a theft of a very large shipment of beef. On a routine check, police stop a truck that is obviously overloaded. They find a large quantity of beef in the truck. They suspect that it is part of the stolen shipment. The driver of the truck decides to cooperate. A policeman travels in the truck cabin and two other officers hide themselves in the back. When the truck arrives at its destination, the police arrest the men waiting to receive the meat who are charged with attempting to receive stolen goods.

33. Conspiracy: Another Inchoate Crime

(a) The Dobells, husband and wife, are charged with conspiracy. No other persons were involved. Can they be convicted?

(b) Dube has been charged with conspiracy with Oscar. Can D be convicted in any or all of the following circumstances:

(a) O has been tried separately and found not guilty;
(b) O has died;
(c) O cannot be found;
(d) O has claimed diplomatic immunity; or
(e) O has a defence of criminal insanity?

(c) Charles owns a hotel in Montreal and, two blocks away, Colin owns a similar hotel. They have very thirsty customers. There is a convention in the district that if friendly Constable O'Reilly is given an incentive on the first of each and every month, there will be no police raids. Unfortunately for all parties concerned, a crusading police chief takes over and discovers the activities of Constable O'Reilly. Charles and Colin are charged with conspiring to bribe a police officer. The Crown chooses this offence rather than the more obvious one of bribery of a police officer because the penalty is greater, and the prosecution case on such a charge would be weak because O'Reilly will not be a very cooperative witness. Charles and Colin argue that they cannot be charged with conspiracy as they have never met and have never discussed the question of bribing O'Reilly by telephone, letter, or in any other way.

(d) On a wall at RCMP headquarters, the narcotics department has a chart that shows a very elaborate pyramidal hierarchy for the illegal marketing of heroin in Canada. This flow chart is based on information, more or less accurate, collected by the intelligence and narcotics departments of the RCMP. The police officers are unable to obtain evidence against every person named on the chart, but they have decided that the following persons are involved in heroin trafficking, based on business partnerships, observed meetings, family relationships, wire-tapped phone calls, the occasional fingerprint, the mention of a particular person in a conversation. In other words, the police have an impressionistic picture of the drug trade, and they would like to use these vaguely connected and interrelated pieces of information that more or less create a relationship (and therefore a conspiracy) between a businessman with a waterfront warehouse in Montreal, a truck driver who lives in Cornwall and drives between Quebec City and Toronto, a known heroin addict in Hamilton who supports his habit by selling a few capsules, a person in Brandon who has been found in possession of a few capsules who happens to be the sister-in-law of a known dope-dealer in Calgary and, finally, a man in Vancouver who seems to have a very flashy lifestyle, does not appear to have a job and spends much of his time in places where heroin dealers and junkies are known to hang out. Could a conspiracy charge succeed against these people and under what circumstances?

(e) Claude is the leader of a radical union and has been causing great agitation by his speeches to members of the union. He has suggested that the only way to achieve their wage demands is sabotage of the employers' truck fleets. John is president of the New Left Club at the university. He has been making speeches advocating sit-ins at the employers' warehouses. Lewis and Ron are rank and file union members who have an informal meeting in a tavern with Keith and Jim, who are university anarchists; after a few drinks, they leave the tavern making noisy declarations that they are going to make bombs to blow up the employers' trucks. All six are charged with conspiracy.

(f) In the last class of the year, Colson, the teacher, suggests that all the students should come to his apartment for a celebratory drink. A student in the class reminds C that parking is illegal on the street where the apartment is located. C suggests that the class ignore the parking prohibition and park their cars illegally. Are C and the students guilty of common law conspiracy under s. 423(2) of the Code?

Some Defences to Criminal Charges

34. *Necessity: The Forces of Nature*

(a) Three men and a cabin boy are shipwrecked and are adrift in a small open boat. The boy is very sick. After many days without food, two of the men agree that the boy should be killed and eaten to save the others.

Is fear of starvation a proper defence to a homicide charge?

(b) After a shipwreck, a lifeboat is in danger of sinking because there are too many people on board. The officer in charge of the lifeboat orders the crew to throw males overboard. Very few of the crew were sacrificed.

Should necessity be a defence in such circumstances and what should be the basis for choosing the victims?

(c) A group of cave-explorers are deep under the earth when there is a very great rock-slide that covers the entrance to the cave. Luckily, radio contact is still possible between the people in the cave and the rescue team on the surface. A group of engineers tells the cavers that even with the use of the most efficient equipment, their rescue cannot be effected for many days. The cavers seek the advice of nutritionists who tell them that the remaining food in the cave will last them much less time than the projected date of rescue. The cavers then seek the advice of a judge as to whether it would be lawful for them to eat one of their number to keep the others alive. Should the judge give such advice? If so, what advice? If the advice is in favour of cannibalism, should the judge set down rules as to the killing of one of the party?

35. *Duress: The Agency of Human Force*

(a) An English actor and his family were interned by the Germans in

1939. The Nazis wanted the actor to broadcast propaganda to England. He refused but finally acceded when they threatened to torture his family or place them in a concentration camp.

Was he guilty of aiding the enemy?

(b) On the threat of serious physical injury if she refused, a wife was forced by her husband to submit to sexual relations with a large dog while her husband watched.

(c) A prisoner in a penitentiary was charged with wilful damage to his toilet bowl. It was broken by him during a prison riot. His defence was that he would have been "dealt with" by the leaders of the riot if he had not complied. He was locked in his cell at the time, but was afraid that the enthusiastic rioters would "fix" him in the exercise yard on the following day.

(d) Druse was asked by two acquaintances to drive them to a store in downtown Ottawa because they intended to commit a robbery there. D at first refused, but one of the two robbers pulled a gun and threatened to kill Druse if he did not accede to their wishes. The robbery took place and an innocent bystander was killed by a bullet fired by one of the robbers.

Are these cases of legal duress?

36. Superior Orders

(a) Dietrich, a soldier working in a Nazi concentration camp, was ordered by his superior—a non-commissioned officer—to deliver prisoners to Doctor Luger. After the war, L was charged before a war crimes tribunal because he carried out experiments on prisoners. Can Dietrich also be convicted of a crime against humanity?

(b) Dorant is an officer commanding a small group of soldiers fighting a guerrilla war. The conventions of international law decree that the prisoners of war must be kept in custody until the end of the war and cannot be shot. A group of enemy terrorists carry out a raid, torturing and killing some of the soldiers' wives. In a fit of rage and revenge, Dorant's superior officer, Major Spencer, orders him to pursue the terrorists and "show them no mercy." Dorant surprises the terrorists in their beds and instead of taking any prisoners, he lines them up, and a firing squad shoots them.

(c) In another war, the mode of fighting is mostly of the guerrilla nature. Soldiers have discovered that seemingly peaceable women and children have been often used to make booby traps and to throw hand grenades at unsuspecting soldiers. Lieutenant Dewar is ordered to go into a particular village (thought to be very sympathetic to the enemy and a place where many soldiers have been killed in ambush by the ordinary citizens) and told to carry out reprisals. He does so with his troops, killing many women and children.

37. *Self-Defence*

(a) Without any prior warning, Vezina started punching Duff. Then Vezina picked up a chair and hit Duff over the head. D fell to the ground but recovered. V had picked up a full bottle of whiskey and was approaching D when D drew a long knife from his pocket and killed V.

Would any of the following have a bearing on your decision to grant D a defence of self-defence:

(a) V was much larger than D;
(b) V was much smaller and weaker than D;
(c) V was attacking with a knife or a gun rather than a bottle;
(d) D did not take the knife from his pocket but just grabbed a knife that was lying nearby; or
(e) D could have escaped at any time but decided that that would have been cowardly or unmanly?

(b) Dave had locked all the doors and he and his wife Wilma had gone to bed for the night. W woke D at 1:00 a.m. to tell him there seemed to be an intruder downstairs. D crept downstairs with his twelve-gauge shotgun. He saw a figure in the living room. He called out but there was no reply. The figure was hiding behind a curtain. He fired one barrel at the curtain from a distance of eighteen feet. There was a yell and a figure dropped to the floor. The deceased was Velcro, a boyfriend of D's teenage daughter Cheryl. C had let V into the house after her parents had gone to sleep. D is charged with murder.

Would your assessment be different if D had given a verbal warning before he started shooting?

38. *The Slain Chicken Thief: Self-Defence or Excessive Self-Defence?*

(a) Darlow lived on a chicken farm just outside the metropolitan area. In the last few years, D and his neighbours had suffered the loss of thousands of chickens by theft. D had decided that he had lost his last chicken. He set up a tripwire in the chicken run. One night, when an intruder tripped on the wire, an alarm bell rang in D's bedroom. The chicken farmer jumped from his bed, grabbed a loaded .22 repeating rifle and ran toward the chicken houses as quietly as possible and spied a human figure crouching in one of them. He crept closer and, without any further warning, fired a shot at the chicken thief. The chicken thief started to run and when he was some yards off, D fired again, causing the thief to drop the stolen chicken and to run faster. At no time did D shout a warning (such as "stop or I'll shoot"), and he kept firing, although he claimed at his trial that he fired to scare or to "wing" the thief. Unfortunately one of D's shots killed the thief, who turned out to be a tramp in search of a free meal.

(a) Should D be acquitted on the grounds of defence of property?

(b) What if D's uncle, who was also a chicken farmer, had been killed some years before by an intruder whom he had disturbed?
(c) Or if stealing chickens were a felony (a serious offence) and citizens could take all reasonable steps in apprehending a felon?

(b) Dean was having a party in Room 801 of a downtown hotel with Pat, Doris, Jake and Alan. The party was a swinging affair, and Dean had invited Julie, who was staying in Room 802, to join the party. Julie was Vince's "woman" and when V heard about the goings-on in Room 801, he decided to investigate. He came into Room 801 and, after a few words with D, warned him that he intended to keep Julie out of D's clutches, by force if necessary. D and V scuffled and V slapped Julie's face and punched Jake when he came to D's aid. V left muttering threats and said he would be back shortly with reinforcements. After ten minutes he returned with four of his henchmen. He kicked open the door of 801 and pointed his .45 automatic at the occupants of the room. Alan threw a chair and a fracas started. At the height of the battle, shots were fired and V dropped to the floor, dead. D and Alan were charged with murder. Ballistics evidence showed that one bullet had been fired from V's gun, and the bullet was found in the plaster above the doorframe. D had fired two shots from his revolver.

(c) Drake was a young man who accepted an invitation from Vanner, an older man, to have a drink in V's apartment one night. Next day, V was found dead. He had been bashed to death with a heavy metal ashtray. When police questioned D, he said that V had made a homosexual pass at him.

39. Provocation

(a) What Colour Is the Reasonable Person?

Degas is a West Indian living in a Canadian city. In a hotel bar one night, he is taunted by a white Canadian who calls him ugly racial names. D becomes so infuriated that he pulls out a knife and kills the white man.

(a) Should D be convicted of murder or of some lesser offence?
(b) If a killing is less than murder when a man is provoked, was D properly provoked within the meaning of s. 215(2) of the Criminal Code?
(c) Would it make any difference if D were
 (i) very drunk; or
 (ii) somewhat impaired by alcohol?

(b) Provocation: Once Again, Who Is the Reasonable Person?

Dermott was a young man of eighteen years. He was impotent and this preyed on his mind. One night he decided to hire the services of a prostitute. He went with her to her room but his impotence prevented him from making much progress. She taunted him, calling him rude names and when he started to wrestle with her, she allegedly kicked him in the genitals. At this point, he claimed that he lost all sense of control and stabbed the prostitute eight times. She died from the wounds.

Does he have a partial defence of provocation that would reduce the crime from murder to manslaughter?

(c) Could Illustration 38(c) be treated as a case of provocation?

40. *Intoxication: What Happens to a Person When Drunk?*

(a) Dan was a nightwatchman who made the hours pass more quickly and pleasurably by having a few shots of whiskey. Vivien, aged thirteen, had been sent to the store by her mother. As she passed by D's place of work, the watchman invited her into his room where, he said, he kept some candy. When V came into the room, D threw her to the ground and raped her. V kept screaming, and to silence her, D placed his hand over her mouth and his thumb was pressed into her throat. D, in his drunken stupor, pressed harder than he intended and V died of asphyxiation.

There was no doubt that he was very drunk at the time. At his trial, the prosecution pressed for a murder conviction, but D's lawyer submitted that rape or even assault was the most serious offence for which he could be convicted and that he, in fact, should be acquitted of murder.

What principle would you formulate in drafting a defence (if any) of intoxication to a criminal offence? Would your principle vary in the following circumstances:

(a) D was a chronic alcoholic;
(b) D had robbed V of her purse (but had not sexually attacked her) and she had died in the struggle; or
(c) D was on a drug trip?

(b) Vane, a lonely thirty-four-year-old secretary, decided to go to a singles' bar. There she met Drucker. He had been drinking all day. Before reaching the singles' bar, D had consumed a twenty-six-ounce bottle of vodka since lunch time. During the evening he had had four double scotches and two beers. Witnesses testified, at his trial, that D was speaking quite rationally and without slurring his words. He was walking without stumbling or swaying. V invited D back to her apartment and two days later she was found there with more than eighty stab wounds in her body. D met a friend of his two or three hours after leaving V's apartment and the friend said that D seemed quite lucid. Over the next few months, D tried to surrender to the police and to confess to the killing of V. He usually did this under the influence of alcohol, and he was dismissed as one of the many cranks who try to draw attention to themselves. When finally arrested, he told police that he could remember standing in V's kitchen and she opened a drawer and he could remember the light shining on a knife blade and that was all he could remember. The rest was "just like a movie script." When news of the discovery of V's body was made known, he said he thought he vaguely remembered something about V but he dismissed it from his mind at that point because the address where the body was found did not seem to be the one to which he had gone with V.

(c) Drovin had been an alcoholic when he was eighteen. He was now thirty-five years old. In the intervening years he had been addicted for a time to heroin and other drugs. He had been married to Vista for a week. On the night in question, he had a little to drink but his brain had so deteriorated over the years that it did not take much alcohol to make him rather confused. He killed V, he said, because he thought she had aborted herself with a coat-hanger. In fact, the unfortunate woman was not even pregnant.

(d) Diver had been in love with Vella but she ditched him and took up with another man. D was sitting in a bar one afternoon. He had had many drinks. His mind was preoccupied with Vella. He remembered that every weekday she sat in her new friend's car at the intersection of X and Y streets waiting for him to finish work. D went to his apartment and collected his shotgun. He went to the intersection and saw a woman sitting in a car. He walked up to the car, poked the gun through the open window and pulled the trigger. He killed the woman in the car but it was not Vella. D went back to his apartment, cleaned his gun and hid it. Two hours later he was arrested by the police and at that time his blood alcohol was .18 (which is more than double what is needed to convict for a driving offence). Evidence showed that he had no further alcohol since the shooting.

41. *Mental Abnormality as a Defence*

Which of the following situations should provide a defence:

(a) Serious and chronic mental deficiency from birth;
(b) A dull to dull-normal intelligence quotient;
(c) A genetic imbalance that affected the brain cells or mental make-up of the accused;
(d) Arteriosclerosis affecting the brain tissue;
(e) Psychopathy or sociopathy;
(f) Psychosis which was known to be in existence and competently diagnosed before the crime was allegedly committed;
(g) The same as (f) except there is evidence that, at the time of the crime, the accused appeared to be going through a lucid "normal" phase;
(h) The accused is usually "normal" but he has one particular delusion;
(i) The accused's behaviour, before and after the commission of the crime, showed no abnormality. He has only been claiming a

defence of insanity since he hired the top criminal defence lawyer in the city;

(j) Psychosis caused by alcohol or drugs;

(k) The accused claims that he suffered a mental blackout. His mind "suddenly went blank" or "everything went blank"—it might be called a catatonic fit or psychomotor epilepsy (compare the case of Jack Ruby).

42. Infancy: The Law's Way of Denoting That the Accused is under the Age of Criminal Responsibility

(J denotes a juvenile who is under the age of criminal responsibility.)

(a) Julie, a child of five years, brings home a tricycle that she found in the playground. Her parents realize that the bike belongs to some other child but do not bother to take it to the police station, and they let her play with it. Her parents are subsequently charged with theft.

Should they be convicted?

(b) James is twelve and a half years old. He is already pubescent and has more than an academic interest in girls. He makes a sexual attack on the eleven-year-old girl next door. J is charged with rape.

Would he be convicted?

(c) Dwight and Jason are friends. D is sixteen years and one month and J is almost the same age, fifteen years and ten months. They are uncontrollable youngsters, particularly J. They both have long juvenile records, although D's tended to reflect youthful exuberance and a spirit of adventure, while J's showed a disturbing tendency toward senseless violence. They decided to plan a big job. J was clearly the leader of the enterprise. They robbed a bank of $1,400. J hit a security guard with a blackjack and the victim has lost his hearing. Because he was over sixteen years, D was sent to the adult court where he was tried by the retributive Judge Nackwurst who gave him a sentence of ten years based, he said, on the need to show an example to other young "punks" and because D had always been antisocial. J was still within the jurisdiction of the juvenile court. The Crown wants the case transferred to adult court but the juvenile court refused to "waive" the case to the criminal court.

Imagine that you are a judge of the Supreme Court who is scheduled to hear the appeal by the Crown against the juvenile court judge's decision. You believe in the rehabilitative ideal of penology and that teenagers like J need help, not long sentences or harsh penal methods. You believe that the Court of Appeal will not reduce D's sentence and, therefore, to order the transfer of J's case will give him a ten-year sentence or perhaps more (because he was the ring-leader).

(d) John is fifteen years old. He has never appeared in juvenile court before. He is charged with theft of sixty dollars. His home life is hopeless.

He has no father and his mother is a neurotic. J has experimented with drugs and is doing very badly in school. He is showing signs of being seriously disturbed. The probation officer who is asked to make a pre-sentence report suggests to the juvenile court judge that he should not remain at home. He points out, however, that he cannot obtain a foster home placement for him. Because of his good record he does not recommend boys' training school. There is no available psychiatric resource in the community for young teenagers unless the youth is referred by adult criminal court.

Should the juvenile court take the risk of giving J the stigma of a criminal record in order to obtain psychiatric help for him?

(e) Jessica is a girl of fourteen. Her parents are rather strict. They don't approve of her boyfriend who is sixteen and a half. She is always coming home after her parents' curfew of 10:00 p.m. They also believe that she is becoming sexually involved with D. J's mother has obtained a confession from her daughter that although they are not indulging in sexual intercourse, the young people are involved in heavy petting. Is J a juvenile delinquent and should she be brought before the juvenile court as a child who is "guilty of sexual immorality or any similar form of vice"? Should D also be charged with contributing to the delinquency of a minor?

(f) Joseph, aged thirteen, sniffs glue. Is he a juvenile delinquent because he is "guilty of sexual immorality or any similar form of vice"? Is he more likely to be guilty under that provision if instead of sniffing glue, he indulged in masturbation?

(g) Jennifer is nineteen years old and is charged with shoplifting. This is her first adult charge in criminal court. The prosecution wants to cross-examine her under s. 12 of the Canada Evidence Act as to her long juvenile record which included six findings of shoplifting. Should this be permissible?

43. Some Related Problems

The following are problems that arise out of the penal jurisdiction of the juvenile court over adults who commit offences against or in relation to children:

(a) Dunster was a professor of education at the university. He despised the official educational system. ("The Establishment Schools," as he called them.) He refused to allow his children to attend such schools and kept them at home where they studied urban planning, municipal politics, existential philosophy and cultural anthropology, painted, made films, performed plays, modelled in clay and read *avant-garde* poetry. The Inspector of Schools charged D with failing to have his children attend school.

Would your verdict be different if the father was a member of a religious sect that did not believe in secular education, rather than an educational radical?

In either instance, should the State interfere with parents' upbringing of their children?

(b) Kate was a divorcee and had one child, twelve-year-old Jane. She and her daughter were staying in a motel during K's vacation. They shared a bedroom in the motel. One night, after J was asleep in bed, K met Drago in the motel liquor lounge. D slept in K's bed that night, although he left before J awoke in the morning. J was never awake while D was in the motel room and never knew of his visit.

Should D be charged with contributing to the delinquency of a minor?

(c) Under what circumstances should the State interfere between child and parent, ranging from ordering social worker visits to the family home to taking the child out of the home—because the parents are immoral, religious extremists, alcoholics, mental defectives, very poor, cruel or psychologically abusive?

Illustrations of Some Criminal Offences

Offences with Sexual Overtones

44. Rape—A Violent Crime

This offence must be distinguished from indecent assault. The latter applies *either* to acts of sexual intercourse where the female partner is not forced but is legally too young to give her consent (see s. 146) *or* cases where the assault is on any female without her consent but in circumstances falling short of sexual intercourse (see s. 149). When the Code is revised, rape and indecent assault are likely to be classified as offences of violence rather than sexual offences because their essence, particularly that of rape, is violence rather than sexual behaviour.

Which of the following constitute rape:

(a) Dustin is almost six feet tall. He weighs one hundred and seventy pounds. He looks quite mature. He attacks a woman in the basement of her apartment and has forcible sexual intercourse with her. Despite his appearance, he is actually only thirteen years and ten months old.

(b) Duke, a big husky fellow, attacks a woman with the intention of raping her. He tries to have intercourse with the woman but

(a) he is impotent; or
(b) he experiences premature ejaculation.

What offence has D committed in each instance?

(c) Dumas met Vernette at a party. V invites D to her apartment for a nightcap. V was willing to have sexual intercourse with D but at a certain stage in the proceedings D wants V to perform an act with him that V considers "kinky." (Note: The exact nature of the act does not matter; but V looked upon it as "kinky.") D persists and performs the act. V has him charged with rape.

(d) Dysart and Vesta met at a party. They both became rather drunk. They had sexual intercourse at V's apartment. V reported D to the police and he is charged with rape. D claimed that he was so drunk that he did not know if V was freely giving her consent or not.

Would your verdict likely be different if any of the following circumstances existed:

(a) Wilson, V's next-door neighbour, was awakened by a frightened and tearful V knocking on his door at 2:00 a.m. of the morning in question.
(b) The event was not reported to the police until V had mentioned the incident to her mother on the following day. Her mother was incensed and called the police.
(c) V did not report the case until a week after the event.

(e) The events are the same as the basic story in (d). D's lawyer seeks to cross-examine V as to her sexual experience and activities.

Should he be permitted to do so?

(f) Dante had three drinking companions. After a few drinks one night, he told them that his wife was great in bed but she was a little "kinky." Her particular form of "kinkiness," according to D, was that she liked to pretend that she was being raped. D guessed that this added to the excitement. D invited his buddies over on the next night to share his wife's favours. He told them that they should not be deterred by his wife's protests; that was part of her "kinky" act. In fact, D was probably the "kinky" one and D's wife had all four men charged with rape.

Could any or all be convicted?

45. *Indecent Assault on a Female*

As stated earlier, indecent assault on a female is a less serious offence than rape. The definition of this crime is rather vague and on occasions a little ludicrous. The following illustrations are not set out for comic effect but to show the potential breadth of the offence.

(a) Dorfman attacked Vickers with some physical force. He had touched her genital area with his hands but before he could remove her underclothing, V managed to stick him with a hatpin and escape.

(b) B is D's secretary. She has often remonstrated with D for making passes at her. She warns him that if he touches her again, she will call the police. D touches one of the following:

(a) her thigh just above the knee,
(b) her buttocks,
(c) her crotch through her clothing,
(d) her breast.

Are any or all these acts indecent assaults?

(c) In this instance, D touches V's body but not in any place that could ever be considered erogenous according to anyone's test. In each case, V had not given any indication that D's attentions are welcome. Instead, D touches V's arm and makes one of the following statements:

(a) How much will it cost to go to bed with you?
(b) You look as if you would be a good lay.
(c) You are very sexy.
(d) You could really have quick promotions in this organization if you played your cards right.
(e) Your place or mine?
(f) You really turn me on.
(g) D says nothing but he is wearing a T shirt on which is printed "Why don't you sit on my head and I could guess your weight?"

Which of these acts are criminally indecent ones? Can you think of a better way to deal with this problem?

46. (a) Reconsider the illustrations in 45(c) where both D and V are male or female.

(b) Dale is a twenty-two-year-old male and Delmonico is a nineteen-year-old male. They are strongly attracted to each other. They have both been very reluctant to acknowledge their homosexual inclinations. They decide to share an apartment and, in this way, to offer the other mutual support in their search for sexual expression. Are they committing a criminal offence?

(c) Auld, Bannon and Cashel belong to the Downsview Steam Bath and Badminton Club. Members of the general public are not admitted. To join the club, one must be nominated by two existing members. There is a joining fee of $100 and annual dues of $250. A, B and C are homosexuals, and they go to the club to have a steam bath and to have sexual relations. The club is raided by the police. Have A, B and C committed any criminal offence? Has anyone committed any offence?

47. Sid and Louise have lived together for the past two years. They would be married but Sid is not yet divorced.

Recently Louise has had an operation and is unable to have sexual intercourse. One night after sharing a bottle of wine, Sid and Louise become amorous and Louise performed an act of fellatio on Sid. Sid and Louise had left the light on and the blind had not been drawn. Constable Voyette saw them and charged them with gross indecency.

Would it make any difference if:

(a) Sid and Louise were only seventeen years old;
(b) They were merely dating;
(c) They were engaged;
(d) It was a one-night stand;
(e) They had the light off and the constable had shone his flashlight into the room;
(f) They had been doing it in an automobile;
(g) They were doing it in a public park;
(h) They had been engaged in cunnilingus or soixante-neuf?

48. Commercial Sex

(a) Dolores was observed outside a hotel by a member of the vice squad. As men left the hotel, she spoke to many of them. The policeman could not hear what she said. He noticed that she did not speak to any women or any men who were with women.

Has D committed any offence? If not, what other evidence would be necessary?

(b) The vice squad knew that Dee was a prostitute. On this night, they had seen her walk up and down the street several times. Finally, Constable Johns, who was dressed in casual clothes and sitting in an unmarked car, called D over to the car and started talking to her and then invited her to sit in the car. After some conversation as to sexual acts and money, he informed her that he was going to charge her with soliciting for purposes of prostitution. Will he be successful?

(c) Dynah is a very well-dressed young lady. She is sitting in the Royalty Cocktail Lounge at the Hotel Ritz. She is not sitting there very long before a prosperous well-dressed man approaches her and soon after they move to the dining room where they have dinner together. He spent the night at her apartment. D is a call-girl and she had been hired by the Mega Corporation to entertain one of that company's most important customers.

Is D guilty of any offence?

(d) Dudley is a lonely single man who decides to go kerb-crawling. He drives his muscle car to a part of the city where he believes prostitutes can usually be found. As he cruises around the block, he notices a woman who seems to be going nowhere in particular. D propositions her.

Has he committed any offence?

(e) The following persons know that Darlene is a prostitute. If it is an offence to live off the earnings of a prostitute, which of the following would be guilty:

(a) her boy-friend with whom she lives and who has no job;
(b) the person who runs her answering service;
(c) her landlord;
(d) the owner of the corner store where she buys her groceries;
(e) her aged mother whom she supports;
(f) the owner of the bar where she picks up men;
(g) the owner of the store where she buys her flamboyant clothes and shoes;
(h) the taxi-driver who sometimes refers customers to her;
(i) the desk clerk of the hotel where she sometimes takes customers?

(f) Which of the following would be considered by the law to be bawdy houses:

(a) the prostitute's one-bedroom apartment where she takes customers every night *or* very occasionally;
(b) an apartment or house in which the prostitute lives and works with four other prostitutes;
(c) a motel where the prostitute has a permanent booking for room 304;
(d) a motel where the prostitute rents whichever room happens to be vacant;
(e) a body-rub parlour where no acts of sexual intercourse are performed but the customers are massaged by masseuses who are naked or partially naked, or where there is masturbation or fellatio;
(f) the same facts as (e), but all persons concerned are of the same gender?

49. Foetus and Child "Killing"

(a) A woman is pregnant. She does not want to have the baby. She wants an abortion and applies to the Abortion Committee at her community hospital. Which of the following factors (as alternatives or in combinations of one, two or three) should convince the committee to grant her request:

(a) She is fourteen;
(b) She is forty-four;
(c) She is unmarried and does not want to marry the father of the child;
(d) She is married and already has three children;
(e) She has a congenital heart disease;

(f) She has a serious kidney disease;
(g) She has syphilis;
(h) She has been exposed to rubella (German measles);
(i) She has taken thalidomide;
(j) She is a chronic alcoholic;
(k) She is addicted to marijuana;
(l) She is addicted to amphetamines;
(m) She is addicted to LSD;
(n) She is addicted to heroin;
(o) She has told her family doctor and the committee that she is so upset she will kill herself if she is refused by the committee;
(p) She has been under the care of a psychiatrist for the past year for severe depression;
(q) A psychiatrist has examined her and is convinced that she may well be suicidal;
(r) She has an I.Q. of 72 and the father of the child has an I.Q. of 80.
(s) She already has two illegitimate children and has treated them so badly that the Children's Aid Society has been forced to take them from her and make them wards of the state;
(t) There is a history of hereditary mental deficiency in her family;
(u) She is an intelligent, responsible woman of thirty-eight years of age with three children—fourteen years, twelve years and nine years. Three years ago, her husband was involved in an industrial accident that has rendered him a permanent invalid. He has not worked in three years and the family has been kept together by the mother working as a teacher in the local high school. If she has this child, she will no longer be able to support the family and will not be able to take proper care of her invalid husband.

(b) A woman had a baby two weeks ago. Soon after she came home from the hospital, her husband noticed that she was very depressed and seemed unable to cope with cleaning house, changing diapers and preparing meals. When the baby had been crying all one afternoon, she became so distraught that she suffocated the child with a pillow. Her family doctor has diagnosed her problem as post-partum depression.

Should she be convicted of infanticide?

50. *Offences Against Property— The Legal Control of Dishonesty*

The fundamental question being constantly asked throughout this section is, Is this behaviour dishonest and is it properly dealt with by the criminal law process? Readers are warned that the actual results in the courts are sometimes quite surprising.

(a) Dabney and his two friends are pranksters and do the following acts:

(a) They take a large political banner belonging to the Tory candidate and tie it to the front fence of the Liberal candidate's house.
(b) They are waiting for a plane and decide to make a souvenir of a large glass ashtray in the departure lounge.
(c) They remove the Israeli flag from that country's embassy in Ottawa and run it up the flagpole at the Libyan embassy.
(d) They take a policeman's motorcycle, ride it around the block and leave it hidden but very close to its original location.

(b) Dutch is a senior at the local high school. He knows all the students in his history class will be wanting a particular book for a project. After he has finished using it, he hides it in the school library, intending to replace it on its proper shelf when the project deadline has passed.

(c) DeMarco rents a car from Visa Car Rental. She told the company that she was renting for one day but she kept it until the company finally tracked down the car a month later. D said that she intended to pay the extra charges when she returned the car. She thought that could be done under the contract.

(d) Dodge is a salesman for a company. He delivered goods to a customer but did not bill the customer because, he said, the pricing policy of his employer was uncertain. His other explanation was that he had granted credit to retain the customer's valuable business. The owner was on vacation at the time, but when he returned he had D charged with an offence.

(e) Drury bought a motorcycle on the "never-never" from Vonda Bikes Ltd.—a conditional sales agreement. The bike became his property only when he had made all the payments. He defaulted on a monthly payment and V repossessed the machine. D went to V's premises and took back the motorcycle.

(f) Vibrant Discount Stores had children's clothes on sale. An outfit consisting of a shirt top and pants bottom was marked at $13.99. The top alone was marked at $6.99. Drax picked up an outfit and removed the $13.99 price-tag and replaced it with the $6.99 tag. He then presented it at the check-out.

(g) Dring pulls into a gas station and asks for ten litres of gas and a litre of oil. The gas-jockey puts the gas in the tank and the oil in the engine. D then says he has no money.

(h) Perry left his car in a parking lot. He did not pay any money for this privilege. Dowson drives a tow-truck and the owner of the lot has a contract with D to tow away any vehicles that are parked without authorization. D tows away P's car which P cannot retrieve without paying the necessary fees. P has D charged with an offence.

(i) Draper pays the city for water on the basis of consumption. D's neighbour has a different arrangement with the city; he pays on a flat rate no matter how much or how little he uses. D decides to hook up to D's neighbour's water supply.

(j) Dubarry delivers milk to supermarkets. He picks up the old milk and replaces it with new milk. He was supposed to pick up fifty containers of old milk and replace them with fifty new containers. Instead he leaves twenty-five of the old containers and puts in twenty-five new ones. D bills the supermarket for fifty.

(k) Duffield goes to a bank with his pay-cheque which was for $423. The bank teller mistakenly gives him $1423. D decides to keep the additional $1000.

(l) Every time Dobson goes by a public telephone, he presses the coin return and sometimes he gets a pay-off.

(m) Denver is a bank teller. He is in debt and would like to find some quick cash. He has a friend who trains harness horses. He tells D that a particular horse is a "dead cert" in the third race next Saturday. On Friday night, D takes home $100 of the bank's money. The horse wins at long odds and D replaces the bank's money on Monday.

As you will see from the text, the above cases have been mostly treated as cases of larceny or theft (the words are interchangeable). The question asked at the head of this group of illustrations related to "dishonesty," not to guilt or innocence in relation to theft. This was for two reasons. The distinction between larceny and false pretences is very vague and technical. Secondly, the Law Reform Commission of Canada recommends that this distinction be scrapped and a crime of dishonesty should replace the mess that the law had created by trying to make distinctions between larceny and false pretences.

The following cases are ones that have traditionally been closer to false pretences than larceny (but be prepared for confusing answers from the courts).

51. (a) Derwent arrived at Verdure's farm looking like the very essence of prosperity and respectability—expensive car, three-piece suit. D offered to buy V's potato crop at a price a little above the going price. D told V that he could not pay him until the end of the month. The potatoes were loaded on trucks and that was the last V saw of them or D.

(b) The same as (a) except D gives V a cheque but D warns V that he would appreciate it if V did not present it to the bank for a week. The cheque "bounces."

(c) The same as (a) except D gives V a cheque that immediately is dishonoured.

(d) The same as (a) except that D gives V a cheque drawn on a non-existent bank account.

(e) The same as (a) except that D gives V a cheque that is drawn on an authentic account but it is not D's account and he has forged the signature.

(f) Dilworth bought furniture on a conditional sales agreement. When the final payment was due and unpaid, the merchant tried to repossess the furniture. D showed a receipt for full payment but in actual fact it was forged.

(g) Dingle bought a car with a postdated cheque. He hoped that when the cheque was presented, he would have received the return of a loan from a friend. Would it make a difference if he signed two or twelve postdated cheques or if it turned out that he was overdrawn by $25 or $2500?

(h) Dorner works for a company. On two occasions, he bought goods from the V hardware store for his boss. He had authority to do this and V simply debited the company. On a third occasion, without authority, he bought goods from V and told V to "put it on the tab."

(i) Davenport lives by his wits. He goes into the Voice Electronic Store which is near a hospital. He is dressed in a white coat and has a stethoscope sticking from his pocket. He gives V his correct name and address and V grants him credit and D takes away with him an expensive piece of electronic equipment. D never actually says that he is a doctor. V assumes it to be the case.

(j) A variation on (i); D has the same real name as a famous person—a hockey player, a movie star, etc. He allows V to think (without actually saying it) that he is the celebrity.

52. The Law Reform Commission admits that some cases of dishonesty do not clearly fall into the categories of larceny or false pretences. The difficulty in these cases is not one of technical detail but a value judgement as to the point where sharp business practice becomes criminal behaviour.

(a) Doucet is a police chief. The person who decides on her salary is Quist, the attorney general, whom she knows quite well through previous political affiliations. Q tells D that he would like to give an increase in salary but that would mean that he would have to grant salary hikes to all the other police chiefs. Q has an alternative plan; he tells D to claim additional travel expenses. She did not have to undertake additional travel but only pretend to do so. She received an additional $150 monthly by filing these travel-expense claims. After a year or so, there is a change of government and D is charged.

(b) Drover is a contractor who has successfully tendered for the building of a stretch of highway. After his tender is accepted, D realizes that he should have included an item for surveying as there is one tricky corner on the highway that will need the services of a surveyor. He asked Roscoe to do the surveying work but explained to R that he could not claim for surveying work. R should submit a bill for his services but call it "hire of a bulldozer." D is charged.

(c) Dashwood bought a small car in Europe. He brought it back to Canada and then decided that he needed a larger car. He agreed with Vipont to swap the small car (which still had European licence plates) for V's larger car. V discovered later that he had to pay import duties on the small car. Has D committed any offence?

(d) Danvers, a used-car dealer, agrees to buy Veck's car. D gives V a downpayment and an IOU for the balance. When V comes to collect the balance owing on the IOU, D says that he did not mean that he would give cash on the IOU but that V could use the balance as a downpayment on another car.

(e) Darwin, a salesperson for a used-car dealer, sold Verney a car for $1000. D told V that the deal could not be closed until tomorrow because it had to be approved by D's boss, Slime, the sales manager. Of course, this was all a subterfuge. D informed S that V was a prospect for "jacking up" as it was called in the trade. When V arrived the next day, S interviewed him and told him that he was very cross with D because he could not possibly sell the car for $1000. S then tried to persuade V to buy another car for $2000.

Note: You can add other versions of the above facts from stories you have heard. Another ploy, popular among appliance dealers, is the loss leader; one item is advertised at a very low (and legitimate) price, although there is only one of them but this is the bait to attract customers who might buy more expensive items.

(f) Dimbleby is starting in the business of buying and selling houses. He puts down a small amount on a house, mortgages the house for the rest and then hopes to make a quick re-sale. D bought a house for $50,000. He put $7500 of his own money into the purchase and approached the bank for a mortgage. He told the bank that he had paid $60,000 for the house; the bank lent him $45,000. When the bank discovered that they had been misled, they had D charged. D never missed a mortgage payment. Evidence at D's trial showed that the house was probably worth $60,000 at the time the bank lent D the $45,000 and it was worth even more at the time of the trial. The bank never had one of its valuers make an appraisal of the house.

(g) Dinsdale is a bank manager. He has instructions that he may make loans to customers who have an "A" credit rating. D lends money to Watt, a customer who is a stranger to him, and has a "C" credit rating. D files false reports that suggests that W has an "A" credit rating. W goes broke and the bank loses its money.

(h) D.H. Dayton applies to the telephone company for a phone. The company has a policy that no new subscriber can have a phone unless he pays a deposit. D allows the company to think that he is the D.H. Dayton who has previously had a telephone. Actually the second D.H. Dayton is the first one's father.

(i) Delafield incorporated a construction company to build houses. He hired salespersons who were paid a high commission when customers signed up to have a house built. D ran into difficulties. He was building houses but was months behind schedule. He had taken orders for sixty houses but only twelve had been completed. Some customers demanded the return of their deposits, but D assured them that he intended to carry out his obligations. D was also in trouble with suppliers of materials. They would not deliver except for cash-on-delivery. D tried to get larger overdrafts from the bank. The police started to receive complaints from D's customers. The fraud squad went to D's bank to enquire about D's financial status; at this point, the bank refused D's company any further credit. An auditor's report prepared for the prosecution showed that even when D knew his company was in serious financial problems, the company's salespersons were still accepting contracts and receiving commissions.

(j) Dufton was a director of the Victory Corporation, a public company, in which he was a major shareholder. He wanted to raise money for a new deal. He wanted to use the assets of V as security for the new loan but he could only do this with the permission of his fellow directors. He failed to do so. He used the assets and later returned them. In the process of using the assets of V, he made a $25,000 profit for V. He was nevertheless charged with fraud.

53. *What is capable of being stolen (or otherwise criminally misappropriated)?*

Which of the following items are recognized by the law as capable of being criminally taken or misappropriated:

(a) a dead body;
(b) real estate;

(c) deeds to real estate;
(d) a doctor's prescripton for a drug;
(e) a physical object that D found;
(f) radio or television time;
(g) radio or television transmissions;
(h) industrial, commercial or artistic ideas;
(i) computer programs;
(j) an item that may be of high sentimental (or perhaps historical) value but has no monetary value;
(k) a person's name or reputation?

Problems of Criminal Procedure and Evidence

54. *The Man Who Had a Few*

Dicey was driving along the expressway at 2:00 a.m. on a Sunday in February. Constable Potter had been following him in a police car and noticed that D's car had been wandering a little from its lane. After a time, P became convinced that the driver was driving in an unacceptable manner and P considered that he had reasonable cause to believe that the driver was impaired. He drove alongside D's car and told him to pull over. He walked over to D's car and told D to step out of the car. D staggered a little as he did so. P asked to see D's licence and told him that he wanted D to accompany him to the police station. At the station, D was given a breathalyzer test, but only after some coercion. The reading was positive and he was charged with impaired driving. He was locked in a cell "to sleep it off," and although D made some mumbled remark about wanting to see his solicitor, no lawyer was called and D was not given an opportunity to make a phone call to his wife, or anyone else for that matter.

The following morning in court, D sought the advice of the Legal Aid Duty Counsel. The lawyer told D that he had a good chance of success because the policeman should not have ordered D to get out of the car, that he only had a right to ask for a driver's licence, that he should have told D that he was arresting him and that he had, in effect, taken D to the police station against his will as defined by law, that he should not have been forced to take a breathalyzer test (without an explanation of the consequences of refusing such a test), that he should have been given a right to make a telephone call and, as a consequence of all these irregularities, the court should throw out any charge of impaired driving that was brought against him.

The reading on the breathalyzer showed a figure of intoxication that was clearly over the acceptable minimum limit. In addition, P's story was corroborated by Squires who was travelling in a following car and who stopped and gave his name to P as a potential witness.

(a) What circumstances should be considered legally sufficient before a police officer:

(i) could stop an automobile and ask the driver for his licence; or
(ii) ask the driver to get out of his car; or
(iii) ask the driver to accompany him to the police station, or
(iv) arrest the driver for impaired driving?

(b) What legal right have the police to force a suspect to submit to a breathalyzer test?
(c) Is the breathalyzer test an infraction of the time-honoured rule that no man is obliged to incriminate himself?
(d) Should the evidence produced by the breathalyzer be treated by the court as decisive of guilt?
(e) Should D have been treated differently at the police station? If there were any deficiencies, should any of them (or a combination of them) secure D's acquittal?

55. *Reasonable and Probable Cause*
(a) Cuthbert, a public-spirited citizen, sees Dobbs committing the following acts:

(a) jaywalking;
(b) hitting D's wife in the Dobbs' apartment;
(c) hitting his child in a supermarket;
(d) shoplifting in a bookstore;
(e) getting into a car with the intention of driving when he is obviously quite drunk;
(f) about to use a brick to smash the jeweller's window;
(g) about to walk away from the teller's wicket at the bank when Dobbs has received an overpayment of $50 or $500;
(h) robbing a store at knife-point.

In which case can he make a legal arrest?

(b) The same facts as (a) except that C did not see the acts being done; he was told by some other person. Can C make a legal arrest?

(c) The same facts as (a) except that C has told a policeman and wants the police officer to arrest D. Would it be legal for him to do so?

56. Here are situations that a police officer may encounter. Would he or she have power to arrest or search?

(a) Two police officers hear on their police-car radio that there have been two break-ins just reported in the neighbourhood of X and Y streets.

Soon after, they are at Z Street about six blocks from X and Y streets, and they see two young men dressed in dark clothes and sneakers walking along Z Street. When asked to identify themselves, they refused to do so. Would your decision be different if they were carrying a large bag, or if it were 2:00 a.m. or if one of the constables recognized one of the young men as a person who had previously been convicted of burglary?

(b) A police officer walks past a warehouse at 11:00 p.m. The warehouse was on a busy city street. Duran was standing outside. He told the police officer that he was waiting for a friend. What if, instead, the time was 2:00 a.m. and the warehouse was on a badly lit and infrequently used street?

57. *Pot, Hash and All That*
Let us imagine that the scene is a so-called hippie area similar to Yorkville Village in the 1960s. Doug is a young man who has left a small rural township to migrate to the bright lights of the big city. He grows long hair and starts wearing the hippie uniform of blue jeans and army surplus jacket. He has never tried marijuana but very soon he hears so much talk among his new friends about pot, grass, Acapulco Gold and Cambodia Red that he decides to try some. He also discovers that many of his friends are making far-ranging experiments with drugs and some of them are very distressed by the use of amphetamines. He starts helping some of his friends who need medical or psychiatric help because of their use of these harder drugs. While engaged in this informal social work, D meets Peter. Peter tells D that he has had some bad trips and wants to keep off the hard drugs. D and P share an apartment and sometimes smoke pot together. P always supplies the marijuana. P tells D that his pot supply has been cut off and asks D to find some pot for a party in the apartment next Saturday night. D willingly offers to buy the pot out of friendship for P. D buys four ounces and returns to the apartment. P immediately identifies himself as an undercover agent for the RCMP and arrests D on a charge of possession of a narcotic for the purposes of trafficking.

(a) What attitude should the courts take toward the use of undercover agents by the police?
(b) Would your answer be different if the drug were heroin rather than marijuana?
(c) Should the courts take a different view if P had "planted" the marijuana in D's suitcase and had then "found" it by accident?

58. Dobell was arrested and charged with possession of hashish for the purposes of trafficking under the Narcotic Control Act. Before being placed in a cell, D was asked if he wished to make a statement but he declined to do so. Prince was an undercover police officer familiar with

the drug scene. He was dressed in blue jeans and cowboy boots and had not had a shave for four days. The officer investigating the case ordered P to share a cell with D. Upon P entering the cell, D remarked that P "looked like a nark." P just laughed. D asked P what he was doing in jail. P said he was there on a traffic ticket. P later told D that he was a truck driver from out of town. P also gave D the impression that P did not know much about drugs but people in his area would be interested in buying. During the conversation D made incriminating statements to P. Should such evidence be admissible?

59. Dowd and Dent were arrested for an alleged criminal offence. They were placed in cells opposite each other and they started talking loudly to each other. A police officer placed a tape-recorder on the floor between the cells. Should the court accept such evidence?

60. *The Odds Maker*

Dion was an illegal bookmaker who worked out of a greasy spoon cafe. He also conducted business from a public telephone outside his apartment. The police were fully aware of his gambling activities but had been unable to find incriminating evidence. They had tapped his telephone but to no avail. They had searched his garbage can but with similar lack of success. They suspected that he was elusive because he wrote his business transactions on flash paper (which is very easily destroyed) and flushed any other evidence down the toilet. To secure evidence, the police decided to make a raid on D's apartment at 2:00 a.m. They broke down the door of his apartment without warning and without a search warrant. They found betting slips and D's record book.

Also consider the following variations on these facts. First, the police had no search warrant but they decided to gain entrance to D's apartment by subterfuge rather than force. Once again, without obtaining a search warrant, a police officer gained entry to D's apartment by representing himself as a city building inspector and found the incriminating evidence. Alternatively, two police officers had a valid search warrant and obtained entry to D's apartment. While one officer engaged D's attention in the kitchen, the other searched the bedroom. He found no evidence of illegal bookmaking, but in searching through a closet he found burglar's tools and an obscene book.

(a) Should the police be able to use force (to break down a door) if they feel that evidence will be destroyed if they adhere to the formalities of using a search warrant?
(b) Should a judge differentiate between a forceful 2:00 a.m. raid without a search warrant and the searching of D's apartment by subterfuge?

(c) Should a court accept evidence which was not contemplated (or described) on the original search warrant?
(d) Should persons be convicted on evidence illegally obtained?

61. *Modern Police Methods*

In the early morning hours of a cold night in February, Jim and Dick are found by police officers in a laneway behind a warehouse. They are both wearing sneakers and gloves. They are not able to give a good account of themselves and they are arrested for attempted breaking and entering.

The officers in charge of the break-in squad suspect that Jim and Dick are members of a group of burglars who have committed many offences in the area. The officers believe that because Jim and Dick are young (eighteen and twenty, respectively), they may be persuaded to give some information. When Jim and Dick arrive at the police station, they are placed in separate interrogation rooms. No one comes near them for forty-five minutes. After this period, Detective Burley started to interrogate Dick. Burley was a very tall, well-built policeman. He used no physical violence on Dick but he spoke very roughly to him and made a few threats which were not very subtle. Burley kept up a barrage of questions that made Dick very confused and frightened. Nevertheless, he told Burley very little of value, but the detective could see that the young man was shaken up. A few minutes after Burley departed, Constable Slope called on Dick. Slope was quiet-spoken, of slight build, and rather fatherly in his approach. He soon gained Dick's confidence by asking how he felt, commiserating with him about the rough tactics of Burley, and generally trying to be understanding. Slope tells Dick that Burley wants "to throw the book at you" but Slope will try to help if only Dick will cooperate by giving some information about the burglary gang. Dick "spills the beans" implicating Jim and four other men. This routine by Burley and Slope, colloquially known as a Mutt and Jeff Act, was of course not spontaneous but carefully planned and executed by two expert investigators.

Jim was kept waiting in another room in a position where he could see Burley's interview with Dick but could not hear it. As soon as Burley had left Dick, he went to Jim's interrogation room and, falsely, told Jim that Dick has confessed to a string of burglaries. At this point, Jim decided to make a statement that was highly incriminating.

(a) Should the police be allowed to use a holding charge while they go on a "fishing expedition"?
(b) Is the Mutt and Jeff Act one which the courts should condone as a lawful method of obtaining incriminating evidence?
(c) Is the deliberate lie told to Jim by Burley sufficient reason for his acquittal?

(d) If the same facts applied but neither Dick nor Jim confessed to the crime but Jim simply told one of the police officers the location of some loot from a previous burglary, should the courts admit it in evidence?

62. *Inspector Migraine Investigates*

Danson had been arrested for a burglary and had been denied bail and kept in custody awaiting trial. On the day of his arrest the dead body of a young woman was found in a small settlement outside the northern Saskatchewan town where D was jailed. Inspector Migraine of the RCMP was brought in to investigate the murder. After making a preliminary investigation at the scene of the murder, he came back to the town. As a matter of routine, he decided to question the men held in the cells. In the third cell, he found D and the following conversation took place:

M: What are you in for?
D: Burglary.
M: Well, you are not much use to me. (Almost as an afterthought.) I don't suppose you know anything about the girl murdered out at Exville?
D: I hit her with a stick.
M: How many times?
D: I can't remember. Maybe ten times. Is she dead?
M: Why did you hit her?
D: I don't know.

At no point in the conversation did Migraine caution D (that he was not obliged to answer any question but that if he made a statement it could be taken down and used in evidence against him) or formally tell D that he may be charged with murder.

Migraine left the cell and went to the front desk and told Constable George that he should take a statement from D. Constable George was not aware that D was implicated in the murder. As soon as D began to make incriminating statements about the murder, Constable George cautioned him. ("I must warn you that anything you say may be taken down and used in evidence.") D continued to make a statement. The following day D was taken to the scene of the crime and he pointed out to Inspector Migraine where the murder weapon and other artifacts of the crime could be found.

(a) Should any parts of the statements made by D be excluded because Migraine failed to give a caution? Alternatively, can we exclude some and admit some?
(b) Why should a caution be given in any event?

(c) Should the rules in relation to interrogation of suspects be different if the suspect is in custody or has been formally charged?
(d) What is the meaning of custody?

5/The STRUCTURE of the CRIMINAL LAW

In the preceding chapters we have seen that the law is a closed system with its own peculiar definition of the social phenomenon known as crime—a definition that differs from that of the philosopher, psychologist or sociologist. When we speak of the criminal law, we must divorce ourselves from many facets of crime which are of interest to physical, behavioural and social scientists. For instance, evidence is often given in court by toxicologists, physiologists, ballistics experts, pathologists, pharmacologists and analytical chemists. These experts may be called by the prosecution or the defence to support or refute the allegation that a crime has been committed or that the accused committed it. These forensic scientists, along with eyewitnesses, provide the proof or disproof at the trial. They add a third dimension to the definition of a crime but their evidence does not form part of the criminal law in any analytical sense.

Similarly, we saw in Chapter 1 that the "real" facts of a case may be very different from the "truth" as it is presented in court. The rules of evidence govern the conduct of the trial in much the same way as the rules of a game govern the conduct of the players. There may be all sorts of data that are "relevant" to the issue at trial, but the evidence may be inadmissible because it is unreliable or prejudicial (or both). Evidence may be disallowed by the judge as unreliable because it is second- or third-hand evidence that cannot be presented by the first-hand witness who is unavailable for testing through cross-examination. (This is the basis of the hearsay rule.) Or the evidence may be first-hand but the judge may decide that, although highly relevant, it is too prejudicial to the accused. (The most obvious example is the inadmissibility of the accused's previous bad character.)

Evidential and procedural questions provide the flesh for the skeletal definition of crime, but we can take little account of it. By the same token, there are analogous questions that are equally outside the ambit of our present discussion. The police, prosecutors and judiciary exercise their discretion widely (and, we hope, wisely) in deciding to make an arrest, lay a charge, proceed with the prosecution, accept a guilty plea to a lesser offence, admit or exclude evidence and set a sentence. These administrative and quasi-judicial acts vitally affect the practical administration of justice. Many sociologists (and some lawyers) believe that the study of these practices would give a truer picture of the criminal law and its administration than any number of appellate court decisions that discuss the "black letter" or technical law. A sociologist might argue that it is crucial to know how often policemen mete out summary justice with their night sticks in a back alley or patrol car in preference to laying a formal charge. The policeman's contribution to informal justice may not be entirely negative; the officer may give a kindly warning or a tongue-lashing to a young person found committing an offence and then allow him to go home. The social scientists are also interested in knowing how often the plea bargaining process is used by prosecutors and defence counsel in negotiating the conviction of an accused for an offence less serious than the one originally charged. These matters are of great importance to lawyers as well as to politicians and social scientists, but they are irrelevant to a study of criminal law theory.

Similarly, behavioural scientists such as psychiatrists, psychologists and, perhaps, social workers may provide data, undertake research or propound theories about the social phenomenon of crime or its causation or prevention, but except within carefully circumscribed limits, they play no part in building or explaining the structure of the criminal law. They may assist at the post-guilt determination stage but have little part in defining the criminal law. Criminologists, penologists or sociologists may have studied the criminal, his social milieu, his treatment, his incarceration or his alleged cure. They may provide data that attempt to explain why crime exists in society but there is little, if any, relationship between these disciplines and the legal conception of crime.

Obviously, the law is a closed system that is, at least in its own estimation, self-sufficient. Unfortunately, the law is a very inexact science or a slightly creative art, depending upon one's point of view. The law has developed its own dogma (and the word is used advisedly).

We must also remember that the idea of the crime was separated from what we know as tort and that this separation was essentially artificial. The notion of crime as a public wrong or a breach of the king's peace was a legal fiction that increased royal authority, centralized power and sought to create social stability or at least to impose conformity.

The concept of *mens rea* or the mental element in a crime is a typical example of this closed approach to human behaviour. In recent years there has been a continuing debate about criminal responsibility, particularly when the crime was committed by those with mental diseases or defects. Very little has been achieved in terms of re-definition despite the active interest of psychiatrists and other behavioural scientists. There has been a dialogue and there has been some rapport between lawyers and members of other disciplines, but as we shall see later, the law still sets the rules of the process.

Some Fundamental Rules

The Principle of Legality

The principle of legality is a fundamental rule built into any democratic system of criminal justice; it may seem so elementary that we need not mention it, but we must always keep it in mind. This self-evident principle can be described as "the rule of law"—fairness in the formulation of the definition of criminal offences, the defences and the rules that govern the determination of guilt. More particularly, we could describe it as *nullum crimen sine lege, nulla poena sine lege*—there can be no crime or punishment unless it is in accordance with law that is certain, unambiguous and not retroactive.

Retroactivity and Vagueness

The most obvious requirement is that criminal law should be prospective and not retroactive; the potential offender is entitled to know beforehand the kinds of behaviour that would attract criminal penalties. Totalitarian regimes often breach this principle. For instance, a Nazi decree of June 28, 1935 provided:

> Punishment shall be inflicted when an act is committed which the law may declare to be punishable or which may appear to be deserving of punishment according to the fundamental idea of a penal law and according to healthy popular feeling. In the event of no penal law applying directly to the act, such act shall be punished under the penal provision whose basic idea is most suited to it.

This law also suffers from another defect that offends against the principle of legality, that is, the law should not be vague. This fault is also seen in the 1934 Soviet Code:

> A crime is any socially dangerous act or omission which threatens the foundations of the Soviet political structure. In cases where the Criminal Code makes no direct reference to particular forms of crime, punishment or other measures of social protection are applied in accordance with those Articles of the Criminal Code which deal with crimes most closely approximate in gravity and in kind, to the crimes actually committed.

A similar provision is found in the Nazi decree "for the protection of the people and the state" which makes it an offence for "whoever provokes or incites to an act contrary to public welfare ... to be punished with a penitentiary sentence, or, under mitigating circumstances, with imprisonment of not less than three months." The terms "contrary to public welfare" and "mitigating circumstances" are inherently vague and should be avoided if we wish to adhere to fundamental fairness.

In more recent times, the South African legislature passed the notorious ninety-day law in 1963:

> Notwithstanding anything to the contrary in any law contained, any commissioned officer may from time to time without warrant arrest or cause to be arrested any person whom he suspects upon reasonable grounds of having committed or intending or having intended to commit any offence under the Suppression of Communism Act, 1950 or under the Unlawful Organizations Act, 1960 or the offence of sabotage, or who in his opinion is in possession of any

> information relating to the commission of any such offence or the intention to commit any such offence, and detain such person or cause him to be detained in custody for interrogation in connection with the commission of or intention to commit such offence, at any place he may think fit, until such person has in the opinion of the Commissioner of the South African Police replied satisfactorily to all questions at the said interrogation, but no such person shall be so detained for more than ninety days on any particular occasion when he is so arrested.

The 1950 Act defined "communism" and included behaviour:

> which aims at bringing about any political, industrial, social or economic change within the Union by the promotion of disturbance or disorder, by unlawful acts or omissions or by the threat of such acts or omissions or by means which include the promotion of disturbance or disorder, or such acts or omission or threat.

The United Nations in 1948 suggested a remedy for these infringements of the principle of legality in article 11(2) of the Universal Declaration of Human Rights:

> No one shall be held guilty of any penal offence on account of any act or omission which did not constitute a penal offence at the time when it was committed. Nor shall a heavier penalty be imposed than the one that was applicable at the time the penal offence was committed.

The Canadian Criminal Code also contains provisions that are very broad and will no doubt be interpreted retroactively to impugn the behaviour of those who are troublemakers, anti-establishment or considered potentially dangerous. Of course, the worst example, the War Measures Act, is found outside the Code. In the recent past we have seen the broad and immoderate use a government in panic, for retribution or propaganda purposes, can make of this broad provision.

The Code purports to embody the rule of law:

> 5(1) Where an enactment creates an offence and authorizes a punishment to be imposed in respect thereof.
>
> (a) a person shall be deemed not guilty of that offence until he is convicted thereof; and
>
> (b) a person who is convicted of that offence is not liable to any punishment in respect thereof other than the punishment prescribed. . . .
>
> 8 . . . no person shall be convicted
>
> (a) of an offence at common law. . . .
>
> (b) of an offence under an Act or in ordinance in force in any province, territory or place before that province, territory or place became a province of Canada.

Section 11 of the Code provides that no person can be punished more than once for the same offence. All these sections are meant to be expressions of the rule of law. On the other hand, it is impossible to describe human behaviour with anything like precision; frequently legislative drafters use words such as "reasonable" or "probable" or "likely to." Ambiguity and uncertainty are inevitable. The offences prescribing theft and fraud contain many vague terms such as "taking without colour of right" or "dishonest" or "mislead with intent." As we have seen, the provisions against obscenity contain phrases such as "deprave and corrupt" and excluding guilt if a publication is for the "public good." The offences that prohibit sexual intercourse with girls under the age of consent sometimes exclude from punishment men who have intercourse with girls who are not of "previously unchaste character."

Unfortunately, other ambiguities seem to be more avoidable. We do not have to look to overtly totalitarian regimes for provisions that seem unnecessarily broad. The following are some examples from the Canadian Criminal Code:

> **Section 46.** Every one commits treason who . . .
> (2)(g) forms an intention to [use force or violence for the purpose of overthrowing the government] and manifests that intention by an *overt* act.
>
> (3) Where it is treason to conspire with any person, the act of *conspiring* is an *overt* act of treason.
>
> **Section 52.** Every one [commits sabotage] who does a prohibited act for a purpose *prejudicial* to
> (a) the *safety, security* or defence of Canada.
>
> **Section 60** tells us that everyone shall be presumed to have a seditious intention who teaches or advocates or publishes any writing that *advocates* the use, *without the authority of law,* of *force* as a means of accomplishing a governmental change within Canada.
>
> **Section 64.** Unlawful assembly
> (2) Persons who are lawfully assembled may become an unlawful assembly if they conduct themselves *with a common purpose in a manner* that would have made the assembly unlawful if they had assembled in that manner for that purpose.
>
> **Section 115.** Every one who, *without lawful excuse,* contravenes an Act of the Parliament of Canada by wilfully doing anything that it forbids or by *wilfully* omitting to do anything that it requires to be done is, unless some penalty or punishment is expressly provided by law, guilty of an indictable offence and is liable to imprisonment for two years.
>
> **Section 168.** Every one who, in the home of a child, participates in adultery or sexual immorality or indulges in habitual drunkenness or *any other form of vice,* and thereby *endangers the morals* of the child or renders the home an *unfit place* for the child to be in, is guilty of an indictable offence and is liable to imprisonment for two years.
>
> **Section 171.** Causing a disturbance
> Every one who *loiters* in a *public place* and in any way obstructs persons who are there.

Section 176.

(2) Every one commits a *common nuisance* who does an unlawful act or fails to discharge a *legal duty* and thereby

(a) endangers the lives, safety, health, property or *comfort* of the public, or

(b) obstructs the public in the exercise or *enjoyment* of any *right* that is common to all the subjects of Her Majesty in Canada.

Section 423

(2) Every one who conspires with anyone

(a) to effect an *unlawful purpose*, or

(b) to effect a *lawful purpose* by *unlawful means*.

The case of *Todd* described in Chapter 3 illustrates one aspect of retroactivity. The English common law—the accretions of centuries of judicial decisions—had given some minor recognition to the crime of "effecting a public mischief." The *Todd* case arose in South Australia in the 1950s, more than one hundred years after that province had been established. There is a convention in the law that English settlers departing for South Australia (or Upper Canada or Newfoundland) metaphorically took the existing law in their suitcases along with seeds for planting, the family bible, maps, books of nursery rhymes and treatises on agriculture. Obviously, they only transported such law as was necessary. In the sunny and primitive South Australia of 1836, they did not adopt laws relating to snow removal or the rules of inheritance to ducal estates. (This is known as the problem of reception.)

The judge in *Todd* decided that the common law of South Australia did not include a crime of effecting a public mischief and that to convict Todd of the offence (which had been recognized by English courts well *after* 1836) would be to convict him of a retroactive offence.

Frey v. *Fedoruk* (1950) was a civil action for wrongful arrest when the defendant arrested the plaintiff who was a Peeping Tom. The B.C. courts decided that Peeping Tommery was a criminal offence at common law, and therefore the plaintiff could be lawfully arrested. The Supreme Court of Canada disagreed. Cartwright J. said:

> I do not think that it is safe to hold as a matter of law, that conduct, not otherwise criminal and not falling within any category of offences defined by the Criminal Law, becomes criminal because a natural and probable result thereof will be to provoke others to violent retributive action. If such a principle were admitted, it seems to me that many courses of conduct which it is well settled are not criminal could be made the subject of indictment by setting out the facts and concluding with the words that such conduct was likely to cause a breach of the peace.

Treason is the ultimate attack on the social order but it does not have to consist of murder of the sovereign or head of state. This crime against public order can consist of conspiracy, that is, a mere agreement to carry out the acts that are described in s. 46 of the Code. In time of war the law of treason is likely to be interpreted broadly against the supposed enemies of the nation. In the 1914 - 1918 war, Sir Roger Casement tried to persuade Irishmen who were prisoners of war in Germany to fight against Britain. He was charged under a five-hundred-year-old statute that defined treason as including ". . . if a man do levy war against . . . the King in his realm, or giving [the King's enemies]: aid or comfort in our realm *or elsewhere. . . .*" The emphasized words led to the execution of Casement. The original meaning of these words was not explored but a few cases decided between 1351 and 1917 were examined for precedent.

William Joyce, better known as the hated propaganda broadcaster Lord Haw Haw, was also convicted of treason and hanged because the English House of Lords in 1946 decided that "allegiance" to the king could be proven by the possession of a current British passport. On the other hand, the court was kind toward *Steane* (Illustration 35(a)); although he had broadcast for the Nazis, the court decided that he had not done it with the *intention* of aiding the enemy.

These offences of conspiracy and treason are frequently used for political or social aims without much regard for the niceties of the principle of legality. We shall see that the law is often content with vagueness if the aim of the prosecution embodies some "higher" principle. In obscenity cases, lawyers for the defence have often tried to persuade courts that the relevant law was "void for vagueness." In the United States they have been successful. In Canada, the courts have not been receptive, as evidenced by the *Isaacs Gallery* case. The "higher" principle—the enforcement of some moral value such as the prohibition of Mark Prent's paintings—triumphed. Lawyers used to say that penal statutes were meant to be construed strictly. This principle no longer holds in the sense of the courts leaning over backwards to acquit the accused if the words of the statute contained any possible ambiguity. That rule may have made sense when the accused had no counsel, no witnesses and no chance to give evidence on his own behalf. The Ontario Court of Appeal recently examined the question of the "strict" interpretation of statutes and defined it as "where a person is charged with an offence created by a statute, or the conduct of that person which gives rise to the charge, or the conduct of someone for which that person may be answerable, must be such as can be clearly and unmistakably demonstrated to fall within the kind of conduct which is proscribed by the statute."

Other Problems of Vagueness

There are some past and present offences that also carry the seeds of vagueness. Illustration 43(b) refers to the case of *Stundon* where the accused was charged under the Juvenile Delinquents Act with contributing to the delinquency of a minor. In addition to having illicit sexual relations with a minor's parent, an adult could conceivably be guilty of the contributing offence by immoderate drinking in the presence of a minor, by setting a bad example for a child by swearing, lying and so on. This problem is also seen in s. 168(1) cited earlier. Quite often, when the law is confronted with such slippery concepts as morality and, in this instance, the problem of deciding what might cause future immoral behaviour, the law avoids precise definition. It certainly does not seek answers from the behavioural sciences (e.g., fifty-one per cent of children who had adult role models who drank alcohol, swore, fornicated, etc., became juvenile delinquents). Instead it leaves the problem to the judge to decide on a case-by-case basis. A similar problem is found in s. 688 of the Code that describes the circumstances in which a criminal can be declared a "dangerous offender" subject to an indeterminate sentence. The criteria are rather indeterminate in themselves:

> (a) (i) a pattern of repetitive behaviour . . . showing a failure to restrain his behaviour and a likelihood of his causing death or injury . . .
> (ii) a pattern of persistent aggressive behaviour . . . showing a substantial degree of indifference . . . as to the reasonably foreseeable consequences to the other person of his behaviour, or
> (iii) any behaviour of the offender . . . that is of such a brutal nature as to compel the conclusion that his behaviour in the future is unlikely to be inhibited by normal standards of behavioural restraint.
> (b) . . . failure to control his sexual impulses and a likelihood of his causing injury, pain or other evil to other persons.

No one can suggest that the problem of the dangerous offender is an easy one. Most penal reformers would agree that a small percentage of offenders should be incarcerated for long periods because they are so dangerous that the public should be protected from them, but how we decide which is the small percentage is the difficult question. Are the words of s. 688 useful? Who should decide on the dangerous criteria? A judge, a panel of psychiatrists or a jury of concerned citizens?

The Law Must Be Accessible

The most Draconian systems have an Alice in Wonderland flavour about them; the hapless citizen has no way of finding out the law until he has already infringed it. The Nazi laws certainly had that quality. Some military codes of discipline have a blanket section advocating punishment of any behaviour "contrary to the good order and discipline" of the armed services.

These problems are closely related to vagueness. Even in our presumably democratic society, there are occasions when the bureaucracy becomes so overburdened with procedures and regulations that it is impossible for the average citizen to have access to the law. A trained law librarian would be severely taxed if he tried to keep on top of the torrent of paper that floods from government departments. The basic rule (found in s. 19 of the Code) is that ignorance of the law is no excuse on the basis that everyone is presumed to know the law. Some courts have held that if it is impossible for the average lay citizen to discover the law, then a reasonable mistake of law might provide a defence despite the ancient rule that "every man is presumed to know the law." *Lim Chin Aik* was a case in which the accused was charged under Singapore law as being a prohibited alien. His defence was that the list of prohibited aliens was unavailable and, in any event, the list was entirely within the discretion of the appropriate minister. He was acquitted.

At one stage the British Columbia government drew up regulations (which were empowered by the initial legislation) but were not published outside the minutes of the legislature. These circumstances would provide an appropriate case for acquitting an accused who infringed the regulations because he had no opportunity of knowing the law (or even being presumed to know it).

There are a few instances where s. 19 does not apply. The decisions in which an accused has been acquitted are rare. *Jollimore,* decided in Nova Scotia in 1961, is such a case. The accused had been convicted of impaired driving. The offence carried an automatic revocation of licence. The magistrate who tried Jollimore did not make an order in court and the Registrar of Motor Vehicles revoked the licence and notified Jollimore by mail. The accused was stopped by a police officer before he reached home where the notice of revocation was awaiting him. He was charged with driving while his licence was suspended; the trial magistrate acquitted and four of five appellate judges agreed. MacDonald J. spoke for the majority in saying that there was "nothing in the enactment to overcome the general presumption that some conscious intention to break the law is essential."

The motor vehicle statute was amended to solve the *Jollimore* problem: the failure of the magistrate to tell the accused that his licence was revoked "shall not affect in any way the validity of the revocation." In another Nova Scotia case, *Villeneuve,* a similar situation arose but after the statutory change. The accused claimed a *Jollimore* defence but the court decided that s. 19 of the Code applied. The trial judge tried to make the difficult and dangerous distinction between the two cases based on mistake of fact in *Jollimore* and ignorance of the law in *Villeneuve.* In the first case, the accused did not know whether his record of conviction had been passed on to the Registrar of Motor Vehicles and this was an administrative fact while in *Villeneuve* the accused was ignorant of the fact that his licence was revoked—this was because he did not know the legal effect of s. 238 of the Code which, therefore, was a clear question of ignorance of law. The Supreme Court in *R.* v. *Prue and Baril* did not agree and decided that Villeneuve was wrong and that the existence of a suspension of a driving licence was a question of fact. Because the accused did not know of the suspension, they had no *mens rea* and should be acquitted.

These cases are really more cases of ignorance of law than pertaining to the accessibility of the law. The appeal court's sympathetic hearing of these cases implicitly suggests that the multitude of law applicable to the ordinary citizen in the complicated society of today means that there will be more cases like *R.* v. *Prue and Baril.*

Maclean (Illustration 23(a)) is a little closer to an accessibility issue. The judge acquitted the accused but pointed out that he was not negating s. 19 but thought that there was a clear distinction between "the discoverability and availability of statutes on the one hand and subordinate legislation on the other." He added:

> Every judge and lawyer knows the difficulty in discovering the exact text of some non-statutory enactments, in particular municipal by-laws, and while federal Government Regulations and other statutory instruments are kept in much better shape and in much more adequate supply, they offer the additional challenge of vast bulk and frequent amendment. Moreover, it is almost twenty years since they were issued in consolidated form.

The judge applied another rider; that he would not have been prepared to acquit if the accused had not also made conscientious and appropriate efforts to discover the law before he drove a vehicle at the airport. In *Potter*, the accused was charged with illegal importation of gambling devices. Before importing them, his employer had asked a customs official if it would be legal to import them. He sent a sample of the device and received no reply. The judge was very sympathetic to *Maclean* and said:

> . . . it is incumbent upon, and the duty of, that Crown officer [of customs] either to give a direct answer if he knows it, which he should, and which the law assumes that he does, or if he does not know it, to find out. This information is readily available to him, but not to a foreign national. By not so advising [Potter's employer], as he should have done, he lulled him into a false sense of security.

He convicted Potter but gave him an absolute discharge. The status of the *Maclean* case is somewhat doubtful since the Supreme Court of Canada decision in *Molis* (which is discussed under mistake of law).

Coincidence of *Actus Reus* and *Mens Rea*

Any legal definition of a crime consists of two elements—the *mens rea* or mental element and the *actus reus* or physical element. The two must exist and co-exist.

Illustration 1 gives the simplest and most obvious example of this principle. No matter how "evil" Donald's intention may be toward Victor, the latter's death in an automobile crash was purely accidental. The law would say that Donald's evil intent was not operating at the time his car collided with the taxi in which Victor was riding. Even if Donald had left a party with an urgent intent to kill his enemy, the situation would be the same providing the collision was accidental.

If Donald had been driving while very drunk, the situation essentially would still be the same. Undoubtedly, he would be convicted of criminal negligence, dangerous driving or driving while impaired. Then his *mens rea* (if one existed at all) would be different and it would not be directed specifically to the death of Victor. Donald could be convicted just as easily of criminal negligence causing the death of the taxi driver or of a pedestrian.

The bizarre facts of *Droste* are of good factual illustration of the above. The Crown alleged that D had planned to impregnate the inside of his car with gasoline, fake an accident and hit his wife over the head with a weighted pipe. He used gasoline on the interior of his car, although it was done in clear view of the neighbours as if he were cleaning the interior. He set off with his wife and two children. While driving at thirty-five miles per hour, the car struck the abutment of a bridge. The car burst into flames and the children (but not D's wife) died in the fire. D claimed it was an accident. His car was in a "terrible state of disrepair." There was uncontradicted evidence that D was devoted to his children. The Ontario Court of Appeal granted a new trial because the trial judge did not make it clear to the jury that although D may have had the *mens rea* to kill Ms. D, he would not necessarily be convicted of first degree murder of the children because the *mens rea* for first degree murder included the ingredients of planning and deliberation.

Illustration 2 requires the same answer; David is not guilty of the murder of Vince. Indeed, he would be acquitted on the grounds of self-defence or justifiable homicide in the killing or the apprehension of a potential criminal found in a dwelling house (*per* s. 40 of the Code so long as he used only "as much force as is necessary").

Illustration 3 is the English case of *Pembliton*, where the accused was acquitted because his *mens rea* was directed to assault but the *actus reus* was damage to property. Yet *Latimer* (described in Illustration 4) resulted in a conviction because his *mens rea* was directed to assault and the *actus reus* was also an assault. The only difference between Dick's intent and the result was the identity of the person assaulted. This is called transferred intent. If, in a variation of Illustration 1, Donald had been stalking Victor with the intention of killing him and Victor, in terror, had fled and been killed by a car as he ran from Donald, the law would probably consider it murder. The verdict would still be murder if D took aim at Victor, missed and killed Vellum or if D thought that Vellum was Victor and deliberately killed him.

In *Faulkner* a sailor, stealing rum from a cask on a ship, started a fire that caused the destruction of the vessel. The court decided that he could be convicted of theft of the rum but that no principle of transferred intent applied that could make him criminally responsible for the loss of the ship.

Transfer of intent applies only if the same kind of crime is committed. Sometimes, however, it is difficult to determine what is meant by the "same kind" of offence.

Illustration 5 describes the case of *Fagan*. Why should there be any question of Dan's guilt? His lawyer argued that, when the car wheel came to rest on the constable's foot, Dan performed the *actus reus* of an offence of assault but at that time he had no *mens rea*. When he had the *mens rea*, that is, when he finally decided to leave the wheel on the foot, he was not committing any *actus reus*. The defence further argued that criminal liability would have been more feasible if Dan's foot had been squashing the policeman's foot because that would have required a continuing willed pressure. The court did not accept this ingenious argument which suggested that there was no coincidence of *actus reus* and *mens rea*. The conviction was upheld on the basis that the *actus reus* was an ongoing one, and when Dan decided that he would not immediately accede to the policeman's request, he committed the *mens rea* as well, and at that point there was coincidence of the two elements.

Glanville Williams has suggested an alternative rule that makes more sense than the legal fiction of the on-going *actus reus* in *Fagan* (above) and *Ashwell* (below):

> ... where the *actus reus* includes an act causing an event, and a person does the act without the mental element specified for the offence, but comes to know that it has caused or may cause the event and that he may be able to prevent the occurrence or limit the continuation of the event, it is his duty to take reasonable steps in that regard, and if he fails to take such steps then: (a) if after acquiring such knowledge he knew that the event or its continuation was practically certain unless action were taken, he is deemed to have acted intentionally in causing it, and (b) if after acquiring such knowledge he was reckless as to the continuation of the event, he is deemed to have acted recklessly in causing it.

In *Ashwell* V gave D a coin while they were in a dark place. V thought it was a silver shilling but it was, in fact, a gold coin of the same size and worth twenty times as much. Later, D discovered the mistake and kept the gold coin. When he was given the coin, D did not intend to steal. The court decided that as soon as D discovered the mistake and decided to misappropriate the coin, he became guilty of larceny. Once again, the court has invented an ongoing *actus reus* that eventually had a point of coincidence or concurrence with the *mens rea*.

Illustration 30(d) is closely related, although it has been treated as a problem of legal causation. In that case, *Thabo Meli*, the accused were convicted as was the accused in the New Brunswick case of *Bernard* where D had intentionally stabbed V but had not killed him and had then run over V with V's own automobile, although this latter act may have been accidental. The stab wounds were serious but the immediate cause of death was the crushing of V under the automobile. The court had no difficulty in upholding a murder conviction because they viewed the driving of the car over V's body as "but one incident in a continuous series of acts in the course of the robbery" and that D "meant to cause bodily harm" to facilitate the robbery or his escape.

Illustration 6 describes the Canadian case of *Ladue*. D argued that he could not be convicted because he had no *mens rea* under s. 178 in that he thought V was alive. One way to approach the problem is to say that his *actus reus* was that of the offence under s. 178 but that he had no *mens rea* and certainly not the intention of committing an offence under s. 178. The British Columbia

Court of Appeal did not accept the submission and convicted D. The court added that if D's contention were accepted, that would mean he was committing rape and could not use a defence that was, in effect, an admission of another offence. In terms of pure theory, this viewpoint is questionable: no one can be guilty of raping a corpse. The *Ladue* case is a different kind of problem because it concerns mistake of fact. We shall return to it later.

The Need for an Act

The most obvious reason for the requirement of an act in the structure of a crime is that the law will not punish mere thoughts. The efforts to describe "an act" in criminal law terms have been generative of much heat but not much light. An "act" can be one of commission or one of omission. A difficult situation in the definitional search is the case of a mere status, e.g., ex-offender, alcoholic, a person addicted to a narcotic, dangerous offender, habitual criminal or vagrant. Similarly, is it an act for a person to fail to fulfil a legal duty?

Philosophers and lawyers have debated the meaning of an act in the criminal law. Roscoe Pound has defined an act as "exertions of the will manifested in the external world." This definition will often include omissions. The Model Penal Code (which is not legislation but the distillation of the best thought on criminal law prepared by the American Law Institute) says that a person is not guilty of an offence "unless his liability is based on conduct that includes a voluntary act or the omission to perform an act of which he is physically capable" (s. 2.01(1)). In answer to Pound's definition, the following are not classed as voluntary acts:

> 2.01(2).
> (a) a reflex or convulsion
> (b) a bodily movement during unconsciousness or sleep
> (c) conduct during hypnosis or resulting from hypnotic suggestion
> (d) a bodily movement that otherwise is not a product of the effort or determination of the actor, either conscious or habitual.

These exceptions may seem a little exotic and we shall return later to a few practical illustrations of the problems posed.

The provisions of the Model Penal Code (M.P.C.) also show that it is impossible to separate the mind from the body or the *mens rea* from the *actus reus*. Though many forests have been sacrificed to a discussion of the distinction, we shall not concern ourselves with it here.

The same section of the M.P.C. discusses "possession," a difficult concept in the law that illustrates the problem of differentiating the mental element from the physical element. The M.P.C. drafters defined "possession" as:

> an act . . . if the possessor knowingly procured or received the thing possessed or was aware of his control thereof for a sufficient period to have been able to terminate his possession.

Illustrations 7 and 8 show problems of possession which we will examine later. At this point, we need only note that D in Illustration 7 was acquitted while D in Illustration 8 was convicted.

Section 3(4) of the Canadian Code defines possession as existing when a person "has it in his personal possession or knowingly":

(i) has it in the actual possession or custody of another person, or
(ii) has it in any place, whether or not that place belongs to or is occupied by him, for the use or benefit of himself or of another person.

Perhaps it would be best to follow Glanville Williams's definition of *actus reus* as "the whole definition of the crime with the exception of the mental element."

The Elements of the Criminal Law

In the following pages we shall be concentrating on the mental element of the criminal law, which must usually be found along with an act before an accused can be convicted. (There are important exceptions to this rule which will be discussed under Illustration 27.) The mental element, or *mens rea,* can consist of intention, recklessness or possibly negligence. Before formulating any more rules, we must remember that the terms "*guilty mind,*" "*intention*" or "*recklessness*" are not to be taken as having the same meaning in the law as they have to the intelligent layperson, the psychiatrist or the philosopher. The psychiatrists' most persistent criticism of the criminal law is that it is based on free will and a theological ethic while the behavioural scientists maintain that human conduct is determined.

Some argue the criminal law was based originally on absolute liability. When harm was done, the kin of the deceased or the aggrieved party himself did not enquire as to frame of mind of the culprit at the time of the wrongdoing. If so, there must have been obvious exceptions because human compassion intervened—as it must in all circumstances where an accident occurred and no one was to blame. The law, through the ingenuity of its lawyers and judges, provided subterfuges or fictions that mitigated the stringency of the punishment or created defences in sympathetic circumstances. The original influence of the canon law was salutary because it tried to regularize the concept of blameworthiness, making a moral contribution to the gradations of liability.

The concept of *mens rea* is based on the Judeo-Christian ethic that man is a willing agent who can control his actions and the thoughts that precede them. A corollary of this is that a man should be punished only for those actions that he has willed. This concept would be quite rational and reasonable if man were simply a mechanism that could be either totally switched on or totally switched off. Even if man could be taught—like a laboratory pigeon—that if he pushed the button marked *mens rea* (or "crime" or "blame") he would receive an electric shock (or punishment or no rewarding pellet of food) and that if he desisted he would gain a reward, we might have a simple, workable system. Unfortunately, it is not that simple; legal guilt is not as mechanistic and obvious as a litmus test because there are grades of guilty intent and shades of blameworthiness that man adopts in all his relations with other human beings.

There is a further complication. The ethos of the criminal law is based on the Old Testament rather than the New. The spirit of *lex talionis* or the Mosaic Code of an eye for an eye or a tooth for a tooth is applied in our system. Of course, it is not applied literally, but we have always lived, and continue to live, in a system where we insist on taking revenge on wrongdoers. Society insists that the criminal suffer degradation or denunciation. At one stage, this consisted of outlawry; at other times the disapproval of the State was expressed by capital punishment and mutilation. Now the offender is exiled to a penal system. The essence of all forms of penal treatment is stigma. The instinctive folk memory, which is only inarticulately expressed, is that there is a difference between those who wilfully transgress codes of behaviour and those who do it accidentally or negligently. Justice Holmes once said that even a dog knows the difference between being kicked and being tripped over. This phenomenon has also been explained by behavioural scientists in a number of ways—the need for guilt to be expiated (which also has been a common stance in Christian theology), the need to punish those who have fallen below standards that we have not yet transgressed or the feeling among the guilty that they should be punished.

We apply moral standards, and even quantitative blameworthiness, in our everyday dealings. If, on an isolated occasion, a child spills his milk at the dinner table, we may patiently wipe it up and console him by saying that it was obviously an accident. If the child manages to spill the milk at every other meal, we may tell him that he is being careless and that he will be punished so that he will be more careful in the future. If he does it at every meal, we may punish him on every occasion—even though we have long ago decided that it does not deter his milk spilling (and even though he protests, "I didn't mean to spill it"). The child does not intend to spill milk, and the thoughtful (and loving) parent may decide that the method of milk distribution must change. The punishment system obviously was not working and the parent may have serious reservations about punishing a child whose behaviour is not intentional because a merely careless actor does not advert to the harm caused and is therefore not deterred. When "careless" behaviour becomes habitual, is it still only careless?

Let us also imagine cases where the milk spilling is not habitual. During a particular meal, there has been great acrimony between parent and child, and as an act of defiance, the child pours his milk on the floor. The parent, a slave to the obvious statement, says, "You did that deliberately." The child has acted intentionally, and the parent has no hesitation in applying punishment. On another occasion, the child is sitting at one end of the table and his brother is sitting at the other. He decides that he would like to throw his dinner roll at his brother. In front of his brother is a glass of milk and the roll thrower realizes that there is a risk that he might hit the glass instead of his sibling but decides that he will take the risk. The milk is spilled and the parent will not listen to protestations of innocence based on the fact that the milk spiller did not really want to knock over the glass. The parent says you saw the danger and you still threw the roll; therefore you were reckless. Finally, we are faced with a situation where a child has been exceptionally mischievous during the meal. The parent is fully aware of the child's past reputation for spilling milk. Before the parent leaves the room, he notices that the child has been gradually moving his glass of milk toward the edge of the table, and the glass is now on the very edge. Soon after leaving the room there is a crash and milk is spilled all over the floor. The parent immediately accuses the milk spiller of deliberately spilling the milk, although he has no direct proof of it. He *infers* guilt from the surrounding circumstances. The parent may have developed an unhealthy preoccupation with the evils of milk spilling or has an unfair bias against this particular milk spiller. The child may have intentionally spilled the milk, or he may have been unlucky in that he wanted to keep the glass on the table but misjudged his balancing trick or his vengeful sibling may have jolted the table causing the glass to fall. The parent knows none of these facts from eye-witness evidence or even from a videotape. There may be other witnesses more or less sympathetic to the alleged milk spiller, which may confirm or refute the parent's inferences.

A child, of course, does not incur criminal liability, and one hopes that parents do not treat milk spilling as a serious domestic crime, but these incidents are fairly accurate metaphors of accident, negligence, gross (or criminal) negligence, intention, recklessness and imputed intent in the criminal law. The first two are not tests of responsibility or blameworthiness in law. The last three are descriptions of *mens rea*. Gross (or criminal) negligence is a strange hybrid which we will examine later. The parent's attitude toward responsibility will depend on many factors: his philosophy of child raising, the size of his family, the incidence of milk spilling, his educational level, the age of the child and the mental and physical health of the child. Many of these ideas can be transposed into the public's attitudes toward alleged criminals who commit acts a little more serious than spilling milk.

As a general statement of *mens rea*, we might adopt the definitions of two commentators. Hall describes the principle of *mens rea* as the "ultimate summation of the moral judgements expressed in the proscription of the voluntary (intentional or reckless) commission of numerous social harms" done by normal adult offenders. Brett sets down an "overriding principle of criminal law, derived from its roots in the community ethic, requiring the presence of moral blameworthiness in every case." Both Brett and Hall stress that the moral connotation relates to the rule that forbids condemnation by the criminal law of a morally innocent person. Considering the earlier discussion of law and morals, some readers might be surprised to find the "moral" ingredient in the definition. In this context, it is not used as indicating a judgement that any particular kind of behaviour should be controlled by the criminal law but rather the way in which we have decided to define the mental attitudes of those who allegedly commit acts that we have already decided should be classed as criminal (as opposed to merely antisocial bad manners, or immoral).

Intention

A typical legal definition of "intention" is found in Turner who says that it "... denotes the state of mind of the man who not only foresees but also desires the possible consequences of his conduct." The test of "intention" should be a subjective one in that the law is interested in the state of mind of the accused himself rather than in an inference that the court might make about his behaviour; that is, what the accused foresees rather than basing liability on some exterior, objective test such as what the reasonable man might have foreseen. As we shall see, there are many exceptions to the subjective rule.

Mens rea, in the form of intention, is not limited to cases where the accused admits he intended to do the prohibited act. The criminal law does not automatically accept the accused's story that he did not intend or desire to do the act. On the other hand, it is only the rare occasion in which police actually observe the crime being committed and see the accused doing it and, even more rarely, receive an immediate confession from the accused. Human behaviour is nearly always more ambiguous than the above situations indicate. Intention is a concept that must often be inferred from the circumstances, but the inference should come from the evidential data produced at trial, not from a supposition of the trier or an implication unsupported by the facts.

The Model Penal Code does not employ the word "intention" but uses the words "purposely" and "knowingly":

> 2.02(2) (a) *Purposely*
> A person acts purposely with respect to a material element of an offence when:
> (i) if the element involves the nature of his conduct or a result thereof, it is his conscious object to engage in conduct of that nature or to cause such a result; and
> (ii) if the element involves the attendant circumstances, he is aware of the existence of such circumstances or he believes or hopes that they exist.
>
> (b) *Knowingly*
> A person acts knowingly with respect to a material element of an offence when:
> (i) if the element involves the nature of his conduct or the attendant circumstances, he is aware that his conduct is of that nature or that such circumstances exist; and

(ii) if the element involves a result of his conduct, he is aware that it is practically certain that his conduct will cause such a result.

The English Law Commission Working Paper on the Mental Element in Crime contains a definition of intention and knowledge:

7. A. (1) A person intends an event not only

(a) When his purpose is to cause that event but also

First Alternative

(b) When he has no substantial doubt that that event will result from his conduct.

Second Alternative

(c) When he foresees that that event will probably result from his conduct.

(2) A person is not by reason only of proposition 7A (1)(b) to be taken to intend the wrongdoing of others.

(3) A person knows of circumstances not only when he knows that they exist but also when

First Alternative

(a) He has not substantial doubt that they exist.

Second Alternative

(b) He knows that they probably exist.

In explanation of these definitions (which are still in a fluid state, thus accounting for the Alternatives), the Working Paper provides a rationale for these formulations:

(a) The law should still accord with the ordinary man's conception of what is just; if it falls below this standard, it will be brought into contempt.

(b) Fairness between individuals requires that persons in like circumstances should be treated in the same way, and that persons who are not in similar circumstances should be treated differently. The degree of fault with which a person of normal capacity commits a prohibited act is generally regarded as an important ground for distinguishing him from other persons of normal capacity who commit the same act with a different degree of fault.

(c) The social interest in economy of punishment requires that a person should not in general be punished for an offence that he does not know he is committing and that he is powerless to prevent, if only because in such cases the threat of sanctions is generally ineffective as a deterrent in relation to his conduct or the conduct of others.

These proposals raise some important points. First, "intention" (or its M.P.C. equivalent) is not limited to the totally subjective mental element of the accused. The law does not automatically accept the accused's explanation ("I didn't mean to do it" or "I never foresaw such harm") if the facts of the case tend to prove otherwise. Such a personal evaluation of *mens rea* would be too narrow, contrary to common sense or socially unacceptable.

The M.P.C. distinguishes between "purposely" and "knowingly." The first term tries to offer further description by using such phrases as "conscious object," "believes" and "hopes." "Knowingly" is elaborated by such terms as "aware" and "practically certain." Similar descriptions are found in the English Law Commission proposals. The Alternatives attempt to offer gradations of foresight—if, indeed, it is possible to talk of gradations in this area of human behaviour.

As Hall has pointed out, *mens rea* comprises knowledge of the material facts and an internal effort, that is, "movement of the will." The formulations of the M.P.C. and the English Law Commission are attempts to put this difficult concept into words describing the accused's mental attitude toward the proscribed harm. It is very difficult to be precise and avoid ambiguity. As we shall see later, the use of such words as "purpose," "motive" or "desire" tends to muddy the waters and introduce elements that are irrelevant or at least confusing. The problem is well illustrated by the House of Lords in *Lang* v. *Lang*:

> If [he] knows the probable results of his acts and persists in them . . . that is enough, however passionately he may desire or request [the opposite result]. His intention is to act as he did, whatever the consequences, though he may hope and desire that they will not produce their probable effect.

The M.P.C.'s use of the phrases "his conscious object" and "he is aware that his conduct is of that nature or that such circumstances exist" reflects the notion that *mens rea* is based on voluntariness and free will. The accused will certainly not be convicted for acts "committed" when he was in the middle of an epileptic fit or when he was acting as an automaton as a result of hypnotic suggestion or somnambulism. These situations result in harm that, in the words of the English Commission, the accused is "powerless to prevent." The accused is not a free agent and his movement is not willed. An enlightened penal policy would suggest that there is no sense in punishing people for acts they do not know they are committing. The simplest reason for withholding punishment is that it would not deter that person or those in similar circumstances. In addition, it is morally right to do so. This point is well stated by Mr. Justice Holmes:

> The reason for requiring an act is, that an act implies a choice, and that it is felt to be impolitic and unjust to make a man answerable for harm, unless he might have chosen otherwise. But the choice must be made with a chance of contemplating the consequence complained of, or else it has no bearing on responsibility for that consequence.

Can we go one step further and decide that the criminal law should not create a test of liability that includes foresight of probable or possible consequence? The accused may say, "Your test says that I should probably have foreseen that my behaviour would result in harm but I am telling you that, in fact, I did not foresee such consequences." The law's answer is that justice and equal treatment of equal cases (mentioned by the English Commission) requires the application of a slightly higher standard than that of the accused. This introduces that fictional personage of the law—the reasonable man—who, *in the place of the accused*, would have foreseen the probability of the consequences. This standard of the reasonable or ordinary man is not that of the stupid person or that of the exceptional person who has extraordinary wisdom or abnormally good eyesight or other senses, reflexes or perceptions. The test is to be used to discover the actual intent of the accused not as a substitute for the intent of the accused. This is well expressed by James Marshall who has described the law as a "codification of experience into expectations of conduct and a declaration of the conditions under which the full coercive power of the State will if necessary be used to enforce those expectations." In applying this, Marshall says:

> If to act intentionally means a free choice of action—even if the only choice is between doing and refraining from doing a specific something—then it must be seen by the actor to be a choice he is capable of acting upon as well as by those who, sitting in judgement, find the act to be intentional, the outcome of an evil choice, *mens rea.*

Subjective and Objective

A clear distinction must be made between these terms as applied to the test of the culpability of the accused and to the assessment of evidence that proves or disproves that guilt. We hope that the trier of fact and law will be objective in the second category in the sense that judgements will be made without bias and with a minimum of consideration given to data that has nothing to do with legal guilt and would only distort the fact-finding.

We have already seen that the current attitudes toward the interrelationship of law and morals suggest that moral judgements about human behaviour should have little effect on the definition of crime. There are, nevertheless, ethical considerations in the rules created for the definition of criminal liability. We cannot be subjective in the sense that we define criminal liability strictly on the basis of the accused's explanation of the event. Similarly, the ethical foundation of the criminal law must be an objective one in the sense, for instance, that we should not differentiate between those of low status in society and those of more exalted position. That is a basic requirement of the principle of legality. This form of objectivity also requires that we take a uniformly neutral ethical stance in deciding liability. Any mitigating or aggravating circumstances, other than legitimate defences recognized in the criminal law, will be taken into account in sentencing only. In theory, at least, we should make rules about criminal liability without regard to the particular personal circumstances of the accused or the events surrounding the alleged offence. The fact that the accused was loved or hated in the community should have no effect on the finding of liability. Similarly, criminal responsibility or blameworthiness should not be affected by the nature of the accused's acts, be they mild or scandalous. These theoretically irrelevant factors may be taken into account only in assessing penalty.

A subjective approach to *guilt* is preferable; that is, a test that judges the culpability of the accused on his *actual* state of mind. The objective test, on the other hand, finds liability on the standard of the "reasonable person." Total subjectivity, as we have seen, is an impossible standard if only because we cannot know the inner workings of the human mind. A liberal penal theorist, however, would argue that we should not punish anyone on some abstract and impossibly harsh standard of objectivity.

We will be subjective in the sense that we will listen to the accused's explanation of the events that led to the charge, but we will then test the accused's perceptions by asking if *he* could have believed the circumstances to be as he described them. This does not mean that his explanation has to be reasonable according to some abstract test, only that *he* actually held those views and entertained those beliefs. In reaching a decision on *his* actual personal guilt, we will perforce make a rational judgement of the evidence in the case, based on the standard of the "reasonable man" who found himself in the circumstances actually confronting the accused—standing in the shoes of the accused and seeing with his eyes.

These problems are usually not of great complexity because what the accused believed or contemplated will often coincide with the view of the reasonable person. Difficulties arise in cases where the accused has made a factual mistake that is "unreasonable" according to an objective test of liability, or in cases where the accused is abnormal but his mental processes are not such that he would have a legal defence of insanity.

Once again, Marshall, who is a keen observer of law and psychology, has put the issue very well:

> ... it is difficult to conceive of a person having free will independent of his experience-conditioned perceptions and his transactions with other people and with objects which compose a given situation in which he interacts. It is equally difficult to accept the thesis that man has no freedom of will to mediate among his own purposes and the people, objects, and culture which compose the field of his interactions. It is not possible for man by his will to eliminate his experience and perceive people or things or interrelationships *de novo* or, if he is not pathological, to ignore the mutuality of his transactions with others.

Motive

Motive, as a general rule, is irrelevant to *mens rea*. In this context motive means the rationale for the accused's actions. The distinction between motive and intention is stated succinctly by Hall:

> ... when we ask questions about a person's motives, we are asking for data relevant to evaluation of his character or at least of the morality of a particular act. Given a motive, a relevant intention can be inferred. But the converse does not apply, *i.e.*, one may be positive that certain conduct was intentional without knowing any motive for it.

A confusion has existed because *mens rea* was once equated with sinfulness or evil at a time when crime had more religious than legal ingredients.

Good motive is as irrelevant as bad motive. In Illustration 26, D's suspicions about the corruption of the mayor are irrelevant, although the prosecution might decide to exercise administrative discretion and not proceed with the charge in such circumstances.

If D had been the head of the fraud squad, the situation would be a little more complicated (and would involve questions that are discussed more fully under procedure). In theory, the case of *Ormerod* pointed out that a police officer who breached the law, even in the course of his perceived duty, could be prosecuted. If his behaviour amounted to entrapment (rather than his merely acting as *agent provocateur*), the accused would have a defence against conviction. In practice, of course, the police officer who acts as a thief to catch a thief is seldom prosecuted. Therefore, in Illustration 26(b) the *de jure* answer is that motive is irrelevant but the *de facto* situation means that the motive of the police officer is all-important.

In Illustration 17 we would not convict D of killing V simply because she was going to benefit under V's will. If that possible bad motive were the only proof of D's intention, then we could not and should not convict, but of course, there is often other evidence of intention, and in such circumstances, motive will be very important as a matter of evidence, although not as a direct contribution to the definition of intention. This is well stated by an Ontario court:

> When a defendant is indisputably shown to be the criminal, evidence of motive is immaterial. Motive relates to a consequence ulterior to the *mens rea* and *actus reus* and, adopting this criterion, motive is irrelevant to criminal responsibility, *viz.*, a man may be lawfully convicted of a crime whatever his motive may be or even if he has no motive. It is, of course, relevant as evidence for if the prosecution can prove that the defendant had a motive for committing the crime it may do so, since the existence of motive makes it more likely that the defendant did in fact commit it.

If D watches V drown without offering aid, should the prosecution be able to prove that D wanted V dead because he had another love or wanted V's job? If there is no legal duty on D to save V's life, then D is not guilty of murder, although we may want to shun D's society and treat him as a moral leper. Some European codes, following Bentham's suggestion, have provisions making it a criminal offence if D fails to act as a Good Samaritan or as a good citizen toward strangers.

In Illustration 8(a), the prosecution persuaded an appeal court to admit evidence that the drugs in the scuba tank were worth many thousands of dollars. Such evidence as to the profit motive would have a very persuasive effect on a jury. If that had been the *only* evidence, of course D should not be convicted.

The moral behaviour or motivation of the accused often has evidential relevance to the question of guilt, although it does not affect the definition of responsibility directly. In Illustration 1, the court would probably admit evidence of D's hatred of V, which would make it more difficult for the trier of fact to be convinced that the automobile collision was entirely accidental. As soon as the accident is proved, however, D must go free no matter how joyful he may seem at the death of his enemy. If V dies under mysterious circumstances that tend to implicate D, then the motive of D for desiring the death of V may be introduced in evidence.

In an Australian case the accused alleged that his wife had drowned while swimming in the sea. There was inconclusive pathological evidence that suggested that the wife's death was not purely accidental and may have been aided by her husband's acts. The court decided that the jury was entitled to hear evidence that the husband had a mistress whom he wished to marry. This rule is not unreasonable and similar evidence is often admitted in a less circuitous fashion; the Crown introduces evidence that, by innuendo, suggests that the husband was not exactly enchanted with his wife and had sought consolation elsewhere. Dr. Crippen's apprehension with Miss LaNeve on an oceanliner bound for New York was corroborative of his intention. Of course, Dr. Crippen or the Australian accused could not be convicted of murder by such evidence alone. There must be some physical or direct evidence pointing to the intent (and act) of the accused.

Revenge, jealousy, hatred or avarice, of themselves, will not convict an accused. The adjective "ulterior" is most apposite to motive in the criminal law. Motive is not strictly an ingredient of *mens rea* but it is frequently possible for the prosecution to tender such evidence to help persuade the trier of fact of the guilt of the accused.

Illustrations 13 and 14 show cases where the accused acted from what they considered to be good motive. In neither case would the law acquit them.

Duty and Motive Compared

In Illustration 17, should we take a different view because D and V were related? In this instance, we are talking about duty rather than motive. The latter is usually only evidential but "duty" is part of the description of the offence and is directly related to intention. Davinia could be convicted of criminal negligence (s. 202) if we decided that there had been "an omission to do anything that it is [her] duty to do." Section 202(2) defines "duty" as a "duty imposed by law." What does "law" mean? An informal contract between D and V that will give D free board and lodging in exchange for D's companionship? Or something more specific such as a provision in a statute that requires children to support their elderly, indigent or sick parents? Or should it be extended to aunts and nieces merely because of a vague moral duty to help or protect one's relations?

If D, standing on the bank of a river, sees his wife and child in danger of drowning and does nothing, can he be convicted of homicide if Ms. D and the child die? The law would say yes, but the answer would be negative if the persons in the water were strangers to D. What would the law say if D did nothing to save V from drowning if V were simply a friend, his fiancée, his mistress or his second cousin? Would the law's attitude be different if D were a doctor or had a gold medal in lifesaving? The harsh rule is that criminal liability will only apply if there is a legal duty, and a mere moral duty based on human emotion, good citizenship or professional ethics would not be enough.

Motive and Criminal Libel

The rule of thumb is that motive is irrelevant—at least that it has no relationship to the definition of criminal responsibility. One of the few unequivocal exceptions is the crime (not to be confused with the civil suit) of defamatory libel that is defined as "matter published, without lawful justification or excuse, that is likely to injure the reputation of any person by exposing him to hatred, contempt or ridicule, or that is designed to insult the person of or concerning whom it is published" (s. 262 of the Code). The libel can be expressed in words or symbols. There are two defences that are based exclusively on motive and these are clear instances where motive is a negation of intent. Publication is not likely to be defamatory libel if the publisher believes, on reasonable grounds, that the statement is true and relevant to the public interest. In most jurisdictions the truth of a statement is a complete defence. Section 279 of the Code provides another clear statement of motive being relevant to criminal liability: it is not defamatory libel to publish defamatory matter "in good faith for the purpose of seeking remedy or redress for a private or public wrong or grievance." (See also ss. 273 to 276.)

Defamatory libel is rarely invoked. One recent case, however, involved a charge against an underground newspaper. A university student who had attended a protest meeting on the steps of the courthouse was charged with loitering near government buildings. The magistrate convicted the student but admitted the loitering law was discriminatory. The newspaper awarded the magistrate the Pontius Pilate Certificate of Justice with the following citation for which the paper was convicted of defamatory libel:

> Eckhardt, Magistrate Lawrence—The Pontius Pilate Certificate of Justice—(Unfairly maligned by critics, Pilate upheld the highest traditions of a judge by helping to clear the streets of Jerusalem of degenerate non-conformists). To Lawrence Eckhardt, who, by closing his mind to justice, his eyes to fairness, his ears to equality, has encouraged the belief that the law is not only blind, but also deaf, dumb and stupid. Let history be your judge—then appeal.

A Closer Look at Intention and Subjective *Mens Rea*

Illustration 7 describes the well-known decision of the Supreme Court of Canada in *Beaver* where the accused was acquitted on the charge of possession of heroin. The majority and minority opinions provide an excellent illustration of differing attitudes toward the meaning of *mens rea*. Cartwright J. for the majority took the attitude that, as a general rule, *mens rea* must exist in any criminal offence, particularly where the penalty is severe, and that the burden is on the prosecution to prove the mental element beyond a reasonable doubt.

If the accused had an explanation and if the prosecution did not refute it successfully, then the accused should be acquitted if he had an honest belief that he was not in possession of a narcotic. In an earlier narcotics case the British Columbia Court of Appeal had said in *Hess* that to constitute "possession" within the meaning of s. 4(1) of the Code, a "manual handling of a thing" must be "co-existent with knowledge of what the thing is." Cartwright J. elaborated in *Beaver*:

> . . . the essential question is whether the belief entertained by the accused is an honest one and that the existence or non-existence of reasonable grounds for such belief is merely relevant evidence to be weighed by the tribunal of fact in determining that essential question. . . . The essence of the crime is the possession of the forbidden substance and in a criminal case there is in law no possession without knowledge of the character of the forbidden substance.

This was an important decision because it reinforced the requirement of *mens rea* in Canadian criminal law. Cartwright J. adamantly refused to exclude the necessity for *mens rea* for three reasons. First, the prosecutor's proof of a guilty mind is a fundamental test of our criminal law. Secondly, if Parliament intended to exclude *mens rea* (that is, impose so-called absolute liability) from the definition of a crime (which it could do), the exclusion should, in the judge's opinion, be stated in unequivocal language. Thirdly, no accused should be convicted of an offence where no *mens rea* is present and where the mandatory penalty is imprisonment (and in this case a lengthy term in prison).

The most significant factor in the *Beaver* decision is that it is the high-water mark of a subjective approach to the definition of *mens rea* that refuses to allow conviction on purely implied intent (in the absence of legislative language to the contrary).

Fauteux J. did not agree. He was of the opinion that the usual presumption of *mens rea* as an essential ingredient of an offence could be rebutted by the subject matter of the offence or by the wording of the legislation. On both grounds Fauteux J. was convinced that Beaver's contention failed.

Fauteux J., for the minority, took the attitude that heroin was such a dangerous substance that the law intended to impose absolute liability without proof of *mens rea* on an accused found in possession of it. Although this dissenting judge admitted that the criminal law usually applied a more lenient rule, the social harm caused by heroin demanded a very stringent policy. He also referred to s. 4(1) of the Narcotic Control Act that described the more serious offences of possession for purposes of trafficking or trafficking in the drug (both of which attracted maximum punishment of life imprisonment). Section 4(1) states that "no person shall traffic in a narcotic *or any substance represented or held out by him to be a narcotic*." Fauteux J.

reasoned that the emphasized part of this legislative provision showed the stringency that the law wanted to apply to this offence and, by analogy, the charge against Beaver for simple possession (under s. 3) should be dealt with in a similar manner. Surely a strong argument could be made for exactly the opposite conclusion: that the possession charge under s. 3 contained no phrase such as that emphasized in s. 4 and, therefore, a reasonable explanation could result in an acquittal on a charge under s. 3.

The Cartwright view established a subjective standard of *mens rea* based on the actual belief of the accused. The majority of the Supreme Court of Canada was not prepared to impute intention where it did not necessarily exist. It was not prepared to deny a defence altogether, as suggested by Fauteux J.'s dissent, which would make a moral decision that heroin possessors have no right to a defence of honest mistake of fact based on a reasonable (believable) explanation given in evidence.

For more than a decade the English courts resisted defence counsel's attempts to rely upon a *Beaver*-type subjective test. The English House of Lords finally succumbed in *Sweet* v. *Parsley* (Illustration 8(c)).

The Crown argued that the offence was one of absolute liability. The House of Lords disagreed. The judges relied upon such basic authority as *Woolmington* v. *D.P.P.* which was said to affirm the principle that the onus lies on the prosecution to prove all the elements of the offence. This did not mean that the "prosecution must call evidence to prove the absence of any mistaken belief by the existence of facts which, if true, would make the act innocent." Of course, Cartwright J. had certainly not gone that far: he had decided the lack of *mens rea* was shown by the accused's honest belief and the reasonable grounds for that belief should be "merely relevant evidence."

This evidentiary point is well illustrated by the remarks of Lord Diplock. The jury is entitled to presume that the accused acted with knowledge of the facts but such presumption can be rebutted by evidence to the contrary and, when there is any such evidence, the jury "after considering it and also any relevant evidence called by the prosecution on the issue of the existence of the alleged mistaken belief, should acquit the accused unless they feel sure that he did not hold the belief or that there were no reasonable grounds on which he could have done so."

Lord Pearce decided that "no real, useful object" would be achieved by imposing liability on innocent persons as would happen if the contention of the Crown had been accepted. D had no control of the circumstances of the alleged offence and "the most that vigilance can attain is advance knowledge of . . . guilt."

Must a Mistake of Fact be Reasonable?

In *D.P.P.* v. *Morgan,* (Illustration 44(f)) the House of Lords was asked to answer the question: "Whether, in rape, a defendant can properly be convicted notwithstanding that he in fact believed that the woman consented if such belief was not based on reasonable grounds."

Although the House of Lords upheld their convictions on a statutory provision similar to the one found in s. 613(1)(b)(iii) of the Canadian Code, the question was answered in the negative. Lord Hailsham laid down a rule very similar to Cartwright J.'s pronouncement in *Beaver*: "Since honest belief clearly negatives intent, the reasonableness or otherwise of that belief can only be evidence for or against the view that the belief and therefore the intent was actually held. . . ." Lord Edmund-Davies (who was dissenting) nevertheless said that honest and genuine belief, even if held on unreasonable grounds, would negate *mens rea*. This judge made explicit reference to the academic cry for a subjective test of *mens rea*. Once again, it is worth reiterating the subjective quality of "honest belief" and the more objective nature of the "reasonableness of the evidence" rule:

> . . . the honest belief of an accused charged with rape that the woman was willing, being wholly inconsistent with the criminal intention necessary to constitute the crime, would call for his acquittal. The more unreasonable such a belief in the proved circumstances of the case, the slimmer the chances of the jury's thinking that it was ever entertained.

Morgan incited great protests from feminists who viewed the decision of the House of Lords as a rapist's charter. One of England's best-known female judges, Rose Heilbron,undertook an investigation and supported the decision. The Heilbron Report stated:

> Morgan's case did not decide, as some critics seem to have thought, that an accused person was entitled to be acquitted, however ridiculous his story might be, nor did it decide that the reasonableness or unreasonableness of his belief was irrelevant. Furthermore it is a mistaken assumption that a man is entitled to be acquitted simply because he asserts this belief, without more.

The Supreme Court of Canada arrived at the same conclusion in *Pappajohn*, another rape case, where Dickson J. said: "It will be a rare day when a jury is satisfied as to the existence of an unreasonable belief. If the claim of mistake does not raise a reasonable doubt as to guilt and all other elements of the crime have been proved, then the trier of fact will not give effect to the defence."

(Rape as an offence will be dealt with at a later stage.)

Recklessness

Recklessness has been redefined by the English Law Commission:

> A person is reckless if,
> (a) Knowing that there is a risk that an event may result from his conduct or that a circumstance may exist, he takes that risk, and
> (b) It is unreasonable for him to take it having regard to the degree and nature of the risk which he knows to be present.

The Commission commented:

> It is accepted that whether or not actual foresight or actual appreciation of the

> risk was present is a matter which in some cases may be difficult to prove, but we are not proposing any departure from the general principle that the court of trial may draw appropriate inferences from what in fact happened in order to reach a conclusion upon these matters.

The Commission did not see the unreasonableness test as a departure from subjectivity. The Working Paper stated:

> The test of unreasonableness comes to be applied only when it is known that there is a risk and in that case the question is: "Did he, the defendant, behave unreasonably in taking the risk of which he knew?" The question is the same whether it is asked of the results of the circumstances of conduct.

The Model Penal Code also formulated a definition of "recklessly":

> A person acts recklessly with respect to a material element of an offence when he consciously disregards a substantial and unjustifiable risk that the material element exists or will result from his conduct. The risk must be of such a nature and degree that, considering the nature and purpose of the actor's conduct and the circumstances known to him, its disregard involves culpability of high degree. [Alternative: its disregard involves a gross deviation from proper standards of conduct.]

We must note that recklessness implies advertence or foresight. If there is no foresight, then a person can be guilty of negligence only—something less than reckless behaviour.

The borderline between the subjective intention of *Beaver* and the (more objective?) recklessness rule was examined in another Canadian drug case which is described in Illustration 8(a).

In this case, *Blondin*, the court convicted the accused and decided that the Cartwright rule in *Beaver* was probably correct but did not apply in these circumstances. The court examined the evidence and decided that Blondin probably knew the scuba tank contained something illegal. If D did not know specifically that it contained hashish, then D had wilfully closed his eyes to the fact that it might contain an illegal drug under the Narcotic Control Act. In other words, Blondin had been reckless, which is a form of *mens rea*. If the accused had thought the tank contained something different, such as counterfeit money or pornography, he would not have been convicted.

Davey C.J.B.C. in *Blondin* said:

> . . . it would be wrong to instruct the jury that proof of knowledge that the substance was one which it would be unlawful to import is itself sufficient to support a conviction. . . . it would be correct to instruct a jury that the existence of that knowledge may be inferred as a fact, with due regard to all the circumstances, if the jury finds that the accused has recklessly or wilfully shut his eyes or refrained from enquiry as to the nature of the substance he imports.

This judgement relied on the remarks of the House of Lords in *Warner* v. *Metropolitan Police Commission* (which also involved a charge of possession of a prohibited drug):

> ... if the accused had a suspicion but deliberately shut his eyes, the court ... is well entitled to hold him guilty. ... it would be pedantic to hold that it must be shown that the accused knew precisely which drug he had in his possession. ... it would be quite sufficient to prove facts from which it could properly be inferred that the accused knew that he had a prohibited drug in his possession.

Some would claim that both these cases involved inferred intent rather than recklessness. The authorities seem divided on this point.

Mens Rea and Homicide Under the Canadian Criminal Code

Members of the public who have had no contact with the criminal courts often think of the criminal law as preoccupied with serious and sensational crimes—particularly murder. In fact, the courts spend most of their time with driving offences and petty thefts but murder has a special fascination. Murder is an atypical crime. It is not a common offence. The victim and the murderer are often known or related to each other. The murderer is not usually a recidivist. Yet this atypical offence is of importance to students of the criminal law because the courts, and particularly the appeal tribunals, pay special attention to the legal problems of this serious crime. *Mens rea*, in the form of intention or recklessness, is examined in depth.

Sections 212 and 213 describe the crime of murder. Section 212(a)(i) is the purest form of intention and need not concern us any further. Sections 212(a)(ii) and 212(b) refer particularly to the problems of the meaning of bodily harm and recklessness which we shall consider later. Section 212(c) is a broader section that has received some judicial attention in recent years. There are phrases in s. 212(c) that indicate something broader than subjective intention, recklessness or foresight of consequences.

We have seen in the discussion of motive that morality is usually irrelevant to an examination and delineation of criminal responsibility. This may seem to be a negation of or a deviation from the "true" Judeo-Christian ethic, but we cannot condemn it so shortly. In the criminal law, judges and lawyers have discovered that the law cannot know or measure the mind of man and cannot have on the legal palette (of the fact-finding process) all colours and shades. Similarly, all the passions, prejudices, virtues, vices and, yes, motives of a person cannot be incorporated into a system that must be as certain and unambiguous as possible and have an overall validity. Furthermore, the law must reflect social values as accurately as possible, which is difficult, and must serve the purposes of society, which can vary widely. Therefore, the law is not always able to attach criminal responsibility to the accused purely on a subjective basis. We cannot always produce eyewitnesses who saw the accused pull the trigger or overheard the accused's plans to set fire to a building. (Direct evidence of this type is often most difficult in the serious crimes.) Similarly, accused persons do not always oblige police investigators by admitting their guilt.

Criminal responsibility cannot always be based on what the accused thought he was doing or what the accused was thinking. The accused, in such circumstances, would always claim that he had no intention of causing the harm that was, in fact, incurred or that he had no idea that the consequences would be so disastrous. The law sometimes takes an objective view, using an external standard of criminal liability. A moment's reflection will convince us that this is not so extraordinary. The father in the milk-spilling cases is not a sadistic, retributive monster when he infers certain facts about his child's behaviour. We all have dealings with other people and interpret human behaviour with such nuances. Some academic lawyers give the impression that all forms of objectivity in the criminal law are creations of the devil and that the test should be solely subjective. This is an untenable position—not only in terms of common sense but also in terms of penal theory. Society would not tolerate a system of criminal justice that would acquit too many defendants because the evidence was non-subjective or inferential, rather than direct and "literal." On the other hand, we have already seen that these objective tendencies must be kept in check and are best restricted to evidential questions rather than tests of culpability.

Objectivity and Constructive Crime

The best opinion in law has always shunned outright objectivity in criminal responsibility. This attitude is consonant with a basic principle summed up in the legal maxim *nulla crimen sine lege*. The State should not define crime retroactively so that any human behaviour could be impugned and punished after its commission if the powers-that-be showed a distaste for it. Total objectivity is as abhorrent as total subjectivity is impossible. Objectivity, which is the external evaluation of criminal responsibility, takes two forms. One, already referred to, is the normative evaluation of criminal responsibility. This must be unobjectionable to all but the strictest behavioural scientists who believe that all criminals are "sick" and in need of reformation on a personal level and that guilt determination is the least important of the problems facing those who must deal with antisocial or deviant members of society. We need tests for defining and controlling antisocial behaviour, and until behavioural scientists can measure and control it a little more exactly than they are presently capable of doing, we must rely on the law with its external and, admittedly, artificial standards.

The more conventional use of objectivity is as a legal concept. In its most pernicious form, it is purely constructive crime. In its most extreme form, it manufactures guilt by association or innuendo. Critics say that the law relating to conspiracy, some status crimes and the broad interpretation of law concerning parties to a crime show these tendencies.

In s. 212(c) the most difficult and potentially damning parts of this definition are the phrases "for an unlawful object," "does anything," "ought to know" and "notwithstanding." These words are imprecise in everyday usage and they have few technical meanings that can be employed by lawyers to narrow their scope. They are bald moral statements or value judgements. A persuasive prosecutor relying on innuendo in addressing a susceptible or willing jury may succeed in "proving" that the accused ought to have known that, once he was engaged on an unlawful object, anything he did should lead to a murder conviction, notwithstanding that he did not mean to kill or cause serious harm.

Illustration 11(b) describes the Ontario case of *Quaranta*. The trial judge had instructed the jury in these terms:

> Counsel for the accused pointed out that clearly they did not anticipate that it was likely that somebody's death would be caused because one of the persons whose death was caused was one of the persons involved in setting fire, so that the accused person should not be found to know or ought to know that it was likely to cause death; and, as such, it ceases to become murder and becomes manslaughter.... strangely enough ... I have never found a case dealing exactly with what they mean by "know or ought to have known" or "know or ought to know." There are some cases that deal with it on the outskirts, as we say, but I think the words have their plain ordinary commonsense meaning when we are dealing with what a person, a reasonable person under the circumstances ought to know under the peculiar facts of this case as they existed at that time....
>
> Ought a reasonable person under the peculiar circumstances of this case as they approached it on that night with the evidence that you have of coming in there and doing the things that they did, ought a reasonable person under those circumstances to know that death was likely to result from their actions?

The Court of Appeal decided that this direction to the jury did not do the accused any injustice and upheld his conviction for murder. The appeal court relied on its own decision in another 1975 case, *Regina* v. *Tennant and Naccarato,* where the court said:

> Liability under s. 212(c) is grounded upon foresight that an act done for an unlawful object is likely to cause death, notwithstanding the offender desires that his object should be effected without causing death or bodily harm to anyone....
>
> Section 212(c) grounds liability for murder upon an objective test, inasmuch as it holds the offender guilty of murder if for an unlawful object he does anything that he knows or ought to know is likely to cause death and thereby causes death....
>
> Where the provisions of s. 212(c) are applicable, the words "ought to know" impose liability for murder where death is unlawfully caused by conduct which a reasonable person, with knowledge of the surrounding circumstances which make such conduct dangerous to life, should have foreseen was likely to cause death....
>
> We have already pointed out, however, that even under s. 212(c) the offender's liability for murder depends upon his knowledge of the surrounding circumstances which make the conduct in question dangerous to life, for example, his knowledge that a pistol which he is brandishing is loaded, or his knowledge of the presence or probable presence of persons in a house to which he sets fire.

To formulate universal rules from the statements of one court in one case is not a very satisfactory mode of analysis, but until further judicial pronouncements are made, the lawyer must often work with meagre tools. Can the last paragraph of the Court of Appeal's quoted remarks be reconciled with the trial judge's direction to the jury which was approved by the appellate court? Can we equate the trial judge's test of "ought a reasonable person under the *peculiar* circumstances as *they* approached it . . . with the evidence that you have . . . to know that death was likely to result from their actions" with the appeal court's use of its *Tennant* dictum that "ought to know" means "conduct which a reasonable person, with knowledge of the surrounding circumstances . . . should have foreseen was likely to cause death"? Probably the trial judge's statement is the more favourable to the accused because he talks about "they" after setting up the test of the "reasonable person." Later in the *Tennant* statement the Court of Appeal does add, however, that "even under s. 212(c) . . . the offender's liability . . . depends upon *his* knowledge of the surrounding circumstances which make the conduct in question dangerous to life."

What exactly then is the test we are applying? Certainly we are not going to acquit D merely because he says, "I did not mean to do it." Similarly, we will not acquit D if he says, "*I* did not foresee *those* consequences." On the other hand, are we going to base a test on the peculiar facts that D clearly did *not* know? Will the answer to that question depend on how "peculiar" the facts might be, for example, if the deceased was not a cleaner in an adjacent building but a person living one block distant who suffered a fatal heart attack when she heard the explosion? Although this person is just as dead as the cleaner, the court is likely to say that it was not foreseeable by that legal abstraction, the reasonable person. Yet a reasonable person observing the accused's acts, which included some precautions about the occupancy of adjacent buildings, may be forced to admit that D, although an arsonist, had otherwise acted reasonably. Given that interpretation, is it not unfair for the courts to then say, "Yes, but a cleaner *was* actually present and that behaviour may have been unexpected but a reasonable person *now* knowing *those* facts would have foreseen that the cleaner might be killed"? If the court tries to apply the personal knowledge of the accused and the constructive knowledge outlined in the last sentence, the court is in an impossible and illogical situation.

Some commentators might say that D was being reckless. If D had told the trier of fact that he and B had calculated that there was only a ten per cent chance that anyone would be in a neighbouring building and an even smaller chance that there would be an explosion and a resulting death, should D be convicted of homicide instead of arson? Could we say that D had intended the death? Or if D and B had been asked about the possibility of the glass front of the store being blown out and of some passer-by being injured or killed, the calculation may have been as high as thirty-three per cent. Should the trier of fact then come to a different decision than when the risk was calculated at ten per cent? If the deceased was the office cleaner and not a passer-by, should D and B's estimate of thirty-three per cent convict them of murder? Of course it seems ridiculous to base criminal liability on mathematical formulae, or actuarial tables. Also consider the remarks of Cross:

1. . . .there should be greater concern with questions of the accused's control of the situation as distinct from his knowledge of relevant circumstances and foresight of relevant consequences. When dealing with incidents which occupy a split second, the question "did the accused contemplate certain results?" is apt to be a little unreal.
2. . . .there is need for discussions of the mental element in crime to be more closely related to moral issues and the theories of punishment. We assume that someone who intentionally causes physical harm to another should, all else being equal, be punished more severely than one who merely exposes his victim to an unassessed risk of harm. Is this only because the latter is less wicked than the former? Would our answer necessarily be the same if deterrent considerations are brought into account?

The Supreme Court of Canada has seldom examined the troublesome s. 212(c) of the Code, but they have recently, in *Vasil,* tried to make some sense of the section. The first difficulty with the subsection is that it is very difficult to imagine its purpose. We shall see in the next discussion that s. 213 is a murder provision that defines constructive murder where the alleged killer was engaged in a crime other than murder and someone died as a consequence. In almost all instances, the other crime was inherently dangerous; in the light of *Quaranta,* we should note that arson is included. The law's policy seems to be that when the person engaged in an inherently or potentially dangerous criminal behaviour that results in death, then he is a murderer rather than a mere rapist, arsonist, robber, etc. What did the drafters of s. 212(c) have in mind? What kind of "unlawful object," other than those in s. 213, would turn a homicide into murder? If a person were doing an unlawful object that was inherently dangerous, then the case need not come within s. 212(c) but could be covered by s. 212(a)(ii) which states that the accused "means to cause him bodily harm that he knows is likely to cause his death, and is reckless whether death ensues or not." Some have said that s. 212(c) was meant to apply to insurrectionists who blew up train tracks or persons performing illegal abortions. If someone blew up a train track that had not been used for three years, that would be very different from blowing up a train track five minutes before a crowded express train was due to pass. Similarly, if a very skilled doctor performed an abortion under the best medical conditions (and the woman's death occurred by a 1000-1 complication), it would be very different from a crude abortion carried out by some unskilled amateur. In each instance, the second cases would indicate recklessness and should result in convictions under s. 212(a)(ii). The judgement of Lamer J. in *Vasil* is a little ambiguous but it seems to say that the unlawful object under s. 212(c) must be an inherently dangerous criminal act and the accused must have known it to be the case.

Cole (1981) was only a charge of manslaughter and the Ontario Court of

Appeal applied a narrow definition to "unlawful act" for the purposes of manslaughter and obviously such a test, *at least*, should be applied to murder under s. 212(c). The accused had given V a large quantity of prescription drugs. It would have been illegal for D to sell such drugs but not to give them away. D had probably given V the drugs with the intention of raping or seducing her. She died of an overdose. The Court of Appeal decided that though D's behaviour in relation to the drugs was morally reprehensible, it was not an unlawful act. The court added that not all unlawful acts resulting in death would support a charge of manslaughter, that there must be an element of dangerousness—doing an intentional act that was likely to subject another person to danger of harm or injury.

Constructive Murder

Section 213 states in statutory form what is called felony-murder at common law—the most constructive form of murder attracting the most objective theory of *mens rea*.

For the purpose of illustrating the idea of constructive crime, let us take the most extreme case under both ss. 212(c) and 213. Under the first of these, let us imagine that we are confronted with the facts in Illustration 18, the case of *Franklin*. (Franklin was not charged actually with murder but with the less serious crime of manslaughter.) Before *Vasil*, an imaginative reading of s. 212(c) would have suggested that we could convict Franklin of murder. Looking at the facts through the eyes of the prosecutor, he seems to fulfil all the ingredients. He had an unlawful object: he was stealing the box, committing a trespass to it and would be liable in tort for the loss of the box. All these acts could possibly be "unlawful objects." Franklin certainly "does anything"—he threw the box into the water. He "ought to have known" that if it hit a swimmer it was "likely to cause death," "notwithstanding that he desires to effect his object without causing death or bodily harm to any human being."

The defence would object that we were stretching the meaning of s. 212(c) to absurd limits. Franklin would argue that "ought to have known" implies some foreknowledge of what was "likely to cause death." The accused would think that a murder conviction was ridiculous because he did not have the foresight of the risk of death. The prosecution might reply that the final part of s. 212(c) includes the phrase "or bodily harm" and that any reasonable man "ought to have known" that bodily harm was a natural result (although this is stretching the meaning of the section).

The essence of constructive crime is found in the imputation of guilt through applying an external standard of guilt—the standard of the reasonable person with little regard to the actual circumstances of the case. The "ought to have known" also implies a moral judgement that overrides the accused's internal or subjective knowledge and accentuates the public's view of the accused's blameworthiness. The objectivists look at the consequences and work backwards.

Perhaps a critic of the above prosecution argument might contend that a conviction for murder would be ridiculous and that no right-minded jury could possibly convict. But, we can counter, what if the victim were the prime minister, a millionaire or, more importantly, the star player in the Stanley Cup finals scheduled for the following week? This should be irrelevant, but would the public have much pity for Franklin or would they object to a severe punishment being imposed on him? The argument is ridiculous and we hope that retribution would not be allowed such free rein. The answer should be that Franklin, at the very limits of criminal liability, was negligent, that he was merely inadvertent—he never adverted to any such danger or potential damage to the victim. The punishment should be minor.

Let us now look at another situation that is less extreme. The facts described in Illustration 9 are fanciful but are similar to several decided cases. The accused were committing a robbery, one of the offences listed in s. 213. That section also requires that the accused causes the death of a human being while in the commission of the crime—whether or not the accused meant to cause death to *any* human being and whether or not he knew that death was likely to be caused to *any* human being. Our accused fit that description quite easily except for one word, "cause." This term is not synonymous with intent and must not be confused with it. The question of causation depends upon proof of the harm being a sufficiently direct result ("not too remote") of the accused's actions. We must consider causation at a later point. At the moment we shall assume that the accused did "cause," in the legal sense, the death of the victim. Do the accused satisfy the other requirements? Certainly they could be brought within the meaning of clause (a) of 213 because they meant "to cause bodily harm" for the purpose of facilitating the commission of the offence. The fact that the eventual victim was not the person at whom the bodily harm was first directed is immaterial. The law has always recognized the principle of transferred intent; if D aims at W and hits V, this does not allow D to escape criminal responsibility. (Intent, however, may not be transferred if the type of harm done differs from that contemplated. See Illustration 3.)

The only objection to conviction under clause (a) is the final causative factor, "and death ensues from the bodily harm." The same problem exists in clause (d), although the preliminary wording of that clause is stronger because it provides that the offence is murder if death results and the accused "uses a weapon or has it upon his person" during the commission of the offence. In this instance there is no direct suggestion that the gun has to be used, hence the "having it on his person." Therefore, the presence of the gun and the assault of the gas station attendant by demanding money may be sufficient nexus to attract criminal liability for murder.

Would it make any difference if the victim had been Darcy or Duggan rather than the gas station attendant? In theory, it should not matter if we go along with the objective constructive theory of criminal liability. The prosecution would argue as follows: the accused started out on a dangerous enterprise, dangerous to himself and to other members of the public; he assumed risks. If he fired a gun or threatened to fire a gun, he is responsible for all the consequences directly flowing from that original wrongful act. The prosecutor would draw the line somewhere but one does not know where. If the accused had held up a gas station and the gas station owner had fired a shot at him but missed and hit a storage truck of gasoline that exploded, would we hold D responsible for all the results that ensued? At this point the idea of responsibility based on a very freewheeling version of causation and objectivity becomes a little ridiculous. Perhaps the whole basis of ss. 212(c) and 213 is equally ridiculous. The accused in the gas station robbery case are going to be severely punished in any event. The constructive theories of criminal responsibility became important only because of society's desire to be retributive and apply capital punishment. The theories of homicide and *mens rea* have become obscure, if not nonsensical, because of capital punishment—the wicked man must be punished says the blood-thirsty public. "Hanging's too good for him" was formerly a common phrase, reminiscent of lynch laws. The public feels a need to label Darcy and Duggan as murderers. The label "robber" or "holdup man" is insufficient. Such attitudes have not only caused grave injustices but have also made a morass of the criminal law.

Constructive theories and retributive punishments sometimes can have a liberalizing effect. The law of murder has produced some of our most severe laws but the courts hearing murder cases have created most of the defences known to the criminal law. Both these effects have been caused, in large measure, by the existence of capital punishment, particularly if mandatory. Judges and juries created defences or partial defences (such as provocation and drunkenness) because death was too harsh a punishment for the accused's acts. On the other hand, when society wanted to show its extreme disapproval of a death that occurred while the accused was engaged in a serious crime, then constructive theories of intent (or the felony-murder rule) were imported into the law.

Perhaps the abolition of capital punishment will have a salutary effect. The strained arguments about constructive objective liability will be minimized because there will be less opportunity for society to be retributive. Capital punishment would not apply to the accused in the gas station case; if they were convicted of armed robbery, which seems inevitable, they could be sentenced under the Code to life imprisonment. What more could the public want? It may not exactly be an expression of the rehabilitative ideal but, at least, it would rid the criminal law of the metaphysics of constructive liability for murder.

Yet the problem remains and these cases are still appearing in the law reports. If Franklin had been "responsible" (in lay terms) for the death of an important person, he could not merely be convicted of stealing a box worth a few cents—at least that is the verdict of public opinion. The case of *D.P.P.* v. *Smith* has caused much discussion. Smith was neither a homicidal maniac nor a dangerous psychopath. He probably was not even a very successful thief but he had the misfortune of being involved in the death of a policeman. The facts of his case are described in Illustration 10. Should Smith be convicted of murder? The trial judge directed that:

> If you feel yourselves bound to conclude from the evidence that the accused's purpose was to dislodge the officer, then you ask yourselves this question: Could any reasonable person fail to appreciate that the likely result would be at least serious harm to the officer? If you answer that question by saying that the reasonable person would certainly appreciate that, then you may infer that that was the accused's intention, and that would lead to a verdict of guilty on the charge of capital punishment.
>
> On the other hand, if you are not satisfied that he intended to inflict grievous bodily harm upon the officer—in other words, if you think he could not, as a reasonable man, have contemplated that grievous bodily harm would result to the officer in consequence of his actions—well then, the verdict would be guilty of manslaughter.

The jury convicted Smith of murder and he appealed. The Court of Appeal quashed the conviction, but in a remarkably inept judgement, the House of Lords restored the murder conviction. (When capital punishment was still applicable in England, there was a convention that before a case was appealed to the judicial side of the House of Lords, the death sentence was commuted. Therefore, the exercise was purely academic. Cases are only allowed to be appealed to the highest tribunal when the case raises legal questions of the highest public importance.)

The reason for the furore over *D.P.P.* v. *Smith* was the re-introduction of a stringent constructive theory of liability. Even if this had been the intention of the Law Lords, it has not had this effect because of the uproar caused, and remedial legislation has been passed.

If the House of Lords had written a well-reasoned judgement, there would have been much less protest. The judgement was not even a good black-letter formalistic one. In addition, the House of Lords gave no thought to penal theory or sociological considerations.

The Court of Appeal quashed the conviction of *Smith* and commented:

> Once mere accident was excluded, the present case became one in which the degree of likelihood of serious injury to the police officer depended on which of the not always consistent versions of the facts given by witnesses for the prosecution was accepted. It was one in which it could not be said that there was a certainty that such injury would result; and it was one in which there always remained the question whether the appellant really did during the relevant ten seconds realize what was the degree of likelihood of serious injury. If the jury took the view that [Smith] deliberately tried to drive the body of the police officer against oncoming cars, the obvious inference was open to them that the appellant intended serious injury to result; if, however, they concluded he merely swerved or zigzagged to shake off the officer, or if they concluded that for

> any reason he may not have realized the degree of danger to which he was exposing the officer, a different situation would arise with regard to the inference to be drawn. In the former case the jury might well have felt they were dealing with consequences that were certain; in the latter only with degrees of likelihood.

The view of the Court of Appeal seems reasonable; the evidence was examined and the jury was to take its own view of the various possible interpretations of the facts. For reasons that are not clear, the House of Lords seemed determined to take a very literal-minded attitude toward criminal responsibility as it was described by the Court of Appeal. In answer to the views expressed by the lower court the House of Lords said:

> This purely subjective approach, involves this, that, if an accused said he did not in fact think of the consequences and the jury considered that that might as well be true, he would be entitled to be acquitted of murder.

The House of Lords thought this was a radical departure from the traditional criminal law. Ironically, it was the House of Lords that was being aberrational. Only someone who had never presided over a trial court or who had never been obliged to make down-to-earth assessments of human behaviour could imagine that the description of subjectivity cited above had any relationship with reality. Juries are not altogether stupid nor do they make decisions in a vacuum. They do not swallow a defendant's story hook, line and sinker. They assess the facts and are perfectly capable of weighing a defendant's story against evidence to the contrary. If the defendant's story is not outweighed by the prosecution's case (or if the prosecution is unpersuasive or incompetent), the defendant's story will be believed and will deserve to be. The burden of proof is on the prosecution and the accused may be acquitted, even if he remains silent, so long as the Crown fails to persuade the jury which acts as sole judge of the facts.

These issues form the core of the criticism directed against the House of Lords in *D.P.P.* v. *Smith.* That judicial body misunderstood the trial or fact-finding process and, while doing so, managed to formulate a very repressive law.

In terms of substantive law, the most thoroughly criticized statement in Viscount Kilmuir's judgement is the following sentence: "The jury must . . . make up their minds on the evidence whether the accused was unlawfully and voluntarily doing something to someone." This is ridiculous. It would allow the jury to convict Franklin of murder—of doing something (unlawfully taking and throwing of a box) to someone (the owner of the box or the swimmer). The immoderate judgement continued: "once . . . the jury are satisfied as to that, it matters not what the accused in fact contemplated as the probable result, or whether he ever contemplated at all, provided [he was not insane]."

The House of Lords took the view that the defendant's story was to be discounted as a matter of law. The trial judge had said to the jury: "The intention with which a man did something can usually be determined by a jury only by inference from the surrounding circumstances including the presumption of law that a man intends the natural and probable consequences of his acts."

This statement is not objectionable except for the bald manner in which the "presumption" is stated. The Court of Appeal had improved upon it and further explained the presumption:

> The law on this point as it stands today is that this presumption of intention means that, as a man is usually able to foresee what are the natural consequences of his acts, so it is, as a rule, reasonable to infer that he did foresee them and intend them. Although, however, that is an inference which may be drawn, and on the facts in certain circumstances must inevitably be drawn, yet if on all the facts of the particular case it is not the correct inference, then it should not be drawn. . . .

The House of Lords did not agree. They took the view that the problem of intention could be solved by reference to the standard of the reasonable person. ("The man on the Clapham omnibus," in England; "John/Jane Q. Public" in North America.) Yet this does not provide a complete answer. If the courts are determined, as was the House of Lords, to formulate a "doing something to someone" rule, then the trial judge must instruct the jury, "Would a reasonable person, who was engaged in acts such as those done by the accused, have realized that doing something to someone would result in death?" This may be innocuous enough had the court not then added, "and a man *must* be presumed to intend the natural and probable consequences of his acts" (emphasis added). This gives the jury the impression that they are obliged to ignore any explanation given by the accused and, looking at the transaction in a vacuum, apply the test of the reasonable person. This is wrong and has always been wrong. The idea of a presumption is simply a shorthand test manufactured by the law and is a short way of asking a jury:

> You have the accused's story; you have heard the external facts of the case; you know the consequences; is it reasonable to convict this person of murder in these circumstances? You may presume that he intended the consequences which followed (in *Smith*, from the acceleration of the automobile) and you will probably do so if you feel strongly enough about the active participation of the accused in the events. However, you may decide that there is insufficient proof, connection, etc., to convict him and remember that the final burden is on the Crown to prove guilt beyond a reasonable doubt.

The jury must be given the option to acquit.

Lord Denning, whose judgement in *Hosegood* v. *Hosegood* was relied on by Smith, was silent in the House of Lords decision in *D.P.P.* v. *Smith*. He later made some *ex cathedra* statements:

> To those who criticize *Smith's* case, therefore, I would suggest that it is wrong to consider it as applying an objective proposition in murder. It is not sufficient to

ask: "Would a reasonable man have known that his act would very probably cause death or grievous bodily harm?" The question is: "Did this man know it?" That is a subjective proposition. But in answering that question the jury are entitled to go by an objective test. "Would any reasonable man in his place have known it?" If any reasonable man would have known it, then the jury may infer that this man knew it, though they are not bound to do so. The familiar direction to the jury—"Must he, as a reasonable man, have known that his act was likely to cause death or grievous bodily harm"—is a telescoped version which combines the subjective proposition with the objective test. "Must he" is the subjective proposition. "As a reasonable man" is an objective test to help the jury towards the answer. . . . Whence comes, then, all this criticism from some of the most respected figures in the academic world? It cannot all be entirely beside the mark. I agree. May it perhaps be that in stressing the test of the reasonable man, that is, the responsible man, the House did not sufficiently point out that it was only a test—a criterion—to help find the intention of the accused man himself, and that ultimately the question is: "Did he intend to cause death or grievous bodily harm?" That is the subjective proposition which underlies the whole discussion. It is still, as before, the essential element of which the jury must be satisfied before they convict the accused of murder.

The criticisms of *Smith* v. *D.P.P.* have continued. The English Criminal Justice Act of 1967 remedied some of the injustices or uncertainties caused by the House of Lords. Section 8 provides:

A court or jury, in determining whether a person has committed an offence,
(a) shall not be bound in law to infer that he intended or foresaw a result of his actions by reason only of its being a natural and probable consequence of those actions; but
(b) shall decide whether he did intend or foresee that result by reference to all the evidence, drawing such inferences from the evidence as appear proper in the circumstances.

Many pages have been devoted to what may seem to some a nonsensical subject. Too often academic lawyers have tried in vain to make sense out of the millions of words uttered by thousands of judges on the subject of *mens rea*. As stated earlier, the abolition of capital punishment has obviated the need for these attempts at microscopic distinctions, and only a society that is preoccupied with retributive justice and the rigid positivistic classification of offences should tolerate such nonsense. And it is nonsense not because tests of *mens rea* are unnecessary but because the criminal law has set itself impossible standards of draftsmanship. Furthermore, too little reliance has been placed on the moral decisions that have to be made by judges and juries with good sense and in good faith. Finally, all this academic concern about *mens rea* takes little account of what actually goes on in a magistrate's court where most criminal cases are tried and where legal expertise, procedure and, unhappily, judicial knowledge are not always of the highest calibre. Decisions are reached there without the rich panoply of justice that accompanies the trial of an accused in a superior court. One could sit in a magistrate's court for days on end and discover that the term *mens rea* was seldom used. The basic question, "Did he do it?" occupies most of the court's attention.

The strictures on *D.P.P.* v. *Smith* acted as a liberal counterbalance to the retributive notions implicit in the House of Lords decision. Every generation or so, it may be necessary to attack those forces that would try to rob the term "responsibility" of any sensible meaning. The attacks, therefore, perform somewhat the same function as the decisions of the U.S. Supreme Court on criminal procedure: they act as a "moral" measuring stick to keep trial judges in line with the "pure" principles of criminal law.

The greatest fault of the House of Lords was the sloppiness of its judgement. A good argument could be made, on deterrent grounds, for applying a stringent test to (a) persons who try to escape from legitimate police inquiries or (b) persons who endanger the life of a policeman or (c) persons who are engaged in a crime and endanger the lives of road users when trying to avoid lawful arrest. This is exactly the problem the House of Lords would not face. The Law Lords were so busy writing a judgement from a doctrinaire viewpoint that they gave no thought to the policy underlying their judgement. Any statement about "doing something to someone" shows a poverty of thought or a cavalier attitude toward criminal law theory.

The members of the English Law Commission were not in total agreement but they all agreed that "there ought to be cases in which intention and knowledge should be imputed where the defendant's state of mind does not amount to intention in the narrowest sense or certain knowledge." The definition of "knowledge" in the Working Paper was meant to reflect the Commission's view that "imputed intention ought to be severely circumscribed, so that foresight of consequences or absence of substantial doubt as to the existence of circumstances ought to be treated as equivalent to intention or knowledge only if the foresight or lack of doubt amounts to practical certainty."

The House of Lords commented further on *Smith* v. *D.P.P.* in the case of *Hyam* which is described in Illustration 11. D was convicted of murder at trial where the judge instructed the jury:

> The prosecution must prove, beyond all reasonable doubt, that the accused intended to (kill or) do serious bodily harm to [V], the mother of the deceased girls. If you are satisfied that when the accused set fire to the house she knew that it was highly probable that this would cause (death or) serious bodily harm, then the prosecution will have established the necessary intent. It matters not if her motive was, as she says, to frighten [V].

The Court of Appeal dismissed the appeal but referred the case to the House of Lords for the following question to be answered:

> Is malice aforethought in the crime of murder established by proof beyond reasonable doubt that when doing the act which led to the death of another the

> accused knew that it was highly probable that the act would result in death or serious bodily harm?

The majority, *per* Lord Hailsham, decided that the murder conviction was proper and proposed the following rules:

> (1) Before an act can be murder it must be "aimed at someone," as explained in *Director of Public Prosecutions* v. *Smith* . . . , and must in addition be an act committed with one of the following intentions, the test of which is always subjective to the actual defendant:
>
> (i) The intention to cause death;
>
> (ii) The intention to cause grievous bodily harm in the sense of that term explained in *Smith*, i.e., really serious injury;
>
> (iii) Where the defendant knows that there is serious risk that death or grievous bodily harm will ensue from his acts, and commits those acts deliberately and without lawful excuse, the intention to expose a potential victim to that risk as the result of those acts. It does not matter in such circumstances whether the defendant desires those consequences to ensue or not, and in none of these cases does it matter that the act and the intention were aimed at a potential victim other than the one who succumbed.
>
> (2) Without an intention of one of these three types the mere fact that the defendant's conduct is done in the knowledge that grievous bodily harm is likely or highly likely to ensue from his conduct is not by itself enough to convert a homicide into the crime of murder.

Lord Hailsham said that the test for liability was now a subjective one but he wanted to retain the *Smith* rule that "the unlawful and voluntary act must be aimed at someone," which seems quite contradictory. Hailsham probably meant that the accused himself must have undertaken and foreseen the risk of at least serious injury to someone. If the foreseeable risk was to W but V actually died, it was still murder so long as the death of V was foreseen.

The dissenting Lord Diplock believed that *Smith* was overruled by the 1967 legislation. He added:

> Intention can only be subjective. It was the actual intention of the offender himself that the objective test was designed to ascertain. So long as the offender was not permitted to give evidence of what his actual intention was, the objective test provided the only way, imperfect though it might be, of ascertaining this. The Criminal Evidence Act 1898 changed all this. A defendant to a charge of felony became entitled to give evidence in his own defence. The objective test no longer provided the only means available in a criminal trial of ascertaining the actual intention of the offender; but it had been so for so long that this House overlooked the historical fact that the objective test did not define the relevant intention as to the consequences of a voluntary act.

Lord Diplock made another important statement in *Hyam* that showed that judge's sensitivity to the history of the law and how a knowledge of our legal past should inform our present decisions. Until the end of the nineteenth century, English and Canadians who were accused of crime were not allowed to give evidence on their own behalf. In such circumstances, an objective test might have made a little more sense because the accused was unable to give his own version of the crime and therefore the court had to infer guilt or innocence from the circumstances and the evidence of third parties. Even when the Canadian Criminal Code became law in 1892, this situation still persisted for another four years. The passing of the Criminal Evidence Act did not mean that the accused's story would be accepted at face value. On the other hand, that bothersome presumption of intention should have lost much of its force as a vehicle for constructive crime. This is well explained by an Australian judge:

> What a man does is often the best evidence of the purpose he had in mind. The probability that harm will result from a man's acts may be so great, and so apparent, that it compels an inference that he actually intended to do the harm. Nevertheless, intention is a state of mind. The circumstances and probable consequences of a man's acts are no more than evidence of his intention. For this reason this Court has often said that it is misleading to speak of a man being presumed always to intend the natural and probable consequences of his acts. And this, I do not doubt is so. . . .
>
> A man's own intention is for him a subjective state, just as are his sensations of pleasure or of pain. But the state of another man's mind, or of his digestion, is an objective fact. When it has to be proved, it is to be proved in the same way as other objective facts are proved. A jury must consider the whole of the evidence of what his intentions were, the jury must weigh his testimony along with whatever inference as to his intentions can be drawn from his conduct or from other relevant facts. References to a "subjective test" could lead to an idea that the evidence of an accused man as to his intent is more credible than his evidence of other matters. It is not: he may or may not be believed by the jury. Whatever he says, they may be able to conclude from the whole of the evidence that beyond doubt he had a guilty mind and a guilty purpose. But always the questions are what did *he* in fact know, foresee, expect, intend. (The emphasis was in the original.)

A better statement of the subjective position would be hard to find and it is not surprising to find Canada's most learned criminal law judge, Martin J.A. of the Ontario Court of Appeal, quoting the above in a recent judgement. Canadian courts have not examined s. 213 very frequently. One reason is that many cases under s. 213 are so obviously murder—if a person commits a brutal robbery or rape and the victim dies then it is rather obvious that great violence in furtherance of a rape could lead to death "whether or not" he means to cause death or "whether or not he knows that death is likely to be caused to any human being." The result in *Vasil* and the lack of *D.P.P.* v. *Smith*-type judgements in Canada, along with the frequent re-affirmation of the subjective rule in *Beaver* would suggest that the objective test is not favoured in this country.

Negligence

Negligence is usually thought of as the basis for liability in tort, the private law concept that decides on the legal obligation of A to pay damages to B for loss and harm suffered, for instance, when A's car negligently comes into collision with B's car and causes property damage and bodily injury or death. Negligence differs from intention and recklessness in that the latter two concepts involve advertence while negligence is a legal term describing inadvertence. By advertence is meant a mental attitude that gives prior thought to the action that is eventually done. The prior thought may be a criminal plan organized over a long period of time or it may be a split-second decision to take a risk and nevertheless undertaking that risk. One cannot advert to negligence. I cannot suggest to you that you should go out and do a negligent act.

Negligence is not, in strict theory, a form of criminal, as opposed to civil, liability. None of the classic crimes, with the possible exception of manslaughter, considers negligence a sufficient mental element for liability. The Canadian Criminal Code contains almost no offences that have negligence as a form of liability. "Criminal negligence" is something of a misnomer, although as we shall see, the courts have had some difficulty in forming clear rules.

Some theorists, notably Hall, argue that negligence, or inadvertence, should not be a basis for criminal liability. The principal aim of the criminal law should be the prevention and discouragement of crime and persons cannot be deterred from committing acts to which they have not adverted.

Others, notably Brett, have replied to this formulation by saying that the separation between intention and negligence is too simplistic, that there are degrees of negligence and that people pay heed in varying amounts to their behaviour. Finally, Brett argues that persons feel guilt (in a non-legal sense) when they are careless and that the threat of punishment does deter some people from being careless. Brett suggests that we need only watch the change in the behaviour of car drivers when a police car starts following them. This does not mean that they will thereafter advert to all facets of their driving behaviour, but it does imply that the drivers will be less inadvertent (if Brett is correct in quantifying lack of care). To accept negligence as a form of criminal responsibility involves the abandonment of a subjective test of *mens rea*. It requires an external test of culpability. Fletcher has stated this well: "If *mens rea* refers not to a specific subjective state, but to the actor's moral culpability without referring to a state of mind ... Whether negligence constitutes *mens rea* depends upon whether negligent conduct is a ground for justly blaming another."

Automobile Offences

Eighty per cent of the criminal courts' time is taken up with highway offences. Most of the offences, such as speeding, are of no theoretical interest.

Similarly, there is a striking lack of jurisprudence on parking offences. We should, however, give some consideration to the two driving offences in the Criminal Code—criminal negligence and dangerous driving—and the closely related offence of careless driving found in the Highway Traffic Act of Ontario and similar legislation in other provinces.

In 1969 the Canadian Committee on Corrections (the Ouimet Committee) showed that between 1901 and 1965 the annual incidence of criminal offences had increased from 42,148 to 4,066,957. Ninety-eight per cent of the increase was found in summary offences, particularly traffic offences that accounted for ninety per cent of the increase. The report also showed that the increase in offences committed by those in the age group of sixteen to twenty-four years was "alarming," and this age group produced a disproportionate number of automobile offenders.

Until the 1960s there was little work done on the criminology of the traffic criminal. One of the earliest and best studies is by Willett who examined "serious" offences in England—offences causing death by dangerous driving, reckless driving, driving under the influence, driving while disqualified, failure to insure and failure to stop after, or to report, an accident. His conclusions are most instructive. His research showed that the common assumption that the serious motoring offender is a respectable citizen who does not commit other (or conventional) crimes is not well founded. Thirty-two per cent of the motor offenders in Willett's study were "known to the police" or had been convicted previously for non-motoring offences. Although Willett's statistical methods incurred the inevitable criticism of sociologists, subsequent studies have confirmed his finding.

As a criminologist, Willett comments:

> The attempt to legislate for every possible contingency in this area of conduct has resulted inevitably in an increasing tendency to rule that motoring offences are absolute prohibitions, since motives are almost impossible to unravel in most cases of motoring misbehaviour, but the effect is mainly to frustrate and irritate the many defendants who are convinced that their behaviour was not only justified but unavoidable.

Of the other hypotheses of Willett, the following findings should be noted:

1. Serious driving offences are viewed quite distinctly—in terms of morality and social ostracism—from "real" criminal offences.
2. Driving offenders are not white-collar criminals. There is, however, a difficulty in this non-finding. Some criminologists would argue that traffic police are less likely to stop a driver who is driving an expensive automobile and who looks prosperous or influential.
3. Recidivism is common among serious driving offenders. In Willett's study, 134 of the 653 offenders had repeated the same kind of offence or committed another equally heinous. One-third of those charged with driving while disqualified had additional convictions for the same offence. One-tenth of the drunk drivers had previous convictions.

4. The sentences are usually very lenient. Before 1957 one hundred per cent of those convicted of motor manslaughter were sent to prison. In 1957 the percentage dropped to forty-four per cent and in 1960 to thirty-one per cent. Other manslaughter offences attracted prison sentences in eighty per cent of the cases.

Willett's second hypothesis has particular relevance to a consideration of the criminal liability of traffic offenders. His study tested the hypothesis that, "The majority of serious motoring offences are derived from accidents, and there is nothing in the offender's personality or background that predisposes him to break the law." Willett discovered that only about fourteen per cent of the offences could possibly be called "inadvertent accidents." His evidence showed that a significant minority of motoring offenders exhibited personality disturbances or behaviour reflecting "selfish, or even ruthless, self-interest."

None of the above analysis is likely to help us formulate a rule about the mental element necessary for the various driving offences. For instance, one of the most serious specific problems of aggression on the road is the man who accelerates when he is being overtaken. Does he do this intentionally, wilfully or recklessly? Or is it simply an "unconscious" reflex action? If the driver who accelerates knows that he is creating a potentially dangerous situation, can we call this intentional behaviour?

Willett thinks the present law is "vague and ambiguous to the point of appearing to be fair to no one." He suggests that no one takes the traffic laws, even those concerning "serious" offences, very seriously. The police do not prosecute or apprehend with the same zeal they apply to "ordinary" criminals, and the courts tend to be more lenient even when the driving offender has obviously done great social harm. The motoring organizations provide a strong political lobby and the general public is also against change, particularly if it would mean greater severity. The police know that more rigorous enforcement would only further damage their public image. The crime of motor manslaughter had its name changed in 1956 to "causing death by dangerous driving." This was done because juries were loath to convict citizens of the crime of manslaughter which sounds so heinous. On the other hand, courts were not so reluctant to impose jail terms on driving offenders who also had an "ordinary" criminal record.

Some solution must be found to the problem of traffic offences. The courts are clogged with trivial offences. The behaviour represented by these offences must be policed, but can it be done more rationally? The public finds it difficult to equate the social damage caused by automobile drivers with the harm perpetrated by thieves, robbers, arsonists or confidence tricksters. Ironically, the rare citizen who has a knowledge of the elements of criminal law may feel that the light penalties attached to dangerous driving (where property damage could amount to several thousands of dollars and physical damage could be as great as death or permanent disability) are proper. This, the citizen may argue, is because the driver did not "mean" to do it and because "but for the grace of God" anyone who owns an automobile could have found himself in a similar position. On the other hand, the informed citizen clearly can see that a thief had the necessary criminal intent (or *mens rea*), although many of us have a little larceny in our hearts and may have been so tempted in the past "but for the grace of God." Similarly, the average citizen, who is worried about crime-in-the-streets has no difficulty in saying that constructive murder should be treated as one of the most serious crimes. Yet a good argument could be made that anyone armed with a lethal weapon (a loaded revolver or a high-powered automobile) who embarks upon a dangerous enterprise (holding up a bank or driving at excessive speed while partially intoxicated) that results in serious harm (death or serious physical impairment) should be treated in a similar fashion by the criminal law. In both instances the law could say that a jury is entitled to take the view that the actor, as a reasonable person, should have known that his behaviour might result in serious harm. A person knows that when he goes to a New Year's Eve party, he usually has too much to drink. As he picks up his automobile keys and drives to the party, can it be said that he intends to drive while intoxicated? Or when he has his third or fourth drink, should he advert to the fact that he is taking a risk of driving while incapacitated? When we examined the case of *Powell* v. *Texas*, we saw that the court measured his liability (for being drunk in a public place) from the time he soberly had his first drink of the day. The courts have not followed this policy with drivers who are charged with criminal negligence.

The cases concerning serious automobile offences are in disarray. The English courts have tried to solve the problem by creating something close to absolute liability. Section 1 of the English Highway Traffic Act (1960) established the offence of causing death by dangerous driving. As explained earlier, this replaced the pre-1956 offence of motor manslaughter which had a maximum penalty of life imprisonment. Juries hesitated to convict and, in any event, the "degree of negligence required to satisfy the law was very high indeed." A famous judicial statement in *Bateman* decided under this earlier law stated in 1925:

> . . . the negligence or incompetence of the accused went beyond a mere matter of compensation and showed such a disregard for the life and safety of others as to amount to a crime against the State and conduct deserving of punishment.

The new offence, which has a maximum punishment of five years' imprisonment, requires only that "a death should be caused in the course of the offence of dangerous driving." In other words, the court looks at the result.

What is "dangerous" or "reckless" driving as defined by s. 2 of the Road Traffic Act? Elliott and Street are not very helpful. Dangerous driving is "more reprehensible" than careless driving. The former suggests "shocking negligence" while the latter is satisfied by a "slighter negligence." The authors attempt to explain further: "is the driving dangerous, viewed objectively in the light of the situation on the road at the relevant time; and the question of the driver's negligence is wholly immaterial." In 1963 the Court of Criminal Appeal further "explained" the situation in *Evans*: "If a driver in fact adopts a manner of driving which the jury thinks was dangerous to other road users . . . then on the issue of guilt it matters not whether he was deliberately reckless, careless, momentarily inattentive or even doing his incompetent best." In other words, if danger has resulted from his driving (and there is no totally exculpating factor such as the driver having a heart attack or the brakes failing due to some unforeseeable, innocent cause), the driver is guilty of dangerous driving. Given the wording of the English legislation, the courts have created a difficult situation. If death results and the accused was driving in an objectively dangerous manner, he can be liable to five years in prison under s. 1 of the Road Traffic Act.

Is the Canadian situation any better? For a few years the crime of dangerous driving was removed from the Canadian Criminal Code. Obviously this left a gap between the crime of criminal negligence and careless driving. Juries no doubt refused to convict on the more serious charge and the prosecution felt that a careless driving conviction under provincial highway legislation was insufficient in many circumstances.

Criminal negligence is found in s. 202 of the Code. Section 203 prescribes that a death caused by criminal negligence is punishable by life imprisonment. Criminal negligence that causes bodily harm is an indictable offence punishable by a ten-year prison term (s. 204). Section 233(1) provides that criminal negligence in the operation of a motor vehicle is either an indictable offence attracting a maximum of five years' imprisonment or a summary offence.

The underlying policy of these sections would seem to be that criminal negligence by motor vehicle is a lesser offence than criminal negligence under ss. 203 and 204. Section 233(1) makes no mention of the result of the negligence. If a criminally negligent motorist slightly injured one person or killed one hundred persons, he would only be liable for a maximum of five years' imprisonment. Under s. 204, if a criminally negligent mine operator, for example, caused one of his employees to be injured, he could be liable for ten years' imprisonment.

Admittedly, this analysis places specific reliance on the penalty provisions of the Code, but a comparison of the provisions suggests that the criminally negligent use of an automobile is to be treated differently from the criminally negligent behaviour of a mine shaft operator or a medical practitioner.

Finally, s. 233(4) of the Code defines dangerous driving as driving "in a manner dangerous to the public, having regard to all the circumstances including the nature, condition and use [of the highway] and the amount of traffic that at the time is or might reasonably be expected to be in such place." Punishment is either summary or, on indictment, imprisonment for two years.

What of the cases? In *O'Grady* v. *Sparling* the Supreme Court of Canada defined recklessness as advertence and negligence as inadvertence and stated that "moral epithets" attached to negligence did not alter the situation of blameworthiness. Most of the decision involved constitutional issues showing that the valid careless driving legislation of the Manitoba Highway Act was concerned with the "regulation and control of traffic." The Supreme Court also took pains to show that the common law offence of manslaughter by "gross," "wicked" or "culpable" negligence has no place in Canadian criminal law. On the question of criminal negligence, the dissenting judgement of Cartwright J. seemed to agree, although he used the unfortunate phrase "advertent negligence" which presumably means "recklessness" (and he used the wording of s. 202 relating to "wanton and reckless disregard" as an overall test for criminal negligence under ss. 202, 203, 204 and 233(1)).

In *Mann* the Supreme Court of Canada reiterated the *O'Grady* v. *Sparling* point that a provincial legislature is not encroaching on the power of federal criminal law by making careless driving a provincial offence. Careless driving ("without due care and attention or without consideration for other persons using the highway") is included in the definition of dangerous driving or criminal negligence under the Criminal Code, but the converse is not necessarily true. The Court also decided that mere inadvertent negligence would not support a conviction for either of the Criminal Code offences and that "something more than mere inadvertence or mere thoughtlessness or mere negligence or mere error of judgement" is necessary.

In *Binus* the appellant was convicted of dangerous driving. The trial judge had told the jury that *mens rea* was not an ingredient of the crime now described in s. 233(4). Laskin J.A. interpreted *O'Grady* v. *Sparling* and a later Supreme Court of Canada case as enunciating that "something more" than inadvertent negligence was necessary for liability in criminal negligence and dangerous driving. In *O'Grady* v. *Sparling* Cartwright J. had said that dangerous driving involved conduct that, while falling short of recklessness, was more than mere inadvertence.

Laskin J.A. thought that it was incorrect to apply the "same test of culpability to criminally negligent driving and to dangerous driving and then seek alleviation on the facts." This seems to be the English approach under "dangerous driving causing death" and "dangerous driving" and, given the wording of the English Road Traffic Act, perhaps it has more justification there. Laskin J.A. preferred to rely on a clear distinction between "negligence" and "recklessness" rather than use the words "inadvertent" and "advertent." Parliament has not left criminal negligence undefined under s. 202 but has imported the element of recklessness and "has clearly shown that it meant to retain a subjective ingredient—the actual foresight of the particular accused as to the prohibited consequences of his conduct. . . ." These *dicta* would make it very difficult to obtain a conviction and Laskin J.A.'s subsequent *ratio decidendi* on dangerous driving set the stage for the latter (revived) offence to become the one which would be successfully prosecuted most often. At the same time Laskin J.A. retained *mens rea* as an element, at least to the extent that the crime of dangerous driving was not an offence of absolute liability. He said ". . . an objective test best comports with the object and the language of the prohibition and with its setting in the scheme of offences of which it is a part." The judge was not saying that this was an offence of absolute liability. Instead, a conviction would be based on "proof of the accused's conduct as allegedly falling below the standard . . . that is, the conduct to be expected from a careful driver, prudent in the care and operation of his vehicle and attentive to the conditions of traffic confronting him."

Finally, Laskin J.A. ruled that the distinction between dangerous and careless driving was "in the prohibited consequences themselves." He added that the "negligence which will support a tort action if damage results may equally support convictions" for either dangerous or careless driving, although the latter "does not necessarily require proof of jeopardy to life or the physical safety of others."

The next chapter in the criminal negligence/dangerous driving saga was *Peda* on appeal to the Supreme Court of Canada from a 2-1 decision of the Ontario Court of Appeal where Laskin J.A. was the dissenter. The accused had been convicted of dangerous driving and the Ontario Court of Appeal dismissed his appeal. Judson J. wrote the majority opinion and soon disposed of the *Mann* decision as not binding and relied upon the reasoning of Laskin J.A. in *Binus*. This creates a strange situation in that the dissenting Court of Appeal judge in *Peda* who would uphold the appeal of Peda is followed for the purposes of dismissing Peda's appeal.

Judson J.'s judgement does not offer us much assistance. He agreed with the trial judge that the essence of the crimes was "to determine the actual behaviour of the driver in the light of [s. 233(4)] and while this will necessarily entail some consideration of the state of mind of the driver, as the car does not drive itself, it does not mean that the jury must find that a given state of mind exists before they can convict." Therefore, he was not prepared to uphold the appellant's contention that the trial judge erred in not telling the jury about the difference between advertence and inadvertence, although Judson J. did not further define the mental element.

Pigeon J.'s judgement presents some difficulties but he was trying to restate the test laid down by Laskin J.A. in *Binus*. He is wrong when he suggests that "wantonness and recklessness of themselves clearly imply the exclusion of mere inadvertence while 'dangerous driving' does not necessarily." From his subsequent remarks, it is obvious he meant that wantonness and recklessness are not needed and that subjective advertence is not necessary in dangerous driving. *Mens rea* is always required but the jury does not always need instructions because the "fact itself is sufficient proof of intention." The jury, therefore, might have acquitted if they "might reasonably have concluded that, although objectively considered, the accused's driving was 'dangerous,' it could be unconsciously so or be attributable to inadvertence." Pigeon J. seems to be suggesting that a test for dangerous driving is a highly objective one based on absolute liability. He confuses the issue by saying that the "driving was actually dangerous" and that a driver "*must* be deemed to intend to do what he is actually doing." Finally, he further muddies the water by saying that "dangerous driving" is a "kind of criminal negligence."

Cartwright J., who was one of three in dissent, did not disagree with Pigeon J., except that he agreed with Laskin J.A. in the lower court that the jury should have been instructed on the difference between advertence and inadvertence. He did not believe that those words should actually be put to the jury but they should be instructed on the separate meaning of dangerous driving. Cartwright J. said:

> So long as it is the law that a necessary ingredient of the offence of dangerous driving is advertent negligence it is essential that the trial judge should so instruct the jury in all cases in which on the evidence they might properly find that the conduct of the accused, while dangerous in fact, did not involve advertent negligence. . . . [the jury] must be satisfied that there was negligence of sufficient gravity to lift the case out of the civil field into that of the Criminal Code . . . something more than mere inadvertence or mere thoughtlessness or mere negligence or mere error of judgement.

Despite this verbal morass created by the highest court of Canada, Laskin J.A.'s formulation in *Binus* seems to stand. The test for criminal negligence (under ss. 202 and 233(1)) is one of recklessness but that mental ingredient must be arrived at subjectively—that is "the actual foresight of the particular accused as to the prohibited consequences of his conduct." "Dangerous driving" will be decided by an objective test of criminal liability. *Mens rea* still applies and dangerous driving is, quite properly, not an offence of absolute prohibition. This is made clear by Laskin J.A. in *Binus* and Judson J. in *Peda*. Laskin J.A. said:

> It is not . . . enough to establish that an accused in fact drove in a manner dangerous to the public if at the same time he has not departed from the standard of conduct expected of a careful driver in the circumstances. For example, a driver may injure pedestrians or other motorists in trying to bring to a stop a car whose brakes have suddenly failed, although he had just had them inspected and they were in good working order.

Other Questions of *Mens Rea*

Crimes other than murder also have problems of *mens rea*. Most of these will be examined in relation to defences to criminal liability. A perusal of the Code will give us some information on defences. Section 8 provides that the

Canadian Criminal Code defines all criminal offences and that there are no common law crimes. We have already seen this in the Peeping Tom case of *Frey* v. *Fedoruk*. Section 8 does not mean that the common law has been totally abandoned. The rules of common law are often incorporated into statutory language and sometimes the Code simply adopts the common law (as with common law conspiracy in s. 423(2)).

Section 7(2) provides that the criminal (common) law of England in force before 1955 still applies to defences but not to offences in Canada. While many defences are defined in the Code, some important defences are omitted and we must resort to the common law; for instance, intoxication must be defined by reference to Canadian and British Commonwealth judicial decisions. Section 7(3) reserves the use of common law defences when the Code is silent or not inconsistent. Sections 16 to 45 contain most of the defences articulated in the Code.

The following provisions of the Code provide some illustrations of offences that incorporate legal terms of art and expressions that infer defences or particular ways to negate *mens rea*. Most of these terms are self-explanatory.

Section 46(1) (e) (Treason): "... *without legal authority*, communicates military or scientific information ... that he knows or *ought to know* may be used ... for a purpose prejudicial to the safety or defence of Canada."

Section 50(1) (b) (Assisting a Traitor): "... does not with *all reasonable dispatch*, inform a justice of the peace ... or make *reasonable efforts* to prevent that person from commiting treason."

Section 58 (Forgery): "... makes a ... statement that *he knows is false or misleading* ..."

Section 64 (Unlawful Assembly): "... *with intent* to carry out any *common purpose* assemble in such a manner or so conduct themselves ... as to cause persons in the neighbourhood of the assembly to fear, *on reasonable grounds that they* ... will by that assembly needlessly and *without reasonable cause provoke* ..."

Section 69(b) (Failure to Disperse): "does not depart ... when he has *reasonable ground to believe* ..."

Section 70 (Neglect by Peace Officer): "A peace officer ... without *reasonable excuse, fails to take reasonable steps* ..."

Section 73 (Forcible Detainer): "... being in actual possession of real property *without colour of right,* he detains it in a manner that is likely to cause a ... *reasonable apprehension of a breach of the peace* ..."
[Note: 73(3) provides that "without colour of right" is a "question of law," which means that the judge, not the jury, decides the issue.]

Section 75 (2) (Piracy): "... does any act *that is likely to endanger the life of another person* ..."

Section 76(3) (Hijacking): "... *without the consent* of the owner.

Section 77 (Duty re Care of Explosives): "is under *a legal duty to use reasonable care* to prevent bodily harm or death."

Section 83 (Possession of Weapon): "... carries a weapon ... for a *purpose dangerous to the public peace* ..."

Section 88 (Delivering Firearm to Prohibited Person): "Every one who sells ... to a person who he knows or *has good reason to believe* ..."

Section 94 (Restricted Weapon in Motor Vehicle): "... *or he* establishes that *he had reason to believe.*"
[Note: The onus of proof is on the accused.]

Section 102 (Finding a Restricted Weapon): "... *has reasonable grounds* to believe has been lost ..."

Section 120 (Perjury): "... with *intent to mislead* gives false evidence, *knowing* that the evidence is false."

Section 133(3) (Escape and Being at Large): "... being at large on his undertaking ... fails, *without lawful excuse, the proof of which lies upon him,* to comply with that condition ..."
[Note: This and section 133(5) are further cases of reverse onus of proof.]

Section 148 (Sexual Intercourse with Feeble-Minded): "... has *sexual intercourse with a female person ... who is and who he knows or has a good reason to believe* is feeble-minded ..."

Section 173 (Trespassing at Night): "Every one who, *without lawful excuse, the proof of which lies upon him,* loiters or prowls at night ..."
[Note: Another reverse onus.]

Section 202 (Criminal Negligence): "... shows *wanton or reckless disregard* for the lives or safety of other persons."

Section 232 (Interfering with Transportation Facilities): "Every one who, with *intent to endanger the safety of any person, places anything upon* or *does anything to any property* ..."

Section 237 (1) (Impaired Driving): "Where it is proved that the accused occupied the seat ordinarily occupied by the driver of a motor vehicle, he *shall be deemed to have had the care or control of the vehicle unless he establishes that he did not enter* or mount the vehicle for the purpose of setting it in motion."

Section 240(1) (Dangerous Operation of Vessel): "... operates a vessel ... *in a manner dangerous* to navigation, life or limb, *having regard to all the circumstances* ..."

Section 246(2) (Assault): "assaults a person *with intent to resist or prevent the lawful arrest* ... of himself or another ..."

Section 249(1) (Abduction of Female Under Sixteen Years): "Every one who,

without lawful authority, takes . . . a female under the age of sixteen years out of the possession of and against the will of her parent . . ."
[Note: Section 249(2) explicitly makes it immaterial, for purposes of subsection 1, that the female consented or that the accused believed that the female was more than sixteen years old.]

Section 254(1) (Bigamy): "*Knowing that another person is married,* goes through a form of marriage with that person."
[Note: Section 254(2) provides that a person is not guilty of bigamy if that person "*in good faith and on reasonable grounds believes*" that his or her spouse is dead.]

Section 260(3) (Blasphemous Libel): "No person shall be convicted . . . for expressing in *good faith* . . . an opinion upon a religious subject."
[Note: See similar reservations in section 281.2(3) on public incitement to hatred.]

Section 285 (Theft by Bailee): ". . . but he does not steal it if his failure to produce and deliver it is *not the result of a wilful act or omission by him.*"

Section 295 (Taking Vehicle Without Consent): ". . . without the consent of the owner, takes a motor vehicle . . . *with intent to drive* . . ."

Section 296 (Criminal Breach of Trust): ". . . converts, with *intent to defraud* and in *violation of his trust,* that thing or any part of it to a use that *is not authorized* by the trust . . ."

Section 302 (Robbery): "steals, and for *the purpose of extorting whatever is stolen* . . . uses violence or threats . . ."

Section 305(1) (Extortion): ". . . without *reasonable justification or excuse and with intent to extort* or gain anything . . ."

The sections quoted are only a sampling of the descriptions of offences in the Code that contain some reference to the mental element or blameworthiness that is required to be proved. The burden of proof will usually fall on the prosecution; the exceptional circumstances, when the accused is required to carry at least part of this burden, have been noted.

There are many sections omitted. Some of these have been cited elsewhere in the text. Some are merely repetitious because they use the word "reasonable," as in "on reasonable grounds." There are other phrases sprinkled through the Code that are meant to provide some adverbial qualification to the acts or intention being described; for example, fraudulently, maliciously, intentionally, lawfully, knowingly, unlawfully, corruptly, with intent to, by unlawful means or without lawful excuse. Courts have written hundreds of thousands of words trying to explain these phrases but their commentaries add little to our knowledge of the criminal law. At best, they assure the civil libertarians, or others who seek adherence to the principle of legality, that *mens rea* is a common ingredient in offences described in the Criminal Code.

These phrases suggest that each criminal offence has a discrete identifiable *mens rea.* The Model Penal Code formulated a common definition of criminal responsibility—either intention or recklessness—which applied to all crimes. We hardly need Code provisions to tell us that "with intent to do grievous bodily harm" does not apply to larceny and "with intent to defraud" does not apply to murder. The most satisfactory code would emulate the M.P.C. and have a General Part that defined General Principles applicable to all crimes and then Rules describing the particular qualities of specific offences. The Canadian Criminal Code unfortunately does not contain a very useful General Part and the Principles of *mens rea* (and defences) are sprinkled throughout the document. There is no overall common definition of intention or recklessness.

Would the courts and lawyers adhere to the definitions of such "ideal" formulations as those of the Model Penal Code? The answer is probably no. Judges seldom heed academic writing. Niceties of language will always cause a problem, particularly with those word merchants, the lawyers. There will often be deep disagreement about the meaning of what seems to be clear and commonplace words. There is also an anti-intellectual attitude among lawyers; they tend to be wary of general definitions that have an underlying philosophy or policy. Canadian judges, in interpreting the Code, have often ignored its actual wording and have relied upon the common law and followed English decisions rather than laying down a distinctly Canadian criminal jurisprudence based on the Code. The lawyers, particularly those trained in the common law, prefer to work on a case-by-case basis. Set definitions with predetermined meanings, they also argue, would rob the law of flexibility, so an accused could be acquitted or convicted where there are extra-legal reasons for wanting a particular verdict on the "peculiar" facts of a case. The arguments against codes are often inconsistent. Some champions of the common law system like to give the impression that its judges are oracles of the law, untainted by emotion or bias, who decide cases by searching thousands of case law precedents, spanning a millennium, and come up with the perfectly just decision. The Continental lawyer, with his Code of General Principles, has no compunction in twisting the law for a particular case and there is no search for absolute consistency under such a system.

Absolute Liability

In many instances the courts have decided that if the prosecution proves that the defendant has committed the proscribed act, he is automatically liable. There is no additional need to prove that the defendant had intention, was reckless or even negligent in relation to the act. This has been variously described as an absolute prohibition, absolute liability, strict responsibility, public welfare or statutory offence (although the term "strict liability" should be avoided because the subsequent discussion will show it leads to great confusion). Most of these offences, which have proliferated greatly in the twentieth century, are found outside the Criminal Code.

The reasons for the recent increase in this type of offence are easy to find. Cities and towns have become massive conurbations. Technology has produced the machinery of "progress"—factories, automobiles, highways and consumer goods. There are laws, regulations and by-laws affecting every facet of our lives—the speed limits on highways, the labelling and processing of foodstuffs, parking, the size and composition of garbage cans, the registration of pets, the control of infectious diseases, zoning regulations and the construction of buildings. The list is endless. The minute regulation of our daily lives is often explained in terms of the complex society in which we live. The rise of the welfare state and the expansion of government bureaucracy have also been contributing factors.

The penalties are usually trivial fines. A conviction does not often result in a criminal record. These offences are not "really criminal" and are sometimes called public torts or ways of enforcing a civil right. Conservative voices tell us that the public sector has expanded to a ludicrous extent and that citizens are over-governed. These criticisms may have some validity but no one is able to suggest which forms of regulation could be abandoned with impunity. Lawyers claim that it is wrong for the legislatures and courts to interpret these laws as absolute prohibitions, that it offends the principle of legality, that no one should be convicted of an offence without the constitutent elements of *mens rea* and *actus reus.*

A sampling of such cases can be found in Illustration 27. The cases are chaotic; some have acquitted on the basis of lack of knowledge while others have admitted no excuses. Readers of these cases would be wrong in thinking that they all resulted in acquittals—or convictions. There appears to be little rationality.

The highest tribunals in both Canada and England have tried to make order out of the contradictory decisions of the past. They have not succeeded but they have, at least, provided some guidelines. Two important decisions have been made in Canada recently.

In *R.* v. *Pierce Fisheries Ltd.* (1970) the accused corporation had been charged under the Lobster Fisheries Regulations with having possession of "any lobster of a length less than that specified." In a catch of more than fifty thousand pounds of lobsters, an inspector found twenty-six undersized lobsters. The defendant company argued that no authorized officer or employee of Pierce Fisheries Ltd. had any knowledge that the undersized lobsters were on the company's premises. The president of the company had instructed his employees not to buy undersized lobsters. Consequently, the accused contended that there should be an acquittal because there was no *mens rea.* The magistrate who tried the case and the Nova Scotia Appeal Court both thought the defendant should be acquitted. A majority of the Supreme Court of Canada thought otherwise.

The starting point for a discussion of the applicability of *mens rea* to "public welfare" offences is that in the criminal law there is a presumption that *mens rea* is "an essential ingredient in every offence; but that presumption is liable to be displaced either by the words of the statute creating the offence or by the subject matter with which it deals, and both must be considered." (The above is a famous statement from *Sherras* v. *DeRutzen*, on which Illustration 27(d) is based.)

Public welfare offences are not found in the Criminal Code but rather in provincial and other federal legislation. Therefore, the common law defences available for Code crimes described in s. 7(2) may not apply. There are some indications that the defences may be available but the burden of proof on the accused may be more onerous.

If the offences (found in this non-Code legislation) contain words or phrases similar to those extracted from the Code (and listed earlier), such as wilfully, knowingly, intentionally, with intent or without reasonable cause, then the wording of the statute will usually persuade the court that this statutory offence was not meant to impose absolute liability and to exclude *mens rea*. This test places unfounded reliance on the accuracy and planning of the legislative draftsman, but it is only meant to be one of several rules of thumb.

The subject matter of the statute is also important. A statutory offence often will not be taken to include the ingredient of *mens rea* in the following circumstances:

1. Where the act is not criminal in any real sense but is prohibited under a penalty in the public interest. Instances of this class have arisen on legislation concerning such matters as food, drugs, liquor, licensing, the operation of motor vehicles.
2. Where the act is in the nature of a public nuisance.
3. Where the proceeding is criminal in form, but it is really a summary mode of enforcing a civil right.

In the Supreme Court of Canada decision in *Pierce Fisheries*, Ritchie J., for the majority, decided that it was an offence of absolute prohibition because the Lobster Fishery Regulations were "obviously intended for the purpose of protecting lobster beds from depletion and thus conserving the source of supply for an important fishing industry which is of general public interest." Perhaps it was only a coincidence that Ritchie J. is the Maritime provinces' representative on the Supreme Court of Canada but he was certainly an appropriate spokesman for the social policy that absolute liability was necessary to protect the Atlantic fisheries.

The Court decided the question as a matter of social policy. The majority also relied, in part, on the wording of the regulations because, while another section contained the phrase "without lawful excuse," the provision relating to undersized lobsters contained no indication that the mental element of the defendant should be considered.

Another important consideration in these cases is the type of penalty that can be imposed by the court. If a jail term is a possible punishment, then *mens rea* should certainly be presumed to apply. If the punishment is a small pecuniary penalty that is meant to deter potential offenders from interfering with the smooth running of society, the mental attitude of the accused is usually considered irrelevant. Parking offences are an excellent example of the latter.

A middle ground, where the courts disagree, are those offences where the accused is not in danger of being imprisoned but is in danger of having his livelihood affected by conviction—a truck driver whose driving licence may be cancelled or a restauranteur who may lose his liquor licence. The courts have also considered the question of administrative convenience. If the granting of acquittals because of legal excuses would result in wholesale flouting of the law or if defended cases would clog the machinery of justice, then the courts might decide, as a matter of expediency, that no excuse would be allowed. This is based on the theory that if the law could not otherwise be satisfactorily enforced, then there will be absolute prohibition. Furthermore, the adherents argue that *mens rea* would be too difficult to prove. (Social policy is said to have dictated the convictions of the defendants in Illustrations 27(e) (f) and (g).)

In contrast, Cartwright J. in dissenting in the *Pierce Fisheries* case said that there was no evidence that the defendant:

> would create so serious a danger of the destruction of the lobster-catching industry as to render it necessary in the public interest that, on the facts as found in this case, one blameless of any intentional wrongdoing and without any guilty mind must be convicted of a criminal offence, albeit not one involving grave moral turpitude.

In addition, Cartwright J. took the view that the displacement of *mens rea* should be very clearly stated and that the onus was on Parliament to displace the requirement of *mens rea* in the most unequivocal terms.

Some courts have taken the view that if a conviction would involve some social stigma, the Crown should prove *mens rea*. Other judges have argued that if there is a moral ingredient in the offence, that is, the alleged behaviour is inherently immoral, an accused can be convicted without a mental element to the offence. This is one possible explanation of the ruling in *Prince*, a nineteenth-century English case where the accused was charged with abducting a girl who was under the age of consent and convicted without *mens rea* because his behaviour was wrong in itself. Yet the court hinted that Prince had been mistaken about obtaining the consent of the girl's parents, rather than in error as to the girl being under age, he might have been acquitted.

Critics argue that offences of absolute prohibition are of little use because there is no deterrent effect if the accused has no defence due to mitigating circumstances. In answer, it is said that the general public is deterred by the mere existence of these prohibitions and is further deterred by the publication of convictions against others. One of the oldest objections to absolute prohibition offences is one of the strongest. Critics complain that public welfare offences offend the principle of legality on the fundamental basis that it is impossible to have prior knowledge of these laws; they are not published and are only obtainable after diligent search by a trained legal researcher.

In most instances the policy underlying offences of absolute liability is one of expediency—the machinery of justice could not function if everyone could claim a *mens rea* defence. In 1974 the Law Reform Commission of Canada examined the problem of these offences. The Commission discovered that the federal laws contain about 20,000 regulatory offences, and each province has a similar number, ninety per cent of which were absolute liability offences. Every year, there are roughly 1,400,000 convictions under these laws. The Commission was concerned that it was very difficult to ascertain which of these thousands of offences were absolute prohibitions:

> The citizen has a right to know the law, and if any part of the law should be clear and certain, the criminal law should. Since criminal law is the law that authorizes state intervention against the individual, liberty demands that the basis and the bounds of that intervention be clearly spelled out, so that we may know exactly what is forbidden and precisely when the state may intervene. Where mystery begins, observed Burke, justice ends. Mystery in the criminal law then is indefensible.

The Commission also was concerned that in seventy per cent of these regulatory offences, imprisonment was a potential punishment. The report pointed to other hazards as well—"the possibility of petty tyranny and administrative oppression."

In assessing the opposing values of justice and expediency, the Commission listed these arguments:

(a) injustice in convicting those not really at fault.
(b) such a practice dilutes the criminal law and leads to cynical disrespect for the law.
(c) care and safety, two of the social values meant to be enshrined in public welfare offences are ignored if the prosecutor does not really have to prove his case or the offender is not obliged to admit fault or provide a reasonable explanation. If the court had to consider a test of liability, then some thought would be given to the extent to which the defendant's behaviour had fallen below community standards.

The Commission rejected the idea of calling public welfare offences by another name and thus seeming to solve the problem. The Model Penal Code had labelled such occurrences "violations" and made provisions that the punishment would be non-penal and that "violators" would not have criminal records. The Commission decided that these regulatory offences were "to promote higher standards of care in business, trade and industry, higher standards of honesty in commerce and advertising, higher standards of respect for the . . . environment and [therefore] the . . . offence is basically and typically an offence of negligence." The laws should be framed in terms of negligence which would be the minimum standard of liability. An "accused should never be convicted of a regulatory offence if he establishes that he acted with due diligence, that is, that he was not negligent." This would place the burden of proving due diligence on the accused without being unfair to the accused, considering the relatively light penalties. Moreover, the rationale of regulatory offences, that is, to regulate, would be maintained.

The Commission consciously did not answer the question of how the test of negligence is to be defined. Is "due diligence" to be assessed in terms of an external standard or by reference to the defendant's internal responses to that standard? The Commission's only further comment was:

> On the one hand it is unfair to punish anyone for things that aren't his fault. Accordingly, the man who falls below the standard of the reasonable man because he can't help doing so should not be convicted. On the other hand to exonerate people who fall below the standard of reasonable care by reasons of their own clumsiness, stupidity or ignorance (albeit unavoidable) may put an undesirable premium on such defects.

There are some good precedents for this viewpoint. One of the best known is the decision of the High Court of Australia (1941) in *Proudman* v. *Dayman*. This case was referred to by Lieff J. in *R.* v. *V.K. Mason Construction Ltd.* where the judge indicated that, in some instances, the law should recognize a halfway house between absolute liability and a full *mens rea* defence. (In the *Mason* case Lieff J. decided that the defendant had not shown due diligence in relation to a charge involving breaches of the building construction safety laws.)

In *Proudman* v. *Dayman* the defendant was charged with permitting "any person not being the holder of . . . a licence to drive a motor vehicle on any road . . . ." Dixon C.J. would have been prepared to give the defendant a defence of reasonable mistake so long as *she* proved it. He said, "the very idea of permission connotes knowledge of or advertence to the act or thing permitted . . . you cannot permit without consenting and consent involves a consciousness or understanding of the act or conduct to which it is directed."

If the accused were simply ignorant of the fact that the driver had no valid driver's licence, there would be no excuse. Similarly, if the accused had made a mistake of fact that was unreasonable, there would be no acquittal. (In such circumstances the accused's frame of mind could be classed as negligent.) If, however, the accused had "an honest *and* reasonable belief in a state of facts which, if they existed, would make the defendant's act innocent affords an excuse for doing what would otherwise be an offence." This presumption would be stronger, in Dixon J.'s opinion, in ordinary criminal offences than in offences of public health and safety where the legislature casts on the "individual the responsibility of so conducting his affairs that the general welfare will not be prejudiced." Therefore, if Ms. Proudman's only explanation was that she forgot to ask if the driver had a licence, then she might not escape conviction. If, however, she specifically asked the driver for his licence and he deceived her by showing her a piece of paper that looked very much like a valid licence, then the Court might well consider that this was a reasonable mistake and that the accused should be acquitted.

A 1960 Canadian case of *Sawicki* came to a similar conclusion. The accused was charged with allowing a vehicle to be operated while it was not equipped with a muffler, contrary to a Saskatchewan statute. The judge observed:

> The appellant may have assumed that someone would install the muffler but that is not enough. The duty to see that the truck was properly equipped before it was put on the road was his and that duty was an absolute one. . . . The appellant, however, took no effective steps to see that the muffler was installed on the truck and made no inquiry or check to ascertain if it had in fact been installed. In my opinion the appellant did not take those precautions which a reasonable or prudent owner should have taken to see that the requirements of the statute had been complied with. Counsel for the appellant contends that *mens rea* is an essential ingredient of the offence with which his client was charged. . . . In my opinion his indifference and the negligence he displayed in disregarding his statutory duty was sufficient to constitute *mens rea* and I so hold. . . .

Illustration 27(h) describes the facts in *Hickey*. For the majority, Galligan J. decided that the offence described by s. 82 of the Ontario Highway Traffic Act was a strict liability offence but that a qualified defence, consonant with the recommendations of the Canadian Law Reform Commission and based on *Proudman* v. *Dayman*, was available. The defence of mistake was qualified to the extent that it was not so broadly based as the rule in *Morgan* and *Beaver*. In the case of an offence that does not have the ingredient of full *mens rea*, the mistake must not only be an honest one but it must also be reasonable and it must be proved by the accused on the balance of probabilities. (The *Hickey* case was overruled by a higher court deciding that speeding was an absolute liability offence that did not require *mens rea*.)

The Canadian courts have now embraced the *Proudman* v. *Dayman* and Law Reform Commission viewpoints with the foundation laid down by Dickson J. in *R.* v. *City of Sault Ste. Marie*. The City had been charged with a pollution offence under Ontario Water Resources Act which could draw a fine up to $5000. The City had contracted with a company to dispose of the city garbage. The garbage was dumped in such a way that a creek was polluted. The City had no knowledge of the Company's operations, and the debate carried on in the many courts that heard this case was whether lack of knowledge (i.e., no *mens rea*) should be a defence to a charge under the Act.

Dickson J. decided that there was a half-way house between full *mens rea* offences and those attracting absolute liability. He described three categories:

1. Offences in which *mens rea*, consisting of some positive state of mind such as intent, knowledge, or recklessness, must be proved by the prosecution either as an inference from the nature of the act committed, or by additional evidence.
2. Offences in which there is no necessity for the prosecution to prove the existence of *mens rea*; the doing of the prohibited act *prima facie* imports the offence, leaving it open to the accused to avoid liability by proving that he took all reasonable care. This involves consideration of what a reasonable man would have done in the circumstances. The defence will be available if the accused reasonably believed in a mistaken set of facts which, if true, would render the act or omission innocent, or if he took all reasonable steps to avoid the particular event. These offences may properly be called offences of strict liability.
3. Offences of absolute liability where it is not open to the accused to exculpate himself by showing that he was free of fault.

Truly criminal offences and public welfare offences that contained words such as "wilfully," "knowingly" and "with intent" would be in the first category. Most public welfare offences would be in the second and the third would be limited to those where the legislation "had made it clear that guilt would follow proof merely of the proscribed act." In deciding on third category offences, Dickson J. suggested that the following criteria should be considered: the overall regulatory pattern of the Act, its subject matter, the importance of the penalty and the precision of the language. In a case similar to Illustration 27(i), the Supreme Court has applied the second category and decided that the relevant regulation was "not a strict prohibition on hunting, [but] rather a hunt controlled within certain limits. . . ." Dickson J. was not sufficiently convinced by the Crown's contention that a second category classification would weaken the efficacy of the legislation. On a practical level, the judge also pointed out that the only way in which a hunter could totally absolve herself would be to search an area within a diameter of half a mile to ensure that no feed had been left for ducks. (*Chapin*) In a subsequent case, *Strasser* v. *Roberge*, the court has again examined the problem. The judgement of the majority is very difficult to follow, and Beetz J. suffers from the misapprehension that *Sault Ste. Marie* allows full *mens rea* crimes to be converted into category 2 offences by placing the onus on the accused. Dickson J. dissented and his view seems preferable. He said the following (which is apposite to a discussion of Illustrations 27(a) (b) and (c)):

> In *Sault Ste. Marie* it was held not to be unfair to place upon the defendant the burden, or . . . the "right and opportunity," of proving that his conduct did not fall below the objective standard of a reasonable man in the circumstances. It did not seem unfair to impose such a burden when the offence would otherwise be

characterized as one of absolute liability and the accused would have no defence whatever. On the other hand, it certainly does seem unfair to reverse the burden of proof where there are strong indications that the offence would otherwise fall within the first category of *mens rea* offences.

Reverse Onus

Dickson J. was referring to a judicial decision by Beetz J. to reverse the onus of proof when the legislative words did not specifically create a reverse onus situation. Can we interpret Dickson J.'s words to declare the Code provisions described in Illustrations 27(a) (b) and (c)? Dickson J. would probably reply that if the Code drafter has used explicit words reversing the onus, then it is not unfair. At least one lower court has already attacked the offence described in Illustration 27(b) and said that taking away the presumption of innocence is contrary to the new Charter of Rights but we have certainly not heard the last of that controversy. A typical reverse onus section of the Code is s. 309 which says "Everyone who, without lawful excuse, the proof of which lies upon him, has in his possession any instrument suitable for house-breaking. . . ." This does not mean that the accused is automatically guilty the minute he is found in possession of a crowbar, a jemmy, five screwdrivers and ten credit cards. If possession of the items and circumstances under which they are found seems incongruous and very suspicious, then the accused will be required to make an explanation. He may be able to convince a policeman, or a court, that he was a carpenter who liked to buy everything on credit but it will be necessary for him to say something in explanation, and such provisions as s. 309 are an erosion of the right to remain silent and the presumption of innocence. The prosecution's answer would be that prevention is better than cure, and such offences are examples of the crime control model of the criminal process.

Some Other Principles of the Criminal Law

Causation

The Canadian Criminal Code does not have a general section describing the principle of causation in the law but s. 209 addresses the problem of causation in homicide:

> Where a person causes bodily injury to a human being that results in death, he causes the death of that human being notwithstanding that the effect of the bodily injury is only to accelerate his death from a disease or disorder arising from some other cause.

In Illustration 30 would D be found guilty of the murder of V? Did D cause the death (as opposed to the bodily injury) of V? Does s. 209 help us solve the problem? D obviously "caused" the bodily injury but did he "only" accelerate the death? We could argue that V's death was only tentatively related to the initial bodily injury because he might have died from penicillin injections following the removal of his wisdom teeth. The prosecution might reply that the foregoing sounds like a convincing argument but, in fact, V was not in the hospital for oral surgery but because he was wounded by V with a knife.

The court acquitted D in Illustration 30(a) (*Jordan*) because the treatment was not normal and, therefore, amounted to an "intervening cause." The treatment was not only abnormal but grossly improper. As we discovered when discussing criminal negligence (and as is true of many other areas of the law), adjectival descriptions of a legal concept, such as "intervening" or "proximate," may solve some questions but usually create as many new ones.

Illustration 30(b), the case of *Smith*, resulted in a conviction for murder and yet the medical treatment was certainly improper. The court decided that the initial wound was a serious one and was still an operating cause in V's death. Illustration 30(d) is based on *Thabo Meli* and D was convicted. The initial injury was still operative and D's misconception as to the cause of death did not matter. These cases, and s. 209, are reminiscent of the eggshell skull rule—if you put the victim in a situation of danger, you must take the victim as you find him. If a mild blow to an ordinary victim may have resulted in a small abrasion or a cut requiring a couple of stitches, an assailant is guilty of murder if the victim happens to have a very thin skull or is a haemophiliac and dies (Illustration 30(*a*)). The assailant assumes the risk and must pay the consequences. This, however, does not solve all problems. What if the unusual medical condition "causes" the death of the victim but only after a lengthy period of time? The law has an answer to this—the ancient and arbitrary rule now found in s. 210 of the Code: V must die within one year and one day "commencing with the time of the occurrence of the past event by means of which he caused or contributed to the cause of death."

Illustration 30(*b*) is not usually viewed as a causation problem. The law would look upon it as a question of recklessness and foreseeability; the accused, and a reasonable person in his place, ought to have realized that if an unconscious person were left in sub-zero conditions then there was a high probability that the victim would die. The same is true of *R.* v. *Black and Mackie* (Illustration 30(c)) because they intended V serious harm and they ought to have foreseen that a drunken person, such as V, might drown.

What if the victim suffers from peculiar psychological, as opposed to physical, susceptibility? What, for example, if V is injured by D in some way and V does some act that immediately "causes" his or her death? D attacks V with intent to rape her and V, in blind terror, leaps from a third story window rather than submit to D and is killed in the fall. V is kidnapped by D and V takes poison. V is injured by D and, rather than endure the pain, V takes his own life. Is D criminally liable in these circumstances? Most courts, particularly in the rape cases, have found D guilty. The liability of D in Illustration 30(e) is unlikely because the acts of S were too remote.

Two recent cases are worth noting because they raise both causation and medical ethical problems. In *Blave*, V had been stabbed but refused a blood transfusion because she was a Jehovah's Witness. The accused was convicted of manslaughter. The appeal judge reiterated the principle of taking your victim as you find her:

> This . . . means the whole man, not just the physical man. It does not lie in the mouth of the assailant to say that his victim's religious beliefs which inhibited him from accepting certain kinds of treatment were unreasonable. [The victim's refusal] did not break the caused connection between the act and death.

In the Canadian case of *R.* v. *Kitching and Adams,* the two accused were bouncers at a night club who dropped V on a sidewalk. The doctors decided that V had no hope of living. V's heart was beating spontaneously but his lungs were only operating with the help of a ventilator. A decision was made to save V's kidneys for transplant. Since doctors prefer to remove kidneys while the body is still "alive," they removed the kidneys and then turned off the ventilator. Thirteen minutes later, V's heart stopped beating. The accused, who were convicted of manslaughter, argued that V's death was caused by the removal of his kidneys. This was rejected on the basis of the law of causation. The Manitoba Court of Appeal did not want to debate medical issues but hoped that the legal and medical criteria could be clarified. (The Law Reform Commission of Canada issued a report in 1981 which sets out criteria including "the irreversible cessation of brain functions . . . determined by the prolonged absence of spontaneous circulatory and respiratory functions.")

In many of these cases we are speaking of the problem of how "remote" a consequence can be before the law will acquit D. D and V decide to hold up a store. V is armed with a gun and he brandishes the gun at A, the store owner. Any observer of the transaction would agree that V (and D) were acting in a violent and threatening manner. Ms. A is also in the store and has a concealed weapon with which she shoots V dead. D was charged with the murder of V, his accomplice. In this particular case, *Almeida,* D was convicted, although in other cases the result has been acquittal. This is an illustration of the constructive murder doctrine that is strongly criticized because it is based on a stringently objective test. Instead, we want to limit homicide during the course of another offence to cases where liability is based on a more subjective rule in the following terms: D embarked on a serious and dangerous crime and in the process caused serious bodily harm to V from which he died. D should have foreseen, as any reasonable person would have adverted, some physical injury to V and is responsible for the direct conseqences. *Almeida* was certainly much broader than that. The Canadian case of *Bernard* was a little closer. D robbed V at his house and hit him, leaving V lying in his yard. In panic, D reversed V's car out of the garage to make a getaway and drove over V. This action probably killed him. Did D "cause" V's death so that he could be convicted of murder? The court's answer was yes. These cases are often confused with causation problems but, it is argued, they are really examples of the difficulty of defining the limits of liability and foresight.

In the light of these decisions should Jordan and Smith be convicted? The courts decided that V's death was too remote a consequence in the former case but not too remote a consequence in the latter.

Tests have been suggested in an attempt to formulate more precisely the remoteness or proximity of consequence:

1. The *sine qua non* or "but for" test; the defendant's act was a necessary condition of the harm caused to V.
2. Most commentators have argued that while this text excludes some persons, it is not sufficiently specific; that it is necessary to qualify it by showing that D's act was a *substantial cause.* In *Smith,* the bayonet wound was still an operating cause when further harm was done to V. Therefore, in Hall's words, we could say that Smith's act was a "*necessary and effective condition.*" That means that D's act was in itself sufficient to produce the harm without intervention.
3. The only thing we need add to "necessary and effective condition" is that D had the necessary *mens rea.*

Silving, in *Constitutent Elements of Crime,* gives us the following:

An event as described by a statute shall be deemed to have been "caused" by a conduct as described by the statute if the concrete event (a) would not have occurred as it did but for that conduct and (b) resulted from those qualities of that conduct that are used in the statute to describe such conduct. . . .

Intervening causes do not exclude causation by the conduct of a defendant, if at the time of their occurrence there was a high probability that without their intervention that conduct would have been followed by consequences as required by the statute, or if these intervening events would not have occurred as they did or would not have had the effect they did but for the situation created by the defendant's conduct.

The Model Penal Code adopts the "but for" test with some important qualifications that are necessary to satisfy the *mens rea* requirements:

(1) Conduct is the cause of a result when:
  (a) it is an antecedent but for which the result in question would not have occurred; and
  (b) the relationship between the conduct and result satisfies any additional causal requirements imposed by the Code or by the law defining the offence.

(2) When purposely or knowingly causing a particular result is an element of an offence, the element is not established if the actual result is not within the purpose or the contemplation of the actor unless:
  (a) the actual result differs from that designed or contemplated, as the case may be, only in the respect that a different person or different property is injured or affected or that the injury or harm designed or contemplated

would have been more serious or more extensive than that caused; or

(b) the actual result involves the same kind of injury or harm as that designed or contemplated and is not too remote or accidental in its occurrence to have a [just] bearing on the actor's liability or on the gravity of his offence.

(3) When recklessly or negligently causing a particular result is an element of an offence, the element is not established if the actual result is not within the risk of which the actor is aware or, in the case of negligence, of which he should be aware unless:

(a) the actual result differs from the probable result only in the respect that a different person or different property is injured or affected or that the probable injury or harm would have been more serious or more extensive than that caused; or

(b) the actual result involves the same kind of injury or harm as the probable result and is not too remote or accidental in its occurrence to have a [just] bearing on the actor's liability or on the gravity of his offence.

These definitions suggest that causation questions are not very far removed from problems of foresight and recklessness in *mens rea.*

Parties to an Offence

There is another area where the law has issued clear warning that it will impute liability and that the subjective mental processes will not always be accepted by the judge (or jury) as the applicable test of criminal responsibility. The law will impute liability, although the accused insists not that he did not intend to do some act but that he was not involved in the completion of the impugned act. The law, in effect, is saying, "We know that, physically, you did not do the act or that you were not involved in the entire completed act. We are, however, going to punish you because (a) your excuse would be too convenient, or (b) your behaviour should be proscribed by the criminal law because of its potential danger or (c) because we would prefer to prevent crime than to solve it." This policy is shown in two types of crime—parties to an offence and inchoate crimes.

Under the common law, there was an elaborate gradation of participation in crime. There were accessories before the fact (that is, the crime), principals in the first degree, principals in the second degree and accessories after the fact. The Canadian Criminal Code has simplified this. In fact, the Canadian criminal law relating to parties is one of the most satisfactory elements of that body of law. The most extreme provision is found is s. 423 of the Code which provides that everyone who "counsels, procures or incites" another to commit an offence, indictable or summary, is guilty of an offence even if the crime is *not* committed. The punishment is severe; the counsellor or incitor is liable to half of the punishment that would have applied to the completed crime. This is a classic case of deterrence—at least that is the hope of the law.

The law takes the attitude that it is better to prevent crime than cure its after-effects. It is better to inform incipient criminals of the penalties that they are likely to suffer than to see an increase in crime. Convictions under this section have been rare, mostly because proof of guilt is extremely difficult unless the counsellee is prepared to inform.

If the crime is actually committed, the counsellor is equally liable, in terms of guilt and punishment, as the perpetrator, even if the offence is committed in a different manner. This is provided by s. 22(1) of the Code and 22(2) provides that the counsellor is a party to "every offence that the other commits in consequence of the counselling or procuring" that the counsellor "knew or ought to have known was likely to be committed."

Under the Canadian law, all other participants in crime, whether active or passive, are treated in the same way in terms of liability and punishment. The only exception is an accessory after the fact—a person who provides a car for escape, who offers shelter or protection, who lends clothes, money or a passport to a criminal on the run. In the technical language of s. 23, an accessory after the fact is one who "knowing a person has been a party to the offence, receives, comforts or assists him for the purpose of enabling him to escape." A spouse, however, is not an accessory after the fact if he or she helps the marriage partner escape detection or arrest (see Illustration 31(k)).

The greatest legal problems are found in s. 21 which makes all other participants in a crime equal partners in criminal responsibility. A person can be guilty of a crime by actually committing, by "doing or omitting to do anything for the purpose of aiding any person to commit it" or by abetting any person. The problem is who does aid and abet? The Code tries to answer this in subsection (2) of s. 21.

In Illustration 31(a) Pan is not guilty of any offence because he did not intend to take part in D's plans. There was no *mens rea*. Illustration 31(b) is more difficult because we must decide how much knowledge we can impute to Pater. Our decision will depend on how objective the courts are prepared to be in *protecting* society from the *potential harm* that Dome might inflict and how the courts will impose on Pater a *constructive knowledge* of any of Dome's enterprises that fall within the general category of serious crime or *dangerous social* behaviour. A subjectivist might complain that the emphasized phrases make it impossible to have any certainty or justice in the law. Illustration 31(b) cannot be easily answered. P is probably not guilty as a party to D's crime of rape because P never contemplated such an offence. If D killed a person while robbing a bank, the court may convict P by saying that P ought to have known that a death could ensue from an inherently dangerous act such as a bank robbery. Presuming for the moment that the victim was not killed by the borrowed automobile, the court might be more willing to acquit P if D had told P that he did not intend to carry any weapon but in fact D walked into the bank armed with a loaded machine gun.

Illustration 31(c) is based on the cases of *Cathro, Chow Bew,* and *Eng Git*

Lee. Is mere presence enough? A short answer is probably not, although it will depend on the type of crime, the number of persons present and their actions preceding the event. A good, although slightly unusual, example is *R. ex. rel. Tomlinson* v. *Hayes*. The appellant was charged with an offence under the old s. 387(d) of the Code in that he attended a cockfight and, in the words of the section, "in any manner encourages, aids or assists at the fighting . . . of birds." His lawyer argued that it would be necessary for his client to have done some physical act such as providing cocks or equipment for the "sport" or helping prepare the cockfight. The Ontario High Court did not agree and held that although his mere presence would not convict, the fact that he went to Hamilton expressly for the purpose of viewing a cockfight and paid an admission fee was sufficient to convict him. (Section 402(4) of the Code now provides that presence at a cockfight makes D a party "in the absence of any evidence to the contrary.") The nineteenth-century case of *R.* v. *Coney* held that the mere presence of a defendant at a prize fight was not conclusive evidence of guilt. In that same case, the court did say that "the surgeon who attends a duel, to save the lives imperilled, attends it as a criminal." It is difficult to distinguish between these cases.

There was a celebrated English case in the 1950s. Craig was legally a juvenile at the time of the offence while Bentley was over eighteen years of age. They were observed breaking and entering a building. Bentley was caught and, while being held by a policeman, called to Craig, who was armed, "Let him have it, Chris." Craig shot "him," the policeman. Bentley claimed that he was advising Craig to give up his gun to the police officer. The prosecutor contended that the phrase had a more vernacular and violent meaning. The cruel irony was that Bentley, as an adult, was tried for murder, convicted and hanged. Craig was treated as a juvenile. Bentley's words helped to hang him. He was ruled to be an aider and abettor (which in Canadian law would make him a party to the offence under s. 21(2)).

In *Cathro* (or "Adam") Taschereau J., who dissented from the majority, agreed that words could be sufficient grounds for conviction. Admittedly, there was some evidence that Cathro had himself used some violence, although it was only limited violence which may have been within the original pre-crime agreement between at least two of the actors. Taschereau J. placed some emphasis on the words spoken by Cathro. The judge did not make it clear when these words were spoken but it appears that they were uttered after Cathro's arrest. Cathro was alleged to have said that, if the victim "put up a fight, he was going to do just what he did," and that "whatever fight the old man would put up, he was ready to overcome it." The judge interpreted ss. 21(2) and 212 and held that "the jury could not reasonably find, in view of the evidence, that the two assailants were not prepared to inflict grievous bodily injury, for the purpose of facilitating the commission of the offence of robbery. In such a case, it is immaterial that they meant or not death to ensue, or knew or not that death would likely ensue."

The majority of the Supreme Court of Canada did not agree. They considered that if the jury had been properly directed, they might have felt there was reasonable doubt that the requirements of 21(2) had been fulfilled to the extent of convicting Cathro of murder. These requirements included "intention in common," "common purpose" and "knew or ought to have known" that the death was a "probable consequence." In the words of Rand J., "... was there such an excess in mode or degree as converted it into an act and an offence so outrageous or so unforeseeable as to be beyond the scope of probable consequence?" Chow Bew (or "Badger") certainly was guilty under s. 212 of the Code, but Cathro should have a new trial.

The court had no trouble in acquitting the third party (Cade) who drove the getaway car. He was too far outside the transaction. Yet if he had been in attendance at the pre-crime discussions, surely he would be guilty on Mr. Justice Taschereau's test—but, of course, that judge was in dissent. The dissenter would go along with the social defence argument or more objective view that anyone who embarks on a dangerous enterprise must take all the consequences. A counter-argument to this stringently objective view is that a reasonable person test, properly interpreted, would not expect that much foresight. Given C's acquittal, Dud would be similarly acquitted.

Illustration 31(d) is based on *Trinneer*. D's lawyer called no evidence at his trial. The appeal was based on the failure of the trial judge to direct the jury that before they could find D guilty, they must find that he knew or ought to have known that the death of V was a probable consequence of carrying out the robbery.

The Supreme Court of Canada decided that such a test would be too favourable to the accused and that under s. 21, D and P had formed a common purpose of robbery and that the death of V was part of the carrying out of that common purpose. If D knew or ought to have known that causing bodily harm to V was a probable consequence of the robbery and death, in fact, ensued from the bodily harm, then D was also guilty of the murder. This test is not very helpful because the key words, once again, are "ought to have known" and "probable consequence." At least in murder cases, the courts seem to be applying a more stringent test.

The problem of s. 21, and other questions relating to *mens rea,* cannot be solved by mere words. The degree of objectivity applied, the value judgements made by the judge and jury about constructive or literal foresight of consequences, the assumption of risk, the protection of citizens from social harm, the application of the punitive principles of retribution and deterrence, all will affect the ambit of blameworthiness and the severity of punishment. Once again, the abolition of capital punishment and the diminution of public importance attached to the crime of murder would obviate some of the problems in s. 21.

The classic Canadian case of *Regina* v. *Roy* provides an excellent illustration of one of the most difficult problems regarding the liability of parties. The easiest defence to a charge of being an aider and abettor might be called the Lord-Nelson-blind-eye-to-the-telescope ploy, or condonation. If the alleged abettor has said to the director or primary participant, "You do what you like, I don't want to know anything about it," is he guilty as a party? In no area of the criminal law are oral and circumstantial evidence as crucial as they are in the law pertaining to parties. If the condoner is a believable witness and the prosecution has little else but suspicion and hearsay to work on, then a conviction is unlikely. On the other hand, if there is no plausible explanation for the condoner being present at the scene of the crime, as in the cockfight case, then a believable explanation should be given if the accused wants to avoid conviction. There is a great difference between merely being present at a hockey match where a serious assault is committed by one player upon another and being a bystander at an inherently illegal duel or bare-knuckle fight.

Ms. Roy was charged with keeping a bawdy house. She owned a house in Montreal and leased it to Florida Lemieux. The prosecution alleged that Ms. Roy knew that Ms. Lemieux was a prostitute, that Ms. Roy herself was a prostitute, that the house had been a brothel before the lease to Ms. Lemieux, that Ms. Roy had visited the house since the start of the lease and must have been aware of the business being carried on there. The Crown had no difficulty proving its case. The judgement is full of phrases that are supposed to be helpful—"knowledge," "concurrence" and, finally, "her conduct in leasing her house with such guilty knowledge would have therefore amounted to active encouragement of the commission of the offence."

The cases raise important issues which have no easy answers. How passive can acquiescence be and still amount to criminal liability? How much culpability should be imputed to the alleged party? What amounts to encouragement? When can an alleged party abandon the alleged joint enterprise and avoid liability? The words of s. 21(2) are all the help we have.

In the two Canadian cases, *Salajko* and *Dunlop*, on which Illustration 31(f) is based, the court acquitted because it decided that mere presence or acquiescence was insufficient. Something more was needed, as Dickson J. said in *Dunlop*:

> ... encouragement of the principal offender; an act which facilitates the commission of the offence, such as keeping a watch or enticing the victim away, an act which tends to prevent or hinder interference with accomplishment of the criminal act, such as preventing the intended victim from escaping or being ready to assist the prime culprit ... prior knowledge of the principal offender's intention to commit the offence or attendance for the purpose of encouragement.

The difficulty of the situation in Illustration 31(f) and in 31(g) is that we only have the story of the accused (who is the alleged party to the offence) and little else. The fact-finder is obliged to rely upon conjecture, suspicion and constructive guilt. The decisions are value-laden, and since the acquittal of the bikers in the rape cases one can hardly imagine a prosecutor being successful if he suggested that Pratt, Potter and Pedder should have run away and phoned the police or at least disassociated themselves from the criminal activities. Such a moral attitude might be appropriate for heroes but it is hardly reflective of ordinary human behaviour. On the other hand, I don't think we would have much difficulty in making the legal (and moral) decision that D1 and D2 had left it a little late to back out of the criminal enterprise. (Illustration 31(j)) If it were a contract rather than a crime, one cannot see a court saying that there was no contract if one party got cold feet when he realized that it was a losing proposition.

The drug cases (some of which are described in Illustration 31(e)) show very clearly that criminal guilt will sometimes depend on time and circumstances. In all three types of cases mentioned in 31(e)—decisions which can be found resulting in guilt and acquittal—a sociologist would argue that if a particular region were worried about the drug problem or if it were a time when the whole country thought Canadian youth were suffering from reefer madness, then a conviction would be registered. The best opinion would result in acquittal in all three instances because the accused in each case was a victim of circumstances and had no *mens rea* for possession of the drug.

The driving cases described in Illustration 31(h) have been uniformly stringent. In *Halmo* (1941) the accused and his chauffeur had been drinking together. Halmo was convicted of reckless driving physically committed by his chauffeur. The court considered Halmo had "charge" and "control" of the automobile—he was the owner of the vehicle, he was the employer of the chauffeur and he was personally present at all material times.

In *Kulbacki* (1965) a young man allowed his sixteen-year-old girlfriend to drive his car at ninety miles per hour on a rough country road. He was charged with dangerous driving. He did or said nothing to stop her from driving in that manner, and on the authority of *Halmo*, he was convicted. The court admitted that not every silent passenger or passive observer was automatically guilty as the passenger may have no control or authority over the driver. In *Kulbacki* the court could not, however, agree with the defence argument that the accused had no duty or "was not under any liability to do anything as long as he did not in some way encourage the commission of the offence." In Illustration 31(i), D was not actually aiding or abetting the offence. At most, he was obstructing the police in the execution of their duty *after* a crime had been committed.

Finally, there are two technical legal points of some interest. If the actual perpetrator of the offence escapes punishment on a technicality that is not available to the aider and abettor, does this mean that a secondary party can be convicted notwithstanding the other acquittal? At least one English case suggests that conviction is proper. This is not the case in Canada. In *Vinette* (1974) the Supreme Court of Canada said:

> Whereas in the case of several persons accused of the same offence, each may be tried before or after the others, plead guilty before or after any of the others, or be convicted regardless of the decision against any of the others, an accessory after the fact may not be tried to tender a valid plea of guilty until the principal is convicted, so that if the latter is acquitted the accessory must of necessity be discharged.

If one party has been convicted of manslaughter, a decision of the Supreme Court of Canada says that the aider and abettor cannot be convicted of the more serious offence of murder.

Inchoate Crime 1: Attempt

Inchoate is an esoteric word used by lawyers, meaning "incomplete." Attempt and conspiracy are the two inchoate crimes. Attempt is not a single crime but is the uncompleted version of any crime and the punishment is usually half that of the completed crime.

Once again, this is an illustration of the law applying a deterrent policy, a salutary aim in terms of social protection. Those who do not succeed (or are caught in the uncompleted act) are almost as troublesome to society as the successful criminals. This point has been well argued by Jerome Hall: "The legal history [of attempt] also discloses that there is an irreducible element of experience in law that cannot be persuasively dissolved in logical analysis and which penal theory must somehow take into account."

Attempt can provide an exception to the rule that a crime must consist of a mental and physical element. The attempt situation may show little manifestation of a physical element, yet the criminal law is loath to punish mere thoughts. This may suit a totalitarian regime but the Anglo-Canadian law of attempt at least pretends to find *mens rea* and *actus reus*.

As Hall shows, the crime of attempt did not emerge as a discrete crime until the beginning of the nineteenth century when there was a resurgence of a repressive attitude toward antisocial behaviour. The stringency of the law can be seen in the following judicial statement from one of the earliest cases:

> So long as an act rests in bare intention, it is not punishable by our laws: immediately when an act is done, the law judges, not only of the act done, but of the intent with which it is done; and, if it is coupled with an unlawful and malicious intent, though the act itself would otherwise have been innocent, the intent being criminal, the act becomes criminal and punishable.

Attempt provides a preventive function in the criminal law—it tries to nip socially harmful behaviour in the bud. Some attempts have become crimes in their own account. The Code is full of these preventive measures, treason being the most obvious example. Traitors or persons engaged in sedition who successfully fulfil their aims are fathers of their country or glorious revolutionaries. George Washington and Fidel Castro have at least that much in common. Other attempt crimes are a little more mundane. Burglary is, in effect, an attempt—it is a breaking and entering of a house with the intent to commit a crime therein. There are several possession offences, such as possession of an offensive weapon, betting slips, house-breaking implements, counterfeiting equipment or explosives, which are, in essence, inchoate crimes. There are also bribery and subornation of witnesses, since it is a crime even if the bribe is merely offered and the intended recipient never planned to take it. The crime of assault is, in some respects, an inchoate crime because contrary to popular misconception, an assault does not always consist of physical damage—it can merely be a threat and put the intended victim in fear of physical injury. The most obvious inchoate offence aiming at crime control is found in s. 175(1)(e) of the Code which makes it a crime for a person previously convicted as a dangerous (sexual) offender to be "found loitering or wandering in or near a school ground, playground, public park or bathing area."

Criminals, or potential criminals, may fail to achieve their ends through ineptitude or bad luck. The law of attempt enables the criminal law to control these acts. The law has not quite reached the point where it is prepared to punish mere thoughts; there must be some manifestation of an act that the law can label blameworthy. The idea of social protection has not gone so far as to punish a man merely because of a hunch, an inkling or a suspicion that he was up to no good. The law tries, in most instances, to allow a man to escape criminal liability if he has had a legitimate change of heart, or *locus poenitentiae*. This does not mean that he can stop his criminal intentions when he finds a policeman breathing down his neck and thereby escape liability. Moreover, a person can be found guilty of attempt even if it was impossible for him to commit the complete crime (s. 24(1)). The Code does not state whether the act must be factually or legally impossible. The common law draws a distinction so that there can be a conviction for an attempt only where it was *factually* impossible to complete the act. In Illustration 32(b) a man can be convicted of attempted murder if he fires into an empty bed, thinking his intended victim is sleeping there. Remoteness (where the intended victim is in another country at the time) or impossibility (where the victim is already dead) may, however, affect liability.

Difficult problems of definitions arise from s. 24(2). What is "mere preparation" and how remote is "too remote"? Attempt cases present fascinating intellectual exercises. Enlightenment has proved elusive and there seem to be more elaborate theories than there are firm rules. Therefore, the question of the evidence produced and its interpretation and evaluation by the fact-finder will be more than usually crucial.

Two tests have been propounded in the last century or so but have certainly not received uniform support. The first—that when an offender is moving toward his objective and has committed some crime (although not the one he intended), he has also committed a criminal attempt—seems to make little sense. The other test was suggested in the English case of *Eagleton*. In Hall's words, the attempt is committed when the "offender no longer controls the agency he has set in motion, when the outcome has become a matter of physics, not volition." Both these tests are unsatisfactory because they are ambiguous. The alleged attempter's behaviour may suggest a number of possible crimes that he did not complete.

Only three of the modern tests propounded by judges and professors will be cited. Perhaps all that any of them is really saying is, "I know an attempt when I see it." The first suggests that the sufficiency of an act will be satisfied only if the act observed is inseparably connected with the crime and not concerned merely with preparation. This is expressed as the "last proximate act," the act that has gone beyond preparation and is sufficiently proximate in space and time so that no further act remains to be done except the actual completion. This test sounds the most satisfactory. It is a good rule for what it includes but it excludes too much. There are many crimes where several acts are performed that go beyond mere preparation but are still some steps away from being the last proximate act. The classic illustration is the man who buys a gun and bullets, draws plans for a suitable vantage point for the killing, goes to that place and is then apprehended. He has not fired an inaccurate shot or even taken a practice aim, yet most would consider him dangerous. Of course, it may make more sense to control him by charging him with possessing an unlicenced firearm, possession of an offensive weapon, watching and besetting or trespass.

Illustration 32(f)(i) is based on the American case of *Rizzo*. There can be little doubt that the police performed a public service in apprehending these men, but were the defendants guilty of attempt? Certainly not under the last proximate act rule. This rule is also impracticable because it suggests that a policeman must use the most precise discretion in stopping a man at the very last moment, which is hardly in the best interests of public safety. No one could sensibly suggest that a potential criminal should only be guilty of attempt when his finger has started to apply pressure to the trigger.

The appellate court in *Rizzo* upset the conviction, deciding that the defendant's acts were mere preparation: "these defendants had planned to commit a crime and were looking around the city for an opportunity to commit it, but the opportunity fortunately never came." A similar Canadian case (*R.* v. *Sorrell and Bondett*) is described in Illustration 32(f)(ii). The trial judge acquitted them and the Court of Appeal agreed. The latter court made a very sensible statement accentuating *mens rea* rather than playing endless mind games with proximate causes, etc.:

> The following passage . . . would tend to support the conclusion that the trial Judge was led into error with respect to the existence of the necessary intent by self-misdirection that the respondents' acts had not gone beyond mere preparation: "It is an extremely fine line, but whether thin or otherwise, if my finding is

> that this line had been crossed beyond mere preparation, the finding—if it were to be made—that the line had been crossed would be sufficient to bring me to a conclusion beyond a reasonable doubt. Nevertheless, the fineness of the line is a bother to me." . . . The issue of intent was basic and, the trial Judge, in our view, could not logically or appropriately make a determination whether the acts of the respondents went beyond mere preparation until he had found the intent with which those acts were done. . . . There was no extrinsic evidence in the form of statements of intention, or admissions by the respondents of intention, or admissions by the respondents showing what their intention was. . . . the acts of the accused, which on their face are equivocal, may be insufficient to show that the acts were done with the intent to commit the crime that the accused is alleged to have attempted to commit, and hence insufficient to establish the offence of attempt.

In essence, the last proximate act test is not a test at all. It is merely a description of the requisites of an attempt. The well-known cases make similar statements: "moving directly toward the commission of the offence"; "the act done must come pretty near to accomplishing that result." Holmes J. in *Commonwealth* v. *Kennedy* also said, "Every question of proximity must be determined by its own circumstances" and "analogy is too imperfect to give much help." This proximity rule has also received further elaboration in *Osborn*, where the judge provided the following simple test in the vernacular: "Was the accused on the job at the time of apprehension?" The *Osborn* test would also take care of cases where the accused had committed preparatory acts but was grossly inept; if for instance, he was trying to kill his victim by a completely inadequate method such as placing two aspirin in the victim's coffee or beating him with a plastic baseball bat. Do these cases differ from one in which the alleged attempter is firing from an impossible range? In all instances, crime control advocates would say the accused was potentially dangerous, but it is very difficult to give a definitive answer based on the case law or the current crop of attempt tests. Once again, we have other crimes with which he could be charged—possession of weapon, discharging firearm, etc.

Another major theory that has attracted much support is the "unequivocality" theory. This test does not try to distinguish between attempt and mere preparation but looks instead at the *mens rea*. The English writer J.W.C. Turner has used a metaphor to describe this rule which is an application of the maxim *res ipsa loquitur* (things speak for themselves). Dr. Turner asks us to imagine that the accused's actions were being filmed and that when he was apprehended or his acts brought to a halt the film was stopped. After seeing this film the jury should be asked to describe the crime that the accused was attempting to commit. If they were able to do so, the attempt charge was made out. Once again, this test has obvious disadvantages. There are many acts that are well on their way to being crimes and are highly dangerous but are also ambiguous and could describe the beginnings of many different crimes.

The unequivocality theory is said to be expressed by Salmond J. in *Barker*, although that may put too narrow an interpretation on the judgement of this eminent jurist. *Barker* is very similar to *Cline*, a 1956 Ontario case. Both cases concerned suspected pedophiles who made statements to young boys and extended ambiguous invitations to them. In *Barker* the accused stopped a boy, a complete stranger, in the street and handed him a note inviting him to meet the accused in a park that evening. The note included a statement that said, "we can have some good fun if you will." He asked the boy to stay with him for a few minutes but the boy refused and promised to return. The boy and his father went to the park that night but the accused did not appear. The next morning the boy received a letter expressing disappointment that he had not kept the appointment and asking him to meet the accused the following night. The unsigned letter also said, "keep this to yourself until after you have seen me." The letter was handed over to the police but the boy kept the appointment. The accused, after asking the boy if he had received the letter, said to him, "Come along the road for a walk." As they walked away, the police arrested Barker.

In *Cline* (Illustration 32(i)) the accused stopped a boy on a street in Hamilton, Ontario, and asked him to carry a suitcase (which he did not have with him at the time). The boy refused and ran away. Cline chased him for some time and finally caught him. He grabbed the boy by the sleeve and told the boy that he did not have to carry the suitcase if he did not want to but, in the boy's words, "he told me not to tell anybody and said they would be after him if I told anybody and he gave me some money." Two weeks later Cline again met the boy and asked him if he wanted to earn a couple of dollars by carrying his suitcase. Again, he had no suitcase with him. The boy refused and the accused went on his way.

Should either of these men be convicted of attempted indecent assault? Both were convicted. Were the facts in the two cases similar and of similar weight? Should the facts in either case be considered sufficiently proximate or unequivocal? The public considers the crime of pedophilia dangerous and abhorrent and wants to prevent its occurrence and protect its children at the earliest opportunity. Therefore, in terms of penal policy, the courts tend to interpret the attempt law loosely.

In *Cline* there was serious question whether the accused could be convicted on the unequivocality test. Laidlaw J.A. expressed his belief that no test was satisfactory in all cases. He added, "each case must be determined on its own facts having due regard to the nature of the offence and the particular acts in question." This test seems to be the one applied in all cases where social protection is considered more important than the principle of legality or strict proof of the elements of a crime, *mens rea* and *actus reus*.

There was a further complication in *Cline*. The court applied the evidentiary rule of "similar facts." This rule provides that if the accused's present acts follow a pattern or show a repeated *modus operandi* (the accused's criminal trademark), then his similar acts on previous occasions can be proved in evidence to establish his guilt on this occasion. Cline was known to have accosted boys previously and to have needed his suitcase carried. The court held that this was relevant and admissible evidence.

Laidlaw J. laid out the rules for convicting Cline in these terms:

> After considering the nature of a criminal attempt and principles as they were developed and established in the common law, together with the cases to which I have referred, and others I state these propositions in my own words to guide me in the instant case: (1) There must be *mens rea* and also *actus reus* to constitute a criminal attempt, but the criminality of misconduct lies mainly in the intention of the accused. (2) Evidence of similar acts done by the accused before the offence with which he is charged, and also afterwards if such acts are too remote in time, is admissible to establish a pattern of conduct from which the Court may properly find *mens rea*. (3) Such evidence may be advanced in the case for the prosecution without waiting for the defence to raise a specific issue. (4) If it is not essential that the *actus reus* be a crime or a tort or even a moral wrong or social mischief. (5) The *actus reus* must be more than mere preparation to commit a crime. But, (6) when the preparation to commit a crime is in fact fully complete and ended, the next step done by the accused for the purpose and with the intention of committing a specific crime constitutes an *actus reus* sufficient in law to establish a criminal attempt to commit that crime.

Laidlaw J.A. would have had difficulty in convicting Cline at all without the "similar facts," although this may not be obvious from the imputations that the judge made in the following statement:

> If the boy had been successfully lured to a destination chosen by the appellant, can there by any reasonable doubt that the crime of indecent assault would have been committed by the accused? If the conduct of the accused did not amount to an attempt to commit that crime, then I know not what it was. The acts of the appellant from the first moment he approached Peter D were not preparation. They were not too remote to constitute an attempt to commit the offence of indecent assault, and I so decide as a matter of law pursuant to s.24(2) of the Criminal Code.

The judge in *Barker* could not use the "similar facts" rule because there was no such evidence.The court was nevertheless convinced of Barker's guilt. Salmond J. considered that the proximate test had been disapproved and that it was "not necessary that the accused should have done his best or taken the last or proximate step toward the completed offence." His next finding is not very useful. The only watertight rule he could find was that "to constitute a criminal attempt the first step along the way of criminal intent is not necessarily sufficient and the final step is not necessarily required." Salmond J. held that the true nature of attempt could only be ascertained by looking at the purpose of the law, although he does not describe this purpose. He then formulated a rule that has become well known as the unequivocality rule:

> An act done with intent to commit a crime is not a criminal attempt unless it is

> of such a nature as to be in itself sufficient evidence of the criminal intent with which it is done. A criminal attempt is an act which shows criminal intent of the face of it. The case must be one in which *res ipsa loquitur.*

On the other hand, an act is not a criminal attempt that is innocent on its face and an accused cannot be convicted by imputed evidence. The criminality, he said, must be "made manifest by the very nature and circumstances of some act done in pursuance of that intent." The acts, he said, must proclaim their guilty purpose. On this basis (without the similar facts evidence), it is difficult to see how Barker or Cline could be convicted. Salmond J. considered that some alleged crimes of attempt cannot be proved because of this innocent quality and it is up to the judge to tell the jury as a matter of law that it is mere preparation. Yet the jury may, in other circumstances, have a right to take account of the words used by the accused which may be "expressive of his criminal purpose" and "may be themselves the means by which he endeavours to fulfil that purpose." In convicting Barker, the judge decided that:

> Such statements are part of the means by which the offence is sought to be accomplished. They are designed to obtain the boy's consent, or to induce him so to act as to afford the accused an opportunity of committing the offence, and they are therefore acts done with intent to commit it. For this reason an open and express invitation or solicitation of another person to submit to an act of sodomy, unlawful carnal connection, or indecent assault is in itself sufficient in point of law to constitute an attempt.

The judge expects us to believe that the statements made by Barker to the boy are incapable of innocent interpretation. This is expecting too much and, on that basis, Rizzo and his confederates should have been convicted.

Barker and *Cline* cases resulted in convictions based on suspicion in the minds of the police and a desire to stop trouble before it started—and not much else. Certainly these convictions bankrupt any theories of attempt and return us to Jerome Hall's suggestion that the crime is rationalized by the law on a case-by-case basis with a view to the type of acts we want to discourage or punish. The hopelessness of finding a universal rule to describe attempt is made obvious by the pedophile cases. The student of the law of attempt will be further confounded when he discovers that the accused in Illustration 32(h) was acquitted of attempted false pretences because he had not filed an insurance claim form which would be the last proximate act. In many attempt cases, it is usually found that the prosecution could have found another offence for which a conviction could be attained. In *Robinson* (Illustration 32(h)), a Canadian court could have convicted him of public mischief under s. 128(c) of the Code for "reporting that an offence has been committed when it has not been committed."

The most we can hope for is more exact legislation. Perhaps the rule of the Model Penal Code on "substantial step" is an improvement (despite a generous sprinkling of negatives):

Conduct shall not be held to constitute a substantial step under subsection (1)(c) of this Section unless it is strongly corroborative of the actor's criminal purpose. Without negativing the sufficiency of other conduct, the following, if strongly corroborative of the actor's criminal purpose shall not be held insufficient as a matter of law:

(a) lying in wait, searching for or following the contemplated victim of the crime;
(b) enticing or seeking to entice the contemplated victim of the crime to go to the place contemplated for its commission;
(c) reconnoitering the place contemplated for the commission of the crime.
(d) unlawful entry of a structure, vehicle or enclosure in which it is contemplated that the crime will be committed;
(e) possession of materials to be employed in the commission of the crime, which are specially designed for such unlawful use or which can serve no lawful purpose of the actor under the circumstances.
(f) possession, collection or fabrication of materials to be employed in the commission of the crime, at or near the place contemplated for its commission, where such possession, collection or fabrication serves no lawful purpose of the actor under the circumstances.
(g) soliciting an innocent agent to engage in conduct constituting an element of the crime.

The question of impossibility in attempt appears to be decided by s. 24(1) which provides that a person is guilty of attempt "whether or not it was possible under the circumstances to commit the offence." This is not a total solution because it cannot include legal impossibility (that is, attempting to commit an act that, in fact, is not a crime; see Illustrations 32(d) and (e)). To convict a person for attempting an act that is not proscribed by the law offends the principle of legality: the accused can only be convicted of acts that have been defined, and been defined previously, by the law.

Factual impossibility is shown in Illustrations 32(a) to (c). Often it is difficult to distinguish factual from legal impossibility (as can be seen by Illustration 32(e)). Perhaps the drafters of the Canadian Criminal Code were trying to abolish the distinction between the two kinds of impossibility but this would be contrary to the common law. Is the Model Penal Code trying to put an end to all this speculation by providing that it is an attempt "if, acting with the kind of culpability otherwise required for commission of the crime, he purposely engages in conduct that would constitute the crime if the attendant circumstances were as he believes them to be"?

Despite the argument above about legal impossibility being contrary to the principle of legality, the distinction does not seem to make much sense. Let's image that D thinks that he is firing a gun at V with the intention of killing V. In the first case, D is unsuccessful because his victim is outside the range of his gun. In the second case, D is unsuccessful because V is already dead. The conventional law would convict in the first and acquit in the second. Or take another set of examples. D tries to steal from the pocket (or cash register) of V but it is empty. In the second case, D tries to steal an umbrella thinking it belongs to V but in fact it is D's own. The verdicts would be guilt in the first and acquittal in the second. If the rationale of the law of attempt is that society is interested in crime prevention, then it is very difficult to see that D is only potentially physically dangerous or a menace to other person's property in the first instances. Yet this appears to be the law. The accused in the empty pocket cases have been convicted in England (*Ring*) and in Canada (*Scott*). The situation has now changed with the English case of *Haughton* v. *Smith* (Illustration 32(j)). The result seems to be similar to the "on-the-job" test mentioned earlier. The House of Lords has left legal impossibility intact but added many of the factual impossibility cases to it, so that the empty pocket, empty bed and empty womb cases (found in Illustrations 32(a) (b) and (c)) would result in acquittals. In other words, the accused will be guilty if the impossibility relates only to the means used but he will not be guilty if the result was impossible. Is this the same rule as the Model Penal Code? No, because the M.P.C. is saying that the situation should be treated as seen through the eyes of the accused. Therefore, if D thinks that V, the corpse, is alive or that the umbrella belongs to V, then D should be convicted of attempt.

The M.P.C. suggestion is similar to the law relating to mistake (which we will examine later). The law of mistake of fact takes the view that the trier of fact must assess the facts as the accused perceived them—subject, perhaps, to the mistake of fact being an honest one. In the present law of attempt, a mistake of fact about an empty pocket that the accused thought contained something does not provide him with a defence.

General principles of criminal law, as expressed in statutory form in s. 19 of the Code, state that ignorance of the law is no excuse. A clear exception is the crime of theft (s. 283 of the Code) which provides a defence if the accused believed he had a "colour of right" to the article allegedly stolen. "Colour of right" is legal shorthand for the accused's belief in a property right in the article. In attempt, however, most of the cases decide that the accused is not guilty of attempted crime if what he was trying to do was not actually illegal.

Ignorance of law under s. 19 has been somewhat eroded, particularly in cases where the error cannot clearly be attributed to ignorance of law or where the error is partly a misapprehension of law and partly a mistake of fact. Similarly, in some cases of attempt such as Illustration 32(b) (v), could it be said that clear factual or legal impossibility exists?

In *Haughton* v. *Smith*, the House of Lords decided that the accused could not be convicted of attempt—not on grounds of remoteness, but because the attempt never could have succeeded as the beef was no longer stolen property but was in the lawful custody of the police. Lord Reid said:

> The crime is impossible in the circumstances, so no acts could be proximate to it. . . . If the facts had been as he believed they were the man would have committed a crime. He intended to commit it. But he took no steps towards the commission of a crime because there was no crime to commit.

There are statements, which are *obiter dicta*, that go even further. These judicial remarks are not authority for future cases but they are strong indications that the English law of attempt will be substantially different from Canadian law. The House of Lords disapproved of the empty pocket case of *Ring*. Lord Reid said that "one cannot just steal, one must steal something," and added:

> A man lies dead. His enemy comes along and thinks he is asleep, so he stabs the corpse. The theory inevitably requires us to hold that the enemy has attempted to murder the dead man. The law may sometimes be an ass but it cannot be so asinine as that.

Lord Reid, along with Glanville Williams, thinks that a conviction in these circumstances would be contrary to the principle of legality because it would convict an accused for mere *mens rea*. Williams would argue that the law was trying to convict a person for an act that was not within the definition decided upon by the legislature.

Another perceptive commentator on the criminal law, Peter Brett, believed that most cases of impossibility should result in conviction because the accused:

> . . . stands in need of punishment or correction or treatment . . . because he has shown that, although he knows that legally he ought not to be doing this thing (or rather, believes this to be the case), he is prepared to defy the law in order to pursue his selfish ends. He thus shows himself to be a dangerous man, prepared to break the law when it suits him.

To add to the confusion, we could ask Brett "What law?"

Inchoate Crime II: Conspiracy, The Crime of the 1960s

Everyone must have heard of the trials of the Boston Five, the Chicago Eight (or Seven without Bobby Seale), the Milwaukee Twelve, the Oakland Seven and, perhaps, the Montreal Twenty-Nine. Headlines from these cases filled the newspapers during the 1960s. It is no coincidence that they all concerned anti-Vietnam war protests, draft resistance or student unrest—the controversial issues of the decade. All were defendants in the United States with the exception of the last group who were students of Sir George Williams University and were tried for conspiring to destroy equipment in the university's computer centre.

All these trials had a political flavour. The crime of conspiracy has always been used as a political weapon and justifiably has been called by some of its critics, "the little darling of the prosecutor's nursery." The crime originated with the Court of Star Chamber, a tribunal that sometimes persecuted religious and political dissenters. In more recent times the crime has been used in an effort to control trade unions or combinations of workers.

Conspiracy, along with attempt, is one of the inchoate or incomplete crimes. The acts required to be proved are minimal. The crime is primarily cerebral and only some inkling of these thoughts has to be translated into overt acts. The essence of the crime is an agreement between two or more persons. This agreement need not be expressed in words; it can be expressed by gesture or implied agreement. The cases show that it is not necessary for the parties to a conspiracy to have met so long as their agreement is implied from their conduct. Since the essence is agreement, the crime requires more than one party. If one of two conspirators is acquitted, the other cannot be convicted. Because the law respects the confidence of a married relationship and views husband and wife as a unit, spouses cannot be convicted of conspiracy unless a third party is also involved. (Illustration 33(a) is based on the Canadian case of *Kowbel.*)

In *Shannon* (1976) the English House of Lords discarded an old rule about conspiracy. S and T were charged with conspiring to handle stolen goods. S, on legal advice, pleaded guilty and was sentenced to four years' imprisonment. T pleaded not guilty to two charges. He was acquitted on a charge of handling stolen goods and a verdict of not guilty was returned on the conspiracy charge when the Crown offered no evidence. S claimed that his conviction for conspiracy should be quashed because his co-conspirator had been found not guilty. The Court of Appeal, following precedent, agreed but the House of Lords restored the conviction. (D would therefore be guilty in all instances in Illustration 33(b).) The esoteric legal argument is well stated by one of the judges of the House of Lords (although some readers may have some difficulty in following or believing the serpentine qualities of the legal mind):

> A general rule of law developed that the acquittal of B on a charge of conspiracy with A involved automatically that A could not be convicted of conspiracy with B, and if so convicted, his conviction would be quashed. The rule was applied even though A's conviction was based on a plea of guilty. But if B were dead, or for any other reason could not be or had not been brought to trial, his presumption of innocence did not serve to exculpate A; for there was then no inconsistency on the face of the record, and the court would not speculate that one might arise.
>
> A comparable rule was applied to the offence of riot, and cross-analogies between riot and conspiracy were drawn in this regard. It takes at least three persons to constitute a riot. If, therefore, A, B and C were charged with rioting together, the acquittal of B or C precluded the conviction of A. . . .
>
> The foundations of this legal superstructure contained, however, a flaw. The law in action is not concerned with absolute truth, but with proof before a fallible human tribunal to a requisite standard of probability in accordance with formal rules of evidence (in particular, rules relating to admissibility of evidence). No doubt, in the realm of the absolute, A could not conspire with B without B also conspiring with A. But it by no means follows that it cannot be proved forensically that A conspired with B (necessarily involving that it is also proved, as against A, that B conspired with him) notwithstanding a total failure of forensic proof, as against B, that B conspired with A (necessarily involving a failure of proof, as against B, that A conspired with him).
>
> Then, adultery is an unlawful meeting of bodies as conspiracy is an unlawful

> meeting of minds. In the realm of the absolute A cannot commit adultery with B without B also committing adultery with A. But it may well be proved forensically that A committed adultery with B (necessarily involving that it is also proved, as against A, that B committed adultery with her), notwithstanding a total failure of forensic proof, as against B, that B committed adultery with A (necessarily involving a failure of proof, as against B, that A committed adultery with him).

In an analogous problem we might ask, Can a corporation be convicted of conspiring with one man who is sole stockholder, chairman of directors and general manager? The case of *O'Donnell* (Illustration 28(c)) seems to say no. This appears to be a little inconsistent. The whole idea of a corporation is that an entrepreneur can create a separate corporate personality—the limited liability company—so that fiscal responsibility is limited to the shareholder's interest in the corporation. Of course, this is a legal fiction but the law recognizes, for some purposes, that the company is quite separate from its officers and shareholders. Should it make a difference if the shares of the company are held by ten thousand investors or one? Or, similarly, should it matter that the company has twenty officers—president, chairman, secretary, treasurer, etc.—or one person who fulfils all these functions and has created the legal fiction to minimize taxes or liability? In *O'Donnell,* the court "pierced the corporate veil" and decided that A.B. Cox and A.B.C. Ltd. were one entity. Perhaps they would not do the same for a larger company with many officers.

Further evidence of the peculiar qualities of the crime of conspiracy can be seen in *R.* v. *Meyrick and Ribuff* (Illustration 33(c)) where the defendants who ran separate night clubs were charged with conspiring to bribe a police officer who should have laid charges against them for breaching liquor licensing laws. The court held that the conspiracy could be viewed as a wheel with the bribed police officer as the hub. Although the conspirators had not met, they had a common goal of bribing a police officer and, therefore, could be convicted of conspiracy.

A chain theory applied in the American case of *Bruno,* where several defendants were charged with conspiring to traffic in narcotics (Illustration 33(d)). The defendants lived in various parts of the United States and allegedly participated, at various levels (wholesaler, intermediate wholesaler, retailer and retailer's salesman), in the drug traffic. The only proved connections among them were a few names or links in a chain of distribution. The evidence concerning the operation was incomplete but the investigators were able to convince the court that the parties had conspired on proof of the isolated links in the chain. The parties had not met and there was no proof from the prosecution that the parties had communicated. The only evidence consisted of the drug transactions, the geographic clues from the transactions and the implication that all the parties must have known they were parts of a larger organization. The court decided that the prosecution did not have to prove all the links in the chain, so long as the evident links gave an impression of a chain of conspiracy. Canadian courts have made similar statements: "On a conspiracy charge the question is not whether there has been participation in acts but in a common design. The acts are links in a chain of collateral circumstances from which the common design may be inferred." Another court made a further explanation of the links saying that they might have "possibly little or no value taken by themselves, but the bearing which one has upon the other must be interpreted; and their cumulative effect, properly estimated in the light of all surrounding circumstances, may raise a presumption of concerted purpose entitling the jury to find the existence of the unlawful agreement." Recent court decisions, such as *R.* v. *Smith and Lang* have shown that the prosecution are finding it more difficult to obtain convictions because the courts are requiring something more than mere surmise. The fact-finders do not feel entitled to make quantum leaps and are insisting on conspiracy being proved on sound evidentiary principles, although the crime is still a vague one.

The following judicial pronouncement gives some idea of the vague nature of this offence and the difficulty of providing proof according to due process of law. Jackson J. of the Supreme Court said in *Krulewitch* v. *U.S.*:

> When the trial starts, the accused feels the full impact of the conspiracy strategy. Strictly, the prosecution should first establish *prima facie* the conspiracy and identify the conspirators, after which evidence of acts and declarations of each in the course of its execution are admissible against all. But the order of proof of so sprawling a charge is difficult for a judge to control. As a practical matter, the accused is often confronted with a hodgepodge of acts and statements by others which he may never have authorized or intended or even known about, but which help to persuade the jury of the existence of the conspiracy itself. In other words, a conspiracy often is proved by evidence that is admissible only upon assumption that the conspiracy existed. . . .
>
> A co-defendant in a conspiracy trial occupies an uneasy seat. There generally will be evidence of wrongdoing by somebody. It is difficult for the individual to make his own case stand on its own merits in the minds of jurors who are ready to believe that birds of a feather are flocked together. If he is silent, he is taken to admit it and if, as often happens, co-defendants can be prodded into accusing or contradicting each other, they convict each other. There are many practical difficulties in defending against a charge of conspiracy which I will not enumerate.

Conspiracy is based on the common law and this has been codified in the Canadian Criminal Code, s. 423(2). The words of the subsection can mean almost anything. The courts have never been able to decide what is meant by "unlawful purpose" or "a lawful purpose by unlawful means"; it seems it would mean more than "unlawfulness" by tort or contract law, although the trade union conspiracies were of that type. (This is now codified and narrowed in ss. 424 and 425 of the Code and analogous sections are found in the Combines Investigation Act.) Certainly "unlawfulness" is wider than some act contrary to the criminal law or the quasi-criminal law found in other federal or provincial statutes, but its limits are rather fuzzy. One doubts if Illustration 33(f) would be a common law conspiracy. Parking in prohibited areas is "unlawful" but a conviction would be stretching the law. One of the more extreme instances is the 1975 case of *Talon*. The defendant company had demolished houses belonging to it without obtaining a permit as required by Montreal by-laws. While the company was contesting the validity of the by-law, the company along with its officers were charged with conspiring to effect an unlawful purpose (contrary to s. 423(2)) by agreeing to demolish a building without a permit. Talon contended that the possible breach of a by-law was not sufficient basis for "unlawful purpose" in s. 423(2). The judge agreed that the definition of "unlawful purpose" was rather vague:

> It must be allowed that not all agreements to infringe provincial statutes or municipal by-laws can be serious enough to justify indictment for criminal conspiracy. The violation of some statutes may involve very minor infractions, and many municipal by-laws are purely regulatory in nature . . . one must look at [the by-law's] nature and purpose and the interest it seeks to protect . . . a general test is . . . that where the violations could cause serious harm or injury to the public or threaten public safety or an important public interest, such violations have been held to be unlawful purposes and the agreements to commit them have been held to be criminal conspiracies.

Demolition of a building might have caused injury or danger to the public and this "unlawful purpose" passed the judge's test. Just about anything can be brought within the crime of common law conspiracy. It is certainly not necessary to have committed the "unlawful act" or pursued "the lawful purpose by unlawful means." A mere "agreement" to do so can be sufficient. In the American political conspiracy cases of the 1960s, often the parties had not met and had done a few separate and isolated acts trying to stop the Vietnam war, to stop the draft or to harass their political opponents at the Democratic Convention of 1968 in Chicago. They had simply made separate statements that had a common purpose. Some of the conspirators had to be introduced to each other, although they were jointly charged with a crime carrying heavy jail terms. The facts in Illustration 33(e) are similar. Common sense prevailed in most of these cases and convictions were registered but reversed on appeal. The crime of conspiracy has nevertheless been used as a form of harassment.

The Canadian Criminal Code has another very tenuous conspiracy offence—the crime of seditious conspiracy found in s. 60(3). Sedition of itself is a vague crime and yet members of the FLQ and other citizens of Quebec were charged with the offence of agreeing to commit sedition.

We have seen that conspiracy is not only a political weapon but also a moral one. The defendant in *Shaw* v. *D.P.P.* was convicted of conspiring to corrupt public morals. The House of Lords took upon itself the role of moral custodian and convinced itself that this version of conspiracy had always been the law of England with precedents dating back to the seventeenth century. On facts quite similar to *Shaw* v. *D.P.P.*, a Canadian court (in *R.* v. *Celebrity Enterprises Ltd.*) has not been so accommodating but of course the Code does not recognize common law crimes but one had assumed that conspiracy in s. 423 would be given a very broad interpretation, but the court in that case said that "unlawful" meant something for which the accused would be convicted. Illustration 33(f) is included for purposes of *reductio ad absurdum*; if unlawful means anything contrary to law, Colson could be convicted of conspiracy.

Conspiracy is a powerful weapon. Much greater punishments can be imposed for mere agreement than for some complete crimes. The criminal law has also allowed an accused to be charged with both the conspiracy and the consummated crime, although convictions on both charges may no longer be possible as the result of the Supreme Court of Canada decision in *Kienapple*. This case decided that an accused cannot be tried twice on the same set of facts. By corollary, an accused should not be convicted twice on the same facts. What is meant by the same facts is not as clear as it might seem. The rationale of conspiracy is one of preventive criminal law—that it is better to punish antisocial actions before they do more harm because this will be beneficial to society at large. This principle, suspect in the law of attempt, has even less validity when applied to conspiracy. Too frequently the courts have virtually created offences retroactively, thus offending the basic principles of the rule of law. If conspiracy is to continue to be part of the law, it should be defined much more precisely so that it no longer can be used as a blatant political weapon.

Conspiracy has often been justified on the basis that there is social danger in numbers. One English judge said, "a combination may make oppressive or dangerous that which if it proceeded from a single person would be otherwise, and the very fact of the combination may show that the object is simply to do harm, and not exercise one's own just rights."

The idea of a combination being more dangerous than a single person's acts has its origin in the State's apprehension about workers combining to defy an employer, to break up machinery or to close a factory. The law of conspiracy should not be used to convict those who cannot be found guilty on the evidence of the acts committed by any one of the conspirators.

The other criticism is the vagueness of the concept. This is well expressed by Francis Sayre:

> A doctrine so vague in its outlines and uncertain in its fundamental nature as criminal conspiracy lends no strength or glory to the law; it is a veritable quicksand of shifting opinion and ill-considered thought.

The 1881 case of *Parnell* also makes an important statement:

> The vagueness of these propositions leaves so broad a discretion in the hands of

> the judge that it is hardly too much to say that plausible reasons may be found for declaring it to be a crime to combine to do almost anything which the judges regard as morally wrong, or politically or socially dangerous.

The House of Lords has had a further opportunity to consider the crime of conspiring to corrupt public morals to which they gave recognition in *Shaw* v. *D.P.P.* We have already discussed the case of *Knuller* but several further comments on conspiracy are worth noting. Lord Reid would have allowed the appeal on the second charge. He did not interpret the liberalized homosexual laws as saying that Parliament intended to decree that indulgence in private adult consensual homosexual acts was not corrupting, but simply that the law would not interfere in such practices. "But," he said, "no licence is given to others to encourage the practice." He added, in reference to *Shaw* v. *D.P.P.*:

> I dissented in *Shaw's* case. On reconsideration I still think that the decision was wrong and I see no reason to alter anything which I said in my speech. But it does not follow that I should now support a motion to reconsider the decision. I have said more than once in recent cases that our change of practice in no longer regarding previous decisions of this House as absolutely binding does not mean that whenever we think that a previous decision was wrong we should reverse it. In the general interest of certainty in the law we must be sure that there is some very good reason before we so act. We were informed that there had been at least thirty and probably many more convictions of this new crime in the ten years which have elapsed since *Shaw's* case was decided, and it does not appear that there has been manifest injustice or that any attempt has been made to widen the scope of the new crime. I do not regard our refusal to reconsider *Shaw's* case as in any way justifying any attempt to widen the scope of the decision and I would oppose any attempt to do so. But I think that however wrong or anomalous the decision may be it must stand and apply to cases reasonably analogous unless or until it is altered by Parliament.

Lord Diplock dissented and would have allowed appeals on both charges. He said:

> Every agreement to do any act which tends to corrupt public morals is a crime at common law. *Shaw's* act of publishing advertisements for prostitutes soliciting fornication tended to corrupt public morals. Therefore *Shaw's* agreement to do that act was a crime at common law.
>
> In English law it is for the judge alone to determine whether the major premise in such a syllogism is true. The truth of the minor premise is a question for the jury, if there is any material upon which a rational being could hold it to be true. I do not criticize the jury's verdict in the instant case upon the minor premise. I deny the conclusion only because I am convinced that the major premise is false.
>
> Civil liability is concerned with the relationship of one citizen to another; criminal liability is concerned with the relationship of a citizen to society organized as a state. Society is now able to express its collective view as to what conduct merits punishment by the state through a legislature now representa-

tive of all adult citizens. It is not, in my view, compatible with the development of English constitutional and criminal law over the past century that your Lordships should assume the role of "the most godly, honourable, wise, and learned persons of the land," and reassert a power to "straine the line of justice beyond the ordinary length and wonted measure, and thereby take exquisite avengement upon" those whose conduct you regard as particularly reprehensible, though Parliament has not found it necessary to proscribe it and no previous precedent for punishing it can be found.

My Lords, it may be rational to hold that there are some kinds of acts which, if done by a number of people acting in concert, have consequences sufficiently harmful to call for punishment by the state, but which, if done by one person acting on his own, have consequences that are not grave enough to demand penal sanctions. But it is the height of sophistry to say that the doing of the acts in concert which alone can have no harmful consequences is not what the law regards as meriting punishment, but that the prior agreement to do them is. This is to turn the common law doctrine of "overt act," which was the origin of the crime of conspiracy, upon its head. In most cases of conspiracy the prior agreement is itself only inferred from the acts which have been done in pursuance of it. They are a consequence of the conspiracy, not a step taken towards it; whereas a conspiracy, like an attempt, became a crime because it was a step taken towards the commission of a crime.

The Defences

At least on a theoretical level, the accused has a right to remain silent. The prosecution must present sufficient facts relating to the charge against the accused to persuade the trier of fact (whether it is a judge or a jury) that the accused should be convicted. If the prosecution evidence is ephemeral or unconvincing, the defence might invite the judge to decide there is "no case to answer" after the Crown has presented its evidence (and the defence has cross-examined the prosecution witnesses). This is an unusual procedure because prosecutors do not often waste their time bringing flimsy cases before the courts.

If the prosecution has a good case, it will be necessary for the accused to answer that case. Sometimes this will consist of a refutation of the prosecution case by means of cross-examination of the Crown witnesses, whose versions of the facts may be shaken or made susceptible to a reasonable doubt. Witnesses for the defence will also provide an alternative version of the facts that might lead to the acquittal of the accused. For instance, the cross-examination of Crown witnesses might successfully challenge the perceptions of those witnesses so that the identification of the accused at the scene of the crime is in doubt. These witnesses might also be shown to be in error as to the identification of the car seen leaving the scene of the crime.

A defence witness might provide the accused with a cast-iron alibi, or might give an explanation of the facts that leads the trier of fact to decide that the accused's acts were, in fact, innocent. The prosecution has the burden of proving guilt beyond a reasonable doubt. The accused is presumed innocent until found otherwise. If the trier of fact has a reasonable doubt about the guilt of the accused, then the accused is entitled to the benefit of the doubt and must be acquitted.

Many acquittals are decided on the facts of the case. We are not concerned with these types of cases. We are most interested in those cases where the accused gives evidence or the defence lawyer puts forward a factual and legal argument that negates *mens rea*. This is the function of the "defence" of mistake of fact which we will discuss presently. In addition, the law has developed a series of rules for circumstances where the accused clearly has carried out the physical act of the crime and was acting voluntarily, but where those acts are subject to certain excuses or justifications that will lead to acquittal. In addition, there are other circumstances, where the law, if it accepts the accused's explanation, will mitigate the grade of the offence (and punishment).

Mistake is not a true "defence" to a charge of crime. In most instances where a criminal charge is laid, the accused admits that he did the act and also admits that he consciously performed the act but claims that his behaviour was justified or should be excused. He says, "Yes I did kill the victim but I acted in self-defence and, therefore, should be acquitted." Or he admits that he did have sexual intercourse with the victim but it was not rape because he thought, in his drunken stupor, that she was consenting. Or the defence claims that the accused should not be convicted of an offence because she was legally insane at the time the alleged crime was committed.

The defences, which either provide full exoneration or partial mitigation, are value judgements that society makes. They decide that the accused lacked free will or that he should not be held criminally responsible. The granting of a defence sometimes recognizes in the accused's behaviour a competing value, such as self-defence or necessity, which society decides is worthy of recognition. The defence may be based on the idea that a person committing an allegedly criminal act in those particular circumstances is not deserving of punishment or should only be punished lightly. Or the law may be saying that a person performing such an act in those circumstances—for example, when suffering from mental disease—cannot be deterred and, therefore, punishment would be ineffectual or inhumane.

Some defences are very old. Self-defence, for instance, has been a legal defence for centuries and recognizes a natural response by human beings when attacked or when their home is invaded. Some aspects of the partial defence of provocation is similarly ancient. Other defences, such as necessity, duress and superior orders, are also of old vintage but are rarely applied.

Many defences were not established until the nineteenth century when major reforms in the criminal law were achieved. Defences were more likely to be raised when the accused was entitled to be represented by counsel or was finally allowed to give evidence in his own defence.

The reforms of Romilly and Bentham not only resulted in the reduction of harsh penalties but also encouraged the courts to be more humane in the assessment of guilt. Until the nineteenth century, for instance, intoxication was not considered a mitigation but an aggravation in determining the accused's responsibility. The same period also saw an amelioration in the law's attitude toward the mentally ill so that the legal definition of insanity has been broadened considerably.

Legal defences are not particularly logical and a sociologist or a behavioural scientist may not be impressed by the law's choice of excuses or the definitions of these excuses. We noticed, when discussing the case of *Powell* v. *Texas*, that the law was prepared to give a narrowly circumscribed definition of intoxication as a defence but was not prepared to recognize social pathology (for example, a poverty-stricken, deprived childhood) as an excuse for criminal behaviour.

The legal defence of insanity is certainly not in accord with the medical concept of psychosis. The law does not grant a defence on the basis that anyone who commits a crime must be "sick."

The defences that are created by the law are usually conservative because legal rules, by definition, are not *avant-garde* but, more often, are a generation behind social mores. For instance, the law gives a partial defence of intoxication when the condition of the accused was caused by alcohol but not when it resulted from the use of some other drug.

Mistake and Ignorance

Mistake is not a true defence in the sense that the law has invented an excuse for the peculiar circumstances in which the accused finds himself: that he intended to do the act and willed the behaviour but claims that he should be excused.

When an accused claims mistake he is saying that he had no *mens rea* because he was acting under a misapprehension about the surrounding circumstances. In legal shorthand, the accused, with a conventionl defence, is saying "*Yes,* I did it *but* I have an excuse," whereas with mistake of fact the accused is saying "*No,* because I was acting under a misapprehension. . . ."

As a general rule, a mistake of fact will lead to an acquittal while ignorance of law will not be an excuse (see s. 19 of the Code). The basic rule is that when the accused has made an honest mistake of fact on reasonable grounds, the law will treat the situation as if the mistaken facts were actually true.

Ignorance of Law

The rationale for disallowing ignorance of law as a defence is that everyone is presumed to know the law, and it would make for an intolerable situation if an accused person could evade criminal liability by showing (or at least proclaiming) that he did not know that the act allegedly committed was contrary to the law. If a person is found with a blood-stained dagger in his hand and, at his feet, the corpse of a person to whom he is known to owe a large gambling debt, he can hardly claim that he should not be convicted because he did not know murder was a criminal offence in that jurisdiction.

But is ignorance of law always to be treated in this way? What if a merchant seaman returns to his home port and is found in possession of a substance (such as a drug) that was perfectly legal when he left but, during his absence, has become a criminal offence with a minimum punishment of three months' imprisonment? Should he be able to raise a defence of ignorance of law? One of the fundamental tenets of a democratic criminal justice system (under the general rubric of the principle of legality) is that the criminal law should not be retroactive and the accused should have prior notice of the provisions of the criminal law if he is to be presumed to have knowledge of it. The citizen might think it would be unfair to convict our sailor when he had no way of knowing about the change in the law, particularly when there is a mandatory jail term attached to it. Some courts have acquitted accused persons in such circumstances. Would that average citizen be prepared to acquit if the punishment were a mere fine? Or would the citizen think it makes no difference because, in both instances, the principle of legality had been breached? This question was recently (1980) addressed by the Supreme Court of the Northwest Territories in *Catholique*. He had been convicted of unlawful possession of liquor under regulations that had never been published in the government *Gazette*. Consequently the judge treated the regulations as a nullity.

Let us imagine another situation: the accused is not a sailor who was physically incapable of finding out about changes in the law. Instead, he is a person of limited education who was charged under a regulation promulgated under an Act, but the regulation has never been published or is almost impossible to discover in the morass of rules, regulations, by-laws and delegated legislation which modern bureaucratic government spawns every year. This situation is similar to that of Illustration 23(a), based on the Nova Scotia case of *Maclean*. The judge, in acquitting the accused, differentiated between *ignorance* of law (as shown in the murder case mentioned above) and *mistake* of law as determined by the facts of the case before him. This is a relatively rare situation but the decision appears to be just.

The judge in *Maclean* made it clear that an acquittal on the basis of mistake of law would be limited to cases where the accused had made conscientious efforts to discover the law and had relied on the advice of an appropriate authority who should have known the state of the law. The case should also be one where the law was very inaccessible. The decision is probably limited to regulations and similar delegated legislation. In further explanation, Judge O'Hearn said:

> . . . s. 19 is not absolute and cannot be applied without reserve to every situation where the essential mistake is one of law. The first (exception) is the case where the conduct is not generally realized to be wrongdoing because people do not categorize it as immoral, or because knowledge of the applicable law is generally

> confined to a small and special circle to which the accused does not belong. To my mind, it might be objected to the latter category, that if an accused wishes to indulge in an activity that requires special knowledge including knowledge of the applicable law, he can fairly be held to be under an obligation to acquire that knowledge.

In the light of the last category mentioned by the judge, *R.* v. *Campbell and Mlynarchuk* is most interesting. The accused was a stripper charged, under s. 163, with taking part in an immoral performance. In her defence she relied upon a decision of a superior court that decided that dancing similar to her performance was lawful. The trial judge refused to accept this defence because in the meantime an appellate court had overruled the decision on which she relied. Ignorance of the law was no excuse. Even though she would have had to read the very latest law reports, the court convicted her because everyone is *presumed* to know the law. The cream of the joke is that the decision on which she relied has been appealed to the Supreme Court of Canada, and the state of the law which she had argued was upheld, and the Alberta Court of Appeal was reversed.

The Supreme Court of Canada has examined the question of ignorance of law—mistake of law on two recent occasions. Neither decision accepts *Maclean* but the decision is not yet totally abandoned. In *R.* v. *Prue and Baril*, the accuseds' driving licences had been suspended for breaches of a provincial statute but they claimed that they did not know the licences had been automatically suspended. They continued to drive (believing that they would receive official notice of suspension) and were charged for driving while under suspension. Laskin C.J. solved the problem by treating the accuseds' lack of knowledge of the suspension as a matter of fact rather than of law. Therefore they were labouring under a mistake of fact that could only result in conviction if *mens rea* were proved. This seems a wise course. Except for cases where the accused's ignorance of the law is blatant ("I did not know it was wrong to beat up my wife in this jurisdiction," etc., as in Illustration 23(c)), the elements of the misapprehension are often a mixture of law and fact. Even where there is a clear case of ignorance of law, the nation's highest court might decide one day that this is excusable if the law is very uncertain (as in the stripper case) or the law is not published or almost inaccessible (as in *Maclean*). In *Molis*, the accused was charged with trafficking in a restricted drug. When he started manufacturing the drug, it was not illegal to do so, but later, the drug in question was added to the list of restricted drugs in Schedule H of the Food and Drug Act by publication of that change in the *Canada Gazette*. Lamer J.'s decision is not very clear; he seems to deny the defence made available in *Maclean* but leaves open a slight possibility that a distinction could be made between ignorance of the law and ignorance (or mistake) as to its meaning, scope or application. He dismisses the appeal but not before adding that the offence was one of due diligence (as in *Sault Ste. Marie*) but "due diligence in relation to the fulfilment of a duty imposed by law and not in relation to the ascertainment of the existence of a prohibition or its interpretation." This not only shows Lamer J.'s talent for making contradictory and fuzzy statements but should lead us to prefer Laskin C.J.'s mixture of law and fact being treated as fact. When law was simple ("thou shalt not kill," etc.) then s. 19 might make sense but when the prohibition is hidden in a government publication, such as the *Gazette*, which is read by a very small percentage of the population, the granting of a defence for ignorance of legal *minutiae* seems a good idea. If we only want to find blameworthy those who acted voluntarily, intentionally or recklessly, then s. 19 needs revision. That section may have made sense when a majority of the population was illiterate but it is no longer useful in a complicated modern society. Lamer J. quoted the Statutory Instruments Act as an example of how Parliament has recognized the problems caused by inaccessible subordinate legislation:

> 11 (2) No regulation is invalid by reason only that it was not published in the *Canada Gazette*, but no person shall be convicted of an offence consisting of a contravention of any regulation that at the time of the illegal contravention was not published in the *Canada Gazette* in both official languages unless ...
>
> (b) it is proved that at the date of the alleged contravention reasonable steps had been taken to bring the purpose of the regulation to the notice of those persons likely to be affected by it.

This hardly seems sufficient. Section 19 is anomalous on two grounds. First, the policy of the criminal law should be to punish the guilty, not those who fall prey to the law through negligence or because they do not have post-graduate legal training. Secondly, the courts have forgotten that mistake is not a true defence but a mere absence of *mens rea*. On both scores, we are likely to see exceptions being made to the absolute rule which supposedly exists in s. 19. While we may not want to make exceptions for the person in Illustration 23(c) because the law cannot take into account every cultural or ethnic difference among recent immigrants, there are many instances where the law has been stretched (if not turned upside down) when the accused were Innuit who claimed they did not understand Canadian or European customs. Does it make any sense to convict persons, such as the stripper, because they are ignorant of the intricacies of the law? We put accused persons in a double bind because it has always been clear law that it is no defence to a criminal charge to say that a lawyer gave faulty legal advice. (This was recently confirmed in *Dunn* where the accused phoned his lawyer from a police station and, following the advice given, refused to take a breathalyzer test with which he was charged.) The same problem arises in the bigamy cases (Illustration 24). Only an expert could say whether D had made a mistake of law or a mistake of fact and yet some of them were convicted because everyone is presumed to know the law. The most sensible decision (which is *Thomas* described in Illustration 24(a)) found that the mistake was mixed law and fact, and therefore D could be acquitted on mistake of fact and absence of *mens rea.*

The rule of law (or the principle of legality) decrees that a person charged with a crime should have prior notice of any law that he has now allegedly broken. How do we reconcile that with the conviction of the bookseller *McAuslane* in Illustration 25(a)? The bookseller (in 25(a)) and the art gallery owner (in 25(c)) argued that they had no way of knowing whether they were in possession of obscene material. They were convicted but *Lee* (25(b)) was acquitted. Perhaps the only explanation is that all three were cases of mistake of fact and only D in 25(b) was not reckless but that is a little difficult to believe.

The law has always specifically recognized one mistake of law and that is found in s. 283 of the Code which defines theft as taking anything belonging to another "fraudulently and without *colour of right.*" The emphasized words are the important ones. We shall examine property offences later but the cases mentioned in Illustration 22, Daisy's case (Illustration 23(b)) and Dalton (23(d)) could result in acquittals if the court were of the opinion that the accused had a *bona fide* belief that he was entitled to take the property in question. The "colour of right" does not have to be a legally legitimate claim to the property but simply a conscientious belief that you have some right to the property.

A recent decision in England is of interest. Of course, it should have no influence on Canadian law but it is significant for two reasons. It purports to rely on the old abduction case of *Prince* which seems quite wrongheaded because the facts in *Austin* (1981) suggest a mistake of law. The case is another sign that the barrier between mistake of fact (which can provide a defence) and mistake of law (which usually can't) is obviously breaking down. *Austin* involved one of those international child kidnapping cases with former spouses fighting over the custody of a child of their marriage. The wife had taken the child out of the United States on the stated purpose of attending a wedding in England. She never returned. The husband obtained a judicial order for custody in a court in the United States. He then hired Austin and his three confederates to nab the child and the husband took her to his home in the United States. Austin and the others were charged with child stealing. That offence contained the word "unlawfully," and the English court, following *Prince,* said that the husband, if he had been charged, would have been acquitted since he had a "lawful excuse" because he had a common law right to possession of the child and particularly when there was no court order affecting that right. Perhaps we should treat this case of child stealing as another example of "colour of right," although the court in *Austin* never mentioned it. Finally, *Austin* is remarkable because the "lawful excuse" was not available to the four defendants as agents of the husband.

Mistake of Fact

We have already examined the fundamental principles of mistake of fact when we discussed *mens rea*. The defence of mistake of fact is best illustrated by the important case of *Beaver* which is described in Illustration 7. The Supreme Court of Canada decided that if Beaver had an honest belief that the substance found in his possession was a harmless substance rather than heroin, as analysis proved, Beaver's belief that the substance was innocent was a good defence so long as it was an honest belief, and the honest quality of his belief was to be decided on a reasonable evidentiary basis.

The question of whether a mistake must be honest and/or reasonable has been an on-going debate. Some early cases such as *Tolson*, described in Illustration 24(d), suggested that the mistake had to be honest *and* reasonable. A recent decision of the English House of Lords, *Morgan*, described in Illustration 44(f), held that the mistake of an accused need only be honest; if the accused in a rape case honestly believed, even if on unreasonable grounds, that the victim was consenting to sexual intercourse, he could be acquitted (but the important word is "could").

This is a subjective test of mistake of fact. The rule is that the facts of a case will be taken as they were perceived by the accused; if the accused thought he was acting innocently, he will be acquitted. Not all courts take such a lenient view and often judge defendants on the basis of an objective test of honest *and* reasonable mistake.

The courts have also taken a less lenient view when the accused claimed mistake of fact but was doing something else illegal (or perhaps immoral). *Kundeus* (Illustration 8(b)) shows this. LSD was a prohibited drug under one part of the Food and Drugs Act, while mescaline was differently described in another part of the same Act. LSD attracted a much larger penalty. Kundeus claimed that his mistake meant that he should not be convicted because he did not mean to sell LSD. The Supreme Court of Canada did not agree and said that he intended to sell *a* drug and that was sufficient *mens rea*.

Ladue (described in Illustration 6) resulted in a conviction because the court was not impressed by the accused's excuse that he made a mistake in thinking that the woman was alive. The court said that the accused could not use that mistake as a defence because the mistaken circumstances would amount to a crime in itself; the accused would then, according to the court, be committing the crime of rape. This is wrong in law because a corpse is not a human being, male or female, and therefore it could not be rape. If Ladue were to be convicted of anything, it would be attempted rape because one can be convicted of attempting the factually impossible.

Sometimes the courts have gone farther and said that if the accused's explanation were merely immoral, then he would still be convicted. In *Prince*, the accused was charged with taking a female under the care and control of her father. He claimed that he thought she was over sixteen. In other words, he said he had made a mistake but the court replied that if this were the case, he was still guilty because his acts were *mala in se*—inherently wrong. Yet the court inexplicably stated that if his mistake had related to a misapprehension about the father's permission, then he might have been acquitted. Such reasoning reflects a moral stance that is rather difficult for us to grasp. The Canadian situation is found in s. 146 of the Code (and Illustration 21); that provision explicitly excludes a defence based on mistake as to age but presumably D would not be guilty if he had some other defence such as alibi or a misconception as to the father's consent.

Illustration 21(b) is based on *McLeod* in which the British Columbia Court of Appeal acquitted the accused of both charges. The court intimated that he could be acquitted of the more serious charge because he was mistaken as to the identity of the victim, who turned out to be a policeman. The court also said that McLeod might have been convicted of the lesser charge because he could be said to be doing something wrong and illegal in assaulting a stranger. He was, however, acquitted of both charges because the court said he had, in fact, no *mens rea* in relation to either charge. They decided he was not guilty of the lesser offence of common assault (of a stranger) because his behaviour might have been innocent since, in a public-spirited way, he was trying to stop the fight from spreading.

The courts have still not given a definitive answer to the scope of mistake of fact. There are three possibilities:

1. Must the accused have been completely innocent of all wrongdoing if the facts were as he mistakenly imagined them to be? Even this question is not completely unambiguous because by "innocent" we could mean devoid of any legal responsibility or lacking any moral fault. Even in *Beaver*, the accused admitted that he was planning to hoodwink or defraud the person who thought he was buying illicit drugs.
2. Should "innocent" have a narrower meaning, signifying that the accused is not guilty of the charge on the indictment or information? If the prosecution has made an error and charged the accused with possession of drug A rather than drug B, or charged the accused with possession of a drug under the Narcotic Control Act while the accused claims that he mistakenly and honestly believed he had possession of a drug prohibited or controlled by the less heinous Food and Drug Act, should we acquit the accused in either case and say that he is innocent *as charged*? The prosecution also made a mistake and should not succeed.
3. Finally, should we subscribe to a rule that if the charge relates to offence A, but the accused says that he thought he was committing the less serious offence B, we should convict him of the lesser offence?

The implication here is that it would be wrong to "trade up" to a more serious offence because the accused was not charged with that offence. In *Ladue*, the accused raised the question of the more serious offence in his defence to a lesser crime.

The cases do not give a clear answer. There are some statements in *McLeod* that would support the first position. The Supreme Court of Canada in *Kundeus* certainly does not support the second or the third position; indeed, the result in that case allows a conviction for a *more* serious offence, although the proper charge would have been attempted trafficking in mescaline for which a conviction could have been obtained, despite the factual impossibility on the evidence.

Necessity

Necessity in its purest form is not a common defence. Self-defence (as we shall see) is a special version of necessity and is more frequently found in criminal cases. The defence of necessity is based on the external forces of nature imposing themselves on the accused. In recent years we have had a few cases that could have evoked the defence of necessity if criminal charges had been laid. (No charges were laid because the necessitous circumstances were certainly obvious and the actors' harrowing experiences were no doubt considered sufficient suffering.) In both instances survivors of a plane crash had eaten the flesh of persons killed in the crash, which technically is an offence under s. 178 of the Code. One of these cases occurred in the Northwest Territories and the other in the Andes.

Cannibalism also occurred in Illustration 34(a) which is the case of *R.* v. *Dudley and Stephens*. The court refused a defence of necessity but convicted the accused only of the lesser homicide offence of manslaughter. They were released after spending six months in prison. The court applied a stringent test, suggesting that the evil avoided must be greater than the evil inflicted. The two defendants tried to justify their behaviour on the basis that they had families dependent on them while the ailing cabin boy was a young lad who might have soon died in any case. The court refused this explanation, commenting that the "sails of rescue" might have appeared on the horizon at any moment. Obviously, rescue did eventuate, but no expert testimony was given by a nutritionist to show that the eating of the cabin boy's flesh was the reason for the survival of the three persons at the expense of one. Similarly the court did not seek any guidance from experts in ethics or maritime lore. The court saw the need to prescribe a standard of behaviour that it admitted might be impossibly high, but mitigated the punishment.

Illustration 34(b) is based on *U.S.* v. *Holmes*.The accused were convicted because the court did not approve of the selection of victims. Unnecessary crew should have been sacrificed before paying passengers, or the drawing of lots would have been a more equitable method of choosing those who were to be saved. The English court in *R.* v. *Dudley and Stephens* did not approve of this method, although it did not offer any better suggestions.

We have all heard of a mountaineering party that has had a mishap and a climber dangling on a rope who is sacrificed to ensure the safety of the others. Can we differentiate such a case because the person wielding the knife cuts the rope and does not directly kill his climbing companion? Such an explanation is not particularly convincing. Similar situations arise when a submarine is trapped on the ocean floor and only some of the occupants can be saved because of time and equipment exigencies. In an analogous situation, hospitals are obliged to establish committees to decide which patients should have the use of scarce equipment (such as dialysis machines) or which person should receive organs for transplant. In wars and on other occasions when there are great numbers wounded or injured, the system of *triage* operates—a decision must be made as to the allocation of scarce resources and personnel so that they are devoted to those who are near death, those who may die if they do not receive immediate attention and those who are quite sick but can survive without immediate attention. Illustration 30(b), the case of *Smith*, had some elements of *triage* in the decisions made by the doctors, although little consideration was given to the faulty use of *triage* in assessing the question of causation. Illustration 34(c) is not a real case but a hypothetical situation composed by a legal philosopher Lon Fuller who wrote a series of fictional judgements with verdicts (of guilty and not guilty) based on the various legal, political and religious views of the judges.

Problems of necessity also arise in more mundane situations where there is no loss of life. A building is blown up or a section of forest is set afire to stop a fire spreading. A fireman or a policeman breaks a window or a door in an emergency situation. An automobile is used without the owner's permission because the situation is urgent. In all of these, the courts would grant a defence of necessity. The law has no difficulty with a defence of necessity that does not depend on the taking of human life. Then, on the other hand, the law was not prepared to acquit Jean Valjean in *Les Miserables* when he stole a loaf of bread to feed his starving child. Nowadays, they would say he should have made application to welfare.

Necessity has been raised in cases of abortion. The gray area between danger to life and danger to health was described in *Bourne*. The defence of necessity was denied in *Morgentaler*: any excuse was to be found in s. 251 of the Code and in the indications considered by a therapeutic abortion committee; the accused doctor could not have recourse to s. 45.

Duress, Coercion or Compulsion

These terms are interchangeable, although the Code uses the last in s. 17 which grants a defence but excludes its use in treason, murder, piracy, attempted murder, assisting in rape, forcible abduction, robbery, causing bodily harm or arson. This is broader than the common law, although most of the cases have concerned murder or treason and the defence has not been granted.

The compulsion imposed on the accused—threats of death or serious injury—is the same at common law and under the provisions of the Code. There must be no chance of escape, the threat must be immediate and the fear must be reasonable.

Other sections of the Code specify some other limitations. Section 18 denies that a wife is automatically acting under the compulsion of her husband simply because he is present. Under s. 150, when a female has committed incest because she acted under the duress of the other party, the court is "not required to impose any punishment upon her."

Duress is very similar to necessity except that the force imposed on the accused is by human agency rather than by Act of God (as an insurance policy might describe the forces of nature).

The best Canadian illustration of an accused raising the defence of duress is *Carker,* described in Illustration 35(c). The appeal court refused Carker's defence because it was held that he was not in immediate danger of death or serious injury, which is the prerequisite of the defence. Carker was locked in his cell at the time and no physical violence could have been immediately imposed. Therefore, he was not forced, in the eyes of the law, to do wilful damage to prison property. This seems a very objective test because, in the closed prison environment, the accused knew that he would surely be dealt with in due course.

Illustration 35(a) is not strictly a case of illustrating the defence, although the case, *Steane,* is often cited as such. The court acquitted the accused on a subjective, liberal interpretation of the legislation under which he was charged—that he did not make the broadcast with the *intent* to assist the enemy. In Illustration 35(b), the English case of *Bourne,* the wife was acquitted on the basis of duress while the husband was convicted.

Paquette, a recent decision of the Supreme Court of Canada, made an important rule about duress in relation to murder. The accused had driven the car while two other persons robbed a store. During the robbery, an innocent bystander was killed. Paquette claimed that, at first, he had refused to drive the robbers but one of them had threatened him with a gun and he was so afraid that he acceded to their wishes (Illustration 35(d)).

Section 17 (which describes the defence of duress or compulsion) speaks of a person who *commits* an offence under compulsion. The Supreme Court decided that this was inapplicable because Paquette did not actually commit the offence. The Crown argued that if an accused could not find a defence of duress under s. 17, the defence did not exist because that section exhaustively codified the law. The Court did not agree and decided that s. 7(3) of the Code provided the possibility of a further common law defence of duress if the person were merely a party to an offence under s. 21(2). For the Court, Martland J. said, "A person whose actions have been dictated by fear of death or of grievous bodily injury cannot be said to have formed a genuine common intention to carry out an unlawful purpose with the person who has threatened him with those consequences if he fails to cooperate." The accused was not present when the murder occurred and did not share in the proceeds of the robbery. The Court disapproved of one of its earlier decisions; in *Dunbar* where it had been decided that duress only referred to motive and not intention.

Duress and Superior Orders

The harm done by the accused as a result of the alleged coercion must usually not exceed the physical danger that the accused was facing. Duress is never a defence to murder. The courts have always taken the attitude that if D were placed in the position that C said he would kill D if D did not kill V, then D has no excuse for the murder of V. The defence of superior orders in warfare is different because the soldier is obliged to obey the lawful orders of a superior. This, of course, begs the question of what is a lawful order and what is permissible behaviour in wartime according to the Geneva Convention or some other international agreement. These problems arose at the Nuremberg trials, the Eichmann trial, in *Breaker Morant* and in the cases of Lieutenant Calley and Captain Medina. (See Illustration 36.)

Robert Jackson was chief U.S. prosecutor at the Nuremberg trials before he became a justice of the U.S. Supreme Court. He said at the time of those trials:

> There is doubtless a sphere in which the defence of obedience to superior orders should prevail. If a conscripted or enlisted soldier is put on a firing squad he should not be held responsible for the validity of the sentence he carries out. But the case may be greatly altered when one has discretion because of rank or the latitude of his orders. And of course, the defence of superior orders cannot apply in the case of voluntary participation in a criminal or conspiratorial organization, such as the Gestapo or the S.S. An accused should be allowed to show the facts about superior orders. The Tribunal can then be allowed to determine whether they constitute a defence or merely extenuating circumstances, or perhaps carry no weight at all. . . .
>
> But none of these men before you acted in minor parts. Each of them was entrusted with broad discretion and exercised great power. Their responsibility is correspondingly great and may not be shifted to that fictional being, the state

The debate about the legality of the Nuremberg trials will never cease. Was the law applied retroactively and therefore in breach of the rule of law or were the allies appealing to a higher law? Marshall makes it quite clear where he says:

> The assumption in both the Nuremberg and Eichmann trials was that Nazi officials had free will to choose between obedience to the Party Line and punishment by the Nazi police. *Actually free will, choice and intent were not necessary elements to the judgements reached in those cases.* The *intent* of the defendants was irrelevant. This does not mean that even defendants in the lower echelons, not soldiers on a firing squad but officers such as Eichmann, and the concentration camp personnel, should not have been found guilty of murder, torture, confiscation and destruction of property. They should have been incarcerated or, if you will, executed for acts which even without intent or choice marked them as dangerous people who could not be permitted to remain at large. The influence of the Nazi value system and the distortions that their cultural norms had performed on them make them unfit to roam freely among other men, although some on the lower levels of the Nazi hierarchy might redeem themselves. (Emphasis in original)

Self-Defence

This defence is a special application of the defence of necessity, although the forces of necessity are usually human agencies. This is one of the oldest defences. Many of the early cases are of little relevance today. Many of the common law rules had been established when the usual weapons were swords rather than firearms which can kill from a distance. Therefore, many of these cases seem more appropriate to tales of the Count of Monte Cristo when they talk of "going to the wall" and retreating as far as practicable. If someone is threatening you with an automatic weapon, retreating to the wall or up the staircase is not likely to stop a bullet which can travel great distance, while in sword-fights, one was safe so long as outside the range of the blade. The retreat rule is important in a symbolic sense; one should not retaliate with deadly force until it is absolutely necessary. These rules are a little academic because often the only witness to the killing (who is still able to give evidence) will be the killer.

Strictly speaking, the phrase "self-defence" is a little narrow because it only applies to defence of one's self. Approximately the same rules apply to apprehension of a dangerous criminal, suppression of a deadly fight and defence of one's loved ones or dwelling house.

Some of the rules will be examined more fully when the law of arrest is discussed but, at this stage, we should note that s. 25 provides that if a person is required or authorized to make an arrest, to take someone into custody or to prevent the commission of an offence, he is justified in using "as much force as is necessary." Also note that s. 25(3) states that such a person is not justified to use force that is intended or likely to cause death or grievous bodily harm unless he reasonably believes that it is necessary to preserve himself from death or grievous bodily harm. Section 25(4) refers specifically to arrest and allows a peace officer to use necessary force to prevent escape. Section 26 provides criminal responsibility if excessive force is used. Section 32 describes further justification for the use of force; this section is concerned with the suppression of riots and authorizes the use of force which is thought necessary, based on reasonable belief, and is "not excessive, having regard to the danger to be apprehended."

The Code has elaborate provisions describing self-defence as a justification. Section 37 justifies force to defend oneself against assault so long as the force used is not more than necessary and is not excessive in relation to the force repulsed. The trier of fact (judge or jury) is obliged to make value judgements and the verdict in Illustration 37(a) may depend less on the facts than on the demeanour of D as a witness and on evidence as to V's character and previous treatment of D. Section 38 makes similar provisions where a trespasser is attempting to take moveable property. Section 39 describes a more common occurrence. The person in possession of moveable property, who believes he has a right to possession, can use "no more force than is necessary" in defending that possessory right. This is important in cases where a bailiff seeks to repossess goods when there is a legitimate counter-claim to the goods.

Section 40 describes the justified behaviour of one in lawful possession of a dwelling house who can use reasonable force to prevent a forcible entry that is without lawful authority. Similarly, s. 41 allows a trespasser to be repelled with reasonable force if the trespasser is seeking forcible entry.

Where excessive self-defence has been recognized as a substantive doctrine, it would appear that the following conditions, at least, are necessary to give rise to that qualified defence:

(a) The accused must have been justified in using some force to defend himself against an attack, real or *reasonably apprehended.*
(b) The accused must have *honestly* believed that he was justified in using the force he did.
(c) The force used was excessive only because it exceeded what the accused could *reasonably* have considered necessary. (Emphasis in original)

Mr. Justice Arnup had no difficulty with (a) in *Reilly*. On (b), the judge found that the accused did not satisfy him as to honest belief. Arnup J.A. said, "... I find it hard to imagine a case where an accused can show his own honest belief ... where he did *not* testify." On (c) the judge took into account that the victim had a knife but was very drunk at the time and had never before threatened D with a knife. V was one hundred and sixteen pounds, and D was one hundred and seventy pounds. D had stabbed her three times, in the front and in the back and with great intensity. (This last factor makes the case similar to *Trecroce* where the victim was shot in the leg, arm and back. He claimed that the shotgun had discharged accidentally.) Nevertheless, the Ontario Court of Appeal in *Reilly* expressly stated that in the appropriate case the qualified defence of excessive self-defence "should be recognized."

Some recent cases involving women have shown the "equitable" nature of this defence of self-defence. The best known is that of Joan Little, who was acquitted when she was accused of killing a jail guard who was trying to assault her sexually. Ms. Garcia was not so fortunate when she used "unreasonable" retaliation against a rapist some time after the event. The equity in that case was taken into account in the relatively light grade of homicide and punishment imposed. A third case, that of Yvonne Wanrow, an Indian woman from Spokane, Washington, has recently been receiving some publicity. Wanrow shot to death a man reported to be a child molester who, at night, entered her house where her children were sleeping. A new trial was ordered because of the reception of illegally obtained evidence at the first trial, and Wanrow has now been released.

The average citizen-householder often asks what are his rights if a trespasser is shot on private premises. If the interloper is merely a trespasser or Peeping Tom, the law will not excuse a killing but may reduce the offence to manslaughter (with an appropriately lighter sentence). If the intruder breaks into the home, the textbook answer raises the Englishman's castle rule. This may be reckless advice, however, because, in these days of fast communications and mobile police forces, the courts may decide that the citizen should be discouraged from taking the law into his own hands. Citizens certainly should be discouraged from a vigilante mentality and firearms should be used by experts such as police officers, if at all.

Excessive Self-Defence

Illustration 37(b) is based on the old English case of *Levett* where the accused was acquitted. A modern court, faced with death by shotgun rather than by sword as in *Levett*, might find D's behaviour unreasonable because we now have fast communication with the outside world, so that the police could be readily summoned. Furthermore, D gave no warning to V that D had a gun. The modern cases talk about reasonable as meaning reasonable in "all circumstances," which is not very helpful and simply means that all the factors mentioned will be weighed. If D's story is totally disbelieved, he will be convicted of murder and if the court decides that the accused's apprehension was justified but his response was disproportionate, then D will probably be found guilty of manslaughter (as was the case in Illustration 38(a), [*McKay*] and Illustration 38(b) [*Barilla*, a Canadian case]).

McKay and *Barilla* are illustrations of the verdict of manslaughter for excessive self-defence. They are compromise decisions that suggest that the accused was partly in the wrong in that he was initially an innocent bystander or that he retaliated with unreasonable force or in a fashion that showed some anger as well as fear. Some of these ideas are built into the Criminal Code in s. 35 that deals with aggression on both sides; s. 34 describes only cases of unprovoked assault.

Barilla was decided in 1944 and while there were several successful Australian attempts to reduce murder to manslaughter by excessive self-defence (*Howe*, *McKay*), the Canadian courts have only re-discovered it in the 1970s. Most of those cases discussed excessive self-defence but did not rely on it. In *Reilly* (1982) Arnup J.A. has specifically recognized the defence and adopted the guidelines set out above.

Provocation

Most cases of self-defence are not clear-cut. Only in the minority of cases is the accused faced with a murderous attack by an axe-wielding homicidal maniac, by an ugly mob storming his peaceful abode or by an armed attacker contemplating rape, robbery or arson. More frequently, the homicide arises from a drunken brawl where both parties have used some violence and it is impossible to say who was the initial aggressor or who was defending whom against what.

In the past, the criminal law has recognized the concept of chance medley or *chaud mêlée*. Any homicide arising from this sudden mutual quarrel would not be the felony of murder but the misdemeanour of manslaughter.

(The terms "felony" and "misdemeanour" are archaic now but the former was certainly more serious because it entailed an automatic death penalty and forfeiture of the convict's landed estates, if he had any.) The law decided that chance medley killing was not "altogether faultless," as the old authority of Hawkins puts it, but "may be intended to proceed from some negligence or at least want of sufficient caution in the party who is so unfortunate as to commit it."

Although sudden quarrels are less frequent than they were in the time when men usually went about armed and when they were more prone to open lawlessness (in the absence of police forces), the idea of an intermediate position between murder and excusable (that is, innocent) homicide still seems to exist. This is shown by the decisions in *Barilla* and *McKay*. There have been several reported cases like Illustration 38(c). The courts have sometimes classed them as excessive self-defence and sometimes as provocation. They are more correctly classified as the former because the retaliation was very excessive under the provocation rules.

The partial defence or mitigation of provocation covers most of this middle ground nowadays. This is covered by ss. 36 and 215 of the Code.

At common law, provocation, which reduces murder to manslaughter, could only consist of blows; words or insults were insufficient. The Code (s. 36) includes all three forms of provocation. At common law the only exception was the so-called unwritten law that allowed a husband (*not* a wife) to have the killing of his wife or her lover reduced to manslaughter if they were caught *in flagrante delicto* performing the act of adultery. (Unwritten lore would have been more appropriate as many persons, mostly males no doubt, thought that such a killing was totally excusable and not just a reduced form of culpable homicide.)

The Code describes the elements of provocation as a mitigation in s. 215.

"A Wrongful Act or Insult . . . Of Such a Nature . . ."

The violent retaliation or response to the provocation must be proportionate to the act or insult. A homicide will not be reduced to manslaughter if the accused responded to a slap on the face by killing the provoker with a deadly weapon. Particularly sympathetic cases can be found that are exceptions: a one-legged man had his crutch kicked from under him and he killed his tormentor with a knife and was convicted only of manslaughter. Indeed, much of the case law on provocation will appear as exceptions to the rule laid down in s. 215(2). The courts have described the rationale for the mitigation of provocation as applying the "benignity of the law" to deserving cases.

". . . To Deprive an Ordinary Person . . ."

Provocation does not exist for the benefit of the super-sensitive or those with extremely short (or unusual) tempers. An "ordinary person" is the average person with normal responses to stress and taunts. The common law used to refer to the "reasonable" person and some cases indicated that the "reasonable" person was an Anglo-Saxon with no physical abnormalities. Illustration 39(a) is a fictional case, but actual cases decided when the English (or Canadian) population was almost exclusively white said that the reasonable person was not from a minority group and racial epithets could not be provocation. This has changed in recent years.

There is an older Canadian case that ruled that the "ordinary" Canadian is Caucasian, but the case was decided before this country had a large increase in Asian and black residents. This is no longer good law. In the *Smithers* case the accused was a black hockey player who had been harassed and insulted during and after a game; he responded to the physical and racial insults with deadly force. He was charged with manslaughter and convicted. Perhaps the prosecution thought that the lesser homicide charge was sufficient mitigation, and provocation has not usually reduced a manslaughter to any lesser offence. Given the courts' strange definitions of an "ordinary" Canadian, one wonders if a native Canadian would receive any special consideration if the victim had made specific insults relating to the accused's ethnic origins.

Illustration 39(b) is based on the more recent English case of *Bedder*, where the court applied an objective test and refused to take into account the peculiar susceptibilities of the accused, announcing that the reasonable person is not impotent. This was an extremely harsh rule and has since been overruled in *D.P.P.* v. *Camplin* (1978) where D killed V with a chapati pan after V had buggered D. The House of Lords decided that D's youth should be taken into account because, in Lord Diplock's words, "to require old heads on young shoulders is inconsistent with the law's compassion of human infirmity." D was fifteen years old. Lord Diplock suggested that, in such a case, the jury should be told:

> The reasonable man ... is a person having the power of self-control to be expected of an ordinary person of the sex and age of the accused, but in other respects sharing such of the accused's characteristics as they think would affect the gravity of the provocation to him, and that the question is not merely whether such a person would in like circumstances be provoked to lose his self-control but also would react to the provocation as the accused did.

The law of provocation is undoubtedly becoming more subjective. Indeed the recent remarks of Lamer J. in the Supreme Court of Canada in *Vasil* has made this explicit.

"... On the Sudden ... Before Time for Passion to Cool"

The accused must act on the spur of the moment while he or she is actually provoked. Legal provocation does not arise as a mitigation if the accused is insulted or receives a blow and rushes halfway across town to fetch a weapon with which to kill the provoker. The accused cannot brood over the insult or blow for days and then seek revenge, calling it a manslaughter on sudden provocation. In a Canadian case an Italian migrant had heard from his home town that while he was trying to become established in his new country, his wife had been unfaithful to him. He paid for her to come to Canada, and when she arrived, he killed her. No matter how provoked he might have been by the affront to his code of honour and even if his anger was rekindled by her arrival, the law would not consider this an appropriate case for mitigation to manslaughter. The Crown often decides that such a case is suitable for commutation of the death penalty (which still existed when this particular case was decided).

Infancy

The problems raised by Illustration 42(a) can be answered easily because s. 12 of the Code provides that no child under seven years can be convicted of an offence. If a child is between seven and fourteen years, s. 13 tells us that he cannot be convicted of an offence under the Code unless "competent to know the nature and consequences of his conduct and to appreciate that it was wrong." The wording of this rule is similar to that of the insanity defence. The rationale is the same: the law is asking whether children between seven and fourteen have capacity or responsibility for their acts.

The English case of *Walters* v. *Lunt* is described in Illustration 42(a). The court decided that the article was *de facto* and not *de jure* stolen and, therefore, the parents could not be convicted of receiving stolen goods. (Compare the case of attempt examined earlier where the accused could not be convicted of handling "stolen" goods when they were already in the lawful custody of the police. Similarly, a wife cannot steal property from her husband because, in most instances during the existence of the marriage, property is deemed to be jointly owned.) Yet in the case of *Bourne* (Illustration 35(b)) the husband was convicted of bestiality despite the acquittal of the wife on the basis of duress.

The juvenile in Illustration 42(b) is exempt from criminal liability by s. 147 of the Criminal Code. This may not make much sense to a biologist or medical doctor but it is one of the few irrebuttable presumptions of the law—a male under fourteen cannot be convicted of rape, attempted rape, incest, or sexual intercourse with a female under fourteen or under sixteen. The attempted rape provision is interesting because it is saying that factual impossibility is a defence.

There are no elaborate tests or case law to explain s. 13. The problem is academic because since early in this century, almost all children under sixteen, seventeen or eighteen (depending on the province) have their cases heard in a separate, private court known as the juvenile court, which is constituted under the Juvenile Delinquents Act (J.D.A.).

The procedure of the juvenile court is as informal "as the circumstances will permit, consistent with a due regard for a proper administration of justice" (s. 17 of the J.D.A.). The same section states that no juvenile court adjudication or disposition will be set aside or quashed "because of any informality or irregularity where it appears that the disposition of the case was in the best interests of the child."

The phrase "best interests of the child" is frequently found in legislation relating to children and is meant to reflect the philosophy that the law should be more interested in protecting children than punishing them, that the spirit of the law is more important than the letter. This is most explicitly expressed in s. 38 of the J.D.A. which lays down that the Act shall be liberally construed to ensure that its true purpose is honoured. Its purpose is described as follows:

> that the care and custody and discipline of a juvenile delinquent shall approximate as nearly as may be that which should be given by his parents, and that as far as practicable every juvenile delinquent shall be treated, not as criminal, but as a misdirected or misguided child, and one needing aid, encouragement, help and assistance.

Juvenile cases can be transferred (or waived) to the adult court if the child is over fourteen years and has allegedly committed an indictable offence. Transfers used to be very unusual and only happened in very notorious cases where the prosecution sought waiver to adult court largely because of the perceived force of public opinion. One of the best known is the case of Steven Truscott who was sentenced to death for the rape-murder of Lynne Harper when he was fourteen. Section 9 of the J.D.A. says that a case should not be transferred unless it is for "the good of the child" or "the interest of the community demands it." Like most sections of the J.D.A., this is a very vague provision. Many cases have been transferred because the juvenile court judge feels that the resources of the juvenile justice system (including the reform institutions) are unsuitable in the case of a particular juvenile. (See Illustration 42 (d).) In other cases, the complexities and legalities of the case have seemed unsuitable for the informality of the court for children. Sometimes public opinion and human curiosity have urged a transfer. Illustration 42(c) is a very difficult case. The trial judge decided not to transfer the case of the juvenile but he was overturned on appeal. We are faced in that case with conflicting values; first, should like cases be treated alike? or secondly, should a juvenile, who has the protection of the J.D.A., be deprived of such lenity? Of course, if we are only thinking of punishment, then J should be transferred.

This idea of the juvenile court as a wise parent is an expression of the ancient concept of the State as *parens patriae* or guardian of all children in need of care or protection. The definition of juvenile crimes includes much more than the adult crimes found in the Code. In addition, it includes offences under other federal Acts (such as drug legislation) and provincial and municipal laws (such as the Highway Traffic Act) and, finally, "sexual immorality or any similar form of vice." The juvenile court also hears cases where the child is alleged to be destitute, neglected, abused or uncontrollable.

Illustration 42(e) would presumably be covered by the blanket provision of the J.D.A. about "sexual immorality." Until recently some provincial statutes also enabled parents to commit their children (particularly females, in another application of the double standard) to training schools for indefinite periods. The females were adjudged to be "in moral danger," and many shocking injustices were done under this power. Parents often used the juvenile court as a way of enforcing morality. A few years ago, teenagers who had been indulging in sexual intercourse would be brought before the court but the charges would be dropped if the boy promised to marry the girl (who usually was pregnant).

Illustration 42(f) seems rather fanciful but an Ontario juvenile court judge decided that glue sniffing was behaviour that came within "sexual immorality or any similar form of vice." Glue sniffing was not illegal and the judge wanted some hook on which to hang a method of controlling the glue sniffer. This was an extraordinary exercise in statutory interpretation but was accepted as a good example of the paternalistic quality of the juvenile court. "Similar form of vice" was undoubtedly meant to control masturbation because Victorian reformers were preoccupied with the "solitary vice."

This paternalistic and rather flexible procedure of the juvenile court has been criticized in recent years. The U.S. Supreme Court (in *Kent* and *Gault*) stated that the juvenile has too frequently been subjected to the informality of a social welfare tribunal that did not protect even the most fundamental rights (such as notice to parents of the charges, right to counsel, properly admissible evidence and so on). Furthermore, it stated that the treatment of the juvenile was often not curative but thinly veiled punishment.

The U.S. courts and the Canadian government have sought to remedy this situation by prescribing basic rights for the juvenile when brought before a court for children. The J.D.A. is being replaced by the Young Offenders Act (Y.O.A.) after many years of debate and consultation. The age of criminal responsibility will be raised from seven to twelve years. All children who perform antisocial acts when under twelve will be dealt with by welfare rather than quasi-criminal legislation. At last, there will be a uniform juvenile age for all Canada—seventeen years. The federal legislation will be limited to juvenile committing offences against the Criminal Code and other federal legislation and regulations. The provinces will have to pass their own statutes to control juveniles who commit offences against provincial or municipal laws. The Y.O.A. will provide machinery for diversion, particularly for less serious offences, so that informal arrangements can be made to dispose of cases by conciliation, orders for restitution and community service. If the youth insists on the more formal procedure of the court, he can opt for that.

The youth court created by the Y.O.A. will be open to the public but the press (presently excluded) will not be able to publish names of young persons. At the moment, juvenile records are admissible in adult court (Illustration 42(g) *Morris*) but under the new Act, such records will be destroyed when the young person has completed the imposed sentence and has committed no further offence for two years (if the offence were summary) and five years (if indictable).

The principles of the Y.O.A. are:

(a) Young persons should be held more responsible for their behaviour but not wholly accountable since they are not yet fully mature.
(b) Society has a right to protection from illegal behaviour.
(c) Young persons have the same rights to due process of law and fair and equal treatment as adults, and that these rights must be guaranteed by special safeguards.
(d) Young persons have special needs because they are dependants at varying levels of development and maturity and therefore also require guidance and assistance.

In relation to (c), the young person has a right to be represented by counsel, to be cautioned and informed of his or her rights and the same rights of appeal as an adult. Of course, we do not yet know the relevance of the Charter of Rights to youths between twelve and seventeen.

6/INSANITY and CRIME

Behavioural scientists look upon the words "sane" and "insane" as imprecise and unscientific when considering problems of mental illness and mental incompetency. The lawyers, however, invent the labels and apply the rules in the criminal law. Mental irresponsibility, as viewed by the courts, and the legal defence of insanity are found in s. 16 of the Criminal Code.

Before considering insanity as a defence, the criminal law may make a preliminary decision that a person should not be tried for a crime because of "unfitness to plead," that the person's mental condition is such that he is incapable of instructing counsel or understanding the proceedings. Such person will be committed to a mental hospital without a trial as to criminal guilt, at that time.

The principle that the criminal law is allegedly based on free will rather than determinism has two consequences. First, the law considers it unjust to punish a man who has done a "criminal" act when incapable of forming the *mens rea* or the mental element of a crime. The criminal law also takes the attitude that punishment after conviction has no value—retributive, deterrent or rehabilitative—if the accused is incapable of understanding the reasons for punishment. The law can hardly look upon him as blameworthy.

The criminal law has not always taken such a charitable view toward the mentally ill but, of course, medical science was also applying barbaric methods less than two hundred years ago. Lunatics and even epileptics were subject to permanent incarceration in such infamous institutions as London's Bedlam. At that time the law's test of insanity was equally unsophisticated. The "wild beast" test, then employed, was derived from the early commentator Bracton who said that "a madman is one who does not know what he is doing, who is lacking in mind and reason and who is not far removed from the brutes." This is not far removed from medieval ideas that the devil possessed some persons. Until the famous *M'Naghten* test of 1843, the tests applied by the courts in the eighteenth and early nineteenth centuries concentrated on the need for a total lack of the power of reasoning or a clear failure to distinguish between right and wrong. The latter was no doubt inspired by a theological approach to mental derangement.

The *M'Naghten* Test and Its Critics

With the exception of a few jurisdictions, the *M'Naghten* rule has lasted for more than a century as the insanity rule on both sides of the Atlantic. In 1843 the court stated that every man is presumed to be sane and

> . . . to establish a defence on the ground of insanity, it must be clearly proved that, at the time of the committing of the act, the party accused was labouring under such a defect of reason from disease of the mind, as not to know the nature and quality of the act he was doing; or, if he did know it, that he did not know he was doing what was wrong.

Since its formulation, the *M'Naghten* rule has been subjected to criticism by psychiatrists and re-examination by lawyers. The rule, however, survived, although it seems, at least, to be in something of a decline. Psychiatry has progressed since 1843; this human science is not exact, and it is not difficult to find examples of deep disagreements among psychiatrists. The social sciences have also added support to the determinist viewpoint but the law, with its emphasis on free will, has not relinquished its hold over the definition of insanity.

Psychiatrists have criticized the *M'Naghten* rule on many grounds. The primary attack is that 1843 ideas on mental illness hardly constitute the current wisdom of behavioural science. They also complain that the legal words impose too much of an ideological straitjacket on psychiatrists who are trying to explain the symptoms of psychosis in the accused's background and behaviour. An allied point is that the psychiatrists feel the conventions of the legal trial, and the skirmishes of the adversary system of trial, impose unrealistic burdens on psychiatrists who are supposed to be appearing as expert witnesses. The adversary system pits one expert against another in an area of human knowledge where black-and-white answers are impossible. There is little doubt that the juries find the conflicting psychiatric evidence confusing.

The psychiatrists, citing phrases such as "*Know* the nature . . ." and "*Know* he was doing . . . wrong," have also complained that the *M'Naghten* test places too much emphasis on the cognitive aspect of mental illness. Not only is there unwarranted reliance on knowledge, but this attitude by the law makes the unreal assumption that there can be a clear dividing line between the emotions and the intellect. Section 16 of the Code uses the word "appreciate" in substitution for "know." The difference was recently discussed by Dickson J. in *Cooper*: "To 'know' the nature and quality of an act may mean merely to be aware of the physical act, while to 'appreciate' may involve estimation and understanding of the consequences of that act." Cooper, in using his hands to choke the victim, may have known the nature and quality of the physical act of choking but not appreciated that it could result in death.

The psychiatrists also criticize the rule because it places too little emphasis on partial psychosis and suggests that the mental illness must be total or non-existent. The insanity rules, including the *M'Naghten* test, also try to make an unreal distinction between the mad and bad or the sick and the wicked.

Yet some judges try to make intelligent distinctions as evidenced by Dixon J.'s classic direction to the jury in *Porter*:

> ... his state of mind must have been one of disease, disorder or disturbance. Mere excitability of a normal man, passion, even stupidity, obtuseness, lack of self-control, and impulsiveness, are quite different things from ... a state of disease or disorder or mental disturbance arising from some infirmity, temporary or of long standing. ... That does not mean ... that there must be some physical deterioration of the cells of the brain, some actual change in the material, physical constitution of the mind, as disease ordinarily means when you are dealing with other organs of the body. ... You are dealing with a very different thing—with the understanding. It does mean that the functions of the understanding are through some cause whether understandable or not, thrown into derangement or disorder.

Some of the more extreme critics, including Dr. Thomas Szasz, contend that the notion of "mental disease" or "defect of reason" is not a scientific judgement but a moral decision. The psychiatrists are only arguing about theories, not fact, and this is inappropriate—because an accused will hire an expert psychiatric witness who will testify that the accused is sick, while the prosecution will find an equally "impartial" witness who will declare that the defendant has criminal responsibility. Even if this view is too extreme, it is true that all definitions of "mental illness" and the like are imprecise and vague, and the courtroom is hardly the place to debate medical diagnoses.

Some critics say that the phrase "disease of the mind" is completely outmoded, but recent Canadian courts have supported the phrase, agreeing with Dixon J. that it is very broad and therefore flexible. Martin J.A. reminded us in *Simpson* that the final decision is a legal one:

> The term 'disease of the mind' is a legal concept, although it includes a medical component, and what is meant by that term is a question of law for the judge. ... It is the function of the psychiatrist to describe the accused's mental condition and how it is considered from the medical point of view. It is for the judge to decide whether the condition described is comprehended by the term 'disease of the mind.'

Dickson J., with his usual clarity, has summed up the definition of disease of the mind as "any illness, disorder or abnormal condition which impairs the human mind and its functioning, excluding, however, self-induced states caused by alcohol or drugs, as well as the transitory mental states such as hysteria or concussion."

Others argue that the "right-wrong" test is based on a knowledge of law that has nothing to do with mental illness. The English case of *Windle* held that "wrong" meant legally wrong. Most American and Australian courts view "wrong" in the *M'Naghten* test as meaning morally wrong. The Canadian courts had decided on both bases until recently, when the Supreme Court of Canada, in a 5-4 decision in *Schwartz*, defined "wrong" as contrary to law. Both sides of the argument have merit. Martland J., speaking for the majority, said that s. 16 of the Code provided "protection to a person suffering from disease of the mind who has committed a crime if, in committing the crime, he did not appreciate what he was doing or, if he did have that appreciation, he did not know that he was committing a crime." In other words, Martland J. was saying that the first part of the test ("appreciate" etc.) was the ethical or moral test and if he passed that one, then he could still be found not guilty on grounds of insanity if he did not know that murder was contrary to law because that would be an obvious symptom of his lack of rationality. The minority, *per* Dickson J., criticized the preoccupation with cognition and accentuated capacity, i.e., the "mental illness so obstructed the thought processes of the accused as to make him incapable of knowing that his acts were morally wrong." Dissecting the words of a statute may be a dangerous occupation but Dickson J. does gloss over the fact that s. 16(2) of the Code talks about "*incapable* of *appreciating* the nature and quality" and "*knowing* that an act is wrong." He approved of the Australian position:

> The question is whether he was able to appreciate the wrongness of the particular act he was doing at the particular time. Could this man be said to know in this sense whether his act was wrong if through a disease or defect or disorder of the mind he could not think rationally of the reasons which to ordinary people make that not right or wrong? If through the disordered condition of the mind he could not reason about the matter with a moderate degree of sense and composure it may be said that he could not know that what he was doing was wrong.

A further criticism is that the *M'Naghten* rule takes no account of "irresistible impulse" or other mental illnesses that are not in an acute form. The accused may know or appreciate the nature and quality or wrongness of the act but be unable to stop himself from doing the act. This defence has seldom been accepted by the courts because it is said to be open to abuse and feigned illness. The English Homicide Act, 1957, section 2, has made some concession in this direction:

> (1) Where a person kills or is party to the killing of another, he shall not be convicted of murder if he was suffering from such abnormality of mind (whether arising from a condition of arrested or retarded development of mind or any inherent causes or induced by disease or injury) as substantially impaired his mental responsibility for his acts and omissions in doing or being a party to the killing. . . .
>
> (3) A person who but for this section would be liable, whether as principal or as accessory, to be convicted of murder shall be liable instead to be convicted of manslaughter.

As we shall see, there are continuing attempts to reformulate legal tests of insanity. The law's abandonment of its grip on the defence of insanity does not seem imminent. The experts are sharply divided. One school, which includes psychiatrists, social scientists (such as Barbara Wootton) and some lawyers, believes that the legal test of insanity should be abolished. They argue that the test is based on free will and retribution, that this is irrelevant to problems of mental illness and that the *mens rea* test should be abandoned in favour of civil commitment, enabling the State to retain control over dangerous persons with mental problems and criminal propensities.

Others, including H.L.A. Hart, maintain that *mens rea* (and the defences which negate it) should be retained and that psychiatric evidence should usually be introduced to decide on punishment and disposition after guilt is determined on legal bases.

There are others who say that if the law is going to take account of legal irresponsibility owing to mental illness, then the law should also negate blameworthiness when the accused has no social responsibility because of economic or social deprivation. (This view was implicit in the minority opinion in *Powell* v. *Texas.*)

The insanity defence is not applied uniformly. Frequently the powerless are found guilty and subjected to penal treatment (including capital punishment in some jurisdictions), but the influential are found not guilty on the grounds of insanity. Even if this is an exaggeration, it is true that the insanity defence is often used as a device to avoid the death penalty (or nowadays, a twenty-five-year "flat" or non-parolable sentence). In most instances, the insanity defence is only raised in serious crimes. The lawyers for accused charged with relatively minor crimes may advise their clients that a short time in jail is preferable to an indeterminate period in some institution for the criminally insane.

The insanity defence is not a true indication of the extent of mental illness among those charged with crime. Once again this is a conscious choice by the law to provide a compromise between the barbarism of punishing the obviously irresponsible and the impracticality of viewing all criminals as "sick" persons who should be treated. The insanity defence allows the jury to be lenient or retributive depending upon the subjective wickedness and overt madness of the accused.

The civil libertarians are not prepared to abdicate jurisdiction to the psychiatrists and other members of the "helping" professions. These lawyers claim that there are insufficient guarantees that only the very dangerous and incurable will come within the statutory definitions of those who should be detained. They also argue that they are dissatisfied with the procedures for release, review of cases and appeal against institutional decisions.

Finally, those in favour of some sort of legal test of insanity claim that its absence would remove two essential qualities of the criminal law. These have been well expressed by Goldstein in his definitive book, *The Insanity Defense*:

> ... the insanity defense can play a part in reinforcing the sense of obligation of responsibility. Its emphasis on whether an offender is sick or bad helps to keep alive the almost forgotten drama of individual responsibility. Its weight is felt through the tremendous appeal it holds for the popular imagination, as that imagination is gripped by a dramatic trial and as the public at large identifies with the man in the dock. In this way, it becomes part of a complex of cultural forces that keep alive the moral lessons, and the myths, which are essential to the

> continued order of society. . . . the heart of the distinction between conviction and acquittal by reason of insanity lies in the fact that the former represents official condemnation. Yet the acquittal is itself a sanction, bringing with it comparable stigma and the prospect of indeterminate detention. If the choice between the two sanctions is to be made in a way that will not only be acceptable to the larger community but will also serve the symbolic function we have noted, it is important that the decision be made by a democratically selected jury rather than by experts—because the public can identify with the former but not with the latter.

Some psychiatrists have reservations too. An eminent one, Dr. Bernard Diamond, has said:

> If and when the time comes when the following conditions are approached, I would freely abandon the adversary system insofar as it applies to problems of mental illness:
>
> (1) Each defendant, rich and poor, rural and urban, in enlightened communities and in backward communities, can be reasonably guaranteed the type of exhaustive clinical investigation that is now available to only a few fortunate defendants.
>
> (2) When all expert witnesses are highly trained and experienced and adept in transmitting their findings to the court.
>
> (3) When observation hospitals are staffed with dynamically oriented psychiatrists who fully appreciate the important role they play in the administration of justice.
>
> (4) When such psychiatrists, through their own enlightenment and self-understanding, can be relied upon to detach themselves from their own prejudice and refrain from homogenizing their moral judgements with their medical opinions.
>
> (5) When our whole profession of psychiatry is less preoccupied with its own omniscience, and sufficiently secure in its public status that it is unafraid to expose its deficiencies of knowledge about some of the most fundamental problems of human nature.
>
> (6) When the forensic psychiatrist is permitted to operate within a legal framework which allows him to apply his professional judgement to appropriate questions of psychological reality and not to philosophical and theological rules and syllogisms—when he can apply his knowledge to human reality instead of legal fiction.
>
> (7) When society is able to leave behind its archaic need for vengeance and retribution and learn that its own best protection is inextricably woven in with the rehabilitation of the individual deviant; that to degrade any member of that society with either the formal vengeance of punishment or the stigmata of legal insanity is to degrade only itself.
>
> Then and only then would I admit the superiority of the impartial expert over the adversary witness. But then, if such a utopia were to be achieved, perhaps there would be no need for experts.

The *Durham* Rule

Only two new tests have received serious consideration since *M'Naghten*. The *Durham* test of 1954 was purposely simple: "an accused is not criminally responsible if his unlawful act was the product of mental disease or mental defect." This was considered a simpler, broader rule that would give the pyschiatrist more freedom to present evidence that reflects modern psychiatric thought. The rule has received more condemnation than recognition. Nevertheless, it has stimulated debate; spawned new rules, such as *Freeman*; and encouraged dialogue between lawyers and behavioural scientists.

Neither of the defendants in these insanity cases had committed homicide which is usually the crime where the defence is raised. Durham had been charged with house-breaking and Freeman with trafficking in narcotics.

Durham had a long history of imprisonment and hospitalization. In 1945, at the age of seventeen, he was discharged from the navy after a psychiatric examination had shown that he suffered "from a profound personality disorder which renders him unfit for naval service." In 1947 he pleaded guilty to violating the National Motor Theft Act and was placed on probation for one to three years. He attempted suicide, was taken to Gallinger Hospital for observation and was transferred to St. Elizabeth's Hospital, from which he was discharged two months later. In January 1948, as a result of a conviction in the District of Columbia Municipal Court for passing bad cheques, the District Court revoked his probation and he served his motor theft sentence. His conduct within the first few days in jail led to a lunacy inquiry in the Municipal Court where a jury found him to be of unsound mind. Upon commitment to St. Elizabeth's, he was diagnosed as suffering from "psychosis with psychopathic personality." After fifteen months of treatment, he was discharged in July 1949 as "recovered" and was returned to jail to serve the balance of his sentence. In June 1950 he was conditionally released but violated the conditions by leaving the district. When he learned of a warrant for his arrest as a parole violator, he fled and during his absence passed a number of bad cheques. When he was returned, the Parole Board referred him to the District Court for a lunacy inquisition and a jury again found him to be of unsound mind. He was readmitted to St. Elizabeth's in February 1951. This time the diagnosis was "without mental disorder, psychopathic personality." He was discharged for the third time in May 1951. The housebreaking took place two months later in July 1951.

According to his mother and the psychiatrist who examined him in September 1951, he suffered from hallucinations immediately after his May 1951 discharge from St. Elizabeth's. Following the last indictment in October 1951, he was adjudged of unsound mind upon the affidavits of two psychiatrists that he suffered from "psychosis with psychopathic personality." He was committed to St. Elizabeth's for the fourth time and given subshock insulin therapy. This commitment lasted sixteen months—until February 1953—when he was released to the custody of the District Jail on the certificate of Dr. Silk, acting superintendent of St. Elizabeth's, that he was "mentally competent to stand trial and . . . able to consult with counsel to properly assist in his own defence." (Note that civil commitment did not absolve him of criminal liability.)

The cross-examination of a defence psychiatrist in *Durham* gives an excellent illustration of the problem of expert psychiatric evidence, the lack of understanding between law and medicine and the difficulty of defining psychiatric terms in legal language (or perhaps defining mental illness in any language). So long as we have the battle of the experts (for prosecution and defence) and the adversary system, we will be burdened with spectacles such as this, which certainly do not add to the sum of our knowledge, psychiatric or legal:

Q: Well, now, Doctor, in forming your opinion, wouldn't the way he attempted to commit suicide, or the means, be important to you to know in forming an opinion?

A: Well, it might. It might not be. It might be important. It might be unimportant.

(This witness is hedging and is going to be an unsatisfactory one. The doctor knows a lot but he is having trouble expressing it in a "yes" and "no" fashion.)

Q: And wouldn't the ways or the means that he attempted suicide be important to you to find out whether or not he was doing it for sympathy?

A: Not after a mental disease had been established, it wouldn't be important.

Q: What do you mean by mental disease?

A: A mental disorder is a condition in which the symptoms of a well-recognized psychosis is present.

(The doctor's answer sounds rather like one he has learned by rote. Also note that "mental disease" has already become "mental disorder.")

Q: Well, what do you mean? Do you mean that the person who has a mental disease will never get well?

(The cross-examiner is taunting the doctor in suggesting that the psychiatric profession does not cure its patients.)

A: Oh, no. I haven't indicated that.

Q: What?

A: I haven't indicated that?

Q: Well now, what is your definition of mental disease again?

A: A mental disorder is the presence of the symptoms of a well-recognized psychosis.

Q: Psychosis.

A: Psychosis being the technical term for unsoundness of mind.

Q: Well now, how did you know whether or not this defendant had a mental defect?

(We have three more terms: psychosis, unsoundness of mind and mental defect.)

A: Well, I think I determined it, yes, sir. I don't know—

Q: What do you mean you determined that?

A: That he at the time I examined him in '48, that he had a psychosis or mental disorder and not—

Q: I am talking about a mental defect.

A: No, I don't believe he had a mental defect.

(Imagine the perplexed state of the jury at this point. Now we are back to "mental defect.")

Q: Well now, you testified as to his symptoms there, I believe.

A: Yes, sir, I do have the symptoms.

Q: Now, don't those symptoms that you have enumerated here indicate a particular type of insanity?

A: No, you asked me the definition of psychopathic personality, Mr. McLaughlin.

Q: That is what I have been talking about all this time.

A: No, not exactly.

(The lawyer and the psychiatrist have been ships passing in the night with no common language or understanding.)

Q: Well, let me ask you this: What is the difference between a psychopathic personality—what are the different symptoms between a psychopathic personality and a person with a psychosis and with a psychopathic personality?

A: Oh, in the person who has psychosis with psychopathic personality—and that must all be present if there is psychosis present—there are symptoms of a well-recognized and definitely classified mental disorder.

(If you were a juror, would you find this useful? Also note that we are back to "mental disorder.")

The *Durham* test was considered too vague. Juries were being presented with many "unlikely" psychiatric explanations that could lead the fact-finders to react with severity. The key problem was the word "product," as psychiatrists could always be found who would say that most forms of antisocial behaviour were "products" of mental disease or defect. "Product" almost allowed the behavioural scientists to talk about *anomie* as a basis for disallowing criminal responsibility! The test gave no guidance as to the meaning of "mental disease," and there was no correlation between "product" and criminal liability.

Soon after *Durham,* the Model Penal Code's definition was published; it was more conventional and many thought better suited to its stated purposes—not for the benefit of psychiatric witnesses but for the guidance of lawyers, judges and juries who were deciding upon the question of criminal responsibility.

The *Freeman* Case And The Model Penal Code

With the exception of the Supreme Court of the United States, the United States Court of Appeals is the highest federal jurisdiction. In a unanimous decision, the Court of Appeals in New York decided that the *M'Naghten* test of criminal responsibility should be abandoned in favour of a rule based on the Model Penal Code of the American Law Institute.

Charles Freeman was found guilty in the trial court of selling narcotics and was sentenced to five years' imprisonment. He had been a drug addict for fifteen years and was a "confirmed alcoholic." The psychiatrist called by the defence testified that Freeman "displayed no depth or variation in his emotional reactions," that his drug habit had caused "frequent episodes of toxic psychosis" as well as "delusions, hallucinations, epileptic convulsions and . . . amnesia." He also said that Freeman "had experienced innumerable brain traumata which produced such organic and structural changes as destroyed brain tissue." The psychiatrist, who had to answer questions on the basis of the *M'Naghten* test (which had been relied upon by the trial court), had to admit, within the strictures of that rule, that although Freeman did not know right from wrong, the appellant "possessed cognition that he was selling heroin." He added, however, that it was his opinion that Freeman was neither aware of the "social implications" of selling heroin nor of the "nature or meaning of what this meant to him."

The prosecution's psychiatric expert stated that Freeman realized the wrongfulness of his acts and "possessed the capacity to enter into purposeful activity" such as the sale of narcotics. The psychiatrist called for the defence testified that Freeman's dullness and vagueness in his thought processes were the "result of a generalized chronic, not overly severe damage to the higher thinking areas of the brain." Dr. Carson, of course, was only concerned at this stage with the question of fitness to stand trial and left open the question of Freeman's "ability to care for himself without rather close supervision."

The trial judge felt himself bound to follow the *M'Naghten* rule which had been generally applied in the federal criminal jurisdictions. He did not consider the alternative *Durham* "product" test. The Court of Appeals did not feel restricted to an application of the *M'Naghten* test and satisfied itself that the U.S. Supreme Court had not ruled conclusively that the *M'Naghten* rule was the true test of legal insanity.

In a learned and far-ranging judgement, Kaufman J. explored the history of the *M'Naghten* rule and the alternatives which have been suggested since 1843. He finally settled on the most recent alternative, the test formulated in the Model Penal Code which states:

> A person is not responsible for criminal conduct if at the time of such conduct as a result of mental disease or defect he lacks substantial capacity either to appreciate the wrongfulness of his conduct or to conform his conduct to the requirements of law.

Judge Kaufman reviewed the rationale of criminal sanctions and asserted that the rehabilitative, retributive or deterrent purposes of punishment were not applicable to those who lacked criminal responsibility. The criminal law (which, in his view, expressed the "moral sense of the community") served no purpose in punishing those who lacked substantial capacity to control their actions. Rehabilitation was not applicable to one who would best be "cured" in a specialized institution; those "who are substantially unable to restrain their conduct or do not appreciate the nature and quality of their actions" could not be expected "rationally to weigh the consequences of their conduct" and, therefore, were not deterrable. Society could not "feel its desire for retribution satisfied when it wreaks vengeance upon the incompetent."

Kaufman J. traced the history of criminal irresponsibility from Lambard, through the "wild beast" test and the enthusiasms for monomania and phrenology, to the trial of Daniel M'Naghten. He described these tests as having been laid down in the "Dark Ages" of psychiatry.

Undoubtedly in 1843 a science of psychiatry was emerging. One of the most significant contributions of the period, Isaac Ray's *Medical Jurisprudence of Insanity*, which had been published in 1838, received a sympathetic hearing at the *M'Naghten* trial. Kaufman J. did not state what specific concepts of Ray were relied upon. He no doubt believed that any worthwhile effects of the trial were obliterated by the "accident of history," as he described the subsequent assembly of judges required to answer five "prolix and obtuse questions on the status of criminal responsibility in England." Kaufman J. regretted the *M'Naghten* rules because they reaffirmed and "froze" the earlier tests of responsibility at a time when they were becoming obsolete. Kaufman J. was right to point out the regrettable fact that the theories of monomania and phrenology were relied upon by the fifteen judges to the exclusion of Dr. Ray's thesis. This does not explain why the United States, which has always been more sympathetic than England to psychiatric knowledge and practice, should not have applied more enlightened views in its courts. Perhaps the consistent and universal conservatism of the legal profession was too strong. The New Hampshire court was the only one that heeded Dr. Ray's work:

> At the trial where insanity is set up as a defence, two questions are presented: First: Had the prisoner a mental disease? Second: If he had, was the disease of such a character or was it so far developed, or had it so subjugated the powers of the mind, as to take away the capacity to form or entertain a criminal intent?

The lawyer who inspired this rule was Judge Charles Doe. He was dissatisfied with the *M'Naghten* rule and had a keen interest in medical jurisprudence. Judge Doe saw insanity as "primarily a problem, not of substantive criminal law, but of evidence." He believed that nineteenth-century American law had done the common law a disservice "by turning facts which should have been decided by the jury into law expounded by the court." Doe J. also held that the jury should be given the best evidence possible. Finally, "his uncompromising dislike of presumptions led him to view the *M'Naghten* rules primarily as unwarranted presumptions of law which presume a man sane unless he is unable to meet a standard of rationality arbitrarily set by the court."

The New Hampshire rule has been misunderstood and equated with the *Durham* "product" test. The latter is a medical test; the New Hampshire rule is basically an evidentiary rule, or in the words of Doe's biographer,

> . . . not so much a definition of criminal responsibility as an affirmation that no

> satisfactory definition can be devised to solve what [the New Hampshire Court] regarded to be a question of fact.

After this historical preamble, the Court of Appeals made specific criticisms of the *M'Naghten* test. The 1843 test was faulted for its "single track emphasis on the cognitive aspect of the personality." As a result, the jury was not allowed to identify those who can distinguish between good and evil but who cannot control their behaviour as being legally irresponsible. Many accused persons were sent to prison and subsequently released when their behaviour required treatment (and perhaps permanent incarceration) in psychiatric institutions. Quite rightly, Kaufman J. saw great potential social danger in this policy. He also added a footnote:

> We recognize our liability to determine at this point whether society possesses sufficient hospital facilities and doctors to deal with criminals who are found to be incompetent. But our function as judges requires us to interpret the law in the best interest of society as a whole. We therefore suggest that if there are inadequate facilities and personnel in this area, Congress, the state legislatures and federal and state executive departments should promptly consider bridging the gap.

The knowledge of the right and wrong test was considered "grossly unrealistic" because mental illness is not a matter of black or white but rather of varying shades of grey.

Judge Bazelon in *Durham* had also been critical of the right-wrong test:

> The fundamental objection to the right-wrong test, however, is not that criminal irresponsibility is made to rest upon an inadequate, invalid or indeterminable symptom or manifestation, but that it is made to rest upon *any* particular symptom. In attempting to define insanity in terms of a symptom, the courts have assumed an impossible role, not merely one for which they have no special competence. As the Royal Commission [on Capital Punishment] emphasizes, it is dangerous "to abstract particular mental faculties, and to lay it down that unless these particular faculties are destroyed or gravely impaired, an accused person, whatever the nature of his mental disease, must be held to be criminally responsible." In this field of law as in others, the fact-finder should be free to consider all information advanced by relevant scientific disciplines.

Another major criticism of the *M'Naghten* rules (including the more recent variations of irresistible impulse) was found in the unrealistic shackles that they placed upon psychiatric testimony. The court cited the criticisms of psychiatrists and defence lawyers. Mr. Justice Frankfurter, appearing before the British Royal Commission on Capital Punishment, had said:

> I do not see why the rules of law should be arrested at the state of psychological knowledge of the time when they were formulated. . . . I think the *M'Naghten* rules are in large measure shams. That is a very strong word, but I think the *M'Naghten* rules are very difficult for conscientious people and not difficult enough for people who say, "We'll just juggle them."

The court in *Freeman* did not forget, however, that the question of legal responsibility is not a medical but a "legal, social or moral" problem. Yet the outmoded *M'Naghten* rule robbed the law, and society, of treating the psychiatrist like every other expert. The expert in mental illness "should furnish the raw data upon which the legal judgement is based." This does not deny the necessary scepticism that the jury often has for some of the theories propounded by psychiatrists; in fact, the present system of trying to fit modern psychiatric knowledge within the *M'Naghten* straitjacket causes juries to scoff at the expert psychiatric evidence. It is in this sense that the Court of Appeals saw the greatest fault in *M'Naghten*: the judge and jury are, at present, deprived of the best knowledge presented in the most meaningful way. Furthermore, psychiatry is more readily accepted today and, therefore, the *M'Naghten* test hardly could be said to represent the "moral sense of the community."

Many of the criticisms described above were answered by the 1954 decision in *Durham*. This test, in turn, was criticized because, as Kaufman J. stated, the criterion of "product" raised "near-impossible problems of causation." Furthermore, the *Durham* test was thought deficient because "it fails to give the fact-finder any standard by which to measure the competency of the accused." Therefore, psychiatric evidence tended to usurp the jury's function by labelling specific acts the "product" of mental aberration. This method of testing criminal responsibility is subject to real dangers. Although psychiatry has made significant advances in the last one hundred years, its practitioners, because of the very nature of their discipline, are notoriously divided as to the diagnosis of various forms of human behaviour—whether abnormal, psychopathic or sociopathic.

The Court of Appeals based its judgement on the Model Penal Code because, although no test was perfect, the test of the American Law Institute had the fewest defects. This test "views the mind as a unified entity and recognizes that mental disease or defect may impair its functioning in numerous ways." The phrase "substantial incapacity" negated the old idea that mental deficiency had to be in absolutely black or white terms. The word "appreciate" was considered a much better word to apply to an examination of criminal behaviour than "know," because

> ... mere intellectual awareness that conduct is wrongful, when divorced from appreciation or understanding of the moral or legal import of behaviour, can have little significance.

Finally, the court believed that, while the new test gave opportunity for an inquiry based on "meaningful psychological concepts," such evidence would be simply expert testimony to assist the jury (and not a "moral or legal pronouncement"). While the test avoided a rigid classification, it was in "sufficiently precise terms to provide the jury with a workable standard when the judge charges in terms comprehensible to laymen." The Court of Appeals added:

> It is desirable, therefore, that the altered standard for criminal responsibility which has been adopted today should not become the *causa sine qua non* of unseemly contest between psychiatric experts. We may anticipate a weakening of public confidence in the value of psychiatric concepts and a reaction against them if this should result.

Many jurisdictions are realizing that the *M'Naghten* rules are outmoded and that they can no longer be patched up and made to last for a few more generations. The Model Penal Code test has been adopted *in toto* or in modified form in several jurisdictions. No doubt further problems will be discovered in this new test but the virtues described by Kaufman J. seem to be important and lasting ones. The law of insanity is merely an exaggerated example of a problem common to all interdisciplinary observations. Semantic problems are created and the non-legal expert will never be content with his less than full acceptance by the law. He finds it difficult to recognize that the law must govern its own house and that the rules and practice of evidence are the final arbiters of the data on which the jury will reach its verdict.

What are the deficiencies of the new formulation? As stated, the science of psychiatry is still in a state of flux: the opposing parties in a criminal trial will still be able to find psychiatrists of opposing views who will conscientiously support the contention of the prosecution or defence.

Can any words solve the problem? Most probably not. Is "appreciate" any better than "know"? The psychiatrists say so and have obviously convinced the drafters of the Model Penal Code.

Perhaps cases will be decided in exactly the same way as before. The jury will simply ask itself, "Do you think that the crime shows the acts of a 'normal' man; do you think that the accused looks like a 'normal' man?" The only difference will be that the jury will have received more information—but will they "appreciate" it or "know" that it is "right"?

The problem of psychiatry and the law will never be solved so long as the moral sense of the community requires that the matter of responsibility must be determined under an adversary system by twelve laymen. That is a problem that the Court of Appeals was neither allowed nor wished to pursue.

The Canadian Position

Canada's definition of the insanity defence, found in s. 16 of the Code, is a modification of the *M'Naghten* test. Many look upon it as an improvement. A Royal Commission in 1956 was asked to re-examine the legal test of insanity. It suggested minor changes but did not recommend the abandonment of the law's attempts to define the "types of abnormal human behaviour which would negate criminal liability."

The key phrase "incapable of appreciating the nature and quality of an act" was thought to incorporate two important changes. In the 1955 revision of the Criminal Code "the act" was replaced by "an act." This was thought to give more flexibility that would lead to a better assessment of the accused's overall mental condition. A more significant difference between the Canadian law and the *M'Naghten* test was the substitution of "appreciating" for "knowing." This alteration was meant to correct the criticism that "know" placed too much emphasis on cognition. "Appreciating" was thought to require a "far-reaching legal and medical consideration" of the accused's state.

The Canadian enquiry agreed with the English Royal Commission on Capital Punishment which argued that *M'Naghten* did not take sufficient account of modern medical knowledge of psychoses such as melancholia, schizophrenia, paranoid states, general paralysis, senile dementia or epilepsy with insanity. In many of these cases, the Commission was told, "the individual's mind is sufficiently clear to know what he is doing, but at the same time the true significance of his conduct is not appreciated either in relation to himself or others." The Canadian report suggested that the substitution of "appreciating" solved some of these deficiencies. (The addition of "natural imbecility" also gave clear recognition that inherent mental abnormality was included along with mental illness that was made manifest some years after birth.)

The Canadians recommended the adoption of the broader meaning of "wrong" in the sense of "something that would be condemned in the eyes of mankind." (This follows the *Laycock* decision rather than the "legally wrong" test of *Cardinal.*) As we have noticed, the Supreme Court disagreed in the 1976 case of *Schwartz.*

The 1956 Royal Commission on Insanity received briefs from medical associations and individual psychiatrists. Many criticized the insanity rules but the consensus of opinion was that the law ought not to be radically changed. The critics could offer no better alternatives. They considered that, in practice, the rules had worked satisfactorily. The essence of the report is perhaps found in the observation that "alternatives that would make for better administration of justice could not be put forward." The test is clearly a legal, not a psychiatric, one; this is well expressed by one of Canada's most eminent counsel, J.J. Robinette, who said:

> ... it has been assumed that the Criminal Code purports to define insanity. It really does not do that at all; it merely purports to define under what circumstances a man shall not be held criminally responsible for his acts or omissions, leaving out any reference to insanity, because I think that that is probably what causes some of the controversy between the medical profession and the legal profession. After all, the Criminal Code is designed to protect the public, and the theory of section 16 is that it excludes those persons who are not responsive, having regard to their mental condition, to the deterrent features in the criminal law.

In administering this law in the courts, the following was suggested as a proper instruction for the jury:

> If you find on a mere preponderance of probability based on the evidence taken as a whole the accused was labouring under natural imbecility or disease of the mind to such an extent as to render him incapable of foreseeing and measuring the consequences of his act or of estimating a right or perceiving the full force of his act, you should find him not guilty on account of insanity; or if on a mere preponderance of probability based on the evidence taken as a whole you come to the conclusion that the accused was labouring under natural imbecility or disease of the mind to such an extent that he was incapable of knowing that the act was wrong (and by that I do not mean merely legally wrong, but wrong in the sense that it was something he ought not to do and for which he would be condemned in the eyes of his fellow men), you should find him not guilty on account of insanity.

The Law in Action

There is a vast chasm between psychiatry and law. There is a similar gap between the law on the books and the law in action. There is also a great difference between the theories of Freud, Jung and Adler and the way psychiatric evidence is produced and received in a criminal trial.

Cynics may take the attitude that only the rich can afford the luxury of an insanity defence. Others may claim that all the jury says to itself is, "Was the guy nuts?" Some may agree with this view of the jury decision-making process but with the reservation that the jury should not acquit if the behaviour of the accused was too monstrous. In these circumstances the thirst for retribution may be too strong and all psychiatric explanations or judicial interpretations of s. 16 of the Criminal Code may be disregarded. Were John Christie, John Haigh, Richard Speck, the Moors Murderers, Jack Ruby, Charles Manson, the Yorkshire Ripper or Son of Sam mad or criminally irresponsible? The courts seem to have taken the attitude that they were more bad than mad.

The following case is not typical. The crime was not a grisly affair. The accused was charged with manslaughter, not murder. The plight of the accused was a pitiful one—*if* the jury believed his story. The trial did not produce a duel between two teams of psychiatrists of equal eminence, both of which were convinced of the positions they postulated. This case was chosen because it raises many interesting points about the insanity defence. The legal points are clearly and simply stated, and the lawyers and presiding judge did not indulge in histrionics but, instead, addressed and instructed the jury in exemplary style.

The transcript of the trial is public property but, because the accused was acquitted and has children who could be hurt by too much public scrutiny, the identity of the case will be disguised. (The case is reported as *K.*)

The accused was charged with manslaughter because he unlawfully killed his wife. The facts of the case could provide material for many psychiatric casebooks. The accused, whom we shall call Douglas, was a man of forty-three years. He was a large man, over six feet tall, weighing two hundred and ten pounds. He was married to Verna who was about thirty-seven, five feet six inches tall and weighed about one hundred and seventy pounds.

Douglas had been married for seventeen years. Before his marriage he had lived at home with his parents. He was the second child of five and the eldest son. When he was fourteen, he had to leave school to support his family because his father had tuberculosis. He was the main breadwinner for his family for four years until his father recovered. Afterwards, Douglas was in partnership with his father in a successful business. He was a devoted son and still has a close and loving relationship with his parents.

Douglas married Verna and had three children. The witnesses, both prosecution and defence, including the wife's mother, were unanimous in assessing the marriage as an ideal one—loving, considerate, a "seventeen-year honeymoon." They also agreed in describing Douglas as a gentle man, a good citizen, a fond father and a dutiful son who was not given to temper or violence.

Not long after his marriage, Douglas bought a farm. It was used in connection with the family business. A year or so before his wife's death, Douglas had been persuaded to sell the farm. The sale realized a great profit for Douglas but after the sale he became increasingly depressed. He sought help from his family doctor who later referred him to a psychiatrist. He had a dozen visits with the psychiatrist before his wife's death.

The family doctor testified that the sale of the farm, which Douglas had loved, seemed to be the cause of the depression:

> . . . he had acquired this farm several years before and he felt that it was a link with reality or a stable, satisfying thing for him to be able to go out there to the farm on occasion, just relax and wander around. He just felt better when he had done this after the burdens of the day's work. . . .
>
> Q: And as a result of the sale of the farm?
>
> A: He felt a great loss, that he lost his touch with tranquillity, as it were, that he was able to obtain prior to this.

In more technical terms, Douglas's private psychiatrist testified that his patient seemed to have "a very severe obsession . . . an obsessive compulsive neurosis." Douglas also testified to his condition:

> Q: Around what did the depression circulate . . .?
>
> A: It was around the sale of the farm, I missed it so badly.
>
> Q: When you say you missed it so badly, what do you mean by that?
>
> A: Well, I had gone out there with my family, and it was no longer part of my work, and it just wasn't there any more.
>
> Q: Looking back on the situation, hindsight today, what do you say as to your attitude, feeling towards the farm?
>
> A: I don't understand how a man who could have given his family happiness and security could become depressed over a situation that could only bring happiness and joy to his family.

Q: Could you tell the jury what your wife's attitude was toward this condition that you had?

A: . . . she said that I should snap out of my depression before school starts or she would leave, and then I became more depressed because I tried harder—I felt that I shouldn't be depressed and I couldn't understand why I was depressed, so I tried harder to get out of this depression: and the harder I tried, it seemed the further I sank into the depression. I just couldn't seem to help myself. . . . I was more depressed because I didn't want to lose the woman I loved, and I became more depressed.

Later he was asked:

Q: . . . did she continue to discuss [her leaving] with you?

A: Yes. And then I would put my arms around her, tell her I loved her and everything was fine, and we would carry on. I always felt that we had such a good relationship, such a close relationship that . . . she would understand and, when I embraced her, hugged and kissed her, everything would be fine.

Q: What was the nature of your relationship with your wife over the years, in terms of embracing generally?

A: I embraced my wife in the morning before I left work and when I came home at night for supper.

After both the husband and wife had been to see the psychiatrist, they decided that they would go to Vancouver to live, to make a fresh start far from the farm which no longer belonged to Douglas. Douglas, however, could not finally make up his mind because he did not want to leave his friends. During this vacillation, Verna announced that she would not go to Vancouver and that she would leave him.

Douglas had been to the bank on the day of his wife's death, possibly to make arrangements for the move to Vancouver. The bank manager found him to be unusually uncommunicative and his conversation did not seem to make sense. In the bank manager's words, "he was there in body but not in mind."

Up to this time he and his wife had not discussed their problem with anyone outside the family. At 8:10 on the evening of the death Ms. S., a friend of the family, called Douglas and told him that his wife had been discussing the matter with her and that Verna was leaving. Douglas's daughter gave evidence of the next occurrence:

> . . . he was really upset and he was sort of stamping with his foot on the floor, and . . . he was saying, "she's going to leave me, I'm losing her. . . ." I think he was crying . . . and he was really upset.
>
> Then my sister and I were sort of, you know, frightened and—not of Dad—just; I don't know, we had never heard him yelling before; and we left and we went over to my girlfriend's.

Ten minutes after the telephone call from Ms. S., Verna was dead. Except for medical evidence, which will be described later, the only testimony as to the death comes from Douglas's evidence at the trial:

> Q: What do you remember next?
> A: I next remember being downstairs and putting my arms around my wife and—excuse me—and saying, "please, honey, don't leave." And I—it's like a dream. Whether I fell, I remember getting up and seeing my wife on the floor, knowing she shouldn't be on the floor, and phoning for help, and—
> Q: When you put your arms around your wife—why do you say you put your arms around your wife?
> A: Because I always embraced my wife, I always would—always.
> Q: Do you recall where you put your arms around your wife?
> A: Like, I would just put my arms around her body, around—just around her body, just to embrace her close to me, like I always did. I did that in the morning and I did it that night.
> Q: And do you remember—do you remember falling?
> A: It's very possible I fell, sir. And I sometimes remember falling and I sometimes remember getting up. It's very difficult, it's—it's very, very hazy. But I remember seeing my wife on the floor and knowing she shouldn't be on the floor, that something was wrong that my wife would be on the floor.

The gist of Douglas's testimony was that he had little recollection of the events of the day of his wife's death, at least not after the lunch with his wife when she said she would not go to Vancouver. The bank manager's evidence showed that his behaviour was quite peculiar. He had a vague recollection of embracing his wife, he also had some recollection of calling Ms. S.'s husband for help a few minutes later, after he saw his wife on the floor.

The police officer who came to Douglas's home soon after the tragedy reported that he asked the accused to explain what had happened, but he couldn't make much sense of his explanation. Douglas kept saying, "Father, father, call my father; I want my father." At other times, "he would grab me by the arms and say "[Verna], I love you." Most of the time Douglas was "just staring, wide-eyed, straight ahead."

Douglas was taken to hospital and placed under sedation. The following day he was questioned there by police officers (after proper cautions had been given). His lawyer was present during the questioning. Douglas stated that he remembered hugging his wife very tightly, he said she squirmed to get away but he held her tight. He said they both fell to the floor and he was on top of her. At one point he mentioned it all seemed like a dream. He said, "I wouldn't hurt my wife for any amount of money."

Douglas continued to say at his trial that his recollection of his wife's death was very hazy. He did not doubt that he had told the police officer that his wife had squirmed to escape but all Douglas could definitely remember was that he had been embracing the wife he loved. On cross-examination by the Crown:

Q: How are you saying to us today then, that you do not remember hugging your wife very tightly?

A: Sir, I embraced my wife, yes, I know I embraced my wife, and then, sir, embracing my wife tightly, and causing—and doing—causing her death, that anyone—there are times that she must have struggled; how could a person just stand there and not move.

Verna was in fairly good health before her death. She had a mild thyroid and a hypothalamic condition. There were also indications that she had attacks of narcolepsy, sudden episodes lasting some minutes where she would be in a twilight sleep approaching unconsciousness. She took large quantities of drugs which had been prescribed by her doctor.

The autopsy showed no abnormalities and the pathologist diagnosed her death as being the result of traumatic asphyxia, which was consistent with strangulation, and/or external pressure on the chest. Verna's death, a result of "air being forcibly prevented from entering the air passages," was more probably a result of external pressure.

If Douglas had intentionally or knowingly tried to hug his wife to death, and the autopsy evidence had persuaded the jury, there would be no reason why the verdict should not have been guilty of murder. Douglas was not charged with murder, but this result was unlikely in any case because there were no signs of violence in Douglas's house or marks of physical force on Verna's body.

The evidence was consistent with traumatic asphyxia but, as the pathologist who appeared for the defence suggested, the evidence was equally, or more, consistent with sudden death. In most cases of traumatic asphyxia, which arise in industrial and road accidents, there is crushing of the ribs and compression of the chest for some considerable time. The prosecution's pathologist admitted that the only recorded case of homicide by traumatic asphyxia had been the Scottish case of *Burke and Hare*. The two accused in that case made their intended victims very drunk and then hugged them to death (before delivering the bodies to an Edinburgh doctor who used them for surgical experiments and anatomical dissections). Douglas had hugged his wife without assistance and Verna was quite sober.

If Douglas had hugged his wife with the intention of doing her bodily harm and she had suddenly died in his arms from a variety of causes, he could still be convicted of manslaughter—if he were not able to prove accident or claim a defence of an unconscious act on his part.

Douglas did not claim the defence of insanity. The prosecution sought to prove that Douglas was suffering from a mental disease at the time of his wife's death. The prosecution's cross-examination of Douglas tried to show that the accused was mentally ill. (The prosecution was half-hearted in his attempt as most of the evidence was presented *via* cross-examination.) Douglas said on cross-examination:

A: And I never felt I was mentally ill; I know I was deeply depressed, and really, mental illness to me was something I read about, I saw on TV.
Q: Right?
A: And it said—you saw an old man sitting in a corner with his head bowed down, and it said, "give to mental health and help these people." To me, I was mentally healthy, I just didn't understand what it meant and what it was.
Q: But my question is, if you were not concerned with this case at all, other than being a—perhaps being a spectator, and you and I were talking about the case and that conversation related to the very facts that had come out before this jury, and I were to perhaps put the question to you and say, "Well, what do you think about that now, about that man?" wouldn't you say, "That man must have been mentally ill?"
His Lordship: Now really, I don't think that that is a proper question, I don't think it is a fair or proper question. I am going to rule it out.

In the cross-examination of the psychiatrists, the Crown also had little success. Douglas's psychiatrist had diagnosed his patient's illness as a neurosis. The defence lawyer had asked the doctor to differentiate neurosis from psychosis (only the latter would come under s. 16 of the Code). The doctor said:

A: Well, a neurosis is a disturbance that occurs in an individual when he is attempting to handle some stress reaction, and he perhaps doesn't do this very well because either the stress is very severe or his methods of dealing with it are not very good. And as a result, he kind of gets himself into difficulties and can't seem to get out of this difficulty. But it pre-supposes that he is still making honest logical efforts to get out of the situation. And so that what he is doing makes very good sense to any casual observer.
Psychosis, on the other hand, where the probable cause of stress is much larger or because his ways of handling it are less adequate, the methods that he uses—they don't make sense to the casual observer. In other words, there is a loss of reality about the way he is attempting to do this.

Another psychiatrist told the judge that Douglas's condition was a neurosis and that it was "a type of mental illness in that sense but not of such a nature and extent as to render him capable of appreciating his acts and the consequences" (and therefore not within s. 16 of the Code).

On cross-examination, the prosecutor asked the doctor:

Q: Now then, considering what he has gone through, that Douglas had suffered from a severe obsessive compulsive syndrome for some months, and he had also been depressed for a period of time in the sense there could have been this disturbing of the thinking process, wouldn't all these be symptoms or signs which could describe mental illness?
A: It depends upon what you define as mental illness; if you say that everybody

is mentally ill who goes to a psychiatrist, well, that's—and it wouldn't fall in that category of mental illness.

Q: I would never suggest that, doctor; but what I am suggesting to you, that if a person is depressed to the extent that you can describe him as being severely depressed, and in addition to that he shows other symptoms or signs of not arranging his thoughts correctly, wouldn't you say that he had mental illness?

A: Yes, if those things were true, I would say that.

Q: Now, then [Douglas] had mental illness?

A: Again, it depends what your definition is.

Q: Wouldn't that be . . . the logical step in the questions that you would come to after answering the questions I have already asked you? You said that if he was depressed and he had thought disorder—

A: You asked me if this would be mental illness, and I would say yes; that doesn't necessarily mean that I would say that mentally—that [Douglas] had mental illness in the strict sense.

Q: Yes?

A: Because I don't think, at least when I was observing him, he did have what I considered to be thought disorder.

Q: Well, what do you call mental illness then?

A: Well, I have difficulty understanding that question because I don't know whether you want me to talk about mental illness from the—as an expression of the man in the street, or whether as an expression that is used in law, or . . . a psychiatric expression?

Q: Well, what about the person who showed very noted mood changes, who was classified as severely depressed and did show this condition over a period of five and a half months and had been to a psychiatrist fifteen times. On the 18th of September, his banker wouldn't do business with him: What about this type of person?

A: Yes, I would think that person would fall certainly into a psychiatric state of mental illness, which is quite a broad one.

Q: Now the last part of my question, doctor, concerns the difference between neurosis and psychosis. A person who has a condition of neurosis, and if it's bad is really a person who is in a more severe mental condition than a person who has a condition of psychosis but it's not too bad, isn't that correct?

A: (*No reply*)

Q: In other words, let's take the severe case of neurosis versus a light case of psychosis?

A: Well, that's the meeting place for these two things and I would imagine they would be classified as being sort of an equal thing, I would say.

Q: And there are several persons with neurosis, who if they have it severely enough, do not know what they are doing, isn't that true?

A: (*No reply*)

Q: In other words, they don't appreciate the acts that they are doing, if they have it that severely?

A: No, I don't think that's so.

Q: You don't think so. Could you tell me why there are several persons with bad cases of neurosis who have been committed to the hospitals?

A: Well, some psychoses take the form of what we call pan-neurosis, in which a patient's every part of his thinking process has a neurotic element to it. Those patients are usually certifiable.

Within two days of Verna's death, Douglas had taken up voluntary residence at the Clarke Institute of Psychiatry. He remained there for seven weeks but he was not certifiable, and the staff doctors at the Clarke considered that he could function in the community and with his family so long as he had consultations with his psychiatrist. The Clarke Institute did not find any indications of psychosis. On cross-examination, one of the staff had said "... mental illness is a layman's term and it's a term that I avoid using. It's something which ... is so broad it at times has no value in terms of meaning." This witness referred to the stresses on Douglas, and how these stresses explained his behaviour. The prosecution asked:

Q: ... the very fact the mind itself, the very mind of [Douglas], that was really the cause for the failure to recall anything that happened. Isn't that right? In other words, it wasn't externally applied on the head, was it?
A: No, but they were external psychiatric factors.
Q: But when you speak about external psychiatric factors, you are immediately speaking about the mind itself, as compared to receiving a blow on the head with a chair, or a person who suffers from epilepsy, and so on?
A: Yes, we are talking psychologically.
Q: So you are saying then that because of the condition of the mind under certain stresses,.... that the mind then is really the cause itself as to what happened, isn't that fair?
A: (*No reply*)
Q: As compared to any other cause?
A: Yes, it's a problem of the mind being overloaded.
Q: And aren't we sort of splitting hairs when we say a person wasn't suffering from some mental disorder or illness?
A: No, I think there's more here than just splitting hairs.

Canada's best-known forensic psychiatrist, Dr. Kenneth Gray (who had legal and medical qualifications), agreed that Douglas was not psychotic, that the earlier diagnosis of "severe obsessive compulsive neurosis" was correct and that the accused did not need institutional care. Dr. Gray considered that Douglas had had "a severe psychological shock" as a result of the phone call from Ms. S. and his wife's plan to leave him. In a word he described the state of mind of Douglas as automatism: "he didn't know really what was happening, with the exception of a few isolated events. And, in my opinion, he had ceased, his mind was no longer in control of his actions to a large extent." The shock was not physical but the effects were similar to a man receiving a sudden blow on the head which caused him to be "stunned or dazed, not unconscious but with little awareness of what was going on around him." Dr. Gray did not believe that this condition was likely to recur.

The Crown cross-examined Dr. Gray, suggesting that the automatism was close to insanity or was temporary insanity. Dr. Gray could not agree and was unable to think of a case of temporary insanity with which he had been associated. In further questioning:

> A: It was a severe psychological blow to [Douglas] because he interpreted it to himself that his wife was leaving him for good.
> Q: Now why is there still some co-relation or relationship between the mind and what he did; in other words, why wouldn't he go out and—well, for example, take the first train to Quebec, or rob a bank, or something. Why is there still the mind somehow being directed to the problems that do exist?
> A: His mind had not stopped functioning completely. He did recognize his wife, he knew that she was his wife and I'm sure that his mind was still concerned about her leaving him.
> Q: Yes?
> A: So—well, peoples' minds just don't work that way, they don't go out and rob a bank if they always lived a law-abiding life, this kind of mind doesn't work out this way. I don't know why.
> Q: But you say that he—his mind wasn't operating?
> A: . . . I didn't say it was not operating at all; I said there was a diminishing consciousness, a diminished awareness of what was going on. He did remember putting his arms around his wife, he knew that she was his wife, he remembers seeing her on the ground, that he should get help.

Specifically, on the question of sane automatism, the following interchange took place:

> Q: Well, as a medical expert then, you don't attach any responsibility at all to a person who is suffering for a particular period of time from sane automatism?
> A: No, and there is a practical reason for that. If this diagnosis is right and you saw the person didn't need to be in a psychiatric or mental hospital as he would be in if it were insane automatism; likewise . . . if the defence of automatism is accepted, if it's a proper one in this case, then obviously he shouldn't be sent to imprisonment either. Therefore it's practical—
> His Lordship: I must intervene, I don't think this is proper at all, or a proper line of cross-examination.
>
> It is for the jury to decide those issues, and it will be for the court, if it is a proper case to leave it to the jury, whether there is an issue of insanity or not, and the consequences of that verdict are not a proper matter for the jury to consider.

And, again, in response to questions put by the judge:

> His Lordship: Q: Well, isn't automatism an unconscious involuntary action?

A: I think Your Lordship's wording is correct, but if I may refer to this glossary, which is published by the American Psychiatric Association, it has a definition of automatism in it—it's about one sentence:

Automatism: Automatic and apparently undirected behaviour that is not consciously controlled.

Q: Well, is it your evidence that, or your opinion that, in embracing his wife the accused had no conscious control of his action?

A: No, I don't think he had any appreciation, My Lord, of the force that he was using. I think he directed his original intention, which is to embrace his wife—he had that much conscious control over his conduct, but I don't think he had any appreciation of the force he was using.

Q: How would you explain his statements attributed to him afterwards. He is reported to have said, "She grabbed me and I grabbed her"; and in the hospital, something to the effect that she was trying to disengage herself?

A: Yes. Well, bearing in mind, My Lord, that he told me that whatever memory he had was very vague and very hazy, it's possible that his wife was making some motions, which he may have some vague recollection of. But I don't think he recognized those efforts on her part to escape from him.

The defence wanted Douglas acquitted on the basis of sane automatism. The prosecution sought a verdict of guilty of manslaughter or not guilty on the grounds of insanity (or specifically insane automatism). When all the witnesses, Crown and defence, had been examined, cross-examined and re-examined, the Crown asked for a judicial ruling that the jury should be able to bring in a verdict of not guilty on the grounds of insanity. The Crown maintained that the issue had been raised at the trial and, therefore, the jury should be able to deliberate on it. Counsel for Douglas argued that:

Firstly, it is my submission that the defence at no time raised the issue of legal insanity by reason of s. 16 of the Criminal Code, and that at no time was there a suggestion by the defence, nor by any witnesses for the defence that [Douglas] ought to be acquitted by reason of the fact that he had a disease of the mind which rendered him incapable of appreciating the nature and quality of his act, or knowing that it was wrong.

During the course of the trial, it is my submission that my learned friend raised the concept of mental illness, disease of the mind, on one occasion with Dr. Gray, and the only occasion that I can recollect when the concept of disease of the mind was raised, was quite properly raised by Your Lordship in the discussion between Your Lordship and Gray.

The defence lawyer also pointed out that Dr. Gray had told the court in his expert testimony that Douglas was not suffering from a disease of the mind and that the question of s. 16 had only been raised by the judge or the Crown. The judge ruled:

> I think the cases are in agreement, that is, is for the judge to decide whether there is evidence to be left to the jury on the defence of automatism. Indeed, I appreciate that any defence that conceivably could be relied on in the evidence, even if not relied upon by the accused as part of his defence, should be placed before the jury. And there is a difficult problem here whether the cause of the involuntary act or the automatism, if such was found to have existed, was due to disease of the mind, then the issue of the insanity should clearly be left to the jury.
>
> After considering these matters and bearing in mind that the alleged defence of automatism does not rest on a blow or other outside factor, and bearing in mind that in the broad general sense the accused had suffered before the 18th of September, 1969, of some disease that could be characterized as a disease of the mind, I feel that it will be necessary for the court to leave the two issues to the jury to bring in three possible verdicts; a verdict of not guilty by reason of insanity. In other words, I feel that it must be determined by the jury in considering the defence of automatism, whether this was a case of insane automatism or a case of sane automatism.

The eloquent submissions to the jury by Douglas's counsel showed that a defence of insanity was not in his trial strategy:

> ... [Douglas] functioned, tried, he was not better but he was functioning; no blackouts or no unconsciousness—functioning! A neurosis, not a psychosis; not out of touch with reality, in touch with reality. Coping, imperfectly but coping. Coping better.
>
> Four days after the event he goes into the Clarke Institute—no evidence of psychosis; neurosis. Functioning.
>
> You remember Doctor Hrab's evidence. A well-ordered man, thoughts in proper motion. Thoughts in proper perspective. No psychosis. No thought disorder. No thought disorder. Dr. Gray. No thought disorder, no psychosis.

He emphasized this again later in his address to the jury: Douglas was not in "a state of unconsciousness, not in any state of diminished consciousness where his mind was not with his body."

The judge's charge to the jury was an excellent one. After quoting s. 16, he told the jury:

> ... the expression, "incapable of appreciating" has been said to mean incapable of foreseeing and measuring, and the words "nature and quality" as used in the subsection do not refer to the moral aspect of what the accused is alleged to have done but refer only to the physical character of his acts or omissions. So it will be seen that the words "incapable of appreciating the nature and quality of an act or omission" have been said to mean incapable of foreseeing or measuring the physical nature and consequences of an act or omission.
>
> You will recall that at the end of the subsection it goes on to say, "or knowing

that an act or omission is wrong." In this connection the word "wrong" should be looked upon as having a broad meaning and not merely confined to the words "wrong in law or illegal." In this context the word "wrong" means that which would be considered by a reasonable man or woman using the ordinary standard of right and wrong. All of which means, that for the purposes of the section, a person is insane—and I only refer here to the second part, which may be relevant here—a person is insane when he has disease of the mind to an extent that renders him incapable of appreciating the nature and quality of his act or omission, or of knowing that the act or omission is wrong. Using those words as I have attempted to define them to you, from the foregoing it will be seen that if after considering all the evidence, the arguments of counsel and my charge you come to the conclusion that the Crown has proved to your satisfaction beyond a reasonable doubt that the accused caused the death, and if you come to the further conclusion that the preponderance of credible evidence shows that he committed the act which constitutes the offence with which he is charged and that when he committed that act he was mentally incapable of appreciating its nature and quality, or if he did appreciate it but he did not know that what he was doing was wrong, then in either such event, it would be your duty to find the accused not guilty by reason of insanity.

When you consider the medical evidence, you must bear in mind that the law of the land is that it is your responsibility and not that of the medical witnesses, no matter how eminent they may be, to determine the question of insanity; if it were otherwise, Parliament would have appointed a panel of medical men to determine such questions and would not have left such matters to the jury. So that is your responsibility.

These remarks to the jury raise two or three interesting points. The most obvious is the difficulty of describing the vague concepts of s. 16 with any more certainty than the original drafters of that provision were able to muster. The final paragraph quoted also raises the related point that whatever the renown and expertise of the psychiatrists for the Crown or the defence, the final decision, on the facts, rests with the jury.

Finally, the problem of burden of proof raised an important issue. The judge stated quite correctly the analomous rule that the burden of proving a defence of insanity is on the defence. Usually the burden of proving the issue in criminal cases is on the Crown—proof beyond a reasonable doubt. Insanity is an exception, although the quantum of proof for the defence is only on a balance of probabilities. In sane automatism, the burden should be on the Crown as this issue has nothing to do with insanity and only goes to the general question of the voluntariness of the accused's allegedly blameworthy behaviour. There was the further complication that the Crown, not the defence, raised the issue of insanity. In such circumstances should the burden be on the Crown and should the quantum of proof be beyond a reasonable doubt? The judge appreciated the dilemma but decided, in answer to comments by the counsel for Douglas, that he could not put it more plainly than was expressed in the passage quoted.

The jury asked a question:

> . . . could we the jury come up with a verdict of not guilty with a recommendation that [Douglas] continue with further treatments?

In answer, the judge directed them that

> there are only three proper verdicts, as I left to you, and that if your verdict of "not guilty," it would be received as an unqualified verdict of "not guilty." However, I see no reason why the foreman, if the unanimous verdict of the jury is "not guilty," and if that verdict is brought in, there is no reason why the court would not receive a recommendation, inasmuch as the evidence points to the fact that the accused is still under treatment, still under psychiatric treatment, and presumably intends to continue receiving those treatments. I would think it would be a very desirable thing that such treatment should continue, but while I am prepared to say that recommendation may be received, it will in no way form part of the verdict and will not be binding on anyone.

This is reminiscent of the decision of the House of Lords in *Bratty* v. *Attorney General for Northern Ireland*: the prosecution has a duty to raise the defence of insanity if the accused may otherwise be acquitted (in that case on the basis of automatism) when there is a real possibility that the accused may be dangerous and needs incarceration or treatment. This returns us to the basic questions: what should be the law's role and how should society deal with the mentally ill who commit crime (or have a propensity to commit crime)? In *Saxell,* the Crown had raised the issue of insanity. The accused argued that to allow the Crown to do so would be a procedure resulting in cruel and unusual punishment because he was denied the right to a short prison term and instead was made liable to a term of indefinite detention. The Ontario Court of Appeal did not agree and decided that "in exercising his discretion whether to permit the Crown to adduce evidence of insanity of the accused, the judge ought to have regard to the nature and seriousness of the offence alleged to have been committed and the extent to which the accused may be a danger to the public."

Douglas was found not guilty on the basis of sane automatism.

Automatism

This troublesome defence has only appeared in the last few decades. Automatism can be of the sane or insane varieties. The former results in outright acquittal and the latter leads to indefinite detention. Some forms of automatism occur through clear physiological causes—somnambulism, brain tumour, concussion, hypoglycemia, epilepsy and insulin shock. (See Illustrations 29(a) and (d).) These cause little difficulty because the physical (or sometimes neurological) cause of the condition can be relatively easily solved. The patient should adhere to a rigorous treatment program—of drugs or surgery—and there will be no recurrence. In terms of penal policy, the public does not feel threatened by such persons. Insane automatism is a more difficult proposition. Many feel that insane automatism is the last refuge of scoundrels because it is too easily faked. ("I had a blackout. Everything went blank and I can remember nothing.")

Two important cases have occurred in Canada in recent years. In both cases, the causes of the alleged automatism was not physiological. The accused had suffered psychological shock (as had Douglas) or they were in a state of disassociation. In *Rabey*, the Crown had appealed because the accused had been acquitted entirely, on grounds of non-insane automatism, and the case was sent back for re-trial after appeal to the Supreme Court of Canada. The debate can be summarized from the remarks of Martin J.A. in the Ontario Court of Appeal whose views were adopted by the majority of the Supreme Court of Canada:

> In my view, the ordinary stresses and disappointments of life which are the common lot of mankind do not constitute an external cause constituting an explanation of a malfunctioning of the mind which takes it out of the category of a "disease of the mind." To hold otherwise would deprive the concept of an external factor of any real meaning. In my view, the emotional stress suffered by [Rabey] ... cannot be said to be an external factor producing the automatism within the authorities, and the dissociative state must be considered as having its source primarily in [his] psychological or emotional makeup. I conclude, therefore, that, in the circumstances of this case, the dissociative state in which [Rabey] was said to be constituted a "disease of the mind." I leave aside, until it becomes necessary to decide them, cases where a dissociative state has resulted from such causes, for example, as being involved in a serious accident although no physical injury has resulted; being the victim of a murderous attack with an uplifted knife, notwithstanding that the victim has managed to escape physical injury; seeing a loved one murdered or seriously assaulted, and like situations. Such external events might reasonably be presumed to affect the average normal person without reference to the subjective makeup of the person exposed to such experience.

In *Revelle* (1979), the accused was acquitted of robbery (and related offences involving firearms) on the basis of non-insane automatism. The Crown appealed successfully and a new trial was ordered. D had become very depressed by the death of his wife due to leukemia. He started to drink very heavily and was placed in a psychiatric hospital. A psychiatrist testified that D suffered brain damage, that alcohol tended to release automatic behaviour in brain-damaged people, that he was grief-stricken and hostile as the result of his wife's death. The Court of Appeal disapproved of the trial judge's decision to leave sane automatism to the jury along with the defences of insanity and drunkenness. Martin J.A. said (and the Supreme Court of Canada agreed):

> ... the dissociative state, if found to exist, was a disease of the mind, and the defence of non-insane automatism was not open to [D]. We take it to be established that a malfunctioning of the mind produced solely by brain damage of a pathological nature as distinct, for example, from a transient state caused by a blow on the head resulting in concussion is a disease of the mind. We are of the view that if the brain damage ... contributed to the dissociated state said to exist, the resulting automatism was insane automatism, notwithstanding that other factors, including drunkenness, contributed to [D's] condition.

These two decisions suggest that the courts are going to become less receptive to the defence of sane automatism.

7/DRUGS: A PROBLEM of LAW and MORALS

More than forty years ago Walter Lippmann wrote *A Preface to Morals.* His comments provide a thought-provoking introduction to the problem of drugs:

> Nothing in the modern world is more chaotic—not its politics, its business or its sexual relations—than the minds of orthodox moralists who suppose that the problem of morals is somehow to find a way of reinforcing the sanctions which are dissolving. How can we, they say in effect, find formulas and rhetoric potent enough to make men behave? . . .
>
> They have misconceived the moral problem, and therefore they misconceive the function of the moralist. An authoritative code of morals has force and effect when it expresses the settled customs of a stable society, the pharisee can impose upon the minority only such conventions as the majority find appropriate and necessary. . . . The moralist cannot teach what is revealed; he must reveal what can be taught. He has to seek insight rather than to preach.

When the average citizen thinks of drugs, he immediately thinks of junkies, hippies "doing up" on pot or hash and speed freaks. He should also include himself as a drug addict if he smokes cigarettes, likes his habitual martini or Scotch before dinner or chews tranquillizers or pep pills before an important meeting. This is best expressed by a Reidford cartoon in the Toronto *Globe and Mail* showing two middle-aged middle-class matrons pushing their supermarket carts. One says to the other, "I am sure I would be on drugs too if it weren't for my tranquillizers."

We live in a drug culture and we cannot avoid the problems by ignoring it or by passing repressive legislation. To what extent is the adult's crusade against youth and its drugs spawned partly by envy and partly by guilt? and to what extent is it spawned by their own immoderate use of drugs? The legal problem of drugs first became obvious when the United States passed the Volstead Act which outlawed the sale of alcoholic beverages. (Canada's folly was called the Scott Act.) The results were disastrous. Prohibition laws were ignored and, in fact, flaunted. A "forbidden fruit" philosophy developed; when liquor was illegal, it became more attractive, evading the revenuers became an exciting game, and an illicit drink was a delightful sin. Organized criminals discovered that good money was to be made out of human vice. Al Capone, for instance, owes his initial success to the prohibition era when he made fortunes out of illegal booze. Many "respectable" law-abiding individuals in Canada made similar fortunes out of bootlegging and rum-running.

Prohibition came about because social reformers, such as Carrie Nation, were convinced that all the evils of the world had emerged from a liquor bottle. The electorate was persuaded and this unpopular, unenforceable law was put into force. Morals triumphed over common sense. The Volstead Act was a clear attempt to legislate morality. The hysterical propaganda of the temperance groups had convinced a majority of the legislators that liquor should be illegal.

Can we say that the Women's Christian Temperance Union and other moralists were wrong when we look at the annual national expenditure on liquor, the convictions for public drunkenness, the lost work-hours because of alcoholism (along with the other effects of this disease such as mental illness, violent crimes, wife beatings, deserted families and economic and emotional suffering)? In the past thirty years, scientists have discovered very little about the effects of alcohol on human physiology or psychology, and scientific evidence has not enabled us to control the drinking habits of many of our citizens. Illustration 40(b) is based on *Swietlinski.* The evidence in that case shows great disagreement between the experts as to the effects of alcohol. In addition, the case shows a naïvete in the experts that would make one believe that they really have little practical contact with alcoholics. The facts of 40(d)—a real case—also show how mechanical tests for alcohol intake are only of limited use in judging the physical behaviour of those under the influence of alcohol.

Furthermore, publicly operated clinics to "cure" alcoholism are found in very few communities. No one has estimated the direct (let alone the indirect) cost of alcohol to the nation—in health costs, traffic accidents, absenteeism or inefficiency. The users of alcohol do not seem to be deterred by any form of social response—whether alcoholism as a ground for divorce, increased premiums for automobile insurance, decreased earning power or the sanctions of the Criminal Code or the Highway Traffic Act.

As we have seen from an examination of *Powell* v. *Texas,* to put an alcoholic in jail does not solve any problem except the very limited one of having physical control over the drunk for a few days. We send Powell to jail because we have no alternative. Powell is not a productive member of society. If a skilled technician or surgeon, a public official, a highly paid sportsman or a brilliant scientist develops a drinking problem, he more or less punishes himself because he loses his job, his income decreases, his status is destroyed or he is incapable of doing skilled work. If such a man becomes dangerous or a nuisance, he can afford to be sent to a private clinic for drying-out or, possibly, cure.

Intoxication as a Defence

Until the second half of the nineteenth century, drunkenness was usually considered to be an aggravation of a criminal offence. The law took the attitude that anyone who became inflamed by drink before committing a crime was more blameworthy than a sober person and, therefore, deserved additional punishment. About one hundred years ago, the English courts decided that in some instances an accused person could have a partial defence, so that murder would be reduced to manslaughter. These reductions in the status of the offence, accorded by the "benignity" of the law, resulted in mitigated punishments.

Of course we are speaking of voluntary intoxication. If alcohol or drugs are given to the perpetrator without his knowledge, he is not accountable for his acts. This shows the continuing importance of volition in the criminal law.

The guidelines of these early cases were hazy and were far from scientific. The intoxication had to be severe and there had to be some sympathy for the accused. (For instance, if he was contrite after he had committed an assault on his own child while in a drunken rage and the court felt that the accused had been partly punished by his own foolishness, the court might mitigate the offence.)

This rule is explained in *Meade* where the English Court of Appeal said in 1909:

> A man is taken to intend the natural consequences of his acts. This presumption may be rebutted—
>
> (i) in the case of a sober man, in many ways;
>
> (ii) it may also be rebutted in the case of a man who is drunk by showing his mind to have been so affected by the drink he had taken that he was incapable of knowing that what he was doing was dangerous—that is, likely to inflict serious injury. If this be proved, the presumption that he intended to do grievous bodily harm is rebutted.

This was narrowed by the House of Lords in *Beard* v. *D.P.P.*, and this 1920 rule is still applied and used by Canadian courts because the Criminal Code does not define the defence of intoxication. The accused had been drinking and raped a thirteen-year-old girl. In the process of raping her, he had placed his hand over her mouth and his thumb on her throat. The girl was asphyxiated and Beard was charged with murder (see Illustration 40).

Two of the rules established by Lord Birkenhead L.C. are clear enough. No one can claim intoxication as a defence if he became drunk simply to give himself false courage. A person whose drinking has caused insanity would be treated as if he were insane. In Canada that will mean he is found not guilty on the grounds of insanity and detained until cured of mental illness.

The third rule is less clear and has stirred much debate. The contentious rule in *Beard* provides that "evidence of drunkenness which renders the accused incapable of forming the specific intent essential to constitute the crime should be taken into consideration with the other facts proved in order to determine whether or not he had this intent."

No one seems at all sure as to the meaning of "specific intent." In *Beard* a special situation existed because the felony-murder rule applied. If an accused were engaged in a felony of violence and death ensued, he was guilty of murder (compare s. 213 of our Code). Perhaps this was the supposed relevance of specific intent. The House of Lords in *Beard* ruled that it was inconceivable in the circumstances that the accused did not know he was forming the "specific intent" to commit rape and, therefore, he was guilty of murder. The latter assessment is probably the more honest legal criterion in *Beard*. The "specific intent" test is not a test at all but a smoke screen of legalese to give weight to an untenable rule. Lord Birkenhead is really saying that the fact of intoxication should be weighed, along with the other evidence, in deciding if the accused had a guilty intent, *mens rea*, blameworthiness or whatever we might wish to call it.

The Canadian courts have taken a similar line. They have refused to follow the more liberal *Meade* rule. In *George*, for instance, the accused had assaulted and robbed the victim but claimed that he was drunk at the time. The trial court convicted him of the lesser charge of assault, but the appeal court held that this was logically unsound. The latter court argued that if he were too drunk to know that he was robbing his victim, he was too drunk to know he was assaulting him. Two subsequent appeal courts, including the Supreme Court of Canada, took the view that it was inconceivable that he was so drunk that he did not know he was striking the victim, and although he may have lacked the "specific intent" to commit robbery, he should still be convicted of assault.

In *Boucher* the British Columbia Court of Appeal disapproved of the Ontario case of *Vandervoort*. In the latter case, the accused was charged with rape. Even on the basis of the nebulous concept of specific intent it was difficult to convict him. Presuming for the moment that the concept has some merit, it has validity only if it means that the defence of intoxication negates some ingredient of the offence. Rape consists of sexual intercourse with a female who is not the wife of the rapist where the sexual act was done without the consent of the female. Vandervoort claimed that he was so drunk at the time of the alleged offence that he did not know that the victim was not consenting. The court accepted his explanation—that he was making a mistake of fact that would put him in the same position as if his mistaken view of the facts were true. Therefore, for the purposes of his trial, he was engaged in the non-criminal act of fornication and should be acquitted.

For reasons that are not entirely clear, the British Columbia Court of Appeal disagreed with this decision and stated that rape was a crime of general, and not specific, intent. In effect, the court disagreed with the result in *Vandervoort* because the trial resulted in complete acquittal while the morality of the crminal law dictates that intoxication shall be only a partial defence. When lack of consent could not be proved in *Vandervoort*, there was no crime left and the accused had to be acquitted. At the moment the law does not want intoxicated persons to be acquitted entirely, although persons who are intoxicated have no exercise of will in the acts that they commit. The law only accepts a partial defence, presumably because a man has committed an immoral act in being intoxicated or, to take a more technical approach, because the accused exercised his will in drinking in the first place. Therefore, the Judeo-Christian ethic is only eroded to the extent that the "conscience" of the law makes a non-specific concession to human frailty. In other words, the intoxication defence is a legal compromise. This seems to be the policy behind the third rule in *Beard*. In terms of *mens rea* or criminal responsibility, the accused does not know what he is doing when he is intoxicated (which seems to be the rule in *Meade*); the law, however, is not prepared to accept that a mind grossly and voluntarily befuddled by alcohol be considered totally lacking in legal responsibility.

The specific intent rule does not make sense. If a person (D) is very drunk and lurches against V and after he has managed to knock down V, he sees V's wallet which—because he is basically dishonest—he unconsciously or subconsciously pockets the wallet. If a person (D) is very drunk and lurches against V and after he has managed to knock down V, D—because he is basically a lecher—unconsciously or subconsciously decides to have sexual intercourse with V. It is difficult to understand why the first case is one of specific intent while the second is not.

The specific intent rule in *Beard* is lacking in logic, and this was acknowledged by the English House of Lords in the 1976 case of *Majewski*, although that august body refused to overrule the 1920 decision. The *Beard* rule was illogical and based on policy, not principle, but the Law Lords decided to leave law reform to the legislators. One would feel happier if the courts would be honest and say that the defence of intoxication was only a modified one because the law wants to make a moral statement about drunkenness.

The Supreme Court of Canada has now followed the *Boucher* rather than the *Vandervoort* rule. In *Leary*, the majority followed very closely the line of argument in *Boucher*. Specific intent is still the important ingredient in the intoxication defence, and rape is looked upon as a crime of general rather than specific intent. The remarks of the dissenting Dickson J. provided one of the most scholarly and thoughtful remarks on the criminal law ever written by a Canadian judge. He has written a very good statement on *mens rea* in general:

> When an accused, in answer to a criminal charge, says that he was so sodden as to be virtually an automaton, incapable of knowing what he was about, his defence is not drunkenness but an absence of voluntariness caused by excessive drinking. The question then is whether the act was voluntary. Likewise, when the offence with which he is charged includes a mental element which must be established by the Crown, such as intention or recklessness, it should be open to an accused to contend that upon all of the evidence the Crown has failed to establish the requisite mental element. The law should take no note of the inducing cause which led to the incapacity or lack of intent. On the other hand, it is generally recognized that the usual effect of drinking is merely to remove

self-restraints and inhibitions and include a sense of self-confidence and, perhaps, aggressiveness. If the accused was drunk at the time of the alleged offence but it is proved that he did the act intentionally or recklessly, it is irrelevant that but for the drinking he would never have done the act. The intent or recklessness, constituting the necessary mental element, is present and the fact that, by reason of drink, his judgement and control relaxed so that he more readily gave way to his instinctual drives, avails him nothing.

From the acts and statements of the accused and all of the other evidence adduced, the jury should be entitled to draw inferences as to the mental state of the accused. The concern is with the mental state of the accused in fact, and not merely his capacity to have the necessary mental state. Intoxication is one factor which, with all of the other attendant circumstances, should be taken into account in determining the presence or absence of the requisite mental element. If that element is absent, the fact that it was absent due to intoxication is no more relevant than the fact of intoxication giving rise to a state of insanity. The jury should be instructed that it is open to them to convict if they find that the accused intended to force intercourse notwithstanding absence of consent, or that he was reckless, in the sense I have indicated, as to whether she consented or not. If the necessary intent or recklessness is there, the fact that he acted in a way in which he would not have acted had he been sober does not assist him at all. The jury should also be instructed that if they are not satisfied beyond a reasonable doubt that the accused had the intent or recklessness required by law, he should be acquitted. In deciding this question, they should have regard to all of the evidence including the ages and background of the accused and the woman, the time and place and circumstances of the encounter, the conduct and statements at the time and following the event, the sobriety of each, and should draw such inferences therefrom as appear proper in the circumstances. In the case of an intoxicated or drugged accused, the jury may have little difficulty in drawing an inference of intent of recklessness in the relevant sense, but that remains an issue of fact for the jury to determine in each particular case.

Intoxication and Insanity

The Supreme Court of Canada also looked at intoxication in 1976 but in a slightly different context. *Mulligan* (Illustration 40(c)) was charged with the murder of his wife. He had been addicted to alcohol since he was sixteen years old and had undergone institutional treatment for alcoholism. He was also addicted to amphetamines. A psychiatrist called by the defence testified that the accused was suffering from dissociative reaction, a disease of the mind, and that alcohol was a factor in his condition but not a major factor. The doctor also said that some alcoholics became disturbed or deranged on a relatively small amount of alcohol.

Mulligan claimed the defences of provocation, insanity and intoxication. He was convicted of murder. The Supreme Court, in a 6 - 3 decision, upheld the conviction. The majority said that when the jury rejected the defence of insanity based on dissociative reaction, it was not necessary for the trial judge to instruct the jury to consider that psychiatric opinion when deciding the defence of intoxication.

The minority judgement of Dickson J. seems to make more sense. The dissenting judge was of the opinion that in considering the intoxication defence, it was necessary to consider the effect of the alcohol "upon the particular accused, at the particular time and in his then mental state. Mental condition is a relevant, indeed essential, consideration to a determination of *mens rea* if, in conjunction with alcohol, it affects capacity to form an intention." In a telling criticism of the majority, he concluded by saying, "A rigid categorization of defences, keeping medical evidence of insanity entirely separate from evidence of drunkenness is not only unrealistic but a departure from all that is embraced in the phrase *mens rea.*"

Dickson J.'s views are preferable but they will not prevail because the Canadian courts will follow the wrongheaded English case of *Gallagher.* They will be strengthened in this view by Martin J.A.'s views on sane automatism.

Intoxication by Drugs

In the 1960s there were several attempts to raise the defence of intoxication when the accused had committed some act while under the influence of a mood-modifying drug such as amphetamine or LSD. The decision in *Spicer* is typical; the trial judge said, "Where an accused voluntarily takes a hallucinatory drug in order to sate his appetite for dreams, and while in that state commits an act repugnant to society, he should not be afforded by law a harbour or refuge from an outraged society by merely saying to the Court, 'I chose to abandon my reason.'" Spicer was convicted of indecent exposure.

Another case, *Vlenko,* did grant a defence in such circumstances but it was only a decision of a trial court and of no great authority. The current mores are tolerant toward alcohol because it is the socially acceptable drug while other drugs are mostly illegal and used only by the deviant and the *avant-garde.*

On the other hand, the case of *King* (Illustration 29(c)) resulted in an acquittal because the drug was the socially acceptable drug administered by a legally qualified and recognized oral surgeon. In this instance (and in all cases described in Illustration 29) we treat the accused as having no mind. In other words, it is a case of sane automatism whether the cause is somnambulism, amnesia, a brain tumour or a blackout. In the *King* case, it could be argued that he had prior knowledge of the likely effects of the drug and voluntarily undertook the risk. The court did not take this view, although Leroy Powell was convicted on a similar argument.

Drunk and Dangerous

If we want to keep the meaning of criminal intent clear and logical, it is necessary to say that voluntary intoxication can be a defence. At the same time society may decide that a man who becomes brutal and enraged when drunk is a danger to other citizens. If such a man has been convicted twice or more for crimes of violence, society may be forced to control him in some way. Obviously, it makes no sense to impose several years in jail, particularly if we offer him no treatment or cure while he is incarcerated. Perhaps a new criminal code should have an offence of "drunk and dangerous" which would not result in long prison terms upon conviction but a compulsory program of rehabilitation. If the inclusion of such classification in the criminal code offends civil libertarians, then the dangerous drunk could be subjected to civil commitment, although the distinction may only be semantic for the subject is still incarcerated. The label over the institution will read "hospital" instead of "penitentiary." In both instances, we should ensure that appropriate and regular review procedures are incorporated in the legislation so that the dangerous drunk is not left to rot in a prison or, euphemistically, an alcoholic rehabilitation centre. If "drunk and dangerous" is included in a criminal code, the drunkenness should be habitual and the antisocial act should be serious and violent.

An alternative formulation would be to create an offence of "culpable intoxication" so that if a person physically commits a serious crime but his mind was befuddled by alcohol, then we could have a reduced offence of committing antisocial acts while intoxicated. In 1982, the Law Reform Commission of Canada had suggested that voluntary intoxication would be a legal excuse (as suggested by Dickson J. in *Leary*) but such person so excused could be convicted of "Criminal Intoxication."

We have already examined the decision in *Powell* v. *Texas* which is an excellent illustration of the theoretical versus the humane and the practical versus the ideal. In conscience, the dissent seems correct in calling public drunkenness a status offence that offends the principle of legality and basic constitutional safeguards. The "wino" or Skid Row type of alcoholic has no way of escaping arrest because, unlike the gentleman in his private club, the street or vacant lot is the only place to get drunk. On the other hand, there are no institutions available to treat the indigent alcoholic even if we had a cure. (Of course the fact that the southern states were not physically able to integrate their schools "with all deliberate speed" did not deter the U.S. Supreme Court from reaching its famous 1954 decision in *Brown* v. *Board of Education*.)

The dissent also made a frontal attack on the idea of criminal responsibility. The ruling of the majority that Powell exercised free will or volition when he took his first drink and was, therefore, criminally responsible is a legalistic argument. Yet all rules about criminal responsibility are equally legalistic and are purely juridical constructs that have little relevance to everyday notions of knowledge or intention. Perhaps one day the behaviourists will be able to provide us with more exact definitions and descriptions of human behaviour so that law courts will no longer be satisfied with a rule of thumb that merely approximates the workings of a man's mind.

Other Drugs

Other drug problems are now emerging and those who work with alcoholics (or perhaps even those who work with cigarette smokers who have been afflicted with lung cancer) have an understandable reaction against the more widespread use of cannabis, amphetamines, LSD, heroin and other drugs. Yet legal measures to curb their use seem to have failed. Attempts to deter the young by imposing heavy jail sentences for possession of cannabis have been ineffective.

Because of the increasing drug problem of the sixties, the Canadian government set up the LeDain Commission to enquire into the non-medical use of drugs. Children were sniffing glue and other solvents, many youths were being convicted of cannabis offences and sentenced to terms of imprisonment for possession and trafficking. Young men and women were dying of overdoses of drugs, including heroin and amphetamines ("speed"). LSD trips were sometimes resulting in death or serious injury. Parents reported that there was a growing drug culture in the schools and adults were concerned that the young people would move on from "soft" drugs such as cannabis to "harder" drugs such as speed or heroin.

Probably the great inducement for an investigation of the laws relating to drugs was that middle-class children were being convicted of criminal offences. The children of many well-known citizens were prosecuted. Graduate students in the universities were sent to jail. There was also a growing use of marijuana among the affluent, respectable middle class. The laws were being flouted, and enforcement became embarrassingly difficult. Citizens who had never concerned themselves with issues of civil liberties suddenly discovered that police investigative activities (they called it "harassment") were unjust and contrary to concepts of fundamental justice.

Because LSD was colourless, odourless and could be transported on a handkerchief in a concentrated form, such offences were difficult to prove. Citizens discovered that amphetamines were potentially more dangerous than cannabis but were available on prescription from doctors. The authorities also discovered that some "dangerous" drugs could be manufactured easily with primitive chemical apparatus. To put it shortly, a "drug culture" was supposedly taking over North American society. The statistics cited in the Interim Report of the LeDain Enquiry would certainly give that impression. In 1968, for instance, Canadians bought almost three billion aspirin tablets. More than 55 million standard doses of amphetamines and 556 million standard doses of barbiturates were produced or imported for consumption in Canada.

Some people forget that alcohol is not only a drug but also the most popular one. In the period from 1951 to 1967 the *per capita* consumption of alcohol increased by twenty-five per cent. In this period the increase of alcoholism was estimated to be sixty-three per cent. In the same period convictions for offences involving alcohol increased one hundred and fifty per cent (from 117,685 to 302,278 offences). Driving offences involving liquor—impaired or drunken driving—also rose drastically, by ninety-two per cent, in those sixteen years.

Unfortunately, comparable statistics on the use of other drugs are not so well documented and are therefore less accurate. The "official" manufacturing statistics for barbiturates and tranquillizers are probably conservative. There is a strong likelihood of large grey and black markets in these prescription drugs.

Perhaps the best indications are found in the effects of the non-medical use of these drugs. We all have some idea of the extent of the alcoholism problem. In addition, we should note that in 1961 there were 197 cases of barbiturate poisoning. Six years later, the number had increased to 478 cases. Similarly, there were 63 cases of tranquillizer poisonings in 1961, and in 1967, the cases had increased to 973.

The social picture for cannabis is much less complete. Marijuana does not seem to cause as much obvious harm as most other drugs including nicotine and alcohol. The incidence of use of cannabis is extremely difficult to gauge. The cannabis debate (and folklore) has often been irrational and hysterical. Its opponents said that it leads to heroin and organized crime, that it makes a man a homicidal maniac, a sexual maniac, a layabout or an imbecile. The potheads, who tended to be rather evangelistic, argued that marijuana makes the smoker a beautiful person, warm, communicative, creative and a generally first-class human being. The LeDain Commission tried to be realistic while working with little firm data; it estimated that if only eight per cent of high school students and only twenty-five per cent of university students have used the drug, then the population of users in Canada would be 215,000. This estimate is probably conservative because it ignores the use of cannabis by the middle class (or the silent non-proselytizing potheads).

The Commissioners were not able to give an accurate picture of the importation and distribution of cannabis. They suspected that these functions of the cannabis scene were not controlled by organized crime but were mostly carried on by users. Sales and distribution was done at the community level and among friends, without any large-scale, professional, well-organized entrepreneurs. (This has changed in the intervening years. There are now large-scale importers but they are not usually criminals who are organized for any purpose other than the importation of cannabis.)

The most interesting chapter in the report is chapter four, "Some Causes of Non-Medical Drug Use." Its authors accurately described it as impressionistic and they provided an excellent extra-legal picture of the drug problem. Quite rightly, the Interim Report stated that "it is idle to seek a single, unifying explanation or theory" of the problem that was "characterized by bewildering diversity and conflicting impressions, but certain dominant themes do seem to emerge."

For instance, the arguments for and against cannabis were well stated. The positive points:

> It is a relaxant; it is disinhibiting; it increases self-confidence and the feeling of creativity (whether justified by objective results or not); it increases sensual awareness and appreciation; it facilitates concentration and gives one a greater

> sense of control over time; it facilitates self-acceptance and in this way makes it easier to accept others; it serves a sacramental function in promoting a sense of spiritual community among users; it is a shared pleasure; because it is illicit and the object of strong disapproval from those who are, by and large, opposed to social change, it is a symbol of protest and a means of strengthening the sense of identity among those who are strongly critical of certain aspects of our society and value structure today.

Those who criticized the drug claimed that "it can dominate a weak personality; it can take too much time; it can become an excuse for procrastination; it lessens the ability to persevere with unpleasant, boring or routine tasks."

The Commission examined the social milieu and discovered the peculiar qualities of this drug generation: "a generalized middle-class affluence; a very rapid rate of technological change; the oppressive, almost foreboding character of certain problems or menaces which cast a serious doubt about man's ability to survive—nuclear power, overpopulation, environmental pollution, racial hostility and the widening gap between wealth and poverty." Youth was also seeking a more hedonistic life because the future will have more emphasis on leisure rather than work. There is a loss of faith in reason and a new emphasis on emotion. There is much discussion in the report of alienation and *anomie.* Two excerpts from the Interim Report reflect the values or anti-values of youth in the drug culture:

> The role which many reject is that of the achievement-oriented male, committed body and soul to the big corporation, and feeling increasingly the need to give proofs of his masculinity. Some have spoken of drugs as dehabituating, desophisticating, and deconceptualizing. . . . They speak of a release or recovery of child-like innocence. . . .
>
> It is a reaction against role and rule—an attempt to find spontaneity, variety and unstructured expression in personality and experience. This reflects again the importance of the dehabituating effect of the drugs—their capacity to break down moulds into which behaviour and personality are threatened with confinement by the various pressures toward conformity.

The drug culture was the core of the new "cult of experience." At its highest it was a new form of religious experience. On a more mundane level it "served "the purpose of relieving the stress and tension that most people, young and old, experience in modern living."

Finally, the Commission said of the cultural aspects of drugs:

> The Commission has very often been told by young people that they reject all that is traditional, conventional and stereotyped, because they consider it to be hypocritical, phony, dehumanizing, threatening and ugly. As a result, they may become alienated and some may be plunged into a frantic search for an identity which may be acceptable to them by their own standards. This search for identity may go in two directions: one leading to a pathological adjustment—the other simply to a non-pathological parting from conformity.

> In the pathological outcome, the individual may substitute a spurious identity for an authentic one, for instance, by accepting his belonging to a drug community as his new identity. Also, by displacing his inner needs, projecting his aspirations and denying his limitations, the person might settle for a drug-induced illusion of false power, rather than real achievement, and for chemically induced comfort, rather than true resolution of conflicts and tensions.

Some of the above reads like ancient history in the neurotic 1980s.

The Law

None of the above has much to do with the law. If only half of the social data quoted has any validity, it can be seen that the law is unlikely to be an appropriate social response to the drug problem. More stringent laws and repressive punishments are even less likely to be effective. This has, however, been the legislative and judicial response in recent years. (See, for instance, the Narcotic Control Act of 1961 which increased the penalties for trafficking and possession for the purpose of trafficking.)

Under the Narcotic Control Act, heroin, morphine and cannabis are all treated on an equal footing. Unauthorized possession of any of these drugs could lead to a maximum punishment of seven years (or a $1000 fine or six months' jail if the charge were dealt with summarily). For the offences of trafficking or possession for the purpose of trafficking, the maximum penalty is life imprisonment. The offence of importing narcotics has the *minimum* of seven years' imprisonment.

Unauthorized possession and trafficking in amphetamines, LSD and similar drugs are dealt with in the Food and Drugs Act. The penalties range from fines to ten years' imprisonment.

To a non-lawyer, the term "possession" seems uncomplicated. The Criminal Code defines it in s. 3(4):

> (a) A person has anything in possession when he has it in his personal possession or knowingly
> (i) has it in the actual possession or custody of another person, or
> (ii) has it in any place, whether or not that place belongs or is occupied by him for the use or benefit of himself or of another person; and
> (b) Where one of two or more persons, with the knowledge and consent of the rest, has anything in his custody or possession, it shall be deemed to be in the custody and possession of each and all of them.

Convictions have sometimes been obtained for possession where the amount found has been a few grains in the corner of a coat pocket. Clause (b) means that constructive possession is included in the definition of criminal responsibility; an accused need not be in physical possession so long as he has control over the forbidden substance or has knowledge of the substance being in the possession of confederates.

In Illustration 7, which is based on *Beaver*, D was acquitted because the

Supreme Court of Canada took a very subjective approach to the *mens rea* of possession. If the charge had been possession for the purposes of trafficking, instead of simple possession, D could have no defence because mere pretence that a substance is a narcotic is sufficient for conviction. If D had had a previous record, the prosecution may have been able to prove the previous convictions as similar acts (or a common *modus operandi*). In those circumstances, the court may not have been so willing to accept his *bona fides* and to presume his innocence.

We have seen elsewhere in a discussion of Illustration 57 that the courts have shown a tolerance for police behaviour in drug cases that would be unacceptable in other areas of the criminal law. Social policy allegedly decrees that the general, blank search warrant—the writ of assistance—gives wide powers to police to break down doors, enter and search without seeking specific permission from a justice of the peace. Of course, the officers are meant to have reasonable cause for carrying out their task but such niceties as seeking peaceful entry, having a list of persons or articles sought or being limited to the descriptions found in an ordinary warrant do not apply when they are acting under the Narcotic Control Act or Food and Drugs Act with the protection of a writ of assistance.

The courts have upheld convictions obtained by means of informers, *agents provocateurs* or entrapment. Once again the courts have been persuaded that the eradication of the evils of the drug market is so crucial to the protection of society that extraordinary powers are permissible.

In *Brezack*, the Ontario Court of Appeal condoned extreme police behaviour where the officers treated the appellant brutally in their attempts to retrieve a capsule of heroin that he had swallowed. He was a drug addict and, presumably, fair game because drugs are a crucial social problem that calls for stern measures.

Too often, the habitual criminal and preventive detention legislation has been used against drug offenders in a vain attempt to stop drug abuse. Repressive police measures and excessive punishments seem to make little sense unless the law enforcers are able to catch the exploitive traffickers and, with the help of lengthy deterrent penalties, are able to stop the supply of the drug. More frequently, the wholesalers go free and the junkies and pushers who support their own drug habit by selling are the victims of the system. We have no effective cure for heroin addiction, and incarcerating these addicts serves little purpose other than social hygiene.

The use of jail terms for possession of cannabis has been equally ineffective, although the courts have been blindly relying on the deterrent value of such sentences. Since August 1969, however, the prosecution has had the option of proceeding by summary conviction in cases of simple possession of cannabis and heroin. The sentences are now mild, usually resulting in conditional or absolute discharge, a probation order, suspended sentence or fine for possession of marijuana, although the sentences for possession of heroin have been less lenient.

The LeDain Commission's report was very much an interim one—partly because of the nature of the problem. The interim nature of the report was essential because public opinion on the drug question has been so changeable.

The social recommendations of the Interim Report are easily summarized—we need more research and more public education. The report showed very clearly that there are serious deficiencies in our knowledge of the effects of drugs and the incidence of drug use. There are similar gaps in the public knowledge of drugs. The first task is to dissipate the fictions and falsehoods that have developed; opponents and adherents of drugs have either given the impression that drugs will convert all users into sexual or homicidal maniacs or that drug users are on the brink of solving the world's problems.

In its report the Commission examined the dichotomy of law and morals and, in particular, the arguments of J.S. Mill, H.L.A. Hart and Lord Devlin. After stating the arguments of these commentators, the Interim Report took an interim position sympathetic to the Hart position:

> The state has a responsibility to restrict the availability of harmful substances—and in particular to prevent the exposure of the young to them—and that such restriction is a proper object of the criminal law. We cannot agree with Mill's thesis that the extent of the state's responsibility and permissible interference is to attempt to assure that people are warned of the dangers. At least, this is our present position, particularly in the light of such recent experience as the thalidomide tragedies. Obviously the state must be selective. It can not attempt to restrict the availability of any and all substances which may have a potential for harm. In many cases it must be satisfied with assuring adequate information. We simply say that, in principle, the state can not be denied the right to use the criminal law to restrict availability where, in its opinion, the potential for harm appears to call for such a policy.
>
> Without entering into the distinction between law and morality, we also subscribe to the general proposition that society has a right to use the criminal law to protect itself from harm which truly threatens its existence as a politically, socially and economically viable order for sustaining a creative and democratic process of human development and self-realization.

The Commission was not convinced by the arguments of the law enforcers that there was a necessary relationship between the cannabis offences of simple possession and trafficking. At the same time, the report would not recommend the total legalization of mere possession, at least until there has been further "study and consideration." The impact on the individual charged with simple possession should nevertheless be reduced "as much as possible" because present enforcement "would appear to cost too much, in individual and social terms, for any utility which it may be shown to have." Furthermore, the report found that the present possession laws "appear to be unenforceable, except in a very selective and discriminatory kind of way." This was considered unsatisfactory and only led to a "strong sense of injustice and a corresponding disrespect for law and law enforcement." The disenchantment with the law was compounded by the use of "extreme methods" of law enforcement. Therefore, the Commission recommended that simple possession of cannabis or a drug listed under the Food and Drugs Act should not be punishable by more than a fine of one hundred dollars.

In terms of the debate on law and morals, the Commission's examination of the cannabis problem is the most instructive. No doubt, the Commission was inundated with briefs in favour of the legalizing of cannabis. The following is a distillation of the most persuasive of those submissions:

1. The use of marijuana is increasing in popularity among all age groups of the population, and particularly among the young.
2. This increase indicates that the attempt to suppress, or even to control, its use is failing and will continue to fail—that people are not deterred by the criminal law prohibition against its use.
3. The present legislative policy has not been justified by clear and unequivocal evidence of short-term or long-term harm caused by cannabis.
4. The individual and social harm (including the destruction of young lives and growing disrespect for law) caused by the present use of the criminal law to attempt to suppress cannabis far outweighs any potential for harm that cannabis could conceivably possess, having regard to the long history of its use and the present lack of evidence.
5. The illicit status of cannabis invites exploitation by criminal elements and other abuses such as adulteration; it also brings cannabis users into contact with such criminal elements and with other drugs, such as heroin, which they might not otherwise be induced to consider.

In answer, the Commission decided against the present legalization of cannabis. A difficult problem of legalization was the age limit under which cannabis could not be sold legally. On a broader level, there was a pragmatic problem:

> How long can society wait for the necessary information? It is very serious that the scientific information concerning cannabis lags so far behind the rapidly developing social problem caused by its illegal status. It is useless to apportion blame. We have referred above to the necessity of research and a fundamental change in the attitude of government towards research. Given a sufficiently comprehensive and aggressive program of research, when are we likely to know enough, one way or the other, to justify a decision on legalization on the basis of potential for harm? It may be that we shall not be able to learn enough in time, at least with respect to potential for long-term harm, before we are obliged to take a decision on another basis—that is, on the basis of calculated risk, or the lesser of evils.

Nevertheless, the Commission decided against legalization for the following reasons:

1. First, it is our impression that there has not yet been enough informed public debate, certainly there has been much debate, but too often it has been based on hearsay, myth and ill-informed opinion about the effects of the drug. We hope that this report will assist in providing a basis for informed debate not only as to the effects, but as to other issues, including the extent to which science is capable of providing a basis for public policy decision on this question.
2. There is a body of further scientific information, important for legislation, that can be gathered by short-term research—for example, the effects of the drug at various dose levels on psychomotor skills, such as those used in driving.
3. Further consideration should be given to what may be necessarily implied by legalization. Would a decision by the government to assume responsibility for the quality control and distribution of cannabis imply, or be taken to imply, approval of its use and an assurance as to the absence of significant potential for harm?
4. A decision on the merits of legalization can not be taken without further consideration of jurisdictional and technical questions involved in the control of quality and availability.

Finally, the Commission made the following recommendations:

1. A moratorium on cannabis would not be a practical measure because it would amount to "*de facto* legalization without government assumption of responsibility for control of availability and quality."
2. Because it is clearly not a narcotic, cannabis should be removed from the Narcotic Control Act and placed under the Food and Drugs Act.
3. The definition of trafficking should be amended so as to exclude the giving, without exchange or value, by one user to another of a quantity of cannabis which could reasonably be consumed on a single occasion. This should be treated only as simple possession.
4. The police should abstain from entrapment and physical violence to obtain evidence. (The Commission regretted the need for the writ of assistance but reluctantly recommended its continued use in controlling trafficking.)
5. That criminal records be annulled after "a reasonable period of time."

The LeDain Commission's final report on cannabis did not differ greatly. More research into the drug's harmful effects was still needed before drastic legislative reform. The Commission expressed concern about the availability of cannabis to minors. Legalized use by adults would make it available to young people as the alcohol experience had shown. In addition, the report stated as a further argument against legalization, that it would be impossible to control potency and encourage moderate use under a licensing system.

The final report shows the Commission caught in a serious dilemma. The cannabis laws had not worked as a deterrent and they were presently too harsh. Their prosecution had also been ineffective because they had not been enforced uniformly. Yet, on the other hand, the Commission did not want legalized cannabis. It recommended that the simple possession of cannabis should be decriminalized. Cultivation of and trafficking in cannabis would continue to be offences but ones of less severity (with a maximum penalty of five years and a minimum as low as a fine). The Commission discussed the decriminalization of simple possession and continued prohibition of distribution:

> The actual perception of harm of cannabis is now so different from that which the law would suggest, that any change in the law could only be recognized as a belated recognition of the facts. It would not be interpreted as the law saying something new and hitherto unknown about cannabis, but the law being obliged to acknowledge what is actually known. The prohibition against distribution would serve to emphasize the continuing concern of the state.
>
> We believe that on balance the marginal effect which a prohibition against distribution can have on availability justifies the costs of continuing to apply it. We recognize that numbers of young people will continue to be involved in trafficking if only as part of the process of supplying their own requirements. But the act of making cannabis available is more serious in our opinion than the act of using it, since it involves facilitating use by others, and there are fewer people affected by the application of the criminal law. In other words, a relatively more effective impact can be made on availability than upon demand with much fewer people adversely affected by the law. The benefit is proportionately greater in relation to the cost.

Since 1972, when the final cannabis report appeared, a Senate committee has held hearings but no new legislation has been passed. In the intervening decade, everyone thought that the drug problem would go away. It hasn't.

8/SEXUAL OFFENCES— and RAPE

Introduction

There is no need to re-argue the question of the relationship between law and morals, although the issue is very obvious when we talk about sexual offences. We might well ask why the State finds it necessary to control sexual behaviour. If the government has difficulty in persuading its weak-willed citizens to control their ingestion of alcohol and other drugs, we can well imagine that it will have even more difficulty with "the sly biological urge," as Noel Coward called it.

The term "sexual offences" as discussed in this chapter will include all the offences related to prostitution and sexual acts that are considered crimes because of the age, gender or status of the "victim." In many instances the existence of a crime will depend on the real or implied lack of consent of the "victim." Rape (and some indecent assaults) must be looked at separately because rape is not so much a sexual offence (although it obviously has sexual components) as it is a crime of violence.

Today when we talk about sexual offences, important consideration must be given to the sexual integrity of one's body, the freedom to choose a sexual partner and the right to decide upon a particular sexual orientation.

In the Elizabethan and early Stuart period, the Church took a very active interest in the regulation of sexual activity as it did over marriage. Until the English Revolution of the seventeenth century, the Church, through its ecclesiastical courts, had a wide quasi-criminal jurisdiction over much sexual behaviour. The Church adopted the Pauline attitude of sexual asceticism—if the higher value of celibacy were beyond the male's moral resolve, then it was "better to marry than burn." St. Paul said that the Kingdom of Heaven would not be inherited by the unrighteous which included fornicators, adulterers, the effeminate and "abusers of themselves." Many branches of the Church still maintain strong opinions on sexual immorality but the punishment for such wrongdoing is limited to ex-communication or future damnation.

Today, many reformers argue that consensual sexual behaviour should not be the concern of the criminal law (of course, they admit that it might become non-consensual because of violence, coercion or exploitation and then the law might intervene). These reformers have had great difficulty in fixing on an age of consent, feeling that any figure chosen was arbitrary and, of necessity, related to chronological age rather than psychological maturity. They have chosen fourteen years as the age of consent for any kind of sexual activity. A quick look at the Canadian Criminal Code shows that the present law is very different; in some instances, factually consensual sexual behaviour with females can be an offence if the female is merely under twenty-one. Yet, in the mid-nineteenth century, sexual offences were limited to rape, abduction and male homosexual crime, and the age of consent for females was twelve years. The Victorian middle classes changed all that.

Attitudes toward sex have not changed. Methods of attempting to control it have simply altered. One perceptive commentator has said that the "history of the control of sex expression . . . has been the history of administrative failures." The sex laws have always reflected male values. Women have been treated as the property of men. There were only two kinds of women—"good" and "bad"—and the male world of the law was only interested in protecting the former. The double standard has been very durable—every man wanted his son to be a stud but to marry a virgin, and of course he expected his own daughter to be *virgo intacta* when she went to the altar.

The laws of the Anglo-Saxons and Normans seem much more interested in property than in protecting women. Women had a bride-price. If a stranger slept with a married woman, then compensation had to be paid to the husband. A law of 1285 decreed that if "women were carried away with the goods of their husbands, the king shall have the suit for the goods so taken away." There was no mention of the fate of the women. The term "ravish" had a very broad meaning and most of the laws concentrated on property rights rather than invasions of personal integrity. For instance, in 1285 a law provided for cases where a child "whose marriage belongeth to another is carried away." The taker was to be punished with imprisonment but only if the "ravisher have no right to the marriage." Another contemporary statute made it an offence to ravish or take away by force "any maiden within age . . . nor any wife or maiden of full age, nor any other woman against her will." The statute added that if the "maiden" were "within age," it did not matter that she consented but neither term was defined.

A century later, there was another law about ravishment; it provided that if "after such rape," the women "do consent to such ravishers," they lost all their property rights. Although the statute is not clear, one gains the impression that rape was an emendable crime (not much more than a tort that would be compensated by money), while adultery and fornication could result in a punishment of the taker with death or mutilation. This should not surprise us because our divorce laws until two decades ago severely punished an adulterous wife so that she lost all claim to support from her former husband (and frequently lost custody of her children).

Women were seen as chattels. They had little or no control over their own property (particularly after marriage and that disability continued until the nineteenth century). They were pawns in the marriage market and if they lost their marketability (i.e., they were deflowered) their value was severely diminished and their reputations permanently tarnished. The males were most interested in protecting their assets as is well expressed in a law of Henry VII (1487):

> Where women, as well maidens, as widows, and wives, having substances, some in goods moveable, and some in lands and tenements, and some being heirs apparent unto their ancestors, for the lucre of such substances been oftentimes taken by misdoers, contrary to their will, and after married to such misdoers, or to other by their assent, or dispoiled, to the great displeasure of God, and contrary to the King's laws, and disparagements of the said women, and utter heaviness and discomfort of their friends, and to the evil ensample of all other.

For the next four hundred years, the law is most concerned with abduction of heiresses and other women with property. In 1557 a law was passed specifically protecting heiresses under sixteen. A heavier penalty applied to any man who deflowered or secretly married such female. The Elizabethan era saw more stringent laws. Rape became a non-clergyable offence meaning that a first offender could no longer escape punishment by invoking the legal fiction that he was a member of the clergy. Another non-clergyable offence was created for any man to "unlawfully and carnally know and abuse any woman-child" under ten. Elizabeth I empowered the quasi-ecclesiastical Court of High Commission to "punish all Incests, Adulteries, Fornications, Outrages, Misbehaviours and Disorders in Marriage." She passed stringent laws to control bawdy houses which were "the cause of many mischiefs, not only to the overthrow of the bodies, and wasting of their livelyhoods, but to the endangering of their soules." There is little evidence that these laws were enforced very vigorously or that the populace was deterred from the proscribed behaviour.

The second half of the nineteenth century produced great changes in the laws to protect young women from sexual acts which hitherto had been consensual. Indeed by the end of that century the law protected young females from *all* sexual acts—at least those that came to the notice of the authorities and the parents. The causes are numerous—the general movement for reform sparked by Benthamite civil servants and philanthropists, the rise of the social gospel and the evangelical movement and the problems caused by increased urbanization. In particular, there was a strong current of reform to protect children and improve their lot in society—Sunday schools, compulsory education, the curtailment of child labour as chimney sweeps and in factories and coal mines, special institutions for children who were orphans, abandoned, neglected, destitute or delinquent. In short, the State became a surrogate parent. The modern idea of the family has its roots in the Victorian era with the rise of the middle class, who were affluent, respectable and ostensibly moral. The wife is idealized as mother, home-maker and helpmate to her busy, prosperous husband. His daughters do not work and emulate their mothers until such time as they marry. They must be protected and chaperoned until they reach the altar. The middle-class reformers wanted to impose their morals on the lower classes, partly out of a wish to do good and partly out of a condescending paternalism. Life for the urban working class was very hard, faced with substandard housing and barely subsistence living. Was it any wonder that girls from the working class would prefer a life of prostitution to the drudgery of being a scullery maid or a working-class mother constantly penniless and pregnant?

The Victorians did not abandon the double standard. The middle class deplored the sexual morals of the lower classes but their own sons were often responsible for deflowering the upstairs maid. They divided the female world into good and bad girls. They had some difficulty in distinguishing between them. They believed that children, particularly girls, should be brought up in total sexual ignorance and were very sentimental about childhood purity. At the same time, the reformers had an unhealthy preoccupation with masturbation. While they wanted to view pubescent girls and young women as angels (potentially good), they constantly worried that they were sexual time-bombs (potentially bad). The most famous statement on Victorian womanhood and sexuality was made by William Acton, a gynecologist and a student of prostitution:

> I should say that the majority of women (happily for them) are not very much troubled with sexual feeling of any kind. . . . Many men, and particularly young men, form their ideas of women's feelings from what they notice early in life among loose or, at least, low and vulgar women. . . . The best mothers, wives and managers of households, know little or nothing of sexual indulgences. Love of home, children, and domestic duties, are the only passions they feel.

The reformers spent the first major effort in improving the lot of the prostitute. In particular Josephine Butler fought against the Contagious Diseases Act which had imposed detention for medical inspection on women merely suspected of being prostitutes. Her motives were a strange mixture of the constructive and sentimental. She wanted women to receive better education so that they did not have to resort to the streets to earn a living. She also wanted to help these women to learn the advantages of a good Christian home influence which would deter them from the attractions of prostitution—idleness, pretty clothes and "a craving for some little affair of the heart to enlighten the insipidity of their lives." She accused the State, by legislation, of degrading women and forcing them to submit to medical attention so that men could indulge in vice with impunity. She pointed out that the Act only applied to the poor; a carefully chaperoned rich girl was never likely to come within the operation of the Act. The efforts of Butler, and other reformers, resulted in the 1871 Royal Commission. She appeared before it and told them of having seen girls bought and sold and demanded that the age of consent be raised to fourteen. Four years later, a bill was introduced to raise the age of consent to fourteen but, in Committee, it was reduced to thirteen. In the House of Lords, Lord Coleridge, one of England's most eminent judges, argued against the change because twelve was the age at which females could marry at common law. The House of Commons won out, and thirteen was the new age of consent.

In the next decade, many attempts were made to increase the age of consent but all were unsuccessful, due to the male monopoly of Parliament and the innate conservatism of lawyers and legislators. Drastic changes were finally made through the sensational yellow-journalism of W.T. Stead, who "exposed" the iniquities of White Slavery and the degradation of young girls. Stead claimed that he had bought a fourteen-year-old virgin from her mother and had spirited her out of the country, implying that she was housed in a Brussels bordello (when in fact she was safely living in a hostel run by the Salvation Army). Stead wrote a set of articles, "The Maiden Tribute of Modern Babylon," telling the story of Eliza. Modern commentators have questioned Stead's motives. Some think that he was a little too interested in the clinical details of proving Eliza was a virgin, a status certified by a midwife and a Harley Street specialist. Others have claimed that he was only interested in increasing the circulation of the *Pall Mall Gazette* of which he was the editor. Stead's articles started a newspaper circulation war and eventually resulted in Stead and an ex-madam, who had helped him, being charged with abduction of Eliza. They were both convicted and sent to prison. This contained a double irony. He was partly convicted because he had only obtained the permission of Eliza's mother but not her father. After his sentence had been served, it was discovered that the man who lived with Eliza's mother and who had not been consulted, was not in fact her father. While Stead was serving his sentence, Parliament passed the Criminal Law Amendment Act which raised the age of consent to sixteen and also made it an offence to procure or harbour young girls for purposes of prostitution.

The Canadian Position

Before Confederation in 1867 and the passage of the Criminal Code in 1892, most Canadian colonies relied upon the common law which provided that the age of consent was ten and it was no offence to have carnal knowledge of females over that age if the act were consensual. The Maritime provinces had passed some Acts. In 1758, Nova Scotia had made twelve years the age of consent. Rape was a non-clergyable offence as was the crime of carnal knowledge with a female under twelve even if she consented. New Brunswick (in 1829) and Prince Edward Island (in 1836) made it a capital offence to have carnal knowledge of a female under ten. If the female was between ten and twelve, it was a much milder offence. These two provisions also made it a crime to abduct a girl under sixteen against the will of her parents. All the colonies mentioned, and the province of Ontario, also had a law making it a misdemeanour to abduct an heiress for the purposes of marriage or sexual activity. There was no upper limit on the age of the heiress but later legislation put the age at twenty-one years. New Brunswick's 1849 laws made crimes of adultery, incest and fornication punishable with two years' imprisonment, but thirty years later, fornication had disappeared and adultery had become a less serious offence which could be punished with the relatively mild punishment of a $100 fine.

After Confederation, in 1869, the criminal law of the colonies was consolidated with a few additions. Procuring a female under twenty-one for purposes of "illicit carnal connection" became a crime. Abduction of females under twenty-one remained a crime but was extended to a female of any age if she had a property interest or was an heiress taken "from motives of lucre and with intent to marry or carnally know her."

The Canadian laws from the 1758 laws of Nova Scotia to the 1869 consolidation acts were not very original and copied the common and ecclesiastical law of England. While the property (and bodies) of heiresses were protected, the age of consent was not raised above twelve. In 1886, Canada partially followed England's Criminal Law Consolidation Act. This legislation, "for the protection of women and girls," was not as stringent as the English model because it only made it an offence to seduce or have illicit connection with a girl above twelve and under sixteen if she was of "previously chaste character." It was also an offence to seduce a female under twenty-one under promise of marriage if, once again, she was of previously chaste character.

The Criminal Code of 1892 provided a remarkably comprehensive system for the sexual protection of females and it was the work of one man—D.A. Watt of Montreal. Watt, as the moving force behind the Society for Protection of Women and Girls, was an indefatigable pamphleteer and lobbyist. For five years, Watt bombarded Ottawa with draft bills, pamphlets and letters. He argued that it was wrong that the law should only protect the heiress from seduction because "the conditions of girl life in Canada are such that the poor and friendless are in greater need of legal protection than the rich and guarded, and not in less need. . . ." He also wanted the age of consent raised from twelve to sixteen because the latter age was "somewhat nearer to civilized decency." Sometimes he enthusiastically but rather unrealistically suggested that the age of consent for all females in all conditions should be twenty-one. He devoted much of his attention to attacking procurers and the evils of prostitution. Watt and his supporters wanted the "better protection of females and the suppression of immorality and vice." They wanted tougher laws on "indecent publications" and adultery should be a misdemeanour. Watt's efforts were richly rewarded in the 1892 Code. Many of the provisions do not seem to have been enforced with any great vigour. Why? Because Watt and other reformers exaggerated the social evil of "white slavery," etc.? Or because the laws deterred the vicious? Or could it be that attempts to impose sexual morality met with public indifference or official corruption? The most likely explanation is that the 1892 Code was passed at a time when the child-saving movement was developing great momentum resulting in comprehensive child welfare legislation and the establishment of public and private social agencies to protect the child. Although the Code of sexual morals in the 1892 Code has been seldom used, nearly all of them are still found in the law today.

The plan of the Code is instructive. Title IV, "Offences against Religion, Morals and Public Convenience," contained Part XIII, "Offences Against Morality," and included sodomy, incest, gross indecency, obscenity, seduction, procuring, defilement, carnal knowledge of "dependent" females such as idiots and the prostitution of Indian females. Title V, "Offences Against the Person and Reputation," contained Part XXI, "Rape and Procuring Abortion": this obviously included rape and various abortion offences but also included defilement (or carnal knowledge) of a girl under fourteen whether or not the defiler believed her to be above that age. (The maximum penalty was life imprisonment with a mandatory whipping.)

Part XIII had a catalogue of offences to protect female virtue. Sections 181 to 184 created offences for seduction of girls over fourteen and under sixteen, of unmarried females under twenty-one under promise of marriage (by males over twenty-one) or seduction of a ward or of an employee under twenty-one. In each instance, with the possible exception of the ward, the seduced party had to be of "previously chaste character." Mr. Watt had wanted protection for immigrant girls travelling on steamships and trains. The second form of conveyance was not covered by s. 184 which made it a crime for anyone employed on a vessel to seduce or have illicit connection with a female passenger (presumably of any age) "under promise of marriage, or by threats, or by the exercise of his authority, or by solicitation, or the making of gifts or presents." In all these offences, except seduction of a ward, "subsequent intermarriage of the seducer and the seduced" was a valid defence and also reinforced the proprieties. Section 185 was a very elaborate section about procuration of females for purposes of prostitution; the females protected were those under twenty-one who were not common prostitutes or of known immoral character.

As stated earlier, sexual and moral offences in the 1892 Code have been changed very little but a couple of subtle amendments should be noted. The 1954 Code moved rape and carnal knowledge of females under fourteen from the classification of "Offences Against the Person" to "Sexual Offences, Public Morals and Disorderly Conduct." The offence of seduction of females fourteen to sixteen was changed in two respects. On the one hand, it was no defence for the male to allege that he thought the female was over sixteen but on the other hand, the court could acquit if "it is of opinion that the evidence does not show that, as between the accused and the female person, the accused is wholly or chiefly to blame." A further gradation of protection of females was added; it made a criminal of any male, who was eighteen years or more, who seduced a female of previously chaste character between sixteen and eighteen.

The Law in Action

The law often has to examine sexual behaviour, not only in criminal law but also in family law. Yet the law is very coy about defining "sexual intercourse." Indeed that term is seldom mentioned in the 1892 Code. It is only used in defining incest ("who cohabit or have sexual intercourse with each other"). Otherwise, the Code speaks of seduction, illicit connection, illicit intercourse, unlawful carnal connection, defilement, unlawfully and carnally knowing, fornication and unlawful carnal knowledge. The consolidation acts of 1861 and 1869 and the Code of 1892 did not define "sexual intercourse" but the 1927 Code provided that "carnal knowledge is complete upon penetration to any, even the slightest degree, and even without the emission of seed." This remains the same in the present Code except "sexual intercourse" has replaced "carnal knowledge." This section was passed mostly for the purposes of rape so that an accused person did not escape because medical examination did not find the presence of semen in the vagina.

The sexual offences created in 1892 have not been prosecuted with equal intensity. Some went through periods of popularity early in the century and are not heard of today. Therefore many of these sections are of mostly historical interest but they do provide an important lesson in the relationship between law and morals.

Defilement

Section 167 of the present Code (s. 187 of 1892 Code) makes it a crime for anyone who owns or controls premises to permit a female under eighteen to be on the premises for "illicit sexual intercourse" with male persons. The 1892 version had no limit as to age. One assumes that this was meant to be an attempt to control the use of houses of assignation which were not well known in English Canada until the advent of the motel. In 1892 there was no bawdy house provision as such. Section 185 of that Code was an elaborate provision but concentrated on procuring, enticing or inveigling any female under twenty-one into prostitution or "unlawful carnal connection." The good girl-bad girl dichotomy was obvious here because, as noted earlier, common prostitutes and women of known immoral character were excluded. D.A. Watt also managed to create further crimes in s. 185 that had nothing to do with prostitution. Subsections (g) (h) and (i) of s. 185 made it a crime to procure a woman under twenty-one for unlawful carnal connection by threats, false pretences or alcohol. Section 186 made it a serious offence for a parent or guardian of any female (no upper age mentioned) to procure such female for carnal connection or to receive the "avails of the defilement, seduction or prostitution" of such female.

The 1892 version of the "defilement on premises" section had referred to any female under sixteen being "unlawfully and carnally known." (The age was raised to eighteen in 1900.) All three reported cases occurred in the first two decades of the Code and all involved Orientals which suggests some discrimination that was certainly prevalent in Canada at that time. In *Karn* (1909) two girls, aged fourteen and eighteen, were brought by the defendent to his store. Karn had sexual relations with one girl, and his clerk with the other. T.C. Robinette, Karn's lawyer, argued that "unlawfully and carnally knowing" meant that the accused's sexual acts had to be contrary to the common or the statute law and not merely against the moral law. The Ontario Court of Appeal did not agree and decided that "unlawful carnal knowledge" and "illicit connection" meant "not sanctioned or permitted by law and as distinguished from acts of sexual intercourse which are not regarded as immoral." The other judges used the rather strange argument that of course the sexual behaviour was unlawful because any offspring from such acts would be unlawful (meaning illegitimate) or that the behaviour was unlawful because any contract to engage in such behaviour would be unlawful. And the final argument gave a very wide range to the meaning of criminality—any sexual intercourse was unlawful if it did not occur between a husband and wife.

The facts in *Sam Sing* (1910) were similar to those in *Karn* except the accused was the only person present. The Ontario Court of Appeal acquitted him. The majority said that the section was only meant to attack houses of assignation and it would be ridiculous if the accused could be convicted of having sexual intercourse on his own premises when it would not be a crime if committed elsewhere. The minority decided on the basis of general immorality but its viewpoint was further discouraged by a B.C. Appellate Court in *Sam Jon* (1914) where the court said that the accused's behaviour was "most deplorable immorality" but it was not a crime either by statute or at common law. This line of cases seemed to have been exhausted by the time of World War I.

Contributing to Immorality and Delinquency

The conservative decision in *Karn* had been strongly influenced by the English case of *Webster* which was decided a year before the Eliza case had inspired the Criminal Law Amendment Act. In *Webster*, a woman was convicted of "knowingly suffering" her fourteen-year-old daughter to be on premises where acts of prostitution took place. The premises happened to be their common home.

Davis arose during the 1914–1918 war. The accused had had sexual intercourse with a woman whose husband was serving overseas. The wife had a three-year old daughter and became pregnant by the accused. He was charged under the Ontario Child Protection Act. The Crown did not allege that the child was poorly cared for but that the mother was indulging in immorality. The appeal court reluctantly overturned the conviction but wished that adultery were a crime under the Code. The drafters of the Code had resisted citizens' suggestions that adultery should be a crime. The closest is the present s. 423(1)(c) which makes it an indictable offence to conspire "with any one to induce, by false pretences, false representations or other fraudulent means, a woman to commit adultery or fornication," although this provision has rusted from disuse.

As late as 1932, a Canadian court was claiming that s. 278(a)(iv), which was primarily concerned with polygamy, made adultery an offence. This subsection made it an offence for anyone "by mere mutual consent . . . who lives, cohabits or agrees or consents to live or cohabit in any kind of conjugal union with a person who is married to another, or with a person who lives or cohabits with another or others in any kind of conjugal union." A year after it was passed, *Liston* had decided this did not make adultery a crime and this was confirmed in *Eastman* (1932). The acquittal of Davis resulted in changes in Ontario law and in 1918 the Code was amended (to incorporate the Ontario law):

> s. 168.
> Everyone who, in the home of a child, participates in adultery or sexual immorality or indulges in habitual drunkenness or any other form of vice, and thereby endangers the morals of the child or renders the home an unfit place for the child to be in . . .

Ducker (1927) resulted in a conviction where the accused lived with a woman who was separated from her husband. There were five children in the house but it is not clear who were the parents. It is well to remember that this is at a time when it was extremely difficult and expensive to obtain a divorce. The court in *Okrainetz* (1929) took a more liberal view, although the facts are so peculiar that they rob the case of any precedent value. Two young persons were of roughly the same age, although the male was the female's uncle. They had a six-month-old child. They were acquitted because they merely lived together, since they could not marry, and the rationale of s. 168 was immorality for the sake of sexual gratification or indulgence. The judge never considered the second issue raised in the section—that the morals of the child had to be endangered but perhaps this is implicit in his first point.

At this time, the federal Parliament passed the Juvenile Delinquents Act 1929 which, by s. 33, made it an offence for any adult to contribute to a child becoming or likely to become a juvenile delinquent. One of the most recent instances of a conviction is *Stundon* which is described in Illustration 43(b). An earlier prosecution, *Strom,* which shows the dangers of mixed bathing, was less successful. The facts are a little cryptic but the judge had photographs to guide him. A mother had been cavorting in the water with the accused who was not her husband. The court offered these morally uplifting comments: "Bathers undoubtedly indulge in frolicsome conduct in the water that they would not think of under other conditions. [The photographs show] evidence of immodesty and indifference to outward appearances but is it conduct inducing juvenile delinquency?"

In *Vahey* (1939) the appellant had been convicted under the predecessor of s. 168 which only mentioned sexual immorality and did not include adultery. The police entered a house and found a woman in bed with a four-year-old boy. Vahey, the father of the child, was not in the bed at the time. The woman was separated from her husband and had lived "in sin" with Vahey for five years. The conviction was thrown out by the appeal court because it did not believe that mere adultery was contemplated by s. 168. Orde J.A. clearly expressed his disapproval of the trial court that "presumably takes the view that the father and mother of an illegitimate child must not be allowed to live together and to maintain and bring up the child and that the home is to be broken up by sending both father and mother to gaol. What is to happen when they come out of gaol? They cannot resume their former mode of living for fear that the law will pounce upon them again." Orde J.A. was unsuccessfully attacked by the trial judge in *Eastman*. He claimed that *Vahey* was limited to long-standing irregular unions but a person could be convicted for "sporadic acts of adultery" merely for the purpose of "gratifying her sexual desires." The trial judge in *Eastman* also wanted to convict because persons in merely "companionate" marriages imposed severe financial burdens on the public treasury because they were "almost entirely immune from civil obligations and criminal responsibility." The Supreme Court of Canada quashed the conviction and the judgement was written by Sedgewick J. who had been one of the drafters of the Code (but not the relevant section which was added in 1918). He did not want to interpret the Code too liberally and decided that "indulgence in sexual immorality" (which is not now the wording of s. 168) meant "giving free course" to sexual immorality. A further reason for allowing the appeal was the lack of proof of the child's morals being endangered. The child-savers and moral busybodies must have had a persuasive lobby because a year after *Eastman*, adultery was specifically added to sexual immorality, and a subsection added (which no longer exists) which created an irrebuttable presumption that a child was in moral danger or that a home was unfit once adultery or sexual immorality was proved. Two years later this very stringent provision was tempered by a proviso that the irrebuttable presumption would not apply to two persons living together with the reputation of being man and wife and if the child were theirs.

As can be seen from *Stundon*, most of the moral vigilantism after the 1930s was limited to "contributing" charges under the Juvenile Delinquents Act. One case, *Linda*, will suffice as an example of the judicial attitudes toward morals and female sexuality. Linda was charged with contributing to the delinquency of a minor; he was not a depraved older man but, himself, a minor. He had had sexual intercourse with a female under sixteen and with her companion (who was over sixteen) in the presence of the younger girl. He argued that he should not be convicted because the younger girl was already a delinquent. The appellate court refused to interfere with the conviction, although the younger girl was a "wanton" and a "sadly depraved girl," that Linda had contributed to her continuing delinquency. Walsh J. said: "I cannot conceive that it was ever intended that because a girl made two or three mistakes in her life, that she should thereafter be beyond redemption, and at the mercy of anyone who might wish to take advantage of her." In most cases, in recent years, the contributing cases have been limited to blatant sexual exploitation of youths and children by predatory strangers. This is despite the fact that in 1935 the following was added to the contributing section of the J.D.A.:

> s. 33(4).
> It is not a valid defence to a prosecution under this section either that the child is of too tender years to understand or appreciate the nature or effect of the conduct of the accused, or that notwithstanding the conduct of the accused the child did not in fact become a juvenile delinquent.

The courts manage to steer their way round this or ignore it. (*MacDonald* (1936) *Hamlin* (1939))

Seduction under Promise of Marriage

These last few cases give some inkling of judicial thoughts about female virtue but the most instructive cases are those where the accused was charged with sexual activity with a female under a specified age where conviction would only result if she were of "previously chaste character." The most common cases are those falling under the present s. 152—seduction under promise of marriage. This provision has remained almost unchanged since its original passage a few years before the 1892 Code. The words "or has illicit connection with" have been struck out. This seems to have been due to a comment in the Senate in 1920 that "You seduce a virtuous girl; you can have illicit intercourse with a prostitute."

The section is never used nowadays but there were several cases in the first twenty-five years of the Code's existence. Only a year after the Code became law, five judges of the Supreme Court of the, then, Northwest Territories heard a stated case of a man over twenty-one years who was charged with seduction, under promise of marriage, of a female under that age who was of previously chaste character. The accused had previously become engaged to the female but had renewed the promise of marriage at the time of the seduction. The judges refused to convict because they believed that the phrase "under the promise of marriage" qualified the word "seduces" and indicated the means by which the seduction was effected.

A decade later, the same court in *Lougheed* considered the situation of a young couple who had "kept company" for a month or two before "illicit connection" occurred under promise of marriage. Intercourse took place on a weekly basis for eighteen months until the female became pregnant. Was she of previously chaste character for the purpose of conviction? The court quashed the conviction but had some difficulty in wrestling with the meaning of "previously chaste character." All of the decisions we will examine show a strange mixture of pontifications on morality and slightly veiled discussions of contract law. Prendergast J. read the object of the Code section as the protection of the chastity and morality of female minors. This did not help him with the phrase "previously chaste character" which seemed to be unique to Canadian jurisprudence. It did not mean previous chaste reputation but pointed to "those acts and that disposition of mind which constitute an unmarried woman's virtue or morals."

Although the judge did not consider that the complainant in *Lougheed* qualified as a female of previously chaste character, this did not mean that a female could not be seduced twice (but obviously fifty or more times was stretching a point). A female who had "once surrendered herself" should not automatically be deprived of the protection of the statute. Prendergast J. prescribed that between the two acts of seduction, the female should exhibit "such conduct and behaviour as to imply reform and self-rehabilitation in chastity." In commenting on the complainant's predicament, the judge said:

> ... this young woman's faith in the accused should have been shaken long before the occurrence in question, and it is rather difficult to believe that this particular promise of September 1902, repeated for the sixtieth or seventieth time under the very same circumstances, was really and truly the inducement to which she allowed herself to yield on that day.

This decision was a liberal one compared with those that followed. A Nova Scotia court found it "almost inconceivable" that the magistrate could acquit the accused because the seduction was independent of the promise of marriage. Townshend C.J. decided that the offence was proved and that there was a "continuing promise." (The accused had proposed to the girl but had later told her that if she got into trouble, "I will marry you before anyone knows about it.") Townshend C.J. had written a very broadly based judgement as a deterrent, not only to the seducers, but also to inferior court judges who adopted a too-liberal attitude. Only Longley J., although concurring, showed any inclination to limit the scope of the offence. He was prepared to convict if the facts showed that the promise of marriage was the super-inducing means of the accused having his way with the female but did add, however, that if the cross-examination of the girl showed that she had "herself sought and desired the act of intercourse," then conviction would not be proper.

The courts were rather coy at deciding on a definition of "previously chaste." In *Comeau*, the court commented that if Parliament had meant *virgo intacta* to be the criterion for s. 152, it would have said so. Instead, the test must be one of reputation (which was also the current thought in the United States) and reputations could be rehabilitated.

The most litigated case in the field was *Magdall.* The Alberta Appellate Division was evenly split and offered very little illumination, although Stuart J. did suggest, perhaps with a glint in his eye, that if a female could be rehabilitated, there might also be a possibility of a "similar change in a male with the strengthening of this virtue and moral purpose." Davies C.J. of the Supreme Court of Canada did not treat the matter so lightly in upholding the conviction:

> I am not able to accept the argument that such a single fall from grace of a woman, engaged to a man to whose solicitations she yields, either because of a weaker will than her or that combined with affection and a hope of their prospective marriage under his promise, necessarily stamps that woman as one of an unchaste character for all future time. That surely cannot be so. There must come a time when repentance and pureness of living can rehabilitate her as a chaste character within the meaning of the statute.

Duff and Brodeur JJ. dissented. The former seemed to write a little more realistically than his Chief Justice:

> . . . evidence of previous conduct could only be admissible as tending to show a reciprocal state of feeling between the two persons concerned making it not only probable that the prisoner would desire to have intercourse with the prosecutrix but a disposition on her part also to yield to him.

To allow the prosecution to rely upon such evidence as a basis for guilt would, in Duff J.'s opinion, "be playing fast and loose with justice."

This problem was solved by an amendment to the Code in 1934 which became s. 301(4): "Proof that a girl has on previous occasions had illicit connection with the accused shall not be deemed to be evidence that she was not of previously chaste character." This addition of course appeared to be a concession to female feelings but there is evidence of the good old male double standard here. As long as the accused, and he alone, had deflowered the virgin, then it was not seduction. The male was not to be burdened with previously used or damaged goods.

Carnal Knowledge Under Fourteen Years

Cases of carnal knowledge of females under twelve or fourteen years of age have generated very little law. This crime is closely related to rape because the law presumes that consent cannot be given by a female of that age. Section 146(1) expressly provides that the accused's belief that the girl is over fourteen is irrelevant. This safeguard was necessary because the nineteenth century cases show that some courts had treated the question of consent as the same whether the charge was assault or carnal knowledge.

The policy of the law is well reflected in the scheme of the 1892 Code. Sexual activity with females under fourteen years was called "defilement" and found with the rape provisions (and carried a maximum penalty of life imprisonment and a whipping). Sexual acts with females between fourteen and sixteen years was called seduction and illicit connection and was only an offence if the female was of previously chaste character. The maximum penalty was only two years' imprisonment.

This arrangement ended with the 1927 Code revision when all sexual activity (including rape) became grouped under the same part. The term applied to sexual activity with females under fourteen years, and fourteen to sixteen years became "carnal knowledge." In 1954, the term became "sexual intercourse." The sexual acts proscribed under s. 146(1) are of little interest to us because no one doubts, not even the most *avant-garde* reformers, that females under fourteen years of age should be protected from sexual predators.

Most of the case law is concerned with corroboration which is not within our present discussion. The punishments inflicted are very far from the potential punishment of life imprisonment. The usual sentence was two years, although a whipping was often added.

Fourteen to Sixteen Years

This seduction—carnal knowledge—sexual intercourse offence can still be committed even if the accused thought that the female was over the age of sixteen years. It seems somewhat inconsistent that, despite the provision negating a defence of mistake of fact, the Canadian Parliament should add an amendment in 1920 which provided:

> . . . the trial judge may instruct the jury that if in their view the evidence does not show that the accused is wholly or chiefly to blame for the commission of said offence, they may find a verdict of acquittal.

This is still in the Code, although the apportionment of blame is described slightly differently—"as between the accused and the female person."

The first reported case under this section resulted in an acquittal because the court held there was insufficient corroboration. One has the impression that the parents were also on trial because they had kept insufficient surveillance over their daughter. The father testified that he had tried to keep himself informed of his daughter's movements, and although he knew she had been in the company of young men, he did not know of any young man "having an opportunity to have improper knowledge of her, and that he could not account for her condition [pregnancy] unless her story was true." The mother gave rather explicit evidence as to her daughter's "courses" (i.e., menstruation) or rather lack of them.

Most of these cases do not show the courts writing highly moralistic sermons about the purity of womanhood and the need to protect the morals of Canada's future wives and mothers. Criminal statistics are sadly lacking here but there is a suspicion that the law was not taken very seriously except by the parents of girls between fourteen and sixteen who were pregnant. There were very few cases of men being charged with the simple deflowering of virgins which suggests that, even in the 1920s, D.A. Watt's age of consent had been set too high for practical purposes. Most cases found the accused claiming that the complainant was not previously chaste and the courts making it clear that the burden of such proof was on the prosecution. Such a case was *Schermer* where seduction was defined as "not only illicit connection but also the surrender by a woman of her chastity to a man as the result of his persuasion, solicitation, promises, bribes or other means without the employment of force." And in *Gasselle,* Mackenzie J.A. said that illicit connection and seduction were not synonymous. On the other hand, a firmer stand was taken in *Stinson* where Martin J.A. decided that consent and submission were not the same. Stephen J. added that "a young child [she was fourteen] who submits to an indecent act no more consents to it than a sleeping or unconscious woman." Stinson's case was made even more difficult after 1934 because the then s. 301(2) of the Code (now 146(2)) was modified with the proviso (already found in s. 211(2)) that the girl could be still of chaste character if she had only had previous sexual acts with the accused.

Sexual Activity of Females between Sixteen and Eighteen

The criminal law has not been very active in prosecuting men for offences under s. 211 (now s. 151). Most of the decisions are concerned with corroboration but one or two judgements contain some purple prose. Langelier J. in *Fiola* consulted his Larousse and resolved to keep the double standard bravely flying:

> Chastity is a virtue which makes one abstain from the prohibited carnal pleasures and repel even the thought of it.
>
> Purity is the most perfect chastity. As far as the words *honour wisdom virtue* are applicable to a woman, it supposes the determination to remain estimable to the eyes of the world; *wisdom* brings the idea of prudence with which a woman must avoid the dangerous occasions; *virtue* suggests the courage with which a woman shall resist the seducer's attacks.

The judge did not necessarily think that "chaste" was limited to cases of physical chastity. If that were the case, "a woman of lewd conversation and manner, guilty of lascivious acts and of indecent familiarity with men is an object of [the statutes'] protection equally with one who is pure in mind and manners." The Code did not mean "constructive chastity" but it meant chastity in fact "according to the practical sense of that word." The result is unclear because the judge also seemed to approve of cases such as *Comeau* which had stated that Parliament would have said *virgo intacta* if it had intended that. He did not actually have to decide the question because he found that the complainant had confessed to two detectives of acts of "gross immorality" with another man which showed a "lewd and lascivious disposition" close to prostitution. Therefore she could not be put on the same footing as a "pure woman" for whom s. 211 was designed.

Section 151 is a frank attempt to control sexual behaviour between males over eighteen and previously chaste females between sixteen and eighteen years. Langelier J. saw the obvious purpose as the protection of pure young ladies. How would the learned judge view a female who was not quite as virtuous? The full bench of the Supreme Court of Alberta considered this problem in *Rioux*. The female concerned had decided to leave home and took up with a woman in a shooting gallery. The woman asked the complainant if she "ever did business" and advised her to enter the "sporting life" and gave her information "how she could avoid trouble as a result of carnal intercourse with men." The younger female took this advice and spent the night with a man who paid her ten dollars. There were other inferences that she had engaged in indecent behaviour with another man who "had possibly gone so far as to have got his private parts in juxtaposition with hers with her consent." The Alberta court affirmed the conviction of the accused. The rationale seemed to be the question of the female's chastity, although the court said that it had expressly refrained from a definition of "previously chaste character" because it was not necessary for the decision. The rationale seems to be that the complainant was *virgo intacta* until her sexual escapade (although there was no admitted evidence that she had had that physical condition). The court viewed her ten-dollar affair as no proof of her unchaste character; instead, the judge said that the accused had appealed to "her avarice and need rather than her passions."

In further explanation, the court said:

> Knowledge of these things comes to all women and . . . long before they have any practical familiarity with them. To impute an unchaste character to this girl because of her understanding of the other woman's talk would be an exceedingly unsafe thing to do, for it would follow that every woman, no matter how pure of mind, who understood the meaning of catch phrases descriptive of impurity, must be similarly branded.

These remarks are rather simplistic. No one would suggest that, even fifty years ago, a woman should be branded as unchaste because she had some knowledge of sexual matters or even if she had a foul mouth. On the other hand, it does not seem to make much sense to penalize the accused. If the criminal law, as opposed to child welfare legislation, should be invoked, it would seem to make more sense to charge the shooting-gallery woman with contributing.

These laws attempting to control sexual activity did not work because they did not protect females (presuming, for a moment, that that was a salutary aim), and they did not prevent such activity. The court in *Rioux* was punishing the female's first customer and was leaving her to the mercy of the sexual market for all future occasions. The law and society did not offer her good guidance to replace the influence of the woman in the shooting gallery and it offered no solution to the girl's economic needs.

Prostitution

Contrary to common belief, being a prostitute or engaging in acts of prostitution are not criminal acts themselves. There have been times in history when that was true; we have already seen the operation of the Contagious Diseases Act which in effect penalized prostitutes (with involuntary hospitalization), although even in that instance it was not a direct penalty for acts of prostitution. In an earlier chapter, we have also noticed the work of the Wolfenden Committee resulting in the Street Offences Act and Shaw's attempt to flout that legislation that had made it an offence for a female in a public place to solicit for the purposes of prostitution.

The Canadian law has tried to control prostitutes who were found in a public place. The essence of the crime was one of maintaining law and order. The wording of the legislation is worth noting in detail. The first Canadian provision was in 1886 and was copied from an English statute of 1775. The section was labelled "What persons shall be deemed loose, idle or disorderly or vagrant" and included prostitutes and "keepers or inmates of disorderly houses, bawdy houses or houses of ill-fame." The definition in 1886 was incorporated into the 1892 Code and remained unchanged until 1954. The loose, idle, disorderly persons included anyone who "being a common prostitute or night walker, wanders in the fields, public streets or highways, lanes or places or public meeting or gathering of people and does not give a satisfactory account of herself." In 1954, the wording lost some of its Victorian flavour and provided that a person committed vagrancy who "being a common prostitute or night walker is found in a public place and does not, when required, give a good account of herself." We have left the fields behind and the less picturesque but all-inclusive "public place" is substituted. Also note that the police are given the additional and positive duty of asking the prostitute's intentions. This was changed in 1972 and the Canadian and English laws are now very similar. Section 195.1 of the Code states that "every person who solicits any person in a public place for the purpose of prostitution" is guilty of an offence.

The important words in the latest prostitution law are "public place," "soliciting" and "person." Illustration 48(b) is based on the recent case of *Hutt* where the Supreme Court of Canada decided that the unmarked police car in which Dee and Constable Johns had their conversation was not a public place but a private one over which Johns had sole control. The Code defined "public place" for the purposes of s. 195.1 as "includes any place to which the public have access as of right or by invitation, express or implied." The last words might suggest that the unmarked police car became a public place when Johns allowed Dee to enter the car, but Spence J. answered by saying that to interpret the words in that way "would mean that if I were to invite anyone to enter my own home then that home would be a public place."

That would have been sufficient to dispose of the case except the Court was also asked to interpret the word "solicit." Dee had exchanged smiles with Johns and then said to him, "Do you want a girl?" and later, "I am a working girl. I am a prostitute." Ritchie J. decided that "solicit" in s. 195.1 "carries with it an element of persistence and pressure and I find no evidence of the existence of such an element in the description of the appellant's activities as contained in the evidence. . . . the police officer's own testimony to the effect that 'one of his duties was to make it appear as if he wanted a girl for sex' is such as to make it more appropriate to characterize the appellant's conduct as 'cooperation' rather than 'solicitation.'" Does this decision mean Dolores in Illustration 48(a) would be acquitted? She was a known prostitute and she was obviously not asking the time of day but the police did not hear what she said. Can "persistence" and "pressure" be implied without knowing the exact words? We have seen the law imply the mental and physical elements of a crime in other contexts and it may be done in prostitution.

The last problem about s. 195.1 is the meaning of "person" because the 1972 version of the Code degendered the section. This issue was faced in Illustration 48(d), and the courts of British Columbia and Ontario have come to different conclusions. In British Columbia, *Dudak* decided that a man could not be convicted of soliciting. The meaning of "prostitution" was discussed and the dictionary definition of "yielding of the body for hire or money" was accepted. Robertson J.A. said:

> A man who offers to pay . . . a prostitute for her services does the reverse of expecting or receiving money. He cannot be said to pay for the use by the woman of *his* body . . . Only she, the proposed or actual recipient of the money, can be said to engage in prostitution. A man who offers to pay . . . does so for the purpose of sexual intercourse.

Not a very convincing argument. The trial judge, whose decision was upheld, at least injected some social policy into the law as he interpreted it: ". . . the evil aimed at was the nuisance of prostitutes loitering and soliciting in public places . . . As far as I know there does not exist a problem of groups of potential customers soliciting and accosting people in public places looking for prostitutes." The Ontario Court of Appeal in *R.* v. *DiPaolo and Palatics* did not agree. In a much more elaborate judgement, Howland C.J.O. decided that a person who solicited a woman to have sex for money was doing it for the "purpose of prostitution" within s. 195.1 He added that such "kerb-crawling" by the accused would be very offensive to other pedestrians if the woman solicited was not a prostitute but "a woman of good moral character who is upset by the man's sexual advances."

Finally, how broad can we interpret the word "person" in s. 195.1? In *Patterson,* the accused flagged down a car and after he had entered the car, discussed with the driver prices for various sexual acts. The accused was in the process of opening the driver's trousers when he was arrested. The police discovered that the accused was a male dressed in female clothes. The court quashed his conviction but the decision has since been disapproved by Howland C.J.O. in *DiPaolo* because s. 195.1 speaks of "*every person* who solicits any person." This is in accord with *Obey* where a B.C. court decided that a male person could be a prostitute for the purposes of s. 195.1. We are in the strange situation that the meaning of the words of the Code, in this case "prostitution," are decided, in part, by the particular dictionary consulted by the judge. In *Obey*, the judge had consulted two very recently published dictionaries that had degendered the word "prostitute."

The problems of living "wholly or in part on the avails of prostitution" (Illustration 48(e)) do not offer easy answers. The decided cases are not very consistent. In many instances, the court was prepared to infer or imply knowledge in the accused that he or she was aware that person was a prostitute and was wilfully blind for the sake of gain. (Also remember the case of *Roy* discussed earlier.) Most readers would have difficulty in convicting the corner-store owner or Darleen's aged mother. The Code provides that:

> s. 195(2).
> Every one who
> (h) for the purposes of gain, exercises control, direction or influence over the movements of a female person in such manner as to show that he is aiding, abetting or compelling her to engage in or carry on prostitution with any person or generally . . .
> (j) lives wholly or in part on the avails of prostitution of another person.

Bawdy Houses

The word "bawdy" suggests immorality and lewdness. The other synonyms, "disorderly house" and "house of ill-fame," reflect the policy behind the law—suggesting lack of law and order. A disorderly house is not limited to sexual behaviour; it can also include a common betting or gaming house but we shall limit our discussion to bawdy houses.

The 1892 Code defined a bawdy house as "a house, room, set of rooms, place of any kind kept for purposes of prostitution." This definition was broadened in 1917 and has not changed much since. The present version found in s. 179 defines it as

> . . . a place that is
> (a) kept or occupied, or
> (b) resorted to by one or more persons
> for the purpose of prostitution or the practice of acts of indecency.

The 1954 Code simplified the location to the simple word "place" and omitted "home, room," etc., and included the word "kept" so that the keeper could be some person who did not occupy but was the landlord or silent partner. Recent events have shown very clearly that "place" can have the very widest interpretation so that a prostitute who committed sex acts in a car-park could be taken as using the car-park as a bawdy house. We also know, if we read the newspapers, that a bawdy house is not limited to the site of acts of sexual intercourse and could include a place where acts of heterosexual fellatio, cunnilingus and masturbation took place and also a place where homosexual acts occurred so long as the place was not private property and involved more than two persons or where one of the participants was under twenty-one. The definition of an indecent act must wait for a later stage.

In the meantime, we must consider the cases found in Illustration 48(f). In *Barrie,* the police had alleged that a Howard Johnson's motel was a bawdy house because sexual acts had taken place there on four dates between June and August, although the officers could only offer evidence of two sex acts (and only evidence of an auditory kind). The judge adopted the Supreme Court of Canada test of a common bawdy house, viz., (1) there is *actual* evidence of continual and habitual use of the premises for prostitution, (2) evidence of the reputation of the premises in the neighbourhood or (3) evidence on which an inference could be drawn that the premises were "kept and occupied" or "resorted to" and such evidence must consist of "frequent or habitual use for prostitution." On the first and third counts, the judge could find no evidence. On the second ground, the judge said he would be somewhat surprised to discover that a Howard Johnson's motel has a neighbourhood reputation as a bawdy house.

We have already seen the definition of "prostitution" and this seemed to involve money. In *Turkiewich,* the accused, who was a clerk at a "warm sheet" hotel, was charged with keeping a bawdy house; he claimed as a defence that there was no proof of intercourse and furthermore, no proof that money had changed hands. The court had no difficulty with the first point because it decided that it could be inferred from surrounding circumstances—hotel guests arriving without luggage, registering in a very vague manner, seeking rooms at unusual hours, guests found in the rooms in the nude and, in one case, in the act of sexual intercourse. On the second point, the court decided that the basis of s. 179 was "to repress ... the keeping of establishments destined to encourage immoral relations between men and women." On these tests, drive-in-theatres and college dormitories are undoubtedly bawdy houses. Admittedly *Turkiewich* was decided in 1963 and more recent cases would throw some doubt on its validity. For instance, *Broccolo* (1975) looked at the issues raised in Illustrations 48(f)(*c*) and (*d*) and decided that the motel owner might be convicted in the first but not the second instance because "the place" of a bawdy house ought to be treated as a "specific spot or area" or a specific room or suite of rooms. *Worthington* (1972) looked at the Illustration 48(f)(*a*) problem and decided that the prostitute's own apartment could be defined as a bawdy house.

We have seen that prostitution is not limited to payment for sex but could also include fornication. Some cases have also suggested that prostitution did not necessarily include sexual intercourse so long as the woman "offered her body commonly for lewdness." Using this definition, the courts convicted operators of massage parlours as keepers of bawdy houses. This view is summarized by the Manitoba court in *Ramberran* (1978):

> ... the evidence of the cost of the massage, the remuneration of the masseuses, the nudity of the participants, the out calls, the shower girl routine, the reverse

> nude massage, the massaging of the breasts of the females, the uncontradicted likelihood and probability of other sexual contact, the customer anonymity and the nude photos lead to one inescapable conclusion—that the accused were operating a bawdy house.

An Ontario court (*R.* v. *Ikeda and Widjaja*) acquitted in somewhat similar circumstances. The Crown had evidence of only a few instances but they did include admissions that the masseuses had performed masturbatory acts. The court followed an earlier case that said: "It is true convictions have been registered and sustained . . . on evidence of a single act of prostitution but always in such cases the surrounding circumstances established the premises had been habitually used for such purpose and in most cases had acquired such a reputation in the community." Of course in bawdy-house cases, the prosecution is not limited to prostitution in any event and can include "the acts of indecency." This explains the convictions in the notorious bath-house cases where Toronto police had raided such premises and found the owners guilty of keeping bawdy houses. Illustration 46(c) describes a borderline situation because the Downsview Steam Bath and Badminton Club is a private rather than a public club but more than two persons were involved, and under s. 158, this would make the acts of A, B and C unlawful and the management of the club operators of a bawdy house.

The Concept of Indecency

There is no definition of indecency in the Code. Section 163 makes it an offence to commit an immoral, indecent or obscene performance. Under s. 169, it is a crime to wilfully do an indecent act in a public place or in any place "with intent to insult or offend any person." It is a crime to be nude in a public place or in public view under s. 170. Nude is defined as "so clad as to offend against public decency or order." Sections 163 and 170 have been used against go-go dancers but the court has had some difficulty in deciding what kinds of "nudity" offended against public decency, and we find cases that state that bottomless or topless dancing does not breach s. 170 or s. 163 but a combination of both has been decided to be indecent. Other cases have suggested that exposure of the genitals is indecent but the courts have not been very helpful in explaining what exposure of the genitals means. Some cases have taken into account the types of audiences that patronize topless or bottomless dancing establishments and the fact that they attended such places for the very reason of seeing such performances. Yet are they typical? and would the ordinary citizen—the reasonable average person—feel the same way?

There are several sections of the Code that proscribe indecency or worse. Section 155 makes it a serious crime to commit buggery or bestiality. Indecent assault on a male (under s. 156) is done with intent to commit buggery or if the actor "indecently assaults" but no definition is given for the latter act. Section 157 makes gross indecency a crime and the use of the adjective would suggest that the latter is the more serious crime, but s. 157 attracts a maximum of five years while "indecent assault" under s. 156 attracts a maximum of ten years. Presumably s. 157 is a lesser offence because it is factually consensual. The 1954 revision of the Code made one important change in that the crime of gross indecency was degendered. We have already discussed the Wolfenden Report and the reform of the law relating to private consensual homosexual behaviour (which is replicated in s. 158 of our Code). Until then women could not be convicted of homosexual or lesbian behaviour, but this is now possible under s. 157. There is little case law on indecent assault by males. The courts have been coy in dealing with this problem. The same is not true of heterosexual indecent assault.

Indecent Assault on a Female

Indecent assault on a female is described in s. 149. It can be a serious crime of violence, and if so, then it is more properly treated as an attempted rape (see Illustration 45(a)) which has a maximum penalty of ten years, which is twice the maximum penalty for indecent assault. There are few prosecutions for indecent assault, although it is often a lesser included offence in a prosecution for rape, and due to plea bargaining, the accused pleads guilty to the lesser offence. Indecent assault should be easy to define: assault plus an ingredient of indecency. We have already noticed that "indecent" is not defined in the Code and is a very loose concept. Most people think of assault as a physical attack on another person. At common law, that is an assault *and* battery. Under the Code, by s. 244, an assault is defined more broadly; either an intentional application of force or an attempt or threat to apply force. What is it that makes an assault indecent? Simple suggestions or gestures may not be sufficient to justify a charge unless they go beyond mere preparation. What if a person touched the arm or shoulder of another? Is that an indecent assault? What if the person merely had an intent that was indecent? Thus we are left in a quandary to decide whether we should adopt an objective or a subjective test. The courts seem to have made the following rules: If the part of the body touched is not one generally associated with sexual gratification, the onus is on the Crown to prove that the assault was intended to be of an indecent nature. If the part of the body is so associated, then the accused will be obliged to offer some evidence as to why it should not be judged an indecent assault.

The case law is, unfortunately, based on the case of *Louie Wong* (1914) which, like the defilement cases looked at earlier, has racial overtones. The accused had followed a fifteen-year-old female, overtook her in an isolated place and, touching her, offered her five dollars to go with him for an "immoral purpose." The girl screamed and he left. In a very short judgement, the court decided that "an act in itself ambiguous may be interpreted [as indecent] by the surrounding circumstances and by words spoken at the time the act is committed." On this basis, all the acts described in Illustration 45(c) would be indecent assaults. If the accused's behaviour is unwelcome, as well as being objectionable and unsubtle, then women have a right to feel affronted in such circumstances. One would hope that males can be taught, by parents, teachers or by reading feminist writings, that there are better ways to organize male-female relationships. Some of the cases in Illustration 45(c) could be dealt with by diverting such problems from the criminal process and have them dealt with as human rights infractions or, in employment situations, by in-house disciplinary proceedings.

One of the essential ingredients of indecent assault is lack of consent. Section 149(2) provides that it is not consent if it were obtained by fraud. Two Canadian cases have examined this question. In *R.* v. *Bolduc and Bird* (1967), Bolduc was a legally qualified medical practitioner. Before carrying out a vaginal examination on a patient, he introduced his friend, who was not a medical doctor, as Doctor Bird, who would watch the examination by Bolduc if the patient did not object. On this introduction of "Doctor" Bird, she consented. They were both convicted of indecent assault but the Supreme Court of Canada quashed the convictions on the basis that there was no fraud as to the "nature and quality of the act" (as expressed in s. 149). In *Maurantonio* (1968), the accused had examined six female patients. They had consented to the treatment because they thought he was a doctor. He was not. He was convicted and in upholding the verdict, Hartt J. said:

> The fraudulent misrepresentation of the appellant that he was a duly qualified and licensed physician was not what induced the complainants to submit to the physical acts entailing the touching of their persons. The false representation which led to consent was that what the appellant was about to do was to conduct a medical examination or administer medical treatment. Since the representation went to the very nature and quality of the act to be performed the consent of each of the complainants, even if given in the full understanding of what physical acts the appellant was about to perform, (was obtained by fraud).

These contradictory cases provide an excellent illustration of different ways of interpreting a statute. The court in *R.* v. *Bird and Bolduc* treated the words "nature and quality of the acts" in a literal fashion. The female patient knew exactly what was being done. She simply did not understand the status of the bogus Doctor Bird. In *Maurantonio,* the patients comprehended the physical act done, but they were hoodwinked into thinking that the physical act was being performed by a professional and if they had known that Maurantonio was a phony, they would not have consented. The words "nature and quality of the act" were interpreted by the court in the latter case to imply "as performed by a medical practitioner" and the fact that *no* doctor took part was a fundamental false representation. Of course Hartt J. had to distinguish the *Bird* case and that explains his opening remarks. If both courts had asked the question "Would the female have consented if she knew the real facts?" would both cases have ended with a conviction?

Rape

The crime of rape is a crime of violence and passion. Much violent and passionate language has been traded between feminists (not all of whom are females) and those who see nothing wrong with the present state of the law and view rape as another sexual offence. In many instances, rape is a very physically violent crime and often comes quite close to murder. Few people, other than psycopathic misogynists, have any trouble seeing rape as a crime that requires the firmest community condemnation. When the rape is a dispute over consent, the issues are more difficult. In such cases, the argument seems to be less about the principles of the law than a discussion of sexual politics. Men fail to realize that their sex organs are weapons, and in many cases, they have been taught, at least by cultural example, to look upon women as sex-objects who exist for the physical gratification of the male.

Taylor's *Medical Jurisprudence* was the great text book in its field in the nineteenth century. In an edition from that period, the author stated that seventy-five per cent of rape charges were spurious. In fact, recent studies have shown that only a small percentage of alleged rapes are reported to the police. There are several reasons for this: the victim's anger and embarrassment, lack of faith in the criminal justice system and, in particular, the fear of being humiliated by investigating police officers and defence lawyers. Clark and Lewis have completed a study of rape in Toronto, *Rape: The Price of Coercive Sexuality*. The authors examined 116 cases. The police had decided that only forty-two were well-founded complaints. Clark and Lewis reached a different conclusion; after examining the files, they decided that only twelve cases out of 116 were unfounded as opposed to the police figure of seventy-four. In summary, they said:

> We believed that a rape had most likely occurred in 104 of the 116 cases we studied. If only forty per cent of all rapes are reported (the highest of all estimated reporting rates), then these 104 represented the approximately 260 rapes which actually occurred. The police classified only 42 of the 116 reported rapes as founded, and arrested 32 suspects. Given an average conviction rate of 51.2 per cent, approximately 17 suspects were probably convicted. Thus only 17 out of approximately 260 rapists are likely to be convicted in Metropolitan Toronto—only seven per cent. That is the highest estimate that any of the figures, at any stage of the process, would justify. As such, it stands as something of a monument to injustice, and a serious indictment of our criminal justice system.

The same Doctor Taylor had a different view: "... aside [from] the cases of infants, idiots, lunatics, and weak and delicate or aged women, it does not appear probable that intercourse could be accomplished against the consent of a healthy adult...." Clark and Lewis give a modern reply:

> ... rape was originally perceived as an offence against one form of property owned by men, and ... it has developed historically and legally within this conceptual framework.... It certainly comes as a shock to most women to learn that attacks on their sexual organs which do not result in physical injury are not illegitimate and will not lead to punishment of their assailants. So far as women are concerned, their sexual organs are no less, and no different, a part of their

> person than their heads, eyes and limbs. . . . it is totally arbitrary to conceptualize female sexual organs as being governed by a different legal framework than that which governs other bodily parts—but for the further reason that rape is always experienced as a potentially *life-threatening* situation.

The Law of Rape

We have seen earlier that the legal definition of rape does not necessarily require full sexual intercourse. That act is complete for the purposes of the Code if there is "penetration to even the slightest degree" and no evidence of emission of seed is necessary. These definitional changes were made necessary by the difficulty of proving "full" sexual intercourse. (See Illustration 44(b) where it is attempted rape in (*a*) and rape in (*b*).)

The Code specifically states that a female rape victim does *not* include the rapist's wife. This law even applies if the couple are no longer living together and is a further manifestation of the female as male property or more particularly, his exclusive property. Oregon and South Australia (and perhaps some others) have abolished this exception.

The core of the crime of rape is consent. Even as late as 1954, we find in the Martin's *Criminal Code* an annotation:

> It has been pointed out many times that a charge of this kind is easy to lay and difficult to disprove. For that reason, the character of the prosecutrix is in issue to some extent, notwithstanding that previous chastity is not an element of the crime. Thus, she may be questioned concerning her relations with men other than the accused. . . .

Consent does not mean that the victim must expressly state her objection to the act of rape. Consent can be proved by submission. In 1852, there was no law specifically making it a crime to have sexual intercourse with the feeble-minded (s. 148 of the present Code). In *Fletcher*, an English court invoked a thirteenth century statute in deciding that it was still rape to have sexual intercourse with a girl of weak intellect who was incapable of giving or withholding consent. In *Firkins* (1977) a Canadian court reiterated the principle—that mere submission does not infer consent. In *R.* v. *Plummer and Brown*, P threatened to do bodily harm to V if she did not have sexual intercourse with him and V submitted. Later B came to P's apartment and seeing V lying on a bed also had sexual intercourse with V. There was no evidence that B knew of the previous threats by P but the court decided it was still a rape by B.

The South Australian legislature has tried to extend the law relating to consent. (This jurisdiction has made other important changes. The crime of rape has been degendered so that male could rape male. The concept of rape has also been extended to include the mouth and anus as well as the vagina.) The new section states:

> A person who has sexual intercourse with another person without the consent of that other person—

> (a) knowing that that other does not consent to sexual intercourse with him; or
>
> (b) recklessly indifferent as to whether that other person consents to sexual intercourse with him
>
> shall be guilty of . . . rape.

A recent New Zealand case decides that a male can commit rape by omission. D and V are engaging in sexual acts. D does something which V does not like. V asks him to stop. He refuses and continues until ejaculation. The court decided this was rape because he failed to stop. V may have asked D to stop because he had struck her, because he was hurting her, because he was doing something "kinky" or because she remembered that she might be ovulating—the reason does not matter. (The accused had an ingenious but unsuccessful defence. He argued that for the purposes of rape, sexual intercourse was complete on the merest penetration and therefore V could not take back her consent.)

Corroboration and the Evidence of the Rape Victim

There is no statutory requirement that the evidence of the rape complainant be corroborated by other independent evidence (as in the law with respect to the unsworn testimony of a child, s. 586 of the Code). Until the 1978 amendment of s. 142, however, the trial judge, in summing up, had to warn the jury that it was "not safe" to convict a person charged with rape without corroborative evidence. This is no longer necessary.

Rape victims have often found the trial of their alleged attacker a humiliating experience because they felt as if they were on trial. Insensitive counsel, taking full advantage of the adversary system, used to cross-examine the rape victim as to her sex life, her methods of birth control and her "immoral" character. Section 142 tries to put limits on this behaviour by the accused's lawyer. This provides that "no question shall be asked by or on behalf of the accused as to the sexual conduct of the complainant with a person other than the accused" unless reasonable notice is given as to the types of questions that will be asked. The judge must hold an *in camera* hearing in the absence of the jury to satisfy himself that "the weight of the evidence is such that to exclude it would prevent the making of a just determination of an issue of fact . . . including the credibility of the complainant." This revision of the Code was meant to be a concession to the submissions of feminists. For instance, Clark and Lewis argued that cross-examination of a rape victim on her sexual history should be inadmissible but they added:

> The defence can always introduce evidence that, in a particular case, such questions should be admissible because they are relevant but the onus should be on the defence to demonstrate the relevance before they can be allowed. *The character of the rape victim is not a matter in issue* and this fact must be clearly articulated within the framework of the criminal law . . .

Section 142 certainly does not answer the objections of Clark and Lewis. The complainant in a rape case can still be asked questions about her general reputation for chastity including questions as to whether she is a prostitute. Similarly she can still be asked questions as to her previous acts of sexual intercourse with the accused. The law has always treated these issues as very relevant to the key issue in rape, viz., consent. On the other hand, questions about her sexual relations with other men could not be pursued if she denied such acts because the law considered the issues in question as "collateral," that is, such data were not directly relevant to the rape victim consenting on this occasion with this man, the accused. If some feminist reader wants to retort, "What has general reputation for chastity or being a prostitute have to do with *this* case of rape?" no persuasive or sensible answer is immediately heard.

Nevertheless, s. 142 only has control over questions about specific sexual relations "with a person other than the accused." In part, the new provision was meant to impose better manners on the accused's lawyer, and "to alleviate the trauma and the humiliation and embarrassment" of the complainant (as Laskin C.J. said in *Forsythe* (1980), the only case on s. 142 heard by the Supreme Court of Canada). The Chief Justice added:

> Section 142 may ... be regarded as balancing the interests of both the complainant and the accused. ... The gain of the complainant is that, whereas she may now be required to answer the question in public, she may not have to do so if the court rules against it, although she may have to submit to the question in private. As for the accused, whereas he could formerly put the question in public without necessarily being entitled to an answer, he now has the right of answer and the right to contradict it if the court rules in his favour in the *in camera* hearing.

In *Forsythe*, the Supreme Court made these findings:

(1) The "particulars" would include time, place and names of other sexual activities of the complainant.
(2) The *in camera* hearing is not limited to legal arguments by counsel on both sides. If the judge decides that witnesses should be called at that stage, he may do so. The complainant would be a compellable witness at that stage. Of course the judge may decide that the evidence he hears is too remote from the issues or too prejudicial.

There will be other decisions on s. 142 but the *Forsythe* ruling is capable of wide interpretation. It does not describe for us the range of questions which could be asked. In *Forsythe*, the judge thought that other sexual behaviour would only be relevant under s. 142 if it happened very close in time to the alleged rape. In *McKenna* (1976) Judge Greco did not construe the ambit of s. 142 quite so narrowly:

> ... evidence as to the prior sexual conduct of the complainant with persons she may have met, at bars, or, ... with persons *she* may have "picked up" at bars, has

> a direct bearing on the issue of consent here, since it is contended that her mode of operating in bars, in the past, was the same as it is alleged to have been on the evening in question. Further it is relevant since it is alleged that the purpose of her attending at bars in the past was to pick up or be picked up by men in order that she could engage in sexual intercourse with them, and here, she did permit herself to be "picked up." (Emphasis in original)

So long as the majority of judges and MPs are male, the rules in such provisions as s. 142 will not lose that male viewpoint that there are "good" and "bad" women and that all women want sex and it is only a question of salesmanship. Illustration 44(c) would strike many men as clearly a case of consensual sexual intercourse because they will not take "No" for an answer. As stated earlier, the examination of the crime of rape is not so much a legal argument as an exercise in sexual politics. At the moment let it suffice to say that it is very difficult to see how evidence of the previous sexual behaviour of the complainant has to do with her "credibility."

The Law Reform Commission of Canada had recommended in its report on Evidence:

> ... evidence of a trait of the character of the victim of a sexual offence that is relevant solely to the disposition of the victim to act or fail to act in a particular manner is inadmissible, unless the judge at the hearing *in camera* is satisfied that the admission of such evidence is necessary for fair determination of the issue of guilt or innocence.

We may be simply playing with words. Is "necessary ... issue of guilt or innocence" really any different from the "credibility of the complainant"?

Reform of the Rape Laws

The Law Reform Commission of Canada has given serious thought to the reform of sexual offences. In effect, the Commission recommended that the crimes of rape and indecent assault should be replaced by a single offence of "sexual assault." This recommendation states:

1. Every one who has sexual contact with a person without that person's consent is guilty of an offence of sexual assault.
2. For the purposes of this section "sexual contact" includes any touching of the sexual organs of another or the touching of another with one's sexual organs that is not accidental and that is offensive to the sexual dignity of that person.
3. In determining the sentence of a person convicted under this section the judge shall consider all of the circumstances and consequences of the offence including whether there has been penetration or violence.

The Commission is attempting to place the emphasis on the violent rather than the sexual qualities of the assault.

The Law Reform Commission of Canada has a reputation for trying to simplify the law, to look at broad concepts and to leave a large discretion to the judge. In contrast, consider the following Model Rape Law that was proposed by feminists who worked with rape victims in a clinic at New York University Law School:

Lack of Consent

Whether or not specifically stated, it is an element of every offence defined in this article that the act was committed without consent of the victim. "Consent" is used to denote meaningful and knowledgeable assent, not mere acquiescence.

A person is deemed incapable of consent when:

1. She or he is less than twelve years old; or
2. She or he is mentally defective, mentally incapacitated, or physically helpless; or
3. If she or he is more than twelve but less than sixteen years old, and the party to be charged is more than five years older than she or he, there shall be a rebuttable presumption that, in fact, there was no consent. For purposes of determining the sufficiency of rebuttal testimony, the greater the disparity of age between the parties involved or where the parties share the same household, or are otherwise related by blood or affinity, the weightier the presumption of coercion, abuse of authority and lack of consent.

Evidence

1. Evidence of prior sexual activity on the part of the victim or previous occasions of consensual sexual activity between the parties involved shall be inadmissible and immaterial to issues of consent and/or injury.
2. Marital relationship between the parties is no defence or bar to prosecution.
3. Evidence of earnest physical resistance to the assault by the victim is not required.

Assault in the Fourth Degree

A person is guilty of *assault in the fourth degree* when, with intent to harass, annoy or alarm another person:

1. She or he strikes, shoves, kicks or otherwise subjects her or him to physical contact, or attempts or threatens to do the same; or
2. In a public place, she or he uses abusive or obscene language, or makes an obscene gesture *or sexual overture*; or
3. She or he follows a person in or about a public place or places; or
4. As a student in school, college or other institution of learning, she or he engages in conduct commonly called hazing; or
5. She or he engages in a course of conduct or repeatedly commits acts which alarm or seriously annoy such other person and which serve no legitimate purpose; or

6. *She or he subjects another to sexual contact, e.g., touching, pinching, goosing.* Assault in the fourth degree is a class B misdemeanour.

Assault in the Third Degree

A person is guilty of assault in the third degree when:

1. With intent to cause physical injury to another person, she or he caused such injury, to such person or to a third person; or
2. She or he recklessly causes physical injury to another person; or
3. With criminal negligence, she or he caused physical injury to another person by means of a deadly weapon or a dangerous instrument; or
4. She or he subjected another person to any sexual contact which tends to immobilize or inhibit her or his freedom of movement however briefly.

Assault in the Second Degree

A person is guilty of assault in the second degree when:

1. With intent to cause serious physical injury to another person, she or he causes such injury to such person or to a third person; or
2. With intent to cause physical injury to another person, she or he causes such injury to such person or to a third person by means of a deadly weapon or a dangerous instrument; or
3. With intent to prevent a peace officer from performing a lawful duty, she or he causes physical injury to such peace officer; or
4. She or he recklessly causes serious physical injury to another person by means of a deadly weapon or a dangerous instrument; or
5. For a purpose other than lawful medical or therapeutic treatment, she or he intentionally causes stupor, unconsciousness or other physical impairment or injury to another person by administering to her or him, without her or his consent, a drug, substance or preparation capable of producing the same; or
6. In the course of and in the furtherance of the commission or attempted commission of a felony, or of immediate flight therefrom, she or he or any other participant if there be any, causes physical injury to a person other than one of the participants; or
7. She or he subjects another person to sexual intercourse.

Assault in the First Degree

A person is guilty of assault in the first degree when:

1. With intent to cause serious physical injury to another person, she or he causes such injury to such person or to a third person by means of a deadly weapon or a dangerous instrument; or
2. With intent to disfigure another person seriously and permanently, or to destroy, amputate, or disable permanently a member or organ of her or his body, she or he causes injury to such person or to a third person; or
3. Under circumstances evincing a depraved indifference to human life,

she or he recklessly engages in conduct which creates a grave risk of death to another person, and thereby causes serious physical injury to another person; or

4. In the course of and in furtherance of the commission of a felony or of immediate flight therefrom, she or he or another participant, if there be any, causes serious physical injury to a person other than one of the participants; or
5. *She or he engages in sexual intercourse with another person which results in serious physical injury.*

9/PROPERTY OFFENCES

Property offences contain a paradox. On the one hand, every citizen would agree that it is obviously both immoral and illegal for someone else to take his property. Similarly if your apartment has been broken into, you have experienced a very clear feeling of invasion of your private space. Yet, the law relating to property offences—theft (larceny), false pretences, burglary, robbery and fraud—are more fraught with legal ambiguity than any other area of the criminal law. While the average citizen may think he knows when his property is wrongfully taken, the courts have not experienced such certainty. The only way to understand this branch of the law is to understand its history.

It is axiomatic that these offences depend upon the type of property available in society for misappropriation, the owners of the property and the way in which the property is protected. Before the rise of mercantilism in England, most of the property was in the hands of the barons and most of their wealth was in the form of land or if they did have property, it was well protected. Those with most property lived in fortified places and had soldiers to guard them. Even in the early part of the nineteenth century, the property resided in the upper and middle classes who were well tended by servants and retainers who protected their property. Compare those situations with the present day when so many of us have so much moveable property that is not well guarded, when the stores have an open design that makes it tempting and easy for goods to be stolen, and when new forms of property are created yearly—so that there are dishonest dealings with cheques and with credit cards, and then the law must grapple with the taking of such intangible items as television signals, industrial secrets or computer programs.

Yet, less than two hundred years ago, the whole basis of property offences, and larceny in particular, was the concept of possession and of trespass. As noticed earlier, at one time most of the property was in the form of real estate and when such property was invaded, the legal process used trespass as a remedy against the wrongdoers. Anything connected with real estate—not just the land itself but also titles to land—were incapable of being stolen, i.e., resulting in a larceny charge. The law had plenty of remedies for those whose land was wrongly dealt with. The essence of trespass was a breach of possession of the land and the importance of possession was carried over into larceny. Larceny applied to all forms of personal property. The formal definition of larceny had the following ingredients: a taking that was a trespass, an offence against possession. If the accused already had possession before he misappropriated the goods, then it could not be larceny. If V allowed D to borrow V's book and D then misappropriated the book, it could not be larceny because D already had possession. This caused great difficulites, and as is so often the case with the law, the problems were solved by fictions, constructs and subterfuges. An employee is charged with larceny of an object of his boss who had given it to him to work on; the employee claimed that he could not be convicted of larceny because he already had possession when it was misappropriated (or "taken"). The same argument was made by a hotel guest who had possessions of the hotel. The law decided that the employee and the guest did not have possession but mere "custody" of the object. This may come as something of a surprise to those who have read the cases on possession of drugs where the court inferred possession or constructive possession, but by now, such readers have abandoned any thought that the law is likely to be consistent.

The law had similar problems with persons who had temporary possession—people who misappropriated while the goods were being transported or stored in a warehouse. Once again the law did not interfere with the basic concept of the law of larceny and in the *Carrier's Case* of 1473 where a carrier had been entrusted with bales of wool and had eventually stolen some of the contents of the bales, the court decided that he had only possession of the bales themselves, and when he "broke bulk," then he obtained possession of the wool itself and took it unlawfully. This legal fiction could not solve cases where the object could not be broken into or broken down into smaller parts. If D was given possession of such an item—e.g., a horse—the decision in *Carrier's Case* could not help. The problem of larceny by bailee was not solved until 1857 when remedial legislation was passed. (Similar crimes are found in ss. 285, 291 and 296 of the Code.)

Further difficulties were encountered when the employee was given something that was meant for his boss but instead he pocketed it. The most obvious example is the bank teller who accepts money for deposit and instead of placing it in the cash drawer, he puts it in his wallet. The money never was in possession of the bank and therefore it was impossible to convict of larceny. This was solved in 1779 with the creation, by statute, of the crime of embezzlement. This did not solve the problem created in the same year of 1779 by *R.* v. *Pear.* He had hired a horse and said he was going to ride it to X. Instead he rode it to Y and sold it. He also lied to the hirer about his residence. He was convicted but the exact basis of the decision is difficult to trace. The better opinion would be that the larceny occurred when he later decided to sell the horse because then he took "real" possession. If the law had said that Pear took possession at the time the hirer physically handed over the horse, this could not be larceny because there was no wrongful possession and no wrongful taking (or trespass) because he had the horse with the consent of its owner. By postponing the possession, the law was able to call it larceny. This legal fiction resulted in that strange hybrid called "larceny by a trick."

The case described in Illustration 51(a) is a little different because there is no question that Verdure intended to pass not only possession but also property in the potatoes to Derwent, and this property passed at the time of the transaction at V's farm. This behaviour was not a crime at common law and only became such by statute in 1767. The law hesitated for a long time to make fraud a crime. The first obvious reason was that the rogue had not interfered with possession by trespass; the victim had willingly given over the goods. The second and probably more important reason was that the economically *laissez-faire* view of the courts was that the commercial principle of *caveat emptor* (or vendor)—let the buyer (or seller) beware—should apply, that a fool and his money are soon parted. In a case where A had obtained money from B by pretending that C had sent him, Holt C.J. had said, "Shall we indict one man for making a fool of another?" The enactment of the false pretences statute did not put a stop to difficulties because the police, prosecution and the courts have difficulty choosing between the offences of theft and false pretence.

Illustration 50(g) is a recent case of *Edwards* v. *Ddin* (1976) where the accused was charged with theft. He was acquitted because the property in the gas and oil had passed and he should have been charged with false pretences. The charge of theft in Illustration 50(f) was dismissed in one case, *Dawood* (1975), but upheld in *Malhotra* (1975), and the legal discussion concentrated on such an abstruse legal point as whether the cashier had authority to pass the property in the goods or only possession. Obviously, the law has not solved its problems.

Finally, the law has had difficulties with the notion of fraud. Where does sharp business practice (with the entrepreneurs maximizing their profits) end and where does criminally illegal behaviour start? Once again, the intricacies of the law of property offences made it necessary to create a new offence of fraud in 1948 because the false pretences crime could only apply to past or present but not future promises. The courts have not been able to reach clearly defined principles on this issue.

Proposals for Reform

The growth of property offences has been the history of expedient measures either achieved by legal fictions or statutory creation of crime. As a problem arose, a solution was found for that pressing issue. The Law Reform Commission of Canada has carefully examined the law of property offences. The Commission agreed with Jeremy Bentham's two-hundred-year-old criticism that the law was suffering from overbulkiness, redundancy, long-windedness and disorderliness. The Commission would like to see Canadian law makers work toward a law a little closer to the simple Biblical commandment, "Thou shalt not steal." Instead the law in the Canadian criminal law has added word upon word and section upon section in an attempt to cover every nuance of language and every possible contingency and fact-situation. The Commission report, *Theft and Fraud,* stated:

> ... we need to escape from the burden of single instances and tyranny of the particular. Just as the physicist doesn't have to record the fall of every individual

> apple, so the lawyer shouldn't have to deal with a separate provision for each different type of property item. Law ... should aim to reflect ... experience arranged in economical order.

As an example of complexity, the Commission quoted s. 290 which in subsection (1) defined theft "by a person required to account" and in further explanation cited subsection (2):

> When subsection (1) otherwise applies, but one of the terms is that the thing received or the proceeds or part of the proceeds of it shall be an item in a debtor and creditor account between the person who receives the thing and the person to whom he is to account for or to pay it, and that the latter shall rely upon the liability of the other as his debtor in respect thereof, a proper entry in that account of the thing received or the proceeds or part of the proceeds of it, as the case may be, is a sufficient accounting therefore, and no fraudulent conversion of the thing or the proceeds or part of the proceeds of it thereby accounted for shall be deemed to have taken place.

The Commission found similar turgidity in the laws describing false pretences and fraud. Crimes were over-described but under-explained. There was great detail but much of it was repetitive and yet such fundamental concepts, as *mens rea,* were neglected. The Commission has drafted a simple law for property offences. For instance, theft is defined as occurring when a person "dishonestly appropriates another's property without his consent." This would cover all kinds of theft of property by whatever means. In explanation of the word "dishonestly," the report points out that it replaces "fraudulently," "without colour of right" and "with intent to deprive" and explains the substitute as having "a common sense meaning, is universally understood and is only definable in less comprehensible terms." In other words, "Did the accused's conduct fall short of the recognized standard of honesty?"

"Appropriating property" was also defined in the Commission's draft as meaning:

> (a) *taking* with intent to treat as one's own, tangible moveables including immoveables made moveable by the taking;
> (b) *converting* property of any kind by acting inconsistently with the express or implied terms on which it is held, or
> (c) *using* electricity, gas, water, telephone, telecommuncation or computer services, or other utilities.

This provision is meant to make sense of the anomalies in the law. The emphasized words show the various ways of dealing with other people's property. One *takes* tangible things, *converts* to one's own intangible things such as the value behind stock certificates and *uses* such intangible substances as electricity.

The report also elaborates on "another's property" as meaning property which another "owns, has possession, control or custody of it or has any legally protected interest in it." This definition is meant to solve any of the problems that were formerly experienced in false pretences, a crime that would disappear. The Commission could not contain all dishonesty under the head of theft, and fraud was a separate crime:

> A person commits fraud who dishonestly by
> (a) deceit
> (b) unfair non-disclosures, or
> (c) unfair exploitation
> induces a person including the public to part with any property or causes him to suffer a financial loss.

Deceit means "any false representation as to the past, present or future," but does not include "puffing" which is "mere exaggerated commendation or depreciation of the quality of anything."

Non-disclosure is defined as unfair where a duty to disclose arises from:

> (a) a special relationship entitling the victim to rely on the offender, or
> (b) conduct by the offender creating a false impression in the victim's mind, or
> (c) circumstances where non-disclosure would create a false impression in the mind of any reasonable person.

and exploitation would be unfair if it exploits

> (a) another person's mental deficiency; or
> (b) another person's mistake intentionally or recklessly induced by the offender; or
> (c) another person's mistake induced by the unlawful conduct of a third party active with the offender.

The Illustrative Cases

The Commission's recommendations are simple and rational but there is little indication that they will become law in the near future. The bench and bar are conservative, and they do not take kindly to new concepts, even in cases where the present law is a morass of detail, confusion and nonsensical fictions. Even if the quoted provisions were passed without too much mauling by ill-informed MPs, there is the serious danger that the lawyers and judges will apply their old common law knowledge to the new concepts and very soon these pristine innovations will be encrusted with anomalies. This will not happen because the lawyers have a great animus toward the provision but rather because they are trained in the common law and think less in terms of general principles than in creating a myriad of special instances that the common lawyers call case precedents.

In the meantime we must struggle with the present chaos and the best way to do this may be to work our way through the illustrations.

Prankster Cases: Illustrations 50(a): (a) (b) (c) (d)

These are all Canadian cases— *Handfield, Kerr, McCormick* and *Wilkins,* respectively. All were acquitted on the basis that they had no criminal intent. A more appropriate charge may have been mischief in which the accused were obliged to pay the costs of investigating, prosecuting and hearing the case (but perhaps such a suggestion shows a serious lack of a sense of humour). The accused in the police motorcycle case could have been convicted of "joyriding" or taking a motor vehicle without the consent of the owner (s. 295). Under the Commission's suggestions, could it be said that the defendants were dishonest? Would the average citizen (as opposed to the "victims") look upon the accuseds' behaviour as criminal?

Temporary Deprivation: 50(b)
The common law definition of theft had an ingredient that the accused had to intend to deprive the victim *permanently* of some object. The 1892 Criminal Code changed this by adding "temporarily" so that Dutch could be convicted. The Law Reform Commission would not necessarily make it a crime of theft for D to move an article from point A to point B which would be a "temporary" taking and it would only become criminal if Dutch had intended to be dishonest and most of D's fellow-students would look upon D's behaviour as criminal.

50(c)
In *DeMarco* (1973), the Ontario Court of Appeal decided that if D honestly believed that V would not object to her keeping the car beyond the rental period, then she would not be guilty because "conduct is not fraudulent merely because it is unauthorized unless it is dishonest and morally wrong." This sounds almost like a rehearsal for the projected laws of the Law Reform Commission. A similar view was expressed in *Sparrow*, where D borrowed V's car without permission but arranged to have V informed as to the car's whereabouts. D went on an alcoholic bender and V was deprived of his car for some days. The court decided he was not guilty because he had no intent to deprive V of the car.

50(d)
The facts of the real case, *Duncan* (1945), are very cryptic and there must be many facts that did not get into evidence. The simple explanation is that neither D's boss nor the court believed his story. The Court of Appeal pointed out that D made no personal profit and if his alleged honest intention had been believed, he would have been acquitted.

50(e)
Under the present law, when a person buys an article on a conditional sales agreement, the article does not become D's property until all payments are made. In *Murphy* (1973) the court acquitted D because he had a "colour of right." As stated in an earlier chapter, "colour of right" is one of the few clear

illustrations in the criminal law where mistake of law can be a defence. D's view of the law need not be accurate law so long as D honestly believes that he has a legal right to do what he did. The Law Reform Commission would scrap "the colour of right" concept and D's guilt would be decided on the dishonesty criterion.

50(f) and (g)

These are the cases of *Dawood* (1975) and *Edwards* v. *Ddin* (1976) which had shown the inanities of trying to make a distinction between larceny (based on trespass to possession) and false pretences (where transfer of property in the object has been achieved by some subterfuge). The case of *Hemingway* (1955) contains some of the elements of 50(e) as well as 50(f) and 50(g). In that case the accused had bought furniture on a conditional sales agreement. He used a name other than his own, although it was the name of another real person and the address he gave was of that other real person. He did not complete his payments and yet declared that he had completed the payments but the receipt he produced was a forgery. He was convicted of false pretences. Hemingway claimed that he could not be convicted of false pretences because property had not passed, but the Supreme Court of Canada examined the Conditional Sales Act of British Columbia and decided that "some" property right had passed and therefore Hemingway could be convicted of false pretences. Other cases such as *Hunter* (1976) have distinguished *Hemingway*, meaning that the later court disapproved of the earlier decision without presuming to overrule a decision of a superior court in the hierarchy. The *Hemingway* decision is probably wrong because the notion of "property" in the law of false pretences should not be based on concepts borrowed from commercial law as found in the Conditional Sales Act.

50(h)

This case was the cause célèbre of *Howson* (1966) which resulted in D's acquittal because he had a "colour of right" as he thought he had a legal right to detain the automobile until P had paid the necessary fees. Laskin J.A. said:

> Although the unreasonableness of a belief, when objectively considered, does not necessarily destroy the honesty of the belief, it may be considered, along with the other evidence in determining whether the Crown had established that a taking or a conversion was without colour of right.

50(i)

Hutton (1911) decided this one in the Crown's favour.

50(j)

This is the case of *Monnink* (1972) who was charged with theft. Once again the problem of the distinction between theft and false pretences was confronted by the Ontario Court of Appeal:

> ... although the appellant was guilty of attempting to obtain property by false pretences ... he is not guilty of theft. There was no theft because the appellant had the right to move the containers from one side of the cooler to the other and he did not deprive the owner, either temporarily or absolutely, of the containers.

The movement issue was raised because s. 283(2) provides that it is theft if a person "with intent to steal anything, he moves it or causes it to move or to be moved, or begins to cause it to become moveable."

50(k)
Middleton (1873) was a celebrated case on these facts. His conviction has been debated; D, it is argued, gained property in the additional $1000 and therefore he could not be convicted of theft. Furthermore, the money was voluntarily given to him. An authority on the history of larceny looked upon this as a landmark decision because there was no clandestine or forceful taking (which had been the essence of theft), and D was convicted because he appeared manifestly guilty of dishonesty and of course this is also the gist of the Law Reform Commission's recommendation.

There was certainly some ambiguity about this question because an additional subsection in s. 283 reads:

> For the purposes of this Act the question whether anything that is converted is taken for the purpose of conversion, or whether it is, at the time it is converted, in the lawful possession of the person who converts it is not material.

In *Brochu* (1950), a Canadian court convicted of theft under s. 283. The manifest criminality that was established in *Middleton* was reiterated in *Ashwell* (1885). D had asked V for the loan of a shilling. It was dark and it was only later, when D and V had parted, that D realized the coin was a sovereign (the same size but was worth twenty times as much). Obviously V had voluntarily given the coin to D. The court decided that D always had possession of the coin (*actus reus*) and when he later realized that he had a more valuable coin and decided to keep the coin, he then intended to appropriate the coin (at this point he had the *mens rea*). This is another legal fiction, analogous to the *Carrier's Case* and *Pear.*

50(1)
What is the quality of the coins in a public telephone that have dropped into the locked coin box? Are they abandoned or do they still belong to the telephone company? If they are abandoned, there is no theft. If they are to be treated as found goods, then different considerations apply. In *Thurborn* (1848), D had found a banknote that someone had accidentally dropped on the highway. He picked it up with intent to keep it. D did not know who owned it and the next day someone told D who owned it but D still decided to keep the note. He was found not guilty, which is not quite incomprehensible in the light of the judge's remarks:

> If a man finds goods that have been actually lost, or are reasonably supposed by him to have been lost, and appropriates them, with intent to take the entire dominion over them, really believing when he takes them, that the owner cannot be found, it is not larceny. But if he takes them with the like intent, though lost, or reasonably supposed to be lost, but believing that the owner can be found, it is larceny.

50(m)

There is no doubt, according to the law, that D is guilty of theft. Compare the facts of Illustration 52(f). Is there any qualitative difference between the two? Perhaps you think both accused should be acquitted. Both cases are "success stories" but imagine that both situations had ended in disaster—the horse did not win and the real estate market had collapsed. Should we only punish failure? Were both accused dishonest?

51(a)

This case is based on *Reid* (1940). The accused was acquitted because he could not be guilty of false pretences as he had made a future promise, and this is not a sufficient criterion for the offence. This is also in accord with the *laissez-faire* notion of *caveat emptor* which has already been discussed. If the Law Reform Commission's recommendations were accepted, D would be convicted of fraud. It is difficult (or impossible) to be quantitative about moral guilt but the accused in this case *seems*, on a visceral level, to be much more dishonest than in the preceding illustration.

51(b)

If D warns that he would not like the cheque presented for a week, this is a future promise and D would not be guilty of false pretence, although one cannot be too categorical because of the wording of s. 320(4) of the Code:

> Where . . . it is shown that anything was obtained by the accused by means of a cheque that, when presented for payment within a reasonable time, was dishonoured on the ground that no funds or insufficient funds were on deposit to the credit of the accused in the bank . . . on which the cheque was drawn, it shall be presumed to have been obtained by a false pretence, unless the court is satisfied by evidence that when the accused issued the cheque he had reasonable grounds to believe that it would be honoured if presented within a reasonable time after it was issued.

What advice should one give a client? That the recipient of the cheque should be given a very specific period before the cheque should be presented for payment, because otherwise he or she might run afoul of s. 320(4)? The intent of D is difficult to assess without the exact facts of the case and the credibility of D (see *Druckman* (1975)).

51(c)

The short answer is that D is more clearly guilty than in 51(b).

51(d)
Morphett (1971) would show that this is clearly a question of guilt.

51(e)
Clear finding of liability here.

51(f)
This is covered by the *Hemingway* case discussed in 50(g).

51(g)
The decision here is very dependent on how the court interprets s. 320(4) of the Code and in particular that slippery legal word "reasonable." The trier of fact must assess what were D's realistic hopes that the cheque would be honoured. If there are twelve, as opposed to two, cheques to be considered and if the deficiency is $2500 rather than $25, these factors will go the credibility of D's story.

51(h)
This is based on *Dvornek* (1962), and the court had no difficulty in convicting D of obtaining credit by false pretence.

51(i) and (j)
False pretences do not have to be verbal. They can also be by conduct. But, on the other hand, did D make any false representation? In fact, D said nothing but he did create an atmosphere that induced V to hand over his goods.

52(a)
In *Lemire* (1965), on which this is based, the accused was convicted. D was not saved by the fact that D was advised by the attorney general, a law officer of the Crown.

52(b)
In *Dumont*, the Quebec Court of Appeal convicted D. The court said:

> D certainly knew that he had no valid claim against the government, that he was not legally entitled to any remuneration, that the account produced and signed by him was fictitious, and that the debt owing to him was non-existent; he knowingly took this devious route, assisted by a departmental employee, to obtain an asset to which he could not have made any legal claim.

52(c)
D was acquitted in *Charters* (1957). The court said:

> It may well be that there was a moral obligation on D to inform V of his knowledge with respect to the liability for customs duties if he sold the car . . . Here there was no misrepresentation or fraud . . . There was non-disclosure of

what was, perhaps, a material fact, but that is not sufficient to justify a conviction.

52(d)

D was convicted of fraud (*Stanley* (1957)). The B.C. Court of Appeal decided that it was fraud because it was a "falsehood for a person to say he will pay when he has no intention to do so," and falsehood was sufficient basis for conviction.

52(e)

This is another case of fraud. One similar example is *R.* v. *McLean and Janko* (1963) where the accused were convicted and the court approved of the decision in *Stanley*. There is very little in the judgement that one can point to as the basis of the decision. This is typical of the fraud cases. The courts seem to convict when they have a moral hunch that the behaviour of the accused was something more than smart business practice; it was false to the point of moral dishonesty.

52(f)

D was convicted in *Dyke* (1977) of false pretences. The trial judge decided that V had lent more than it would have done but for the misrepresentation of D. D was not saved from criminal liability merely because V got some value for its money. He also said: "The deceit was not simply to induce a state of mind in the lender but quite obviously the deceit was for the sole purpose of inducing a course of action, i.e., to have the lender part with its money." The court decided that D had made false statements that caused V to be "defrauded." That hardly seems a layperson's usage of the word defraud. An economist might say that V was induced to lend an unreasonable amount of that precious resource, money, which meant that it decreased the entrepreneurial choices it could make about the allocation of other economic resources.

52(g)

D was convicted in the case of *Roy* (1922). The court decided that D had acted in bad faith and disobeyed the instructions of his superiors.

52(h)

In *Linton* (1975), D was convicted. He was fraudulent and he had obtained an advantage from V (although it was not at all sure that a financial loss is always necessary). The fraud is more important. The courts have been very vague about this.

52(i)

This is very close to the case of *R.* v. *Zaritec Industries Ltd.* (1976), where D was finally acquitted but cases can be found going both ways. The dilemma facing the courts is to separate the rogues from those accused persons who had simply shown bad business judgement.

The following is taken from another judgement that was followed in *Zaritec*:

> That the business was not adequately financed is readily apparent from the evidence. It may be properly inferred that the appellant may have lacked the necessary competence to bring it into successful operation and that he may have been over-optimistic with respect to his abilities, but in my judgement this conclusion does not necessarily lead solely to the conclusion that he intended to make no deliveries [and therefore defraud V].

The court decided that D's behaviour was as compatible with innocence as with guilt, and on evidentiary rules, D deserved to be acquitted. The cases in this area give the impression that the fraud must be egregious and have a deeply seated immoral quality to defraud and deceive. The courts have often said that the criminal law should not be used by disappointed clients to apply criminal sanctions when they could not obtain satisfaction in the civil courts (on breach of contract, etc.).

52(j)

This is the rather unusual case of *R.* v. *Ben Smith and Harry Smith* (1963). Remember the case of 50(m); there was a risk to V and the courts seem to think that is enough when there is a very obvious fraudulent scheme. D in 50(m) took money from the bank's cash drawer. D in this case used resources of the V Corporation in clear contravention of the law. The court in *Smith* cited J.F. Stephen as to the essential elements of fraudulent intent: "deceit or an intention to deceive or in some cases mere secrecy; and, secondly, either actual injury or possible injury or an intent to expose some person either to actual injury or to a risk of possible injury by means of that deceit or secrecy."

53

The problems in this illustration are examples of the law of property (which is even a mystery to many lawyers). The answers are deeply rooted in legal history which means that they may have made sense in their original context or to the medieval mind but modern minds may have some trouble comprehending them. The crucial question here is the words in s. 283, "anything whether animate or inanimate."

53(a)

A dead body is clearly inanimate and would seem to fit with the definition of "anything" but any first-year law student could tell you that no one can own a dead body and therefore it cannot be stolen, although this may not apply to Egyptian mummies or, possibly, anatomical specimens, but we have no cases on the subject.

53(b) and (c)

As explained earlier, there are historical reasons why real estate and real-estate documents cannot be subject to larceny charges. Real estate, of course, could not be "asported," i.e., taken away. The same applied to "fixtures," e.g., things attached to the real estate. We have seen the case of D who decided to take away some decorative tiles from a fireplace. D could not remove them because they become part of the fixtures. There is no rational reason why deeds or titles to real estate should also be excluded from things capable of being stolen, and the Code seems to have amended the common law by providing in the definition of "property" in s. 2: "real and personal property of every description and deeds and instruments relating to or evidencing the title or rights to property, or giving a right to recover or receive money or goods." Of course there are other offences, created by statute that apply to deeds—fraudulent dealing, forgery, etc. Yet in *Scallen* (1974), D was not successful in his argument that he had not stolen "anything" when he had, with the help of electronics, transferred three million dollars from Bank A to Bank B.

53(d)

In *Falconi* (1977), D was acquitted of fraud under s. 338. The judge decided that a doctor's prescription would not come within the definition in s. 2 (above) and mere words, even if written on a prescription, are not capable of being "property" or "anything" so as to constitute a property offence.

53(e)

Larceny by finder has been dealt with earlier.

53(f) to (i)

With some hesitation, all these items could be said to be stolen or fraudulently misappropriated, although the courts have had some difficulty with computer programs, but this is probably only due to the unfamiliarity of the judges. There is no difference between an electronic transfer of bank funds (as in *Scallen*) and the stealing of computer time. Indeed, it is easy to put a price on computer time.

53(j)

Probably no liability unless it can be proven that it has commercial value.

53(k)

This is not the concern of the criminal law. Such misappropriation may be a subject of a civil action.

10/CRIMINAL EVIDENCE and PROCEDURE

Historical Background

We have already seen some of the interrelationships between law and religion. The influence of religion is also clearly seen in the procedures of the criminal trial. From the earliest times the law has been interested in proof rather than truth, although our ancestors once thought that an appeal to a supreme deity might result in the coincidence of truth and proof. In the last millennium, they have not sought truth in the entrails of some sacrificed beast, but superstition, in the guise of religion and in the pursuit of "truth," has often imposed terrible hardship on accused persons. Some of the tests had a grim logic—usually heavily weighted in favour of the State. One such method was trial by ordeal. A woman accused of being a witch was lowered into water, and if she floated, her unnatural and guilt-ridden state was considered proved; she then could be burned. Until the thirteenth century, this trial was supervised by a priest who besought the water not to accept a liar. The procedure was not restricted to trials for witchcraft.

The ordeal also took other forms often surrounded by religious trappings. The suspect might be branded with red-hot irons, be forced to ingest poisons or, in an elaborate eucharistic ceremony, be given the holy morsel to swallow. If the burn did not heal, if the poison killed or if the suspect choked on the morsel, these were clear indications of divine displeasure and guilt was proved. In 1215 the Lateran Council decreed that priests should not participate in such superstitious rites and alternate methods of proof had to be found.

The loss of trial by ordeal created a vacuum in the methods of proof. Trial by battle was one alternative, derived from the feud and usually limited to private rather than public wrongs. In any event, it was popular only among the most robust, although "champions" were hired in some instances to do the fighting. In cases of serious crimes or "felonies" against the Crown, the question of liability could not be solved by the use of a "champion" in lieu of the real parties to the dispute. Trial by battle was still law until the nineteenth century, although it fell into disuse. An attempt to revive it occurred in 1836 in *Ashbury* v. *Thornton*. In this case a young woman had died in mysterious circumstances and her brother brought an appeal of murder against Thornton. (An appeal was a private prosecution with some overtones of a civil suit.) When asked to plead, Thornton said he was not guilty and that he was ready to defend with his body. He then took off his glove and threw it upon the floor of the court. In other words, he threw down the gauntlet.

Ashbury asked for a few days' adjournment, and when he returned, he said he would not fight, and Thornton went free. The law was soon changed to prevent further attempts to revive medieval custom.

Another method of proof closely allied to religion was the system of compurgation or use of oath takers. If a party to a legal dispute could produce credible witnesses to testify on his behalf, he would win. This method obviously relied very heavily on the participants' (and judges') faith in oath-making and the moral consequences of lying.

These witnesses did not testify as to the truth or falsehood of the allegations against the accused but simply acted as guarantors of his veracity. This method of proof became absurd when the "trial" developed into a swearing match between two groups of compurgators. It became useless when reverence for the oath decreased and there was a deterioration in the belief in divine retribution for lying.

The gap left by trial by ordeal was filled, after much confusion and experimentation, by trial by jury. Of course, the grand jury had been in operation for centuries. That investigative body was responsible for "presenting" suspects before the royal officers—the coroner and the shire-reeve (or sheriff) and, in due course, the royal judge on assize. At first the petty jury, or trial jury, fulfilled the function of witnesses rather than triers of fact; they decided the facts in issue from their own peculiar, local knowledge of events and places. By the fourteenth century, however, the function of the petty jury became separate from that of the grand jury and acted more as an objective fact-finder. The jury evolved from a group of local citizens summoned to tell everything they knew of the alleged crime to a randomly chosen twelve people who had no prior knowledge of the incident.

Before the eighteenth century it would be too optimistic to believe that there was a fair and full presentation of the facts. Conviction was much more probable than acquittal because the trial was weighted so heavily against the accused. The "trials" were very short and were less trials (with a presumption of the innocence of the accused) than they were confirmatory of the communal hunch that they had the right culprit in these circumstances, and because of the pervading influence of religion, the court wanted a confession. The confession would not only confirm the strongly held suspicion but it would ensure the accused's soul some respite in the "life" he would have after execution. Many accused refused to plead because of the near certainty of conviction. If they so refused, they were imprisoned and, in effect, tortured until they pleaded to the indictment. This process was known as *peine forte et dure*; increasingly heavy weights were placed on the chest of the accused until he confessed or died. If the accused died without confession, he did not die a convicted felon and his property (particularly land) was not forfeited to the Crown. This process was finally abolished in 1772 when a refusal to plead was taken as a guilty plea. (In 1827 this was reversed and no plea was presumed to be a not guilty plea.)

Trials were less than "due process" for another reason. Until the seventeenth century the same jurors sat on the presentment (or grand) and trial juries. At that time the accused was confined before trial and could be fully questioned about the charge against him. Witnesses were examined in the absence of the accused; he could not confront or cross-examine them, and he was not allowed to read copies of their evidence. The accused had no counsel and could call no witnesses.

At the beginning of the eighteenth century there was some improvement when an English act of 1708 allowed the prisoner to have a list of witnesses and jurors ten days before the date set for the trial. It was not until 1836 that the Prisoners' Counsel Act made it possible for alleged felons to have counsel. The accused, however, was still not allowed to speak on his own behalf. This "privilege" was finally granted in England by the Criminal Evidence Act, 1898. (Upper Canada made earlier changes in the law. In 1849 anyone but the parties could give evidence in both civil and criminal trials, and only two years later, this disability was removed from litigants in civil suits. Between 1852 and 1893 there were inconclusive efforts to make the accused immune from being asked questions about his crime; this innovation was finally achieved in the latter year by the Canada Evidence Act.)

Many lawyers like to give the impression that the strength of the English law has been its fundamental fairness from time immemorial. In 1937 England's highest court found it necessary to re-examine this false assumption. The House of Lords in *Woolmington* v. *D.P.P.* declared that a "golden thread" has always run through the law, that a man is presumed innocent until proven otherwise and that the burden of proof beyond a reasonable doubt is on the prosecution. This thread has worn rather thin at times. The resurgence of "due process" (declared but hardly acted upon in the Canadian Bill of Rights) and the presumption of innocence in the 1960s, particularly as seen in the decisions of the U.S. Supreme Court, were no doubt an attempt to make the romantic fiction a reality.

The Trial Process Today

Laymen often imagine that most criminal charges are heard by a judge and jury with lawyers on both sides, examining and cross-examining witnesses, making objections that are overruled or sustained, making eloquent pleas to the jury to convict or acquit the accused. These trials do occur in Canadian courtrooms but not as frequently as in crime novels or on television programs. More than ninety per cent of the criminal trials in Canada are heard before justices of the peace, magistrates or provincial court judges, some of whom are not even legally trained. Most of these accused persons plead guilty, and some of them are not represented by counsel. (Lack of representation is no longer common in provinces that have comprehensive legal aid plans.)

When anyone is accused of a criminal offence he may be notified by summons (sworn out before a justice of the peace) to appear in a particular court at a specified time. The summons sets out the bare details of the offence alleged against him. Alternatively, the alleged offender can be arrested without a warrant on the sole authority of a police officer. He will be taken to a police station where he will be "booked." If the offence charged is an indictable one, he can also be fingerprinted and photographed.

If the arrested person has no friend or lawyer who can make application for and raise bail, he will remain in custody until the following morning, when he will be brought before a judge or magistrate. At this stage he can plead guilty and the case will probably be disposed of immediately—with a fine, a jail term or a probation order. The judge can also remand him pending a pre-sentence report (prepared by a probation officer) which will assist the sentencer in making the most suitable disposition.

If the accused pleads not guilty, he will be remanded in custody until the date set for his trial unless he has been able to arrange bail. He can be tried in various ways depending on the type of offence. If the offence is a summary one, a magistrate (or provincial court judge) will have sole jurisdiction. Unless there is a specific provision to the contrary, the maximum penalty on summary conviction is a fine of five hundred dollars or six months' imprisonment or both (as provided by s. 722 of the Code).

Indictable offences are usually more serious crimes and can be tried in several ways. There are some over which the judges of the lower courts have exclusive jurisdiction. With others, the accused can consent to be tried by a magistrate (for the purpose of having a speedier trial or in the hope that the magistrate will give a lighter sentence than a superior court). Otherwise, these offences can lead to a preliminary hearing and if a *prima facie* case has been made out by the prosecution, a county court or other superior court will try the case. Finally, there are those crimes, such as murder and rape, that are completely outside the jurisdiction of a magistrate.

Bail

The criminal process is supposedly geared to the security of the community. If the police are convinced that the accused will appear voluntarily at court, a simple summons will be issued. This, of course, is the method used to notify most traffic offenders that their alleged infraction of the highway traffic legislation is being heard.

If the policeman, in his discretion, takes the view that the accused must be kept in custody to ensure attendance in court, the alleged criminal is arrested. There has been much criticism in recent years that too many of those arrested are not granted bail; this leads to unnecessary overcrowding of the jails, loss of employment for the person incarcerated and hardship for the accused and his family when the trial is delayed. Bail is meant to serve the same purpose as a summons. It enables the accused to carry on his normal life pending his trial. If the accused is not dangerous, is more likely than not to appear on the date set for a further hearing, does not have a long criminal record or has not previously absconded bail, he should be granted bail. Studies during the 1960s, however, showed that excessive bail was set in many instances, that bail was frequently granted on a mere ability to pay and was therefore discriminatory, that many of those who were kept in custody because they could not raise the stipulated amount would have appeared at trial if released on their own recognizance. In short, the wrong people were too frequently granted bail—or denied it. The Ouimet Committee Report of 1969 recommended that the justice of the peace to whom application for bail is made should make a thorough investigation of the reasons for granting or withholding bail. The committee also recommended that in some cases one or more of the following conditions would be appropriate: that the accused will

(a) report at designated intervals to the police or other designated persons;
(b) give notice of any change of address;
(c) reside at a certain place;
(d) remain away from the complainant;
(e) not intimidate witnesses or engage in criminal misconduct;
(f) surrender his passport; *or*
(g) not leave or attempt to leave the jurisdiction.

Bail has been subject to much research. It was one of the first areas in the criminal process in which lawyers took an interest in empirical studies and their findings have resulted in important changes in the law. The State has saved money by having fewer accused persons awaiting trial in jail. More persons charged with criminal offences are free on bail and, therefore, able to work and support themselves and their families. In addition, they are better able to prepare their defence to the charges they are facing. Perhaps most importantly, the accused persons have not suffered the psychologically and physically debilitating effects of long periods of idleness awaiting trial in holding jails, which are frequently the worst in the country.

These changes in the law are embodied in the Bail Reform Act 1970 (and are described below under the Arrest section).

Police Power

The role of the policeman is one of the most difficult and anachronistic in the criminal law process. He has little or no training in the law but has to make some of the most crucial decisions—whether to stop and question, whether he has reasonable cause to suspect that a crime has been or is about to be committed, whether to issue a summons or make an arrest, when to take into custody, when and how to interrogate a suspect within the rules of due process and when to caution a suspect as to his legal rights.

At the same time the police protect law-abiding citizens by apprehending criminals, controlling traffic and providing emergency services. Police must learn to endure provocative behaviour. They are subjected to violence and yet must refrain from unnecessary and unlawful violence to the citizen.

The policeman also has wide discretion to follow up an inquiry, lay a charge, issue a warning, ignore an infraction and, within limits, to decide on the gravity of the charge laid.

We must ensure that we have the best possible police forces. This can be achieved only by good salaries, careful screening processes for recruitment, wise leadership and an intelligent and forward-looking approach to in-service training and education.

The Power to Question

Walter Lippmann once said, when talking about journalists in search of a story, that there is no such thing as an indiscreet question, only indiscreet answers. The same could be said for police questioning. A civil libertarian would immediately advise any citizen that there is an overriding right to remain silent but, of course, that does not stop a policeman from asking questions.

A policeman may ask questions for the mere purpose of obtaining information—about the facts surrounding a crime, about witnesses to a crime and, of course, to obtain evidence for a subsequent trial.

Later, we will be examining the law relating to confessions. Most accused persons convict themselves by talking too much. The policeman has a psychological advantage because the average citizen feels compelled to answer questions put by a policeman. If a citizen is ignorant as well as frightened, he is at a further disadvantage. If the citizen knows his rights, the confrontation is on a more equal basis. The police may obtain less information but the information will be obtained fairly and will not be disallowed by the courts because it was extracted by unfair means. The evidence is also likely to be more reliable.

In Illustration 54 Harry must stop his car when so requested by the police officer. Under most provincial traffic legislation, he also has an obligation to identify himself by producing a valid driver's licence. Harry did not have to step out of his car. The policeman was not wrong to ask him to do so; Harry was simply indiscreet in acquiescing. A lawyer, in a similar position, may have challenged the police officer to arrest him or lay a charge against him on the basis of the evidence already available, erratic driving, for example. As soon as Harry corroborated the officer's suspicions by staggering, the officer was convinced that a charge should be laid and an arrest made. Technically, the police officer had no right to request Harry to accompany him to the police station. Harry could have refused until such time the officer announced he was arresting Harry for impaired driving and planned to lay a formal charge. If the police officer had requested Harry to take a breathalyzer test at the police station, Harry could have refused but, of course, could have been charged for the refusal.

Discretion should be exercised on both sides. The police discretion or judgement is obvious, although often difficult to apply in practice. If a driver, on the other hand, rolls down his window an inch or so, hands over his licence, studiously avoids the possibility of the officer smelling his breath, the officer's suspicions may be sufficiently aroused for him to lay a charge. If a citizen ceremoniously stands on his rights, he may cause the officer to become suspicious (or at least antagonistic). If the officer makes a mistake, he may be subject to a civil suit for false arrest, and if it is a serious mistake, his superiors may also discipline him.

There are too many instances of police officers whose perceptions of reasonable suspicion or bases of decision to arrest have been distorted by their prejudices. They take the attitude that anyone with a beard, long hair, wearing love beads, having overtly homosexual mannerisms, from a particular ethnic group or riding a motorcycle and wearing a leather jacket should be watched more often and more closely. Too often police officers believe that the discretion to invoke the criminal process can be exercised more precipitously in such cases. The police were somewhat chastened by the decision in *Koechlin* v. *Waugh and Hamilton* (which was a civil suit for damages for false arrest). The arresting officers claimed that there had been burglaries in the neighbourhood. The plaintiff and his companion were wearing sneakers and windbreakers on a public street at night. They refused to identify themselves. The court held that, on these facts, the police did not have reasonable and probable grounds for arrest without a warrant within s. 450 of the Canadian Criminal Code. Consequently, the police officers were obliged to pay damages to the plaintiff (see Illustration 56(a)). The young men were within their rights in not identifying themselves and this no doubt aroused the police's suspicions but that is an occupational hazard for an officer. If they had been carrying a large bag and it was 2:00 a.m., the situation would not be changed unless there were other pieces of behaviour that raised reasonable grounds for suspicion. In theory, a previous conviction for burglary should make no difference. In practice, the court may have some sympathy for the police if such evidence could be put before the court. In Illustration 56(b), the problem would appear to be on safer ground in arresting, at least in the second example. Common sense would suggest suspicious circumstances.

The fear of violence on the streets and the increase in crime in the United States has caused some state legislatures to pass "stop and frisk" laws. An officer can, on mere suspicion, stop and frisk any citizen who arouses the officer's curiosity because of his appearance or behaviour. These rules go much farther than the common law or the statutory law of Canada. Few people in this country feel that such extreme measures are needed here. Similarly, we do not have laws that allow police officers to detain a person as a material witness or merely for the purposes of interrogation.

Arrest

Many people believe that police officers' powers of arrest are much greater than those of private citizens. While police officers have additional powers, they are not extraordinarily powerful, and there is a historical explanation for this. Before organized full-time police forces were created one hundred and fifty years ago, citizens were responsible for the apprehension of criminals. These citizens' powers have now been partially delegated to the police. In a western movie we see this process in reverse. The sheriff delegates citizens as deputies and the posse is a modern version of the ancient custom of "hue and cry" to pursue and bring the wrongdoer to justice. Two centuries ago every citizen had a duty to apprehend criminals, particularly felons. The "hue and cry," symbolized by the call of "Stop Thief!" was the warning alert that a criminal was in flight from the scene of his crime.

The modern law of arrest is codified in the Canadian Criminal Code where it is provided in s. 449(1) that:

> *Any one* may arrest without warrant a person who, on reasonable and probable grounds, he believes
> (i) has committed a criminal offence, and
> (ii) is escaping from and freshly pursued by persons who have lawful authority to arrest that person.

Anyone, private citizen or police officer, can arrest, without a warrant, a person whom he finds committing an indictable offence (ss. 449 and 450 of the Code). The important words here, other than "anyone," are "finds" and "indictable." This miscreant must have been in the act of committing the offence (or escaping after committing it). The average citizen may have some difficulty recognizing an indictable offence but, in shorthand terms, it is usually a serious offence.

In Illustration 55(a), jaywalking (*a*) is definitely not indictable, and Cuthbert could not arrest. At the other end of the scale, drunk driving (*e*), burglary (*f*), false pretence (*g*) and robbery (*h*) are clearly indictable and a citizen could arrest. The assaults (*b*) and (*c*) and the theft (*d*) would depend on the seriousness of the assault or the value of the goods shoplifted. If Cuthbert does not see them being committed, then the citizen cannot make any arrest (Illustration 55(b)). If Cuthbert tells a policeman, the officer can make an arrest in all instances of indictable offences, although he may simply give some of the suspects an appearance notice (Illustration 55(c)).

A peace officer has wider powers. The definition of a peace officer (found in s. 2 of the Code) is not limited to police officers and includes mayors, sheriffs, justices of the peace, jail officials, customs officers and a pilot in charge of an aircraft in flight. A peace officer is empowered to arrest without a warrant a person who has committed an indictable offence or "who, on reasonable and probable grounds, he believes has committed or is about to commit an indictable offence." Finally, a peace officer has the additional power that he can arrest without warrant anyone he finds committing *any* criminal offence. (Section 449(2) of the Code gives the same power to the owner or caretaker of property in relation to offences against that property.)

Arrest by Warrant

Arrest by warrant is subject to judicial supervision and is, therefore, sufficiently circumscribed by law and causes little difficulty unless the warrant was obtained or issued illegally.

Warrants of arrest are usually used only when the peace officer was not able to make an immediate arrest or has decided that a summons to appear in court would be inadvisable because, for instance, he believes that the accused may not appear voluntarily.

Anyone who, on reasonable and probable grounds, believes that a person has committed an indictable offence, may lay an information in writing and under oath before a justice. The justice will hear and consider the information and hear witnesses if necessary. He may issue a summons or a warrant for the arrest of the accused. He will issue a summons unless the hearing on the information discloses "reasonable and probable grounds to believe that it is necessary in the public interest to issue a warrant for the arrest of the accused" (s. 455.3(4)).

The justice may, unless the offence is too serious, issue a warrant but endorse the warrant for the release of the accused (s. 455.3(6)) for subsequent appearance at trial.

A summons or warrant must never be issued in blank. A summons must be addressed to the accused and describe the alleged offence and must state a time and place at which the accused must attend (s. 455.5(1)).

A New Scheme for Speedier Release

A new provision, s. 452(2), provides new rules where a peace officer arrests without a warrant in relation to the following offences:

(a) an indictable offence mentioned in s. 483 (which refers to relatively minor offences within the absolute jurisdiction of magistrates or provincial court judges).
(b) an offence which may be tried by indictment or punishable on summary conviction. This would exclude treason (and similar offences found in sections 49, 51) incitement to mutiny, sedition, piracy, hijacking, judicial corruption, bribery of officers of justice, rape, causing death by criminal negligence, murder and manslaughter. In addition, attempts or conspiracies to carry out any of these offences.
(c) or an offence punishable on summary conviction.

In these situations the peace officer is usually obliged to release the person from custody and to ensure the suspect's appearance at trial by means of a summons. Alternatively, the officer can issue an appearance notice to the person and then release him (an appearance notice could be described as an instant summons).

The peace officer is not required to release the suspect if he has reasonable and probable grounds to believe that it is necessary in the public interest that the person be detained in custody (at least until a full judicial determination is made on this issue). The "public interest" is determined by looking at "all the circumstances" including

(i) the need to establish the identity of the person,
(ii) the need to secure or preserve evidence of or relating to the offence,
(iii) the need to prevent the continuation or repetition of the offence or the commission of another offence, or
(iv) the officer has reasonable and probable grounds to believe that, if released, the person will fail to attend in court at his trial.

Under ss. 453 and 453.1 the decision to release a suspect may be made by an "officer in charge" rather than a lower-ranking officer. The same provisos apply about "the public interest" and looking at "all the circumstances" and reasonable belief in the trustworthiness of the suspect. This procedure applies to the same offences plus any other offence punishable with less than five years' imprisonment. This procedure is meant to keep more people out of prison and to unclog court procedures. The officer in charge may release the person with the intention of issuing a summons, release on a mere promise to appear, release on the suspect's own recognizance (or promise) without sureties, providing the suspect pledges a sum of up to $500. No money or valuable security need be provided at that time, unless the suspect is a stranger to the province or lives at some distance.

Finally, s. 454(3) contains a broad discretion:

> A peace officer or officer in charge having the custody of a person who has been arrested without warrant as a person about to commit an indictable offence shall release that person unconditionally as soon as practicable after he is satisfied that the continued detention of that person in custody is no longer necessary in order to prevent the commission by him of an indictable offence.

Judicial Decision As to Release

Section 454 also makes provision for those cases in which the peace officer has not previously released the person who has been arrested with or without a warrant. In such instances, the person must be taken before a justice within twenty-four hours or as soon as possible. The justice may then decide to release or detain the accused.

When the accused is brought before the justice, and is not charged with murder or treason, the justice may release the accused on a mere promise to appear. The prosecutor may contest this decision by showing why the accused should not be released. Alternatively, the justice may release on conditions, such as reporting to a police station, notifying any change of address, depositing his passport, not communicating with certain persons or "such other reasonable conditions" (s. 457(4)). The accused can also be asked to enter into a recognizance with or without sureties.

According to s. 457(7), the accused will be detained if the prosecutor shows that:

(a) his detention is necessary to ensure his attendance in court, and
(b) his detention is necessary "in the public interest or for the protection or safety of the public, having regard to all the circumstances including any substantial likelihood that the accused will, if he is released from custody, commit a criminal offence involving serious harm or an interference with the administration of justice."

In arriving at his decision, the justice must not examine the accused as to the offence charged. The prosecutor, on the other hand, may produce evidence that the accused has a previous criminal record, is awaiting trial on other charges or has previously committed an offence under s. 133 (escape from lawful custody).

A 1975 amendment, inspired by criticisms of the bail reform measures mentioned earlier, has provided more stringent provisions. These apply if the accused is charged with an indictable offence that he allegedly committed while at large awaiting trial for another indictable offence, if the accused is usually a non-resident or not a citizen of Canada or if he is charged with escaping from lawful custody. In these circumstances, "the justice shall order that the accused be detained in custody until he is dealt with according to law, unless the accused, having been given a reasonable opportunity to do so, shows cause why his detention is not justified." Note that the onus is squarely placed on the accused.

If an accused has been released by a justice on "interim release," and subsequently there are reasonable and probable grounds for believing that he has violated or is about to violate his undertakings, or has committed an indictable offence, a warrant may be issued for his arrest or he may be arrested by a peace officer without a warrant.

The Use of Force by Police Officers

We shall see presently that police officers are not allowed to use force to obtain a confession from a suspect. Policemen are, nevertheless, sometimes obliged to use force to subdue an obstreperous suspect, but the force must be reasonable in the circumstances (s. 25 of the Code).

In recent years, there have been occasions when the public has been concerned when persons being arrested by police have died in somewhat questionable circumstances. There has been talk of "trigger-happy cops" when it was discovered that the deceased was unarmed. Some have felt that the indiscriminate use of firearms must be curtailed, particularly in crowded city streets. The Ouimet Report recognized this problem and proposed an amendment to s. 25 that would "prohibit the use of firearms by a peace officer or other person lawfully assisting him in order to prevent the escape of a person who has taken to flight to avoid arrest, notwithstanding the arrest sought to be made is lawful, unless:

(a) The person who has taken to flight to avoid arrest is believed on reasonable and probable grounds to have committed or attempted to commit a serious offence involving violence.
(b) There are reasonable and probable grounds for believing that there is a substantial risk that the person whose escape is sought to be prevented may seriously endanger the public if his escape is not prevented.
(c) Such escape cannot be prevented by reasonable means in a less violent manner.

The Power to Search

Unlike arrest, the power to search a person or his dwelling is an extraordinary power and should be strictly controlled. The law takes the attitude that an Englishman's home is his castle. By statute, a search warrant can only be obtained by swearing on oath before a justice of the peace or magistrate that there are sufficient facts and belief for a warrant to issue. In other words, it must be a judicial act, not a mere legal formality or ministerial order. In addition, the power is a discretionary one. The justice of the peace or magistrate must have a *prima facie* case placed before him; he must not issue a warrant without first considering the case on its merits and being satisfied that sufficient grounds exist. Although the officer need not state the sources of his information, he cannot expect a magistrate to issue the warrant on a bald statement that he has cause to believe certain facts to exist without stating the bases for such belief.

In one case where a search warrant was quashed, the appeal court said that a search warrant should only be issued with "great care and circumspection" because the warrant enables the police to take "great liberties" with the person and property of others. An appeal court will not usually overturn the discretion of the magistrate for some minor technical fault in the warrant even if the appeal court judges themselves would not have issued a warrant. They will overturn it, however, if "some grave injustice" has been done to the citizen whose privacy has been invaded. An appeal court will invariably invalidate a warrant when the information does not state, either specifically or by strong inference, the offence that is suspected to have been committed by the person whose property is to be searched.

The Code does not provide a comprehensive set of procedural rules on the powers of search (see ss. 443-446). We are reliant on the common law and some specialized legislation.

During the prohibition era, almost a complete jurisprudence on the law of search warrants was developed and, perhaps because of the subject matter, the judge's decisions were remarkably liberal. On the other hand, four pieces of Canadian legislation (concerned with narcotics, customs, excise, food and drugs) empower peace officers to use the writ of assistance, which is a blank or general warrant.

At common law, a police officer who has arrested anyone has the power to search him for evidence or a weapon. Similarly, a police officer may search premises or an automobile as an incident of the arrest but not otherwise, unless he has a warrant.

Search warrants may be issued by a justice of the peace to a peace officer who has reasonable grounds for believing that a building contains "anything" connected with a criminal offence that is suspected, or that is likely to be committed.

The warrant is only good for search by day unless endorsed otherwise. The search must be carried out in strict accordance with the terms of the warrant. Most challenged warrants have been declared illegal by the courts because of their vagueness. The property to be searched must, for instance, be carefully, although not meticulously, described. If the property is a boarding house or an apartment building, a mere street address is insufficient; the room or apartment number should also be specified.

The reasonable suspicion must point to a specific offence and the objects to be searched out must also be described with some particularity. For instance, in a recent Saskatchewan case the police suspected a lawyer X of fraud and obtained a search warrant that simply empowered the police to search the files and premises of the law firm "X, Y and Z." This was sufficiently vague and general for the appeal court to comment that the Canadian law relating to search warrants did not envisage that "those executing the warrant would have *carte blanche* to open and to read the private papers of clients and of partners in the hope of finding something therein that might, in the sole judgement of those searching, have evidentiary value relevant to the charge made."

This was not a new rule as the Ontario High Court had earlier stated that "the fundamental thing is that the purpose of the search warrant is to secure things that will, in themselves, be relevant to a case to be proved, not to secure an opportunity of making observations regarding the use of things and thereby obtain evidence." In other words, mere "fishing expeditions" are not permissible.

The officer must also act reasonably when he is embarking on a search. Although the issue of a warrant may have been legal, the search may become illegal by its manner of execution. Officers should not break down doors or smash windows in making a search—at least not until they have made a formal demand for admittance. In any event, they must use no more force than is necessary.

The Consequences of an Illegal Search

What is the significance of a court decision that a search warrant has been illegally issued or executed? If the victim of the illegal search warrant makes a legal attack on the document before the police have executed it, no harm is done. The police will be ordered by the court to proceed by a valid warrant. If the warrant has been executed and evidence seized, the courts seem to have said that the evidence should be inadmissible, and if decisive as to guilt, the prosecution should fail.

Yet these pronouncements by appeal courts seem to contradict the recognized principle that illegally obtained evidence is, in fact, admitted to prove guilt in Canada. If the police had unlawfully obtained an oral confession from an accused by means of coercion, the substance of the incriminating statement would not be admitted in evidence at trial. If, however, the accused had told the police about the whereabouts of the stolen goods or the weaspon used, that physical evidence could be used against him (see Illustration 61(d)). Furthermore, the rule in *Kuruma*, which has received some recognition in Canada in *Attorney General for Quebec* v. *Begin*, decided that illegally obtained evidence is generally admissible. This means that a police officer would be better off if he did not seek to exercise power by a search warrant but simply acted illegally by indiscriminately searching. This seemingly ridiculous state of affairs perhaps is solved, in practice, by a judge's use of discretion to declare as inadmissible evidence obtained in circumstances that show a grave injustice to the accused. One could be more cynical and say that a judge will only admit such evidence when otherwise convinced of guilt. The *Kuruma* decision added a rider that evidence would be admitted even if obtained illegally unless obtained by a "trick," although this term was not defined further. As a general rule, such evidence will probably not be admitted if it sufficiently offends the susceptibilities of a liberal-minded judge.

The Ouimet Committee considered this problem and decided that an "inflexible rule" that rejected all evidence illegally obtained is "neither necessary or desirable," yet it believed that there would be circumstances where such evidence should be rejected. Therefore, the Committee recommended that:

1. The court may in its discretion reject evidence which has been illegally obtained.
2. The court in exercising its discretion to either reject or admit evidence which has been illegally obtained shall take into consideration the following factors:
   (i) Whether the violation of rights was wilful or whether it occurred as a result of inadvertence, mistake, ignorance or error in judgement.
   (ii) Whether there existed a situation of urgency in order to prevent the destruction or loss of evidence, or other circumstances which in the particular case justified the action taken.
   (iii) Whether the admission of the evidence in question would be unfair to the accused.

3. The legislation should provide that the discretion to reject evidence illegally obtained provided for by such legislation does not affect the discretion which a court now has to disallow evidence if the strict rules of evidence would operate unfairly against an accused.

The decision of the Supreme Court of Canada in *Wray* suggests that the meaning of "trick" would have to be very broad before the courts would exclude the evidence. Mere subterfuges to take the suspect off his guard will obviously not be enough to outlaw the evidence. The decision in *Wray* seems extraordinarily tolerant of questionable police behaviour. The evidence obtained by an overbearing attitude of a polygraph operator resulted in police obtaining evidence about the location of the murder weapon. In strict terms, this was not a search case but the principle that illegal means will be accepted by the court applies equally to unlawfully obtained evidence, whether it is an oral confession or information leading to the production of physical evidence.

The Writ of Assistance

This additional, and more extraordinary, power to search has received much attention in recent years because of the controversy over drugs. The victims of the drug laws complain that the use of the writ of assistance by members of the RCMP under the authority of the Narcotic Control Act is an unjust invasion of privacy and contrary to the provisions of the Canadian Bill of Rights. Their complaints have not aroused judicial sympathy.

The use of the writ of assistance is not limited to the Narcotic Control Act but is also found in the Excise, Customs and Food and Drug Acts. The writ is of ancient origin and was used in England and colonial America. The earliest statutory reference is found in a 1662 Act of Charles II. The writ is no longer used in either of those jurisdictions. The American colonists, and John Otis in particular, found in the use of the writ by British agents one of their major grievances against British rule. In *Stanford* v. *Texas* the U.S. Supreme Court said:

> The hated writs of assistance had given customs officials blanket authority to search where they pleased for goods imported in violation of the British Tax Laws. They were denounced by James Otis as the worst instrument of arbitrary power, the most destructive of English liberty, and the fundamental principles of law, that ever was found in an English law book. . . .

The Canadian Narcotic Control Act provides for the use of a search warrant but also for the writ of assistance. Section 10(1) states:

> A peace officer may, at any time,
> (a) without a warrant enter and search any place other than a dwelling house and, under the authority of a writ of assistance or a warrant issued under this section, enter and search any dwelling house in which he reasonably

believes there is a narcotic by means of or in respect of which an offence under this Act has been committed;
(b) search any person found in such place; and
(c) seize and take away any narcotic found in such place, anything in such place in which he reasonably suspects a narcotic is contained or concealed, or any other thing by means of or in respect of which he reasonably believes an offence under this Act has been committed or that may be evidence.

The wording is almost identical in all the relevant federal acts. The writ can be executed without notice and by night as well as by day. There are no technical rules about particularity of description of buildings, etc. The present scope of the writ is difficult to ascertain; statistics on its use are not published. In 1962, the minister of justice, in response to a question in Parliament, told the House that members of the RCMP held 2047 writs. Twelve hundred of these "blanket" search warrants had been issued in the preceding four years (118 were held under the narcotics legislation, 118 under the Food and Drugs Act, 836 under the Customs Act and 975 under the Excise Act). Undoubtedly, the numbers issued under all these Acts, and particularly the drug legislation, have increased considerably in the last decade. More recent questions in Parliament have drawn similar responses.

The writs are issued by the Federal Court of Canada. They are issued to particular officers. The writ is given to an officer for a specific task and is returned to the officer's superior on completion.

The case law is sparse and mostly dates from the era of prohibition. Judicial opinion has been divided. Most courts refused to declare the operation of the writ illegal. The writ has rarely been challenged successfully and then on the basis of the outrageousness of the police behaviour. Many courts took the view that they could not review the use of the writ. Others said that the writ was so general that its use should be closely scrutinized (although few did anything about it). Some decided that the writ was designed to be used when a search warrant was not applicable (at night, for example) and was therefore not subject to the same strictures as a search warrant. Others believed that the extraordinary quality of the writ meant that its use must be more restricted than that of the search warrant. In one of the few cases since 1950 the Exchequer Court said that the writ confers authority upon the person named therein to exercise the wide powers of search throughout his whole career and without limit as to place.

The RCMP convinced the Ouimet Committee that the writs are used sparingly and circumspectly, that "a system for recording their use has been developed so that any abuse thereof is more visible" (and therefore subject to parliamentary scrutiny).

The Ouimet Report also noted that "the principal areas in which they are granted involve matters of vital public interest, namely, the protection of the revenue and the suppression of traffic in narcotic drugs." Therefore, after "careful consideration," the report did not recommend their abolition.

Criminal Procedure on Both Sides of the 49th Parallel

The laws of Britain, Canada and the United States share many common characteristics such as an adversary system of justice, trial by jury, rules relating to illegal arrest and unlawful searches and evidentiary rules that exclude hearsay evidence and testimony obtained in a confidential relationship. The administration of these laws and their interpretation in the context of the United States Constitution, however, create a great divergence between the two systems.

The founding fathers of the United States were more influenced by the French Enlightenment than by the British model of law and government. They adopted a written constitution and, in some jurisdictions, a codified criminal law. In terms of the substantive criminal law (that is, the law that describes the criminal offences and defences), this system worked no better than it has under the Canadian Criminal Code. The judges did not discover universal principles in the criminal codes but, instead, tended to build from the common law, including the English common law. The story of the procedural criminal law (that is, the rules that regulate the proof of the substantive criminal law) is very different. The strength of the U.S. Supreme Court in interpreting criminal procedure has only emerged in the last twenty years, when the United States Constitution has been construed as applying "due process" standards to state as well as federal criminal trials and police procedures.

The Canadian Bill of Rights

Since 1960 Canada, too, has had a Bill of Rights and perhaps Canada will eventually follow the American example, rather than the consensual, unwritten, "subtle" English constitutional safeguards. At the moment, with the limited exception of the *Drybones* decision, the Supreme Court of Canada has not used the fundamental rights seemingly embodied in the Bill of Rights—at least not in relation to criminal law or procedure. The Canadian constitutional situation is complicated by the constitutional fact that s. 92 of the British North America Act gives to the provinces "property and civil rights within the province." In the criminal law field, the administration of criminal justice is a responsibility of the provinces, although the definition of criminal law and procedure is a federal power.

The Manitoba Court of Appeal held in *Ballegeer* that right to counsel in criminal cases is unequivocally guaranteed by the Bill of Rights. The Supreme Court of Canada had previously refused to recognize that principle and has only applied the Bill of Rights in the *Drybones* case. Although this is not a criminal procedure case, it may have far-reaching and significant effects.

Joseph Drybones was charged under the provisions of the Indian Act with being an Indian unlawfully intoxicated off a reserve. The accused did not dispute the facts but claimed that this legislation discriminated against

Indians and was therefore contrary to s. 1 of the Canadian Bill of Rights:

> It is hereby recognized and declared that in Canada there have existed and shall continue to exist without discrimination by reason of race, national origin, colour, religion or sex, the following human rights and fundamental freedoms, namely,
> (a) the right of the individual to life, liberty, security of the person and enjoyment of property, and the right not to be deprived thereof except by due process of law;
> (b) the right of the individual to equality before the law and the protection of the law;
> (c) freedom of religion;
> (d) freedom of speech;
> (e) freedom of assembly and association; and
> (f) freedom of the press.

Drybones did not rely on "due process" in clause (a) but "equal protection of the law" in clause (b). The Canadian Supreme Court, in a 6-3 decision, agreed with the contentions of Drybones.

This is not strictly a criminal law case and this first recognition of the Bill of Rights by Canada's highest court does not mean that this decade will produce a "Warren Court" for Canadian civil liberties lawyers. Only one judge mentioned the phrase "due process" and he was dissenting. The majority wrote a narrow judgement that was legalistic rather than sociological. One of the concurring judgements made approving reference to the 1954 decision of the U.S. Supreme Court in *Brown* v. *Board of Education of Topeka* (the school integration case) and agreed that the earlier principle in *Plessey* v. *Ferguson* of "separate but equal" educational facilities for blacks was wrong.

The majority refused to limit the significance of the Canadian Bill of Rights to a mere device for construing the words of federal statutes. Ritchie J. saw the Bill as a "statutory declaration of . . . fundamental human rights and freedom." He also said:

> . . . without attempting any exhaustive definition of "equality before the law" I think that s. 1(b) means at least no individual or group of individuals is to be treated more harshly than another under the law, and I am therefore of opinion that an individual is denied equality before the law if it is made an offence punishable at law, on account of his race, for him to do something which his fellow Canadians are free to do without having committed any offence or having been made subject to any penalty.

The dissenters, and particularly Pigeon J., did not want to apply the safeguards of the Bill to strike down provincial or federal legislation which had been passed before 1960. These judges were content to rely on parliamentary supremacy. They saw dangers in the broadsword approach of the majority which could render inoperative many legislative schemes including the administration of Indian Affairs. Such expressions as "due process of the law," "equality before the law," "freedom of religion" were viewed with scepticism because they are "largely unlimited and undefined." Pigeon J. was afraid that if the role of law reform was not left to Parliament, "according to individual views and the evolution of current ideas, the actual content of such legal concepts is apt to expand and to vary as is strikingly apparent in other countries."

This humble start in applying "due process" to Canadian criminal procedure is likely to continue. The decisions of the U.S. Supreme Court have been widely discussed and have inspired liberal lawyers, law professors and law students to seek similar protections in Canada. Several civil liberties bodies are extremely active. In the law schools many professors have been won over to the idea of an activist and "creative" appellate court. Some of their students are now trying to put these ideas into practice.

The Charter of Rights

Anything that is said about the Charter of Rights has to be tentative at the present time because the document has not received serious attention from the courts, and in particular, the provincial Courts of Appeal and the Supreme Court of Canada have not handed down any decisions. A number of judicial pronouncements have been made by the lower courts such as the Ontario Provincial Court. Judges of those courts have cast doubt on the validity of the reverse onus found in the possession for purposes of trafficking in narcotics, a similar provision in the Code relating to possession of house-breaking tools and the breathalyzer tests for persons suspected of drunk driving.

These cases will no doubt be appealed and the instrinsic merits of these decisions are not important but the mere fact that they have occurred is interesting and perhaps significant. While offering no disrespect to the judges concerned, it should be pointed out there is little empirical evidence that the Canadian judiciary has been very enthusiastic about civil libertarian issues. What, then, has brought about the change? Canadians seem to be aware of the Charter of Rights in a way that was never true of the twenty-year-old Bill of Rights. Somehow, the Charter has caught the public imagination or sunk into the collective national consciousness. This may be due to the great amount of publicity given to the patriation process—debates in the House of Commons in Ottawa, the Supreme Court of Canada decision on the constitutional reference, the final legislative acts of the Mother of Parliaments at Westminster and the symbolic bringing home of the Constitution. Perhaps Canadians feel that they, at last, have a *real* constitution with a Charter that is really entrenched. This does not make much legal sense on a practical level but in cultural, anthropological or symbolic terms, it obviously is important.

Historical explanations are seldom uni-causal, and the decisions on the Charter of Rights cannot be explained by attributing them to the enthusiasm of the Canadian public and a few members of the judiciary. The climate in which this has happened may be much more important. For instance, the Canadian population is much more diverse than it was twenty years ago and a blind belief in all things British (including a trusting attitude toward the official discretion of police and judges) may have become eroded. The public, particularly the television-watching public, may have become convinced that Canadians' rights are not as well protected as those of the United States and that a fundamental constitutional document is a desirable addition to our law. In those twenty years, legal education has been very drastically changed. The methods of teaching in the nation's law schools have deserted the black-letter approach of the past and have become more critical and questioning of the *status quo*. The legal education of the public has been expanded enormously so that citizens are more aware of their rights and liberties. In that same period, the personnel teaching in law schools have changed from imported English teachers to being mostly home-grown products who have had their post-graduate training in the United States rather than England. The quality of the Canadian judiciary has been steadily improving in the last two decades and there will be further changes in the next period because the next crop of judges will be the first who have had academic rather than "trade school" legal training. Finally, the provision of universal legal aid has meant that many more lawyers are practising criminal law and are arguing sophisticated law before more enlightened judges. Therefore the interest in the Charter of Rights may well be due to a new awareness among Canadians and a culmination of twenty years of important social and legal change.

The relevant provisions of the Charter of Rights are:

8. Everyone has the right to be secure against unreasonable search or seizure.
9. Everyone has the right not to be arbitrarily detained or imprisoned.
10. Everyone has the right on arrest or detention
    (a) to be informed promptly of the reasons therefor;
    (b) to retain and instruct counsel without delay and to be informed of that right; and
    (c) to have the validity of the detention determined by way of *habeas corpus* and to be released if the detention is not lawful.
11. Any person charged with an offence has the right
    (a) to be informed without unreasonable delay of the specific offence;
    (b) to be tried within a reasonable time;
    (c) not to be compelled to be a witness in proceedings against that person in respect of the offence;
    (d) to be presumed innocent until proven guilty according to law in a fair and public hearing by an independent and impartial tribunal;
    (e) not to be denied reasonable bail without just cause;
    (f) except in the case of an offence under military law tried before a

military tribunal, to the benefit of trial by jury where the maximum punishment for the offence is imprisonment for five years or a more severe punishment;

(g) not to be found guilty on account of any act or omission unless, at the time of the act or omission, it constituted an offence under Canadian or international law or was criminal according to the general principles of law recognized by the community of nations;

(h) if finally acquitted of offence, not to be tried for it again and, if finally found guilty and punished for the offence, not to be tried or punished for it again; and

(i) if found guilty of the offence and if the punishment for the offence has been varied between the time of commission and the time of sentencing, to the benefit of the lesser punishment.

12. Everyone has the right not to be subjected to any cruel and unusual treatment or punishment.

13. A witness who testifies in any proceedings has the right not to have any incriminating evidence so given used to incriminate that witness in any other proceedings, except in a prosecution for perjury or for the giving of contradictory evidence.

15. (1) Every individual is equal before and under the law and has the right to the equal protection and equal benefit of the law without discrimination and, in particular, without discrimination based on race, national or ethnic origin, colour, religion, sex, age or mental or physical disability.

The U.S. Approach

The successful submission of denial of "due process" in American law has a more direct and drastic effect than does the judicial recognition of procedural irregularities in the Canadian criminal process. "Due process" is an imprecise and elastic term, the meaning of which varies with time and place. Basically, it suggests fundamental fairness and tries to apply that concept to all parts of the criminal process. The breadth of the concept depends upon the subjective view of the American courts, particularly the U.S. Supreme Court. In the last twenty years "due process" has included protections against self-incrimination, coerced confessions, illegal searches, denial of counsel or jury trial and unregulated eavesdropping. In the American system a judicial finding that law enforcement officials have offended due process will result in a complete exclusion of the impugned evidence and will usually result in the acquittal of the accused.

The American approach to due process and constitutional guarantees has been criticized on three bases. First, it places enormous powers in the hands of judges who are merely appointed, have life tenure and are not answerable to any constituency. Second, the constant judicial interpretation and re-interpretation of a written constitution is fraught with the danger of nonreviewable judicial discretion and denies the certainty that many hope to find in a written constitution. Third, the critics of "judicial legislation" argue that the U.S. Supreme Court acts like a super-legislature that is too responsive to the current moods of society and particularly the demands of the most visible or persistent minorities. Unfortunately, much of the criticism is less intelligent and more emotive.

The U.S. Supreme Court does sometimes act as an ultimate "legislative" body. Its defenders claim that its decisions are necessary and salutary because, in a country as heterogeneous as the United States, it would be otherwise impossible to maintain a uniform control over state criminal procedures; furthermore it would be unlikely that any consensus could be arrived at by the legislative process. It may well be that the United States, with its huge population, widespread dissensions and constant social flux, needs a "super-legislature" to lay down rules that can be later adapted to local conditions. The U.S. Supreme Court sets up minimum standards for the administration of justice at the local level where the criminal process is plagued by political influence, elected judges and prosecutors, inferior, undermanned or over-worked police forces and by a prejudiced local populace that is likely to discriminate against some ethnic or socio-economic groups.

The recent criminal cases on due process which have caused so much controversy have not produced the drastic effects feared by police chiefs. The same types of suspects are still "spilling the beans" no matter how many warnings they are given as to their right to remain silent. The court has succeeded in enforcing a level of morality on the police forces that had previously been acting in a brutal fashion or otherwise disregarding the fundamental rights of accused and suspected persons. The exclusion of evidence illegally obtained by the denial of due process was, for instance, punishing police forces that were inefficient or corrupt.

The critics of the court say that the incidence of crime in the United States is so great that the country cannot survive civil libertarian rules made by an appellate bench whose members have seldom been trial judges, who do not know the *realpolitik* of local crime administration and whose principles are unworkable except on an abstract level. President Nixon appointed "strict constructionalists" to the vacancies on the court, and that court has slowed down and, in some instances, reversed the liberal interpretation of "due process."

A Canadian Comparison

Canadians do not see their judicial institutions as omnipotent, with the super-legislature image of the American court. (Whether the Charter of Rights will change this is not yet determined.) The most drastic reforms in this country have been proposed by Royal Commissions, departmental enquiries, and law reform commissions, although their recommendations have only infrequently passed into law. In Ontario, for instance, the Honourable J.C. McRuer, who had been Chief Justice of Ontario, was chairman of a Royal Commission on Civil Rights in Ontario. While on the bench Chief Justice McRuer had been conservative of the *status quo*. Royal Commissioner McRuer was much more liberal and more critical of the laws purportedly protecting the civil rights of citizens. Few of his recommendations have been put into practice but, in due course, as political expediency and social pressure dictate, these ideas will be introduced slowly into the law.

The Canadian (and British) courts have not taken a drastic attitude toward exclusion of evidence. In the Canadian Criminal Code, s. 613, subsection (1)(a) provides that a court of appeal may allow the appeal where the court decides:

(i) that the trial verdict is unreasonable or cannot be supported by the evidence;
(ii) that the trial verdict was wrong on a question of law; or
(iii) that there was a miscarriage of justice.

Section 613(1)(b), however, qualifies this power to upset a conviction. Clause (iii) provides that an appeal court can refuse to quash a conviction if "notwithstanding that the Court is of the opinion that on any ground mentioned in (613(1)(a)(ii)) the appeal might be decided in favour of the appellant, it is of the opinion that no substantial wrong or miscarriage of justice has occurred."

The Canadian appeal courts have used this proviso to uphold convictions—presumably on the basis that although there may have been irregularities in the fact-finding process (arising from the wrongful behaviour of police, prosecutor or trial judge), the appeal court, in its discretion, has decided that the accused was probably guilty and it would be doing an injustice to the criminal process to allow the accused to escape on a "technicality."

One should not gain the impression that the Canadian courts are the modern successors to the Spanish Inquisition. The appeal courts are not doing grave injustices, but the Anglo-Canadian law is not in favour of absolute rules. They have more faith in the exercise of judicial discretion—or a limiting rather than expansive variety. They do not regard judges as political animals and do not see the function of the courts as handing down "policy" decisions. Of course, all courts decide legal issues on questions of policy but the Canadian judge prefers to disguise his policy in case-law precedent and leave articulated policy to the provincial legislatures and federal Parliament.

Once again an anthropological analogy seems apposite. The United States system was born out of revolution. The colonies in 1776 wanted to break away from English ways of viewing the law. They were attracted by the abstractions (and the notions of liberty) propounded by the French and Scottish *philosophes* of the Englightenment and neither of those groups was particularly enamoured of English institutions. Power was to be distributed so that, with a system of "checks and balances," no one group—legislative, administrative or judicial—could be predominant. Instead they would have controls on each other. (Watergate shows this system in operation.) Implicit in the revolutionary background and in the structure of the constitution was the idea that no one public functionary should be entrusted with power or trusted with unbridled power. The ethos of its people was to admire the constitution but at the same time to proclaim the individual citizen's right to challenge the State if the citizen felt aggrieved. In practical terms, this has meant that the U.S. Constitution has taken on some of the qualities of Holy Writ and it is interpreted as a basic document that will override other law, written or common. In this climate it is not surprising to find the U.S. Supreme Court giving almost religious significance and interpretation to "due process," the right against "self-incrimination" or "equal protection under the law."

If the Battle of Waterloo were won on the playing fields of Eton, one could equally argue that the "super-legislation" of the U.S. Supreme Court under Warren C.J. was inspired by the legal education instilled in future lawyers when they were students at Yale Law School (and other schools). United States legal education had been academic for many decades, and its treatment of the law was much more critical and imaginative than the instruction found in Anglo-Canadian law schools.

Hugh MacLennan once said that Canada was made up of three defeated races—the Scots, the Irish and the French. Presumably such people are used to obedience to their English masters, although they may do it rather grudgingly. In addition, many of the most influential settlers after 1763, and 1776, were American colonists who were loyalist, royalist and wanted to adhere to English ways. In Upper Canada, for instance, they were aided in this aim by the prime Anglophile Lieutenant-Governor Simcoe. In most provinces, the first judges were former English barristers or United Empire Loyalists. The colonial mentality had a serious effect on the law. The judges were slaves to precedent, particularly to English cases. The legislatures copied English Acts. Legal education was based on an apprenticeship system that was uncritical and tended to replicate the present system, handing down values from master to student. Canada used an English court (Judicial Committee of the Privy Council) as a final court of appeal until World War II. The ethos seems to be trust of authority. In practical terms, this means that there is a presumption that the authorities—the police, the prosecutor, the judge—will do the right thing. Therefore we should give them the authority to exercise their discretion. This can be seen in the use of s. 613 of the Code. This is partly based on a more rigid class system that exists in England (and Canada?) than is the ideology of the United States. The Anglo-Canadian lawyer and judge is steeped in the common law and does not have an affinity for absolute rules (such as the U.S. exclusionary rule) and tends to be somewhat suspicious of the enunciation of fundamental principles in a written constitutional document.

Some Fundamental Principles of Criminal Procedure

The basic principle of the criminal trial is the presumption of innocence—the law presumes that a man is innocent until the contrary is proved. The burden of proving guilt is on the prosecution and the trier of fact (judge or jury) must be convinced "beyond a reasonable doubt." No attempt will be made to give an exact definition of "reasonable doubt." Many trial judges have suffered rebukes from appeal courts for their attempts to qualify or explain the term. As a bare minimum, it can be said that the jury must not acquit because the prosecution case has a miniscule flaw in its reasoning or because there is some small flicker of uncertainty in the unexplained or insufficiently explained facts of the case. The jury does not have to be one hundred per cent convinced that the accused did not do the act. The jury will seldom be presented with a "watertight" case and it can hardly expect to see a movie film of the occurrence, with the accused in full view. The accused must, however, be given the benefit of the doubt.

The second fundamental rule, related to the burden of proof being on the prosecution, is that the accused is not obliged to say anything in his defence. (Until the nineteenth century, the accused was not allowed to speak in his own defence.) Other than pleading "guilty" or "not guilty," the accused need not utter a word in court or at any time—on arrest, on being charged, etc. Of course, if the prosecution has anything like a case, the accused is in serious danger of being convicted, but the burden of proving guilt is on the Crown and remains there. We must remember that our system is not seeking truth in an absolute sense, any more than it is seeking absolute knowledge as to the accused's "real" mental processes at the time of the crime.

The Adversarial Form of Trial

The Anglo-American system of trial, criminal and civil, is an adversarial not an inquisitorial one. Under Continental law the judge acts as inquisitor and is the leading actor in the trial. He can ask questions and generally direct the proceedings. The accused is obliged to answer questions put to him. The burden to some extent is on the accused to exonerate himself. Under the adversary system the trial can be perceived as a battle, or a morality play, depending on one's perspective. The judge in this system is discouraged from taking an active role and instead is more like a referee in a game. The side that wishes to prove the point at issue (in civil cases, that the defendant is liable in negligence or for breach of contract and, in criminal cases, that the accused is, in fact, blameworthy, culpable or guilty of the offence charged) must present its case. The other side (the defendant or the accused) must do its best to disprove the case for the Crown or the plaintiff. The Crown produces witnesses—eyewitnesses, police officers, expert forensic witnesses, alleged accomplices—who present their evidence in question-and-answer form. After each Crown witness has presented his evidence, from his own knowledge and without the prompting of pointed "leading" questions from the Crown, the defence has the right to cross-examine the witness. The cross-examiner tries to discredit the story of the Crown witness in the hope that inconsistencies will encourage the trier of fact to find that the accused is not guilty "beyond a reasonable doubt." The Crown has a right to re-examine each witness hoping to rectify or amplify ambiguities or uncertainties created by the cross-examination.

After the Crown's case is closed, the defence lawyer may present his defence. The scope of this defence will vary widely depending on the forum (magistrate, judge and/or jury), the type of offence and the character and demeanour of the accused. As stated earlier, the defence can choose to say nothing, but this is unusual unless the Crown case is weak. (If the Crown case is particularly weak, the case may never be brought to trial or the judge may be asked to stop the trial at the end of the Crown presentation because there is "no case to answer.") The defence lawyer may decide that he does not want to present any evidence and does not want to subject his client to a cross-examination by the Crown.

The usual procedure is for the defence to produce witnesses who are examined, cross-examined and re-examined. The accused, in these circumstances, will take the stand and be subjected to cross-examination. The trier of fact is likely to be strongly influenced by the demeanour and credibility of the accused on the stand.

After all witnesses have been heard, the Crown and the defence counsel will make their final submissions to the judge (in the absence of the jury) on questions of law. They then address the jury (if there is one), summarizing the evidence and trying to persuade the trier of fact, on the strength or weakness of the evidence, to convict or acquit the accused. If there is a jury, the judge will address them. His address should be balanced and unbiassed, although the judge must direct the jury that he is the sole judge of the law and must advise the jury on the law. He must not give them a distorted picture of the facts of which they are the sole arbiters.

The Jury

It is probable that laymen have gained the impression from television and films that the ordinary criminal trial is conducted with a judge and jury. This is not the usual case in Canada, where ninety per cent of the trials are conducted before a judge who acts as trier of both fact and law. This system is not universally approved. Some critics argue that one of the most important jobs in the administration of justice is given to poorly paid political appointees who are sometimes not even legally trained or, at best, were obscure practitioners who have been rewarded for performing political tasks for the party in power.

This situation seems to be improving—the inferior bench is now attracting better appointees. Governments are realizing that these courts perform some of the most crucial functions in the criminal process. The task cannot be left to appointees who are political hacks. A second criticism is a little more abstract. The admirers of the jury system deplore the decreasing use of that institution; they believe that the collective common sense of twelve jurors from diverse backgrounds may provide a leaven of equity or mercy to the law. Many times the jury is more attuned to everyday affairs than a judge who may be middle-aged (or older) and insulated, because of his position, from prevailing social mores and customs. In short, the jurors may be better judges of credibility and social accountability.

The jury is a dying institution in Canada, and whatever its virtues and vices, it now seems irrelevant to argue for its retention or abolition. Some lawyers however, have recently, and unsuccessfully, invoked the Canadian Bill of Rights, claiming that their clients have a fundamental right to be tried by a jury of their peers. Supporters of the jury like to remind the bench that trial by jury was supposedly guaranteed by Magna Carta in 1215. Perhaps the Charter of Rights will revive this fine institution.

Evidence: Truth and Proof

The evidence that is produced at a trial is not the "truth" as it might be seen by the man-in-the-street, a gangster, a clergyman, psychologist, sociologist, psychiatrist, historian or philosopher. There is no way in which we can be assured that all the facts are before a court; criminals seldom commit offences in public view and even less often are they posing before television cameras at the time. (Holdup men in banks and department stores, however, have discovered that hidden television cameras are making this more likely.)

Human acts and events cannot be proved on an absolute level; truth is relative. All the disciplines mentioned have their own ideas about truth and its revelation. The law's time-honoured methods of arriving at the "truth" may be puzzling to a psychologist or a communications expert because they offend basic principles of human psychology. A police officer may dislike the legal rules of evidence which exclude hearsay and other evidence, thereby "coddling" criminals, offending common sense and excluding the very strong (but unprovable) suspicion that the officer has of the accused's guilt. On the other hand, the civil libertarian will be equally vehement in his protestations that the police and the courts are "railroading" accused persons because of repressive rules of evidence. Finally, the behavioural scientist or humanitarian may tell us that the court is only interested in the dry analysis of the legal facts and ignores the social data that would "really" show why the accused committed this act that the law has termed a crime (childhood spent in an orphanage, drunken parents, interrupted schooling, constant ill health, poverty).

Therefore, it is well to remember that legal evidence of a crime is just as relative as legal descriptions of human behaviour which the Criminal Code defines as crimes. No one is suggesting that guilt is to be equated with sinfulness or that the facts of a crime as described in court are the true state of affairs in the unfortunate accused's life. Conversely, a verdict of innocence does not necessarily mean that the accused did not do some act that the community considers reprehensible. It simply means that the Crown did not satisfy the fact-finder that the accused's behaviour fell within the legal definition of crime or that the admissible data produced by the Crown provided insufficient proof of the alleged crime.

The law has laid down rules that exclude all but the "best" evidence ("best" being a technical term, a legal term of art). This means that the court will not usually convict an accused on the basis of mere innuendo or third-hand gossip, particularly if it cannot be tested on cross-examination. This is the basis of the hearsay rule, although it has many exceptions. For instance, if a man is dying (and knows it) the law takes the view that such a man is more likely to tell the truth than to lie. If a man makes a statement that is contrary to his pecuniary interests, it is also thought more likely to be true. Sometimes statements that are relevant and usually admissible are excluded because of the circumstances under which they are made. For instance, some statements are privileged because of the relationship between the auditor and the speaker; in most instances, one spouse cannot be compelled to divulge any conversation with the other spouse during the marriage. In some jurisdictions confidential conversations between lawyer and client, doctor and patient, social worker and client, priest and penitent are not compellable evidence in court unless the giver of the confidence permits the receiver to divulge the contents. At common law, the only fully privileged communication was between lawyer and client, although as a matter of discretion, most judges would excuse a priest, and perhaps a psychiatrist, from answering an indelicate question. (There was a recent case in Ontario, however, where a psychiatrist was cited for contempt of court because of his refusal to divulge a confidential but unprivileged communication between his patient and himself.)

Modern psychological theories may show that the rationale of the law of evidence is faulty. There may be other anomalies in the law because it does not make allowance for twentieth-century methods of gathering, storing and retrieving information. This problem is suggested by the English decision in *Myers* v. *D.P.P.* The accused were, allegedly, a gang of well-organized car thieves. They bought cars that had been wrecked in accidents and thereby obtained legitimate registration papers. They then would steal an identical car—at least identical in every way except for serial numbers. They erased the serial numbers from the engine blocks and frames of the car and replaced the numbers of the wrecked cars. The Crown sought to prove the real identity of the cars by calling production personnel from the automobile factories. The judge refused to accept the evidence of production supervisors because the serial numbers were stamped on the cars and recorded on worksheets by production line operatives who frequently could not be located to give evidence. The court held that the evidence of the supervisors was less than the "best" evidence and was hearsay. The House of Lords agreed. Lord Pearce, in dissent, argued that this ruling did not take into account the modern methods of recording data or the problems of mass manufacture. His dissenting opinion suggested the problems of proving exactly who was responsible for programming each piece of data fed into a computer where much of the process may be automatic or partially anonymous.

The law has also decided that evidence is not admissible if the witness is incapacitated in some way; if the witness is too young, mentally deficient, psychotic, drunk or senile, the court will not accept the evidence or will only accept the evidence with reservations.

There are instances where the court will accept evidence only on the proviso that the trier of fact will not convict on that evidence alone or only if the evidence of guilt is clearly proved. For instance, there are many sexual offences (such as rape, indecent assault of the feeble-minded or of girls under the age of consent) where the law provides that no accused should be convicted or it is considered very dangerous to convict on the uncorroborated evidence of the complainant. These laws have been amended in relation to rape. Similar warnings apply to cases where the only evidence against the accused is the uncorroborated testimony of accomplices to a crime.

Self-Incrimination

Most of the rules already discussed apply, with only minor variations, in both the British Commonwealth and the United States. The same is not true of the rules relating to self-incrimination and confessions. Everyone has heard of Americans "pleading the Fifth" which refers to the Fifth Amendment to the American Constitution. This rule, based on the right to silence, provides that, no man is obliged to incriminate himself and this is an absolute rule. Critics of this rule suggest that resort to the protection of the Fifth Amendment has reached an absurd point so that a witness will refuse to answer any question other than providing his name. This practice, they argue, amounts to an obstruction of justice and makes it difficult to control organized crime or to conduct government enquiries into pressing social problems.

The Canadian law also has a Fifth—s. 5 of the Canadian Evidence Act, a federal statute that governs the rules of evidence in criminal trials. It is not an absolute rule. Section 5(1) provides that "no witness shall be excused from answering any question upon the grounds that the answer . . . may tend to incriminate him" or make him liable in any civil suit. In other words, the witness must answer the questions. There is, however, basic protection against self-incrimination in that s. 5(2) provides that, although the witness is obliged to answer the incriminating question, "the answer so given shall not be used or receivable in evidence against him in any criminal trial . . . other than a trial for perjury."

The use of the *subpoena* (a summons to appear as a witness) is enforceable by law and therefore a witness cannot refuse to appear at a trial and give evidence. He must answer questions put to him, but the proviso in s. 5(2) saves the witness from having this evidence used at a subsequent trial when the witness is the accused. Therefore, there is some safeguard but there are several situations that make the privilege against self-incrimination less than complete. First, the witness or his counsel must claim the right before the evidence is given. Secondly, the privilege does not extend to all quasi-judicial hearings. (Although *Batary* v. *A.G. for Saskatchewan* holds that a person charged with murder cannot be compelled to testify as a witness at a coroner's inquest into the death of his alleged victim.) The law is not so clear where a person is subpoened to appear before a judicial enquiry, departmental committee or Royal Commission. The protection of s. 5 of the Canada Evidence Act (or of the provincial evidence legislation) was not afforded to a witness appearing before the judicial enquiry into the financial disaster of the Atlantic Acceptance Corporation. Therefore any testimony presented to the enquiry could be used at a subsequent trial of the witness. Some argue that this ruling by the Ontario Court of Appeal means that such a witness will, to say the least, be less than candid before a judicial enquiry or Royal Commission and, therefore, that the proper function of the extraordinary fact-finding body will be compromised.

The third reservation is not only the most nebulous but also the most dangerous for the person claiming the privilege. Who is to say what evidence is incriminating—the judge, the witness, his counsel or the cross-examiner? Furthermore, an answer that, on face value, may not be incriminating may give factual leads to the police, enabling them to discover evidence that is perfectly admissible. The import of this has resulted in the American rule that a witness refuses to answer all questions except "name, rank and serial number."

Stephen, who certainly was not a great liberal advocate of the criminal's rights, nevertheless said:

> This is one of the most characteristic features of English Criminal procedure and it presents a marked contrast to that which is common to, I believe, all continental countries. It is, I think, highly advantageous to the guilty. It contributes greatly to the dignity and apparent humanity of a criminal trial. It effectually avoids the appearance of harshness, not to say cruelty, which often shocks an English spectator in a French Court of Justice; and I think that the fact that the prisoner cannot be questioned stimulates the search for indepen-

> dent evidence. During the discussions which took place on the Indian Code of Criminal Procedure in 1872, some observations lead native officers to apply torture to prisoners. An experienced civil officer observed, "There is a great deal of laziness in it. It is far pleasanter to sit comfortably in the shade rubbing red pepper into a poor devil's eyes than to go about in the sun hunting up evidence." This was a new view to me, but I have no doubt of its truth. The evidence in an English trial is, I think, usually more full and more satisfactory than the evidence in such French trials as I have been able to study.

Wigmore said the real objection is that "any system of administration which permits the prosecution to trust habitually to compulsory self-disclosure as a source of proof must itself suffer morally thereby." He added:

> If there is a right to an answer, there soon seems to be a right to the expected answer—that is, to a confession of guilt. Thus the legitimate use grows into the unjust abuse; ultimately, the innocent are jeopardized by the encroachments of a bad system. Such seems to have been the course of experience in those legal systems where the privilege was not recognized.

And G. Arthur Martin, when leader of the criminal bar and before his appointment to the Ontario Court of Appeal, said:

> . . . the real truth seems to me to be that the privilege has its source in the need to strike a just balance between the collective power of the state and the rights of the individual and it draws its life blood from deep feelings which are a product of history, of humanitarian ideals and the concept of the dignity and value of the individual.

Martin also believes that this privilege is being eroded by special statutory provisions such as those found in the Ontario Securities Act:

> This is not the place to make an exhaustive study of the privilege against self-incrimination. This problem is a further manifestation of the ambivalence which is found in the Canadian courts' attitudes toward the rights of the accused and the standard of behaviour that we expect from our law enforcers. Furthermore, the provisions of the Canada Evidence Act (e.g., section 5 relating to self-incrimination and section 12 regarding previous convictions) are so drafted or have been construed in a way which tends to erode principles inherent in the "due process" of law.

Confessions

The law of confessions is an exception to the right of silence rule. It is also an exception to the hearsay rule. A man is not obliged to say anything when interrogated, stopped, suspected, arrested or charged by a police officer. Under some provincial legislation he may be obliged to show his driver's licence or some similar documentary evidence. As a general rule, he need say nothing. Most accused persons convict themselves by talking unnecessarily; as has been said, people tend to hang themselves with their long tongues.

The Canadian statute law does not incorporate any rules on confessions.

Instead, we find the rules in the common law and in administrative directives that have been drawn up for the guidance of policemen. While there are many areas where Canada has followed the American rather than the English pattern—labour law and penal administration, for example—this has not been the case with the laws of confessions. Perhaps this can be explained in cultural terms. The Canadian police forces have followed the English model rather than the gun-toting, allegedly corrupt, crime-busting stereotype of the American "cop." Canada has not had the violent history that has plagued the United States. Furthermore, Canada has not had a gun culture. The urban problems of the United States have not been repeated with the same intensity in this country. Some chauvinists might also argue that Canadians have inherited some of the traditional English respect for the law, and consequently a better type of citizen has been recruited into the police forces.

While Americans have been formulating increasingly stringent rules about confessions, Canadians have maintained a standard rule for many decades. The basic Canadian rule states that a statement is not voluntary when it is made to a person in authority who has offered hope of advantage or fear of punishment in exchange for the statement. The most important word is "voluntary" because that is the essence of the rule. Under the Canadian system of allowing judicial discretion to decide on voluntariness, the judge will ask himself, in effect, "is it fair, is it relevant—if so, admit it in evidence." A "person in authority" is not necessarily a policeman; he may be a customs officer, a superior officer in the armed services, a school principal or an employer. "Hope of advantage" does not mean merely a monetary payment held out as an inducement. If the confession is made to a policeman, the court may hold, depending on the circumstances, that an improper inducement could consist of statements such as "We will make it easier for you," "You might get a better deal from the judge," "It would be better for you to tell the truth" or "You might as well tell us that you did it." Similarly, punishment does not necessarily mean that the police have done anything as unsubtle as bearing down on the suspect with a truncheon or thumbscrews. The police, or other authority figure, may simply have said, "You will get the book thrown at you if you don't . . . ," "You are going to be a very sorry young man if you don't . . . ," or "I don't think you would like it in the Hole but that is where you will go if you don't. . . ."

The voluntariness of a confession is not decided by the jury but by the judge in the absence of the jury. The judge conducts a *voir dire* or "a trial within a trial" to decide if the confession was obtained voluntarily. (He hears the evidence before he hears the contents of the confession.) The judge questions the policeman or other "person in authority" and discovers the circumstances under which the confession was made, including the method of recording the confession. In *Boudreau* the Supreme Court of Canada said that the trial judge, in deciding upon the voluntariness of the statement, must look at "all the surrounding circumstances." This rule is not a do-or-die rule and is subject to judicial discretion; some Canadian lawyers believe that it is more satisfactory than the total exclusionary rule set down by the American courts.

Before we embrace an American interpretation of the Charter of Rights, it would be wrong to ignore totally much of the exclusion of questionable evidence that is performed by trial judges at the *voir dire* level. These decisions are not reported and therefore receive little notice. In recent years, there has been increasing use of the *voir dire* as a modified vehicle for exclusion of inadmissible evidence. This has occurred because of improvements in the quality of the judiciary, more frequent presence of lawyers (and better trained lawyers) in the criminal courts and a growing scepticism about the unfailing veracity of police witnesses.

The voluntariness depends on the circumstances and these may vary widely. The courts do not take the attitude that the circumstances should be the same in every case. The decision as to admission may depend on the time of day the confession was obtained (was it 3:00 p.m. or 3:00 a.m.?) and on the length of time the subject had been under interrogation. If the confession had been obtained at the seemingly reasonable hour of 3:00 p.m. but after ten hours of continuous interrogation, which began at 5:00 a.m., the court, looking at "all the circumstances," may rule that this amounts to unfair police tactics.

Many of the "circumstances" may be coincident in one case. The court may be interested in the status or condition of the confessor. Was the suspect young (twelve, fourteen, sixteen or eighteen), old, female (if questioned by male police officers), tired, distraught (particularly if in this state for reasons other than being apprehended or caught in the act), drunk, mentally deficient (and yet legally sane)? For how long was the suspect interrogated? What is a reasonable length for an interrogation—two hours, four hours, six hours? Under what physical condition did the interrogation take place? Was it in the comfort and security of the suspect's home, in a police car, on a public street, before his parents, in a cold and uncomfortable police station office or in a cell? What material comforts were afforded the suspect? Was he or she given refreshments, and if so, how frequently and of what kind? Was the subject given the chance to go to the toilet?

Most of these problems are now academic because police forces are better trained than they used to be and do not make fundamental mistakes. Therefore, if a sixteen-year-old was arrested at 11:00 p.m., interrogated by rotating teams of police detectives for six hours until 5:00 a.m., not allowed to go to the toilet, offered no refreshments and if his parents were not told of his arrest, the court would have little difficulty, "in all the circumstances," in not admitting the confession. Usually the circumstances are less obvious than those given. Furthermore, police interrogation and detection techniques are now more subtle than they were. Electronic eavesdropping, entrapment, the employment of *agents provocateurs* and paid informers are devices more frequently used than beatings with rubber hoses.

Illustration 61 shows one of the more subtle police techniques. Is a confession so obtained one that the judge should admit in evidence? Such techniques have been incorporated in police manuals and most courts would admit such evidence unless the subject was exceptionally vulnerable. On the *voir dire* in *R.* v. *McLean and McKinley* police officers intimated that they did not believe the accused's story after speaking with the complainant. They told the accused falsely that his co-accused had made a statement. They gave him the necessary caution, and after a delay of ten minutes, he told them a different story implicating himself in the crime. The police explained that if the accused had insisted upon his innocence despite what his co-accused had said, they would have been inclined to believe his first story.

The British Columbia Supreme Court relied on *Boudreau* and agreed with the judge in *Sim* that "Police officers are forbidden from inducing a confession by deliberately lying or inventing situations to an accused which have no shadow of truth."

A well-known commentator has been critical of the British Columbia decision:

> Relying on *R.* v. *Boudreau* and *R.* v. *Fitton*, the learned trial judge excluded the statement on the ground that it was not free and voluntary, the accused having been tricked into making it. With respect, this attitude seems unrealistic when viewed in the light of the problems facing our police forces. Dressing a police officer in plain clothes or otherwise disguising him has never been regarded as an abuse of the citizen's private rights. What possible infringement of such rights is involved in telling a citizen, in custody and charged with an offence, that a co-accused has made a statement which incriminates him? Where is the unreliability of a confession made in answer to such a statement? To permit a self-confessed criminal to go free, save for some cogent reason, is surely to cut off one's nose to spite one's face. It is not only the police officer who played the cunning trick who is penalized when the true confession is rejected; indeed it is unlikely that he will be the next victim of a sexual attack.

Professor Morton's sympathy for the overworked police is understandable, but perhaps we should ask, "When *do* an accused's rights become sufficiently infringed that the statement would be ruled involuntary?" Would this not come within the *Kuruma* "trick" rule? Or are verbal admissions different from other types of evidence? The confession situation should be stronger, not weaker; the public should more readily believe the cold hard facts of two cartridges illegally taken by the police (in *Kuruma*) than a statement made by an accused while overborne by one or more interrogators in the oppressive atmosphere of a police station.

Why do we single out confessions for special attention? Prosecutors complain that some judges have now reached a frame of mind where they exclude all confessions obtained under colourable circumstances. Are the courts paying too little attention to the public's interest in being protected against criminal activity? Should the protection of the accused's private rights be subject only to civil remedies against those who have abused them?

Should the only deterrents imposed on the police be their own sense of decency, the internal discipline of the force and the threat of an inquiry or court action?

Rothman (described in Illustration 58) is ostensibly about self-incrimination but is also an important statement of policy. The court decided that this was not a case where the privilege against self-incrimination was applicable because it only applied when an accused was a witness. This is in line with other decisions of the Supreme Court of Canada that have stated that an involuntary breath sample was not self-incrimination. The other issue was the voluntariness of the confession. The Supreme Court had declared confessions inadmissible in *Horvath* (where the accused had made statements after being in a hypnotic state) and in *Alward* (where the police had lied to the accused that the victim had regained consciousness). Martland J. in *Rothman* decided that those two cases could be distinguished because, in those instances, there was reasonable doubt that the confession was the "utterance of an operating mind." In *Rothman*, however, the judge decided that there was no evidence that:

> the mind of the accused was affected by the actions of the police officer. No person thought by the accused to be in authority sought by oppression to coerce, or even to persuade, the accused to make a statement. His statement was made freely, and it was volunteered by him. The circumstances of this case show only that the accused was mistaken as to the identity of the person with whom he was talking. The accused thought that person was a fellow prisoner who presented himself as a sympathetic listener.

A vigorous dissent was written by Estey J. (with Laskin C.J. concurring). He said:

> The rules of evidence in criminal law, and, indeed, in civil law, are all concerned with relevancy, reliability and fairness, as well as other considerations, such as the reasonable economy and efficiency of trial. The rules with reference to confessions have an additional element, namely, the concern of the public for the integrity of the system of the administration of justice. If the reliability of an accused's statements were the only consideration in determining their admissibility, the courts would not have adopted distinctive principles applicable only to statements to persons in authority and not to statements against interest generally. Reliability cannot be the ticket for admission, because statements may have enough of the appearance of reliability to ensure reference to the trier of fact but still have been excluded by the confession standard.

An additional factor must decide the issue of voluntariness of confessions in criminal cases—their admission will be denied if to do so would bring the administration of justice into disrepute. And Estey J. added:

> It is also necessary to adopt these basic rules for the higher reason that ethical precepts are a vital ingredient in a system of justice if it is to command the respect and support of the community it serves, particularly in a judicial

> structure which embraces the concept of the jury. In this appeal the first encounter of significance was with a person in authority, that is, the authority to whom the accused communicated his decision or election not to give a statement. It is that incident which, in the circumstances here concerned, started the process which, in my view, leads to the exclusion of the statements thereafter obtained by the authorities.
>
> The analysis need go but one step further. To be voluntary, a statement must be volunteered by the speaker, in the sense that the statement must be the product of a conscious *volens* on the part of the speaker. The *volens* must relate not only to the mechanics of speaking, that is, the articulation of the ideas of the speaker. Where the speaker has, as here, already refused to give a statement to the authorities, the test of voluntariness must include an appreciation of the circumstances in which the statement is made, including an awareness that his statement is being "volunteered" to a person in authority. To apply the rule otherwise in the circumstances we have here not merely would permit but would encourage the deliberate circumvention by the authority of the accused's announced exercise of his right not to give a statement to the authorities.

In summary, the judge said:

(a) The exclusionary confession rule applies to statements given before trial by an accused to persons in authority.
(b) The basic reason for the rule is a concern for the integrity of the criminal justice system. Such a system necessarily requires the support and respect of the community it purports to serve. That support and respect can be maintained only if persons in authority conduct themselves in a way that does not bring the administration of justice into disrepute in the community.
(c) The rule and its administration strike a delicate balance between the need to secure the conviction of the guilty and, above all, the avoidance of the conviction of the innocent.
(d) In the realm of confessions, this standard of conduct is reflected in the requirement that an accused's statement be given "voluntarily."
(e) In this appeal, an expressed decision to remain silent was made by the accused to a policeman who was, in the mind of the accused as well as in fact, a person in authority.
(f) The statement ultimately obtained and tendered in court was the product of a trick and lies by persons in authority, calculated to subvert the appellant's expressed decision to stand mute.
(g) Such a determined subversion by the police of an expressed right to refuse to make any statement brings the administration of justice into disrepute. Accordingly, such a statement given in these circumstances cannot get over the hurdle of the exclusionary rule.
(h) This appeal is not concerned with the gathering of evidence by any other means, nor with the circumstance where an accused has not announced to persons in authority that he did not wish to make a statement.

One hopes that this dissent will soon become the majority view of the law in Canada in relation to the admissibility of confessions.

Electronic Eavesdropping

If we must set a liar to catch a liar, how much latitude can we allow the police? Should electronic eavesdropping be permitted or does it violate a fundamental right of privacy or property? Until recently the only protection in the United States had been some state legislation, some ambiguous provisions in the communications legislation and some vague judgements about property rights. The U.S. Supreme Court (in *Katz*) and the Canadian criminal law now favour electronic eavesdropping judicially supervised by the issuance of warrants in appropriate circumstances.

Section 178.11(1) of the Criminal Code provides that everyone who wilfully intercepts a private communication by electronic (or similar) means is guilty of an indictable offence and liable to five years' imprisonment. Section 178.18 provides that possession, sale or purchase of "bugging" equipment will be a criminal offence unless it is possessed, sold or purchased by a police officer or other person with permission to use such equipment.

Section 178.11 does not apply to:

1. A person who has permission from the sender to intercept such message.
2. A person who intercepts a private communication in accordance with an authorization or any person who in good faith aids in any way a person whom he has reasonable and probable grounds to believe is acting with any such authorization.
3. An employee of a telephone or telegraph service who is acting within his ordinary employment.

Under s. 178.12, an application for authorization can be made to a judge of a superior court of criminal jurisdiction by the attorney general of any province or the solicitor general of Canada. The application is to be accompanied by an affidavit in which a peace officer will swear as to the following facts:

(c) the facts relied upon to justify the belief that an authorization should be given together with particulars of the offence;
(d) the type of private communication proposed to be intercepted;
(e) the names and addresses, if known, of all persons, the interception of whose private communications there are reasonable and probable grounds to believe may assist the investigation of the offence, and if not known, a general description of the place at which private communications are proposed to be intercepted or, if a general description of that place cannot be given, a general description of the manner of interception proposed to be used;
(f) the period for which the authorization is requested; and
(g) whether other investigative procedures have been tried and have failed or why it appears they are unlikely to succeed or that the urgency of the matter is such that it would be impractical to carry out the investigation of the offence using only other investigative procedures.

The judge will give authorization if

> ... satisfied that it would be in the best interests of the administration of justice to do so and that
> (a) other investigative procedures have been tried and have failed;
> (b) other investigative procedures are unlikely to succeed; or
> (c) the urgency of the matter is such that it would be impractical to carry out the investigation of the offence using only other investigative procedures.
> (2) An authorization shall
> (a) state the offence in respect of which private communications may be intercepted;
> (b) state the type of private communication that may be intercepted;
> (c) state the identity of the persons, if known, whose private communications are to be intercepted and where the identity of such persons is not known, generally describe the place at which private communications may be intercepted or, if a general description of that place cannot be given, generally describe the manner of interception that may be used;
> (d) contain such terms and conditions as the judge considers advisable in the public interest; and
> (e) be valid for the period, not exceeding thirty days, set forth therein.

Section 178.16(1) provides that any communication intercepted without authorization will be inadmissible, but subsection (2) states:

> (2) Where in any proceedings the judge is of the opinion that any private communication or any other evidence that is inadmissible pursuant to subsection (1)
> (a) is relevant, and
> (b) is inadmissible by reason only of a defect of form or an irregularity in procedure, not being a substantive defect or irregularity, in the application for or the giving of the authorization under which such private communication was intercepted or by means of which such evidence was obtained, or
> (c) that, in the case of evidence, other than the private communication itself, to exclude it as evidence may result in justice not being done,
>
> he may, notwithstanding subsection (1), admit such private communication or evidence as evidence in such proceedings.

The Commission of Inquiry into the RCMP recommended that the RCMP should be empowered to open mail but only after obtaining judicial authorization and only in relation to narcotic and drug offences.

Escobedo and *Miranda*

The decisions of the U.S. Supreme Court in *Escobedo* and *Miranda* were concerned with the morality of police practices. They are not limited to narrow debates about confessions or the privilege against self-incrimination. They are manifestoes in the continuing dialogue on law and order.

The clearest expression of the *ratio decidendi* of these cases is found in Warren C.J.'s opinion in *Miranda*:

> ... the prosecution may not use statements, whether exculpatory or inculpa-

tory, stemming from custodial interrogation of the defendant unless it demonstrates the use of procedural safeguards effective to secure the privilege against self-incrimination. By custodial interrogation, we mean questioning initiated by law enforcement officers after a person has been taken into custody or otherwise deprived of his freedom of action in any significant way. (This is what we meant in *Escobedo* when we spoke of an investigation which had focussed on an accused.) As for the procedural safeguards to be employed, unless other fully effective means are devised to inform accused persons of their right to silence and to assure a continuous opportunity to exercise it, the following measures are required. Prior to any questioning, the person must be warned that he has a right to remain silent, that any statement he does make may be used as evidence against him and that he has a right to the presence of an attorney, either retained or appointed. The defendant may waive effectuation of these rights, provided the waiver is made voluntarily, knowingly and intelligently. If, however, he indicates in any manner and at any stage of the process that he wishes to consult with an attorney before speaking there can be no questioning. Likewise, if the individual is alone and indicates in any manner that he does not wish to be interrogated, the police may not question him. The mere fact that he may have answered some questions or volunteered some statements on his own does not deprive him of the right to refrain from answering any further inquiries until he has consulted with an attorney and thereafter consents to be questioned.

In a historical survey the majority referred to the 1896 decision of *Brown* v. *Walker* which epitomizes the heritage that the Chief Justice saw in the American law:

> The maxim *Nemo tenetur seipsum accusare* had its origin in a protest against the inquisitorial and manifestly unjust methods of interrogating accused persons, . . . and . . . for the protection of the people against the exercise of arbitrary power. . . . the ease with which the questions put to [an accused] may assume an inquisitorial character, the temptation to press the witness unduly, to browbeat him if he be timid or reluctant, to push him into a corner, and to entrap him into fatal contradictions . . . made the system so odious as to give rise to a demand for its total abolition. . . . So deeply did the inequities of the ancient system impress themselves upon the minds of the American colonists that the States, with one accord, made a denial of the right to question an accused person a part of their fundamental law, so that a maxim, which in England was a mere rule of evidence, became clothed in this country with the impregnability of a constitutional enactment.

Warren C.J.'s opinion was aimed at a total eradication of improper police practices which he considered an affront to human dignity. The court examined the manuals of police techniques that are now "psychologically rather than physically oriented." They stress the need for privacy in the interrogation, for questioning a suspect away from his home where friends or family might lend him moral support. The police are instructed to "display an air of confidence" so that the "guilt of the subject is to be posited as a fact." The use of the "friendly-unfriendly" approach is advocated: one officer acts as the relentless investigator who has a great reputation for obtaining convictions by the use of overbearing tactics, while his colleague provides the alternative, sympathetic approach (see Illustration 61). Another manual recommends that officers offer legal excuses for the suspect's actions while seeking to obtain the full factual story. False legal advice is sometimes given. A fake line-up is suggested in another passage; fictitious witnesses or victims "identify" the suspect, with the help of previous coaching from police.

Extracts from the manuals well illustrate modern psychological techniques. One states:

> In the preceding paragraphs emphasis has been placed on kindness and stratagems. The investigator will, however, encounter many situations where the sheer weight of his personality will be the deciding factor. Where emotional appeals and tricks are employed to no avail, he must rely on an oppressive atmosphere of dogged persistence. He must interrogate steadily and without relent, leaving the subject no prospect of surcease. He must dominate his subject and overwhelm him with his inexorable will to obtain the truth. He should interrogate for a spell of several hours pausing only for the subject's necessities in acknowledgement of the need to avoid a charge of duress that can be technically substantiated. In a serious case, the interrogation may continue for days, with the required intervals for food and sleep, but with no respite from the atmosphere of domination. It is possible in this way to induce the subject to talk without resorting to duress or coercion. This method should be used only when the guilt of the subject appears highly probable.

Another police manual was pertinent to *Miranda* and describes one of the most successful psychological ploys where the interrogator has conceded the right to remain silent. This ploy is effective because the suspect is "disappointed in his expectation of an unfavourable reaction on the part of the interrogator" and the police officer "impresses the subject with the apparent fairness of his interrogator." After this atmosphere is created, the officer says:

> Joe, you have a right to remain silent. That's your privilege and I'm the last person in the world who'll try to take it away from you. If that's the way you want to leave this, OK. But let me ask you this. Suppose you were in my shoes, and I were in yours and you called me in to ask me about this and I told you, "I don't want to answer any of your questions." You'd think I had something to hide, and you'd probably be right in thinking that. That's exactly what I'll have to think about you, and so will everybody else. So let's sit here and talk this whole thing over.

The U.S. Supreme Court commented that:

> Even without employing brutality, the "third degree" or the specific stratagems described above, the very fact of custodial interrogation exacts a heavy toll on individual liberty and trades on the weakness of individuals.

Therefore, in reviewing police methods, the Court came to the conclusion that:

> ... the defendant was thrust into an unfamiliar atmosphere and run through

> menacing police interrogation procedures. . . . in none of the cases did the officers undertake to afford appropriate safeguards at the outset of the interrogation to insure that the statements were truly the product of free choice.
>
> It is obvious that such an interrogation environment is created for no purpose other than to subjugate the individual to the will of the examiner. . . . The current practice of incommunicado interrogation is at odds with one of our nation's most cherished principles—that the individual may not be compelled to incriminate himself. . . . We can readily perceive an intimate connection between the privilege against self-incrimination and police custodial questioning.

Furthermore, the Court called this privilege "the essential mainstay of our adversary system," based on the principle that "the respect of government . . . must accord to the dignity and integrity of its citizens." The privilege must be "guaranteed," not merely available, and must be applicable during a period of custodial interrogation.

The Court was seeking a "protective device to dispel the compelling atmosphere of the interrogation," which was stated by the majority in these terms:

> The presence of an attorney, and the warnings delivered to the individual, enable the defendant under otherwise compelling circumstances to tell his story without fear, effectively and in a way that eliminates the evils in the interrogation process. Without the protections flowing from adequate warning and the rights of counsel, all the careful safeguards erected around the giving of testimony, whether by an accused or any other witness, would become empty formalities in a procedure where the most compelling possible evidence of guilt, a confession, would have already been obtained at the unsupervised pleasure of the police.

The majority stated that "the right to have counsel present at the interrogation is indispensable to the protection of the Fifth Amendment." A mere warning would "not alone be sufficient to accomplish that end." Preliminary advice given to the accused by his lawyer could be "swiftly overcome by the secret interrogation process." Waiver of constitutional rights did not arise simply by a failure to ask for a lawyer and was only effective if specifically made after a direct unequivocal warning had been given. The Court noted that the police should not take advantage of the indigence or ignorance of an accused who may be the very person who most needs counsel.

The Supreme Court, *per* Warren C.J., set out some possible effects of a lawyer being present:

> If the accused decides to talk to his interrogators, the assistance of counsel can mitigate the dangers of untrustworthiness. With a lawyer present the likelihood that the police will practice coercion is reduced and, if coercion is nevertheless exercised, the lawyer can testify to it in court. The presence of a lawyer can also help to guarantee that the accused gives a fully accurate statement to the police and that the statement is rightly reported by the prosecution at trial.

If an accused indicates that he intends to exercise his Fifth Amendment privilege, questioning must stop. If a suspect says he wants to see his lawyer, interrogation must be postponed until the lawyer arrives. If questioning continues after the suspect has asked to consult his lawyer, "a heavy burden rests on the government to demonstrate that the defendant knowingly and intelligently waived his privilege against self-incrimination and his right to retained or appointed counsel."

The following pronouncement of the Court can be compared with the operation of s. 5 of the Canada Evidence Act:

> ... where in-custody interrogation is involved, there is no room for the contention that the privilege is waived if the individual answers some questions or gives some information on his own prior to invoking his right to remain silent when interrogated.

In the final portion of Warren C.J.'s opinion, he gave the social justification for the decision. The *Miranda* rule was "not intended to hamper the traditional function of police officers in investigating crime." When a suspect is in custody on probable cause, the police may, of course, seek out evidence in the field. Similarly, the decision was not meant to affect "general on-the-scene questioning of citizens in the fact-finding process."

In answering the recurrent argument that "society's need for interrogation outweighs the privilege," the Court's opinion is quoted from the well-known dissent of Brandeis J. in the wiretapping decision, *Olmstead* v. *United States*:

> Decency, security, and liberty alike demand that government officials shall be subjected to the same rules of conduct that are commands to the citizen. In a government of laws, existence of the government will be imperilled if it fails to observe the law scrupulously. Our government is the potent, the omni-present teacher. For good or for ill, it teaches the whole people by its example. Crime is contagious. If the government becomes a lawbreaker, it breeds contempt for law; it invites every man to become a law unto himself; it invites anarchy. To declare that in the administration of the criminal law the end justifies the means ... would bring terrible retribution. Against that pernicious doctrine this court should resolutely set its face.

The Court reiterated its concern for the burden carried by law enforcement officers but believed that the need for confessions was often overstated (a view shared by J.F. Stephen, quoted earlier). In the cases under appeal, the Court stated there was no need to interrogate for periods as long as five days because there was "considerable" independent evidence against each accused.

As a further justification for the views expressed in the majority opinion, Warren C.J. set out the information obtained from the Federal Bureau of Investigation on the methods used by that agency. The policy of the FBI coincides with the decision in *Miranda* with the important exception, noted by the dissent, that the interrogation (after proper warnings as to self-incrimination and right to counsel) does not take place in the presence of the suspect's counsel. The FBI directives to its personnel include:

> When the person who has been warned of his right to counsel decides that he wishes to consult with counsel before making a statement, the interview is terminated at that point. It may be continued, however, as to all matters other than the person's own guilt or innocence.

The *Escobedo* and *Miranda* rules have been strongly criticized by police chiefs in the United States and Canada. There have been jeremiads about the dangers to society, the erosion of "law and order" and the frustrations of police forces when dangerous criminals go free because of the aberrational decisions of the U.S. Supreme Court. These fears are exaggerated and the prognostications are quite possibly unwarranted. The police were never able to obtain confessions from the most important professional criminals, partly because they were unable to obtain sufficient evidence to make an arrest and partly because those arrested were fully aware of their constitutional rights—particularly the right to remain silent. They said nothing without consulting their lawyers.

Studies of the effects of *Escobedo* and other decisions have shown that the new Supreme Court rules have not resulted in fewer admissible confessions or fewer convictions. The same types of people were confessing as had been doing so before the Supreme Court decisions. The compulsion to confess is such that no number of warnings or U.S. Supreme Court decisions would persuade the beneficiaries to keep silent and perhaps avoid a conviction.

A study conducted by Yale law students showed that educated and sophisticated students who had been thoroughly briefed as to their legal rights under the United States Constitution still made incriminating statements to educated and sophisticated interrogators who questioned them after their arrests arising out of peace demonstrations. Education may have little to do with the promptings of suspects' consciences. Alternatively, academic achievement may be no antidote to the subtle probings and patient tactics of a skilled interrogator even if he has taken the precaution of warning the suspect that he has the right to remain silent. If, however, the suspect is angry, uneducated, stupid or scared, warnings of constitutional safeguards will have even less effect.

The most remarkable study was carried out by a prosecutor in Los Angeles County where the district attorney's office has the heaviest caseload in the United States. Two studies reported in 1968 showed that "suspects will talk regardless of the warnings." The district attorney offered some explanations. First, people will confess in cases where their guilt is obvious, when, for example, they are caught red-handed. Second, "in every human being, however noble or depraved, there is a thing called conscience."

The most important finding, already suggested by a New York study, was that a confession is needed for a successful prosecution in less than ten per cent of criminal cases. The Los Angeles district attorney was "amazed" by the findings because "like most prosecutors I had assumed that confessions were of the utmost necessity in the majority of cases"; he discovered that it "isn't so all-fired important whether they talk or not."

Perhaps we shall eventually reach the view held by the draftsmen of the Indian Evidence Code that confessions should not be admitted at all.

The Judges' Rules: The British and Canadian Experience

The British, unlike the American, system of criminal justice does not adopt the absolute exclusionary rule. The Anglo-Canadian law of criminal procedure is based partly on judicial discretion and partly on administrative directives known as the Judges' Rules.

These rules were formulated by a committee of judges for the guidance of police officers. They do not have the precise force of law, but an officer who ignores them will be in serious danger of having his evidence declared inadmissible.

The first set of rules (now called the Old Judges' Rules) was first laid down in 1918 and revised in 1964. Many police forces in Canada are still acting under the Old Rules. The New Rules, which are in force in England, made some important changes. With some exceptions, the New Rules provide the same safeguards as do the recent decisions of the U.S. Supreme Court.

The rules are concerned with police interrogation procedures and the voluntariness and admissibility of confessions. The confession is an exception to the fundamental rule of Anglo-Canadian justice that no man is obliged to be a witness against himself or to incriminate himself. A basic protection against self-incrimination is that a suspect must be cautioned, in these familiar words: "I must warn you that anything you say can be taken down and used in evidence. . . ."

The Caution Rule

The caution rule does not mean that the police are forbidden to ask any questions from the moment they have their first contact with the suspect. That would unnecessarily hinder police interrogation. The New Rules provide that a police officer investigating a crime may question any person, whether suspected or not, from whom useful information may be obtained. Under the Old Rules, any person "in custody" could not be questioned without a caution being given. The meaning of "in custody" had caused difficulties; if a police officer merely "suggested" that a suspect might accompany him to the station, was he "in custody"? Under the New Rules, it does not matter if the person is in custody as long as he has not been charged with the offence or told that he may be prosecuted. Would admissibility of evidence be affected if the suspect had been charged with one offence but suspected of another? *Christie* v. *Leachinsky* ruled that if the first charge was a mere subterfuge, the arrest was probably illegal and the judge may therefore exercise his discretion to exclude evidence so obtained.

A caution must be given as soon as the police officer has sufficient evidence to lay a charge or has, in fact, charged the suspect. Additional cautions must be given if the police officer wishes to ask further questions after the charge is laid or if the accused informs the officer that he wishes to make a statement. In the first of these instances, the New Rules lay down that questions should be put to a charged person only in exceptional circumstances. The questions must be designed to prevent or minimize harm or loss to some other person or to the public (for example, discovery of the location of a wounded victim or the place where a dangerous object may have been hidden) or for "clearing up an ambiguity in a previous answer or statement." This is wider than the Old Rule which flatly stated that the accused could not be cross-examined except to remove an ambiguity inherent in what had already been said. This was unreasonable and was more often breached than obeyed.

The courts believe that a caution is necessary to ensure the voluntary quality of a statement, but they do not believe that the need for a caution should be slavishly obeyed in all possible circumstances. In *Boudreau*, Kerwin J. said:

> The mere fact that a warning was given is not necessarily decisive in favour of admissibility but, on the other hand, the absence of a warning should not bind the hands of the Court, so as to compel it to rule out a statement. *All the surrounding circumstances must be investigated* and if upon their review the Court is not satisfied of the voluntary nature of the admission, the statement will be rejected. Accordingly, the presence or absence of a warning will be a factor and, in many cases, an important one (emphasis added).

And on the same point, Rand J. said:

> It would be a serious error to place the ordinary modes of investigation of crime in a straitjacket of artificial rules; and the true protection against improper interrogation or any kind of pressure or inducement is to leave the broad question to the Court. Rigid formulas can be both meaningless to the weakling and absurd to the sophisticated or hardened criminal; and to introduce a new rite as an inflexible preliminary condition would serve no genuine interest of the accused but add an unreal formalism to that vital branch of the administration of justice.

In other words, the basic rule is: in all circumstances, was the confession voluntary and therefore admissible? This, of course, is not the only consideration. The police behaviour cannot be assessed in a vacuum governed by rules abstractly applied. When the police have obtained sufficient evidence to lay a charge, have they then proceeded to hunt for all the other relevant evidence? Is the evidence so gathered consistent with the alleged confession? Does it tend to corroborate the truth of the statement made by the accused or is it inconsistent?

Many of the New Rules are administrative but some are important. These include detailed instructions about keeping records of statements made as to time and place of questioning, the duration of the questioning and the persons present. The record must be made contemporaneously and signed by the person making the statement. The statement must be read by the suspect and must be made on standard forms. The statement must not be translated into "official language" because "this may give a misleading impression of the genuineness of the statement." Records must be kept of breaks in the questioning process and refreshments provided. Special rules are also made for the interrogation of children and those who cannot speak English.

The Jurisprudence of the New Rules

The most surprising parts of the New Judges' Rules are found in the Preamble, which is a non-enforceable Bill of Rights for the administration of justice.

Clause (a) states, "That citizens have a duty to help a police officer to discover and apprehend offenders." This sounds like an innocuous exhortation to public spirited citizens, but it has serious implications. In recent years the public has been apathetic or antipathetic toward police officers. Many citizens seem determined to make the policeman's job more difficult. They distrust the law enforcers or they do not want to "get involved." Admittedly, a law-abiding pedestrian (as compared to an automobile driver) whose actions are not suspicious is not legally obliged to volunteer any information. On the other hand, he may arouse the policeman's suspicions by being uncooperative or obstructive. If the citizen is found in an unlikely place at an unlikely time and offers no explanation or no satisfactory explanation, the officer may feel that he has reasonable cause to suspect that the citizen was committing or was about to commit a crime. If the policeman exercises his discretion and makes an arrest, he takes the risk that he may be making a mistake that may lead to discipline from his superiors or a civil suit brought by the aggrieved citizen for wrongful arrest.

Some of the civil liberties organizations which, by definition, want to protect individual rights, advise citizens to be courteous to police and not to make exaggerated, dogmatic or pedantic assertions of their rights.

Motor traffic legislation has extended the rights of the police officer to ask for identification including motor vehicle registration or driving licence. Failure to identify oneself in such circumstances and to produce the required documents has become an offence in some provinces.

Clause (b) of the Preamble provides, "That police officers, otherwise than by arrest, cannot compel any person against his will to come to or remain in any police station." This point has been discussed already in relation to Illustration 54. Frequently people are hoodwinked into custody because an officer "invites" them to come down to the station. They are probably not under compulsion but the citizen interprets the "request" of the police officer as an ultimatum. Once citizens fall into the habit of acceding to such requests, the police take the attitude that someone would only refuse if he had something to hide. The citizen who refuses or raises objections is either presumed to be guilty (or to be a law student who is unnecessarily flaunting his new-found knowledge).

Clause (c) of the Preamble could be a pronouncement of the U.S. Supreme Court:

> That every person at any stage of an investigation should be able to communicate and to consult privately with a solicitor. This is so even if he is in custody provided that in such a case no unreasonable delay or hindrance is caused to the processes of investigation or the administration of justice by his doing so.

The "in custody" provision is also incorporated into the New Rules themselves (in Rule II(a)).

This is reminiscent of *Gideon* v. *Wainwright* and *Escobedo* v. *Illinois*. The latter provides that a man in custody has a right to consult with counsel when "the process shifts from investigatory to accusatory—when its focus is on the accused and its purpose is to elicit a confession." The time of the "shift" is ambiguous, must always be so and is dependent on the good judgement and good faith of the interrogating officer. Presumably, the New Judges' Rules envisage the accusatory stage as starting when the police have "evidence which would afford reasonable grounds for suspecting that a person has committed an offence"; a charge will be laid (or the person is notified that a charge will be laid).

Despite all the criticism of the Warren Court and the *Escobedo* decision, that court made clear that the constitutional rule enunciated was conditional on necessary and reasonable police investigations being unimpeded.

The Preamble's direction that an accused be able to consult with his solicitor depends, of course, on the availability of counsel. Legal aid plans are not of a uniformly high quality throughout Canada, and in some provinces, the accused is not able to obtain help until his case reaches the court stage and sometimes then only if the offence is a serious one. If our system of criminal justice is really interested in maintaining the principle that the State must prove its case and that a man has a right to silence, the Preamble provides the only sound rule, because the major damage to an accused's case is often done at the interrogation stage. The wealthy man or the professional criminal either has his lawyer by his side when he is arrested or he is so experienced that he does not help the policeman by volunteering information. The inexperienced, naive, nervous and distraught are likely to tell all. Self-incriminating and sometimes inaccurate stories and falsehoods are uttered out of nervousness or to please the overbearing interrogator.

The New Rules also provide:

> That when a police officer who is making enquiries of any person about an offence has enough evidence to prefer a charge against that person for the

> offence he should without delay cause that person to be charged or informed that he may be prosecuted for the offence.

The rules go on to state that interrogation should continue after this point only in exceptional circumstances. This is also in accord with the *Escobedo* rule about the shift from the investigatory to the accusatory stage.

On the other hand, the guilty do have a "compulsion to confess." In the words of Wigmore, one of the greatest authorities on evidence:

> The nervous pressure of guilt is enormous; the load of the deed done is heavy; the fear of detection fills the consciousness; and when detection comes, the pressure is relieved; and the deep sense of relief makes confession a satisfaction. At that moment, he will tell all, and tell it truly. To forbid soliciting him, to seek to prevent this relief, is to fly in the face of human nature. It is natural, and should be lawful, to take his confession at that moment—the best one. And this expedient, if sanctioned, saves the state a delay and expense in convicting him after he has reacted from his first sensations, has yielded to friends' solicitations and comes under the sway of the natural human instinct to struggle to save himself by the aid of all technicalities.

"Unfair" Police Tactics

Is it fair for the police to create a state of tension resulting in a confession? For the police to feign friendship, comfort or sympathy? For the police to imply, by playing one of their cards, that they know all the facts?

What about cases where there is bald trickery on the part of the police? Is it illegal (or immoral) for the police to use marked money to catch a thief, to employ an undercover agent to break a vice ring, to have a policewoman pose as a pregnant woman in search of an abortionist? Perhaps these are not considered reprehensible by most fair-minded lawyers who believe that the means justify the end of protecting the law-abiding members of society. Or are they contrary to fair play and are they likely to result in the public's loss of confidence in the police? On the other hand, is police morale adversely affected if their hands are too securely tied? Even if we are prepared to live with these practices, are we satisfied with the use of eavesdropping? Can we condone actions that would be struck down as instances of entrapment in the United States? Much of this evidence will be obtained before arrest and a formal charge. Therefore, should the suspect's lawyer be present before the client is required to answer any questions? This is a point raised and left ambiguous in the Preamble to the New Judges' Rules. The problem strikes at the very heart of our "sporting theory of justice" and the right to remain silent. Glanville Williams believes:

> A police officer goes a little further when he says:
> But it is a question that a crime-beset society such as ours will have to face for itself before long, and answer. For despite what may be said to the contrary by the academics and the theorists, the law exists for the benefit of the community. It is not an elaborate game of chequers governed by rules of absolute ethical validity so much as a means, admittedly imperfect, by which society can protect

> itself from the socially inconvenient consequences of such prohibited acts of self-indulgence as murder, rape, theft, disorder and so on. It must, therefore, be drafted in terms of human nature and, if you like, of human weaknesses. The procedures it contemplates for determining whether a particular crime must be capable of operation by the agencies employed by society for the purpose. Police officers may therefore find some reassurance in the reflection that, though the high winds of academic controversy and complaint may be noisily ruffling the branches above their heads, they stand in relative quiet below, with their feet on the ground, surrounded by strong trunks of judicial understanding. For it is to the courts that the police must look for control and guidance in their difficult duties. The judges, and the Bar from which the judges come, are practical men, and know well that the police have a job to do, and that if they are prevented from doing it reasonably effectively, it is society which must pay the price.
>
> This is not to say that the police can safely try their best to secure convictions by outmanoeuvring the guidance the judges have given them in the form of the Judges' Rules. They must continue to act fairly and justly within the general terms of their duty to keep crime within reasonable limits.

The 1981 Commission of Inquiry into the RCMP considered these questions and surveyed the Canadian law. The *Wray* case has decided that if the evidence were admissible (meaning relevant and probative of the facts in issue), then the majority of the Supreme Court of Canada was "not concerned with how it was obtained." Martland J. added a rider that judicial discretion could always relax the strict rule of admissibility if the evidence "would operate unfairly against an accused," but this would not be done if the evidence was only of trifling importance. The English House of Lords has agreed and gone further. In *Sang*, Lord Diplock said that if evidence were illegally obtained, the accused could always sue the policeman who might also be subject to departmental disciplinary proceedings but excluding such evidence in a criminal trial was no part of the judicial function. The Australian courts have agreed with the use of judicial discretion but warned that use of unlawful and unfair methods by the police is dangerous to individual liberty and convictions obtained by such methods may be done so "at too high a price."

The Commission set out the arguments in favour of the judicial use of illegally obtained evidence (the bracketed portions have been added as commentary):

1. Exclusion of such evidence "would divert a criminal trial away from its essential function of discovering the truth and making a correct finding as to the guilt or innocence of the accused." (This is a very strange statement because it tends to equate truth and proof, and they are not synonymous. The Commission seems to realize this and tries to explain it away with the rather vapid comment: "whether the social value in issue is sufficiently important to justify the suppression of relevant evidence and whether the suppression of relevant evidence is an efficacious manner of achieving the social value.")
2. Exclusion would reduce the effectiveness of law enforcement. (The Com-

mission suggests that it would make more sense to change the law of search and seizure than have "intentional and serious" police law-breaking.)
3. The state should "fight fire with fire." (The Commission did not agree with this because it could mean murder would be fought with murder, etc.)
4. If the police "know" a person is "guilty" but exclusion of illegally obtained evidence would result in acquittal, this encourages police officers to lie. (The Commission thought this argument was an unacceptable foundation for the law. In addition, it did not believe RCMP officers lied.)
5. Release of persons acquitted when they are "really" guilty would "shock the conscience of the community." (The Commission seemed to be in agreement with this.)

The arguments for an exclusionary rule were:

1. The need to "protect the integrity of the judicial process." The public "may be outraged" by flagrant police illegality. (The Commission quoted Holmes J. in *Olmstead* v. *U.S.* who said, "I think it is a less evil that some criminals should escape than that the government should play an ignoble part." Spence J. had made a similar comment in dissenting in *Wray* when he referred to an "almost riotous disregard for the administration of justice." The Commission would have some difficulty agreeing with this argument when it seemed to agree with point 5 among the "against" arguments. The report fudges and says that the judges quoted seem to think that the public cannot "disassociate the courts from the rest of the government machinery for the detection, investigation and prosecution of crime." This strange comment seems to be premised on the Blackstone school of judicial philosophy—that the judges are oracles of the law who—rather like the three monkeys—see, hear and speak no evil but have attained almost supernatural powers by something approaching apostolic succession. The Commission does not believe that judges read newspapers or, as Mr. Dooley said, read the election results.)
2. The exclusionary rule "serves to educate people, including the police, as to the serious commitment which our society has to the proper and restrained exercise of power." (The Commission believes the RCMP already believes this.)
3. An exclusionary rule will deter the police from breaking the law. (The Commission found *some* evidence for this view.)

The Commission decided that the U.S. absolute rule should not be applied but a discretionary rule should be adopted. Its reasons are the following:

1. "The state's commitment to due process would be seriously diluted if the court in the most serious of crimes were to exclude evidence that was obtained as a result of the most trivial breaches of the law of search. Rather than demonstrating the commitment of the law to principle, such a result would confirm in the minds of many members of the public the commitment of the law to technicality and in their minds would bring the law into disrepute." (The Commission does not supply us with examples from the U.S. Suprme Court where "trivial" breaches have resulted in the operation of the exclusionary rule.)

2. The rationale of deterrence (Reason 3 in the "for" rules above) does not differentiate between intentional breaches of the law and cases where the police officer simply made an error of judgement.

The Commission wished to adopt the draft of the Law Reform Commission of Canada:

1. Evidence shall be excluded if it was obtained under such circumstances that its use in the proceedings would tend to bring the administration of justice into disrepute.
2. The determining whether evidence should be excluded under this section, all the circumstances surrounding the proceedings and the manner in which the evidence was obtained shall be considered, including the extent to which human dignity and social values were breached in obtaining the evidence, whether any harm to an accused or others was inflicted wilfully or not, and whether there were circumstances justifying the action, such as a situation of urgency requiring action to prevent the destruction or loss of evidence.

The Commission added to this a couple of riders: That if the affront to human dignity or harm inflicted showed wilful acts or an "inexcusable ignorance of the law," then the evidence should more likely be excluded. The other factor that would help the court arrive at its discretionary decision would be "the seriousness of the breach of the law in obtaining evidence as compared with the seriousness of the offence with which the accused is charged."

Entrapment: Police Morality and Crime Prevention

Entrapment is another instance where United States courts exclude evidence while Canadian judges condone or ignore such police behaviour. The American rule was firmly established in *Sorrells,* where a revenue officer investigating the bootleg liquor business met a man, Sorrells, whom he suspected of being a bootlegger. The "victim" was not, at first, interested in selling bootleg liquor. The officer kept asking Sorrels, and after a few drinks and reminiscences about common wartime experiences and many more requests, Sorrells gave in and agreed to sell the liquor. He was charged and convicted. The Supreme Court of the United States threw out the conviction on the basis that the behaviour of the law enforcement officer was reprehensible.

The principle was refined in *Sherman.* The appellant who had been a narcotic addict was attending a clinic in the hope of curing his addiction. There he met Kalchinian who was a fellow addict but also a government informer. Kalchinian told Sherman that his cure was not going well and he needed a "fix." After several "accidental" meetings, the informer asked Sherman to buy heroin for him. After several refusals and much hesitancy, Sherman bought heroin which he shared with his new "friend." After a few transactions narcotics agents observed a sale and arrested Sherman. The U.S. Supreme Court quashed the conviction. Warren C.J. said:

> The function of law enforcement is the prevention of crime and the apprehension of criminals. Manifestly, that function does not include the manufacturing of crime. Criminal activity is such that stealth and strategy are necessary weapons in the arsenal of the police officer. However, a different question is presented when the criminal design originates with the officials of the government, and they implant in the mind of an innocent person the disposition to commit the alleged offence and induce its commission in order that they may prosecute. Then stealth and strategy become as objectionable police methods as the coerced confession and the unlawful search. Congress could not have intended that its statutes were to be enforced by tempting innocent persons into violations.

The Chief Justice was laying down a universal rule on entrapment—that if the offence was a product of the creative activity of the police, the evidence so obtained would be excluded and the prosecution would fail. Can we have a rule of entrapment which could be applied to all circumstances? Does the rule depend on the amount of persuasion required? Should the court ignore (and studiously ignore) the previous criminal record of predisposition of the "victim"? What is the exact meaning of police "creativity"? If the police believe that the accused has been engaged in criminal activity, should this be taken into account? Does the criminal activity have to be of the same kind as the present charge? Need it have occurred in the recent past or must it be concurrent? The police argue that they have a right (or is it a duty?) to set a thief to catch a thief, that they are merely simplifying the question of proof.

Mr. Justice Frankfurter wrote a concurring judgement from a different perspective. He believed that mechanical rules could not answer the problem of entrapment. Innocence or criminal predisposition were irrelevant if the police behaviour was intolerable. Frankfurter J. cited Holmes J. who had said (in a dissenting judgement in a wire-tapping case) that it is "less evil that some criminals should escape than that the government should play an ignoble part." In agreement, Frankfurter J. said that the "courts have an obligation to set their face against enforcement of the law by lawless means or means that violate rationally vindicated standards of justice, and to refuse to sustain such methods by effectuating them." In essence, this view is similar to the judicial discretion of the Canadian courts.

Therefore, the imprecise U.S. law on entrapment is that the police cannot act in a blatantly immoral manner as they did in *Sorrells* or *Sherman*. If the police are being lawless by creating offences, the courts will declare the conviction of the accused a nullity. This does not mean that the police cannot use subterfuges to trap a suspected criminal. In some of the "victimless" crimes—such as homosexuality, prostitution and abortion—police frequently act as *agents provocateurs*, posing as potential customers, and the courts have not quashed convictions on this basis. The accused was willing to commit the crime, and the police simply provided a further opportunity on this particular occasion.

The Canadian courts, with few exceptions, have refused the defence of entrapment. In recent years defendants have frequently pleaded entrapment in drug trafficking cases, but *Shipley* is the only reported case where a court acquitted. The acquittal, however, resulted from an abuse of process rather than the explicit defence of entrapment. The judge described the facts in these words:

> We have a young fellow, naive, lacking in experience, perhaps, and the officer working undercover. . . . the officer had won his friendship and his respect and the lad looked up to him. I think it is fair to say that, without the inducements held out by the officer, the accused would not have indulged in an offence against the Narcotic Control Act . . . and the inducements were that the officer wishes, for perfectly proper reasons, to ascertain if Shipley had drug suppliers and, if so, who they were. Among other inducements he was told quite frankly that he would not get his money back until the transaction went through.

The judge saw a clear legal distinction between entrapment and the activities of an *agent provocateur.* The judge described an entrapment situation as one where "an agent . . . instils in the mind of a man . . . the idea of committing an offence that he otherwise would not have intended and then persuades and encourages him to carry out that intent." (*Shipley* is Illustration 57.)

Shipley does not establish a universal entrapment rule for Canada. That has not been the judicial style of this country. The Ottawa judge has, however, shown that police behaviour that could be described as "entrapping" has some recognition in Canada. The appellate courts have not made an authoritative ruling and have not invoked the Canadian Bill of Rights for the "entrapee." *Ormerod,* where the accused claimed that he had been entrapped, is an instructive exercise in the judicial process and also shows some of the unsolved problems of Canadian criminal procedure. How should a judge decide on Ormerod's guilt? Should he simply suggest that Parliament must give serious thought to outlawing entrapment or the use of *agents provocateurs* in a comprehensive statute on criminal procedure? Should the trial judge or the appeal court apply the Canadian Charter of Rights on an exclusionary basis and declare that such police behaviour offends due process? Or should the judge limit the effect of his decision by exercising his discretion to rule the police practices unfair in this one case? Should the judge take the view that the answer must be found in the substantive criminal law of *mens rea* and *actus reus*? Should the judge take a pragmatic look at police practices and rule that there is a *de facto* immunity for entrappers and *agents provocateurs,* and therefore, there should be a *de facto* defence for the accused? Or, finally, should the judge recognize the serious social problem caused by drugs and strictly construe the Narcotic Control Act, taking into account the wide powers of police officers under the Act (for instance, the use of the writ of assistance) and the supposition that the dangers of drug trafficking militate against a liberal interpretation.

Canada has no Code of Procedure and this country's judges are loath to be innovative or lay down firm procedural rules. They are more likely to take up the first suggestion—that if Canada wants to outlaw entrapment, it is the task of the legislature, despite the curious lack of procedural legislation since the passage of the Canadian Criminal Code.

The Bill of Rights was fraught with problems, real and imaginary, constitutional and practical, and the past nine years show that the courts were not likely to apply the principles of that document to problems of criminal procedure. We are yet to see the effect of the Charter of Rights.

In explaining his decision to disallow the defence of entrapment, Laskin J.A. said in *Ormerod*:

> To uphold the defence ... it would be necessary for the courts to exercise a dispensing jurisdiction in respect of the administration of the criminal law. There is no statutory warrant for such a jurisdiction, but that does not mean that a Court is powerless to prevent abuses, be they abuses in the launching of the prosecution itself or in the establishment of the foundation for the prosecution.

Ormerod was a nineteen-year-old youth from a rural community who moved to Toronto to take up employment. He said that he became concerned about drug abuse and particularly about the use of drugs by a friend. After Ormerod had assisted policemen in finding two missing girls, these officers arranged a meeting between Ormerod and Sergeant Rozmus of the RCMP who was told that the appellant wanted to supply information on marijuana traffickers in the Yorkville area. Rozmus gave Ormerod telephone numbers and a code name to use and advised him not to tell anyone that he was working for the RCMP. In his evidence Rozmus further stated:

> The accused appeared to be quite sincere in what he was saying albeit he had a tendency to exaggerate; and he indicated that although he could not offer the accused any protection he could perhaps "help" him, if the accused was in a place innocently, but not if he was himself in possession of drugs or took an active part in marijuana activities.

In one of his first meetings with Rozmus, Ormerod had mentioned "Dennis from the Race Track" who supplied drugs. After approximately six telephone conversations in the first week, Rozmus discovered that "Dennis" was, in fact, Constable King of the RCMP working undercover. Rozmus terminated the relationship after a few weeks because he discovered Dennis's true identity and because Ormerod's information was not useful. The appellant claimed that the communications with Rozmus ceased on the request of Ormerod's father.

Ormerod was accused on two counts of trafficking in marijuana under the Narcotic Control Act. Both transactions were with King. The first occurred before Rozmus knew the true identity of "Dennis" and the second was subsequent to such knowledge.

The third charge was one of trafficking in a controlled drug contrary to the Food and Drugs Act. These pills were also sold to King.

The appellant claimed that Rozmus told him he could buy hashish from a third party and recover his money by reselling, but Rozmus denied this. Another police officer had allegedly told Ormerod that he should not be surprised if he discovered that "undercover agents sometimes buy, sell and use drugs to get information."

The facts seen through Ormerod's eyes may be a little difficult to believe, and McGillivray J.'s assessment may have been correct:

> There was also the possibility that he might be seeking some established relation with the police in order to disarm observation of his own activities.

Unfortunately, we do not know enough about police practices to make a judgement on Rozmus's alleged dealings with Ormerod. It seems unlikely, however, that a police force of the RCMP's sophistication would explicitly tell a callow youth that he was an agent with a licence to buy drugs. We must remember, on the other hand, that although Laskin J.A. may have shared McGillivray J.A.'s suspicions, for the purposes of judicial reasoning, His Lordship was "prepared to assume" Ormerod considered his activities were "*bona fide* . . . to be in furtherance of the police agency." Ormerod was convicted on all three charges and sentenced to six months' imprisonment. The trial judge told the jury that even if they accepted Ormerod's story that he honestly believed he had entered a working relationship with the police, this was no defence. The Ontario Court of Appeal was asked to decide on the propriety of this direction.

Before the appellate court, Ormerod argued three issues: that he had committed no offence because he was acting as an agent (or honestly believed himself to be doing so); that he had no *mens rea* because he had no illicit purpose; and that, even if he had trafficked, he had been entrapped by the police.

Although Laskin J.A., for the purposes of his decision, did not question the *bona fides* of Ormerod, he would not give the appellant a defence of public duty. The judge decided that Ormerod had no defence on this basis because police officers have no such defence in similar circumstances. In strict law, this seems to be the correct decision. From a practical point of view, it is questionable because we all know that police officers are not, in fact, charged in such circumstances. To Ormerod, at least, it seems dishonest to suggest that police officers are going to be treated in the same way because it is simply not true.

The Ontario Court of Appeal rejected Ormerod's second defence, lack of criminal intent or *mens rea,* because motive is irrelevant in most criminal cases (see Illustration 26). If the criminal law accepted every worthy story put before the fact-finders by accused persons, there would be no rules but simply a string of special instances. The law usually prefers an external or objective test of liability. Yet this seems to be a flimsy argument in the present case. Ormerod's *bona fides* was never questioned by Laskin J.A. Few of the cases cited by the appeal court were helpful, although in *Benjoe,* a Saskatchewan court acquitted an Indian counsellor who had taken possession of liquor from an Indian youth in the honest belief that he had a right to hold and "possess" liquor for these limited purposes in his capacity as counsellor.

The criticism has been made that it seems inappropriate to discuss *mens rea* as being totally separate from the public duty concept. The cliché that one can commit crime for the best of motives is just that—a cliché. No one doubts that a Robin Hood who steals from the rich and gives to the poor is nevertheless guilty of crime. One who teaches practical sex education to young girls from narrow puritanical family backgrounds will also be punished for his benevolence. A man who takes it upon himself to expose municipal fraud in his home town will nevertheless be guilty of attempted bribery despite his alleged public-spiritedness (see Illustration 26). Surely, these cases differ from cases in which properly constituted authority has established a police force and has allowed its officers to act as undercover agents and hire informers for the purpose of detecting crime. To say that the police officer may not act illegally, that he will be liable to prosecution if he does so and that the informer can only indulge in illegality with similar risks is stating the law on a very abstract level. The occasions on which police officers are prosecuted in such circumstances are rare. No one can suggest that the trial judge or appellate court can do anything about this situation, but if policeman are not, in fact, charged, does this mean the courts should formulate new rules about "public duty," its effect on *mens rea* and the formulation of rules on entrapment?

In *Ormerod* Laskin J.A. decided that there was no need to come to a decision on entrapment because it did not exist in that case. The judge thought there was a wide factual divergence between *Sherman* and *Ormerod.* Was Ormerod more or less entrapped than Sherman? In that case, the U.S. Supreme Court said:

> When the criminal design originates with the officials of the government, they implant in the mind of an innocent person the disposition to commit the alleged offence and induce its commission in order that they may prosecute.

Who was the originator of the scheme in Ormerod? Was it Rozmus, who acquiesced in Ormerod's behaviour, or are we to imagine that a man starts committing a crime when he offers to help the police convict him of a crime that has not yet been committed? Another passage may offer us a little more light:

> . . . the fact that government agents "merely afford opportunities or facilities for the commission of the offence does not" constitute entrapment. Entrapment

occurs only when the criminal conduct was "the product of the creative activity" of law enforcement officials.

Laskin J.A. took the view that it was not entrapment:

... merely because an undercover policeman provides the opportunity or gives the occasion for an accused to traffic in narcotics. Moreover, I cannot say that there was any such calculated inveigling and persistent importuning of the accused by Dennis ... as to go beyond ordinary solicitation of a suspected drug seller.

There are problems with this analysis. If we believe Ormerod's story, which may be a little far-fetched, and his *bona fide* belief was at least accepted by the Court of Appeal, the true entrapper was not "Dennis" but Rozmus. Ormerod continued his operations entirely because of Rozmus who, during at least one drug transaction, did not know of Dennis's existence or identity.

At the end of his judgement, Laskin J.A. recognized that Canadian courts did not follow the U.S. example and that the Bill of Rights was not, as yet, the vehicle for wholesale changes in criminal procedure.

I do not, of course, say that these would be the findings if the evidence was evaluated against the background of a principle of an overriding judicial discretion to stay a prosecution because of police complicity in the events which led to it. Nor do I say that such a principle must be recognized. It may, however, be arguable that it should be, but I leave consideration thereof to an occasion when it is squarely raised.

The Canadian courts are still sufficiently British that they will try to solve problems of criminal procedure (or due process) by means of substantive criminal law. This is obvious from the case of *Lemieux*, which was not decided as an entrapment case but as a decision based on technical arguments about the elements of a crime.

Lemieux drove the getaway car when he and two others (including the informer) forced their way into a house for the purpose of committing larceny. The break-in did not happen according to the letter of the law because the police had chosen the house with the help of the informer and the owner had consented to his house being used for the purposes of trapping Lemieux and his confederates. Lemieux was totally unaware of these plans. The following remarks by Judson J. comprise the total jurisprudence of the case:

For Lemieux to be guilty of the offence with which he was charged, it was necessary that two elements should co-exist, (i) that he had committed the forbidden act, and (ii) that he had the wrongful intention of so doing. On the assumption on which the appeal was argued *mens rea* was clearly established but it was open to the jury to find that, notwithstanding the guilty intention of the appellant, the *actus* which was in fact committed, was no crime at all.

This seems to dispose of the case as it would in the case of *Ormerod*. Laskin

J.A. said of the facts in *Lemieux*: "The accused had no intention of committing such an offence until approached by the informer who was acting under police instruction." The distinction between this and *Ormerod* is hard to follow. Ormerod had even less *mens rea* than Lemieux because the latter did not know he was involved in a police trap and went ahead with his "intention."

Mens rea, therefore, seems to be the basis of *Lemieux* and yet there is an enigmatic statement by Judson J.A.:

> Had Lemieux in fact committed the offence with which he was charged, the circumstances that he had done the forbidden act at the solicitation of an *agent provocateur* would have been irrelevant to the question of his guilt or innocence. The reason that his conviction cannot stand is that the jury were not properly instructed on a question vital to the issue, whether any offence had been committed.

Therefore, a technical legal argument provided a defence to Lemieux, with scant discussion of police ethics, while Ormerod was convicted. Laskin J.A. took the view that in *Lemieux* Judson J. was saying that "even assuming *mens rea* . . . it was open to the jury to find that there was no wrongful act." This could be found only on the basis that there was no *actus reus* because of the artificial quality of the transaction. Yet does this situation not also apply to *Ormerod*? Judson J.A. said that "solicitation of an *agent provocateur* would have been irrelevant to guilt or innocence." What difference is there between an owner of a house giving permission for a crime to be committed on his premises and a police officer allowing goods to be sold to him? If we are talking about social danger, there is no difference between *Ormerod* and *Lemieux*.

Whatever rule we have for entrapment or similar police practices, we are faced with a debate between control of crime and the civil liberties of citizens. Do we want a society where the law itself is in bad odour because policemen are allowed to resort to subterfuges? Will subterfuges lead to worse police acts such as extortion, blackmail and bribery? The argument goes that the law and its administrators and enforcers must not stoop to the level of the practitioners of crime because this would destroy the moral fabric of society. On the other hand, the police argue that they must set a thief to catch a thief, and they can only catch some criminals by using underhand methods.

If ephemeral notions of "national security" or fears of "organized crime" are involved, the public may be prepared to give greater latitude to entrapment, police decoys or *agents provocateurs* than in moral offences and "victimless" crimes where the damage to society may not be as great.

The police have always used "stool pigeons" and many Canadian police forces have "fink funds" that are used at the discretion of senior police officers who pay for information. Should this be stopped? Probably not, because quite often the stool pigeons are merely petty criminals who provide information leading to the conviction of more dangerous or successful criminals. Similarly, informers are used in courts everyday when one participant in a crime gives evidence against another to avoid prosecution or in exchange for a lesser conviction or punishment.

The Bill of Rights has been raised and is raised continuously, particularly by young lawyers who have been influenced by American law. While a few isolated courts have recognized the application of the Bill of Rights to right to counsel and, recently, to the prohibition of "cruel and unusual punishment" (in the cocaine case *Shand*), the nation's highest court has only recognized the Bill of Rights as applying specifically in the *Drybones* case. *Shand* has been overruled on appeal.

In the lower courts, there is a growing body of cases that recognize the principle of "abuse of process," which is not specifically mentioned in the Bill of Rights. These cases have usually involved behaviour by police or prosecutors that the judges have considered unconscionable. The accused have been harassed by unreasonable delays, vexatious prosecutions or shady practices to such an extent that the judge considered the accused as being persecuted rather than prosecuted. Abuse of process has received sympathetic treatment from the lower courts. The appeal courts have not been so enthusiastic. In *Osborne* and *Rourke,* the Supreme Court of Canada has not given its blessing to abuse of process but has not closed the door to its invocation when the appropriate facts present themselves on appeal. Of course the Charter of Rights may make abuse of process outdated.

The Commission of Inquiry into the RCMP recommended the establishment of a defence of entrapment. It equates the behaviour of *agents provocateurs* with entrapment. In the light of its recommendations in relation to illegally obtained evidence, the Commission's comments are interesting, although somewhat inconsistent, for instance:

> We think that it is unacceptable that a police force should be tacitly encouraged by the law to tolerate instigation by its members of crime by others when that instigation goes well beyond mere solicitation. If members of the RCMP engage in such conduct, we think it is not surprising if they should regard such conduct as being tolerated by the courts and thus implicitly approved of; as the record shows, the same reasoning applies, in the minds of at least some members of the RCMP to illegal methods of obtaining evidence.

The defence would read:

> The accused should be acquitted if it is established that the conduct of a member or agent of a police force in instigating the crime has gone substantially beyond what is justifiable, having regard to all the circumstances, including the nature of the crime, whether the accused had a pre-existing intent, and the nature and extent of the involvement of the police.

POSTSCRIPT

The "New" Sexual Offences

The federal government proclaimed Bill C-127 in January 1983. Its definitions are not so revolutionary as those of the Law Reform Commission of Canada. The feminists had lobbied for reform which would emphasize the violent qualities of rape and minimize the sexual aspects of that and related crimes. They had been most vehement in their demands for changing the rule in *Pappajohn*. An initial reading of the changes found in C-127 would suggest that the feminists will not be happy. Indeed the only persons who will enjoy this new legislation might be lawyers who specialize in criminal appeals; they should have plenty of work.

Section 17, which describes the defence of compulsion by threats, has been amended. The phrase "assisting in rape" (among the exceptions to the defence) has been deleted and replaced by "sexual assault, sexual assault with a weapon, threats to a third party or causing bodily harm, aggravated sexual assault" and some new abduction offences (including parental "kidnapping" in defiance of a lawful custody order). The omission of "assisting" may be significant. *Paquette* would suggest there is a general rule that aiders and abettors do not lose the defence of compulsion even for offences usually within the exceptions. *Bergstrom* is a little "elliptical" but it seems to distinguish *Paquette* for the purposes of any participation in the crime of rape. Therefore the dropping of the "assisting" phrase may be significant.

Section 18 has been degendered so that no married *person* can claim a presumption of compulsion on the basis of a married relationship. (Married person is not defined more specifically and probably is limited to the narrow definition found in the provincial Marriage Acts.)

The new legislation abolishes the crime of rape and attempted rape (ss. 143 to 145 of the Code), sexual intercourse with the feebleminded (s. 148), indecent assault on a female (s. 149), indecent assault of a male (s. 156). These offences have been replaced by the sexual assault sections which will be discussed below. The age of consent for heterosexual behaviour has not been changed despite the Law Reform Commission's recommendation that it be reduced to fourteen years. While much degendering has gone on in the new sexual offences, the drafters have, for some reason, left buggery and bestiality (s. 155) and gross indecency (s. 157) on the books. One can only presume that public opinion militated against wholesale and sensible reform. Section 146 has been left intact; that section makes it an offence for any male to have sexual intercourse with a female under fourteen years (maximum punishment of life imprisonment) and sexual intercourse with a female over fourteen but less than sixteen years of age. An accused charged with either offence cannot claim, as a defence, that he thought the female was over fourteen or sixteen respectively. The provision in s. 146(2) that the female between fourteen and sixteen was of "previously chaste character" has been retained. This is a little surprising because that phrase has a strange Victorian quality which has caused judges some difficulty in the past. This quaint phrase is also found in s. 151 (seduction by a male of eighteen or more of a female between sixteen and eighteen) and s. 152 (seduction, under promise of marriage, of a female under twenty-one by a male over twenty-one), and s. 153(b) (illicit intercourse with a female employee). These provisions have not been removed, although they seem to be dead letters. Section 140 has been left intact at least as it applies to females under fourteen; a male cannot claim a defence that the under-fourteen female consented to the act of sexual intercourse. This means that there is a defence of consent for a male person who has sexual intercourse with a female between fourteen and sixteen (or charged with an offence under s. 149 or 156).

Section 139 has been repealed and this is a welcome change. The section had been a grab bag of provisions reflecting moralistic views; for instance, s. 139(2) secured the acquittal of a male charged with seduction under promise of marriage, illicit intercourse with a female employee and seduction of female passengers if such male married the victim. Section 139(3) placed on the accused the burden of proving the previously *unchaste* character of the female when the male was charged under ss. 146(2), 151, 152 or 153(b). Subsection (4) of 139 had provided that in prosecutions under ss. 146(2), 151 and 153(b), evidence that the accused had had prior sexual intercourse with the female in question was not to be deemed evidence negativing previously chaste character. One moralistic judgement has been left standing in s. 146(3); where an accused is charged under s. 146(2), the accused could be acquitted if the court decided that the evidence "does not show that, as between the accused and the female person, the accused is more to blame than the female person."

Finally, s. 139(1), which forbade convictions under ss. 148, 150, 151, 152, 153, 154 or 166 unless the evidence was "corroborated in a material particular by evidence that implicates the accused," has also been repealed. Indeed, corroboration, as an evidential requirement, has disappeared from all sexual offences including the new sexual assaults. This does not affect the need for judicial remarks on corroboration of the evidence of unsworn child witnesses where that would arise in sexual assault cases.

The term "prostitute" is, for the first time, defined in the Code (in s. 179(1)) as "a person of *either* sex who engages in prostitution." Section 182 (search for a woman in a bawdy house) and s. 183 (examination of persons arrested in disorderly houses) have been repealed. Section 195 is repealed and replaced but the only changes amount to a degendering of the section so that the section now refers to "persons" rather than merely "female persons" who are procured for purposes of prostitution or illicit sexual intercourse in a common bawdy or house of assignation, etc.

The most controversial sections relate to assault and sexual assault. Sections 244, 245 and 246 are repealed and replaced with more extensive definitions. The assault section (244) does not change the definition of assault but a new subsection (244(2)) applies the definition to the sexual assaults. Subsection (3) codifies the rule in *R.* v. *Firkins* and *R.* v. *Plummer and Brown* that mere submission does not amount to consent in sexual offences.

The most difficult new provision is s. 244(4) which is meant to codify the rule in *Pappajohn* (and inferentially *Morgan*). Or is it meant to change that rule? The provision states:

> Where an accused alleges that he believed that the complainant consented to the conduct that is the subject matter of the charge, a judge, if satisfied that there is sufficient evidence and that, if believed by the jury, the evidence would constitute a defence, shall instruct the jury, when reviewing all the evidence relating to the determination of the honesty of the accused's belief, to consider the presence of absence of reasonable grounds for that belief.

This provision seems to make no change in the law but it is possible that the drafters thought that they were changing the law. In *R.* v. *Beaver,* Cartwright J. set out a test of subjective *mens rea* which has become recognized as the standard for subjective criminal responsibility. The decision stated that an accused could be acquitted on the basis of mistake of fact if he had an honest belief based on reasonable evidential grounds. It is *not* a test of honest *and reasonable* belief (which would apply in a case of due diligence such as *R.* v. *Sault Ste. Marie*).

It may seem pedantic but the placement of the word "reasonable" is very important. If it is used to qualify the word "belief," then it forms part of the definition of the substantive law describing the defence to a criminal charge. If the formulation is as stated in *R.* v. *Beaver,* then the reasonableness simply goes to the evidential question of what facts should satisfy the jury as to conviction or acquittal. That is not a revolutionary statement of the law; it is simply making a formal statement of the common-sense view that if the accused claims an honest belief which would exonerate him, then it must have a reasonable evidential basis. The reasonableness should not be based on what the *jury* would have believed in the circumstances but what the *accused* believed and what reasonable evidential grounds he had for doing so. That seems to be all that the new s. 244(4) says. Will it make any difference that the word "reasonable" has now been enshrined in statutory language? When courts are faced with the word "reasonable" in a statute, they tend to apply a more objective test. The words "reasonable grounds" in s. 244(4) should not be treated as anything more than an evidential test. Every decision by a judge or a jury is objective in the evidentary sense but that is inevitable unless the accused decided his own fate. That is not the way in which "objective" is used here. The jury as objective (i.e., impartial, outside) observers should decide what reasonable grounds the *accused* himself (i.e., subjectively) had for his alleged honest belief.

A scheme of assault offences is created by s. 245. Section 245.1(2) defines bodily harm in a sensible fashion as "any hurt or injury to the complainant that interferes with his or her health or comfort and that is more than merely transient or trifling in nature." (This makes sense in the light of the Lord Diplock's enlightening remarks on the history of the law (and medical treatment) in *Hyam.*)

The same gradation of offences has been created for both assault and sexual assault. Assault can be punished summarily or, on indictment, with a maximum of five years. If the assault is committed while the accused "carries, uses or threatens to use a weapon or imitation thereof" *or* causes bodily harm, the offence is indictable with a maximum of ten years (s. 245.1). (The latter provision relating to bodily harm is repeated in s. 245.3 for no obvious reason.) Section 245.2 defines aggravated assault as one which "wounds, maims, disfigures or endangers the life of the complainant." The maximum penalty is fourteen years. The crimes of attempted murder (s. 222) and causing bodily harm with intent (s. 228) do not appear to be repealed. This is not of great lament (except for possible confusion) because s. 228 carries the same penalty as s. 245.2. Attempted murder carries a maximum of life imprisonment but presumably the drafters of our various codes have always seen a distinction between wounding with intent to . . . "endanger life " (s. 228) and attempted murder (s. 222).

Finally, s. 246 has been repealed but the new section is exactly the same but for the omission of the old s. 246(1) which made it an offence to assault with intent to commit an indictable offence. This seldom used section was probably thought otiose. The crime of attempt would cover most situations.

As stated earlier, the sexual assault sections are replicas of the ordinary assault sections with the addition of the adjective "sexual" which is not defined. The crimes of rape and indecent assault have disappeared. The scheme is as follows:

(1) Section 246(1) makes *sexual assault* an assault punishable summarily or on indictment with a maximum of ten years' imprisonment.

This is not quite the sexual equivalent of "common assault" because the maximum is double for sexual assault (if tried on indictment).

Nowhere in the new provisions is the word "sexual" defined. We can only presume that the old ingredients of indecent assault will be called into use. This is regrettable because it means that the creaky old test in *Louie Chong* (which has been affirmed in recent years) will still apply. Therefore a touching (or trespass) to the erogenous zones will be a sexual assault if the complainant was not consenting. Determining what are the erogenous zones may require help from Drs. Masters and Johnson but we can assume it means the crotch (but how far down the thigh?), the lower belly (but how far up the belly?), the buttocks and the breasts (but only if the complainant is female). One wonders if the lips and mouth are included? Alternatively, the complainant could be touched on a non-erogenous zone so long as the behaviour of the accused was accompanied by some "indecent" or overtly sexual remark. Does such remark have to be merely sexual and uninvited or must it be insulting, undignified and gross? In other words, are we trying to define the mating (or at least dating) habits of Canadians? What kind of "pass" will the courts consider legitimate as opposed to one that is illegal, sexual and assaultive? If the accused touched the complainant on a non-erogenous zone and said one of the following: "How much do you charge?", "Wanna fuck?", "You look easy," "I'm horny," "Your place or mine?", "You turn me on," "I think you are very sexy," "What are you doing after the show?", "Aimez-vous Brahms?", or "I would like to have a meaningful relationship," which one would amount to a crime under s. 246.1?

When the Victorians (particularly W.T. Stead in England and D.A. Watt in Canada) made important changes to sexual offences in the nineteenth century, they were interested in protecting young females of virtue from sexual predators, raising the age of consent and improving morals. At a distance of almost a century, their major aim seemed to be the imposition of moral standards *via* the criminal law. Is the aim of the new legislation a little different? Are the new laws an educational exercise in sexual politics? Or, to put it more simply, is it an exercise in teaching people better sexual manners? If I am at a party and having had too much to drink put my arm round a stranger while making a crude sexual invitation or remark, is that different from another sober person who touches another person on the arm and says, "I would very much like to have sexual intercourse with you"? To make it even more polite, the alleged assaulter could substitute "make love" for "have sexual intercourse." Subtlety seems to be an important ingredient in the law of pornography and perhaps it will be the same with the new sexual offences. If an advertiser blatantly said, "Want to get laid? Then buy Bloggs panty hose," that would shock the populace much more than a subtler TV commercial which merely suggested that you are more sexually attractive if you use a particular brand of lingerie, perfume or wine.

Another difficulty, not answered by the new provisions, is the test to be applied to sexual assault. Is it to be judged as "indecent" or "sexual" as seen through the eyes of the complainant or through the eyes of a reasonable trier of fact or are we limited to the intent of the accused? *Louie Chong* seems to favour the second.

(2) Sexual assault will be more serious and is an indictable offence, punishable with a maximum of fourteen years if the accused
   (a) carries, uses or threatens to use a weapon or imitation thereof;
   (b) threatens to cause bodily harm to the complainant;
   (c) causes bodily harm to the complainant *or*
   (d) is party to the offence with any other person.

This is the second most serious sexual assault and it accentuates the *threat* of violence while the most serious offence of aggravated sexual assault incorporates *real* violence. Subsection (b) is a little strange because ordinary assault is a threat to cause bodily harm and yet this same ingredient is found in sexual assault attracting a maximum punishment of fourteen years. Subsection (d) has a salutary aim but the drafting is a little foggy. The intended policy was to penalize group sexual assault more seriously. The subsection is badly drafted if it is meant to state policy. Alternately, why was subsection (d) needed when s. 21, describing parties to crime, is already in existence?

(3) The most serious offence is aggravated sexual assault which is indictable and punishable with a maximum of life imprisonment. This offence is defined as a sexual assault which involves wounding, maiming, disfiguring or endangering the life of the complainant.

None of these terms is defined in the Criminal Code but one can presume that the harm done will be at least "grievous bodily harm." The punishment is the same as for attempted murder but, given the sexual ingredient, the physical harm would not be as serious as for attempted murder.

Section 246.1 has a subsection (2) which tells us that it is not a defence under these three sexual assault sections for the accused to prove that the complainant consented to the alleged acts if the complainant is under fourteen years unless the accused is less than three years older than the complainant. This makes little sense because the drafters seem to have forgotten that "assault" was defined in s. 244(1) as including an act done by an accused who "without consent . . . applies force intentionally. . . ." Of course it may mean that the assault definition in s. 244(1) does not apply to the various sexual assaults but this seems unlikely. What the drafters meant is that persons charged with sexual assaults on females under fourteen years cannot raise the defence of consent. They also seem to have forgotten that they did not repeal s. 146 of the Code. Admittedly s. 149 (indecent assault on female) has been repealed and the new sexual assault offences do not make any mention of sexual intercourse.

The greatest difficulty will be encountered with the further reforms of the law of evidence in relation to sexual offences. Section 246.4 provides that no corroboration is required for conviction under s. 150 (incest) 157 (gross indecency) and the new sexual assault laws. To make it absolutely clear, the section stated "and the judge shall not instruct the jury that it is unsafe to find the accused guilty in the absence of corroboration." Section 246.5 states that "the rules relating to evidence of recent complaint in sexual assault cases are hereby abrogated." On a practical note, will this stroke of a drafting pen really put an end to all cross-examination questions about the complainant's behaviour after the alleged offence? Will the judge stop any counsel who presses a complainant with questions as to why she did not tell anyone for a week, or took three days to telephone the police, or only made a complaint after talking to her mother or her best friend? Will the defence counsel claim that he cannot make full answer and defence unless he can fully question the complainant so as to test her credibility?

Section 142 has been repealed. That section has attracted much appellate court attention and we can only live in the vain hope that the new s. 246.6 fares better. The "reasonable notice" provision in s. 142(1)(a) has been left intact. Section 142(1)(b) has been replaced by s. 246.6(3) and seems to clarify some of the problems caused by s. 142(1)(b). There will still be a hearing *in camera* and the absence of the jury. The new law suggests that no evidence will be heard in the *in camera* hearing until the judge has heard submissions by counsel and the complainant will not be compelled at that point (which is contrary to the decision in *Forsythe*). Counsel will try to persuade the judge as to the question of "reasonable notice," the relevance of the evidence hoped to be submitted by defence counsel and that such evidence satisfies the requirements of s. 246.6(1) which is the most crucial part of the overall evidentiary scheme. Section 246.6(1) describes the limitations on the evidence which could be "adduced by or on behalf of the accused concerning the sexual activity of the complainant with any person other than the accused." This section does not change the law concerning previous sexual activity with the accused and the usual rules of evidence and judicial discretion will apply. The defence will only be able to adduce evidence of other sexual activity in the following circumstances:

(a) evidence that rebuts evidence of the complainant's sexual activity or absence thereof that was previously adduced by the prosecution.

This and the subsequent provisions are all completely new and are meant to clarify some of the problems raised by *Forsythe* and similar cases. If the prosecution had elicited in examination-in-chief that the complainant was previously *virgo intacta* (if female) or a person of the greatest moral and sexual virtue, then the defence is given an opportunity to rebut. Presumably the prosecution would only produce such evidence in rare circumstances and on the strongest indications as to its truth. Once again, sexual politics raises its head and one can imagine shy or intimidated complainants wanting to conceal sexual activities from members of the family or from the prying eyes of the public and then being attacked on cross-examination. Perjury is also a possibility. But is it more of a danger when the defence counsel is able to put on the stand the accused's friends who will be strongly influenced by male bonding or male boastfulness?

(b) evidence of specific instances of the complainant's sexual activity tending to establish the identity of the person who had sexual contact with the complainant on the occasion set out in the charge.

This is a strange subsection and its purpose is not very clear. The phrase "sexual contact" appears for the first time. This phrase is found in the report of the Law Reform Commission of Canada in a set of recommendations which were much broader than the recently enacted law. "Contact" is a rather neutral word and seems more appropriate to a law about VD. The drafters did not want to use the words "sexual intercourse," but by avoiding them the phrase "sexual contact" could be taken to mean something less than sexual intercourse—that the complainant had indulged in "heavy petting," etc. That is not the most difficult or puzzling ingredient. The word "identity" in this context can only refer to a situation where various persons had "sexual contact" with the complainant—such as a sex orgy at a bikers' gathering—and the defence's wish to cast doubt on her ability to identify the party accused as her (or his) assaulter. The subsection should be of limited use.

> (c) evidence of sexual activity that took place on the same occasion as the sexual activity that forms the subject matter of the charge, where that evidence relates to the consent that the accused alleges he believed was given by the complainant.

This is the most difficult provision. What is meant by the "same occasion"? Does this mean the same day, at the same party or in the same hour? One hopes that the remarks of Greco, Prov. Ct. J. in *R.* v. *McKenna, McKinnon and Nolan* which suggests that females who go to singles bars for the purposes of picking up or being picked up are not a test of admissible evidence. If a person seemed to be receptive to potential suitors A, B and C, it does not necessarily mean that he or she is not going to be rather abrupt with D and his solicitations. The complainant may have told D that he or she found D an unattractive person. Similarly, the mere fact that the complainant had consensual "sexual contact" with A, B and C does not necessarily mean that the complainant wanted anything to do with D. These provisions, and particularly s. 246.6(1)(c), are difficult to reconcile with s. 246.7 which provides that in any trial of a sexual offence "evidence of sexual reputation, whether general or specific, is not admissible for the purpose of challenging or supporting the credibility of the complainant." This is a change, at least on paper, from s. 142(1)(b) which allowed the judge, *in camera*, to consider the admission of evidence of previous sexual activity and one factor to be taken into account was the credibility of the complainant. Is previous sexual activity different from "sexual reputation"? Is rebutting the prosecution case (and being given full opportunity to make full answer and defence) different from a "mere" attack on credibility? The difference is a very fine one.

The only other provisions which need concern us are the following:

1. Section 246.8 makes it possible for a spouse to be convicted of a sexual assault offence on the other spouse even if they are living apart at the time of the offence.
2. The new legislation has unfortunately omitted any specific mention of the mental element of recklessness in the sexual assault offences. This was

included in the recommendations in the report of the Law Reform Commission of Canada and is in accord with the recent New Zealand case where there was a conviction for rape by omission.

Glossary

This list of terms is not meant to be a substitute for reading the text to discover the meaning of *mens rea, actus reus* or the definition of a legal concept. The index, the Canadian Criminal Code or even the dictionary should also be useful. This glossary is only meant to be helpful in explaining abstruse legal terms and ordinary words which have a special meaning in the law.

Absolute (Liability)
Applied to offences, usually of a minor nature, where there can be a conviction without the Crown having to prove the ingredient of *mens rea.*

Adversary System
The procedural method used in our criminal trials where the ideal judge is a non-interfering umpire and the opposing lawyers use their forensic skills in examining and cross-examining the witnesses for the Crown or the defence. The European countries use the inquisitorial method where the judges play a more active role in adducing evidence.

Agent Provocateur
A person, usually a police officer or police informer, who acts as a catalyst in the commission of a crime. This is different from entrapment where the crime is almost the total creation of the police officer or entrapper.

Appellant
The person who has initiated an appeal to a higher court. In most countries an appeal can only be brought by an accused who is convicted but in Canada the Crown (or prosecution) can appeal an acquittal. The other side is the respondent.

Arson
The crime of deliberately setting fire to property.

Assault
This crime can be either a physical attack on another person or a mere threat of violence.

Bail
A process which enables a person charged with crime to remain at liberty pending trial or the outcome of an appeal.

Bigamy
Going through a form of marriage when already married.

Blasphemy
Usually associated nowadays with "blasphemous libel"; any act or speech which would be scandalous to current religious values.

Burglary
This crime is often misinterpreted. Technically, the crime consists of breaking and entering a building (usually a house) with intent to commit a felony inside. The felony (or serious crime) can be of any kind but is usually theft.

Capital offence
One which used to attract the death penalty.

Caveat Emptor
Literally means "let the buyer beware" or, more idiomatically, could be translated as "a fool and his money are soon parted" or "never give a sucker an even break."

Civil action
A piece of litigation or a court case where one private citizen sues another for damages or to enforce a private right. A criminal case usually involves the State as one of the parties.

Civil law
The system of law found in Europe and partially in Quebec, Scotland and South Africa.

Code
A body of law which is more than a mere statute and embodies all the principles and rules of law applicable to a particular segment of human affairs. The Canadian Criminal "Code" is not a true code.

Corporation
An artificial legal entity created by incorporation under statute and with the approval of the government.

Criminology
The study of criminals, crime and its causes and the institutions which are connected with crime—police, prisons, courts, etc.

Damages
Money (or other valuable thing) awarded to the successful party in a civil action.

Defence
Any circumstance which can provide partial or complete exemption from criminal liability.

Deviance
A sociological term describing behaviour or human acts which veer from societal or community norms.

Diversion
A process which substitutes informal settlement or treatment of criminal behaviour without recourse to the usual courts or other institutions.

Due Process
A term found in seventeenth-century England and in eighteenth-century United States which describes a proper observance of the niceties of process—in describing the charge, arresting, interrogating, trying and punishing the accused.

Excusable
Criminal behaviour which will not attract liability, although once it required a royal pardon.

Extra-judicial
A process which would not require the intervention of a court.

Felony
No longer relevant to Canada but once used to describe serious crimes which were tried by a jury and were punished by hanging. The term was abolished in Canada in 1892 and replaced by the term "indictable offence."

Grievous Bodily Harm
The outcome of an aggravated form of assault which would seriously interfere with the health of a victim, often resulting in maiming or wounding with the breaking of the skin.

Heresy
Deviation from the religious norm.

Homicide
Not to be confused with murder: simply any kind of killing, some culpable and some non-culpable.

Inchoate
Incomplete, usually applied to the crimes of attempt and conspiracy.

Infancy
Relating to a defence of a person who is under the age of criminal responsibility—seven years or older, depending on the circumstances.

Indictable
Crimes which are initiated by an indictment (or charge) and are, usually, relatively serious crimes and sometimes cannot be tried by the lower courts, such as the provincial courts. (*See* felony.)

Justifiable
Behaviour which is completely exonerated by the criminal law and never required a pardon. (*See* excusable.)

Libel
A written statement which is scandalous, degrading or demeaning to the person or group described. (A spoken statement would be slander in the law of torts.)

Malice aforethought
The mental element (or *mens rea*) required for the crime of murder. A very ambiguous term which cannot be taken literally.

Misdemeanour
A minor criminal offence often triable in a summary (see below) fashion. The term was abandoned in Canada in 1892.

Nuisance
A legal term of art which means much more than an annoyance. A legal nuisance is one which causes damage or inconvenience to another person.

Offence
An alternative name for a crime.

Parens patriae
Literally means "parent of the country" and used to describe the philosophy of the juvenile court which is dedicated to the "best interests of the child" rather than taking a punitive attitude.

Party
A participant in a crime.

Penology
The study of prisons and punishment.

Perjury
Giving false testimony in a court proceeding.

Presumption
A legal artifice which assumes, in whole or part, the truth of a statement without proving in full.

Ratio-decidendi
The principle of law for which a court case is an authority.

Real
Describes property relating to the land rather than moveable "personal" property.

Relevance
Facts or events which will be accepted in a court case within the conventions of the law of evidence.

Respondent
See appellant.

Responsibility
Could also be described as "blameworthiness," "guilt" or "criminal liability"; it is a term which describes the proof of the *actus reus* and *mens rea* of a crime.

Reverse Onus
A procedure where the burden of proving an issue in a criminal case is placed on the accused rather than on the prosecution (Crown).

Stare decisis
Literally means "let the decision stand." The courts in a common law precedent system tend to follow previous decisions of higher courts in their own hierarchy.

Strict
A form of liability used to describe offences which are not full *mens rea* crimes but result in conviction if there is no proof of "due diligence" by the accused. *Cf.* absolute.

Summary
Refers to less serious offences which can be tried before lower courts and can attract a maximum punishment of a $500 fine or 6 months' imprisonment or both.

Summons
A document which informs citizens that their presence is required in court.

Usury
The act of lending money at excessive rates of interest.

Vagrant
A transient who has no fixed address, no method of supporting himself or is loitering in a public place.

Vi et armis
Literally means "by force and arms" and describes the basis of the law of trespass and assault.

Voluntary
Refers to the notion of "free will" as the basis for liability under the criminal law. The accused intended or willed his or her behaviour and was not hampered by intoxication or insanity which would have hampered his or her free choice to do the act alleged and could afford a partial or full defence to a criminal charge.

Warrant
Applied to a legal document used by a law enforcement or peace officer and obtained, under oath, from a minor judicial officer called a Justice of the Peace and empowers the officer to arrest or search.

Wrong
Used as a noun, this usually applies to private wrongs or torts which can result in a civil action for damages.

Bibliographic Notes

Footnotes have been avoided in the text. The following should provide sufficient bibliographical detail to identify the authorities cited. On occasion, some suggestions for further reading have been included.

page vii (and others)	*Our Criminal Law,* Law Reform Commission of Canada, Ottawa, 1977.
page 2	The most crucial volume of Blackstone for our purposes is William Blackstone, *Commentaries on the Laws of England,* Volume IV, *Of Public Wrongs,* London 1796, published in facsimile in 1979. A useful one-volume work is Gareth Jones (ed.), *The Sovereignty of the Law: Selections from Blackstone's Commentaries on the Laws of England,* Toronto, 1973.
page 5	George Wheelock Burbidge, *A Digest of the Criminal Law of Canada (Crimes and Punishments).* Founded by Permission on Sir James Fitzjames Stephen's *Digest of the Criminal Law,* Toronto, 1891.
page 6	John Robinson, *Honest to God,* London, 1958; Sexual Law Reform Society, *Working Party on the Law in Relation to Sexual Behaviour,* London, 1974.
page 9	James Fitzjames Stephen, *A General View of the Criminal Law,* London, 1863.
page 10	H.L.A. Hart, *Punishment and Responsibility: Essays in the Philosophy of Law,* Oxford, 1968, particularly chapters vii and viii; Barbara Wootton, *Crime and Criminal Law,* London, 1963.
page 11	For a history of penal reform, see James Heath, *Eighteenth Century Penal Reform,* Oxford, 1963, which includes exerpts and editorial commentary on penal theorists which include Montesquieu, Beccaria, Blackstone, Eden Howard, Bentham and Romilly.
page 11	Hugh Stretton, *The Political Sciences,* London, 1969.
page 12	Jerome Skolnick, *Justice Without Trial,* 1966.
pages 12 and 13	For a survey of criminological thought, see Hermann Mannheim (ed.), *Pioneers in Criminology,* 2nd ed., Mont-

clair, 1972; also see Taylor, Walton and Young, *The New Criminology,* 1973; also see Georg Rusche and Otto Kirchheimer, *Punishment and Social Structure,* New York, 1939.

page 13 Howard Becker, *Outsiders,* New York, 1963.

page 14 Richard Quinney, *Class, State and Crime: On the Theory and Practice of Criminal Justice,* New York, 1977. Also see Michael E. Tigar, *Law and the Rise of Capitalism,* New York, 1977.

page 15 Roscoe Pound, *Jurisprudence,* St. Paul, 1959.

page 20 For a history of prisons and punishment, see Harry Elmer Barnes, *The Evolution of Penology in Pennsylvania: A Study in American Social History,* Indianapolis, 1927; E.C. Wines, *The State of Prisons and Child-Saving Institutions in the Civilized World,* Montclair, 1968; R.S.E. Hinde, *The British Penal System, 1773-1950,* London, 1951; Orlando F. Lewis, *The Development of American Prisons and Prison Customs, 1776-1845,* Montclair, 1967; John Kidman, *The Canadian Prison: The Story of a Tragedy,* Toronto, 1947; J.M. Beattie, *Attitudes towards Crime and Punishment in Upper Canada, 1830-1850,* Toronto, 1977; Michael Ignatieff, *A Just Measure of Pain: The Penitentiary in the Industrial Revolution, 1750-1850,* London, 1978; Michel Foucault, *Discipline and Punish: The Birth of the Prison,* New York, 1977.

page 21 Herbert L. Packer, *The Limits of the Criminal Sanction,* Stanford, 1968; Alf Ross, *On Guilt, Responsibility and Punishment,* London, 1975.

page 29 Paul Radin, *The World of Primitive Man,* New York, 1971.

page 31 John Gregory Dunne, *True Confessions,* New York, 1976.

page 32 For early English laws, see F.L. Attenborough (ed.), *The Laws of Earliest English Kings,* New York, 1963. For further history see James Fitzjames Stephen, *A History of the Criminal Law of England,* London, 1883; Carleton Kemp Allen, *The Queen's Peace,* London, 1953.

page 34 For a history of some criminal law, see Graham Parker, "The Evolution of Criminal Responsibility" (1970) 9 *Alberta Law Review* 47.

page 34 — The excerpts from the book of Exodus are taken from *The New English Bible*, Oxford, 1961.

page 36 — For a history of methods of proof, see Henry Charles Lea, *Superstition and Force*, Philadelphia, 1892.

page 39 — Edward Coke, *Institutes*, III; Matthew Hale, *The History of the Pleas of the Crown*, London, 1736; William Hawkins, *A Treatise of the Pleas of the Crown*, London, 1716. These laws are described in Graham Parker, "Case Comment" (1982) 60 *Canadian Bar Review* 502.

page 40 — Macaulay's work is described by John Clive, *Macaulay: The Shaping of the Historian*, New York, 1973. Also see *The Complete Works of Edward Livingston on Criminal Jurisprudence*, 2 volumes, Montclair, 1968.

page 41 — S.F.C. Milsom, *Historical Foundations of the Common Law*, 2nd ed., London, 1981; Douglas Hay et al., *Albion's Fatal Tree: Crime and Society in Eighteenth Century England*, London, 1975.

page 43 — Regarding Becarria and Bentham, see Heath *op. cit.* at page 11 *supra.*

page 44 — See Graham Parker, "The Origins of the Canadian Criminal Code," in David H. Flaherty (ed.), *Essays in the History of Canadian Law*, Toronto, 1981, 249-280.

page 45 — See authorities cited for page 20 and Leon Radzinowicz, *A History of English Criminal Law*, 4 volumes, London, 1948-1968.

pages 47-48 — On the G.E. price conspiracy, see Monrad Paulsen and Sanford Kadish, *Criminal Law and Its Processes*, Boston, 1963.

page 50 — Gordon Hewart, *The New Despotism*, London, 1928.

page 52 — Patrick Devlin, *The Enforcement of Morals*, London, 1965; H.L.A. Hart, *Law, Liberty and Morality*, London, 1968.

page 53 — Richard Wollheim, "Crime, Sin and Mr. Justice Devlin" (1959) 34 *Encounter* 40.

page 54 — For further history and explanation of *Shaw v. D.P.P.*, see Ian Brownlie and D.G.T. Williams, "Judicial Legislation in Criminal Law" (1964) 42 *Canadian Bar Review* 561.

page 54 — On obscenity, see Donald Thomas, *A Long Time Burning: The History of Literary Censorship in England,* London 1969; Charles Rembar, *The End of Obscenity,* New York, 1968; C.H. Rolph, *The Trial of Lady Chatterley,* London, 1961.

page 56 — *Todd* is discussed by Brownlie and Williams, mentioned at page 54.

page 64 — *Sexual Offences,* Law Reform Commission of Canada, Ottawa, 1978. *Rape and Other Sexual Offences* (Special Report of Criminal Law and Penal Methods Committee of South Australia), Adelaide, 1972; *I Know What I Am: Gay Teenagers and the Law,* Joint Council for Gay Teenagers, Liverpool, 1980; Roy Walmsley and Karen White, *Sexual Offences, Consent and Sentencing* (Home Office Research Study No. 54), London, 1979.

page 79 — American Law Institute, *Model Penal Code: Proposed Official Draft,* 1965.

page 79 — Donald Horne, *The Lucky Country,* Sydney, 1967.

page 80 — U.S. Congress, *The Report of the Commission of Obscenity and Pornography,* Washington, 1970.

page 81 — *Obscenity: A Study Paper,* Law Reform Commission of Canada, Ottawa, 1972.

page 82 — Andrea Dworkin, *Pornography: Men Possessing Women,* New York, paperback edition, 1981. Gloria Steinem is quoted at page 199.

page 87 — Harold J. Berman (ed.), *Soviet Criminal Law and Procedure: The RSFSR Codes,* Cambridge, Mass., 1966.

page 89 — "If the law supposes that," said Mr. Bumble . . . "the law is a ass, a idiot," Charles Dickens, *Oliver Twist,* chapter 51.

page 139 — Mens rea and other general principles of criminal law can be best studied in greater detail in the following works: Leon Radzinowicz and J.W.C. Turner (eds.), *The Modern Approach to Criminal Law,* London, 1948, especially pages 195 to 261; Jerome Hall, *General Principles of the Criminal Law: A Treatise,* Toronto, 1982; *Studies on Strict Liability,* Law Reform Commission of Canada, Ottawa, 1974; *Criminal Law: The General Part: Liability and Defences,* Law Reform Commission of Canada, Ottawa, 1982. This last document has only recently been published and includes the following definitions of criminal liability:

Definitions of offences shall be so interpreted that, unless otherwise provided, no one commits an offence
(a) by reason of an act unless in doing it he knows the circumstances specified in the definition of that offence;
(b) by reason of an omission unless he fails to perform a duty imposed by law and knows the circumstances giving rise to such a duty;
(c) by reason of any other situation (including possession) specified in the definition of that offence unless he knows the circumstances specified in that definition;
(d) by reason of a consequence specified or implied in the definition of that offence unless he knows that he might cause that consequence; or
(e) by reason of a purpose specified in the definition of that offence unless in fact he has that purpose.

page 141 — The best available text-book on the criminal law, which is frequently quoted in these pages, is Jerome Hall, *General Principles of the Criminal Law*, 2nd ed., Indianapolis, 1960.

page 141 — J.K. Pollock and H.J. Heneman, *The Hitler Decrees*, 2nd ed., Ann Arbor, 1934; South African Legislation, Act No. 37 of 1963.

page 144 — J.E. Cote, "The Reception of English Law" (1977) 15 *Alberta Law Review* 29.

page 145 — B.L. Reid, *The Lives of Roger Casement*, New Haven, 1976.

page 150 — Glanville Williams, *Criminal Law: The General Part*, 2nd. ed. London, 1961.

page 154 — Peter Brett, *An Enquiry into Criminal Guilt*, Sydney, 1963.

page 156 — English Law Commission, *Working Paper on the Mental Element in Crime*, London, 1968.

page 157 — Oliver Wendell Holmes, Junior, *The Common Law*, 1881.

page 158 — James Marshall, *Law and Psychology in Conflict* and *Intention, in Law and Society*, New York, 1968.

page 161 — The motive case is based on *Smith* [1960] 2 Q.B. 423.

page 162 — The Pontius Pilate case is based on *R.* v. *Georgia Straight Publishing Co.* 6 C.R. 150.

page 165 — The Report of the Advisory Group on the Law of Rape (The Heilbron Report), 1975 Cmnd. no. 6352.

page 171 On *Vasil,* see Graham Parker, "Case Comment" (1982) 60 *Canadian Bar Review* 502.

page 177 A.T. Denning, *Responsibility Before the Law,* Jerusalem, 1963.

page 181 The Australian case is taken from *Vallance* (1961) 108 C.L.R. 56.

page 183 Roger Ouimet (chairman), *Toward Unity: Criminal Justice and Corrections,* Ottawa, 1969.

page 183 Terrence Willett, The Criminal on the Road, London, 1964.

page 185 D.W. Elliott and Harry Street, *Road Accidents,* London, 1968; also see William Plowden, *The Motor Car and Politics, 1896-1970,* London, 1971.

page 197 *The Meaning of Guilt: Strict Liability,* Law Reform Commission of Canada, Ottawa, 1974. Also see Keith Jobson, "Far From Clear" (1975-1976) 18 *Criminal Law Quarterly* 294.

page 201 H.L.A. Hart and A.M. Honoré, *Causation in the Law,* Oxford, 1959.

page 203 *Criteria for the Determination of Death,* Law Reform Commission of Canada, Ottawa, 1981.

page 204 Helen Silving, *The Constituent Elements of Crime,* Springfield, 1968.

page 225 Francis B. Sayre, "Public Welfare Offenses" (1933) 33 *Columbia Law Review,* 55.

page 238 See the Postscript for changes in the law.

page 246 See Graham Parker, "The Appellate Court View of the Juvenile Court" (1969) 7 *Osgoode Hall Law Journal* 155; "The Juvenile Court Movement" (1976) 26 *University of Toronto Law Journal,* 253.

page 249 Donald J. West and Alexander Walk, *David McNaughton: His Trial and the Aftermath,* Ashford, Kent, 1977.

page 253 Abraham S. Goldstein, *The Insanity Defense,* New York, 1967.

page 254 Bernard Diamond, "The Fallacy of the Impartial Expert" (1959) 3 *Archives of Criminal Psycho-Dynamics,* 221-226, 234-236.

page 259 Isaac Ray, *A Treatise on the Medical Jurisprudence of Insanity*, Boston, 1838.

page 259 John Reid, *Chief Justice: The Judicial World of Charles Doe*, Cambridge, Mass., 1967.

page 260 Great Britain, *Royal Commission on Capital Punishment*, London, 1949-1953, Cmnd. 8932.

page 262 J.C. McRuer (Chairman), *Royal Commission on the Law of Insanity as a Criminal Defence*, Ottawa, 1955.

page 279 Walter Lippmann, *A Preface to Morals*, New York, 1929.

page 285 *The General Part—Liability and Defences*, Law Reform Commission of Canada, Ottawa, 1982.

page 290 Gerald E. LeDain, (Chairman) *Interim Report of the Commission of Inquiry into the Non-Medical Use of Drugs*, Ottawa, 1970.

page 297 Keith Thomas, "The Double Standard" (1959) 20 *Journal of the History of Ideas*, 195-216.

page 299 There is extensive literature on this topic. The following are representative but not exhaustive: Leo Markun, *Mrs. Grundy: A History of Four Centuries of Morals in Great Britain and the United States Intended to Illuminate Present Problems*, New York, 1930; Ernest A. Bell, *War on the White Slave Trade*, reprinted, Toronto, 1980; Clifford G. Roe, *Panders and Their White Slaves*, New York, 1910; Ronald Pearsall, *The Worm in the Bud*, London, 1969; Steven Marcus, *The Other Victorians*, London, 1966; Fraser Harrison, *The Dark Angel: Aspects of Victorian Sexuality*, New York, 1978; Glen Petrie, *A Singular Iniquity: The Campaigns of Josephine Butler*, London, 1971; William W. Sanger, *The History of Prostitution and Victorian Society*, New York, 1913; Michael Pearson, *The Age of Consent: Victorian Prostitution and Its Enemies*, Newton Abbot, 1972; Charles Terrot, *Traffic in Innocents: The Shocking Story of White Slavery in England*, New York, 1960; Judith R. Walkowitz, *Prostitution and Victorian Society: Women, Class and the State*, New York, 1980; Kellow Chesney, *The Victorian Underworld*, London, 1970; Janet Murray (ed.), *Strong-Minded Women and Other Lost Voices from Nineteenth-Century England*, New York, 1982; D.A. Watt, *Moral Legislation: Prepared for the Information of the Senate*, Montreal, 1890; Frederic Whyte, *The Life of W.T.*

Stead, London, 1925; G.J. Barker-Benfield, *The Horrors of the Half-Known Life: Male Attitudes Toward Women and Sexuality in Nineteenth-Century America*, New York, 1976; Jeffrey Weeks, *Sex, Politics and Politics and Society: The Regulation of Sexuality Since 1800*, London, 1981.

page 301 See the history of the Canadian Criminal Code cited with page 44.

page 320 Lorenne Clark and Debra Lewis, *Rape: The Price of Coercive Sexuality*, Toronto, 1977; Susan Brownmiller, *Against Our Will: Men, Women and Rape*, New York, 1975; Duncan Chappell, Robley Geis and Gilbert Geis (eds.), *Forcible Rape: The Crime, The Victim and The Offender*, New York, 1977.

page 324 *Evidence*, Law Reform Commission of Canada, Ottawa.

page 325 The Model Rape Law is reproduced with the permission of the Rape Study Group of New York University Law School.

page 328 For a history of property offences (and a full description of the law) see Jerome Hall, *Theft, Law and Society*, 2nd. ed., Indianapolis, 1952; George P. Fletcher, *Rethinking Criminal Law*, Boston, 1978.

page 330 *Theft and Fraud: Offences*, Law Reform Commission of Canada, Ottawa, 1977.

page 341 On Ashford v. Thornton, see Charles Rembar, *The Law of the Land: The Evolution of Our Legal System*, New York, 1980. On trial by battle generally, George Neilson, *Trial by Combat*, Glasgow, 1890.

page 361 On the Charter of Rights, see Peter Hogg, *The Canada Act Annotated*, Toronto, 1982.

page 370 James Fitzjames Stephen, *A History of the Criminal Law of England*, 1883.

page 370 G. Arthur Martin, "The Privilege Against Self-Incrimination Endangered" 5 *Canadian Bar Journal* 6.

page 374 J. Desmond Morton, Letter to the Editor, 38 *Canadian Bar Review* 292.

page 384 "Interrogations in New Haven: The Impact of Miranda" (1966-67) 76 *Yale Law Journal*, 1519.

page 388 Glanville Williams, "Questioning by the Police: Some Further Points—2" [1960] *Criminal Law Review* 352.

page 389 *Freedom and Security Under the Law, Commission of Inquiry Concerning Certain Activities of the Royal Canadian Mounted Police*, Second Report, 2 vols. 1981. Compare an earlier document prepared by the R.C.M.P. itself: *Law and Order in Canadian Democracy: Crime and Police Work in Canada*, revised edition, 1952, Ottawa. Also see Alan Grant, *The Police: A Policy Paper*, Law Reform Commission of Canada, Ottawa, 1980; Lee Paikin, *The Issuance of Search Warrants: A Manual Prepared for the Law Reform Commission of Canada*, Ottawa, 1980.

page 393 On Ormerod, see Graham Parker, "Case Comment" (1970) 48 *Canadian Bar Review*, 178.

Index of Cases

Single names and names joined by "and" rather than "v" indicate criminal cases which are usually prefixed by *"Rex v."* or *"Regina v."*

Subject Index